Teacher Edition

LEVEL 7

Contents

HOUGHTON MIFFLIN

Boston • Atlanta • Dallas • Denver • Geneva, Illinois • Palo Alto • Princeton

Grateful acknowledgment is given for the contributions of

Student Book

Rosemary Theresa Barry
Karen R. Boyle
Barbara Brozman
Gary S. Bush
John E. Cassidy
Dorothy Kirk
Sharon Ann Kovalcik
Bernice Kubek
Donna Marie Kvasnok
Ann Cherney Markunas
Joanne Marie Mascha
Kathleen Mary Ogrin
Judith Ostrowski
Jeanette Mishic Polomsky
Patricia Stenger
Annabelle L. Higgins Svete

Teacher Book
Contributing Writers

Dr. Judy Curran Buck
Assistant Professor of Mathematics
Plymouth State College
Plymouth, New Hampshire

Dr. Richard Evans
Professor of Mathematics
Plymouth State College
Plymouth, New Hampshire

Dr. Mary K. Porter
Professor of Mathematics
St. Mary's College
Notre Dame, Indiana

Dr. Anne M. Raymond
Assistant Professor of Mathematics
Keene State College
Keene, New Hampshire

Stuart P. Robertson, Jr.
Education Consultant
Pelham, New Hampshire

Dr. David Rock
Associate Professor,
Mathematics Education
University of Mississippi
Oxford, Mississippi

Michelle Lynn Rock
Elementary Teacher
Oxford School District
Oxford, Mississippi

Dr. Jean M. Shaw
Professor of Elementary Education
University of Mississippi
Oxford, Mississippi

Printed in the U.S.A.

ISBN: 0-395-98547-1

123456789-B-05 04 03 02 01 00 99

HOUGHTON MIFFLIN

MathSteps

In Step With Today's Classroom

What is *MathSteps*?

- **MathSteps** is a Kindergarten through Middle grades mathematics program that ***explicitly teaches*** all the essential content covered at your grade level.
- **MathSteps** is the one program ***designed*** to focus specifically on the development of skills and sub-skills, so that all students can be successful.
- **MathSteps** is the ***highly systematic,*** step-by-step instructional plan that's easier for students to follow—and easier to implement efficiently and effectively in any classroom.
- **MathSteps** is the comprehensive program that even offers a fully integrated, ***easily managed*** Tutorial for intervention and remediation.
- **MathSteps** is the ***right step*** for teachers and students alike, to improve skills mastery, build confidence in mathematics, and rise to higher standards of success.

What does *MathSteps* offer?

- **MathSteps** uses an explicit instructional approach that clearly develops the mathematical content. Operations, thinking skills, problem solving, estimation, data, statistics, geometry, and probability are emphasized appropriately at all grade levels.

- **MathSteps'** instructional philosophy is incorporated into Workbook texts that provide a consistent, easy-to-use format.

- **MathSteps** follows a simple structure, supporting a natural teaching and learning style with:

  - Clear, unambiguous teaching models that begin each lesson, helping teachers convey procedures and rules.

  - Carefully selected exercises that provide practice of new learning and lead students toward mastery of skills.

  - Two Problem Solving lessons in every unit that teach a systematic problem solving plan.

  - Frequent "Quick Checks" that provide ongoing assessment opportunities and integrate fully with the Tutorial kit.

What is the *MathSteps* Skills Tutorial?

- **The Skills Tutorial** is an individualized diagnostic and prescriptive program designed to help all students master computational skills. It is a total package that includes all the materials you need for pre- and post-testing, instructional practice, and record keeping.
- **The Skills Tutorial** is organized by grade level, by strand, and by skill, with a:
  - Teaching Card for each skill
  - Practice Sheet for each skill
  - Comprehensive Teacher Manual
  - Diagnostic Computation Test
- For your convenience, the entire **Skills Tutorial** is available on CD-ROM.

MathSteps:

What every student needs!

Lesson Support Contents

Unit 1 • Introduction to Algebraic Thinking

Annotated Student Book

The annotated Student Book for Unit 1 may be found on pages 1–30.

Lesson Support Contents

Unit 2 • Number Theory, Decimals, and Fractions

Annotated Student Book

The annotated Student Book for Unit 2 may be found on pages 31–72.

Lesson Support Contents

Unit 3 • Measurement

Annotated Student Book

The annotated Student Book for Unit 3 may be found on pages 73–96.

Lesson Support Contents

Unit 4 • Ratios, Proportions, and Percents

Annotated Student Book

The annotated Student Book for Unit 4 may be found on pages 97–126.

Lesson Support Contents

Unit 5 • Applications of Percent

Annotated Student Book

The annotated Student Book for Unit 5 may be found on pages 127–150.

Lesson Support Contents

Unit 6 • Data, Statistics, and Probability

Annotated Student Book

The annotated Student Book for Unit 6 may be found on pages 151–178.

Lesson Support Contents

Unit 7 • Geometry

Annotated Student Book

The annotated Student Book for Unit 7 may be found on pages 179–214.

Lesson Support Contents

Unit 8 • Integers and Rational Numbers

Annotated Student Book

The annotated Student Book for Unit 8 may be found on pages 215–240.

Lesson Support Contents

Unit 9 • Algebra: Expressions and Equations

Annotated Student Book

The annotated Student Book for Unit 9 may be found on pages 241–274.

Lesson Support Contents

Unit 10 • Using Formulas in Geometry

Annotated Student Book

The annotated Student Book for Unit 10 may be found on pages 275–314.

Lesson Support Contents

Unit 11 • The Coordinate Plane: Graphs and Transformations

Lesson Support

Introduction to Algebraic Thinking

Vocabulary

base (of a power) The number that is used as a factor when evaluating powers

equation A number sentence that says that two expressions have the same value. It may be true, false, or open.

exponent A number that tells how many times a base is to be used as a factor.

formula A general rule or relationship expressed in symbols.

order of operations The rules that define the order in which the operations in an expression are to be evaluated. They are:

1. Work within parentheses; 2. Evaluate powers; 3. Multiply and divide from left to right; 4. Add and subtract from left to right

power A number that can be expressed using a single base and exponent.

variable A letter that is used to represent one or more numbers

variable expression An expression that contains one or more variables

Unit Objectives

- **1A** Use line plots to find mean, median, mode, and range
- **1B** Write and evaluate algebraic expressions
- **1C** Use properties and order of operations to simplify expressions
- **1D** Solve equations with whole numbers
- **1E** Use formulas to find perimeter, area, and volume
- **1F** Use formulas to solve multi-step problems; use Write an Equation and other strategies to solve problems

About This Unit

The support pages that follow provide more information on prerequisite skills, methods for teaching skills and concepts, daily routines, tips on classroom management and materials, and useful dialogue techniques.

Prerequisite Skills and Concepts

Students should be able to

- use place value through billions, including expanded notation with powers of ten.

If not, use prerequisite Reteach Worksheet 1.

Assessments

Use Beginning of the Year Inventory for entry-level assessment.

Ongoing Evaluation Quick Checks, Reteach Worksheets, the Skills Tutorial Inventories, and the Midyear Test help ensure that students are progressing adequately to meet the standards.

Summative Evaluation Use Test Preps, Unit Review (p. T26), Cumulative Review (p. T27), Reteach Worksheets, and the Computation Skills Tutorial to assure that students have achieved the standards for the unit.

Diagnosing Errors The Quick Checks highlight common errors and provide remediation. See also the **Teaching Strategies Handbook** pp. T16–T19, where short discussions labeled Common Misconceptions appear as needed with the strategies for key concepts.

Homework and Family Involvement

Home Note In the Student Book, the Dear Family home note provides objectives, vocabulary, and a sample skill discussion for family participation. (**Teaching Strategies Handbook** pages also provide homework and family involvement tips.)

Education Place Refer families to Houghton Mifflin's EduPlace Web site at **http://www.eduplace.com**; for resources and activities for students at **http://www.eduplace.com/math**; and additional resources and activities at **http://www.eduplace.com/parents**.

Helping Your Children Learn Math This book has activities for children ages 5–13 and tips for getting involved in children's mathematics education. (Houghton Mifflin, 1994)

Lessons	Student Pages	Teacher Pages	Resources	State or Local Objectives	State or Local Assessment
1.1 Whole Numbers and Data	3–4	**T20**	Unit 1 Pretest; Reteach 2		
1.2 Expressions	5–6	**T20**	Reteach 3		
1.3 Order of Operations	7–8	**T21**	Reteach 4; Extension 1		
1.4 Solving Addition and Subtraction Equations	9–11	**T21**	Reteach 5		
1.5 Solving Multiplication and Division Equations	12–13	**T22**	Reteach 6		
1.6 Problem Solving Strategy: Write an Equation	14–15	**T22**			
1.7 Properties	16–18	**T23**	Reteach 7		
1.8 Using the Distributive Property	19–21	**T23**	Reteach 8		
1.9 Expressions with Exponents	22–23	**T24**	Reteach 9		
1.10 Using Geometric Formulas	24–26	**T24**	Reteach 10		
1.11 Problem Solving Application: Using a Formula	27–28	**T25**	Unit 1 Posttest		

Teaching Strategies

Math Background — Introduction to Algebraic Thinking

Students continue building the bridge from arithmetic to algebra at this level. Review with them the order of operations and mathematical properties with numerical expressions and equation; then, apply these concepts to algebra. Post the chart on page T19 that shows the relationships among some of the arithmetic and algebra concepts in this unit.

When Students Ask, Why Learn This?
Thinking algebraically will become a very useful problem solving tool for your students. Ask them, *How many $15 CDs could be purchased with $75?* By writing an algebraic equation to model the problem, students can find the solution. Let c equal the number of CDs.

$$c \cdot \$15 = \$75$$
$$c = \$75 \div \$15$$
$$c = 5$$

As your students' algebraic thinking skills grow, their confidence in solving problems will grow as well.

A Positive Start
Students are proud to say they are "doing algebra." Give them a good start by being sure that they have a complete understanding of the order of operations. An expression such as $-2 + -3 \times 4$ can be ambiguous. Explain that an agreed upon order was developed to specify how expressions are to be combined. This is a key element in the study of algebra. Spend extra time, if necessary, to make sure students making the critical transition from simplifying numerical expressions to simplifying algebraic expressions. Make it a challenge to "get the variable by itself" when solving equations.

Linking Past and Future Learning

By looking back at the topics students covered in Level 6, you can better focus your instruction for this year. This will help prepare your students for success at Level 8.

Concept/Skills	Last Year	This Year	Next Year
Simplifying Expressions	Use the order of operations to evaluate numeric and variable expressions, some containing exponents	Use the order of operations to simplify numeric and variable expressions, some containing exponents	Simplify numeric and variable expressions containing rational and irrational numbers
Solving Equations	Solve addition, subtraction, multiplication, and division problems using inverse operations	Isolate the variable, then solve one- and two-step equations; understand difference between an equation and a formula	Solve quadratic equations
Using Formulas	Use formulas to find area, perimeter, discount, surface area, volume, circumference	Use formulas to find area, perimeter, surface area, volume, circumference; solve percent problems	Use formulas to solve problems involving measurement and money applications

Methods and Management

You'll find that the strengths and weaknesses of students are different from year to year. Before beginning any new unit, encourage students to talk about their understanding of the concepts in the unit. Talk to the Level 6 teachers to find out how students did with similar concepts last year.

Teaching Strategy: Simplifying Expressions

Simplifying algebraic expressions is made easier when students see the relationship between numerical expressions and algebraic expressions.

- Write the numerical expression $3^2 - (5 + 5) \div 2$ on the board.

▶ ***Ask:*** *What operation would you perform first? Second? Third? Fourth?* Have students explain their responses; then, have them simplify the expression.

- Write the algebraic expression $x^2 - (z + z) \div y$ on the board. Again, ask students for the order of operations and to simplify the expression.

▶ ***Then ask:*** *How are $3^2 - (5 + 5) \div 2$ and $x^2 - (z + z) \div y$ alike? How are they different?*
To simplify both expressions, the same order of operations needs to be followed. The only difference between the expressions is that the algebraic expression uses letters and the numerical expression uses numbers.

▶ ***Vocabulary Development*** Encourage students to use the complete names of mathematical properties in class discussions. Have them identify the properties they use in the first few exercises of each lesson.

▶ ***Common Misconceptions*** Some students may make mistakes when simplifying algebraic expressions, such as $y + y$. They may think that $y + y = y^2$. Students can check their answers by replacing the variables with numbers.

Check $y + y = 2y$. Let $y = 5$.
$5 + 5 = 2(5)$
$10 = 10$ It checks.

Check $y + y = y^2$. Let $y = 5$.
$5 + 5 = 5^2$
$10 \neq 25$ It doesn't check.

Teaching Strategy: Solving Equations

The key objective in solving one-step equations is to isolate the variable. This means getting the variable alone on one side of the equation.

- Have students complete these statements about solving equations. *Whatever you do to one side of an equation,* _____. (you must do to the other side) *To undo an operation, use the* _____. (inverse operation)

▶ ***Ask:*** *How can you isolate the variable in each of these equations?*

$4 + x = 9$ $n \div 7 = 4$ $40 = s \cdot 8$ $9 = 17 - t$

Show how to use the inverse operation on each side of each equation.

▶ ***Common Misconceptions*** Students may rush into applying an operation to each side of an equation, without taking enough time to determine the operation they really should be using. It may help them to note the original operation, by symbol, next to their work.

Calculators Collect different types of calculators. Have students enter $2 + 3 \cdot 4$ in each calculator to see if all of the calculators follow the order of operations. Point out to students that not all calculators do.

Memory Trigger Some teachers use the phrase "*P*lease *E*xcuse *M*y *D*ear *A*unt *S*ally" as a tool to remember the order of operations. The first letter of each word stands for an operation.

P	Parentheses
E	Exponents
M	Multiplication
D	Division
A	Addition
S	Subtraction

A caution, however:
Multiplication and division have equal priority, and addition and subtraction have equal priority. These pairs of operations are done from left to right in the order they appear.

Daily Routine Start each class by having students simplify an algebraic expression. Include different operations, parentheses, and exponents in the expressions. Then, have student volunteers explain the steps they followed to find the answer.

Pacing Although some students will be able to solve one-step equations using mental math, don't underestimate the importance of the concept of isolating the variable to solve equations. It is an essential prerequisite skill for solving multi-step equations later on.

Connecting Suggest that students look through science and geography books for other examples of formulas. Then, have them share with the class how the formulas are used.

Questioning Tips When students have difficulty coming up with the correct response to a question, ask other questions to lead them in the right direction. Offer hints or tips that will guide their thinking. Use encouraging phrases such as "Daryl is leading us in the right direction. Can anyone else offer a solution?" or "The first part of your solution will work. Let's take a closer look at the second part."

Teaching Strategy: Using Formulas

Formulas are algebraic equations that state a fact or rule. Though students have used formulas, they may not realize that they were actually using algebraic equations.

▶ ***Show This:***

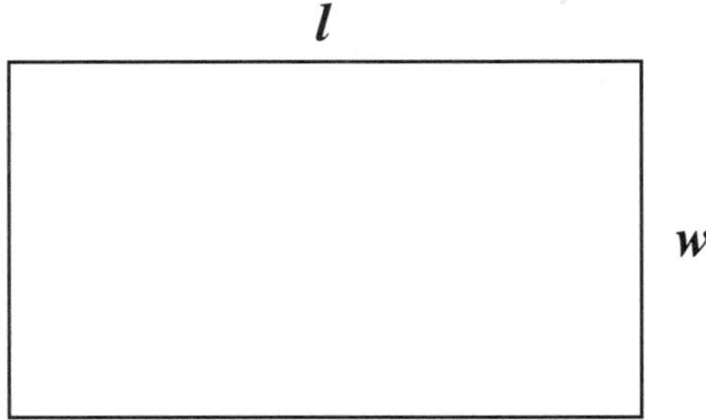

Have students write a formula for the perimeter of the rectangle. Some may write $l + l + w + w = P$; others may write $2(l + w) = P$. Explain that a formula allows them to find the perimeter for any rectangle.

▶ ***Common Misconceptions*** When students try to solve equations such as solving for m in $F = ma$, they may think they are supposed to get a single letter for a solution, because they always got a single number when solving equations previously. Use the examples to help them overcome this misunderstanding.

Solve for m:	Solve for w:
$F = ma$	$A = lw$
$(m = F \div a)$	$(w = A \div l)$

Opportunities to Assess

Observation

Classroom observation is a valuable tool for informal assessment. It helps you determine how to pace your lessons and what to plan for remedial or extension activities. Watch students as they interact with each other and as they work independently. Do they seem confident with the topics in the lesson, or do they seem to be struggling? Jot notes to yourself about your observations. Then, use your notes to help plan for tomorrow's lesson.

Family Involvement

Some family members may not feel confident enough about their understanding of algebra to communicate with your students. Encourage students to play the role of teacher at home. Have students explain to their family members what they learned about the relationship between arithmetic and algebra. This will not only help boost the confidence of the family, but it will also help to reinforce students' understanding of algebra concepts.

Teacher/Student Dialogue

How to Talk About Math

When discussing math topics with students, motivate them to try different solutions and encourage them to explain the reasoning behind their responses.

Teacher: Let's try to solve the equation $14x = 98$. Our goal is to get x all by itself on one side of the equation. How can we get x alone? Hal?
Student: *Get rid of the 14.*

Teacher: How can we get rid of the 14? Remember, whatever you do to one side of an equation you have to do to the other side. Beatriz?
Student: *Subtract 14 from each side?*

Teacher: Let's look at the equation again. What operation is being performed on x?
Student: *Multiplication.*

Teacher: So to undo the multiplication, what must I do?
Student: *Divide?*

Teacher: Yes. Vic, can you tell me why to divide?
Student: *Because division is the "inverse" of multiplication. To "undo" multiplication by 14, you need to divide by 14.*

Teacher: Great. Michi, which side do I divide by 14?
Student: *Don't you divide each side by 14?*

Teacher: Yes. On the left side of the equation, I divide 14 by 14. What is that?
Student: *1.*

Teacher: So I have "$1x$" on the left side of the equation. Is that what I wanted to get on the left?
Student: *Yes. 1x is the same as x. So x equals 98 divided by 14, or 7.*

Visual Aids

Use tables, charts, and posters in this unit and future units to help strengthen students' algebra skills.

	Arithmetic	*Algebra*
Order of Operations	$2 + 3 \cdot 4$ Multiply first. $2 + 12$	$x + y \cdot z$ Multiply first. $x + yz$
Associative Property	$3 + (6 + 1) = (3 + 6) + 1$	$r + (s + t) = (r + s) + t$
Distributive Property	$4(2 + 5) = 8 + 20$	$a(b + c) = ab + ac$

What to do

When

If a lesson doesn't go as well as you had hoped, realize that all teachers have times like these. Reflect back on what you might have done to make the lesson go more smoothly and make notes. If you make a habit of noting what goes well and what doesn't from lesson to lesson, when you have a "rough" lesson, you'll have improvement ideas at hand.

Unit 1 Introduction to Algebraic Thinking

LESSON 1
PAGES 3–4

OBJECTIVE
To identify the mean, median, mode, and range of a set of data

PREREQUISITES
Concepts
- Understand whole-number operations
- Understand scales on a graph

Skills
- Perform computations with whole numbers
- Read scales on a graph

VOCABULARY
mean, median, mode, range, line plot, bar graph, line graph

Whole Numbers and Data

Presenting the Lesson
Introduce the Skill Have students come to the board and write the number of members of their immediate families. Discuss ways they could display this data. Make a line plot of the data on the board. Discuss which typical value (range, mean, median, or mode) is most representative of this population sample.

Check Understanding *At Lincoln Middle School, students were asked which sport was their favorite, and the responses were baseball 108 votes, soccer 79 votes, football 37 votes, basketball 257 votes, and swimming 42 votes. Would you display this data using a line plot, bar graph, or line graph? Explain.* (bar graph, since the categories are not numerical.)

Guided Practice
Have students do exercises 1 and 6 through 8 on pages 3 and 4. Be sure students can read the line graph correctly in order to name the three warmest months.

Independent Practice
Have students complete pages 3 and 4 independently.

Closing the Lesson *What kind of graph might you construct if you recorded the temperature every hour for the next 48 hours and wanted to display your data?* (a line graph, so you could see what happens to the temperature over time)

LESSON 2
PAGES 5–6

OBJECTIVE
To evaluate numerical and algebraic expressions containing whole numbers and decimals

PREREQUISITES
Concepts
- Understand the four basic operations with whole numbers
- Understand the meaning of a variable
- Understand grouping symbols

Skills
- Perform computations with whole numbers

VOCABULARY
variable, evaluate, expression, numerical expression, variable expression

Expressions

Presenting the Lesson
Introduce the Skill Write $3 + (12 - 8)$ and $3 + (12 - n)$ on the board and ask the students, *What kinds of expressions are these?* ($3 + (12 - 8)$ is a numerical expression and $3 + (12 - n)$ is a variable expression.) Ask them how to simplify the first expression.

Check Understanding *To evaluate the expression $16 + 4(9 - 3)$, what would you do first? Explain.* (You would evaluate what is grouped with parentheses first ($9 - 3 = 6$); then, you would multiply 4×6 (24) and add 16 to get 40.)

Guided Practice
Have the students do row 1 and the first exercise in rows 3 and 6 on page 5 and row 7 on page 6. Check that students are substituting for the variables correctly.

Independent Practice
Have students complete pages 5 and 6 independently.

Closing the Lesson *If $m = 6$ and $p = 7$, how would you evaluate $3(m + p)$?* (Substitute 6 for m and 7 for p, add them together, since they are in parentheses, and then multiply by 3, obtaining 39.)

LESSON 3
PAGES 7–8

OBJECTIVE
Use order of operations to simplify numerical and algebraic expressions

PREREQUISITES
Concepts
- Understand the four basic operations with whole numbers
- Understand the meaning of variable
- Understand grouping symbols

Skills
- Perform computations with whole numbers
- Evaluate expressions by substituting for variables

VOCABULARY
order of operations, left to right rule

MATERIALS
Copymasters
Reteach 2, 3, 4, pp. 72–74

Order of Operations

Presenting the Lesson

Introduce the Skill Write *12 − 4 × 2* on the board and have a student evaluate it by performing the operations as they appear left to right (12 − 4 = 8 and 8 × 2 = 16). Have another student evaluate it by multiplying first (4 × 2 = 8 and 12 − 8 = 4). Point out the need to have an agreement about what operations will be done first.

Check Understanding *Who can evaluate 12 ÷ 4 × 3?* (12 ÷ 4 = 3 and 3 × 3 = 9) *Why didn't you multiply first and then divide?* (The left to right rule states you do multiplication and division as they appear left to right.) *How do you evaluate the expression 16 − 4 × 2 + 3?* (4 × 2 = 8, and 16 − 8 = 8 and 8 + 3 = 11)

Guided Practice

Have students do the first exercise in rows 2, 4, 12, and 13 on page 7. In row 4 check that students simplify the parentheses first, and in row 13 be sure they substitute correctly.

Independent Practice

Have students complete pages 7 and 8 independently.

Closing the Lesson *What does the left to right rule mean?* (Possible answer: You do multiplication and division as they appear going left to right, and do addition and subtraction as they appear going left to right.)

LESSON 4
PAGES 9–11

OBJECTIVE
Solve whole-number equations using addition and subtraction

PREREQUISITES
Concepts
- Understand equations
- Understand that addition and subtraction are inverse operations

Skills
- Perform computations with whole numbers

VOCABULARY
equation, inverse operations

MATERIALS
Film container and counters
Overhead projector

Copymasters
Teaching Resource 20, 21 (Equation-building cards), pp. 210–211
Extension 1, p. 177

Solving Addition and Subtraction Equations

Presenting the Lesson

Introduce the Skill On the overhead show 4 cubes and a film container with 5 counters followed by an equal sign. On the other side of the equal sign put 9 counters. Write the equation $b + 4 = 9$ below. Ask students how they might find out how many counters are in the container. (Remove 4 counters from both sides of the equation.) Now, open the container and dump out the 5 counters. Solve several one-step addition and subtraction equations symbolically. Stress that in solving these equations, you "undo" what was done to the variable.

Check Understanding *If you wanted to solve the equation $x - 3 = 5$, what would you do, and why would you do it?* (Add 3 to both sides of the equation, because adding 3 undoes the operation of subtracting 3.)

Guided Practice

Do exercises 1, 5, and 9 on pages 9–11 and have the students check their answers. Check to see that they are doing the correct inverse operations for each problem.

Independent Practice

Have students complete pages 9–11 independently.

Closing the Lesson *What do you do to solve an addition equation?* (Answers will vary: You subtract the number that was added to the variable from each side of the equation.)

LESSON 5
PAGES 12–13

OBJECTIVE
Solve whole-number equations using multiplication and division

PREREQUISITES
Concepts
- Understand equations
- Understand that multiplication and division are inverse operations

Skills
- Perform computations with whole numbers

MATERIALS
Film container and counters
Overhead projector

Copymasters
Teaching Resource 20, 21 (Equation-building cards), pp. 210–211

Solving Multiplication and Division Equations

Presenting the Lesson

Introduce the Skill Put 4 counters in 3 film containers on the overhead with an equal sign and 12 counters on the other side of the equal sign. Write the equation *3n = 12*, and ask your students what they could do to solve the equation. (Make 3 equal groups from the 12 counters. Then, take 1 film container and 4 counters away. Do this twice.) Discuss the idea that division undoes multiplication and vice versa.

Check Understanding *What would you do to solve the equation* $\frac{b}{4} = 8$*?* (Multiply both sides by 4, getting $b = 32$.)

Guided Practice
Have students do the first exercise in rows 1, 4, 5, and 7 on pages 12 and 13. Check to see that they are using the correct inverse operation for each equation.

Independent Practice
Have students complete pages 12 and 13 independently.

Closing the Lesson *What would you do to solve* $\frac{m}{3} = 7$ *and why would you do that?* (Multiply both sides by 3, because multiplying by 3 is the inverse of dividing by 3.)

What is the inverse operation of subtraction? (Addition)

LESSON 6
PAGES 14–15

OBJECTIVE
Use Write an Equation or other strategies to solve problems

PREREQUISITES
Concepts
- Understand variables and equations
- Understand vocabulary related to the four basic operations
- Understand the four steps of problem solving—Understand, Decide, Solve, and Look back

Skills
- Perform computations with whole numbers
- Solve one-step equations
- Translate words into symbols

Problem Solving Strategy: Write an Equation

Presenting the Lesson

Introduce the Strategy Point out that in this lesson students will write equations to solve problems.

Model the Four-Step Problem Solving Process Pose the following problem to the class. *Four friends each paid the same amount to buy a gift for another friend. If they paid a total of $56.00 for the gift, how much did each person pay for the gift?*

- **Understand:** What is known? (4 friends each paid the same amount totaling $56.) What are you trying to find? (How much each person paid)
- **Decide:** How could you solve the problem? (Write an equation and solve it.)
- **Solve:** $4f = 56$, thus dividing both sides by 4 gives $f = 14$
- **Look back:** Does $4 \times 14 = 56$?

Check Understanding *Write an equation to solve this problem. If Mary worked for 17 hours and got paid $102.00, how much did she make each hour?* ($17p = 102$)

Guided Practice
Have the students solve problems 1 and 2 on page 15. Check that they write an equation.

Independent Practice
Have students complete page 15 independently.

Closing the Lesson *Write a problem that could be solved by this equation:* $\frac{m}{3} = 14$. (Solutions will vary: Maria divided her marbles into three groups of 14 each. How many marbles did Maria start with?)

LESSON 7
PAGES 16–18

OBJECTIVE
To review properties of whole numbers and use them in mental computations

PREREQUISITES
Concepts
- Understand the four basic operations
- Understand variables and equations

Skills
- Perform computations with whole numbers

VOCABULARY
commutative, associative, and identity properties for addition and multiplication; zero property of multiplication

MATERIALS
Copymasters
Reteach 5, 6, 7, pp. 75–77

Properties

Presenting the Lesson

Introduce the Skill Ask your students how they could find the following product: 25 × 17 × 4. Show how they could do the computation mentally by first using the commutative property: 25 × (17 × 4) = 25 × (4 × 17) and then the associative property: 25 × (4 × 17) = (25 × 4) × 17. Discuss the properties. Do several problems to illustrate their value and use in doing computations.

Check Understanding *What property is illustrated by (17 + 16) + 24 = 17 + (16 + 24)?* (associative) What property is illustrated by this: 5 × (19 × 4) = 5 × (4 × 19)? (commutative property of multiplication).

Guided Practice

Do the first exercise in rows 1, 8, and 19 on pages 16 and 17. Check that students recognize the properties and that the properties don't hold for subtraction and division.

Independent Practice

Have students complete pages 16–18 independently.

Closing the Lesson *Why is it important to know and be able to use these properties?* (Answers will vary: They help you do computations quickly and easily, even in your head; they simplify the work you may need to do.)

LESSON 8
PAGES 19–21

OBJECTIVE
Use the distributive property in mental computations and to simplify and evaluate expressions

PREREQUISITES
Concepts
- Understand the order of operations with grouping symbols
- Understand variables

Skills
- Perform computations with whole numbers involving grouping symbols
- Simplify and evaluate expressions

VOCABULARY
distributive property of multiplication over addition, distributive property of multiplication over subtraction, like or similar terms

Using the Distributive Property

Presenting the Lesson

Introduce the Skill Put the expression *15 × 17 + 15 × 13* on the board and ask the class to find its value. Have two volunteers come to the board to do it. If both ways [15 × 17 + 15 × 13 = 255 + 195 and 15 × 17 + 15 × 13 = 15 (17 + 13)] were not done, show the class how to do it both ways. Point out the advantage of the second format: 15(17 + 13) = 15(30) = 450. Discuss how to use the property in the multiplication algorithm 7 × 23 = 7 × 3 + 7 × 20, in adding fractions $\frac{1}{5} + \frac{2}{5} = \left(\frac{1}{5}\right) \times (1 + 2)$, when using the addition algorithm by lining up the ones, tens, hundreds, etc., and when simplifying algebraic expressions by adding like terms $3x + 2x = (3 + 2)x$.

Check Understanding *How do you use the distributive property to simplify 6 × 7 + 6 × 93?* [6(7 + 93); 600] *How would you simplify* $3(t - 4) + 5$? [$(3 \cdot t - 3 \cdot 4) + 5$; $3t - 12 + 5$; $3t - 7$]

Guided Practice

Have students do the first exercise in rows 1, 7, 10, 13, and 21 on pages 19–21. Check to see that the students multiply through the expression when simplifying in row 1. Check also to see that students combine like terms in row 21.

Independent Practice

Have students complete pages 19–21 independently.

Closing the Lesson *What are like terms?* (Possible answer: Like terms have the same variable raised to the same power, such as $3t$ and $5t$.) *Is division distributive over addition?* (Answers will vary: No, because $8 \div (4 + 2) \neq 8 \div 4 + 8 \div 2$.)

LESSON 9
PAGES 22–23

OBJECTIVE
Use the order of operations to simplify expressions containing exponents

PREREQUISITES
Concepts
- Understand the order of operations
- Understand variables

Skills
- Perform computations with whole numbers
- Simplify and evaluate expressions

VOCABULARY
exponent, power, base, evaluate powers, factor

Expressions with Exponents

Presenting the Lesson

Introduce the Skill Write on the board $3 \times 3 \times 3 \times 3$, and have someone volunteer to write it using exponents. (3^4) Discuss how 3 is called the base and 4 is called the exponent. Do several more examples like that. Ask students what $5x^3$ means. ($5 \cdot x \cdot x \cdot x$; only the x is cubed.) Have a volunteer come to the board and evaluate $3n^4 - 5$ when $n = 2$. (43) Do a couple of examples like this.

Check Understanding *How could you simplify* $3 \cdot x \cdot x \cdot y \cdot x \cdot y$*?* ($3x^3y^2$) *What does* $2x^2$ *equal if* $x = 3$*?* (18)

Guided Practice

Have students do the first exercise in rows 1, 5, 8, and 10 on pages 22 and 23. Check to see that students are substituting and evaluating correctly in exercises 8 and 10.

Independent Practice

Have students complete pages 22 and 23 independently.

Closing the Lesson *How could you simplify* $y \cdot y \cdot 5 \cdot y \cdot y$*?* ($5y^4$) *What does an exponent tell you?* (how many times the base is used as a factor.)

LESSON 10
PAGES 24–26

OBJECTIVE
Use formulas to compute length, area, and volume of plane or space figures

PREREQUISITES
Concepts
- Understand the four basic operations
- Understand the units of measure for length and area
- Understand variables

Skills
- Perform computations with whole numbers
- Simplify and evaluate expressions

VOCABULARY
perimeter, circumference, formulas, area

MATERIALS
Graph paper

Copymasters
Reteach 8, 9, 10, p. 78

Using Geometric Formulas

Presenting the Lesson

Introduce the Skill Have students draw the following rectangles on their graph paper: 3 by 4, 6 by 2, and 5 by 3. Discuss finding the area of a figure by counting squares. Have the students find the perimeters and areas for those rectangles. Discuss finding the perimeters and areas of common figures through the use of formulas. Ask someone if they can figure an easy way to get the perimeter of a rectangle. ($P = 2\ell + 2w$, where ℓ is length and w is width) How would you find the area of a rectangle? ($A = \ell\, w$)

Discuss the fact that the perimeter of a polygon is the distance around the polygon, so for a triangle add the lengths of the three sides ($P = S_1 + S_2 + S_3$). The area of a triangle is found by thinking of a triangle as half of a rectangle. Thus, $A = \frac{1}{2}\, b \cdot h$. Give the formulas for the circumference (perimeter) of a circle and the area of a circle.

Check Understanding *What is the perimeter of a figure?* (The distance around the figure.) *What is the perimeter of a square with a side measuring 6 cm?* (24 cm) *What is its area?* (36 cm^2)

Guided Practice

Have students do the first exercises in rows 1, 4, 5, and 8 on pages 24–26. Check to see that students use the correct formulas for each problem.

Independent Practice

Have students complete pages 24–26 independently.

Closing the Lesson *If an equilateral triangle has a perimeter of 36 cm, what is the length of one side?* (12 cm) *How did you get that?* (Since an equilateral triangle has 3 equal sides, I divided 36 by 3.)

LESSON 11
PAGES 27–28

OBJECTIVE
Use formulas to translate verbal descriptions into mathematical language

PREREQUISITES
Concepts
- Understand the four basic operations
- Understand variables and formulas

Skills
- Perform computations with whole numbers
- Simplify and evaluate expressions

Problem Solving Application: Using a Formula

Presenting the Lesson

Introduce the Focus of the Lesson Explain to students that in this lesson they will need to decide what formula they can apply to the problem.

Model the Four-Step Problem Solving Process Work through with students the problem of the distance traveled by the baseball on page 27.

Discuss the Problem Solving Tips Point out to students that the four Problem Solving Process steps—Understand, Decide, Solve, and Look back—are listed in the box on page 27. Discuss how formulas save time and effort in solving problems. Make sure students understand that each problem solving step is distinct from the others.

Check Understanding *How would I find the time it took to travel a distance of 18 miles at a rate of 2 miles per hour?* (Use the formula $d = rt$, substitute for d and r, and solve for t.)

Guided Practice

Have students do problems 1 and 2 on page 27.

Independent Practice

Have students complete pages 27 and 28 independently.

Closing the Lesson *In which step of the problem solving process does the use of a formula arise?* (In the second step when deciding on a strategy to solve the problem.) *How do you change a rate from distance per hour to distance per second?* (Multiply by $\frac{1}{3{,}600}$ or divide by 3,600, since there are 3,600 seconds in an hour.)

UNIT 1 REVIEW

Page 29

Item Analysis

Items	Unit Obj.
1–4	1A
5–10	1B
11–13	1C
14–16	1D
17–20	1C
21–22	1E
23	1F

Answers to Unit 1 Review items can be found on page 29 of the Teacher's Annotated Edition.

Administering the Review

This page reviews concepts and skills taught in this unit. Be sure students understand all direction lines. You may want to do the first example in each section cooperatively to ensure understanding.

Scoring Chart

Number Correct	23	22	21	20	19	18	17	16	15	14	13	12
Score	100	96	91	87	83	78	74	70	65	61	57	52

Number Correct	11	10	9	8	7	6	5	4	3	2	1
Score	48	43	39	35	30	26	22	17	13	9	4

After the Review

- The Item Analysis chart on the left shows the Unit 1 objective(s) covered by each test item. This chart can help you determine which objectives need review or extra practice.
- For additional assessment, use the Posttest for Unit 1, Copymaster Book, p. 14.
- To provide extension opportunities, use Copymaster Book, p. 177.

UNIT 1 CUMULATIVE REVIEW

PAGE 30

Item Analysis

Items	Unit Obj.
1–2	1A
3	1B and 1E
4–5	1B and 1D
6	1C

Answers to Cumulative Review items can be found on page 30 of the Teacher's Annotated Edition.

Administering the Review

This page reviews concepts and skills from earlier levels as well as providing practice with standardized test formats. Students may circle their answers, or you may prefer to duplicate and distribute the answer sheet, Copymaster Book, p. 91. This page may be assigned as homework or as classwork.

Test-Taking Tip If a problem seems confusing, relax and reread it.

Scoring Chart

Number Correct	6	5	4	3	2	1
Score	100	83	67	50	33	17

After the Review

The Item Analysis chart on the left shows the unit objective covered by each test item. This chart can help you to determine which objectives need review or extra practice.

Number Theory, Decimals, and Fractions

Vocabulary

composite number A number with three or more factors

greatest common factor (GCF) The greatest number that is a factor of each of two or more numbers

least common multiple (LCM) The least number that is a common multiple of two or more numbers

prime factorization Expressing a number as a product of prime numbers

prime number A whole number greater than 1 that has exactly two factors, itself and 1

reciprocals Two numbers whose product is 1. They are also called multiplicative inverses.

repeating decimal A number whose decimal expression shows a repeating pattern of digits.

terminating decimal The decimal expression of a fraction whose denominator can be written using only powers of 2 and 5.

tree diagram An organized way of listing all the possible outcomes of an experiment

Unit Objectives

2A Add, subtract, and multiply decimals, fractions, and mixed numbers
2B Divide with decimals, fractions, whole numbers, and mixed numbers
2C Use prime factorization to find the greatest common factor and the least common multiple of two or more numbers
2D Write a fraction in simplest form and write equivalent fractions
2E Use properties and order of operations to simplify expressions with decimals and fractions
2F Compare and order decimals, fractions, mixed numbers, and decimals; use Draw a Picture and other strategies to solve problems

About This Unit

The support pages that follow provide more information on prerequisite skills, methods for teaching skills and concepts, daily routines, tips on classroom management and materials, and useful dialogue techniques.

Prerequisite Skills and Concepts

Students should be able to

- find factors and prime numbers.
- find multiples and LCM.

Assessments

Use Beginning of the Year Inventory for entry-level assessment.

Ongoing Evaluation Quick Checks, Reteach Worksheets, the Skills Tutorial Inventories, and the Midyear Test help ensure that students are progressing adequately to meet the standards.

Summative Evaluation Use Test Preps, Unit Review (p. T43), Cumulative Review (p. T44), Reteach Worksheets, and the Computation Skills Tutorial Inventory to assure that students have achieved the standards for the unit.

Diagnosing Errors The Quick Checks highlight common errors and provide remediation. See also the **Teaching Strategies Handbook** pp. T30–T34, where short discussions labeled Common Misconceptions appear as needed with the strategies for key concepts.

Homework and Family Involvement

Home Note In the Student Book, the Dear Family home note provides objectives, vocabulary, and a sample skill discussion for family participation. (**Teaching Strategies Handbook** pages also provide homework and family involvement tips.)

Education Place Refer families to Houghton Mifflin's EduPlace Web site at http://www.eduplace.com; for resources and activities for students at http://www.eduplace.com/math; and additional resources and activities at http://www.eduplace.com/parents.

Helping Your Children Learn Math This book has activities for children ages 5–13 and tips for getting involved in children's mathematics education. (Houghton Mifflin, 1994)

Lessons	Student Pages	Teacher Pages	Resources	State or Local	
				Objectives	Assessment
2.1 Comparing and Ordering Decimals	33–34	T34	Unit 2 Pretest		
2.2 Rounding and Estimating Decimals	35–36	T34	Strand 8, Skill 2		
2.3 Adding and Subtracting Decimals	37–38	T35	Strand 8, Skill 8, 10 Reteach 11		
2.4 Multiplying Decimals and Powers of Ten	39–41	T35	Strand 8, Skill 11		
2.5 Dividing Decimals and Powers of Ten	42–44	T36	Strand 8, Skill 12		
2.6 Prime Factorization, GCF, and LCM	45–46	T36	Strand 5, Skill 6, 9, 11, 12		
2.7 Equivalent Fractions	47–48	T37	Strand 5, Skill 7, 10		
2.8 Equivalent Fractions and Decimals	49–50	T37	Strand 8, Skill 3-6; Extension 2		
2.9 Comparing and Ordering Fractions	51–52	T38	Reteach 12		
2.10 Adding Fractions and Mixed Numbers	53–54	T38	Strand 6A, Skill 1–5		
2.11 Subtracting Fractions and Mixed Numbers	55–56	T39	Strand 6B, Skill 1–6		
2.12 Problem Solving Application: Use a Diagram	57–58	T39			
2.13 Multiplying Fractions and Mixed Numbers	59–61	T40	Strand 7A, Skill 2–6		
2.14 Dividing Fractions and Mixed Numbers	62–64	T40	Strand 7B, Skill 2–6		
2.15 Problem Solving Strategy: Draw a Diagram	65–66	T41			
2.16 Algebra: Expressions with Fractions and Decimals	67–68	T41			
2.17 Algebra: Solving Equations with Fractions and Decimals	69–70	T42	Reteach 13, 14; Unit 2 Posttest		

Teaching Strategies

Math Background — Number Theory, Decimals, and Fractions

Your students should be familiar with set models, area models, and measurement models that show the relationship between the parts and the whole represented by fractions and decimals. At previous levels, students used these models to compare, order, and operate with fractions and decimals. At this level, these topics will be reinforced and then extended to algebraic applications of evaluating expressions and solving equations.

The teaching strategies on these pages focus primarily on fractions. You'll want your students to visualize fraction operations to fully understand the algorithms. Have fraction circles, rectangles, counters, and paper strips on hand as possible models to illustrate fractions concepts. Limit the size of denominators in initial examples. Review connections between the symbolism and the models. It is crucial for students at this level to strengthen their understanding of fractions and fraction symbols and a return to models as needed is important support.

When Students Ask, Why Learn This?
Fractions and decimals grew out of the need to describe parts of wholes. Suggest that students make a list of everyday activities in which they use fractions and decimals. Some possibilities include sports, music, cooking, and carpentry. In addition to daily activities, fractions and decimals are used in many professions such as building, banking, medicine, and science, just to name a few.

A Positive Start
Students should be comfortable with decimal operations but perhaps not with fraction operations. Don't be concerned; this is a common reaction at all levels. To increase your students' conceptual understanding of fractions and decimals, ask them to "think and visualize" before working. Focus attention on lessons 6 and 7. By mastering the concepts in these lessons, students will be well prepared for fraction operations.

Linking Past and Future Learning

You can better focus your instruction this year by being aware of what your students learned last year, and what they will learn at Level 8. Refer to the chart below frequently as you progress through this unit.

Concept/Skills	Last Year	This Year	Next Year
Equivalent Fractions	Rewrite fractions with a common denominator to find equivalent fractions	Use cross multiplication and common denominators to find equivalent fractions	Simplify fractions with polynomials in the numerator and denominator
Operations with Fractions	Add, subtract, multiply, and divide with fractions and mixed numbers	Add, subtract, multiply, and divide with fractions and mixed numbers; understand that a fraction is another way of expressing division	Add, subtract, multiply, and divide rational expressions and functions
Solving Equations with Fractions	Evaluate expressions and equations containing fractions	Evaluate numerical and algebraic expressions and equations containing fractions	Evaluate numerical and algebraic expressions and equations containing rational and irrational numbers

Methods and Management

Get to know your students by finding out their prior knowledge. As you plan your lessons, build on that knowledge using the strategies and tips below.

Teaching Strategy: Equivalent Fractions

Equivalent fractions are fractions that represent the same part of a whole.

- To decide whether two fractions are equivalent, students can use cross multiplication or rewrite both fractions with a common denominator and compare the new numerators.

▶ ***Ask:*** *Is $\frac{24}{42}$ equivalent to $\frac{4}{6}$? How can you find out?*

Have students explain how they found the answer. Some students may check the equivalency by using mental math. This is an acceptable method.

▶ ***Ask:*** *What fraction is equivalent to $\frac{24}{42}$?*

Some students will divide the numerator and denominator by the same number to find an equivalent fraction. Others will multiply the numerator and denominator by the same number to find an equivalent fraction. Students can share with the class their answers and the methods they used to find them.

▶ ***Common Misconception*** The term *reducing* is frequently used to describe the process of finding the simplest form of a fraction. However, this term can be misleading, because the fraction is not actually being reduced in size.

▶ ***Vocabulary Development*** *Simplest form* and *lowest terms* are phrases that can be used interchangeably. A fraction is in simplest form, or lowest terms, when the greatest common factor of the numerator and denominator is 1.

Teaching Strategy: Operations with Fractions

Everyone can make mistakes with fraction operations. What's important is for students to recognize their mistakes. Encourage them to use estimation to check the reasonableness of their answers.

▶ ***Ask:*** *When you add $\frac{2}{3}$ and $\frac{1}{4}$, will the sum be more or less than 1?*

When you divide 12 by $\frac{1}{2}$, will the quotient be more or less than 12?

If students have difficulty answering these questions, have volunteers draw number lines on the board. The rest of the class can offer suggestions on how to set up the number lines.

▶ ***Common Misconception*** The most common misconception about multiplying and dividing fractions is that "multiplication makes bigger" and "division makes smaller," when in fact the opposite is true. Show students several examples like the following to correct this misconception.

$$6 \div \frac{1}{2} = 12 \qquad 12 > 6$$

$$8 \times \frac{1}{2} = 4 \qquad 4 < 8$$

Teacher Tips

Management Meeting the individual needs of every student is never easy. But there are things that you and your students can do to meet this challenge. Have students of different abilities work together in small groups. This will give the students who are strong in math the opportunity to help other students. Encourage advanced students to take on projects such as developing alternative methods for teaching math topics or researching interdisciplinary math connections. This will give you more time to spend with students who need your individual attention.

Good Routine For lessons 9 through 14, begin each class with a quick warm-up on equivalent fractions. Have student volunteers lead the warm-up.

Real-Life Have students think of real-life situations that can be represented by equivalent fractions; for example, 6 out of 12 eggs is equivalent to $\frac{1}{2}$ dozen eggs, 45 out of 60 minutes is equivalent to $\frac{3}{4}$ of an hour. Invite a music teacher or a music student to speak to the class about how fractions are used in music.

Helpful Hints Keep one part of the board available for students to record math tips they think might be helpful to other students. You may want to have students vote for their favorite "Tip of the Week."

Good Routine Have student volunteers present a real-life problem solving situation to the class at the end of each lesson. For example: *How much flour is needed to triple a recipe that requires $\frac{3}{4}$ cup?*

Flexibility If you feel that your students are falling behind in this unit or any other unit, be flexible. Ignore your lesson plans for the day and take time to review previously taught skills.

Materials Students can use graph paper to solve equations with fractions. This will help them better organize their written work.

Connecting Encourage students to always try to apply what they already know to new concepts. For example, the rules for solving equations with fractions are the same as the rules for solving equations with whole numbers.

Reasoning Ask students to explain the reasoning behind their answers. This will benefit all of the students in the class and will help you refocus your questions as needed. If students seem to be confused by a question, you may need to use a simpler question that leads to the same concept. Using visual aids, when possible, can help to illustrate your question. Draw a diagram, or write the question on the board.

Teaching Strategy: Solving Equations with Fractions

Students at this level need to develop the idea that a fraction is another way of expressing division.

▶ ***Show This:*** $\frac{x}{4} = 12$

Point out that the symbol ÷ stands for "divided by." Read the sentence as *"x divided by 4 equals 12."*

- Explain why $\frac{1}{4} \cdot x = \frac{x}{4}$.

▶ ***Show This:*** $\frac{1}{4} \cdot x = \frac{x}{4}$

$\frac{1}{4} \cdot \frac{x}{1} = \frac{1x}{4}$, or $\frac{x}{4}$

- Ask students to make up other examples like the ones shown above and share them with the class.

▶ ***Common Misconception*** Some students may write $\frac{1}{4} \cdot x$ as $\frac{1}{4} \cdot \frac{1}{x}$.

Reinforce the concept that $1x$ is equivalent to x with examples such as the following:

$a = 1a$

$1y = y$

Opportunities to Assess

Observation

Go beyond marking students' answers right or wrong. Look for error patterns. This takes more time now, but it will greatly benefit the students and save time and mistakes in the future.

Homework

Have each student bring a recipe to school that includes ingredients measured in fractional units. Have each student exchange their recipe with a classmate and find the amount of ingredients needed to double, triple, or halve the recipe.

Family Involvement

Send notes home to alert family members of error patterns in student work. This can be a gentle reminder that a student needs help with a particular concept. Family members can then be on the lookout for the error when they help with homework or provide tutoring.

Teacher/Student Dialogue

How to Encourage Student Participation

When students are given the opportunity to verbalize math concepts, they are better able to stay focused on the lesson.

Teacher: Let's solve the equation $\frac{3}{4} \cdot x = 12$. Who has an idea of how to solve this?
Student: *Divide both sides of the equation by $\frac{3}{4}$.*

Teacher: Explain why you think that's the way to go, Sean.
Student: *Because x is being multiplied by $\frac{3}{4}$ and dividing by $\frac{3}{4}$ would reverse that.*

Teacher: Does everyone agree with Sean?
Students: *Yes.*

Teacher: What is $\frac{3}{4}$ divided by $\frac{3}{4}$?
Student: *I'm not sure.*
Student: *Ugh, I don't know.*

Teacher: I'll write it out on the board from left to right the way you're used to seeing it: $\frac{3}{4} \div \frac{3}{4}$. Dyna?
Student: *Now I get it.*

Teacher: Noel? How do you divide $\frac{3}{4}$ by $\frac{3}{4}$?
Student: *Multiply $\frac{3}{4}$ by $\frac{4}{3}$.*

Teacher: Melissa, can you finish that for us?
Student: *You'd get $\frac{12}{12}$, or 1.*

Teacher: So class, what do you have on the left side of the equation now?
Students: *1x.*

Teacher: And what does 1*x* equal?
Students: *x.*

Teacher: So you have what you need on the left side. What do you need to do on the right-hand side?
Student: *Divide 12 into $\frac{3}{4}$.*

Teacher: Be careful. You need to divide $\frac{3}{4}$ into 12. I think you knew what you were supposed to do, but you're saying it backwards. I'll write it on the board. It should be $12 \div \frac{3}{4}$. Class, finish it at your seats.

What to do

Everyday

Involve as many students as possible in class discussions. Don't just rely on the students who always raise their hands. Call on other students for their opinions about a topic. Even if they don't know the answer, their comments can lead the discussion in the right direction.

What to do

When

If students don't do homework assignments or turn in homework assignments late, spend a few minutes speaking to the whole class about what your expectations are. Explain assignments clearly and write the assignment on the board along with the due date.

Unit 2 Number Theory, Decimals, and Fractions

LESSON 1
PAGES 33–34

OBJECTIVES
To compare and order decimals

PREREQUISITES
Concepts
- Understand decimals
- Understand what "greater than" and "less than" mean and the symbolism for both

Skills
- Read and write decimals
- Understand how to order whole numbers

VOCABULARY
compare

MATERIALS
Copymasters
Teaching Resource 9 (Hundredths Square)

Comparing and Ordering Decimals

Presenting the Lesson

Introduce the Skill Write a decimal such as *2.38* on the board and ask the students how to read the decimal. Ask them how to write the decimal "two and forty-three thousandths." Write the decimal *34.582* and ask them what digit is in the hundredths place, tens place, thousandths place. Do this for several more decimals.

Ask students which is greater, 238 or 85. Confirm that 238 is greater because the first number has two hundreds and the second has zero hundreds. Say that the same is true when comparing decimals. Do this for a set of four decimals such as 0.25, 0.5, 0.2, and 0.52.

Check Understanding *Who can read these two decimals to me: 4.38 and 0.894?* (four and thirty-eight hundredths and eight hundred ninety-four thousandths) *Which of them is greater and how do you know that?* (4.38 because $0.894 < 1$)

Guided Practice

Have students complete the first exercise in rows 1, 4, and 10 on pages 33 and 34. Check that students are starting from the left when comparing place values.

Independent Practice

Have students complete pages 33 and 34 independently.

Closing the Lesson *What are some real-life uses for decimals?* (Answers will vary: Possible answers: money, measuring distances, measuring time, batting averages)

LESSON 2
PAGES 35–36

OBJECTIVE
To round and estimate with decimals

PREREQUISITES
Concepts
- Round whole numbers to the nearest unit

Skills
- Read and write decimals

VOCABULARY
round, estimation

MATERIALS
Copymasters
Teaching Resource 9 (Hundredths Square), p. 199

Skills Tutorial
Strand 8: Skill 2

Rounding and Estimating Decimals

Presenting the Lesson

Introduce the Skill Draw a number line showing 0.2480, 0.2481, . . . 0.2489, 0.2490 with equally spaced intervals. Ask someone to write where 0.24848 would go on the number line. Ask the class whether it is nearer to 0.248 than to 0.249. Do this for several more examples. Do some examples that involve rounding with money.

Check Understanding *If I round 2.483 to 2.5, to what place would I have rounded?* (tenths) *To what place would I have rounded if I had written 2.48?* (hundredths)

Guided Practice

Have your students do the first exercise in each section on pages 35 and 36. Check that students are rounding the numbers in the correct place value.

Independent Practice

Have students complete pages 35 and 36 independently.

Closing the Lesson *Can you think of some times when you might need to round decimals?* (Answers will vary: When calculating averages like batting averages and field goal averages, when dividing two numbers that do not have a simple quotient, or when estimating distances to the nearest tenth of a meter.)

LESSON 3
PAGES 37–38

OBJECTIVE
To add and subtract decimals

PREREQUISITES
Concepts
- Rounding a decimal to the nearest whole number

Skills
- Adding whole numbers

VOCABULARY
vertical form (for an addition exercise)

MATERIALS
Copymasters
Reteach 11, p. 81

Skills Tutorial
Strand 8: Skill 2, Practice 1–4
Skill 10, Practice 1–3

Adding and Subtracting Decimals

Presenting the Lesson

Introduce the Skill Ask students to round the sum of 2.71 and 5.23 (8) Explain that to find the exact sum, you would put them into the **vertical form** with their decimal points **lined up.** To subtract 2.05 from 5.6, show students how to write a zero at the end of 5.6, then subtract. Do several more examples.

Check Understanding *How do you add 5.47 to 3.8?* (Check that students write a zero in the empty column and can explain why.) *What is the difference between 7.23 and 2.579?* (4.651) *What do you need to do in order to subtract decimals?* (Line up the decimal points.)

Guided Practice Have your students do the first exercise in rows 1, 3, 5, and 8 on pages 37 and 38. Check to see that the students are lining up the decimal points correctly.

Independent Practice Have students complete pages 37 and 38 independently.

Closing the Lesson *Why is estimating first a good idea?* (It gives you a way to check if your answer is reasonable.) *When in real life would you add or subtract two decimals?* (Answers will vary: When you are working with money and you need to add or subtract, as with a check book, or when computing distances using the odometer of a car.)

LESSON 4
PAGES 39–41

OBJECTIVE
To multiply with decimals and powers of ten

PREREQUISITES
Concepts
- Multiplication
- Finding the area of rectangles

Skills
- Multiplication of whole numbers

MATERIALS
Overhead transparency

Copymasters
Teaching Resource 9 (Hundredths Squares)

Skills Tutorial
Strand 8: Skill 11

Multiplying Decimals and Powers of Ten

Presenting the Lesson

Introduce the Skill Use a transparency of hundredths squares and ask the students: If the whole grid represents one, what would one row represent? What would one square represent? Mark off a square which is 0.6 long and 0.6 wide. What is the area of the square? After having done this for a couple of rectangles, lead into the algorithm for multiplying decimals.

If the area of an 8 cm x 14 cm rectangle is 112 cm^2 what would be the area of an 0.8 cm x 1.4 cm rectangle? (1.12 cm^2)

Check Understanding *Who can explain how to multiply 5.8 by 0.43?* (Have student come to the board and explain.)

Guided Practice

Have students do the first exercise in each of the sections on pages 39–41. Check that students are placing their decimal points correctly.

Independent Practice

Have students complete pages 39–41 independently.

Closing the Lesson *How is multiplying decimals similar to multiplying whole numbers? How is it different?* (Possible answer: First, you multiply the numbers just like whole numbers but then you must place the decimal point in the product.)

LESSON 5
PAGES 42–44

OBJECTIVE
To divide with decimals and powers of 10

PREREQUISITES
Concepts
- Division

Skills
- Division of whole numbers

MATERIALS
Overhead transparency

Copymasters
Teaching Resource 9 (Hundredths Squares)

Dividing Decimals and Powers of Ten

Presenting the Lesson

Introduce the Skill Using an overhead transparency with hundredths squares, ask students how you could divide 0.48 evenly into three groups. Show them how to divide 0.48 by 3 using the algorithm for division. Tell them the key idea is to line up the decimal point in the quotient with the decimal point in the dividend.

Check Understanding *If you divide 3.67 by 8, is your answer greater than one? Explain.* (Since $8 > 3.67$ the quotient is less than 1.) *What do you do to divide a number by 100?* (You move the decimal point in the dividend two places to the left.)

Guided Practice

Have students do the first exercise in each section on pages 42–44. Check that students are placing their decimal points correctly.

Independent Practice

Have students complete pages 42–44 independently.

Closing the Lesson *When might you want to divide a decimal by a whole number or by a power of 10?* (Answers will vary: When you are writing metric measurements using other metric units or when doing unit pricing and comparative shopping.)

LESSON 6
PAGES 45–46

OBJECTIVE
To use prime factorization to find the GCF and LCM of two or more numbers

PREREQUISITES
Concepts
- Division
- Factors
- Multiples

Skills
- Factor a number

VOCABULARY
prime number, composite number, prime factorization, tree diagram

MATERIALS
Skills Tutorial
Strand 5: Skills 6 and 9
Strand 8: Skills 11 and 12

Prime Factorization, GCF, and LCM

Presenting the Lesson

Introduce the Skill Show students how to factor 36 using a factor tree or tree diagram. Point out that no matter how you start to factor the number, it will break down to the same factors. Have students find the prime factorization of 56 using a tree diagram.

Ask the students if they remember what is meant by the greatest common factor and the least common multiple of two numbers. Find the GCF for 24 and 36 by writing the prime factorization of the numbers and picking out the factors which are in common. Find also the LCM for 24 and 36 by examining the prime factorization of the numbers. Do both processes for 20 and 24 and one or two other pairs of numbers.

Check Understanding *How can you find the GCF of 40 and 24?* (Factor the two numbers into prime factors, and then select all the factors in common.) *What is the LCM of 40 and 24?* (120)

Guided Practice

Have the students do the first exercise in each section on pages 45 and 46. Check that students are factoring the numbers correctly and finding the LCM and GCF correctly.

Independent Practice

Have students complete pages 45 and 46 independently.

Closing the Lesson *When would you ever use the GCF or LCM of two numbers?* (Answers will vary. GCF: when simplifying fractions, and LCM: when finding a common denominator)

LESSON 7
PAGES 47–48

OBJECTIVE
To simplify fractions and write equivalent fractions

PREREQUISITES
Concepts
- Greatest common factor

Skills
- Multiplication of whole numbers

VOCABULARY
equivalent fractions, simplest form

Equivalent Fractions

Presenting the Lesson

Introduce the Skill Give students several examples like $\frac{3}{4} = \frac{?}{12}$. Ask them what the denominator was multiplied by to obtain an equivalent fraction; then, have them multiply the numerator by the same number to obtain an equivalent fraction. Illustrate how to simplify a fraction like $\frac{12}{16}$ by dividing the numerator and denominator by the GCF of 12 and 16, namely 4, to obtain an equivalent fraction of $\frac{3}{4}$.

Check Understanding *Can someone name me a fraction equivalent to* $\frac{3}{5}$*?* $\left(\frac{12}{20}\right)$ *Who could simplify* $\frac{18}{30}$ *for me?* $\left(\frac{3}{5}\right)$

Guided Practice

Have students do the first exercise in each section on pages 47 and 48. Check that students are multiplying or dividing the numerator and denominator by the same number to get equivalent fractions.

Independent Practice

Have students complete pages 47 and 48 independently.

Closing the Lesson *What are equivalent fractions?* (fractions that name the same value.) *How do you find equivalent fractions?* (Multiply or divide the numerator and denominator by the same whole number.)

LESSON 8
PAGES 49–50

OBJECTIVE
To write equivalent fractions and decimals

PREREQUISITES
Concepts
- Fractions
- Decimals

Skills
- Dividing by a whole number

VOCABULARY
terminating decimal, repeating decimal

MATERIALS
Copymasters
Extension 2, p. 178

Equivalent Fractions and Decimals

Presenting the Lesson

Introduce the Skill Take the fractions $\frac{3}{4}$ and $\frac{5}{12}$ and write each as a decimal. Point out that $\frac{3}{4}$ terminates and that $\frac{5}{12}$ repeats. Have the students do a few of these. Then, have a student explain how to do each one. Show students how to write a terminating decimal as a fraction by writing the digits over the appropriate power of ten. For example, $0.48 = \frac{48}{100}$. Have the students do a few of these at their desks. Ask students which is greater, 0.6 or $\frac{2}{3}$, or are they equal? Tell them they could change 0.6 into $\frac{6}{10}$ and $\frac{2}{3}$ into $\frac{6}{9}$. Thus, since $\frac{1}{9} > \frac{1}{10}$, $\frac{6}{9} > \frac{6}{10}$.

Check Understanding *What would 0.235 become when written as a fraction?* $\left(\frac{235}{1000}\right.$, which could be simplified as $\left.\frac{47}{200}\right)$

Guided Practice

Have students work the first exercise in rows 1, 4, and 7 on pages 49 and 50. Check that they are writing fractions as decimals correctly and vice versa.

Independent Practice

Have students complete pages 49 and 50 independently.

Closing the Lesson *Why is it important to be able to change fractions to decimals and vice versa?* (Answers will vary: You may need to change from one to the other to make computation simpler.)

LESSON 9
PAGES 51–52

OBJECTIVE
To compare and order fractions

PREREQUISITES
Concepts
- Understand how to rewrite fractions with a common denominator
- Understand the meaning of the symbols $=$, $>$, and $<$

Skills
- Know basic multiplication and division facts
- Find a common multiple of two numbers
- Write equivalent fractions

VOCABULARY
comparing fractions, ordering fractions

MATERIALS
Copymasters
Reteach 12, p. 82

SKILLS TUTORIAL
Strand 5: Skills 7 and 10
Strand 8: Skills 3 and 4

Comparing and Ordering Fractions

Presenting the Lesson

Introduce the Skill Ask students to find which is greater, $\frac{2}{3}$ or $\frac{3}{4}$, without looking at models. Review with students how to find a common denominator and write equivalent fractions for $\frac{2}{3}$ and $\frac{3}{4}$ to show which is greater.

Check Understanding *Which is greater, $\frac{2}{3}$ or $\frac{3}{5}$?* ($\frac{2}{3}$ is greater because when you use common denominators, $\frac{2}{3} = \frac{10}{15}$ and $\frac{3}{5} = \frac{9}{15}$.)

Guided Practice

Have students do the first exercise in rows 1 and 7 on pages 51 and 52. Check that they are finding a common denominator correctly.

Independent Practice

Have students complete pages 51 and 52 independently.

Closing the Lesson *Why are common denominators important?* (Answers will vary but might include the following: You need them to add and subtract fractions.)

LESSON 10
PAGES 53–54

OBJECTIVE
To add fractions and mixed numbers

PREREQUISITES
Concepts
- Understand the meaning of equivalent fractions
- Understand the meaning of mixed numbers

Skills
- Write equivalent fractions
- Simplify fractions and mixed numbers

Adding Fractions and Mixed Numbers

Presenting the Lesson

Introduce the Skill Write the fractions $\frac{3}{8}$ and $\frac{1}{3}$. Explain that in order to add these two fractions, we must have the same denominators. Change $\frac{3}{8}$ to $\frac{9}{24}$ and $\frac{1}{3}$ to $\frac{8}{24}$. Now, the denominators are the same size, so we can add the numerators and get $\frac{17}{24}$. Continue by adding two mixed numbers: $3\frac{1}{6} + 5\frac{1}{3}$. Mention how it is often easier to add the whole number parts first; then, add the two fractional parts. Do several examples of this.

Check Understanding *What is the first step in adding $\frac{1}{3}$ and $\frac{3}{5}$?* (Find the LCD (15) and change $\frac{1}{3}$ to $\frac{5}{15}$ and $\frac{3}{5}$ to $\frac{9}{15}$.) *What do we do if the sum of the fractions is greater than one?* (Write it as a mixed number, reducing the fraction to its simplest form.)

Guided Practice

Have students do the first exercise in rows 2 and 5 on pages 53 and 54. Check that students are finding common denominators before adding.

Independent Practice

Have students complete pages 53 and 54 independently.

Closing the Lesson *How do you add mixed numbers with different denominators?* (Find the LCD, write equivalent fractions with the LCD as denominator, add the fractions, add the whole numbers, and simplify if necessary.)

LESSON 11
PAGES 55–56

OBJECTIVE
To subtract fractions and mixed numbers

PREREQUISITES
Concepts
- Understand the meaning of equivalent fractions
- Understand the meaning of mixed numbers

Skills
- Write equivalent fractions
- Simplify fractions and mixed numbers

Subtracting Fractions and Mixed Numbers

Presenting the Lesson

Introduce the Skill Illustrate how to subtract $\frac{1}{4}$ from $\frac{5}{6}$ by finding common denominators and subtracting the numerators. When subtracting mixed numbers, if students need to regroup, this can be done by taking 1 from the whole number part and rewriting it as a fraction with the appropriate denominator.

Check Understanding *How do you subtract $2\frac{3}{4}$ from $5\frac{1}{6}$?* (Rewrite $5\frac{1}{6}$ as $4\frac{14}{12}$, and $2\frac{3}{4}$ as $2\frac{9}{12}$. Then, subtract the fractions from one another and the whole numbers from one another.)

Guided Practice

Have students work the first exercise in rows 2 and 5 on pages 55 and 56. Check that students are finding common denominators correctly.

Independent Practice

Have students complete pages 55 and 56 independently.

Closing the Lesson *When might you need to subtract mixed numbers or fractions?* (Answers will vary: When you are finding the difference between two measures such as lengths, heights, or times.)

LESSON 12
PAGES 57–58

OBJECTIVE
To draw a number line and locate the position of fractions, mixed numbers, and decimals

PREREQUISITES
Concepts
- Number line
- Venn diagrams
- Understanding of problem solving

Skills
- Add and subtract decimals and fractions

Problem Solving Application: Using a Diagram

Presenting the Lesson

Introduce the Focus of the Lesson Explain to students that in this lesson they will need to use a diagram that can be applied to the problem.

Model the Four-Step Problem Solving Process Set up the problem on page 57 about four friends living on the same avenue that is a straight path.

Discuss the Problem Solving Tips Point out to students that the four Problem Solving Process steps—Understand, Decide, Solve, and Look back—are listed in the box on page 57. Make sure students understand that each problem solving step is distinct from the others.

Check Understanding *Why is drawing a diagram a good strategy?* (Answers will vary: It helps you visualize what is given and what you need to find.)

Guided Practice

Have students try problem 5 on page 58. Have them draw a picture of each route.

Independent Practice

Have students complete pages 57 and 58 independently.

Closing the Lesson *When do you think it would be a good time to use a diagram?* (Answers will vary: When a lot of information is given and you need to visualize it in order to solve the problem.)

LESSON 13
PAGES 59–61

OBJECTIVE
To multiply fractions and mixed numbers

PREREQUISITES
Concepts
- Understand that multiplying fractions is finding a fraction of a fraction

Skills
- Know basic multiplication and division facts
- Write a mixed number as an improper fraction
- Simplify fractions

MATERIALS
Skills Tutorial
Strand 6A: Skills 1–5
Strand 6B: Skills 1–5
Strand 7A: Skills 1–5

Multiplying Fractions and Mixed Numbers

Presenting the Lesson

Introduce the Skill Point out how in multiplying fractions, the product is always less than either of the two factors. When working with mixed numbers, students will need to change the mixed numbers to improper fractions before multiplying. Show them how simplifying before they multiply will save them a lot of work.

Check Understanding *How can you simplify* $\frac{2}{3} \times \frac{15}{22}$ *before multiplying?* (Divide out 2 from 2 and 22. Divide out 3 from 3 and 15, leaving $\frac{1}{1} \times \frac{5}{11} = \frac{5}{11}$.)

Guided Practice

Have students work the first exercise in rows 1 and 7 on pages 59 and 60. Show how simplifying can be used in exercise 7.

Independent Practice

Have students complete pages 59–61 independently.

Closing the Lesson *Explain how to multiply two mixed numbers.* (Change the mixed numbers to improper fractions, simplify if possible, multiply the numerators, multiply the denominators, and simplify if needed.)

LESSON 14
PAGES 62–64

OBJECTIVE
To divide fractions and mixed numbers

PREREQUISITES
Concepts
- Understand multiplication of fractions
- Understand the relationship between multiplication and division

Skills
- Write a reciprocal
- Multiply whole numbers and fractions

VOCABULARY
reciprocal

Dividing Fractions and Mixed Numbers

Presenting the Lesson

Introduce the Skill Ask a volunteer to write the division sentence $\frac{6}{8} \div \frac{3}{8}$ on the board and show how multiplying by the reciprocal of the divisor will give the answer. Have the students divide several other pairs of fractions by multiplying by the reciprocal. Show students that to divide two mixed numbers, they need to write each mixed number as an improper fraction; then, write the reciprocal and multiply.

Check Understanding *What is the meaning of 20 ÷ 5?* (How many 5's are in 20? Answer: 4) *What is the meaning of* $\frac{3}{4} \div \frac{2}{5}$*?* (How many $\frac{2}{5}$'s are in $\frac{3}{4}$? Answer: $1\frac{7}{8}$)

Guided Practice

Have students work the first exercise in rows 1, 7, and 11. Make sure students multiply by the reciprocal of the divisor, not the dividend.

Independent Practice

Have students complete pages 62–64 independently.

Closing the Lesson *How do you divide a mixed number by a mixed number?* (Write each mixed number as an improper fraction and then write a multiplication sentence using the reciprocal of the divisor. Remember to simplify, if possible, before multiplying. Simplify the result also, if possible.)

LESSON 15
PAGES 65–66

OBJECTIVE
To use the strategy of drawing a diagram or other strategies to solve problems

PREREQUISITES
Concepts
- The four-step process of solving a problem—Understand, Decide, Solve, and Look back

Skills
- Add, subtract, multiply, and divide whole numbers, fractions, and decimals

Problem Solving Strategy: Draw a Diagram

Introduce the Strategy Point out that in this lesson students will draw diagrams to help them solve problems.

Model the Four-Step Problem Solving Process Present the problem of finding out how many different rectangles you can make by placing 12 toothpicks end-to-end.

- **Understand** Make sure students understand how the perimeter, but not the shape, of the rectangle is determined by the number of toothpicks.
- **Decide** Note how soon students realize that you don't need to use actual toothpicks and that diagrams will do.
- **Solve** Emphasize the importance of an organized approach so that a definite solution emerges.
- **Look back** Make a table of the dimensions of all the possible rectangles.

Check Understanding *In the problem solving steps, what does the step "Decide" mean?* (Decide on a method you will use to solve the problem.)

Guided Practice
Have the students try problem 3. Check whether they are using the rectangle that was divided into eighths. If not, suggest how they might use it.

Independent Practice
Have students complete pages 65 and 66 independently.

Closing the Lesson *When might you want to use this strategy?* (Answers will vary: When there are many possibilities and drawing a picture will help you organize those possibilities, or when geometric figures or measurements are involved.)

LESSON 16
PAGES 67–68

OBJECTIVE
Use order of operations to simplify algebraic expressions containing decimals and fractions

PREREQUISITES
Concepts
- Understand the use of grouping symbols
- Evaluating algebraic expressions involving whole numbers

Skills
- Know basic addition, subtraction, multiplication, and division facts
- Square a whole number

VOCABULARY
order of operations

Expressions with Fractions and Decimals

Presenting the Lesson
Introduce the Skill Write the expression: $\left(\frac{4}{5}\right)^2 - \frac{3}{10} \times \frac{2}{5}$. Ask, What operations are used in this expression? (multiplication, subtraction, and squaring) What grouping symbols are used? (parentheses) Work through the example demonstrating the correct order of operations.

Check Understanding *What is the function of parentheses in an expression?* (Parentheses tell you to perform the operation within parentheses first.)

Guided Practice
Have students work the first exercise in rows 1 and 5 on pages 67 and 68 and compare answers.

Independent Practice
Have students complete pages 67 and 68 independently.

Closing the Lesson *In what order are the operations to be done in an expression?* (Work in parentheses, simplify powers, multiply and divide in order from left to right, add and subtract in order from left to right.)

LESSON SUPPORT

LESSON 17
PAGES 69–70

OBJECTIVE
Solve one-step equations containing decimals and fractions using all four operations

PREREQUISITES
Concepts
- Equations
- Properties of equality

Skills
- Solving one-step linear equations involving whole numbers
- Add, subtract, multiply, and divide fractions and decimals

MATERIALS
Copymasters
Reteach 13,14, pp. 83–84

SKILLS TUTORIAL
Strand 7B: Skills 1–5

Solving Equations with Fractions and Decimals

Presenting the Lesson

Introduce the Skill Remind students of how they solved equations involving whole numbers in Unit 1. List the properties of equality. Put the equation $n + \frac{2}{5} = \frac{3}{4}$ on the board and ask them how you could solve it. $\left(\text{Subtract } \frac{2}{5} \text{ from both sides.}\right)$ Ask how to simplify the right hand side. (Find a common denominator and subtract.) Do a few more similar examples. Do some that involve multiplying or dividing both sides of the equation by the same number.

Check Understanding *In the equation $x - 5.3 = 8.25$, what should you do to solve it?* (Add 5.3 to both sides and simplify.) *What should you do to solve the equation $\left(\frac{3}{4}\right)p = 6$?* (Multiply both sides by $\frac{4}{3}$ and simplify.)

Guided Practice

Have the students do the first exercise in rows 1 and 5 on pages 69 and 70. Check to see that they are solving the equations by using the inverse operation and that they are applying the operation to both sides of the equation.

Independent Practice

Have students complete pages 69 and 70 independently.

Closing the Lesson *What is the secret to solving one-step linear equations?* (Apply the inverse operation to both sides of the equation and simplify.)

UNIT 2 REVIEW

Page 71

Item Analysis

Items	Unit Obj.
1–12	2A
13–15	2B
16–18	2C
19–21	2D
22	2E, 2F

Answers to Unit 2 Review items can be found on page 71 of the Teacher's Annotated Edition.

Administering the Review

This page reviews concepts and skills taught in this unit. Be sure students understand all direction lines. You may want to do the first example in each section cooperatively to ensure understanding.

Scoring Chart

Number Correct	22	21	20	19	18	17	16	15	14	13	12
Score	100	95	91	86	82	77	73	68	64	59	55

Number Correct	11	10	9	8	7	6	5	4	3	2	1
Score	50	45	41	36	32	27	23	18	14	9	5

After the Review

- The Item Analysis chart on the left shows the Unit 2 objective(s) covered by each test item. This chart can help you determine which objectives need review or extra practice.
- For additional assessment, use the Posttest for Unit 2, Copymaster Book, p. 16.
- To provide extension opportunities, use Copymaster Book, p. 178.

UNIT 2 CUMULATIVE REVIEW

PAGE 72

Item Analysis

Items	Unit Obj.
1	2A and 2F
2	2A and 1A
3	2B
4	1D
5	1F
6	2E
7	2D

Answers to Cumulative Review items can be found on page 72 of the Teacher's Annotated Edition.

Administering the Review

This page reviews concepts and skills from earlier units as well as providing practice with standardized test formats. Students may circle their answers, or you may prefer to duplicate and distribute the answer sheet, Copymaster Book, p. 191. This page may be assigned as homework or as classwork.

Test-Taking Tip Use mental math or estimation to check answers for reasonableness.

Scoring Chart

Number Correct	7	6	5	4	3	2	1
Score	100	86	71	57	43	29	14

After the Review

The Item Analysis chart on the left shows the unit objective covered by each test item. This chart can help you to determine which objectives need review or extra practice.

Teacher Notes

Measurement

Unit Objectives

3A Measure length, area, volume, capacity, mass, and temperature in both metric and customary systems

3B Change from one unit of length, area, volume, capacity, mass, weight, or time to a larger or smaller unit within a measurement system

3C Identify needed information in problems; use Make a Table and other strategies to solve problems

About This Unit

The support pages that follow provide more information on prerequisite skills, methods for teaching skills and concepts, daily routines, tips on classroom management and materials, and useful dialogue techniques.

Prerequisite Skills and Concepts

Students should be able to

- read and use a ruler to mm.
- read a thermometer in both scales (match picture with appropriat temperature).

If not, use prerequisite Reteach Worksheets 15 and 16.

Assessments

Use Beginning of the Year Inventory for entry-level assessment.

Ongoing Evaluation Quick Checks, Reteach Worksheets, the Skills Tutorial Inventories, and the Midyear Test help ensure that students are progressing adequately to meet the standards.

Summative Evaluation Use Test Preps, Unit Review (p. T57), Cumulative Review (p. T58), Reteach Worksheets, and the Computation Skills Tutorial to assure that students have achieved the standards for the unit.

Diagnosing Errors The Quick Checks highlight common errors and provide remediation. See also the **Teaching Strategies Handbook** pp. T48–T51, where short discussions labeled Common Misconceptions appear as needed with the strategies for key concepts.

Homework and Family Involvement

Home Note In the Student Book, the Dear Family home note provides objectives, vocabulary, and a sample skill discussion for family participation. (**Teaching Strategies Handbook** pages also provide homework and family involvement tips.)

Education Place Refer families to Houghton Mifflin's EduPlace Web site at http://www.eduplace.com; for resources and activities for students at http://www.eduplace.com/math; and additional resources and activities at http://www.eduplace.com/parents.

Helping Your Children Learn Math This book has activities for children ages 5–13 and tips for getting involved in children's mathematics education. (Houghton Mifflin, 1994)

Lessons	Student Pages	Teacher Pages	Resources	State or Local Objectives	State or Local Assessment
3.1 Metric Units of Length	75–76	**T52**	Unit 3 Pretest; Reteach 17		
3.2 Metric Units of Capacity and Mass	77–78	**T52**	Reteach 18		
3.3 Metric Units of Area and Volume	79–80	**T53**	Reteach 19; Extension 3		
3.4 Problem Solving Application: Too Much or Too Little Information	81–82	**T53**			
3.5 Customary Units of Length	83–84	**T54**	Reteach 20		
3.6 Customary Units of Capacity and Weight	85–86	**T54**	Reteach 21		
3.7 Customary Units of Area and Volume	87–88	**T55**	Reteach 22		
3.8 Algebra: Temperature and Line Graphs	89–90	**T55**	Reteach 23		
3.9 Time	91–92	**T56**	Reteach 24		
3.10 Problem Solving Strategy: Make a Table	93–94	**T56**	Unit 3 Posttest		

Teaching Strategies

Math Background — Measurement

Measurement originally used natural, nonstandard units. Length was measured by the width of a finger or hand span. Mass was based on the weight of a grain of wheat. Units of measurement have now been standardized. The United States has adopted the customary system. Most other countries, as well as the scientific and industrial communities in the United States, have adopted the metric system. The metric system is based on powers of 10, which allow for easy conversion from one unit to another.

The metric system uses the basic units of meter, gram, and liter and forms other units by using powers of 10. It is now the official system of almost every country. The United States uses the customary system officially, but many people use the metric system so that their work is compatible internationally.

When Students Ask, Why Learn This?
Most objects around us are standardized by measurement—the sizes of windows, beds, cartons and other containers; the length and width of rooms, stairs, ramps, and so forth. Students usually recognize the need for measurement skills. However, they may want to know why they need to know two systems of measure. Ask students how many of them have family members who work in medicine, science, or companies that buy or sell products internationally. These jobs usually require using both measurement systems.

A Positive Start
The study of measurement allows students to integrate math in other disciplines such as science, geography, and art. As students use units of measurement, graph temperatures, calculate elapsed time, and solve measurement problems, they will be reviewing their fraction and decimal skills.

Linking Past and Future Learning

What do students already know about measurement? Plan your instruction based on what students have already learned and targeted toward what they will need to know.

Concept/Skills	Last Year	This Year	Next Year
Metric Measurement	Measure length, mass, and capacity in the metric system and write measurements using different units	Write equivalent metric measures of length, mass, capacity, area, and volume	Solve problems of length, mass, capacity, area, and volume involving metric measurement
Customary Measurement	Measure length and write measurements of length, mass, and capacity in different customary units	Write equivalent customary measures of length, capacity, weight, area, and volume; understand and use precision in measurement	Solve problems of length, mass, capacity, area, and volume involving customary measurement
Temperature and Time	Calculate elapsed time; determine equivalent times for different time zones; use Celsius and Fahrenheit scales	Determine equivalent times for different time zones; use a 24-hour clock; write equivalent Celsius and Fahrenheit temperatures	Plot functions of temperature and time in a scatter plot

Methods and Management

Planning ahead establishes goals and ensures that all essential content will be included in your lessons. Daily planning in conjunction with unit planning will help you determine the best sequence in which to introduce the material. Once you have a plan, stay flexible. Plans can and should change when students need more time on a topic.

Teaching Strategy: Metric Measurement

To write measurements using other units, students need to know how to order metric units of measurement from greatest to smallest units: kilometer, hectometer, decameter, meter, decimeter, centimeter, and millimeter.

▶ **Ask:** *How would you write a measurement using a smaller unit? What would you multiply by? To write a measurement using a greater unit, would you multiply or divide?*
Point out how powers of 10 are used.

▶ **Ask:** *How would you write 0.9 kilometers in meters? How would you write 12 centimeters in decameters?*
Work with students to find the answers. Ask student volunteers to demonstrate their solutions on the board. Use mistakes or omissions as teaching opportunities.

- Avoid overemphasizing formulas. Plugging numbers into formulas does not involve students in actual measuring and thereby defeats the purpose of developing measurement understanding.

▶ ***Vocabulary Development*** Learning the meanings of the metric prefixes will facilitate students' understanding of the metric system. Ask students questions like *What would we mean by a "kilodollar"?* or relate prefixes to common computer usage, such as the meaning of the word *kilobyte*, and the recent habit of classified ads of stating salary figures in the form 50K.

Teaching Strategy: Customary Measurement

There are times when precision in measurement is not important, and phrases such as *a little less than 4 feet* are appropriate. There are other times, when precision is necessary, and smaller units of measurement need to be used. Smaller units of measurement make possible a greater degree of precision.

▶ **Ask:** *Which measurement is more precise: $3\frac{1}{4}$ in. or $3\frac{3}{8}$ in.?*
What range of measures would be reported as $3\frac{1}{4}$ in.? $3\frac{3}{8}$ in.?
The more precise measure is $3\frac{3}{8}$ in. Lengths between $3\frac{1}{8}$ and $3\frac{3}{8}$ would be reported as $3\frac{1}{4}$ in.; lengths between $3\frac{5}{16}$ and $3\frac{7}{16}$ would be reported as $3\frac{3}{8}$ in. Use a number line divided into eighths to illustrate this concept.

▶ **Say:** *Here are a few examples of when precision is important. Which unit of measurement would you use to make each of these measurements? How precise would the measurement be?*

- *your height*
- *the weight of a newborn baby*
- *the time it takes the winner of the Boston Marathon to complete the race*

Teacher Tips

Visual Aid Put this reminder on the board. Encourage students to copy it so they will have it for reference when they're doing homework.
- To write a metric measurement using a smaller unit, multiply by a power of 10.
- To write a metric measurement using a unit to a larger unit, divide by a power of 10.

Visual Aid II Students may have difficulty remembering the order of the metric units. Hang a paper strip showing the order from greatest to smallest in your classroom.

Pacing Plan on spending more time studying the metric system than the customary system of measurement. The customary system is familiar to students and will be mastered easily.

Daily Routine At the beginning of each class, have a student point to an object in the room and estimate its length, mass, or volume. Then have another student find the actual measurement.

Developing Concepts To introduce the concept of area, have students approximate the area of their handprints or footprints on graph paper.

Hands-On Have students bring boxes of different sizes to school and put them in order, based on their best estimate, from greatest volume to least volume. Then have them find the actual volume of each box. They may be surprised by the results!

Connections Students will find an interdisciplinary unit on time and clocks interesting. Have them research types of clocks. Then have students make a clock of their choice. Some good possibilities include a sundial, pendulum, or sand clock.

Every Day Have students name the time they participate in different daily activities using a 24-hour clock. Vary the activities from day to day. Some possibilities include having dinner, going to a friend's house, and going to soccer practice.

Special Project Have students research the history of time-keeping in different cultures. Books, magazines, and the Internet are great resources for information.

Teaching Strategy: Temperature and Time

In Europe and in the military, time is measured using a 24-hour clock, with no repeating hours for A.M. and P.M. The day begins at 0000, which is 12:00 A.M.., or midnight. It ends at 2400 hours, or midnight again. 9:00 A.M. is 900 hours, noon is 1200 hours, 3:00 P.M. is 1500 hours, and so on.

- Have students work in groups to make 24-hour analog clocks with hour hands and minute hands. Have them notice the difference between this clock and a standard 12-hour clock when reading minutes. Encourage them to find the generalization: Divide the number by 2 and multiply by 5. For example when the minute hand points to 16, it is $(16 \div 2) \times 5$ or 40 minutes past the hour. Then have them use their clocks to answer questions similar to the following.

▶ ***Ask:*** *What time is 8:00 P.M. on a 24-hour clock? What time is 11:45 A.M. on a 24-hour clock?*

▶ ***Ask:*** *What time is 3 hours after 11:00 P.M. on a 24-hour clock? What time is 9 hours after 4:00 P.M. on a 24-hour clock?*

▶ ***Common Misconception*** Finding elapsed time is easy on a 24-hour clock. But students may experience difficulty finding elapsed time on a standard 12-hour clock. Allow for extra time on this topic when you do your lesson plans.

Opportunities to Assess

Observation

Assessment involves more than a student's ability to demonstrate mastery of skills. It also involves the student's ability to reason, think logically, and analyze problems. By monitoring the progress of your students in these areas, you can better tailor your instructional methods and questioning techniques to meet your students' individual needs.

Homework

Have students measure the length and width of any room in their home, then draw a floor plan of the room on graph paper, showing the location of doors, windows, etc. Display their drawings on a bulletin board in the classroom.

Family Involvement

Encourage students to solicit the help of family members with their homework assignment. In doing so, families will be aware of what the student is studying in school, and will feel involved in the educational process.

Teacher/Student Dialogue

How to Introduce a Lesson

Getting students involved and motivated from the start will help the lesson run smoothly.

Teacher: When you measure area, you are finding how many units will cover a surface. If you were to measure the area of the floor in this room using square units, would you use big squares or small squares and explain why. Marta?

Student: *Big squares, because small squares would take too long and probably not be accurate.*

Teacher: How big? What would the dimensions of your square be?

Student: *A yard on each side.*

Teacher: That's what is called a square yard. Everyone, write down an estimate for the number of square yards it would take to cover this floor. *(Students write their estimates)* How did you find your estimate? Lance?

Student: *I estimated the number of yards across and down the room. Then I multiplied.*

Teacher: Any other methods? Elena, you first, then Yokio.

Student: *I estimated the number of square yards that would fit in each part of the room. Then I added the square yards together.*

Student: *I just counted the number of square yards I thought would fit.*

Teacher: Those are all good solutions. Let's measure the room and see how close your estimates are. *(Student volunteers measure the room and compare their estimates to the actual estimates.)*

Questioning Techniques

Teachers tend to ask questions that have very specific answers, such as, *What is the area of this figure?* To obtain more information about your students' understanding of concepts, probing and more open-ended questions are needed, such as, *Can someone explain how to find the area of this room?* After the first response, you can continue to assess other students' understanding by asking *Does anyone else have a suggestion?*

What to do

Every Day

Students can use an instrument of their own design to record the daily precipitation over a given period of time. Have a guest meteorologist talk to the class about how to obtain precise measurements. Graph the data and compute daily and weekly averages. If there is little or no precipitation at this time of year in the area where you live, have students choose a location they would like to follow, and use the newspaper or Internet for precipitation data.

What to do

When

A student is not paying attention. Make eye contact to get the students' attention, or simply stand by the students' chair as you proceed with the lesson. These silent gestures are often enough to get the student back on task.

Unit 3 Measurement

LESSON 1
PAGES 75–76

OBJECTIVE
To use multiplication or division to write metric measures using other metric units

PREREQUISITES
Concepts
- Understand the size and relationships of linear metric units
- Understand decimals

Skills
- Multiply and divide decimals by powers of 10

MATERIALS
Centimeter ruler

Metric Units of Length

Presenting the Lesson

Introduce the Skill Make a table like the one in your text on page 75 on a transparency and put that on the overhead projector. Discuss each of the categories: the unit of measure, its symbol, its relation to a meter, and some familiar approximations with each unit. Mention common instances of a mm (thickness of a dime), cm (thickness of a finger), and m (height of a doorknob above the floor). When having students do conversions, stress that multiplying by 10 moves the decimal point one place to the right and dividing by 10 moves it one place to the left.

Check Understanding *A line segment measures 58 cm. How many millimeters is that?* (580) *About how thick is a dime?* (1 mm) *How many meters are there in a kilometer?* (1,000) *What portion of a meter is a centimeter?* (0.01)

Guided Practice
Have students do exercises 1, 5, 11, and 13 on pages 75 and 76. Check to see that students select reasonable units to measure the objects in number 1.

Independent Practice
Have students complete pages 75 and 76 independently.

Closing the Lesson *What would be an appropriate metric unit with which to measure the length of the school building?* (meters) *How many centimeters is 3.64 m?* (364 cm)

LESSON 2
PAGES 77–78

OBJECTIVE
To review metric units of capacity and mass, and use multiplication or division to change from larger to smaller units or vice versa

PREREQUISITES
Concepts
- Understand powers of 10
- Understand relationships of metric units
- Understand the size and relationships of metric units of mass and capacity

Skills
- Multiply and divide by powers of 10

Metric Units of Capacity and Mass

Presenting the Lesson
Introduce the Skill Show the students how much a liter is, then have them estimate how much various containers (mayonnaise jar, frozen orange juice can, teaspoon, etc.) will hold. Fill the containers and measure what they hold using a kitchen measuring cup.

Check Understanding *If a fishtank held 5 L of water, how many mL of water does it hold?* (5,000 mL) *If a metric ton is 1,000 kg, how many kilograms is 4.32 metric tons?* (4,320 kg)

Guided Practice
Do exercises 1, 3, and 7 on pages 77 and 78. Check that students correctly change to other units in exercises 3 and 7.

Independent Practice
Have students complete pages 77 and 78 independently.

Closing the Lesson *A container has a capacity of n liters. How many kL is that?* ($\frac{n}{1,000}$) *An object has a mass of n milligrams. How many cg is that?* ($\frac{n}{10}$ cg)

LESSON 3
PAGES 79–80

OBJECTIVE
To review metric units of area and volume, and use multiplication or division to change from larger to smaller units or vice versa

PREREQUISITES
Concepts
- Understand area and volume
- Understand relationship of metric units

Skills
- Multiply and divide by powers of 10

MATERIALS
A cubic decimeter
A cubic centimeter

Copymasters
Teaching Resource 6 (Centimeter Squared Paper)
Reteach 17–19, pp. 87–89
Extension 3, p. 179

Metric Units of Area and Volume

Presenting the Lesson

Introduce the Skill Ask the class what they would multiply by to write square meters as square centimeters. (10,000) Stress that when changing metric units of area, they must multiply or divide by 100 instead of 10, since area has two dimensions. Ask them what they would multiply or divide by to change from one metric unit of volume to another, such as cubic meters to cubic decimeters. (Multiply by 1,000) Stress that when working with units for volume, you are counting three dimensions.

Check Understanding *A floor has an area of 14 m^2. How many square centimeters is that?* (140,000 cm^2) *A refrigerator has a volume of 1,800 dm^3. How many cubic meters is that?* (1.8 m^3)

Guided Practice
Have students do the first exercise in rows 1, 3, 6, and 9 on pages 79 and 80.

Independent Practice
Have students complete pages 79 and 80 independently.

Closing the Lesson *Why do we multiply by 100 when changing from a larger unit of area to the next smaller unit of area?* (It takes 100 of the smaller area units to make the next larger area unit.) *A cubic meter has how many cubic centimeters in it?* (1,000,000)

LESSON 4
PAGES 81–82

OBJECTIVE
To identify information needed to solve problems

PREREQUISITES
Concepts
- Understand the four-step problem solving process
- Understand operations with rational numbers

Skills
- Perform computations with rational numbers

Problem Solving Application: Too Much or Too Little Information

Presenting the Lesson

Introduce the Focus of the Lesson Explain to students that in this lesson they will need to decide whether there is enough information, or maybe unnecessary information, in the statement of the problem.

Model the Four-Step Problem Solving Process Work through the problem on page 81 with your students.

Discuss the Problem Solving Tips Point out to students that the four Problem Solving Process steps—Understand, Decide, Solve, and Look Back—are listed in the box on page 81. Ask for volunteers to read the tips aloud. Make sure students understand the purpose of each step.

Check Understanding *Can you solve the following problem, and if not, why not? "A 16-ounce bag of candy costs $2.49, and a smaller bag of candy costs only $1.79. Which bag is the better buy?"* (You need to know how many ounces the second bag contains before you can determine the better buy.)

Guided Practice
Have students do problems 1 and 2 on page 81.

Independent Practice
Have students complete pages 81 and 82 independently.

Closing the Lesson *How can you know whether a problem has too little or too much information?* (Read the problem very carefully.)

LESSON 5
PAGES 83–84

OBJECTIVE
To review customary units of length, and use multiplication or division to change from larger to smaller units or vice versa

PREREQUISITES
Concepts
- Understand relationships of customary units

Skills
- Multiply and divide whole numbers, fractions, and mixed numbers

MATERIALS
$\frac{1}{16}$-inch rulers for all students
Blank piece of paper

Customary Units of Length

Presenting the Lesson

Introduce the Skill Have students draw a line segment that is $1\frac{5}{16}$ inches long and another that is $3\frac{3}{4}$ long. Have them swap with their neighbors and check their work. Review changing from inches to feet and yards, feet to yards, and feet and yards to miles. Discuss how in the customary system they do not use a base of ten. Remind them that if, in adding and subtracting linear distances measured in inches and feet, they need to regroup, there are 12 inches in one foot. Have a volunteer subtract 2 ft 9 in. from 5 ft 2 in. Do several similar examples.

Check Understanding *Into how many equal parts is each inch divided on your ruler?* (16) *How many $\frac{1}{16}$-inches are in $\frac{1}{4}$ inch?* (4) *How many feet are in 4 yards?* (12 feet)

Guided Practice

Have students do the first exercise in rows 1, 3, 6, and 9 on pages 83 and 84. Check that when, in rows 3 and 6, they regroup linear measures, that they regroup in 12s.

Independent Practice

Have students complete pages 83 and 84 independently.

Closing the Lesson *From a board measuring 9 ft 3 in., you need to cut off a piece 2 ft 8 in. long and another that is 4 ft 10 in. How much of the original board will be left?* (1 ft 9 in.)

LESSON 6
PAGES 85–86

OBJECTIVE
To review customary units of capacity and weight, and use multiplication or division to change from larger to smaller units or vice versa

PREREQUISITES
Concepts
- Understand the relationship between customary units of capacity and weight

Skills
- Multiply and divide whole numbers

MATERIALS
Measuring containers with various capacities

Customary Units of Capacity and Weight

Presenting the Lesson

Introduce the Skill Have a student fill a measuring cup with water and pour it into a pint container and repeat this until the pint container is full. Have other students show, in a similar manner, the relationships among the units of capacity. Make a chart similar to the one in the pupil's text based on the class work. Write the equivalent measures of weight on the board. Add two weights involving ounces and pounds: 2 lb 10 oz + 4 lb 9 oz = 7 lb 3 oz. Mention that fluid ounces used in measuring capacity are different from the ounces used in measuring weights.

Check Understanding *Which is greater, 10 quarts or 2 gallons?* (10 quarts, because it equals $2\frac{1}{2}$ gallons) *If a truck weighed $4\frac{1}{4}$ tons, how many pounds would it weigh?* (8,500 pounds)

Guided Practice

Have students do row 1, exercises 5–8, and exercises 5 and 14 or page 85. Check that students are adding correctly in exercise 18.

Independent Practice

Have students complete pages 85 and 86 independently.

Closing the Lesson *How many cups are in a gallon?* (16) *If a gallon of a certain fluid weighed 24 pounds, how much would one pint of that fluid weigh?* (Since there are 8 pints in a gallon, then one pint would weigh $\frac{24}{8} = 3$ lb.)

LESSON 7
PAGES 87–88

OBJECTIVE
To review customary units of area and volume, and use multiplication or division to change from larger to smaller units or vice versa

PREREQUISITES
Concepts
- Understand area
- Understand relationship of customary units
- Understand the relationship between units of volume

Skills
- Multiply and divide whole numbers, fractions, and mixed numbers

MATERIALS
Copymasters
Reteach 20–22, pp. 90–92

Customary Units of Area and Volume

Presenting the Lesson

Introduce the Skill Ask a student to draw a square about a foot on each side on the board and to label the sides 12 in. Then write the area of the square in square inches. (144 in.^{2}) Ask, *If a rectangle had an area of 3 ft^2, how many square inches would it be?* (432 in.^{2}) Ask, *What would you have to multiply by to write square yards as square feet?* (9) Do two exercises involving cubic measures. Discuss why the measures are in cubic units for volume (three dimensions) and in square units for area (two dimensions).

Check Understanding *If a refrigerator has a volume of 12 ft^3, is that more or less than the volume of refrigerator with a volume of $1\frac{1}{2}$ yd^3? Explain.* (Since 1 yd^3 = 27 ft^3, then $1\frac{1}{2}$ yd^3 = $40\frac{1}{2}$ ft^3, so the second refrigerator is much larger.)

Guided Practice

Do the first exercise in rows 1, 3, 6, and 9 on pages 87 and 88. In doing row 3 make sure students divide, and when doing exercise 9 make sure they multiply.

Independent Practice

Have students complete pages 87 and 88 independently.

Closing the Lesson *The price of linoleum at Dad's Floors is \$1.30 per ft^2, and the price for the same linoleum at The Floor Store is \$12.50 per yd^2. Which is the better buy? Explain.* (Dad's Floors: \$1.30 per ft^2 × 9 ft^2 per yd^2 = \$11.70 per yd^2)

LESSON 8
PAGES 89–90

OBJECTIVE
To learn to rewrite Celsius temperatures in Fahrenheit units and vice versa

PREREQUISITES
Concepts
- Understand systems for measuring temperature

Skills
- Read scales and graphs

VOCABULARY
Celsius and Fahrenheit scales
Line graph

Temperature and Line Graphs

Presenting the Lesson

Introduce the Skill Draw a big thermometer on the board. Ask students what temperatures they know about. As they mention things like water freezing at 32° Fahrenheit, put a mark on the thermometer and write the temperature down next to it. Ask for the corresponding temperature in degrees Celsius. Discuss the rules for approximating Fahrenheit temperatures from Celsius temperatures, and vice versa. Show a line graph of the stock market for the last week. Ask questions about the line graph, such as what was the highest point it reached, when did it drop the most from one day to the next, etc.

Check Understanding *The high temperature reported for Sydney today was 34°C. About how much is that in degrees Fahrenheit?* (98°) *If you were given a temperature in degrees Fahrenheit, what would you do to get an approximation in degrees Celsius?* (Subtract 30 and divide by 2.)

Guided Practice

Have students do rows 1, 5 and 8 on pages 89 and 90. Check that they are reading the line graph correctly in exercise 8.

Independent Practice

Have students complete pages 89 and 90 independently.

Closing the Lesson *When is a line graph a good graph to use?* (Possible answer: when you want to show a trend over time)

LESSON 9
PAGES 91–92

OBJECTIVE
To understand the relationships of time zones, and the use of a 24-hour clock

PREREQUISITES
Concepts
- Understand relationships of the units of time

Skills
- Perform the four basic operations with rational numbers

MATERIALS
Map with time zones for United States

Copymasters
Reteach 23–24, pp. 93–94

Time

Presenting the Lesson

Introduce the Skill Show students how to find the number of seconds in $3\frac{1}{2}$ minutes, hours in 4 days, days in 6 weeks, etc. Then show them a map of the United States with the four time zones indicated. Discuss the fact that the time is earlier by one hour as you move west through each time zone and later by one hour as you move east. Ask students questions such as, *"If it is 6:00 A.M. in Boston, what time is it in Denver?"* Discuss how, in the 24–hour system, A.M. times are between 0000 and 1200 and P.M. times are between 1200 and 2400. Ask, *If it is 1400, what time is it using the 12-hour clock?* (2:00 PM)

Check Understanding *Using a 24-hour clock, what time is it if it is 4:30 P.M.?* (1630)

Guided Practice

Have students do rows 1 and 11 and the first exercise in rows 17 and 19 on pages 91 and 92.

Independent Practice

Have students complete pages 91 and 92 independently.

Closing the Lesson *How would you calculate how many minutes are in 3 weeks?* (3 weeks = 21 days = 504h = 30,240 min)

LESSON 10
PAGES 93–94

OBJECTIVE
To use Make a Table or other strategies to solve problems

PREREQUISITES
Concepts
- Understand the four-step process of solving a problem

Skills
- Read a table
- Perform computations with rational numbers

Problem Solving Strategy: Make a Table

Presenting the Lesson

Introduce the Strategy Point out that in this lesson students will make a table to help them solve problems.

Model the Four-Step Problem Solving Process Present the problem on page 93.

- **Understand** Help students realize that it's not immediately obvious from the "raw" data what the answer to each question is.
- **Decide** Emphasize the basic purpose of the table.
- **Solve** Point out that totalling each column gives the three-year record.
- **Look Back** To find the best year, compute the percent of games won.

Check Understanding *What role does a table play in solving problems?* (Possible answer: It helps you organize the information so that you can see a pattern between the variables.)

Guided Practice

Have students do problem 1 on page 94. Have them look for common differences between the terms in the table.

Independent Practice

Have students complete pages 93 and 94 independently.

Closing the Lesson *Can you think of places where tables are used to display information?* (Possible answer: Sports data often appear in tables.)

UNIT 3 REVIEW

Page 95

Item Analysis

Items	Unit Obj.
1–3	3A
4–25	3B
26–28	3A
29–30	3C

Answers to Unit 3 Review items can be found on page 95 of the Teacher's Annotated Edition.

Administering the Review

This page reviews concepts and skills taught in this unit. Be sure students understand all direction lines. You may want to do the first example in each section cooperatively to ensure understanding.

Scoring Chart

Number Correct	30	29	28	27	26	25	24	23	22	21	20	19	18	17	16
Score	100	97	93	90	87	83	80	77	73	70	67	63	60	57	53

Number Correct	15	14	13	12	11	10	9	8	7	6	5	4	3	2	1
Score	50	47	43	40	37	33	30	27	23	20	17	13	10	7	3

After the Review

- The Item Analysis chart on the left shows the Unit 3 objective(s) covered by each test item. This chart can help you determine which objectives need review or extra practice.
- For additional assessment, use the Posttest for Unit 3, Copymaster Book, p. 18.
- To provide extension opportunities, use Copymaster Book, p. 179.

UNIT 3 CUMULATIVE REVIEW

PAGE 96

Item Analysis

Items	Unit Obj.
1	3A
2	3A
3	3B
4	3B
5	2A, 2B
6	1E
7	1A
8	2E
9	2E

Answers to Cumulative Review items can be found on page 96 of the Teacher's Annotated Edition.

Administering the Review

This page reviews concepts and skills from earlier units as well as providing practice with standardized test formats. Students may circle their answers, or you may prefer to duplicate and distribute the answer sheet, Copymaster Book, p. 191. This page may be assigned as homework or as classwork.

Test-Taking Tip To be sure you're on track when performing a complex task, reread the directions after making your first calculations.

Scoring Chart

Number Correct	9	8	7	6	5	4	3	2	1
Score	100	89	78	67	56	44	33	22	11

After the Review

The Item Analysis Chart on the left shows the unit objective covered by each test item. This chart can help you to determine which objectives need review or extra practice.

Teacher Notes

Ratios, Proportions, and Percents

Vocabulary

cross products In a proportion $\frac{a}{b} = \frac{c}{d}$, the cross products are ad and bc. If these products are equal, the proportion is correct.

direct proportion A relationship between two quantities such that both increase simultaneously.

inverse proportion A relationship between two quantities such that as one quantity increases, the other decreases.

rate A comparison by division of unlike quantities

ratio A comparison of two like quantities using division

scale drawing An enlargement or reduction of a picture in which each distance is in the same proportion as the corresponding distance in the original.

scale factor The ratio in a scale drawing that compares the scale drawing dimensions to the actual dimensions

unit price The cost of a single unit of an item

unit rate A rate whose second term is a single unit

Unit Objectives

4A Write the ratio of two quantities in simplest form
4B Write and solve proportions
4C Use direct and indirect proportion to compute rates
4D Use proportions to read and make scale drawings
4E Write fractions and decimals as percents
4F Write percents as fractions and decimals
4G Use fractions, decimals, and percents to estimate and solve problems
4H Use dimensional analysis to check reasonableness; use Work Backward and other strategies to solve problems

About This Unit

The support pages that follow provide more information on prerequisite skills, methods for teaching skills and concepts, daily routines, tips on classroom management and materials, and useful dialogue techniques.

Prerequisite Skills and Concepts

Students should be able to

- know the meaning of a percent.
- write ratios as fractions.

Assessments

Use Beginning of the Year Inventory for entry-level assessment.

Ongoing Evaluation Quick Checks, Reteach Worksheets, the Skills Tutorial Inventories, and the Midyear Test help ensure that students are progressing adequately to meet the standards.

Summative Evaluation Use Test Preps, Unit Review (p. T72), Cumulative Review (p. T73), Reteach Worksheets, and the Computation Skills Tutorial to assure that students have achieved the standards for the unit.

Diagnosing Errors The Quick Checks highlight common errors and provide remediation. See also the **Teaching Strategies Handbook** pp. T62–T65, where short discussions labeled Common Misconceptions appear as needed with the strategies for key concepts.

Homework and Family Involvement

Home Note In the Student Book, the Dear Family home note provides objectives, vocabulary, and a sample skill discussion for family participation. (**Teaching Strategies Handbook** pages also provide homework and family involvement tips.)

Education Place Refer families to Houghton Mifflin's EduPlace Web site at **http://www.eduplace.com**; for resources and activities for students at **http://www.eduplace.com/math**; and additional resources and activities at **http://www.eduplace.com/parents**.

Helping Your Children Learn Math This book has activities for children ages 5–13 and tips for getting involved in children's mathematics education. (Houghton Mifflin, 1994)

Lessons	Student Pages	Teacher Pages	Resources	State or Local	
				Objectives	Assessment
4.1 Ratios	99–100	**T66**	Unit 3 Pretest; Strand 9, Skill 1		
4.2 Algebra: Unit Rates	101–102	**T66**	Strand 9, Skill 6		
4.3 Algebra: Solving Proportions	103–104	**T67**	Strand 9, Skill 3		
4.4 Algebra: Direct Proportion	105–106	**T67**			
4.5 Algebra: Inverse Proportion	107–108	**T68**			
4.6 Problem Solving Application: Is the Answer Reasonable?	109–110	**T68**			
4.7 Scale Drawing	111–113	**T69**	Reteach 25–27; Extension 4		
4.8 Percents, Decimals, and Fractions	114–116	**T69**	Strand 10, Skills 6–7		
4.9 Fractional and Decimal Percents	117–118	**T70**	Strand 10, Skills 3-4		
4.10 Percents Greater than 100%	119–120	**T70**	Strand 10, Skills 3, 4, 5, 7		
4.11 Estimating with Fractions, Decimals, and Percents	121–122	**T71**	Reteach 28		
4.12 Problem Solving Strategy: Work Backward	123–124	**T71**	Unit 4 Posttest		

Teaching Strategies

Math Background — Ratios, Proportions, and Percents

In previous levels, students have gradually developed proportional reasoning skills. Proportional reasoning is a way of thinking that involves the ability to compare ratios and produce equivalent ratios. This thinking is a shift from much of the work done previously this year. The focus with these concepts is on the relationship between numbers, not the numbers themselves.

When Students Ask, Why Learn This?
Proportional reasoning skills will help students solve problems. Whenever students compare quantities, they are using proportional reasoning skills. They encounter ratios and proportions in many different forms and in many different contexts—"three for a dollar," "twice as far," "half as much," "feet per second," and "seconds per minute." Ask students to consider a statement such as, "Four out of five dentists recommend it." The specific number of dentists involved is unknown, but the relationship between the number of dentists that recommend it to the total number of dentists is known. Explain to students that with proportional reasoning, they can make conclusions about the recommendation.

A Positive Start
Ratio, proportion, and percent should be taught as connected ideas. This connection will enhance your students' understanding of the concepts. Activities should focus on these concepts in familiar contexts, such as comparison pricing and using scales on maps.

Linking Past and Future Learning

Link students' prior knowledge to what they'll learn about ratios, rates, and percents. Note how the concepts in the unit support what students have already learned about proportional reasoning and what they'll learn next year.

Concept/Skills	Last Year	This Year	Next Year
Ratios	Find and write equal ratios; use equal ratios to solve problems using scale drawings	Write ratios in three ways; write rates as ratios and find unit rates; write equal ratios	Name simple trigonometric ratios
Proportions	Write and solve proportions; use the Cross Product Property; determine if a proportion is true	Write and solve proportions; solve problems involving direct and inverse proportions	Solve direct and inverse variations
Percents	Show the relationship among fractions, decimals, and percents; use percent as a factor to calculate interest	Show the relationship among fractions, decimals, and percents; locate on a number line	Show percents as rational numbers; use in estimation, computation, and application

Methods and Management

New teachers are often learning or relearning some of the mathematics right along with their students. Every now and then, you may work through a problem with your students without necessarily knowing the right answer. Show students that you are not afraid to explore new mathematical situations, and model perseverance as you work your way through solution steps.

Teaching Strategy: Ratios

A ratio is a comparison by division between two like or similar quantities.

- A ratio can be a comparison of one part to another part, such as comparing the number of cups of raisins in a recipe to the number of cups of nuts in the same recipe.
- A ratio can also be a comparison of a part to the whole, such as comparing the square footage of the lakes in a state park to the square footage of the entire state park.
- Ratios are expressed as *a* to *b*; *a*:*b*; or $\frac{a}{b}$.

▶ ***Ask:*** *If a basketball team is made up of two forwards, two guards, and one center, what is the ratio of forwards to centers? What is the ratio of guards to all players? Suppose two basketball teams are on a court. What is the ratio of all players to centers? What is the ratio of guards to forwards?*

Point out that because a ratio can be expressed as a fraction, finding equivalent ratios is similar to finding equivalent fractions. Demonstrate on the board the relationships among teams and players.

▶ ***Vocabulary Development*** A *rate* is a comparison by division of quantities measured in two different units. When expressing rates, the word *per*, meaning "for each," is often used. For example, the ratio of calories burned to hours of running is 210 calories to 1 hour, or "210 calories per hour."

▶ ***Common Misconceptions*** Students should be comfortable expressing ratios that compare a part to the whole. They may find expressing ratios that compare one part to another part more challenging. If this happens, encourage students to name the parts and the whole before writing the ratio.

Teaching Strategy: Proportions

A proportion is an equation which states that two ratios are equal.

- Finding one number in a proportion, when given the other three, is called solving a proportion. Begin by having students solve a proportion in a problem solving setting: *Jim walked 4 miles in 60 minutes. At the same rate, how many miles will he walk in 90 minutes?*

▶ ***Show This:*** $\frac{4 \text{ miles}}{x \text{ miles}} = \frac{60 \text{ minutes}}{90 \text{ minutes}}$

▶ ***Ask:*** *What does x represent? How can we find the value of x?*

Write each step on the board as students describe how to cross-multiply to solve a proportion.

$$\frac{4}{x} = \frac{60}{90} \quad \Rightarrow \quad \begin{aligned} 4 \cdot 90 &= 60 \cdot x \\ 360 &= 60x \\ \frac{360}{60} &= \frac{60x}{60} \\ 6 &= x \end{aligned}$$

He will walk 6 miles.

Teacher Tips

Prior Planning Before you begin this unit, collect articles or clippings from newspapers and magazines that mention ratios, proportions, or percents. After a few lessons, have students look for examples. Use examples to generate problem solving situations.

Good Routine At the start of class, ask questions about the concepts discussed in the previous class. You will be reviewing, as well as assessing students' knowledge.

Familiar Contexts Have students write facts about a sport that could be used to write ratios, such as *The Steelers scored 6 points for a touchdown, 3 points for a field goal, and 2 points for a safety, all in one game. What is the ratio of points for the touchdown to all points scored in the game?*

Extend Write a ratio such as 55:100 on the board. Have students write a scenario that the ratio could represent. (55 students out of 100 students are girls.) Repeat this activity with other ratios.

Connection Connect to the previous unit by having students write a ratio for the length of one side of a square to the perimeter of the square.

Family Project: Have your students go to the grocery store with a family member and do some unit pricing. See if they can find family-size packages that cost more per unit than a smaller package, as well as the most expensive item in the store per pound or per gram. Hint: Spices are one of the most costly items per pound in a grocery store.

Teacher Tips

Words of Experience Allow more than one approach to solving a problem. By using different methods to solve problems, students' reasoning skills will grow.

Math Journal Have students describe real-life applications of proportions, such as the amount of time spent studying for a test to the grade on the test or the number of hours at gymnastics practice to the scores received in competition.

Common Difficulty Students may have difficulty knowing where to put the numbers when setting up a proportion. Draw a simple table to organize their thinking. Here is one example: *Beth can run 200 miles in 12 seconds. If she continues at this pace, how long will it take her to run 600 miles?*

Time	12 s	n s
Distance	200 mi	600 mi

Materials A meterstick is a good tool for illustrating percent because it is divided into both 100 (cm) and 1000 (mm) parts. Have students name the number of centimeters or millimeters in different percents. For example, 15% of a meter is how many millimeters? (150) What percent of a meter is 86 centimeters? (86%)

Connection Because a dollar is made up of 100 cents, it provides a natural connection to percents. For example, $.25 is 25% of a dollar, and $1.50 is 150% of a dollar. Give students many opportunities to make this connection.

Other methods for solving this proportion include mental math and patterns.

▶ ***Vocabulary Development*** Have students practice reading proportions out loud. For example, the proportion $\frac{2}{5} = \frac{10}{25}$ is read as *2 is to 5 as 10 is to 25,* or *2 and 5 have the same ratio as 10 and 25.*

Teaching Strategy: Percents

Percent is a type of ratio that represents a part to whole relationship, the whole being 100. Percents can be less than or greater than 100.

▶ ***Ask:*** *What percent does $\frac{45}{100}$ represent? Write $\frac{45}{100}$ as a percent and a decimal. What percent does 1.05 represent? Write 1.05 as a percent and a ratio.*

- Give students many experiences at showing the relationship between percents, decimals, and fractions.

▶ ***Vocabulary Development*** The words *percent* and *percentage* are often confused. *Percent* represents a part of the whole being 100. *Percentage* is the result of multiplying a percent by a number. For example, in the equation $10\% \cdot 500 = 50$, the percent is 10% and the percentage is 50.

▶ ***More Vocabulary Considerations*** When the ratio between two quantities is always the same, we say the quantities *vary proportionally*. For example, feet and yards vary proportionally because the ratio of the number of feet to the number of yards in any measurement is always 3 to 1.

When an increase (decrease) in one of the quantities means an increase (decrease) in the other quantity, the ratios form a *direct proportion.*

When an increase (decrease) in one of the quantities means a decrease (increase) in the other quantity, the ratios form an *inverse proportion.*

Opportunities to Assess

Homework

Have students and their families collect as many different examples of percents off sales data as they can find in outside sources, and then estimate how much they would save by buying items on sale. In class you might discuss how accurate the estimates are compared to the actual sale prices.

Family Involvement

Family members may enjoy helping students find applications of fractions, decimals, and percents in newspapers and magazines at home. Have students classify what they find according to topics such as consumerism, science, etc., and share it with the class.

Teacher/Student Dialogue

Linking Ratio to Proportion

In this dialogue, the teacher connects an understanding of ratio to proportion and can continue this thread with percents. Students can see that the percent of students in the school wearing red is the same as the percent of students in the class wearing red, if the proportions are the same.

Teacher: I want everyone wearing red today to stand at their seats. Okay, let's count how many people are standing and how many are still seated. *(Students count)* What's the count? Cheryl, what did you get?

Student: *8 standing, 14 seated.*

Teacher: Everyone agree? You may be seated. What was the ratio of people standing to people seated? Raul?

Student: *8 to 14.*

Teacher: Raul, come up and write that on the board. Who would like to write the ratio in a different way? *(Calls on students who write different representations)* Now, suppose there are 280 students in our school. Given the ratio in our own class, what would you guess is the number of students in the whole school wearing red? In other words, if there is the same *proportion* of students wearing red in our class as wearing red in the whole school, how many students in the school are wearing red? *(Writes both questions on the board)*

Questioning Techniques

Students exhibit an understanding of ratio, proportion, and percent when they can use these concepts in many different ways. Ask questions not only in various contexts but from different angles. Here are a few twists on a typical question:

- *If I have read $\frac{1}{4}$ of a book, what percent of the book have I read?*
- *How much more do I have to read?*
- *If a book has 300 pages, and I've read 150 of them, what percent have I read?*
- *If I complete the 300-page book, what percent of the book have I read?*

What to do

Every Week

Encourage students to do special math projects on their own. Here are suggestions for topics:

- Choose a famous mathematician and write a report about his or her contribution to the field.
- Research local, state, and national math competitions, and report back to the class how they could become involved.
- Search the Internet for math Web sites created by students and share your findings with the class.

What to do

When

If your students need a break from being asked questions, have them work in small groups to write their own questions about a topic for a quiz. Compile the best and most creative questions and use them for a class quiz.

Unit 4 Ratios, Proportions, and Percents

LESSON 1
PAGES 99–100

OBJECTIVE
To write and simplify ratios

PREREQUISITES
Concepts
- Understand fractions
- Understand units of quantities

Skills
- Write a fraction
- Find equivalent fractions

VOCABULARY
rate, ratio

MATERIALS
Skills Tutorial
Strand 9: Skill 1

Ratios

Presenting the Lesson

Introduce the Skill Write the following expressions on the board: *4 bananas for $1.00, 100 feet in 12 seconds*, and *12 times per hour*. Explain that these represent rates because they compare one quantity to another quantity with different units. Now, write on the board the following: *Max has scored 42 points and Pablo has scored 26 points in the three games their team has played.* Ask, *What is the ratio of Max's points to Pablo's points in the three games?* (42 to 26 or 21 to 13) Discuss how when comparing two quantities with the same unit of measure, we usually call it a ratio.

Check Understanding *What are two other ways to write the ratio* $\frac{2}{5}$? (2 to 5 and 2:5)

Guided Practice

Have the students do the first exercise in rows 1, 3, 7, and 11 on pages 99 and 100.

Independent Practice

Have students complete pages 99 and 100 independently.

Closing the Lesson *Can ratios be simplified?* (Possible answer: Ratios can be simplified because they can be written as fractions.) *Name three things you do that involve rates.* (Possible answers: buying food or goods at a store; getting paid for work; etc.)

LESSON 2
PAGES 101–102

OBJECTIVE
To use proportional thinking to compute the simplest form of a rate such as unit price

PREREQUISITES
Concepts
- Understand the four basic operations
- Understand rates

Skills
- Perform calculations using the four basic operations

VOCABULARY
unit rate, unit price, per

MATERIALS
Skills Tutorial
Strand 9: Skill 6

Unit Rates

Presenting the Lesson

Introduce the Skill Pose the following problem: *Manuel was paid $78.00 for working 13 hours for his neighbor. What was Manuel's hourly wage?* ($6.00 per hour) Discuss with the class how the $6.00 per hour is a unit rate. *If Barry Sanders gained 120 yards on 15 carries of the football, what was his rate per carry?* (8 yards per carry) Pose the following question: *If a ten-pound bag of potatoes costs $1.60 and a five-pound bag of the same potatoes costs $.75, which would be the better buy?* (The smaller bag; the larger size is not always the better buy.)

Check Understanding *If someone types at a rate of 320 words in five minutes, how many words can they type in one minute?* (64 words)

Guided Practice

Have the students do the first exercises in rows 1, 4, and 9 on pages 101 and 102. In row 9, check to see that they divide by the 200 and 75 to get the cost per foot for each size foil.

Independent Practice

Have students complete pages 101 and 102 independently.

Closing the Lesson *If 6 bananas cost $1.50, what would the cost be per banana?* (25 cents per banana) *At this rate, how many bananas could you buy for $1.00?* (4 bananas)

LESSON 3
PAGES 103–104

OBJECTIVE
To write and solve proportions

PREREQUISITES
Concepts
- Understand equivalent fractions
- Understand common denominators
- Understand one-step linear equations

Skills
- Know basic multiplication and division facts
- Multiply fractions
- Understand how to find common denominators
- Understand how to solve one-step linear equations

VOCABULARY
proportion, cross product

MATERIALS
Skills Tutorial
Strand 9: Skill 3

Solving Proportions

Presenting the Lesson

Introduce the Skill Write the proportion *6 is to 15 as n is to 45* on the board. Ask a volunteer to write it as two equivalent fractions ($\frac{6}{15} = \frac{n}{45}$). Ask a volunteer to solve for n by writing both fractions with the same denominator. ($\frac{6}{15} = \frac{18}{45}$, therefore $n = 18$) Students know already that multiplying both sides of an equation (or proportion) by the same quantity preserves the equality. For example, in the proportion $\frac{2}{5} = \frac{6}{15}$, you could multiply each side by the product of the denominators (75) and get $\frac{2}{5} \cdot 75 = \frac{6}{15} \cdot 75$, which after simplifying is equivalent to $2 \cdot 15 = 6 \cdot 5$. In this form of the proportion, each numerator has been multiplied by the denominator of the other fraction (or cross-multiplied). Have students use this method to solve $\frac{20}{p} = \frac{15}{18}$.

Check Understanding *Write as many different proportions as you can from the cross-products $3 \times 6 = 9 \times 2$.* $\left(\frac{3}{9} = \frac{2}{6}; \frac{9}{3} = \frac{6}{2}; \frac{9}{6} = \frac{3}{2}; \frac{6}{9} = \frac{2}{3}\right)$

Guided Practice

Do the first exercise in rows 1, 4, and 8 on pages 103 and 104. Check to see that they set up the proportion correctly in number 1.

Independent Practice

Have students complete pages 103 and 104 independently.

Closing the Lesson *When you use the Cross Products Property, what are you really doing?* (Possible answer: multiplying both sides of the equation by the product of the two denominators)

LESSON 4
PAGES 105–106

OBJECTIVE
To write equations for problems in which the quantities are related by direct proportion

PREREQUISITES
Concepts
- Understand ratios and proportions
- Understand equations

Skills
- Solve a proportion
- Perform computations with rational numbers

VOCABULARY
direct proportion

Direct Proportion

Presenting the Lesson

Introduce the Skill Write this problem on the board: *At 60 mph, how long will it take a car to travel 150 miles?* Show students the two ways they could set up a proportion to solve this problem: 60 miles is to 1 hour as 150 miles is to h hours, or 60 miles is to 150 miles as 1 hour is to h hours

Check Understanding *If 50 is to n as 4 is to 18, what can you tell me about n?* (Possible answer: $n \neq 18$ since $4 \neq 50$.)

Guided Practice

Have students try exercises 1 and 5 on pages 105 and 106.

Independent Practice

Have students complete pages 105 and 106 independently.

Closing the Lesson *Can you think of any formulas which are direct proportions?* (Possible answer: The circumference of a circle and its radius are directly proportional ($C = 2\pi r$).

LESSON 5
PAGES 107–108

OBJECTIVE
To write equations for problems in which the quantities are related by inverse proportion

PREREQUISITES
Concepts
- Understand direct proportions

Skills
- Solve proportions

VOCABULARY
inverse proportion

Inverse Proportion

Presenting the Lesson

Introduce the Skill Review that in a direct proportion, as one term increases so does the other. Explain that in an inverse proportion, as one term increases the other term decreases. Write this problem on the board: *Jill drove to town at a rate of 40 mph and took* $1\frac{1}{2}$ *hours. She returned through heavy traffic and averaged 30 mph. If she traveled the same route, how long did it take her to get home?* In this case, as the speed is decreased the number of hours needed to go the same distance increases.

Check Understanding *In an inverse proportion, what happens between the variables involved?* (Possible answer: As one variable increases, the other decreases.)

Guided Practice

Have them answer problem 1 on page 107. Check to see that students set up an inverse proportion in the correct order.

Independent Practice

Have students complete pages 107 and 108 independently.

Closing the Lesson *Is this an example of an inverse proportion? Explain. Stephanie's Health Store usually buys 480 health bars, which come in 12 boxes. This month she only bought 9 boxes. How many health bars did she get?* (No, this is a direct proportion. Since the number of boxes is decreasing, so will the number of health bars.)

LESSON 6
PAGES 109–110

OBJECTIVE
To use unit analysis to check the reasonableness of solutions to rate problems

PREREQUISITES
Concepts
- Understand systems of measurement
- Understand relationships between units of measure
- Understand ratios
- Understand the four-step problem solving process

Skills
- Perform computations with rational numbers
- Solve proportions

VOCABULARY
dimensional analysis

Problem Solving Application: Is the Answer Reasonable?

Presenting the Lesson

Introduce the Focus of the Lesson Explain to students that in this lesson they will need to use dimensional analysis (or unit analysis) in order to check the reasonableness of answers to the problems.

Model the Four-Step Problem Solving Process Work through the problem on page 109 with the students.

Discuss the Problem Solving Tips Point out to students that the four Problem Solving Process steps—Understand, Decide, Solve, and Look back—are listed in the box on this page. Ask for volunteers to read the tips aloud. Make sure students understand that each step is distinct from the other steps.

Check Understanding *To change miles to feet, what unit ratio would you use?* (5,280 ft/1 mi) *Why?* (So the miles unit in the denominator cancels the miles unit from the miles you are rewriting.)

Guided Practice

Have students do the problem on page 109.

Independent Practice

Have students complete pages 109 and 110 independently.

Closing the Lesson *If you change from feet per hour to feet per minute, should you expect more or fewer feet than you have?* (Fewer, since time is shorter.)

LESSON 7
PAGES 111–113

OBJECTIVE
To learn to construct and interpret scale drawings

PREREQUISITES

Concepts
- Understand ratio and proportion

Skills
- Set up a proportion
- Solve a proportion

VOCABULARY
scale drawing, scale factor, scale

MATERIALS

Copymasters
Teaching Resource 6 (centimeter squared paper)
Reteach 25–27, pp. 95–97
Extension 4, p. 180

Scale Drawing

Presenting the Lesson

Introduce the Skill Have the students draw the following figure using a piece of centimeter squared paper and starting in the lower left-hand corner. Move 4 cm right, 6 cm up, 4 cm right, 4 cm up, 8 cm left, and 10 cm down. Now have them repeat this process at the corner opposite the figure just drawn, and move half the distances given before and trace a new figure. Discuss how this new figure is a scale drawing of the original with a scale factor of $\frac{1}{2}$.

Check Understanding *If a map had a scale factor of 2 cm to 5 mi, what would that mean?* (Possible answer: Every 2 cm on the map corresponds to an actual distance of 5 mi.)

Guided Practice

Have the students do exercises 1 and 7 on pages 111 and 112. Check to see that they are setting up the proportions correctly.

Independent Practice

Have students complete pages 111–113 independently.

Closing the Lesson *If the scale factor is $\frac{2}{3}$, what would be the length of a side in a scale drawing if the original side is 9 cm?* (6 cm)

LESSON 8
PAGES 114–116

OBJECTIVE
To understand the relationships among fractions, decimals, and percents

PREREQUISITES

Concepts
- Understand fractions
- Understand that 1 whole can be written as $\frac{100}{100}$
- Understand decimals

Skills
- Simplify fractions
- Write equivalent fractions with a denominator of 100
- Perform computations with rational numbers

MATERIALS

Copymasters
Teaching Resource 6 (centimeter squared paper)

Skills Tutorial
Strand 10: Skills 6–7

Percents, Decimals, and Fractions

Presenting the Lesson

Introduce the Skill Write *43%* on the board and explain how to change it to a decimal by first changing it to the fraction $\frac{43}{100}$, because the % sign means division by 100. Then, divide 43 by 100. Stress the idea that percent means per 100 or division by 100. Explain that the process of changing a percent to a fraction has already been done above. The only thing they need to be concerned with is simplifying the fraction whenever possible. However, the process of changing a fraction to a percent requires rewriting the fraction with a denominator of 100. Have the class change $\frac{3}{20}$ to a percent. $\left(\frac{3}{20} = \frac{15}{100} \text{ and } \frac{15}{100} = 15\%\right)$

Check Understanding *If a hundredths squared grid has 63 squares shaded, what percent is shaded? Not shaded?* (63%; 37%) *How do you change 62% to a decimal?* ($62\% = \frac{62}{100}$ and $\frac{62}{100} = 0.62$)

Guided Practice

Have the students do exercises 1, 13, 16, 19, and 22 on pages 114, 115, and 116. Check to see that when changing from percents in numbers 13 and 19, they change the percent to a fraction first.

Independent Practice

Have students complete pages 114–116 independently.

Closing the Lesson *How do you change $\frac{1}{5}$ to a percent?* (Possible answer: Rewrite $\frac{1}{5}$ as $\frac{20}{100}$ and $\frac{20}{100} = 20\%$.) *What does percent mean?* (division by 100)

LESSON 9
PAGES 117–118

OBJECTIVE
To use percents that are fractions or decimals

PREREQUISITES
Concepts
- Understand terminating decimals
- Understand the relationships between fractions, decimals, and percents

Skills
- Know how to change terminating decimals to percents and vice versa
- Know how to change fractions whose denominators are factors of 100 or 1000 to percents and vice versa

MATERIALS
Skills Tutorial
Strand 10: Skills 3–4

Fractional and Decimal Percents

Presenting the Lesson

Introduce the Skill Write *$33\frac{1}{3}$%* on the board and ask the class how to change it to a decimal. Explain that they need to change the fraction $\frac{1}{3}$ to the repeating decimal $0.\overline{3}$; then, multiply by 0.01. Ask the class how they could change 6% to a fraction. (remove the % sign and multiply by $\frac{1}{100}$) Discuss with the class the idea that to change from a fraction to a percent, do the reverse, namely, multiply the fraction by 100 and annex the % sign. Have the class change $\frac{2}{3}$ to a percent and $8\frac{1}{3}$% to a fraction.

Check Understanding *How is $\frac{2}{9}$ written as a percent?* ($22\frac{2}{9}$%) *Write $\frac{2}{3}$ as a decimal and as a percent.* ($0.66\frac{2}{3}$ or $0.\overline{6}$, $66\frac{2}{3}$%)

Guided Practice

Have the students do the first exercise in rows 1 and 5 on pages 117 and 118. Check that they multiply by 0.01 in number 1 and by 100 in number 5.

Independent Practice

Have students complete pages 117 and 118 independently.

Closing the Lesson *How do you change a fractional percent to a decimal?* (Remove the % symbol, write the fraction as a decimal, and multiply this decimal by 0.01.) *How do you write a decimal as a percent?* (Multiply the decimal by 100 and add the % symbol.)

LESSON 10
PAGES 119–120

OBJECTIVE
To use percents that are greater than 100%

PREREQUISITES
Concepts
- Understand percents, fractions, and decimals
- Understand the relationships between fractions, decimals, and percents

Skills
- Know how to change percents less than 100% to a fraction or decimal and vice versa

MATERIALS
Skills Tutorial
Strand 10: Skills 3, 4, 5, 7

Percents Greater than 100%

Presenting the Lesson

Introduce the Skill Discuss the fact that percents can be greater than 100%. Ask a volunteer to explain how to change a percent to a decimal. (Remove the % sign and multiply by 0.01 or divide by 100, which is the same as moving the decimal point two places to the left.) Have the class change 143% to a decimal. (1.43)

Check Understanding *Write 175% as a fraction or mixed number in simplest form and as a decimal.* $\left(1\frac{3}{4}, 1.75\right)$

Guided Practice

Do the first exercise in rows 1, 3, and 4 on pages 119 and 120. Check to see that they multiply by 0.01 or $\frac{1}{100}$ when doing rows 1 and 3, respectively.

Independent Practice

Have students complete pages 119 and 120 independently.

Closing the Lesson *How would you write 110% as a decimal?* (First, remove the % symbol → 110. Then, multiply by 0.01 (or divide by 100) → 1.10.)

LESSON 11
PAGES 121–122

OBJECTIVE
To use percents, fractions, and decimals in estimation, computation, and applications

PREREQUISITES
Concepts
- Understand estimation and compatible numbers
- Understand decimals, fractions, and percents and the relationships between them

Skills
- Round fractions, decimals, and percents to numbers that are easy to work with
- Find compatible numbers
- Round whole numbers

VOCABULARY
compatible numbers

MATERIALS
Copymasters
Reteach 28, p. 98

Estimating with Fractions, Decimals, and Percents

Presenting the Lesson

Introduce the Skill Write fractions such as $\frac{12}{67}$, $\frac{13}{40}$, $\frac{27}{51}$, and so on. Ask students to round these to fractions that are easy to work with, such as $\frac{1}{6}$, $\frac{1}{3}$ and $\frac{1}{2}$, respectively. Then, write percents on the board such as 18%, 32%, and 81%. Ask students to round the percents to the nearest 10%. Show how to estimate 32% of 78 by rounding 32% to 30% and rounding 78 to 80. 32% of 78 is about $3 \times 10\%$ of $80 = 3 \times 8$ or 24. Ask them how to estimate 0.52×68. (Round to $0.5 \times 70 = 35$.)

Check Understanding *How would you estimate 7% of 123?* (Think 10% of 120 is 12; 7% is a little more than half that; so 8 would be a good estimate.)

Guided Practice

Do the first exercise in rows 1, 4, 7, and 10 on pages 121 and 122.

Independent Practice

Have students complete pages 121 and 122 independently.

Closing the Lesson *Explain what the general strategy is in estimating fractions, decimals, and percents.* (Possible answer: Round the fractions, decimals, and percents to numbers easy to use, round the whole number to a compatible number, and multiply.)

LESSON 12
PAGES 123–124

OBJECTIVE
To use Work Backward or other strategies to solve problems

PREREQUISITES
Concepts
- Understand the four-step problem solving process

Skills
- Perform computations with rational numbers

Problem Solving Strategy: Work Backward

Presenting the Lesson

Introduce the Strategy Point out that in this lesson students will work backward to help them solve problems.

Model the Four-Step Problem Solving Process Present the problem of computing how much the total birthday money was originally.

- **Understand** Help students realize that what the remainder was after the spending stage becomes the starting point of your computation.
- **Decide** Emphasize that the basic technique of this method is to reverse each stage of the spending process by applying inverse operations.
- **Solve** Make sure to have students share in identifying what operations the question marks represent.
- **Look back** Have students write a similar problem.

Check Understanding *When is it a good idea to try to use the method of working backward?* (When you have an end result but do not know what you started out with.)

Guided Practice

Have the students try exercise 1 on page 123. Check their inverse operations.

Independent Practice

Have students complete pages 123 and 124 independently.

Closing the Lesson *How is solving the equation $\frac{x}{3} = 12$ similar to working backward?* (Possible answer: You reverse what was done to the variable.)

UNIT 4 REVIEW

Page 125

Item Analysis

Items	Unit Obj.
1–4	4A
5–7	4C
8–11	4B
12–15	4C
16–21	4F
22–27	4E
28	4H
29	4G, 4H

Answers to Unit 4 Review items can be found on page 125 of the Teacher's Annotated Edition.

Administering the Review

This page reviews concepts and skills taught in this unit. Be sure students understand all direction lines. You may want to do the first example in each section cooperatively to ensure understanding.

Scoring Chart

Number Correct	29	28	27	26	25	24	23	22	21	20	19	18	17	16	15
Score	100	97	93	90	86	83	79	76	72	69	66	62	59	55	52

Number Correct	14	13	12	11	10	9	8	7	6	5	4	3	2	1
Score	48	45	41	38	34	31	28	24	21	17	14	10	7	3

After the Review

- The Item Analysis chart on the left shows the Unit 4 objective(s) covered by each test item. This chart can help you determine which objectives need review or extra practice.
- For additional assessment, use the Posttest for Unit 4, Copymaster Book, p. 20.
- To provide extension opportunities, use Copymaster Book, p. 180.

UNIT 4 CUMULATIVE REVIEW

PAGE 126

Item Analysis

Items	Unit Obj.
1	4D
2	4D
3	4C
4	4B
5	1C
6	1D
7	4G
8	4E

Answers to Cumulative Review items can be found on page 126 of the Teacher's Annotated Edition.

Administering the Review

This page reviews concepts and skills from earlier units, as well as providing practice with standardized test formats. Students may circle their answers, or you may prefer to duplicate and distribute the answer sheet, Copymaster Book, p. 191. This page may be assigned as homework or as classwork.

Test-Taking Tip Work the problem. Jot down your solution. Then, look at the answer choices and find the one that matches your solution.

Scoring Chart

Number Correct	8	7	6	5	4	3	2	1
Score	100	88	75	63	50	38	25	13

After the Review

The Item Analysis chart on the left shows the unit objective covered by each test item. This chart can help you to determine which objectives need review or extra practice.

Applications of Percent

Vocabulary

base (number) The part of a percentage statement that represents the entire original amount.

commission The part of the total selling price that is paid to the sales person.

discount A reduction in the original price of a product.

interest The amount of money charged for a loan or earned on a savings account. Interest that is allowed to accumulate and be added to the principal at regular intervals is compound interest. Otherwise, it is simple interest.

net price The price of an item after a discount has been deducted from the list, or original, price.

percentage The result obtained by multiplying a quantity by a percent

principal (of a loan or savings account) The amount of money that is borrowed or deposited.

Unit Objectives

5A Use the percent equation to find percentage, base number, or rate percent.

5B Compute percent of increase or decrease.

5C Compute discount, list price, net price, and commission.

5D Compute simple and compound interest.

5E Use a withholding tax table; use Conjecture and Verify and other strategies to solve problems.

About This Unit

The support pages that follow provide more information on prerequisite skills, methods for teaching skills and concepts, daily routines, tips on classroom management and materials, and useful dialogue techniques.

Prerequisite Skills and Concepts

Students should be able to

- use inverse operations to solve equations.

If not, use prerequisite Reteach Worksheet 29.

Assessments

Use Beginning of the Year Inventory for entry-level assessment.

Ongoing Evaluation Quick Checks, Reteach Worksheets, the Skills Tutorial Inventories, and the Midyear Test help ensure that students are progressing adequately to meet the standards.

Summative Evaluation Use Test Preps, Unit Review (p. T85), Cumulative Review (p. T86), Reteach Worksheets, and the Computation Skills Tutorial to assure that students have achieved the standards for the unit.

Diagnosing Errors The Quick Checks highlight common errors and provide remediation. See also the **Teaching Strategies Handbook** pp. T76–T79, where short discussions labeled Common Misconceptions appear as needed with the strategies for key concepts.

Homework and Family Involvement

Home Note In the Student Book, the Dear Family home note provides objectives, vocabulary, and a sample skill discussion for family participation. (**Teaching Strategies Handbook** pages also provide homework and family involvement tips.)

Education Place Refer families to Houghton Mifflin's EduPlace Web site at **http://www.eduplace.com**; for resources and activities for students at **http://www.eduplace.com/math**; and additional resources and activities at **http://www.eduplace.com/parents**.

Helping Your Children Learn Math This book has activities for children ages 5–13 and tips for getting involved in children's mathematics education. (Houghton Mifflin, 1994)

Lessons	Student Pages	Teacher Pages	Resources	State or Local Objectives	State or Local Assessment
5.1 Algebra: The Percent Equation: Solving for the Percentage	129–130	**T80**	Unit 5 Pretest; Strand 10, Skill 8		
5.2 Algebra: The Percent Equation: Solving for the Base	131–132	**T80**	Strand 10, Skill 10		
5.3 Algebra: The Percent Equation: Solving for the Percent	133–134	**T81**	Strand 10, Skill 9		
5.4 Problem Solving Strategy: Conjecture and Verify	135–136	**T81**			
5.5 Percent of Increase or Decrease	137–138	**T82**			
5.6 Algebra: Discount	139–140	**T82**			
5.7 Algebra: List Price and Net Price	141–142	**T83**	Reteach 30, 31, 32		
5.8 Algebra: Commission	143–144	**T83**			
5.9 Algebra: Simple and Compound Interest	145–146	**T84**	Reteach 33, 34; Extension 5		
5.10 Problem Solving Application: Use a Table	147–148	**T84**	Unit 5 Posttest		

Teaching Strategies

Math Background — Applications of Percent

In this unit, students focus their attention on real-world problem solving—discounts, net prices, commissions, and interest. To find solutions to these types of problems, students are given a solid foundation in working with the percent equation in the first three lessons of the unit. The classic percent problem is "_______ is ______ percent of _____." This is the basis of percent equations in which two of the numbers are given and students are asked to find the third number. Students will solve for the percentage, 25% of $460 = x$; for the base number, 25% of $w = 115$; and for the rate percent, n% of $200 = 50$.

Students may be familiar with the "rule" of changing a decimal to a percent by moving the decimal point two places to the right. This can be confusing. Be sure to equate hundredths with percent, orally and in notation, as in 0.65 is the decimal equivalent to 65%. It will be more meaningful to students to learn that the decimal identifies the hundredths position just as the percent symbol designates hundredths.

When Students Ask, Why Learn This?
Few mathematical topics have more practical applications than percents. As consumers, most students have been exposed to percents used in discounts. Students who have savings accounts are aware of percents and interest, and those with after-school or summer jobs will be familiar with percent and taxes. Suggest that students research percents in real-world situations by collecting examples from magazines and newspapers. Allow them to share their findings with the class and to form groups to create bulletin boards on the topic.

A Positive Start
Students are motivated to work on the topics covered in this unit because they either use these applications now, or know they will use them in the future. Spend extra time, if necessary, on the first three lessons; the concepts developed in these lessons are the backbone for the rest of the unit.

Linking Past and Future Learning

Get to know your students' mathematics background from Level 6. Then look ahead to the concepts your students will address next year. With this knowledge, you will be able to establish realistic goals in your instructional program.

Concept/Skills	Last Year	This Year	Next Year
Percent Equations	Solve problems by computing discount and interest	Write and solve percent equations involving discounts or commissions	Write percent equations to solve real-world problems
Percent of Increase or Decrease	Use percents to find discounts	Compute the percentage a quantity has been increased or decreased	Understand exponential growth and decay
Monetary Application of Percent	Compute discount and sale price; compute simple interest	Understand simple and compound interest, sales commissions, and discounts	Use the compound interest formula to solve problems

Methods and Management

Before you begin a lesson, decide how much time should be spent on each part of the lesson. Judge the relative importance of the parts in terms of the time available and the background your students have with each topic.

Teaching Strategy: Percent Equations

A percent diagram can help students find meaning in percent equations and it can give them guidance in setting up the correct proportion to solve the problem.

▶ ***Ask:*** *If Francine buys a CD for $16.00 that is marked 30% off, how much will she save?*

▶ ***Show This:***

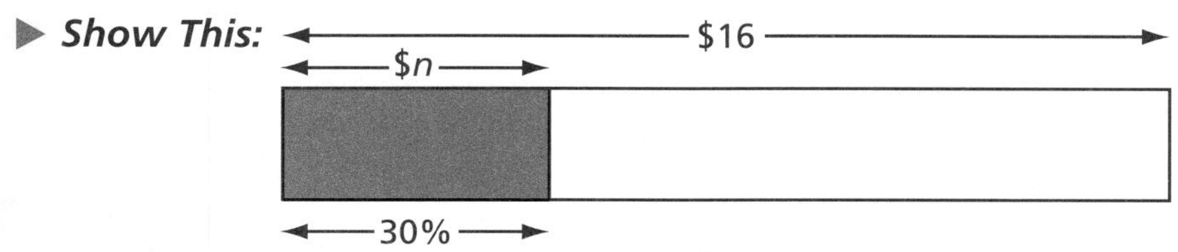

The bar represents 100% of the whole, or \$16. The shaded part of the bar represents 30% off, or \$$n$ in savings. Use the diagram to set up and solve a proportion:

$\frac{30}{100} = \frac{\$n}{\$16} \rightarrow 0.3 = \frac{\$n}{\$16} \rightarrow \$16 \cdot 0.3 = n \rightarrow \$4.80 = n$

Francine will save \$4.80 by buying the CD on sale.

- Encourage students to offer other solutions to the problem. Some may suggest: $\frac{\$16}{100\%} = \frac{\$n}{30\%}$. Others may say to organize the information in a table. While others may write an equation the way they did in Unit 1: $30\% \cdot \$16 = y$.

▶ ***Vocabulary Development*** Point out to students that the whole is always 100%, because percent is a comparison to 100.

▶ ***Common Misconceptions*** Students may confuse the part of the whole and the whole in the percent equation. Have them label the whole, part of the whole, and percent, in the first few exercises of each lesson.

Teaching Strategy: Percent of Increase or Decrease

Percent increase is a comparison of the amount of an increase to the original amount. Percent decrease is a comparison of the amount of a decrease to the original amount. Both comparisons are expressed as ratios in percent form.

- Point out that $\frac{2}{10} = 20\%$ could compare an increase of 2 hours of homework to an original 10 hours of homework, or a 20% increase; and that $\frac{1}{10} = 10\%$ could compare a decrease of 1 hour of homework to an original 10 hours of homework, or a 10% decrease.

▶ ***Ask:*** *If a salary is raised \$.20 from \$5.00 per hour, what is the percent increase?*

Have students identify the change in salary and the original salary, then have them compare the amounts using a ratio. Ask volunteers to offer different solutions for writing the ratio as a percent.

Teacher Tips

Communication Have students justify their solutions with a drawing or an explanation. It is better to assign 3 exercises that require an explanation, than 15 exercises that require only the answer.

Mental Math Provide students with mental computation practice such as *Ten is what percent of 20?* and *Fifty percent of 30 is what?*

Connections Make a connection to geometry by having students draw and shade parts of geometric figures using percent to describe the part that is shaded.

Make It Easy Ratios made up of whole numbers can be easier to work with than ratios made up of decimals. Point out to students that by changing ratios with decimals to ratios with whole numbers, the percent equivalents are the same. For example, $\frac{\$.20}{\$5.00} = 4\%$ and $\frac{\$20}{\$500} = 4\%$.

Reading Math Have students read aloud percent increases and decreases expressed as ratios. For example, read $\frac{\$.02}{\$1.12}$ *as a decrease or increase of \$.02 per gallon compared to the original cost of \$1.12 per gallon.*

Calculator Use When doing monetary calculations in dollars and cents, students should be allowed to use a calculator so they can focus on doing the appropriate operations.

Vocabulary Your students should be able to say in their own words what is meant by simple interest and compound interest. Have them give examples of simple interest and compound interest situations that involve borrowing money or saving money.

At Home Have students check the newspaper for ads from banks and mortgage companies. Then, have them report back to class how each bank is compounding interest.

Reminder When you calculate simple interest for less than a year, write the amount of time as a fraction of a year. For example, 1 month is $\frac{1}{12}$ of a year and 4 months is $\frac{4}{12}$, or $\frac{1}{3}$, of a year.

▶ ***Common Misconceptions*** Some students may not understand that percent increase and percent decrease are actually comparisons. Display these equations:

$$\frac{\textit{amount of increase}}{\textit{original amount}} = \textit{percent increase} \qquad \frac{\textit{amount of decrease}}{\textit{original amount}} = \textit{percent decrease}$$

Have students substitute values in these equations as they complete exercises.

Teaching Strategy: Monetary Applications of Percent

Interest is the cost of borrowing money or the income from saving money. The amount of interest paid or earned depends on the principal (the amount of money saved or borrowed), the interest rate, and the length of time.

- *Simple interest* is calculated using the original principal. *Compound interest* is calculated using the original principal and any previously earned interest. Interest can be compounded annually, semi-annually, quarterly, monthly, or even daily.

▶ ***Show This:***

Year	Simple Interest	Compound Interest (compounded anually)
Beginning of Year 1	$100	$100
End of Year 1	$105	$105
End of Year 2	$110	$110.25
End of Year 3	$115	$115.76

The table shows what would happen to a deposit of $100 left in the bank for 3 years, earning 5% each year.

- Students can add rows to the table to show how the principal would grow in each account for the next seven years. Show how the account would grow in an account that pays compound interest semi-annually, and monthly.

▶ ***Common Misconception*** Students may confuse the intervals at which interest is compounded. Encourage them to organize problems in a table format in which rows and columns are labeled with the appropriate information.

Opportunities to Assess

Communication

Getting students to communicate effectively about mathematics will increase their mathematical power. Get started by adding follow-up questions to the problems you use for assessment, such as "Explain how you got this answer" or "What would be the savings if the discount doubled?"

Family Involvement

Some students' family members or family friends may have first-hand experience with being paid on commission. Ask your students to interview them and give a summary to the class about the advantages and disadvantages of being paid on commission.

Teacher/Student Dialogue

Building Confidence

You play a key role in building your students' confidence. Take advantage of every opportunity to do so.

Teacher: I would like everyone to think about this problem, take notes, and decide how you would find the answer. *Brandy is saving up for a new skateboard. The one she wants costs $45 including tax. She makes $8 a week with her paper route. If she saves 75% of earnings each week, in how many weeks will she have enough to buy the skateboard? (Reads problem again)* Discuss your solution with the person sitting next to you. *(Waits)* Who thinks they have a good approach to the problem? Leasa, do you want to come up and show the class what you would do?

Student: *First, I drew a diagram so I could find out how much Brandy saved each week.* (Draws on the board) *The bar stands for the $8 she makes every week. Next, I estimated what 75% of the bar was, and shaded it in. Then I made this proportion: 75% is to 100% as n is to 8.*

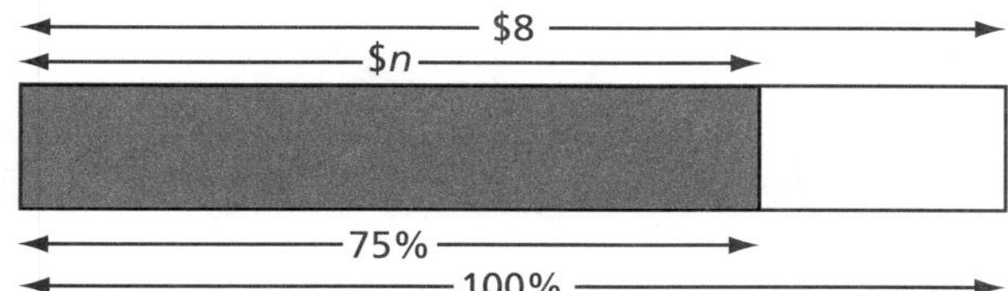

Teacher: Class, is her method okay so far? Looks like you're doing well. Keep going.

Student: *Then I solved for n . . . $\frac{75}{100}$ is the same as $\frac{3}{4}$. I want a ratio the same as $\frac{3}{4}$ with a denominator of 8. That means I should multiply the 3 by 2 and I got 6.*

Teacher: Show me where 6 would be on the diagram. Good, can everyone see how she got 6? Okay, now what does the 6 mean, Leasa?

Student: *That's how much Brandy saves each week. So she would have to do this for eight weeks, and 8 times $6 would be $48. Seven weeks wouldn't be enough.*

Teacher: You did a great job. Does anyone want to ask Leasa a question? No? Did someone else do the same problem differently? *(A few students raise their hands)* Jess, show us your solution, please.

Questioning Techniques

Encourage students to share ideas with a classmate before presenting their solutions to the whole class. This strategy helps students gain the self-confidence necessary to participate in class. A personal exchange of ideas will provide students with the opportunity to "practice" explaining their solutions.

What to do

When

Everyone seems to be talking out of turn. Review with students the classroom courtesy guidelines. Be a model for your students. Give recognition to students who do not interrupt and to those who wait to be called on.

What to do

Every Day

Identify mental math exercises appropriate for the lessons. Take a few minutes each day for oral mental math practice.

Unit 5 Applications of Percent

LESSON 1
PAGES 129–130

OBJECTIVE
To understand the three elements of the basic percent equation and how to solve for the percentage

PREREQUISITES
Concepts
- Understand percents
- Understand equations and variables

Skills
- Perform computations with rational numbers
- Solve one-step equations

VOCABULARY
percent equation, rate, base, percentage

MATERIALS
Skills Tutorial
Strand 10: Skill 8

The Percent Equation: Solving for the Percentage

Presenting the Lesson

Introduce the Skill Ask students, *What is 20% of 70?* You may have to give them a hint to rewrite the percent as a decimal. Discuss the words *is, of,* and *what.* Have the students solve the equation $0.2 \times 70 = n$. (14)

Check Understanding *What is the formula for the percentage?* ($r \times b = p$) *What is the difference between a percent and a percentage?* (A percent is a rate and a percentage is some amount of the base.)

Guided Practice

Have students do the first exercise in rows 1, 4, and 9 on pages 129–130. Check to see that they change the repeating decimal to an improper fraction correctly when calculating the percentage in number 9.

Independent Practice

Have students complete pages 129 and 130 independently.

Closing the Lesson *What would you do to find 18% of 240?* (Change the 18% to a decimal, 0.18, and multiply by 240 obtaining 43.2.)

LESSON 2
PAGES 131–132

OBJECTIVE
To solve a percent equation for the base number

PREREQUISITES
Concepts
- Understand percents and the percent equation
- Understand equations and variables

Skills
- Perform computations with rational numbers
- Solve one-step equations

MATERIALS
Skills Tutorial
Strand 10: Skill 10

The Percent Equation: Solving for the Base

Presenting the Lesson

Introduce the Skill Ask students, *30% of what number is 18?* Ask students to use the percent equation and translate the question into an equation. Ask the class to solve the percent equation for b (60) Do several other examples similar to this, being sure to use a rate that involves a repeating decimal in at least two of them. Check for reasonableness of the answers.

Check Understanding *How could I solve the following equation: If $16\frac{2}{3}$% of a number is 12, what is the number?* (Change $16\frac{2}{3}$% to a fraction and substitute into the percent equation, obtaining $(\frac{1}{6})b = 12$. Now divide both sides by $\frac{1}{6}$, obtaining 72.)

Guided Practice

Have students try the first exercises in rows 1 and 10 on pages 131–132. Check to see that they changed $33\frac{1}{3}$% to $\frac{1}{3}$ in number 10.

Independent Practice

Have students complete pages 131 and 132 independently.

Closing the Lesson *If you use the form $r \times b = p$ and r is written as a decimal, what do you do once you have substituted into the equation in order to solve for b?* (Divide by r.)

LESSON 3
PAGES 133–134

OBJECTIVE
To solve a percent equation for the percent

PREREQUISITES
Concepts
- Understand percents and the percent equation
- Understand equations and variables

Skills
- Perform computations with rational numbers
- Solve one-step equations

MATERIALS
Skills Tutorial
Strand 10: Skill 9

The Percent Equation: Solving for the Percent
Presenting the Lesson

Introduce the Skill Write the following problem on the board and ask students to write the percent equation in a way that can be used to solve for the rate: *What percent of 80 is 32?* (r% of 80 is 32 or $r \times 80 = 32$) Have them solve the equation for r and then have a volunteer explain how to do it on the board. (40%) When solving for r, they will get 0.4. Discuss that this is not 0.4%, but 40%. Remind them that when they found 40% of 80, they first changed the 40% to a decimal. Thus, when we solve for r, it is as a decimal and needs to be changed to a percent.

Check Understanding *If the percentage is greater than the base, what can you tell me about the rate?* (It is greater than 100%.)

Guided Practice
Have students do the first exercise in rows 1, 5, and 8 on pages 133–134. Check to see that they are substituting correctly for the base and percentages in all three exercises.

Independent Practice
Have students complete pages 133 and 134 independently.

Closing the Lesson *If we use the percent equation $r \times b = p$, what do we do to solve for the rate?* (Possible answer: Substitute the base and percentage into the equation, and divide both sides by the base. The rate is given as a decimal, so we need to change the decimal to a percent.)

LESSON 4
PAGES 135–136

OBJECTIVE
To use Conjecture and Verify or other strategies to solve problems

PREREQUISITES
Concepts
- Understand the four-step process for solving problems
- Understand how to solve equations

Skills
- Perform computations with rational numbers
- Be able to translate a written expression into an algebraic expression or equation

Problem Solving Strategy: Conjecture and Verify
Presenting the Lesson

Introduce the Strategy Point out that in this lesson students will use Conjecture and Verify in order to solve problems.

Model the Four-Step Problem Solving Process Present the problem on page 135.

- **Understand** Remind students that they need to translate the words "three more . . . than . . ." into a mathematical phrase.
- **Decide** Assure students that guessing is a genuine problem solving tool.
- **Solve** Emphasize that once the suggested quantities in the conjecture match up with the known total money spent, a solution has been reached.
- **Look back** Have students check answers for reasonableness.

Check Understanding *What is another way of saying conjecture and verify?* (guess and check)

Guided Practice
Have the class try problem 1 on page 136.

Independent Practice
Have students complete pages 135 and 136 independently.

Closing the Lesson *When is the strategy of conjecture and verify good to use?* (Possible answer: When you can do a quick calculation to see if the numbers you guessed are consistent with the data or not.)

LESSON 5
PAGES 137–138

OBJECTIVE
To learn to compute by what percent a quantity has increased or decreased

PREREQUISITES
Concepts
- Understand percents and the percent equation
- Understand how to set up and solve word problems and equations

Skills
- Perform computations with rational numbers
- Determine the percent one number is of another or the rate in a percent equation

VOCABULARY
percent of increase, percent of decrease, percent change

Percent of Increase or Decrease

PRESENTING THE LESSON

Introduce the Skill Write the following problem on the board: *If a pair of sneakers originally cost $72.00, but were on sale for $54.00, what was the percent of decrease in the price?* Ask the class what you would need to do first in order to solve the problem. (Find the amount of decrease = $18.) Ask them, *Now that we have found the decreased amount, what do we do?* (We divide the $18 by $72, the original amount, to get the percent of decrease, which is 0.25 or 25%.)

Check Understanding *If the price of a mountain bike went from* $280 *in* 1998 *to* $322 *in* 1999, *how would I find the percent of increase?* (Subtract $280 from $322, obtaining $42 as the increase in the price. Now divide that by $280 to get 0.15. So the percent of increase was 15%.)

Guided Practice
Have the students do exercises 1 and 12 on pages 137–138. Check to see that the students find the amount of increase in exercise 12 first and that they divide it by 200 to find the percent of increase.

Independent Practice
Have students complete pages 137 and 138 independently.

Closing the Lesson *What is the general process you use to find percent of change?* (Possible answer: You need to find the amount of increase or decrease first, then divide that by the original amount.)

LESSON 6
PAGES 139–140

OBJECTIVE
To solve the percent equation in the context of discounts

PREREQUISITES
Concepts
- Understand percents and the percent equation
- Understand how to set up and solve word problems and equations

Skills
- Perform operations with rational numbers
- Solve equations and problems involving rates and percents

VOCABULARY
discount, list price

Discount

Presenting the Lesson
Introduce the Skill Ask the class to calculate the discount on a shirt costing $12.00 if it is reduced 20%. ($2.40) Now discuss with students the term *discount rate.* Ask the class to solve for the discount rate on an item costing $34.00 if it is to be discounted $5.10. (15%) Do another problem similar to this one. Check each of the problems for the reasonableness of the answers.

Check Understanding *How do you calculate a rate of discount.* (Divide the discount by the original price.)

Guided Practice
Have students do the first exercises in rows 1 and 7 and problem 13 on pages 139–140. Check to see that in problem 13 they take 25% of (3 × $7.50), or $22.50, not just 25% of $7.50.

Independent Practice
Have students complete pages 139 and 140 independently.

Closing the Lesson *If you know the original price of an item and the discount rate, how do you find the discounted amount?* (Possible answer: Change the percent into a decimal or fraction and multiply by the original price.)

LESSON 7
PAGES 141–142

OBJECTIVE
To solve the percent equation in the context of discounts for the net price of the item after discount

PREREQUISITES
Concepts
- Understand percents and the percent equation
- Understand how to set up and solve word problems and equations

Skills
- Perform operations with rational numbers
- Solve equations and problems involving rates and percents
- Solve for the amount of discount and the discount rate using the percent equation

VOCABULARY
net price

MATERIALS
Reteach 30–32, pp. 100–102

List Price and Net Price

Presenting the Lesson

Introduce the Skill Discuss the fact that if you subtract the amount of discount from the original price you obtain the net price. Ask the class to solve this problem, *A pair of skis cost $380.00. If they are being discounted 30%, what would be the net price you would have to pay to purchase them?* Discuss the fact that since the skis were discounted 30%, you paid 70% of the original price. Thus, one way to find the net price is to find the percent you will *pay* for the item and multiply by the original price. (0.7 × $380 = $266.)

Check Understanding *How would you find the discount rate if you knew the original price and the net price?* (Divide the net price by the original price to find what percent of the original price you paid for the item. Now subtract that percent from 100%.)

Guided Practice

Have students do problems 1 and 15 on pages 141–142. Check to see that they subtract the rate they paid for the coat in problem 15 from 100% to find the discount rate.

Independent Practice

Have students complete pages 141 and 142 independently.

Closing the Lesson *How can you find the net price given the discount rate and the original price?* (Possible answer: Find the amount of discount by multiplying the discount rate by the original price. Subtract this amount from the original price to determine the net price, or, subtract the discount rate from 100% and multiply the result by the original price.)

LESSON 8
PAGES 143–144

OBJECTIVE
To use the percent equation in the context of sales commissions

PREREQUISITES
Concepts
- Understand percents and the percent equation
- Understand how to set up and solve word problems and equations

Skills
- Perform operations with rational numbers
- Solve equations and problems involving rates and percents
- Solve for the percentage, base, and rate, using the percent equation

VOCABULARY
commission, net proceeds

Commission

Presenting the Lesson

Introduce the Skill Ask: *If Marsha sells an automobile for $16,800.00, what is her commission if the rate is 5 %?* ($16,800 × 0.05 = $840.) Discuss how the difference between the sale price and the commission is the net proceeds.

Check Understanding *In the percent equation $b \times r = p$, what quantity represents the commission?* (It is *p*, the percentage.)

Guided Practice

Have students do numbers 1 and 10 on pages 143–144. Check to see that students are finding the net proceeds by subtracting the commission from the sale price.

Independent Practice

Have students complete pages 143 and 144 independently.

Closing the Lesson *If you know the commission and the commission rate, how could you find the sales price?* (Substitute the commission for the percentage and the commission rate for the rate in the percent equation and solve for the base, which corresponds to the sales price.)

LESSON 9
PAGES 145–146

OBJECTIVE
To understand the difference between simple and compound interest and use the simple interest formula

PREREQUISITES
Concepts
- Understand percents
- Understand how to set up and solve word problems and equations

Skills
- Perform operations with rational numbers
- Solve equations and problems involving rates and percents
- Solve for the percentage, base, and rate using the percent equation

VOCABULARY
simple interest, compound interest, principal, rate, time, amount due

MATERIALS
Reteach 33, 34, pp. 103–104
Extension 5, p. 181

Simple and Compound Interest

Presenting the Lesson

Introduce the Skill Introduce the simple interest formula $I = prt$ and discuss each of the variables in the formula. Ask the class to solve the following problem: *If you borrow $500 for 6 months at an annual interest rate of 9%, how much will you have to pay in interest for the loan?* ($I = prt$, so $I = \$500 \times 0.09 \times 0.5$, and $I = \$22.50$.) Discuss the idea of compound interest and the concept of interest compounded monthly and quarterly.

Check Understanding *If you borrowed* $2,500.00 *at* 8% *simple interest for one year, what would be the interest due at the end of the year?* (Substitute into the formula $I = p \cdot r \cdot t$ for the principal = $2,500.00, the rate = 0.08 and the time = 1 and compute the interest. $I = \$200$.)

Guided Practice

Have students do problems 1 and 9 on pages 145–146. In problem 1, check to see that they add the interest to the principal to determine the amount due.

Independent Practice

Have students complete pages 145 and 146 independently.

Closing the Lesson *What is the difference between simple interest and compound interest?* (Possible answer: With simple interest you only earn interest on the principal, but with compound interest, you earn interest on the principal plus previous interest.)

LESSON 10
PAGES 147–148

OBJECTIVE
To apply Use a Table to the understanding of income tax

PREREQUISITES
Concepts
- Understand how to read a table
- Understand the problem solving process

Skills
- Perform computations with rational numbers

MATERIALS
Overhead transparency of the Tax Withholding Table for married people

Problem Solving Application: Use a Table

Presenting the Lesson

Introduce the Focus of the Lesson Explain to students that in this lesson they will need to use tables in solving some problems.

Model the Four-Step Problem Solving Process Work through the example problem on tax withholding.

Discuss the Problem Solving Tips Point out to students that the four Problem Solving Process steps—Understand, Decide, Solve, and Look back—are listed in the box on page 147. Make sure students understand that each step is distinct from the other steps.

Check Understanding *If a married person with three exemptions pays a tax of* $28.60, *then how much might he or she earn per week?* (an amount between $270 and $280)

Guided Practice

Have students do exercise 1 on page 147. Check to see that they read the table correctly.

Independent Practice

Have students complete pages 147 and 148 independently.

Closing the Lesson *Do you know any other tables in which information is given?* (Possible answer: bus schedules)

UNIT 5 REVIEW

Page 149

Item Analysis

Items	Unit Obj.
1–7	5A
8–9	5B
10–14	5C
15–16	5D
17	5E

Answers to Unit 5 Review items can be found on page 149 of the Teacher's Annotated Edition.

Administering the Review

This page reviews concepts and skills taught in this unit. Be sure students understand all direction lines. You may want to do the first example in each section cooperatively to ensure understanding.

Scoring Chart

Number Correct	17	16	15	14	13	12	11	10	9
Score	100	94	88	82	76	71	65	59	53

Number Correct	8	7	6	5	4	3	2	1
Score	47	41	35	29	24	18	12	6

After the Review

- The Item Analysis chart on the left shows the Unit 5 objective(s) covered by each test item. This chart can help you determine which objectives need review or extra practice.
- For additional assessment, use the Posttest for Unit 5, Copymaster Book, p. 22.
- To provide extension opportunities, use Copymaster Book, p. 181.

UNIT 5 CUMULATIVE REVIEW

PAGE 150

Item Analysis

Items	Unit Obj.
1	2C
2	5A
3	5A
4	5C
5	2E
6	3B
7	4A

Answers to Cumulative Review items can be found on page 150 of the Teacher's Annotated Edition.

Administering the Review

This page reviews concepts and skills from earlier units as well as providing practice with standardized test formats. Students may circle their answers, or you may prefer to duplicate and distribute the answer sheet, Copymaster Book, p. 191. This page may be assigned as homework or as classwork.

Test-Taking Tip There may be more than one way to solve the same problem. Ask yourself what alternative strategy you could try.

Scoring Chart

Number Correct	7	6	5	4	3	2	1
Score	100	86	71	57	43	29	14

After the Review

The Item Analysis Chart on the left shows the unit objective covered by each test item. This chart can help you to determine which objectives need review or extra practice.

Teacher Notes

Data, Statistics, and Probability

Vocabulary

box-and-whisker plot A graphic way of showing how data are distributed by using the median, quartiles, and maximum and minimum values

compound event The combination of two or more single events

dependent events Two or more events such that the results of one influences the results of the others

independent events Two or more events whose outcomes do not affect each other

outlier An item of data that is significantly greater than or less than all the other items of data

quartiles The three numbers that divide a data set into four equal groups. The middle quartile is called the median. The other two points are the upper and lower quartiles.

scatter plot A graph of ordered pairs that shows two measurements for each item of a set

stem-and-leaf plot A way of arranging data in order from least to greatest by making the last digit of each number a leaf and the other digits of each number the stem.

Unit Objectives

- **6A** Make and interpret line plots, histograms, stem-and-leaf plots, box-and-whisker plots, and scatter plots
- **6B** Identify median, quartiles, and maximum and minimum values of a data set
- **6C** Identify and interpret misleading graphs
- **6D** Make predictions using a line graph
- **6E** List and count permutations and combinations
- **6F** Compute probabilities of dependent and independent events
- **6G** Organize and analyze data using tables and graphs; use Make a List and other strategies to solve problems

About This Unit

The support pages that follow provide more information on prerequisite skills, methods for teaching skills and concepts, daily routines, tips on classroom management and materials, and useful dialogue techniques.

Prerequisite Skills and Concepts

Students should be able to

- express outcomes as fractions or percents.

If not, use prerequisite Reteach Worksheet 35, p. 105.

Assessments

Use Beginning of the Year Inventory for entry-level assessment.

Ongoing Evaluation Quick Checks, Reteach Worksheets, the Skills Tutorial Inventories, and the Midyear Test help ensure that students are progressing adequately to meet the standards.

Summative Evaluation Use Test Preps, Unit Review (p. T100), Cumulative Review (p. T101), Reteach Worksheets, and the Computation Skills Tutorial to assure that students have achieved the standards for the unit.

Diagnosing Errors The Quick Checks highlight common errors and provide remediation. See also the **Teaching Strategies Handbook** pp. T90–T93, where short discussions labeled Common Misconceptions appear as needed with the strategies for key concepts.

Homework and Family Involvement

Home Note In the Student Book, the Dear family home note provides objectives, vocabulary, and a sample skill discussion for family participation. (**Teaching Strategies Handbook** pages also provide homework and family involvement tips.)

Education Place Refer families to Houghton Mifflin's EduPlace Web site at http://www.eduplace.com; for resources and activities for students at http://www.eduplace.com/math; and additional resources and activities at http://www.eduplace.com/parents.

Lessons	Student Pages	Teacher Pages	Resources	State or Local	
				Objectives	Assessment
6.1 Line Plots and Histograms	153–154	**T94**	Unit 6 Pretest		
6.2 Stem-and-Leaf Plots	155–156	**T94**			
6.3 Box-and-Whisker Plots	157–158	**T95**	Reteach 36, 37, 38		
6.4 Scatter Plots	159–160	**T95**	Extension 6		
6.5 Misleading Graphs	161–162	**T96**			
6.6 Algebra: Making Predictions from a Graph	163–164	**T96**	Reteach 39, 40, 41		
6.7 Problem Solving Strategy: Make a List	165–166	**T97**			
6.8 Permutations and Combinations	167–168	**T97**			
6.9 Probability: Independent Events	169–170	**T98**			
6.10 Probability: Dependent Events	171–172	**T98**	Reteach 42, 43, 44		
6.11 Problem Solving Application: Use Graphs and Tables	173–174	**T99**	Unit 6 Posttest		

Teaching Strategies

Math Background — Data, Statistics, and Probability

The process of collecting, organizing, displaying, describing, and interpreting data and using it to make decisions or predictions has become a basic skill in today's society. Statistics and probability are important links to social science, science, medicine, politics, and the world of business. Statistics and probability make use of numbers, measurement, estimation, and problem solving in real-life contexts. Tables and graphs are common in newspapers, magazines, and other forms of the media, including topics such as weather reports, public opinion polls, and population growth.

When Students Ask, Why Learn This?
Being able to interpret information correctly is fundamental to making decisions. Point out to students that throughout their lives, they will rely on their knowledge of statistics and probability to inform their decisions about what candidate to vote for or what career to pursue, for example. In this unit, they use data in tables and graphs to make predictions and draw conclusions. And while exploring these topics, students will continue to exercise the mathematical concepts and skills studied in previous units.

A Positive Start
Investigations surrounding the concepts of probability and statistics will stimulate enthusiasm in your class as your students become actively involved in the entire process: formulating key questions to answer; sampling the population; collecting and organizing the data; representing the data in graphs, charts, tables, mean, median, and mode; analyzing the data; making conjectures and predictions; and communicating their findings in a convincing manner. Students will apply previously learned skills and extend their problem solving and reasoning skills as they work through this unit.

Linking Past and Future Learning

What types of graphs did your students study last year? What probability topics have they covered? The chart below answers these questions for you. Refer to the chart often to help plan your instruction so your students will be well-prepared for Level 8.

Concept/Skills	Last Year	This Year	Next Year
Data Displays in One Variable	Organize data in appropriate graphs; use graphs to make inferences and predictions; identify and discuss gaps, cluster, and outliers	Read and draw histograms, line plots, stem-and-leaf plots, and a box-and-whisker plots; detect misleading graphs	Linear functions
Data Displays in Two Variables	None	Represent two variables on a scatter plot	Nonlinear functions
Probability	Use samples; determine experimental and theoretical probability; find outcomes of a compound event; discuss dependent and independent events	Use permutations and combinations to determine number of outcomes; use Make a List and other strategies to solve probability problems	Use counting strategies and principles to find the number of solutions for a situation

Methods and Management

Students mirror many of the attitudes and beliefs of teachers. With a positive attitude about mathematics, an appreciation for the usefulness of the subject, and an inquisitive mindset, you can have a major influence on how your students approach their studies.

Teaching Strategy: Data Displays in One Variable

At this level, student broaden their data analysis skills using line plots, histograms, stem-and-leaf plots, and box-and-whisker plots. Students should be able to identify which type of graph is most appropriate for displaying a given set of data and to use the graphs to draw conclusions, describe trends, and make predictions.

- *Box-and-whisker* plots provide the most information about the "spread" of data sets. Students should be aware that each section of the box-and-whisker plot contains $\frac{1}{4}$, or 25% of the data.
- The height of bars in *histograms* represent data or percentages. Intervals, or the width of the bars, should always be the same size. Histograms are used mostly to display *discrete* data, as in the number of people attending a movie. Line graphs are generally used for *continuous* data, as in time or temperature.
- Show examples of the graphs listed above.

▶ ***Ask:*** *Which graph would you use to show the finishing times of a marathon? Why? Do you see a trend in any of the graphs? Describe the trend.*

▶ ***Common Misconceptions*** Encourage students to look carefully at the range and intervals on graphs. These elements can be manipulated to make a graph misleading. Students should develop a healthy skepticism when examining graphs. They need to learn when information is accurately portrayed.

Teaching Strategy: Data Displays in Two Variables

Scatter plots demonstrate relationships between two quantities that vary, for example, age and height. Each point on a scatter plot represents an ordered pair. The first coordinate in an ordered pair is a value for one quantity, such as age, and the second coordinate is the corresponding value of the other quantity, such as height. Trends can often be seen by drawing a line that corresponds to the ordered pairs through a scatter plot. These trends can be used to predict values beyond the range of the plotted points. Use questions like the following to guide students as they explore scatter plots.

Ask: *Can you make any predictions based on the curve of the data in the scatter plot? Explain your answer. What relationship do you see between the coordinates?*

Common Misconceptions A common mistake students make is to assume that a graph is a realistic picture of a situation. A velocity-versus-time graph of a roller-coaster ride will not look at all like the path the roller coaster takes. Many distance-versus-time graphs don't look like the actual events either.

Technology Several different graphs with the same data can be constructed using software or graphing calculators. Ask students from a local high school to show your class graphs they have created using technology.

Project Provide opportunities for students to collect their own data. Then, have them decide how to best represent the data graphically. This could be an individual or group project.

Think Ahead An understanding of graphs such as scatter plots, which show relationships, will serve students well in algebra and beyond.

Be Creative Remove the labels from graphs, and have students describe situations the graphs could represent.

Words to the Wise To show how data in graphs is sometimes distorted to make a claim, show your students graphs containing the same information but with different scales and intervals.

Visual Aid Tree diagrams are helpful to illustrate the possible outcomes for repeated events, such as tossing coins and rolling number cubes.

Materials Coins, number cubes, and spinners are commonly used for experiments in probability. Spinners can be easily made by spinning a large paperclip around the tip of a pencil held on a piece of paper that has the divisions of the spinner marked on it. (See Teaching Resource 10 (circle/spinner), p. 200.)

Teaching Strategy: Probability

Probability describes the likelihood of an event occurring. Provide students with opportunities to model examples of probability.

- Have students simulate this situation.

▶ ***Ask:*** *How many different ways can 3 students stand in a line? 7 students?*

- Use a tree diagram to model this situation.

▶ ***Ask:*** *How many different sundaes containing one flavor of frozen yogurt and one topping can be made if 3 flavors of frozen yogurt and 2 different toppings are available?*

- Compare experimental and theoretical probabilities and fairness using number cubes, cards, or spinners.

▶ ***Ask:*** *Is the game fair or unfair? If unfair, how could the rules be changed to make the game fair?*

▶ ***Vocabulary Development*** Give students many opportunities to use appropriate probability terminology. For example, ask: What term describes the set of possible outcomes when rolling a number cube? (sample space) How would you describe the relationship between choosing a boy's name from a hat, then choosing a girl's name? (dependent events)

▶ ***Common Misconceptions*** Students sometimes think that if a coin comes up heads two times in a row, it is more likely that it will come up tails the next time. In reality, the probability remains $\frac{1}{2}$, despite what has already happened.

Opportunities to Assess

Grading

Selection and interpretation of graphs rarely involves one right answer. To grade student's graphs, award points for critical features—labels on the axes, appropriate scale, etc. Make your own list of what's crucial.

Homework

Students should show evidence of being able to make reasonable judgments based on the graphs they make. Ask them to write a paragraph giving an overall summary of the graph or ask questions that require more explanation than a quick answer, such as *How could you use this information to support your opinion about ________?* or *What other types of graphs could we use to represent this data?*

Family Involvement

Have students identify an issue that is important to them and survey their family members for their opinions on the issue. They can then select an appropriate graph to make and share with the class.

Teacher/Student Dialogue

Discussing Outcomes

Talking about probability as a group will allow students to hear ways of thinking that are different from their own.

Teacher: I am holding a regular number cube in my hand. How many different outcomes are possible when I toss it? Cara?
Student: *6—1, 2, 3, 4, 5, or 6.*

Teacher: Are all outcomes equally likely? Buck?
Student: *Yes.*

Teacher: Samuel, what's the probability that I will roll a 3 when I toss it?
Student: *1 out of 6.*

Teacher: Yes, we would say $\frac{1}{6}$. What would it be as a decimal? Patrice, use your calculator and tell us.
Student: *(Punches numbers into calculator) Point one, six, six, six . . . lots of sixes and then a seven.*

Teacher: What would be the probability of rolling an even number? Who would like to answer. Jasmine, you have your hand up.
Student: *3 out of 6.*

Teacher: *(Writes* $\frac{3}{6}$*)* Or—?
Student: *One out of two; or one over two.*

Teacher: The decimal notation would be 0.5, right? Can you explain how you got that probability?
Student: *There are 3 even numbers—2, 4, and 6. So 3 over 6.*

Teacher: Good. Adon, what's the probability of rolling a number greater than 6?
Student: *Zero over 6.*

Teacher: Which is equal to?
Student: *Zero.*

Teacher: And the probability of rolling a positive number less than 7?
Student: *6 over 6, which is 1.*

What to do

When

Your students just don't seem to grasp a concept you are teaching. Look back at the previous level and identify the prerequisite skills. Take some time to review those skills with your students; then, proceed with the new concept. Ask some experienced teachers how they teach this concept. Perhaps an alternative teaching strategy will work better.

What to do

Every Day

Encourage students to learn from their mistakes. Talking about an answer that is incorrect can lead students to the correct answer as well as a better understanding of the concept.

Unit 6 Data, Statistics, and Probability

LESSON 1
PAGES 153–154

OBJECTIVE
To read and draw histograms and line plots

PREREQUISITES
Concepts
- Understand how to read line plots
- Understand the mean, median, mode, and range for a data set

Skill
- Calculate the mean, median, mode, and range for a data set

VOCABULARY
line plot, mean, median, mode, range, frequency table, histogram

Line Plots and Histograms

Presenting the Lesson

Introduce the Skill Tell students that you've written a secret number taken from the sequence 19–33. Then, have them write on the board the number they think it will be. Have the class make a line plot of the data and find the mean, median, mode, and range for the data. Discuss what the line plot and typical values tell them about their guesses. Now, group the data in intervals of three units (e.g. 19–21, 22–24, etc.). Show students how to construct a histogram based on the data. Mention that there is a bar for each of the intervals in the frequency table. Label this graph. (Possible name: Histogram of Numbers Guessed, 19–33 Inclusive) Discuss what the frequency table and histogram tell them about the data generated. Now, randomly select one of the pieces of paper and compare it to the graphs and statistics generated.

Check Understanding *What is an interval frequency table?* (It is a table that tallies the data in intervals.) *Can you tell what each score is from an interval frequency table?* (No, but you can tell how many scores there are in any given interval.)

Guided Practice

Do exercises 1 and 6 on pages 153 and 154. Check to see that the intervals chosen in exercise 6 cover the range of the scores and that the interval contains 10 points.

Independent Practice

Have students complete pages 153 and 154 independently.

Closing the Lesson *If you used intervals to construct your histogram, what does the height of the bar in the histogram indicate?* (It tells you how many scores are in that interval.)

LESSON 2
PAGES 155–156

OBJECTIVE
To organize a set of data using a stem-and-leaf plot

PREREQUISITES
Concepts
- Understand how to read line plots and bar graphs
- Understand the mean, median, mode, and range for a data set

Skills
- Calculate the mean, median, mode, and range for a data set

VOCABULARY
stem-and-leaf plot, back-to-back stem-and-leaf plot, outlier

Stem-and-Leaf Plots

Presenting the Lesson

Introduce the Skill Have everyone in the class find his or her height in centimeters using a meterstick. Have them make a list of their heights on the board. Now, show them the three-step process of making a stem-and-leaf plot: (1) figure out what the stems should be, (2) write each score as it appears in the list on the board, and (3) order each of the leaves in ascending order. Also, discuss how easy it is to find the median, mode, and range using a stem-and-leaf plot.

Check Understanding *Who can explain to me what a stem-and-leaf plot is for?* (It is a very easy way to organize and order data.)

Guided Practice

Have the students do exercise 1 on page 155. Check to see that they are using the tens digit as the stem and the units digits as the leaves.

Independent Practice

Have students complete pages 155 and 156 independently.

Closing the Lesson *What are some reasons for using a stem-and-leaf plot to display the data?* (Possible answer: The original data is not lost and the median, mode, and range are easy to find.)

LESSON 3
PAGES 157–158

OBJECTIVE
To use the median, quartiles, and maximum and minimum values of a data set to make a box-and-whisker plot

PREREQUISITES
Concepts
- Understand how to read and organize data sets
- Understand the median for a data set
- Understand percents

Skill
- Calculate the median of a data set

VOCABULARY
box-and-whisker plot, first quartile, second quartile, third quartile

MATERIALS
Number cubes

Copymasters
Reteach 36, 37, 38, pp. 106–108

Box-and-Whisker Plots

Presenting the Lesson

Introduce the Skill Have each student roll a number cube five times and add up the scores. Have students write their sums on the board. Use that data to make a box-and-whisker plot. Mention that you need to find five values: the greatest and least number, and the first, second, and third quartiles. Relate quartiles to the idea of quarters. Draw the box-and-whisker plot and discuss the fact that the box contains 50% of the data, that below the first quartile is 25% of the data, etc.

Check Understanding *What does the third quartile represent?* (The score that has 75% of the scores below it and 25% above it.) *How do you find the third quartile?* (Arrange the data in ascending order. Divide the data set in half; then, find the median for the upper half of the data set.)

Guided Practice

Have the students do numbers 1 and 3 on page 157.

Independent Practice

Have students complete pages 157 and 158 independently.

Closing the Lesson *If a score is in the box of a box-and-whisker plot, what can you tell me about that score?* (Possible answer: It is in the middle 50% of the scores.)

LESSON 4
PAGES 159–160

OBJECTIVE
To represent two variables on a scatter plot and determine what sort of correlation they show

PREREQUISITES
Concepts
- Understand ordered pairs

Skill
- Plot ordered pairs

VOCABULARY
scatter plot, ordered pairs, positive, negative, no correlation

MATERIALS
Rulers and metersticks
Graph paper and overhead
Transparency of graph paper

Copymasters
Teaching Resource 5 (Quarter-inch squared paper)
Extension 6, p. 186

Scatter Plots

Presenting the Lesson

Introduce the Skill Have students take off their shoes and measure their height and their right foot's length to the nearest centimeter. Have each of the students write an ordered pair (foot length, height) on the board. Using the grid paper, have them make a scatter plot of the data collected, with the horizontal axes showing the foot length and the vertical axes showing the height. Discuss any trends the class may see. (e.g.: As one's foot length gets bigger, so does one's height.) Discuss the idea of positive, negative, and no correlation and what it would look like in a scatter plot.

Check Understanding *If you were to graph the height of a child versus age in years to age 15, what kind of correlation would you expect, and why?* (Positive, because the child will be growing during those years.)

Guided Practice

Do exercises 1A, 1B, 3A, and 3B on page 159. Check to see that the students are graphing the ordered pairs correctly in exercise 3.

Independent Practice

Have students complete pages 159 and 160 independently.

Closing the Lesson *What would you expect for a correlation between number of hours of sleep and alertness in class the next day?* (positive)

LESSON 5
PAGES 161–162

OBJECTIVE
To learn to detect how graphs can be visually misleading

PREREQUISITES
Concepts
- Understand and analyze graphs

Skills
- Be able to read and construct graphs

Misleading Graphs

Presenting the Lesson

Be sure to explain to students that graphs can be deliberately made misleading in order to support a particular argument or viewpoint. Mention that the most common methods or gimmicks for doing this are: use of an inappropriate scale as in the monthly sales example, use of a broken (noncontinuous) scale as in the favorite ice cream example, and visual tricks, such as using the thickness of the bars in a bar graph, to exaggerate differences as in the Internet Subscribers' example.

Check Understanding *Why would someone create a misleading graph?* (Possible answer: to support a particular viewpoint)

Guided Practice

Do exercises 1 and 2 on page 161. Check to see if the students recognize why one graph is misleading.

Independent Practice

Have students complete pages 161 and 162 independently.

Closing the Lesson *What might you do to make a misleading graph?* (Possible answers: Don't begin the vertical axes at zero; Don't show the trends over a sufficient amount of time; Make the size of the icons disproportionate to the actual data.)

LESSON 6
PAGES 163–164

OBJECTIVE
To use a linear graph to make predictions

PREREQUISITES
Concepts
- Understand and analyze graphs

Skills
- Be able to read a graph

MATERIALS
Copymasters
Reteach 39, 40, 41, pp. 109–111

Making Predictions from a Graph

Presenting the Lesson

Introduce the Skill You are planning a party and would like to purchase 5 pounds of meat, and want to know how much it would cost. Ask students what you might do to find the cost for 5 pounds.

One way is to use the unit price, if you know it; you can multiply the unit price by 5. Another way: Suppose a graph is already available that shows the prices for various amounts of meat. Since the price of the meat and its weight are in direct proportion, the points on the graph appear to be in a straight line. So holding a straightedge along the line of points, you can find 5 on the "pounds" axis, read vertically up to the straightedge, and read horizontally left to the "cost" axis for the price of 5 pounds of meat.

Discuss the fact that connecting the points of the graph with a straight line is just a method of estimating based on the graph. Go over the two sample graphs on page 163.

Check Understanding *Data from the Olympics indicate that the time needed to swim 50 meters has been decreasing at about 1.3 seconds every five years. Must this trend continue for the next 100 years?* (Possible answer: No. Swimmers will reach a limit and times will level off, or maybe will decrease in minute amounts.)

Guided Practice

Have the students do exercises 1 and 3A on page 163.

Independent Practice

Have students complete pages 163 and 164 independently.

Closing the Lesson *What assumptions are you making when you make predictions based on graphs?* (Possible answer: You are assuming that the trend will continue in the same fashion and that the prediction makes sense in terms of a real-life situation.)

LESSON 7
PAGES 165–166

OBJECTIVE
To use Make a List or other strategies to solve probability problems

PREREQUISITES
Concepts
- Understand the four-step problem solving process

Skills
- Be able to find the areas of triangles
- Be able to make a tree diagram

Problem Solving Strategy: Make a List

Presenting the Lesson

Introduce the Strategy Point out that in this lesson students will make a list to help them solve problems

Model the Four-Step Problem Solving Process Present the problem on page 165.

- **Understand** Remind students to consider all possibilities.
- **Decide** Emphasize that a tree diagram is a very useful preliminary.
- **Solve** Point out the significance of a probability of $\frac{1}{8}$.
- **Look back** You may want to discuss repeated trials.

Check Understanding *When would it be a good idea to make a list in order to solve a problem?* (Possible answer: when it is important to consider all possible combinations or outcomes)

Guided Practice
Have the class try problem 1 on page 166.

Independent Practice
Have students complete pages 165 and 166 independently.

Closing the Lesson *What does a list help you do?* (Anticipate all possible outcomes.)

LESSON 8
PAGES 167–168

OBJECTIVE
To use permutations and combinations to count the number of ways an event can happen

PREREQUISITES
Concepts
- Understand how to make organized lists

Skills
- Be able to multiply

VOCABULARY
permutation, combination

Permutations and Combinations

Presenting the Lesson

Introduce the Skill Write the sample problem on page 167 on the board: *There are four players remaining in a tournament. In how many different ways can the four finish in the standings?* Discuss how the problem involved a permutation because it was a listing or ordering of objects in which the order was important. Relate this to the multiplication rule that states that if you can do the first thing in *m* ways and the second thing in *n* independent ways, you can do the two things together in *mn* ways. Write this problem on the board: *Two people are to be selected from a group of four people to be on a committee. How many different committees could be formed?* Discuss how this problem is called a combination because it is a listing in which the order is not important.

Check Understanding How many different ways could you select three people from a group of four? (4)

Guided Practice
Have the students do the exercises 1 and 3 on page 167.

Independent Practice
Have students complete pages 167 and 168 independently.

Closing the Lesson *What is the difference between a permutation and a combination?* (Possible answer: A permutation is an arrangement of elements in which the order is important, and a combination is an arrangement in which the order of elements is not important.)

LESSON 9
PAGES 169–170

OBJECTIVE
To calculate the probability of simple events and independent events

PREREQUISITES
Concepts
- Understand rational numbers

Skills
- Compute with rational numbers

VOCABULARY
probability of an event, independent events, "and", "or"

Probability: Independent Events

Presenting the Lesson

Introduce the Skill Pose the following problem to the class: *If you were to flip a coin and then roll a number cube, what is the probability you would get a head followed by a 2?* Explain that these are what we call independent events since the outcome of the first event does not affect the outcome of the second event. One way to solve this is to make a list of all the possible outcomes and see how many of them are successes.

H1 (H2) H3 H4 H5 H6 T1 T2 T3 T4 T5 T6

There is only one success out of the 12 possible outcomes, all of which are equally likely. Since these events are independent, we could multiply the two probabilities. $P(H) = \frac{1}{2}$ and $P(2) = \frac{1}{6}$, thus the $P(H, 2) = \frac{1}{2} \times \frac{1}{6}$ or $P(H, 2) = \frac{1}{12}$.

Check Understanding A spinner is divided into 6 equal sections numbered 1–6. *What is the probability of landing on 1 or 2?* ($\frac{2}{6}$ or $\frac{1}{3}$)

Guided Practice

Have the students do exercises 1, 8, and the first one in row 6 on pages 169 and 170.

Independent Practice

Have students complete pages 169 and 170 independently.

Closing the Lesson *If all the outcomes are equally likely, how do you find the probability of an event?* (Possible answer: You divide the number of successful outcomes for the event by the total number of events possible.)

LESSON 10
PAGES 171–172

OBJECTIVE
To calculate the probability of dependent events

PREREQUISITES
- Understand rational numbers
- Understand simple probability and independent events

Skills
- Compute with rational numbers
- Compute the probability of simple events and independent events

VOCABULARY
compound event, dependent event

MATERIALS
Copymasters
Reteach 42, 43, 44, pp. 112–114

Probability: Dependent Events

Presenting the Lesson

Introduce the Skill Tell students that a bag contains 12 marbles—4 green, 3 blue, 3 red, and 2 yellow. Ask them questions like these: *If I draw a marble at random, replace the marble, and draw another marble, what is the probability that I draw a red marble followed by a blue marble?* (These are independent events, so $P(R) = \frac{1}{4}$ and $P(B) = \frac{1}{4}$, so $P(R, B) = \frac{1}{4} \times \frac{1}{4}$ or $\frac{1}{16}$.) *If I don't replace the first marble, but instead set it aside, what is the probability of getting a red followed by a blue?* (These are dependent events, thus $P(R) = \frac{1}{4}$ and $P(B \text{ after drawing a red}) = \frac{3}{11}$, thus $P(R, B \text{ after a red}) = \frac{1}{4} \times \frac{3}{11}$ which equals $\frac{3}{44}$.)

Check Understanding *When are two events dependent events?* (when the outcome of one event affects the outcome of the other event)

Guided Practice

Have the students do exercises 1 and 2 on page 171.

Independent Practice

Have students complete pages 171 and 172 independently.

Closing the Lesson *How do you find the probability of two dependent events?* (Possible answer: Find the probability of the first event; then, find the probability of the second event based upon the success of the first event having occurred. Now, multiply those two probabilities together.)

LESSON 11
PAGES 173–174

OBJECTIVE
To use graphs and tables to organize, represent, and analyze data

PREREQUISITES

Concepts
- Understand the four-step problem solving process
- Understand how to read and construct tables and graphs

Skills
- Be able to read and analyze tables and graphs and use them to make predictions

Problem Solving Applications: Use Graphs and Tables

Presenting the Lesson

Introduce the Focus of the Lesson Explain to students that in this lesson they will need to use graphs and tables to help them organize and interpret data in order to solve problems.

Model the Four-Step Problem Solving Process Work through the problem of the sales graph on page 173 with your students.

Discuss the Problem Solving Tips Point out to students that the four Problem Solving Process steps—Understand, Decide, Solve, and Look back—are listed in the box on page 173. Make sure students understand that each step is distinct from the others.

Check Understanding *What are some of the reasons for using graphs instead of tables?* (Graphs will give you a quick picture of the total data set. It is easy to see trends, high points, low points, and make predictions or comparisons.) *What are some disadvantages of using graphs?* (Sometimes the exact data are lost; specific data are hard to distinguish.)

Guided Practice

Have the students do problem 1 on page 173. Check to see how students are estimating three times the combined bars of Vincent and Xavier.

Independent Practice

Have students complete pages 173 and 174 independently.

Closing the Lesson *What are some reasons for using tables over graphs?* (The representation of data is more precise and accurate. You can tell specific differences between various points, and you can find specific details you may be interested in.) *What are some disadvantages of using tables?* (Trends in the data may be harder to see; you need to scan all the data to find where high and low points may occur.)

UNIT 6 REVIEW

Page 175–177

Item Analysis

Items	Unit Obj.
1–6	6A, 6B
7–10	6A, 6B
11–13	6A, 6B
14–15	6C
16–20	6A, 6D
21–24	6E
25	6G
26–30	6F

Answers to Unit 6 Review items can be found on pages of 175–177 of the Teacher's Annotated Edition.

Administering the Review

This page reviews concepts and skills taught in this units. Be sure students understand all direction lines. You may want to do the first example in each section cooperatively to ensure understanding.

Scoring Chart

Number Correct	30	29	28	27	26	25	24	23	22	21	20	19	18	17	16
Score	100	97	93	90	87	83	80	77	73	70	67	63	60	57	53

Number Correct	15	14	13	12	11	10	9	8	7	6	5	4	3	2	1
Score	50	47	43	40	37	33	30	27	23	20	17	13	10	7	3

After the Review

- The Item Analysis chart on the left shows the Unit 6 objective(s) covered by each test item. This chart can help you determine which objectives need review or extra practice.
- For additional assessment, use the Posttest for Unit 6, Copymaster Book, pp. 26–28.
- To provide extension opportunities, use Copymaster Book, p. 182.

UNIT 6 CUMULATIVE REVIEW

PAGE 178

Item Analysis

Items	Unit Obj.
1	6A
2	2B
3	5A
4	4E
5	4C
6	5D
7	2E
8	3B

Answers to Cumulative Review items can be found on page 178 of the Teacher's Annotated Edition.

Administering the Review

This page reviews concepts and skills from earlier units as well as providing practice with standardized test formats. Students may circle their answers, or you may prefer to duplicate and distribute the answer sheet, Copymaster Book, p. 191. This page may be assigned as homework or as classwork.

Test-Taking Tip When reading a bag graph, place a ruler or the edge of a piece of paper across the top of the bar to make sure you read the correct label.

Scoring Chart

Number Correct	8	7	6	5	4	3	2	1
Score	100	88	75	63	50	38	25	13

After the Review

The Item Analysis chart on the left shows the unit objective covered by each test item. This chart can help you to determine which objectives need review or extra practice.

Unit 7 Planner

Points, Lines, and Angles

Vocabulary

angle A geometric figure formed by two rays with a common endpoint

central angle An angle whose vertex is the center of a circle

congruent figures Figures that have exactly the same size and shape. In congruent polygons, corresponding angles are congruent and corresponding sides are congruent.

coplanar Two or more points, lines, or figures that are in the same plane

corresponding angles Two angles in the same position in relation to two lines and a transversal

polygon A plane figure composed of line segments that meet only at their endpoints. The segments must form a closed figure.

polyhedron A closed figure in space whose faces are all polygons

quadrilateral A polygon that has four sides

transversal A line that intersects two or more other lines in the same number of points as there are lines

vertical angles Two opposite angles formed by two intersecting lines

Unit Objectives

7A Identify basic elements of plane and space figures

7B Measure angles

7C Identify angle relationships such as vertical and corresponding angles

7D Construct congruent angles and segments, angle and segment bisectors, and perpendicular lines.

7E Identify parts and properties of triangles, quadrilaterals, congruent polygons, and circles

7F Use central angles to make and interpret circle graphs

7G Use geometric representations to draw diagrams; use Find a Pattern and other strategies to solve problems

About This Unit

The support pages that follow provide more information on prerequisite skills, methods for teaching skills and concepts, daily routines, tips on classroom management and materials, and useful dialogue techniques.

Prerequisite Skills and Concepts

Students should be able to

- classify polygons.

If not, use prerequisite Reteach Worksheet 45, p.115.

Assessments

Use Beginning of the Year Inventory for entry-level assessment.

Ongoing Evaluation Quick Checks, Reteach Worksheets, the Skills Tutorial Inventories, and the Midyear Test help ensure that students are progressing adequately to meet the standards.

Summative Evaluation Use Test Preps, Unit Review (p. T115), Cumulative Review (p. T116), Reteach Worksheets, and the Computation Skills Tutorial to assure that students have achieved the standards for the unit.

Diagnosing Errors The Quick Checks highlight common errors and provide remediation. See also the **Teaching Strategies Handbook** pp. T104–T107, where short discussions labeled Common Misconceptions appear as needed with the strategies for key concepts.

Homework and Family Involvement

Home Note In the Student Book, the Dear Family home note provides objectives, vocabulary, and a sample skill discussion for family participation. (**Teaching Strategies Handbook** pages also provide homework and family involvement tips.)

Education Place Refer families to Houghton Mifflin's EduPlace Web site at http://www.eduplace.com; for resources and activities for students at http://www.eduplace.com/math; and additional resources and activities at http://www.eduplace.com/parents.

Helping Your Children Learn Math This book has activities for children ages 5–13 and tips for getting involved in children's mathematics education. (Houghton Mifflin, 1994)

Lessons	Student Pages	Teacher Pages	Resources	State or Local	
				Objectives	Assessment
7.1 Points, Lines, and Angles	181–182	**T108**	Unit 7 Pretest		
7.2 Planes	183–-184	**T108**	Extension 7		
7.3 Measuring Angles	185–186	**T109**	Reteach 46, 47, 48		
7.4 Angle Relationships	187–188	**T109**			
7.5 Angle Relationships of Parallel Lines	189–190	**T110**			
7.6 Triangles	191–192	**T110**	Reteach 49, 50, 51		
7.7 Problem Solving Strategy: Find a Pattern	193–194	**T111**			
7.8 Constructing Congruent Segments and Angles	195–196	**T111**			
7.9 Constructing Bisectors	197–198	**T112**			
7.10 Polygons and Congruent Figures	199–201	**T112**	Reteach 52, 53, 54		
7.11 Circles and Central Angles	202–203	**T113**			
7.12 Making and Interpreting Circle Graphs	204–206	**T113**			
7.13 Polyhedrons	207–208	**T114**	Reteach 55, 56, 57		
7.14 Problem Solving Application: Use a Diagram	209–210	**T114**	Unit 7 Posttest		

Teaching Strategies

Math Background — Geometry

Geometry is essential to the design of every human-made structure. Both the arts and the sciences use geometry as a bridge between ideas and physical reality. Spatial abilities are positively correlated to mathematical abilities and to academic success in general. Research suggests that the development of geometric ideas progresses though four levels: recognizing shapes; observing and defining properties of shapes (for example, "The opposite sides are parallel."); recognizing relationships between shapes; and making simple deductions or proofs.

In learning geometry, students draw, measure, and interpret figures. They compare, look for patterns, and generalize. The ideas students explore in this unit will help them develop their logical reasoning skills and prepare them for the challenge of geometric "proofs" in the future.

In this unit, students examine two- and three-dimensional figures. They extend their work with geometric topics from Level 6 to help determine characteristics of geometric figures as well as relationships between those figures. Students make use of tools such as rulers and protractors to gather information about figures and to construct new figures.

A Positive Start
Fill the classroom with geometric figures and construct posters of geometric facts and relationships. These will be resources you can use over and over again. Students are naturally interested in geometry and its visual, constructive nature. Those students who struggle with number concepts may excel in geometry. This is an excellent opportunity to reward their mathematical efforts.

Linking Past and Future Learning

Being aware of how concepts are covered in the earlier and later levels is useful when preparing lessons. Use the chart below to help you plan your instruction.

Concept/Skills	Last Year	This Year	Next Year
Angle Relationships	Use degree measure to classify angles; find the sums of the angles of a polygon; give rule to determine sum of angles for any polygon	Construct and compare angles; observe and identify angles with special relationships	Analyze angles; describe and compare angles
Congruent Polygons	Identify similar and congruent polygons	Identify and construct congruent polygons	Prove basic theorems involving congruence
Circle Graphs	Construct and interpret circle graphs; determine central angles	Apply central angles, measuring angles, and percents	Determine when it is appropriate to display data in a circle graph

Methods and Management

Review the entire unit and note how the lessons progress. Throughout the unit, the focus will be on determining characteristics of geometric figures and developing clear definitions of figures. Use this common thread as an organizational structure.

Teaching Strategy: Angle Relationships

There are many interesting relationships between pairs of angles. Look at the relationships of angles that result from a third line intersecting a pair of parallel lines.

▶ ***Show This:***

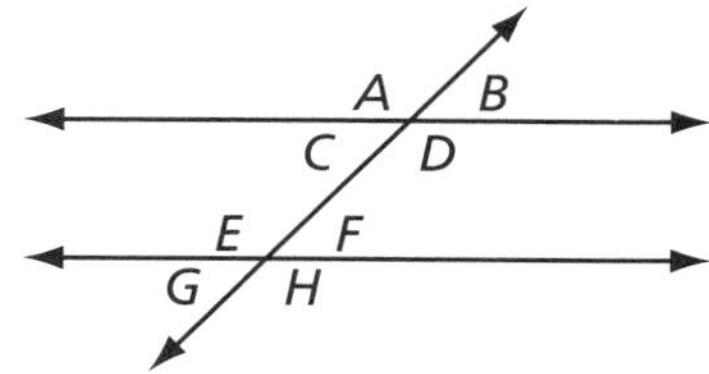

- Explain that the opposite angles are called vertical angles. Angles *A* and *D* are vertical angles.

▶ ***Ask:*** *What other vertical angles can you find in this diagram? What do you notice about the angle measures of each pair of vertical angles?* Help students see that vertical angles are congruent. They can verify this by measuring the angles with protractors.

▶ ***Common Misconceptions*** Many protractors show a "double row" of angle measures so that angles opening either from the left or right can be measured. Some students may read the wrong row. Have them estimate angle measures before they measure.

Teaching Strategy: Congruent Polygons

Focus on the characteristics of angle measure and side length when determining whether or not two polygons are congruent.

▶ ***Show This:***

▶ ***Ask:*** *Are the quadrilaterals congruent? Why or why not?* These quadrilaterals are not congruent because two of the corresponding sides are not the same length.

▶ ***Show This:***

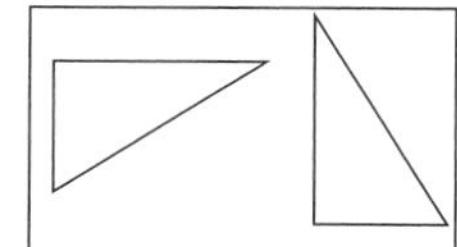

▶ ***Ask:*** *Are the triangles above congruent?* They are. Even though the triangles are in different positions in the plane, they have all the characteristics of congruent figures.

▶ ***Common Misconceptions*** Students may not see that the two triangles in the second example are congruent. Have them measure the sides and angles to verify their answers. Congruency is more difficult to determine when one figure has been rotated or flipped.

Teacher Tips

Visual Aids Post examples of angles being measured using a protractor. Be sure to include examples of measuring angles opening both from the left and from the right.

Materials To keep track of tools such as rulers and protractors that can easily be lost, label them with numbers assigned to each student. That way, when something turns up missing, it will be easier to trace.

Communication The language of geometry is precise, and the symbols used to express geometric ideas are numerous. The more clearly you express geometric vocabulary and use geometric symbols, the easier it will be for your students.

Pacing Drawing and measuring angles and polygons takes time. Make sure to plan enough time in your lessons for these activities.

Vocabulary In this unit, students should become comfortable using the symbol $\angle$ to represent the word *angle*. Students should also regularly use the $^\circ$ symbol to represent degrees. For example, a pair of vertical angles could be expressed as, $\angle ABC$ and $\angle DEF$ are each 135°.

Help from Home When comparing congruent figures, it is useful to have many cut-out figures for each student. Enlist the help of families to cut out preprinted figures at home to save some time.

Management Students often make mistakes when they measure figures. It is sometimes useful to have students work in pairs so they can each measure a figure independently and then verify his or her partner's results.

Real World Seek out circle graphs in newspapers and magazines for students to interpret. This will help students see that circle graphs are a widely used method of illustrating information.

More Materials A compass is a very useful tool for helping students construct a circle. Students can also use fraction circles or other templates to sketch circles.

Math Connections Help students see the relationships between fractions, percents, and central angle measures by having them start with a fraction, find its percent equivalent, and determine what angle measure would represent that percent of the 360 degrees in the full circle. They should also be encouraged to work through this process in the reverse direction.

Graph Practice Ask, *If 25% of the people surveyed about favorite pets said they liked birds, 25% liked cats, and 50% liked dogs, how would you show this in a circle graph? What central angle measures would there be?* As students suggest that 180° would represent one half of the circle and 90° would represent one fourth of the circle, prompt them to determine a way to translate any percent to its related angle measure.

Teaching Strategy: Circle Graphs

Circle graphs can combine angle measures, ratios, and percents. Students will benefit from interpreting circle graphs before constructing their own.

▶ ***Show This:***

Favorite Frozen Yogurt

▶ ***Ask:*** *What percent of the people surveyed about favorite frozen yogurt flavors chose mint?*

The angle measures given can be used to find the ratio between 45° and 360°. So the question can be rephrased as *What percent of 360 is 45?* Students can then determine that 45 is $\frac{1}{8}$ of 360, or 12.5%.

▶ ***Common Misconceptions*** When determining what percent of the circle a certain angle measure represents, some students will simply determine that if the angle measures 20°, then that portion is 20% of the circle. To help students overcome this obstacle, consistently rephrase the question to ask, *What percent of the 360 degrees of the circle would 20 degrees be?*

Opportunities to Assess

Observation

Classroom observations are a vital assessment tool. As you observe students' geometric constructions, make note of what steps give them difficulties and include some suggestions for overcoming these difficulties in your next lesson or in a concluding whole-class discussion.

Homework

Homework not only keeps students engaged in mathematics outside the classroom but also provides a means of communicating to family members about the current topics of study. In geometry, homework may include finding examples of geometric figures, congruent figures, and/or similar figures at home.

Teacher/Student Dialogue

Guiding Students to Build Definitions

Students should be asked to look at geometric figures and determine how they are similar and how they are different. The more they are able to identify and explain, the clearer geometric definitions will become.

Teacher: *(Holds up pictures of a square and a rectangle)* Can someone explain how these figures are alike and how they are different? Amy?

Student: *They both have four sides, but in the square, all the sides are the same size, and in the rectangle, they aren't.*

Teacher: I agree with you. Are there other ways they are alike or different? Cal?

Student: *Well, they both have right angles.*

Teacher: Be more specific about that.

Student: *Well, they each have four angles and all four angles are right angles.*

Teacher: Good. John, if you were to define a square and define a rectangle, what characteristics of these figures would you have to be clear about?

Student: *Their sides and their angles.*

Teacher: Okay, define a rectangle, and then a square.

Student: *A rectangle is a 4-sided figure where all four sides are not the same length, but where all four angles are right angles. A square is a 4-sided figure where all four sides are the same length and all four angles are right angles.*

Teacher: Okay, everyone, let's look at a couple more figures and see if we need to alter these definitions at all. *(Holds up a trapezoid and a parallelogram)*

Questioning Techniques

It is always a good idea to prepare key questions in advance. In the dialogue above, the teacher was ready with a question that focused the student on the figures' attributes, subtly weaving in the very important notion that defining a geometric figure essentially depends upon describing its most important and distinguishing characteristics.

What to do

When

In each class, there is usually at least one student who has a tough time sitting still. This is particularly difficult when students are working with tools such as a ruler or protractor. The tools can become further distractions for the student. It is good to involve this student in the whole-class setting, perhaps having him or her perform a measurement or construction for the whole class to analyze. This way, the student has the sense of having accomplished a related task, making the new task easier to jump into.

What to do

Every Day

Have a prepared "question of the day" ready to present to students at the beginning of the lesson. It could be a question related to the previous lesson or a question to stimulate their thinking for today's lesson. For example, *Yesterday we discussed similarities and differences between a square and a rectangle. What was the primary difference between them?*

Unit 7 Geometry

LESSON 1
PAGES 181–182

OBJECTIVE
To identify basic elements of plane geometric figures

PREREQUISITES
Concepts
- Understand linear measure

Skills
- Be able to measure the length of objects

VOCABULARY
point, line, line segment, ray, vertical, horizontal, collinear, angle, vertex

MATERIALS
Straight edge or ruler

Points, Lines, and Angles

Presenting the Lesson

Introduce the Skill Discuss how a point only occupies space and has no dimensions, so we represent it with a dot. Explain that a line continues forever in each direction but is represented by any two points on the line. Discuss line segment, ray, horizontal and vertical lines, and angles. Stress that, when reading an angle, the vertex is the middle letter if three letters are used. Remind students that three or more points on the same line are said to be collinear.

Check Understanding *Draw an angle on the board and label it ABC. Discuss the different ways to name the angle. How could you name the rays containing the angle?* ($\overrightarrow{BA}$ and $\overrightarrow{BC}$)

Guided Practice

Have students do numbers 1 and 5 on page 181. Check to see that students recognize that there are an infinite number of lines that pass through a given point.

Independent Practice

Have students complete pages 181 and 182 independently.

Closing the Lesson *How does a segment differ from a line?* (A line is infinite in length and a segment has a finite length.)

LESSON 2
PAGES 183–184

OBJECTIVE
To examine the properties of planes and how two or more objects can be related in space

PREREQUISITES
Concepts
- Understand basic elements in geometry

Skills
- Be able to label basic geometric figures appropriately

VOCABULARY
plane, coplanar

MATERIALS
Copymasters
Extension 7, p. 183

Planes

Presenting the Lesson

Introduce the Skill Point to the wall and ask students what geometry idea is represented by the wall. (a plane) Tell them we name a plane by listing at least three points of the plane that are not on the same straight line. Points, lines, segments, etc., that are on the same plane are said to be coplanar. Ask students: *When two planes intersect, what do they have in common?* (A line; Look at two intersecting walls.) *Can three planes intersect?* (Yes; Look at the corner of a room.) *What is in common where the three planes meet in a corner of a room?* (a point) *Do two planes always intersect?* (No; Consider the ceiling and floor.)

Check Understanding *Can three planes intersect so that they have a line in common?* (Yes; As in a book, the binding is the line in which all the pages meet.)

Guided Practice

Have the students do exercises 1, 7, and 12 on pages 183 and 184. Check to see that the two planes in exercise 12 have a line in common.

Independent Practice

Have students complete pages 183 and 184 independently.

Closing the Lesson *If two different planes have two different points, A and B, in common, what can you tell me about the two planes?* (They intersect in line *AB*.)

LESSON 3
PAGES 185–186

OBJECTIVE
To use a protractor to measure angles

PREREQUISITES
Concepts
- Understand rays and angles

Skills
- Be able to name angles and rays

VOCABULARY
protractor, degree, congruent, acute, right, obtuse, straight angle

MATERIALS
protractors and overhead transparency with angles drawn on it (You could demonstrate them with a large protractor on the board.)

Copymasters
Teaching Resource 11 (protractors)
Reteach 46, 47, 48, pp. 116–118

Measuring Angles

Presenting the Lesson

Introduce the Skill Have students draw an acute angle of 40° using their protractor. Do the same for a right angle and an obtuse angle of 110°. Have them draw two intersecting lines and measure the various angles created. Have them label the angles by putting points on each of the rays and labeling them and the vertex. Have them swap with a neighbor to see if they agree with the measurements obtained.

Check Understanding *What sort of angle is greater than a right angle and less than a straight angle?* (obtuse angle) *What can you tell me about two right angles?* (The sum of their measures is 180°; they are congruent.)

Guided Practice

Have them do the first exercise in rows 1 and 4 on pages 185 and 186. Check to see that they are placing the protractor's center on the vertex and the 0° line along one side of the angle.

Independent Practice

Have students complete pages 185 and 186 independently.

Closing the Lesson *Why is it important to know how to measure angles?* (Possible answer: When surveying land or building a house, you need plans that accurately describe how things look.)

LESSON 4
PAGES 187–188

OBJECTIVE
To identify types of angles and their relationships

PREREQUISITES
Concepts
- Understand measurement of angles

Skills
- Be able to measure angles using a protractor
- Compute using rational numbers

VOCABULARY
adjacent and vertical angles complementary and supplementary angles

MATERIALS
Protractors

Copymasters
Teaching Resource 11 (protractors)

Angle Relationships

Presenting the Lesson

Introduce the Skill Draw a pair of adjacent angles on the board whose sum is an acute angle. Label the angles so that they can be distinguished. Discuss with students how the two angles are adjacent angles because they share a common vertex and a common side and their interiors have no points in common. Define complementary and supplementary angles and give examples of each. Have students draw two intersecting lines and label them. Now, have them measure the four angles. Explain that the two that are "opposite" each other and that have the same measures are called vertical angles.

Check Understanding *If two angles are supplementary, what can you tell me about the sum of their measures?* (They add up to 180°.)

Guided Practice

Do the first exercise in rows 1, 5, and 13 on pages 187 and 188. In exercise 1, make sure they are naming adjacent angles.

Independent Practice

Have students complete pages 187 and 188 independently.

Closing the Lesson *What can you tell me about vertical angles?* (Possible answers: They are the opposite angles or non-adjacent angles formed when two lines intersect; They are congruent to one another.)

LESSON 5
PAGES 189–190

OBJECTIVE
To identify the relationships between angles where two or more lines are cut by a transversal

PREREQUISITES
Concepts
- Understand adjacent, supplementary, and vertical angles

Skills
- Be able to measure angles

VOCABULARY
transversal, parallel lines, corresponding and alternate interior angles

MATERIALS
Protractor

Copymasters
Teaching Resource 11 (protractors)

Angle Relationships of Parallel Lines

Presenting the Lesson

Introduce the Skill Have students draw two non-parallel lines and two parallel lines and draw a transversal for each pair. Have them label the lines and intersection points. Identify corresponding angles on each set of lines and have the students measure the angles. *What relationships, if any, did you discover about the corresponding angles?* (The ones formed by parallel lines are congruent.) Now, explain what alternate interior angles are. Have students measure the alternate interior angles in each set of lines. *What did you discover about alternate interior angles?* (If the lines are parallel, the alternate interior angles are congruent.)

Check Understanding *What are corresponding angles of parallel lines?* (angles on the same side of the transversal and in a corresponding position with the lines, either above the lines or below the lines.)

Guided Practice

Do exercises 1, 4, and 7 on pages 189 and 190.

Independent Practice

Have students complete pages 189 and 190 independently.

Closing the Lesson *What are alternate interior angles?* (angles on the opposite sides of the transversal and interior to the two lines)

LESSON 6
PAGES 191–192

OBJECTIVE
To classify triangles and compute the sum of the angle measures

PREREQUISITES
Concepts
- Understand angle measure and the classification of angles by their measures

Skills
- Be able to measure angles and distances

VOCABULARY
right, acute, and obtuse triangles; congruent sides; equilateral, isosceles, and scalene triangles

MATERIALS
Protractor and ruler

Copymasters
Teaching Resource 11 (protractors)
Reteach 49, 50, 51, pp. 119–121

Triangles

Presenting the Lesson

Introduce the Skill Have everyone draw a triangle and cut it out. Then, have them snip off the three angles of the triangle and line up the sides and vertices. They should form a straight angle showing that the sum of the angles of a triangle is 180°. Now, draw three triangles that are scalene, isosceles, and equilateral. Have three volunteers come to the board to measure the three sides in each triangle one at a time. Define the triangles based on the number of congruent sides they have.

Check Understanding *Can a triangle be isosceles and right at the same time?* (Yes.) *Can a triangle be equilateral and a right triangle at the same time?* (No.) *Can a triangle have a right angle and an obtuse angle in it?* (No, because the sum of the angles would then be greater than 180°.)

Guided Practice

Have students do the first exercise in rows 1, 3, and 5 on page 191.

Independent Practice

Have students complete pages 191 and 192 independently.

Closing the Lesson *There are seven possible ways of classifying a triangle. What are those seven ways?* (scalene right, scalene acute, scalene obtuse, isosceles right, isosceles acute, isosceles obtuse, equilateral acute)

LESSON 7
PAGES 193–194

OBJECTIVE
To use Find a Pattern or other strategies to solve problems

PREREQUISITES
Concepts
- Understand the four-step problem solving process

Skills
- Perform computations with rational numbers

Problem Solving Strategy: Find a Pattern

Presenting the Lesson

Introduce the Strategy Point out that in this lesson students will look for patterns to help them solve problems.

Model the Four-Step Problem Solving Process Present the handshake problem described on page 193.

- **Understand** Remind students to identify some basic numbers.
- **Decide** This step, together with the following step, applies four strategies for one problem.
- **Solve** Emphasize how important number sense is in searching for the pattern.
- **Look back** Discuss what strategies were combined to solve the problem

Check Understanding *What was the basic idea of the strategy used?* (finding a pattern.)

Guided Practice

Do exercise 1 on page 194. Check to see that they extend the pattern.

Independent Practice

Have students complete pages 193 and 194 independently.

Closing the Lesson *What is the next number in this pattern?* 2, 5, 10, 17, . . . (26)

LESSON 8
PAGES 195–196

OBJECTIVE
To use compass and straightedge to construct congruent segments and congruent angles

PREREQUISITES
Concepts
- Understand the congruence relation for angles and segments

MATERIALS
Compass and straightedge

Constructing Congruent Segments and Angles

Presenting the Lesson

Introduce the Skill Draw a line segment on the board and ask students to draw one on a piece of paper. Show them how to construct a line segment congruent to the one you drew. Mention that, when doing constructions, you can only use a compass and unmarked straightedge. Have them construct a line segment congruent to the one they originally drew on their papers. Ask them how they could construct a line segment twice as long. Have them do it, and then have someone come to the board to demonstrate how to do it.

Check Understanding *If you were going to construct a line segment three times as long as a given segment, what would you do?* (Construct a segment congruent to the original segment. Then, from the outer endpoint, construct another segment congruent to the original segment and repeat this step.)

Guided Practice

Do exercises 1, 4, and 9 on pages 195 and 196. In exercise 4, check to see that the students start the second segment from the outer endpoint of the first one.

Independent Practice

Have students complete pages 195 and 196 independently.

Closing the Lesson What is a geometric construction? (a construction done using only compass and straightedge)

LESSON 9
PAGES 197–198

OBJECTIVE
To use compass and straightedge to construct bisectors and perpendicular lines

PREREQUISITES
Concepts
- Understand right triangles, angle measure, and basic constructions

Skills
- Be able to construct congruent segments and angles
- Be able to use a compass, straightedge, and protractor

VOCABULARY
perpendicular

MATERIALS
Compass, straightedge, and protractor

Copymasters
Teaching Resource 11 (protractors)

Constructing Bisectors

Presenting the Lesson

Introduce the Skill Draw an angle on the board and ask the class how they might divide the angle into two equal parts. Some students may suggest that you measure the angle with a protractor, compute half of that measure, and set up an angle with that measure within the original one. Explain that a geometric construction must be independent of that kind of measurement and is, in fact, more accurate. Discuss the same ideas relating to the task of bisecting the segment. Explain carefully the stages involved in bisecting the angle and in bisecting the segment.

Check Understanding *When you bisect a segment, what other geometric figure do you construct?* (a line that is perpendicular to the segment.)

Guided Practice

Have students do construction 1 on page 197. Check to see that students used the correct centers when drawing the second and third arcs.

Independent Practice

Have students complete pages 197 and 198 independently.

Closing the Lesson *Can you think why it might be important to be able to bisect a segment?* (Possible answer: When you want to find the exact midpoint of the segment.)

LESSON 10
PAGES 199–201

OBJECTIVE
To identify types of quadrilaterals and the properties of congruent polygons

PREREQUISITES
Concepts
- Understand the congruence relation for angles, segments, and triangles

Skills
- Be able to measure angles and linear distances

VOCABULARY
quadrilateral, parallelogram, rhombus, regular polygon, congruent polygons

MATERIALS
Grid paper, overhead transparency of dot paper

Copymasters
Teaching Resource 3 (square dot paper)

Polygons and Congruent Figures

Presenting the Lesson

Introduce the Skill Ask students what kinds of quadrilaterals they know about. Have them draw a parallelogram on their dot paper. Discuss the fact that the opposite sides are parallel and congruent and that the opposite angles are congruent. Have them draw a rectangle, square, and a non-square rhombus as you draw it on the overhead. Discuss the properties of each and the fact that they are all parallelograms. Discuss the fact that a square is both a rectangle and a rhombus.

Check Understanding *If a polygon has all of its sides congruent is it a regular polygon?* (Not necessarily; a rhombus has all of its sides congruent.)

Guided Practice

Have students do exercises 1, 5, 7, and 12 and the first line in exercise 11 on pages 199–201. Check to see that they classified the square in exercise 5 as a parallelogram, rectangle, rhombus, and square.

Independent Practice

Have students complete pages 199–201 independently.

Closing the Lesson *Is every square a rhombus?* (Yes, because it is a parallelogram with four congruent sides.) *Are all rhombuses squares?* (No, because a rhombus need not have right angles.)

LESSON 11
PAGES 202–203

OBJECTIVE
To identify the parts of a circle and find the measures of arcs and central angles

PREREQUISITES
Concepts
- Understand angle measurement and rational numbers

Skills
- Perform calculations using rational numbers

VOCABULARY
circle, diameter, arc, central angle

Circles and Central Angles

Presenting the Lesson

Introduce the Skill Define what a central angle is and draw several of them in a circle. Point out that we measure arcs in degrees and that the measure of an arc equals the measure of the central angle that intersects its endpoints. Draw a central angle measuring 60°. Mention that the ratio of the measure of a central angle to 360° is used in the making of circle graphs.

For this case it is $\frac{60°}{360°} = \frac{1}{6}$.

Check Understanding *If a central angle is* 120°, *what portion of the circle does it enclose?* ($\frac{1}{3}$)

Guided Practice

Have students do numbers 1, 8, and 11 on pages 202 and 203.

Independent Practice

Have students complete pages 202 and 203 independently.

Closing the Lesson *If the arc intercepted by a central angle is* 80°, *what portion of the circle is enclosed by the central angle and its arc?* ($\frac{80°}{360°} = \frac{2}{9}$)

LESSON 12
PAGES 204–206

OBJECTIVE
To make a circle graph and use it to represent percentages

PREREQUISITES
Concepts
- Understand percent and fractional relations

Skills
- Be able to read and analyze graphs
- Perform computations with rational numbers

VOCABULARY
circle graph

MATERIALS
Copymasters
Teaching Resource 10 (circle spinner)

Circle Graphs

Presenting the Lesson

Introduce the Skill Pose the following problem: *Maria has to pay 20% for taxes and another 10% for benefits, 25% for rent, 30% for food and other household goods and 15% percent for retirement and savings.* Have students find out how large the central angle should be for each portion in a circle graph that shows Maria's expenses.

Check Understanding *If one portion of a circle graph is* 15%, *what is the size of the central angle?* (54°) *If a central angle is* 120°, *what fraction of the total circle does it enclose?* ($\frac{1}{3}$)

Guided Practice

Have students do exercises 1, 6, and 12 on pages 204 and 206. Check to see that students are finding the percents correctly in exercise 1.

Independent Practice

Have students complete pages 204–206 independently.

Closing the Lesson *If a central angle of a graph is* 108°, *how would you find what percent of the circle is enclosed in that central angle and its arc?* (Possible answer: Divide 108° by 360°, obtaining 0.3. Now, change that to a percent by multiplying by 100 and writing the percent sign.)

LESSON 13
PAGES 207–208

OBJECTIVE
To identify various types of space figures

PREREQUISITES
Concepts
- Understand polygons

Skills
- Be able to name polygons by the number of their sides and angles

VOCABULARY
polyhedron, prism, pyramid, net, faces, edges and vertices of polyhedrons, diagonals

Copymasters
Teaching Resources 12–16 (nets)
Reteach 55, 56, 57, pp. 125–127

Polyhedrons

Presenting the Lesson

Introduce the Skill Show students a simple box and discuss what its faces, edges, and vertices are. Be sure to point out that it is a prism. You may want to have students build the polyhedrons found on Teaching Resources 12–16 before completing the tables on page 207.

Check Understanding *What is a polyhedron?* (a three-dimensional figure whose sides are polygons)

Guided Practice
Have students complete the table for prism 1 (exercise 1) and pyramid 1 (exercise 2) on pages 207 and 208. Check to see that they counted the parts correctly.

Independent Practice
Have students complete pages 207 and 208 independently.

Closing the Lesson *What are some examples of where polyhedrons are used in everyday life?* (Possible answer: Most boxes are prisms.)

LESSON 14
PAGES 209–210

OBJECTIVE
To use construction and other drawing tools to draw diagrams to solve problems

PREREQUISITES
Concepts
- Understand length, area, and the four-step problem solving process

Skills
- Be able to use construction tools

Problem Solving Application: Use a Diagram

Presenting the Lesson
Introduce the Focus of the Lesson Explain to students that in this lesson they will need to draw diagrams to solve problems.

Model the Four-Step Problem Solving Process Work through the problem of the hexagonal frame and the cord on page 209 with your students.

Discuss the Problem Solving Tips Point out to students that the four Problem Solving Process steps—Understand, Decide, Solve, and Look back—are listed in the box on page 209. Make sure students understand that each step is distinct from the others.

Check Understanding *What is the altitude or height of a triangle?* (It is a line drawn from the opposite vertex perpendicular to the side chosen as the base.) *How does the picture help you solve the problem?* (Possible answer: It helps you visualize relationships that you might not recognize without the picture.)

Guided Practice
Have students do problems 1 and 2 on page 209. Check to see that students do the construction correctly.

Independent Practice
Have students complete page 210 independently.

Closing the Lesson *What kinds of diagrams and tools can you use to solve problems?* (Possible answers: construction tools (straightedge and compass), rulers, protractors, number lines, grid paper, lined paper)

UNIT 7 REVIEW

PAGES 211–213

Item Analysis

Items	Unit Obj.
1–7	7A
8–14	7B, 7C
15–20	7A
21–25	7E, 7F
26–29	7F
30–32	7A, 7E
33–35	7B
36	7E
37–39	7A, 7E
40–42	7C
43–44	7D
45–46	7G

Answers to Unit 7 Review items can be found on pages 211–213 of the Teacher's Annotated Edition.

Administering the Review

This page reviews concepts and skills taught in this unit. Be sure students understand all direction lines. You may want to do the first example in each section cooperatively to ensure understanding.

Scoring Chart

Number Correct	46	45	44	43	42	41	40	39	38	37	36	35	34	33	32	31
Score	100	98	96	93	91	89	87	85	83	80	78	76	74	72	70	67

Number Correct	30	29	28	27	26	25	24	23	22	21	20	19	18	17	16	15
Score	65	63	61	59	56	54	52	50	48	46	43	41	39	37	35	33

Number Correct	14	13	12	11	10	9	8	7	6	5	4	3	2	1
Score	30	28	26	24	22	20	17	15	13	11	9	7	4	2

After the Review

- The Item Analysis chart on the left shows the Unit 7 objective(s) covered by each test item. This chart can help you to determine which objectives need review or extra practice.
- For additional assessment, use the Posttest for Unit 7, Copymaster Book, pp. 32–34
- To provide extension opportunities, use Copymaster Book, p. 183

UNIT 7 CUMULATIVE REVIEW

PAGE 214

Item Analysis

Items	Unit Obj.
1	7A
2	7C
3	5D
4	4B
5	7C
6	5C
7	3B
8	5A

Answers to Cumulative Review items can be found on page 214 of the Teacher's Annotated Edition.

Administering the Review

This page reviews concepts and skills from earlier units as well as providing practice with standardized test formats. Students may circle their answers, or you may prefer to duplicate and distribute the answer sheet, Copymaster Book, p. 191. This page may be assigned as homework or as classwork.

Test-Taking Tip When drawing pictures to help you find a solution, always reread the problem after making your sketch.

Scoring Chart

Number Correct	8	7	6	5	4	3	2	1
Score	100	88	75	63	50	38	25	13

After the Review

The Item Analysis chart on the left shows the unit objective covered by each test item. This chart can help you to determine which objectives need review or extra practice.

Teacher Notes

Integers and Rational Numbers

Vocabulary

absolute value The distance of a number from zero on the number line, regardless of direction

integer The set of numbers containing all the whole numbers and their opposites

irrational number A number that cannot be expressed as a ratio of two integers

opposites Two numbers whose sum is 0. They are also called additive inverses.

rational number A number that can be expressed as the ratio of two integers

Unit Objectives

- **8A** Use a number line to recognize, model, compare, order, and find the absolute value of integers and their opposites
- **8B** Add and subtract integers
- **8C** Multiply and divide integers
- **8D** Add, subtract, multiply, and divide rational numbers
- **8E** Use positive and negative rationals to draw graphs; use Draw a Picture and other strategies to solve problems

About This Unit

The support pages that follow provide more information on prerequisite skills, methods for teaching skills and concepts, daily routines, tips on classroom management and materials, and useful dialogue techniques.

Prerequisite Skills and Concepts

Students should be able to

- identify positive and negative numbers.
- compare and order integers.

If not, use prerequisite Reteach Worksheets 58 and 59, p. 128–129.

Assessments

Use Beginning of the Year Inventory for entry-level assessment.

Ongoing Evaluation Quick Checks, Reteach Worksheets, the Skills Tutorial Inventories, and the Midyear Test help ensure that students are progressing adequately to meet the standards.

Summative Evaluation Use Test Preps, Unit Review (p. T129), Cumulative Review (p. T130), Reteach Worksheets, and the Computation Skills Tutorial to assure that students have achieved the standards for the unit.

Diagnosing Errors The Quick Checks highlight common errors and provide remediation. See also the **Teaching Strategies Handbook** pp. T120–123, where short discussions labeled Common Misconceptions appear as needed with the strategies for key concepts.

Homework and Family Involvement

Home Note In the Student Book, the Dear Family home note provides objectives, vocabulary, and a sample skill discussion for family participation. (**Teaching Strategies Handbook** pages also provide homework and family involvement tips.)

Education Place Refer families to Houghton Mifflin's EduPlace Web site at **http://www.eduplace.com**; for resources and activities for students at **http://www.eduplace.com/math**; and additional resources and activities at **http://www.eduplace.com/parents**.

Helping Your Children Learn Math This book has activities for children ages 5–13 and tips for getting involved in children's mathematics education. (Houghton Mifflin, 1994)

Lessons	Student Pages	Teacher Pages	Resources	State or Local	
				Objectives	Assessment
8.1 Integers	217–220	**T124**	Unit 8 Pretest		
8.2 Adding Integers	221–222	**T124**			
8.3 Subtracting Integers	223–224	**T125**	Reteach 60, 61, 62		
8.4 Problem Solving Strategy: Draw a Diagram	225–226	**T125**			
8.5 Multiplying Integers	227–228	**T126**			
8.6 Dividing Integers	229–230	**T126**	Extension 8		
8.7 Rational Numbers on the Number Line	231–232	**T127**	Reteach 63, 64, 65		
8.8 Algebra: Adding and Subtracting Rational Numbers	233–234	**T127**			
8.9 Algebra: Multiplying and Dividing Rational Numbers	235–236	**T128**	Reteach 66, 67		
8.10 Algebra: Problem Solving Application: Use a Graph	237–238	**T128**	Unit 8 Posttest		

Teaching Strategies

Math Background — Integers and Rational Numbers

Integers are the set of whole numbers and their opposites; for example, 546, $^{-}2$, and 0 are all integers. Rational numbers are the set of numbers that can be written as the quotient of two integers ($^{-}31$, 0, $\frac{-2}{3}$, $\frac{14}{1}$, $^{-}0.25$, and 0.333 are all rational numbers). Integers are part of this set; so are fractions and decimals.

In this unit, students will learn about the relationship between the set of integer numbers and the set of rational numbers. They will compare integers and other rational numbers on a number line and learn how to perform addition, subtraction, multiplication, and division with both positive and negative rational numbers.

When Students Ask, Why Learn This?
Your students are exposed to many situations in their daily lives that involve positive and negative numbers. They observe rising and falling temperatures in their environment, read about government surplus and debt in the newspaper, and encounter undersea and space exploration in science class. The knowledge they acquire working with rational numbers will help them better understand and appreciate these real-life situations.

A Positive Start
You'll be surprised at how many situations your students will think of that can be expressed using positive and negative numbers. Stimulate their creative thinking by asking them to describe situations about football games, hot-air balloon rides, and mountain climbing, or other sports that could be expressed with positive and negative numbers. Then, have them come up with some ideas of their own.

Linking Past and Future Learning

Knowing what students learned the previous year can help you guide their introduction to new topics. The following chart offers a comparison of related topics taught last year, as well as topics for next year.

Concept/Skills	Last Year	This Year	Next Year
Adding and Subtracting Integers	Compare and order integers; determine when integer addition or subtraction is appropriate	Strategies for integer addition and subtraction; using a number line	Work with integers at all levels
Rational Numbers on the Number Line	Rational numbers and their properties	Compare integers and rational numbers	Explore rational and irrational numbers
Multiplying Rational Numbers	Multiplying decimals, fractions, and mixed numbers	Multiplying and dividing positive and negative rational numbers	Operationing with rational and irrational numbers

Methods and Management

Working with integers and rational numbers can be challenging for students. Be prepared to offer a variety of models for students to use. Consult with colleagues, at your level and at the previous level, about models that they find to be successful.

Teaching Strategy: Adding and Subtracting Integers

Students will benefit from using number lines and two-color counters for adding and subtracting integers. Two-color counters are valuable because of their connection to algebraic thinking and the inverse property of integers.

- With two-color counters, let black represent positive numbers and white represent negative numbers. Ask, How can I show $^{-}5 - (^{-}3) = {}^{-}2$?

▶ ***Show This:***

Ask a student volunteer to explain the model to the class. Next, have students solve $^{-}4 - 2 = {}^{-}6$ using counters. A positive counter and a negative counter together are worth zero. Add two positive and two negatives to the model and the value of the counters is still $^{-}4$. Take away two positive counters. How many are left?

▶ ***Common Misconceptions*** Students are usually taught the rule that subtracting a negative number is like adding a positive number. That rule certainly works, but students often remember it incorrectly or misuse it. Make sure that you provide your students with the rationale behind the rule.

Teaching Strategy: Rational Numbers

One of the most interesting facts about rational numbers is the density property. The density property means that between any two rational numbers on a number line, there is an infinite number of rational numbers.

▶ ***Show This:***

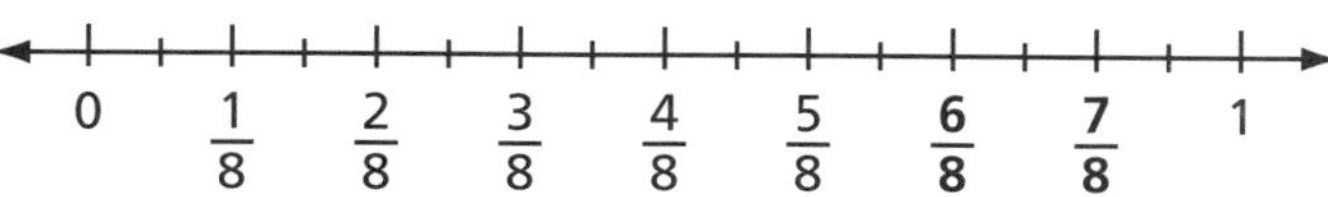

▶ ***Ask:*** *How can I find some rational numbers between $\frac{6}{8}$ and $\frac{7}{8}$?*

Encourage students to try this: Convert $\frac{6}{8}$ and $\frac{7}{8}$ to the equivalent fractions $\frac{12}{16}$ and $\frac{14}{16}$. Because $\frac{13}{16}$ is between $\frac{12}{16}$ and $\frac{14}{16}$, $\frac{13}{16}$ is between $\frac{6}{8}$ and $\frac{7}{8}$.

▶ ***Ask:*** *Does this strategy work when finding a rational number between $\frac{1}{3}$ and $\frac{1}{2}$?*
Students may change $\frac{1}{3}$ and $\frac{1}{2}$ to the equivalent fractions $\frac{2}{6}$ and $\frac{3}{6}$ and worry that this won't give them an answer. Encourage them to find other equivalent versions of the fractions, such as $\frac{4}{12}$ and $\frac{6}{12}$. Another approach would be to find the midpoint between $\frac{1}{3}$ and $\frac{1}{2}$ by adding $\frac{1}{3}$ and $\frac{1}{2}$ and dividing the sum by 2.

Teacher Tips

Visual Aids Display horizontal and vertical number lines labeled with positive and negative values in your classroom. Students will be able to refer to these to help them visualize relationships among rational numbers.

Good Routine Encourage students to get in the habit of sketching a number line when reasoning through problems. This will be a useful tool throughout their mathematics schooling.

Management To avoid developing a static classroom environment, move students around periodically. Relocating their seats in the room can keep the class from feeling predictable and encourage them to interact with different classmates.

Pacing Spend the time to make sure students are comfortable with performing operations with integers in lessons 2, 3, 5, and 6. A relaxed pace during these lessons will set the stage for a smooth progression through lessons 8 and 9.

More Materials Grid paper is very useful when students construct number lines. It is also handy for illustrating multiplication with arrays.

Help from Home Have students bring different types of thermometers to class. Check in the library for maps that show sea levels. These materials can provide some connections for students as they work with integers.

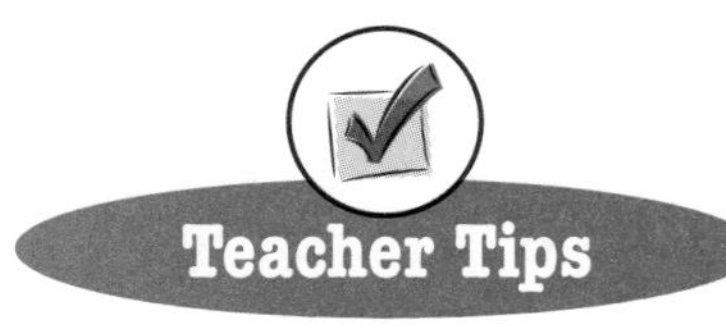

Teacher Tips

Planning Ahead Make sure that you provide students with the opportunity to work with vertical numbers lines as well as horizontal number lines. The vertical number lines are particularly helpful when analyzing rises and falls in temperature or stock prices. This will familiarize students with viewing positive and negative numbers in both directions, which will help prepare them for coordinate graphing in Unit 11.

Real World Your students will probably be interested in applications that involve money. Have the class keep track of the stock market as it rises and falls. They may each want to choose a few different stocks to follow.

Vocabulary Discussion of finding rational numbers on a number line should elicit vocabulary associated with comparing and ordering fractions, such as *equivalent* and *midpoint.*

Memory Trigger To help students remember that numbers to the right of zero on a horizontal number line are positive, tell them to think of "feeling positive." To help them recall that the numbers "up" from zero on a vertical number line, they can think of "feeling up."

Showing, Describing These two stages come together most dramatically when trying to help students see the "why" behind the multiplication of one fraction by another. Provide many examples of multiplying one fraction by another, illustrating the factors using the array model. Ultimately, students will begin to more clearly see what happens when you multiply rational numbers.

Teaching Strategy: Multiplying Rational Numbers

Multiplication of rational numbers can best be visualized with an array model through paper folding or sketching a rectangle.

- **Ask:** *How can you show that $\frac{1}{3} \times \frac{1}{2}$ is $\frac{1}{6}$?*
- **Show This:**

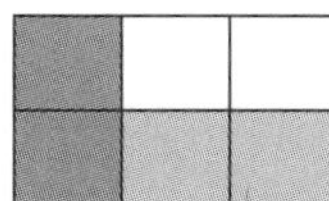

Divide one side of a rectangle in thirds; the other in halves. Shade one of the thirds and one of the halves. The overlap of shading shows the product of $\frac{1}{3}$ and $\frac{1}{2}$, or $\frac{1}{6}$.

- ***Vocabulary Development*** When multiplying a fraction less than one by another fraction less than one, students should express the multiplication as finding a fraction of a fraction. For example, $\frac{1}{3}$ multiplied by $\frac{1}{2}$ can be expressed as $\frac{1}{3}$ of $\frac{1}{2}$. Students will then be better able to see that the answer has to be less than $\frac{1}{2}$.
- ***Common Misconceptions*** Some students have particular difficulty understanding how to explain why the product of a negative rational number multiplied by a negative rational number is a positive rational number. Use a number line to illustrate the combination of facing the negative direction and moving "backward." Point out that two negative actions can "undo" each other and produce a positive result.

Opportunities to Assess

Observation

Have students work in small groups to model addition and subtraction of integers on a number line. Have them illustrate, in particular, what happens when they subtract a negative number. These tasks will quickly show you who understands these topics and who needs more practice.

Homework

Homework can reinforce skills learned during the school day. For this unit, homework can include challenging students to explain the reasoning behind an integer transaction such as: A boy bought a bike for $50, then sold it for $60. Then, he bought it back again for $70 and finally sold it again for $80. What is the net profit or loss from this series of transactions?

Family Involvement

Ask students to find at least three different examples at home or on the news of where they might encounter positive and negative integers. Have them record their observations and bring them to school to share.

Teacher/Student Dialogue

How to Conclude a Lesson

Summarizing a lesson can be a vital step in making sure students understood key concepts. A whole-class discussion can be a very effective means of summarizing what was learned that day, as well as uncovering any misconceptions.

Teacher: Let's look back on today's lesson. Describe something you learned today, Mason.

Student: *One thing I learned was that integers are also rational numbers.*

Teacher: Why are integers considered rational numbers?

Student: *Because they can be rewritten as fractions. Like 2; it can be written as 2 over 1.*

Teacher: So from your example can you make a statement about what makes a number a rational number?

Student: *Sure. A rational number is a number that can be rewritten like a fraction where the numerator and denominator are both integers.*

Teacher: Good. What else did you discover today?

What to do

When

Students have difficulty identifying the location of negative rational numbers on a number line. Help them remember that as they move to the left on the number line, the value of the number gets smaller. So when trying to locate $^{-}3.25$ on a number line, they should indicate a point between $^{-}3$ and $^{-}4$, closer to $^{-}3$.

What to do

Every Day

Give students the opportunity to subtract integers every day. Have a volunteer report the high and low temperature in Alaska or some other area where temperatures go above and below zero during the day. Then, have the class determine how much the temperature changed over the course of the day.

Unit 8 Integers and Rational Numbers

LESSON 1
PAGES 217–220

OBJECTIVE
To use a number line to model integer concepts (including absolute value)

PREREQUISITES
Concepts
- Understand the meaning of the distance (or number of intervals) of a number from 0 on a number line
- Understand the meaning of a variable

Skills
- Locate whole numbers on a number line

VOCABULARY
integer, positive integer, negative integer, opposites, absolute value

MATERIALS
Copymasters
Teaching Resource 7 (number lines)

Integers

Presenting the Lesson

Introduce the Skill Discuss absolute value (and absolute value notation) in relation to the pairs of numbers $^{-}10$ and 10, 32 and $^{-}32$, and others, and ask the class to guess the absolute value of 0. Discuss other situations in which positive and negative numbers would be used: a positive bank account balance versus a negative one, etc.

Check Understanding *For what type of integer would its opposite be positive?* (The opposite of a negative integer is positive.) *For what type of integer would its absolute value be negative?* (None. The absolute value of an integer is always greater than or equal to zero.)

Guided Practice

Have students do exercises 1, 3, 8, 12, 16, 22, and 26 on pages 217–220. Be sure students list two numbers for the answer to each of the exercises 16 and 22.

Independent Practice

Have students complete pages 217–220 independently.

Closing the Lesson *What is an integer?* (Any number in the set {. . . $^{-}3$, $^{-}2$, $^{-}1$, 0, 1, 2, 3. . . . .})

LESSON 2
PAGES 221–222

OBJECTIVE
To add two integers

PREREQUISITES
Concepts
- Understand the meaning of positive and negative integers
- Understand whole number addition and subtraction

Skills
- Locate integers on a number line
- Perform addition and subtraction of whole numbers
- Solve equations involving missing addends

MATERIALS
Copymasters
Teaching Resource 7 (number lines)

Adding Integers

Presenting the Lesson

Introduce the Skill Use a simple procedure to introduce a way to find the sum of a positive integer and a negative integer: To find the sum of 2 and $^{-}5$, start at 0, move 2 intervals to the right, and then move 5 intervals to the left; the sum is $^{-}3$. Try a few more examples to show that the sum of a positive integer and a negative integer may be positive, negative, or zero: $4 + {}^{-}1$, ${}^{-}3 + 3$, ${}^{-}7 + 8$, ${}^{-}10 + 8$.

Check Understanding *How can you predict the sign of the sum of a positive integer and a negative integer?* (If the two integers have the same absolute value, the sum will be zero. Otherwise, the sum will have the same sign as that of the integer whose absolute value is larger.)

Guided Practice

Have students do the first problem in exercises 1, 2, 5, 8, and 11 on pages 221 and 222. Check to see that students' answers are correct in sign and in value.

Independent Practice

Have students complete pages 221 and 222 independently.

Closing the Lesson *Indicate the sign of each of these: the sum of two positive integers* (positive), *the sum of two negative integers* (negative), *the sum of a positive integer and a negative integer* (could be positive, negative, or zero; depends on the absolute values of the two integers being added).

LESSON 3
PAGES 223–224

OBJECTIVE
To subtract integers

PREREQUISITES
Concepts
- Understand the meaning of positive and negative integers
- Understand addition of integers

Skills
- Locate integers on a number line
- Identify the opposite of an integer
- Perform addition of integers

MATERIALS
Copymasters
Teaching Resource 7
Reteach 60, 61, 62, pp. 60–62

Subtracting Integers

Presenting the Lesson

Introduce the Skill Review the concept of an integer's opposite. Discuss the idea that subtracting an integer is the same as adding its opposite and use this idea to rewrite each of these subtraction problems as an addition problem: $1 - 3$, $2 - {}^{-}6$, ${}^{-}5 - 1$, ${}^{-}3 - {}^{-}10$, ${}^{-}2 - {}^{-}2$. Emphasize that addition and subtraction are inverse operations.

Check Understanding *For each of these, find the difference: ${}^{-}8 - 3$ and ${}^{-}4 - {}^{-}6$.* (${}^{-}11$, 2)

Guided Practice
Have students do exercises 1, 3, 6, 7, and 11 on pages 223 and 224.

Independent Practice
Have students complete pages 223 and 224 independently.

Closing the Lesson *Why do we call ${}^{-}3$ and 3 additive inverses of each other?* (Because their sum equals zero, which is the additive identity element.)

LESSON 4
PAGES 225–226

OBJECTIVE
To use Draw a Diagram to apply positive and negative integers to problem situations

PREREQUISITES
Concepts
- Understand addition and subtraction of integers
- Understand the four steps of problem solving—Understand, Decide, Solve, and Look back

Skills
- Perform addition and subtraction of integers
- Translate words into diagrams

Problem Solving: Draw a Diagram

Presenting the Lesson

Introduce the Strategy Point out that in this lesson students will draw diagrams to help them solve problems.

Model the Four-Step Problem Solving Process Present the problem of computing the total distance traveled by the particle.

- **Understand** Explain that what is required is the total distance.
- **Decide** Emphasize that the basic technique of this method is to be able to visualize the distances involved as the particle moves from one position to another.
- **Solve** Make sure that students add distances (which are all positive), not integers.
- **Look back** Remind students that what they added were absolute values.

Check Understanding Have students work through the problem (exercises 1 and 2) on page 226 and check their answers.

Guided Practice
Have students solve exercise 3 on page 226.

Independent Practice
Have students complete page 226 independently.

Closing the Lesson *Describe several problems for which it would be helpful to draw a diagram to solve the problem.* (Answers will vary.)

LESSON 5

PAGES 227–228

OBJECTIVE

To multiply integers

PREREQUISITES

Concepts

- Understand the meaning of positive and negative integers
- Understand subtraction of integers
- Understand whole number multiplication

Skills

- Perform multiplication of whole numbers

Multiplying Integers

Presenting the Lesson

Introduce the Skill On the board, write the patterns of multiplication problems listed at the top of page 227 and ask the class to find a pattern in the answers: In the case of the problems involving 4, the product decreases by 4 each time. Have the students use this pattern to find the answers to the remaining products: $4 \times {}^{-}1$, $4 \times {}^{-}2$, $4 \times {}^{-}3$, $4 \times {}^{-}4$, $4 \times {}^{-}5$ (${}^{-}4$, ${}^{-}8$, ${}^{-}12$, ${}^{-}16$, ${}^{-}20$) and generalize to see that the product of a positive integer and a negative integer is a negative integer. Then, in a similar way, develop the fact that the product of two negative integers is a positive integer.

Check Understanding *Find each of the following products:* $7 \times {}^{-}3$, ${}^{-}4 \times {}^{-}5$, ${}^{-}4 \times 6$, ${}^{-}1 \times {}^{-}9$, 4×8. (${}^{-}21$, 20, ${}^{-}24$, 9, 32)

Guided Practice

Have students do exercises 1, 5, 6, and 8 on pages 227 and 228.

Independent Practice

Have students complete pages 227 and 228 independently.

Closing the Lesson *What can you say about the product of two integers?* (The product may be positive if both integers have the same sign, negative if one integer is positive and one integer is negative, or zero if at least one of the integers is zero.)

LESSON 6

PAGES 229–230

OBJECTIVE

To divide integers

PREREQUISITES

Concepts

- Understand the meaning of positive and negative integers
- Understand subtraction and multiplication of integers
- Understand whole number division

Skills

- Perform division of whole numbers
- Perform multiplication of integers
- Solve equations involving missing divisors or missing dividends

MATERIALS

Copymasters

Extension 8, p. 184

Dividing Integers

Presenting the Lesson

Introduce the Skill Emphasize that multiplication and division are inverse operations. Help the class develop these rules for dividing integers: If both integers in the division problem have the same sign, their quotient is positive. If the two integers in the division problem have opposite signs, their quotient is negative. Point out the similarities between these rules and the rules for integer multiplication. Do several examples of integer division, including problems in which the integers have the same sign and problems in which they have different signs.

Check Understanding *Find each of the following quotients:* ${}^{-}20 \div {}^{-}4$, $15 \div {}^{-}5$, $8 \div 2$, ${}^{-}24 \div 4$. (5, ${}^{-}3$, 4, ${}^{-}6$)

Guided Practice

Have students do exercises 1, 4, 6, 8, and 10 on pages 229 and 230.

Independent Practice

Have students complete pages 229 and 230 independently.

Closing the Lesson *Describe how to find the quotient of two integers, including how to determine whether the quotient will be positive, negative, or zero.* (It is similar to finding the quotient of two whole numbers, except that with integers the quotient may be positive (if both integers have the same sign), negative (if one integer is positive and one integer is negative), or zero (if the dividend is zero).)

LESSON 7

PAGES 231–232

OBJECTIVE

To use a number line to compare positive and negative rational numbers

PREREQUISITES

Concepts

- Understand the meaning of positive and negative integers
- Understand the meaning of the opposite of an integer
- Understand division of integers

Skills

- Perform division of integers
- Identify the opposite of an integer

VOCABULARY

rational number

MATERIALS

Copymasters

Teaching Resource 7 (number lines)

Reteach 63, 64, 65, pp. 133–135

Rational Numbers on the Number Line

Presenting the Lesson

Introduce the Skill Have students come to the board and determine the sign of each of these rational numbers and simplify them (by eliminating unnecessary parentheses and 2 symbols, if possible): $\frac{^-2}{^-5}, \frac{2}{^-7}, {^-}(\frac{1}{^-3}), {^-}(\frac{^-9}{^-2}) \cdot (\frac{2}{5}, \frac{^-2}{7}, \frac{1}{3}, \frac{^-9}{2})$.

Check Understanding *Consider the following numbers:* $\frac{^-7}{^-6}$, *and* ${^-}(\frac{^-7}{3})$. *For each, name the closest two integers that the given number is between.* ($\frac{^-7}{^-6} = \frac{7}{6}$ and it is between 1 and 2; ${^-}(\frac{^-7}{3}) = \frac{7}{3}$ and it is between 2 and 3).

Guided Practice

Have students do exercises 1, 4, and 6 on pages 231 and 232.

Independent Practice

Have students complete pages 231 and 232 independently.

Closing the Lesson *Given a rational number, how can you determine the closest two integers that the given number is between?* (Locate the number on the number line.)

LESSON 8

PAGES 233–234

OBJECTIVE

To add and subtract positive and negative rational numbers and decimals

PREREQUISITES

Concepts

- Understand the meaning of positive and negative rational numbers
- Understand addition and subtraction of integers, decimals, and fractions

Skills

- Perform addition and subtraction of integers, decimals, and fractions
- Determine the absolute value of a number

Adding and Subtracting Rational Numbers

Presenting the Lesson

Introduce the Skill Remind students: When subtracting two rational numbers, change the problem into an addition problem—subtracting a number is the same as adding its opposite—and follow the rules for addition. Have students come to the board to solve example problems involving the subtraction of positive and negative rational numbers. Review the addition and subtraction of fractions and decimals as needed.

Check Understanding *Solve the following:* $\frac{^-1}{6} + \frac{^-5}{9}$. *Explain how you solved the problem.* (Find a common positive denominator and add: $\frac{^-1}{6} + \frac{^-5}{9} = \frac{^-3}{18} + \frac{^-10}{18} = \frac{^-13}{18}$.)

Guided Practice

Have students do exercises 1 and 3 on pages 233 and 234. Be sure that students change each subtraction problem to an addition problem.

Independent Practice

Have students complete page 234 independently.

Closing the Lesson *Describe how to subtract one rational number from another.* (Change the subtraction problem to an addition problem. Instead of subtracting the number, add its opposite or additive inverse. Then, solve the resulting addition problem.)

LESSON 9
PAGES 235–236

OBJECTIVE
To multiply and divide positive and negative fractions and decimals

PREREQUISITES
Concepts
- Understand the meaning of positive and negative rational numbers

Skills
- Perform multiplication and division of integers, decimals, and fractions

MATERIALS
Copymasters
Reteach 66, 67, pp. 136–137

Multiplying and Dividing Rational Numbers

Presenting the Lesson

Introduce the Skill Ask the class to describe how to determine the sign of the product or quotient of two integers—Put some examples on the board to help them recall the rule. (If the two integers have the same sign, the product or quotient will be positive. If one of the integers is positive and the other is negative, the product or quotient will be negative.) Point out that the same rule applies when multiplying or dividing positive and negative rational numbers, and give some examples.

Check Understanding *Find the value of each:* $\frac{^-1}{6} \times \frac{^-5}{2}$ $(\frac{5}{12})$, $\frac{^-2}{3} \div \frac{^-5}{11}$ $(\frac{^-2}{3} \times \frac{^-11}{5} = \frac{22}{15})$.

Guided Practice
Have students do exercises 1, 4, and 7 on pages 235 and 236.

Independent Practice
Have students complete pages 235 and 236 independently.

Closing the Lesson *What can you say about the product of rational numbers?* (If the two numbers have the same sign, the product or quotient will be positive. If one of the numbers is positive and the other is negative, the product or quotient will be negative.)

LESSON 10
PAGES 237–238

OBJECTIVE
To apply Use a Graph and other strategies to solve problems

PREREQUISITES
Concepts
- Understand the four basic operations with rational numbers
- Understand bar graphs
- Understand the four steps of problem solving—Understand, Decide, Solve and Look back

Skills
- Construct bar graphs
- Read information from bar graphs

Problem Solving Application: Use a Graph

Presenting the Lesson

Introduce the Focus of the Lesson Explain to students that in this lesson they will need to apply the use of graphs to the solving of problems.

Model the Four-Step Problem Solving Process Work through the favorite food survey problem with the students.

Discuss the Problem Solving Tips Point out to students that the four Problem Solving Process steps—Understand, Decide, Solve, and Look back—are listed in the box on page 237. Ask for volunteers to read the tips aloud. Make sure students realize that these steps are distinct from one another.

Check Understanding *If a bar graph represents the results of a survey of automobile owners, how can you determine the number of people that participated in the survey?* (Determine the total number of people in each category by estimating the height of each bar. Add these category totals to determine the total number of people that participated in the survey.)

Guided Practice
Have students complete exercises 1–4 on page 237. Have them design at least two additional questions that could be answered using information from the graph.

Independent Practice
Have students complete page 238 independently.

Closing the Lesson *Describe several situations in which you might use a graph to solve a problem.* (Answers will vary. Possible answer: information in newspapers and magazines, in scientific and business reports, and in other real-world settings)

UNIT 8 REVIEW

Page 239

Item Analysis

Items	Unit Obj.
1–6	8A, 8D
7–18	8B, 8D
19–27	8C, 8D
28	8E
29	8B, 8C
30–31	8D

Answers to Unit 8 Review items can be found on page 239 of the Teacher's Annotated Edition.

Administering the Review

This page reviews concepts and skills taught in this unit. Be sure students understand all direction lines. You may want to do the first example in each section cooperatively to ensure understanding.

Scoring Chart

Number Correct	31	30	29	28	27	26	25	24	23	22	21	20	19	18	17	16
Score	100	97	94	90	87	84	81	77	74	71	68	65	61	58	55	52

Number Correct	15	14	13	12	11	10	9	8	7	6	5	4	3	2	1
Score	48	45	42	39	35	32	29	26	23	19	16	13	10	6	3

After the Review

- The Item Analysis chart on the left shows the Unit 8 objective(s) covered by each test item. This chart can help you determine which objectives need review or extra practice.
- For additional assessment, use the Posttest for Unit 8, Copymaster Book, p. 36.
- To provide extension opportunities, use Copymaster Book, p. 184.

UNIT 8 CUMULATIVE REVIEW

PAGE 240

Item Analysis

Items	Unit Obj.
1	8A
2	5B
3	8D
4	7B
5	1D
6	1F
7	2E
8	7E

Answers to Cumulative Review items can be found on page 240 of the Teacher's Annotated Edition.

Administering the Review

This page reviews concepts and skills from earlier units as well as providing practice with standardized test formats. Students may circle their answers, or you may prefer to duplicate and distribute the answer sheet, Copymaster Book, p. 191. This page may be assigned as homework or as classwork.

Test-Taking Tip When time permits, revisit difficult problems and use the answer you chose to begin working backward.

Scoring Chart

Number Correct	8	7	6	5	4	3	2	1
Score	100	88	75	63	50	38	25	13

After the Review

The Item Analysis chart on the left shows the unit objective covered by each test item. This chart can help you to determine which objectives need review or extra practice.

Teacher Notes

Algebra: Expressions and Equations

Unit Objectives

- **9A** Use number properties, order of operations, and rules for exponents to simplify monomial and polynomial expressions
- **9B** Evaluate polynomials in one variable over the integers
- **9C** Use scientific notation
- **9D** Solve one- and two-step equations with rational numbers
- **9E** Use symbols, equations, and inequalities to represent verbal phrases and sentences
- **9F** Solve two-step inequalities
- **9G** Use equations to solve multi-step problems; use Write an Equation and other strategies to solve problems

About This Unit

The support pages that follow provide more information on prerequisite skills, methods for teaching skills and concepts, daily routines, tips on classroom management and materials, and useful dialogue techniques.

Prerequisite Skills and Concepts

Students should be able to

- multiply with decimals and powers of ten.

If not, use prerequisite Reteach Worksheet 68, p.138.

Assessments

Use Beginning of the Year Inventory for entry-level assessment.

Ongoing Evaluation Quick Checks, Reteach Worksheets, the Skills Tutorial Inventories, and the Midyear Test help ensure that students are progressing adequately to meet the standards.

Summative Evaluation Use Test Preps, Unit Review (p. T144), Cumulative Review (p. T145), Reteach Worksheets, and the Computation Skills Tutorial to assure that students have achieved the standards for the unit.

Diagnosing Errors The Quick Checks highlight common errors and provide remediation. See also the **Teaching Strategies Handbook** pp. T134–T137, where short discussions labeled Common Misconceptions appear as needed with the strategies for key concepts.

Homework and Family Involvement

Home Note In the Student Book, the Dear Family home note provides objectives, vocabulary, and a sample skill discussion for family participation. (**Teaching Strategies Handbook** pages also provide homework and family involvement tips.)

Education Place Refer families to Houghton Mifflin's EduPlace Web site at http://www.eduplace.com; for resources and activities for students at http://www.eduplace.com/math; and additional resources and activities at http://www.eduplace.com/parents.

Helping Your Children Learn Math This book has activities for children ages 5–13 and tips for getting involved in children's mathematics education. (Houghton Mifflin, 1994)

Lessons	Student Pages	Teacher Pages	Resources	State or Local Objectives	State or Local Assessment
9.1 Exponents and Roots	243–245	**T138**	Unit 9 Pretest		
9.2 Operations with Monomial Expressions	246–247	**T138**			
9.3 Operations with Polynomial Expressions	248–249	**T139**	Reteach 69, 70, 71		
9.4 Evaluating Polynomial Expressions	250–251	**T139**			
9.5 Problem Solving Application: Choose an Equation	252–253	**T140**			
9.6 Scientific Notation	254–256	**T140**	Reteach 72, 73		
9.7 Solving Equations with Rational Numbers	257–259	**T141**			
9. 8 Solving Two-Step Equations	260–262	**T141**	Reteach 74, 75		
9.9 Equations and Inequalities	263–265	**T142**			
9.10 Problem Solving Strategy: Write an Equation	266–267	**T142**			
9.11 Solving Inequalities	268–270	**T143**	Reteach 76, 77, 78; Extension 9; Unit 9 Posttest		

Teaching Strategies

Math Background — Algebra: Expressions and Equations

Algebraic reasoning is the foundation for solving fundamental, as well as complex, mathematical problems. Algebraic concepts are greatly expanded at this level. Students will develop algebraic expressions, equations, and inequality statements from given situations. They will learn to solve equations and inequalities that require two steps. They'll also move beyond linear equations and learn to work with polynomials, using exponent notation.

When Students Ask, Why Learn This?
Algebraic reasoning is key in situations in which there is a known relationship and you want to know what might happen in a particular situation. Here is a typical situation your students may encounter: "A store charges a one-time $10 membership fee for movie rentals plus a $3 charge per movie. Suppose you joined and rented some movies. It's time to return the movies, but you can't remember how many you rented. You do remember your bill was $22. How many movies did you rent?" Algebraic reasoning helps students set up and solve an equation to find the answer.

A Positive Start
From movie rentals, to train schedules, to ticket sales, students encounter algebra every day, even if they are unaware of it. Your creative ideas can increase their awareness of the algebraic world around them. You can help them see that algebra is a practical and useful method of solving interesting problems.

Linking Past and Future Learning

What algebraic concepts did your students learn last year? What should you do to prepare them for next year? Knowing the scope of the unit's basic conceptual goals can help you focus your instruction.

Concept/Skills	Last Year	This Year	Next Year
Exponents and Roots	Evaluate expressions containing exponents; linear equations	Evaluate expressions containing positive and negative exponents; find square roots	Use rational number exponents
Evaluating Polynomial Expressions	Solve one-step linear equations	Solve for one variable across the set of integers	Solve for two variables across the set of rational numbers
Solving Inequalities	Using inequality symbols to express relationships	Derive inequality statements; solve two-step inequalities	Solve and graph solutions to inequalities

Methods and Management

In this unit, students will be encouraged to make use of number properties, order of operations, and rules for exponents to simplify expressions. Ultimately, they will make connections between these concepts and solving a variety of one- and two-step equations with rational numbers. A key to success will be organization—clear and consistent approaches to setting up and solving algebraic problems.

Teaching Strategy: Exponents and Roots

Teaching students to work with exponential notation can be fun. Be sure to make connections to the order of operations, emphasizing that exponents indicate the number of times a number is multiplied by itself.

▶ ***Ask:*** *How much is 10^1? What is 10^2? What is 10^3?*
Students should determine the answers to be $10^1 = 10$, $10^2 = 10 \times 10 = 100$, and $10^3 = 10 \times 10 \times 10 = 1{,}000$.

- Explain to students that our number system is called a base 10 system because all of our place values are based on "powers of 10." Ask, What do you think is meant by the phrase "powers of 10?" Help students express the phrase "powers of 10" as: *Each place value can be expressed as the number 10 raised to some exponential power.*

▶ ***Vocabulary Development*** Help students distinguish between "power," "exponent," and "base." A power is an expression that contains both a base and an exponent. For example, 64 can be written as a power in three ways: 8^2, 4^3, and 2^6.

▶ ***Common Misconceptions*** Sometimes students solve an exponential problem by multiplying the base by its exponent. Practice and showing their work usually helps students see exponents as the number of times they are to multiply the base by itself.

Teaching Strategy: Evaluating Polynomial Expressions

The concept of order of operations is a key element when evaluating polynomial expressions. Emphasize that operations enclosed in parentheses are done first, followed by exponential operations, and then multiplication, division, addition, or subtraction.

▶ ***Say:*** *Evaluate the expression $x^2 + 7$, when $x = 2$.*
Students may rewrite the expression as $2^2 + 7 = 4 + 7 = 11$. This is a good process. However, they may have difficulty doing the same sort of re-write to evaluate $5x^2 + 4$, when $x = 3$.

- As students attempt to rewrite this expression by substituting 3 for x, they need to be careful to indicate the operation of multiplication that is implied by the coefficient, 5. They should rewrite this expression as: $5 \times 3^2 + 4 = 5 \times 9 + 4 = 45 + 4 = 49$.

▶ ***Common Misconceptions*** The most common error students make is to forget the correct order of operations. Refer to the Memory Aid in Unit 1 Teacher Tips to help students avoid this mistake.

Teacher Tips

Visual Aids Post a picture of a balanced scale as a model of an equation. On the scale, show some examples of solving equations. This visual model will reinforce the notion of maintaining equality on both sides of an equation during the solution process.

Pacing Structure class time so that some time is available for students to look over assigned homework and ask questions, if necessary.

Showing, Describing Provide students with many opportunities to demonstrate and explain their solutions to problems. Avoid emphasizing your ability to solve problems; instead, focus on your students' abilities to solve problems.

Time Savers Write the materials needed for the day on the board before class begins. As students enter the classroom, they can look at the board and know what materials to have ready when the lesson begins.

"Off Task" Talking Students at this level can be very social in class. Over time, you will be able to distinguish levels of acceptable and unacceptable socializing during class. Talk to experienced teachers about how they handle too much talking when students are supposed to be working together.

Vocabulary Help students make connections between phrases such as "no more than" and "at most" and interpret those phrases as "less than" situations. Similarly, phrases such as "no less than" and "at least" indicate "greater than."

Taking Stock Make sure that at the end of each lesson you take the time to note what went well and what did not go as expected. You will appreciate these brief notes as you prepare future lessons.

Teaching Strategy: Solving Inequalities

Many problem solving situations call for finding an amount that never goes over or under a certain amount. These types of problems can be solved by setting up inequalities.

▶ ***Ask:*** *Suppose you collect $25 to purchase special pens through a catalog. Each pen costs $1.50. The shipping cost is $3, no matter how many pens you order. What is the greatest number of pens you can order?*

Let the letter p stand for the greatest number of pens. Guide students to set up an expression that represents the cost in dollars of ordering pens: $1.5p + 3$. Set up an inequality that explains the problem: $1.5p + 3 < 25$.

- Students should progress through the steps solving the inequality by subtracting 3 from each side, and then dividing each side by 1.5 to determine that p must be less than 14.67. Part of a pen can't be ordered, so the greatest number of pens that can be ordered is 14.

▶ ***Common Misconceptions*** Although the process of solving inequalities is much like that of solving equations, it often poses difficulties for students because it is tough to picture how to maintain an inequality. One way to deal with this problem is to construct less-than and greater-than scales that are slightly off balance. These models can help students see that the goal of solving inequalities is to maintain the less-than or greater-than relationship.

Opportunities to Assess

Observation

Observe students demonstrating algebraic solutions on the board. Be conscious of the discomfort students may feel when standing in front of the class alone. Consider sending students to the board in teams so that one student does not feel singled out in front of the class.

Homework

Students should have sufficient opportunities on their own to practice problems similar to those done in class. Don't assign so many problems that the task becomes overwhelming. Rather, divide up a set of homework problems among different members of the class. They can prepare solutions to share with the class and benefit from seeing the solutions to other problems solved by their classmates.

Family Involvement

Family members will often comment that they were "never any good at algebra." Send a note home to families asking them to provide as much encouragement and positive reinforcement as possible so that your students can eventually say, "I'm great at algebra!"

Teacher/Student Dialogue

Encouraging a Reluctant Participant

Occasionally, you will encounter students who do not participate in class discussions. Encouraging them may not gain complete participation, but little by little these students become more involved.

Teacher: Let's look at the equation $1 = \frac{3}{4}x + \frac{5}{4}$. What should we do to solve the equation? Roberto, what do you think?

Student: *I don't know.*

Teacher: You may not think you know, but I'm certain you can figure it out. Suppose we had the equation $1 = \frac{3}{4}x$, how would you solve for x?

Student: *I don't remember.*

Teacher: Suppose I suggest that you multiply both sides of the equation by a number so that instead of $\frac{3}{4}x$ you have x on the right side. What would you multiply by?

Student: *I guess $\frac{4}{3}$.*

Teacher: Correct. Okay, suppose you have the equation $1 = x + 5$. How would you solve for x?

Student: *Just subtract 5 from both sides.*

Teacher: Good. So in one case you had to subtract something from both sides, and in the other case you had to multiply both sides by the same number. Now, do you have any ideas how you could solve $1 = \frac{3}{4}x + \frac{5}{4}$?

Student: *Yeah, you just subtract $\frac{5}{4}$ from both sides and then multiply both sides by $\frac{4}{3}$.*

Teacher: I agree. Would everyone try the steps Roberto suggested and see what solution you get?

Questioning Techniques

Some students simply do not think it's "cool" to participate in class. They think that by saying "I don't know", you will move on to someone else. Don't give up after one or two negative responses. It is likely that students will eventually determine that it is easier to engage in conversation than to continue not participating.

What to do

When

Some students love participating in class to the point where they dominate conversations. To keep this from becoming a problem, you might want to establish a routine of rotating from table to table or row to row for responses to questions.

What to do

Every Day

Because algebra is a topic about which some students ask the question, *When am I ever going to use this?*, it might be fun to challenge them to create a bulletin board titled "Practical and Career Uses of Algebra." Begin each class by having students add something new to the board. There are many sources for these ideas: high-school students, teachers, guidance counselors, the Internet, and books about careers.

Unit 9 Algebra: Expressions and Equations

LESSON 1
PAGES 243–245

OBJECTIVE
To understand the relationship between exponents and roots

PREREQUISITES
Concepts
- Understand the meaning of positive integer exponents
- Understand the properties of positive integer exponents

Skills
- Add, subtract, multiply, and divide integers and rational numbers
- Simplify expressions using properties of positive integer exponents

VOCABULARY
exponent, base, power, negative exponent, square roots, principal square root

Exponents and Roots

Presenting the Lesson

Introduce the Skill Write the following on the board:

$2^4 = 2 \cdot 2 \cdot 2 \cdot 2 = 16$ $\quad 2^2 = 2 \cdot 2 = 4$

$2^3 = 2 \cdot 2 \cdot 2 = 8$ $\quad 2^1 = 2$

Ask the students what pattern they see and to predict the value of 2^0. ($16 \div 2 = 8$, $8 \div 2 = 4$, $4 \div 2 = 2$. 1, because $2 \div 2 = 1$) Then, continue with these terms and have students predict the answers:

$2^{-1} = ?$ $(\frac{1}{2}^1 = \frac{1}{2})$ $\quad 2^{-2} = ?$ $(\frac{1}{2}^2 = \frac{1}{4})$ $\quad 2^{-3} = ?$ $(\frac{1}{2}^3 = \frac{1}{8})$ $\quad 2^{-4} = ?$ $(\frac{1}{2}^4 = \frac{1}{16})$

Do another example using 3 as the base. Then, define b^0 and b^{-n} for $n > 0$. Have students evaluate $(-3)^{-2}$, $(\frac{1}{5})^{-3}$, $(-\frac{2}{3})^{-1}$, 99^0, and others. Remind students of the properties of exponents and do several examples, such as $a^{-3} \cdot a^5 \cdot a^{-4} = a^{-2}$. Illustrate how to find the principal square root of a number, using examples such as $\sqrt{49}$ and $\sqrt{\frac{9}{121}}$ (7 and $\frac{3}{11}$).

Check Understanding *What is $(-5)^{-11}(-5)^{-9}$ when simplified?* $(\frac{1}{25})$ *Find* $\sqrt{\frac{256}{25}}$. $(\frac{16}{5})$

Guided Practice
Have students do exercises 1, 3, 7, 12, and 14 on pages 243–245.

Independent Practice
Have students complete pages 243–245 independently.

Closing the Lesson *Simplify $b^{-3}b^4 \div b^{-4}$.* (b^5) *Find* $\sqrt{\frac{25}{64}}$. $(\frac{5}{8})$

LESSON 2
PAGES 246–247

OBJECTIVE
To apply all four operations to monomials

PREREQUISITES
Concepts
- Understand the meaning and properties of integer exponents
- Understand the distributive property

Skills
- Add, subtract, multiply, and divide integers
- Simplify expressions

VOCABULARY
monomial, polynomial, like terms, unlike terms, coefficient, power, distributive property

Operations with Monomial Expressions

Presenting the Lesson

Introduce the Skill Write on the board these pairs of terms: $3a$, ^-8a; $4x^2$, $3x^2$; ^-2x, $11x$; by^5, $7by^5$. Ask students what each pair has in common. (Both terms in the pair have the same exponent and the same base.) Identify these pairs as **like terms.** Give examples of unlike terms and ask students to explain why they are **unlike.** Write on the board $4x + 13x$, and ask a student what the total number of x's will be. ($17x$) Illustrate the use of the distributive property to simplify $4x + 13x = (4 + 13)x = 17x$. Ask students to do examples, such as $2y^3z - 7y^3z$. ($^-5y^3z$) Mention that we can multiply or divide monomial expressions, even if the expressions are unlike terms.

Check Understanding *Simplify:* $^-8xy - {}^-3xy$ *and* $\frac{(54c^5d)}{(9c^3)}$ (^-5xy and $6c^2d$).

Guided Practice
Have students do exercises 4 and 6 on pages 246 and 247.

Independent Practice
Have students complete page 246 and 247 independently.

Closing the Lesson *When can two monomials be added or subtracted?* (The monomials must have like terms.) *Can you simplify* $(^-2ab^4)(3a^2b^6)$, *even though the two factors do not have like terms?* (Yes, because this is multiplication, not addition or subtraction.)

LESSON 3
PAGES 248–249

OBJECTIVE
To use order of operations and exponent properties to simplify polynomial expressions

PREREQUISITES
Concepts
- Understand the meaning of like terms
- Understand operations with monomial expressions

Skills
- Add, subtract, multiply, and divide integers and monomial expressions

VOCABULARY
associative property, commutative property

MATERIALS
Copymasters
Reteach 69, 70, 71, pp.139–141

Operations with Polynomial Expressions

Presenting the Lesson

Introduce the Skill Write on the board $3y + 2x^2\ {}^-7y + 10x^2$. Remind the class that they can add or subtract like terms and ask students which terms in that expression can be added or subtracted. ($3y$ and ^-7y are like terms, as are $2x^2$ and $10x^2$) Illustrate how to simplify $3y + 2x^2\ {}^-7y + 10x^2$, using number properties to justify each step:

$$\begin{aligned} 3y + 2x^2\ {}^-7y + 10x^2 &= 3y + 2x^2 + {}^-7y + 10x^2 \\ &= 3y + {}^-7y + 2x^2 + 10x^2 \\ &= (3 + {}^-7)y + (2 + 10)x^2 \\ &= {}^-4y + 12x^2. \end{aligned}$$

Ask a student how to rewrite x^5x^2 (x^7). Illustrate how to simplify: $4ax^5 \cdot 6a^3x^2 = 24a^{1+3}x^{5+2} = 24a^4x^7$. Illustrate division of a polynomial by a monomial:

$$\frac{18b - 12b^2}{3b} = \frac{6b(3 - 2b)}{3b} = \frac{3b(2)(3 - 2b)}{3b} = 2(3 - 2b) = 6 - 4b.$$

Check Understanding *Simplify* $(7x - 4y + 2z) - (3x + y - 8z)$ and $^-3c(c^2 + 5c - 1)$. ($4x - 5y + 10z$ and $^-3c^3 - 15c^2 + 3c$)

Guided Practice

Have students do exercises 1, 8, 10, and 14 on pages 248 and 249. Check that students get $3ab + 1$ (not $3ab$) in the first exercise in row 14.

Independent Practice

Have students complete pages 248 and 249 independently.

Closing the Lesson *Simplify* $xz^3(10x^2 - 3z) + {}^-4xz^4$. ($10x^3z^3 + {}^-7xz^4$) *How do you divide a polynomial by a monomial?* (Factor the numerator, then divide.)

LESSON 4
PAGES 250–251

OBJECTIVE
To use a table of values or spreadsheet to evaluate polynomial expressions

PREREQUISITES
Concepts
- Understand the meaning of a variable

Skills
- Perform addition, subtraction, and multiplication of integers

VOCABULARY
spreadsheet, cells

Evaluating Polynomial Expressions

Presenting the Lesson

Introduce the Skill Remind students that they can evaluate expressions like $6x^2$ and $x + 7$ for different values of x. Ask a student to evaluate $^-2x^4 - 5x + 3$ for $x = {}^-1, 0, 2$. (6, 3, $^-39$) Be sure that they use one column for each term. Then, have the class work through the spreadsheet exercise on page 251.

Check Understanding *Evaluate* $x^4 - 3x^2 + 6x - 1$ *for* $x = 2$. (15) *Do you get the same answer when you use* $x = {}^-2$*?* (No. For $x = {}^-2$, the answer is $^-9$.)

Guided Practice

Have students do exercises 1, 2, 9, and 10 on pages 250 and 251.

Independent Practice

Have students complete pages 250 and 251 independently.

Closing the Lesson *Given a polynomial expression, describe how to evaluate it for* $x = {}^-4$. (Evaluate each term of the expression by substituting $^-4$ for x. Then, combine these results by adding or subtracting to get the final answer.)

LESSON 5
PAGES 252–253

OBJECTIVE
To choose the appropriate equation to solve a problem

PREREQUISITES
Concepts
- Understand the meaning of a variable
- Understand equations

Skills
- Add, subtract, multiply, and divide integers and rational numbers
- Evaluate polynomial expressions

Problem Solving Application: Choose an Equation

Presenting the Lesson

Introduce the Focus of the Lesson Explain to students that in this lesson they will need to choose the right equation to solve the problem.

Model the Four-Step Problem Solving Process Work through the problem of the monthly car-rental cost on page 252 with your students.

Discuss the Problem Solving Tips Point out to students that the Problem Solving Process steps—Understand, Decide, Solve, and Look back—are listed on page 252. Make sure students understand that each step is distinct from the others.

Check Understanding *For "Three times a number increased by 4 is 8 times the number," choose an equation:* $3x + 4 = 8x$ *or* $3(x + 4) = 8x$. ($3x + 4 = 8x$)

Guided Practice

Have students do exercises 1 and 2 on page 252.

Independent Practice

Have students complete page 253 independently.

Closing the Lesson *Which operation does each of these phrases suggest? "more than"* (addition), *"increased by"* (addition), *"quotient"* (division), *"less than"* (subtraction), *"product"* (multiplication), *"decreased by"* (subtraction).

LESSON 6
PAGES 254–256

OBJECTIVE
To read, write, and compare rational numbers in scientific notation

PREREQUISITES
Concepts
- Understand the meaning of integer exponents
- Understand decimals and place value
- Understand the use of scientific notation to represent large numbers

Skills
- Represent large numbers using scientific notation
- Multiply and divide decimals and rational numbers

VOCABULARY
scientific notation

MATERIALS
Copymasters
Reteach 72, 73, pp.142–143

Scientific Notation

Presenting the Lesson

Introduce the Skill Ask a student to write 5,200 in scientific notation (5.2×10^3) and remind the class that when we multiply 5.2 by 10^3, the exponent 3 means move the decimal point 3 places to the right. Then, show this example: $6.3 \times 10^{-4} = 6.3 \times \frac{1}{10}^4 = 6.3 \times \frac{1}{10000} = 0.00063$. Point out that when we multiply 6.3 by 10^{-4}, the exponent $^-4$ means move the decimal point 4 places to the left. Illustrate how to express numbers like 0.05 in scientific notation ($0.05 = 5 \times 0.01 = 5 \times \frac{1}{100} = 5 \times \frac{1}{10}^2 = 5 \times 10^{-2}$). Present the two-step method for expressing a small number in scientific notation (see page 254). Ask students to help you do several more examples.

Check Understanding *Express 0.00251 in scientific notation.* (2.51×10^{-3}) *Is* 0.64×10^{-1} *in exact scientific notation?* (No. The first number must be between 1 and 10. This number is 6.4×10^{-2} in scientific notation.)

Guided Practice

Have students do exercises 1, 4, 7, and 12 on pages 254 and 255. Check to see that the decimal point is in the correct place.

Independent Practice

Have students complete pages 254–256 independently.

Closing the Lesson *Given a decimal number between 0 and 1, describe a way to express it in scientific notation.* (Two steps: (1) "Move" the decimal point to the right so that there is one non-zero digit to its left. (2) Count the number of places that you moved the decimal point and use this as a negative exponent of the base 10.)

LESSON 7
PAGES 257–259

OBJECTIVE
To solve equations with rational numbers

PREREQUISITES
Concepts
- Understand equations
- Understand the additive inverse and the multiplicative inverse properties

Skills
- Solve addition, subtraction, multiplication, and division equations involving whole numbers
- Perform addition, subtraction, multiplication, and division of integers and rational numbers
- Evaluate polynomial expressions

VOCABULARY
substitution

Solving Equations with Rational Numbers

Presenting the Lesson

Introduce the Skill Remind the students that the additive inverse property can help them to solve equations involving addition and subtraction. Write on the board $x + 9 = 2$. Explain that to solve the equation they must isolate x on one side of the equation. Solve ($x = {}^-7$) and then check the solution. Ask students to solve several other equations involving addition and subtraction, such as $x - \frac{5}{2} = {}^-1$ ($x = \frac{3}{2}$), and have them check by substitution. Next, write on the board $12x = {}^-22$ and ask the class what they can do to both sides of the equation to solve it. (Multiply both sides of the equation by $\frac{1}{12}$, the reciprocal of 12.) Ask students to solve several other equations involving multiplication and division, such as ${}^-7 = \frac{d}{5}$, and have them check each answer by substitution.

Check Understanding *Solve and check* ${}^-9 = \frac{4}{x}$ *and* $n - 2 = {}^-7$. ($x = {}^-\frac{4}{9}$ and $n = {}^-5$)

Guided Practice
Have students do exercises 1, 3, 7, and 12 on pages 257–259.

Independent Practice
Have students complete pages 257–259 independently.

Closing the Lesson *Given a subtraction equation such as* $x - 7 = 12$ *or* $d - \frac{1}{3} = \frac{8}{3}$, *what should be done to solve the equation?* (Add the same number to each side of the equation.) *Given a multiplication problem such as* $2x = 6.8$, *what should be done to solve the equation?* (Divide each side of the equation by the same number.)

LESSON 8
PAGES 260–262

OBJECTIVE
To solve two-step equations

PREREQUISITES
Concepts
- Understand the additive inverse and the multiplicative inverse properties

Skills
- Solve equations involving rational numbers
- Evaluate polynomial expressions
- Follow the order of operations

VOCABULARY
complex equation, two-step equation

MATERIALS
Copymasters
Reteach 74, 75, pp. 144–145

Solving Two-Step Equations

Presenting the Lesson

Introduce the Skill Review the order of operations with students. Then, explain that when we solve an equation, we "undo" the operations in the opposite order in which they were done. Ask a student to solve the equation $8x - 21 = 19$. Have the student tell the order of the operations on the left side of the equation and tell what operation he/she will "undo" first. Have the student show how to check the answer. ($x = 5$) Have students do several other problems (like those on pages 260–262, including ones involving multiplication and addition as well as multiplication and subtraction) on the board and explain their work in a similar way.

Check Understanding *Solve* $4x - 21 = {}^-6$ *and* $3.5 = 2n + 9.5$. ($x = \frac{15}{4}$ and $n = {}^-3$) Be sure that students check their answers by substitution.

Guided Practice
Have students complete row 3 and do exercise 7 on pages 261 and 262.

Independent Practice
Have students complete pages 260–262 independently.

Closing the Lesson *Solve this two-step equation and describe your steps as you solve it:* $12x + 6 = 1$. (Add the opposite of 6 to each side of the equation: $12x + 6 + {}^-6 = 1 + {}^-6$. Simplify to get $12x = {}^-5$. Multiply each side of this equation by the reciprocal of 12: $(\frac{1}{12})12x = (\frac{1}{12})(^-5)$. Thus, $x = {}^-\frac{5}{12}$.)

LESSON SUPPORT

LESSON 9
PAGES 263–265

OBJECTIVE
To use variables and operations to write an equation or inequality from a verbal description

PREREQUISITES
Concepts
- Understand the meaning of a variable
- Understand equations and inequalities and symbols that describe each of these
- Understand vocabulary related to operations with integers and rational numbers

VOCABULARY
word phrase, equation, inequality, number sentence

MATERIALS
Copymasters
Extension 9, p. 185

Equations and Inequalities

Presenting the Lesson

Introduce the Skill Write the following word phrases on the board and ask students to write them using symbols: *the product of 4 and x, the difference between a and 5, 2 more than the quotient of y divided by 7.* ($4x$, $a - 5$, $\frac{y}{7} + 2$) Ask them to translate these symbols into word phrases: $x + 8$ and $6(b - c)$. (the sum of x and 8, 6 times the difference between b and c) Then, give examples of English sentences (such as *The product of 3 and c is less than 4.*) and ask students to write them as mathematical sentences. ($3c < 4$)

Check Understanding *Write as an equation: One third of a number equals the number decreased by 5.* ($(\frac{1}{3})x = x - 5$) *Write as an equation or inequality: A number squared is greater than or equal to 3 more than the number.* ($x^2 \geq x + 3$)

Guided Practice
Have students do exercises 1, 4, 6, 9, 13, 20, and 25 on pages 263–265.

Independent Practice
Have students complete pages 263–265 independently.

Closing the Lesson *Translate into a sentence: $2d + 1 < 3d$.* (Twice a number increased by 1 is less than three times the number.)

LESSON 10
PAGES 266–267

OBJECTIVE
To use Write an Equation to solve problems

PREREQUISITES
Concepts
- Understand equations and the symbols used in them

Skills
- Translate word phrases into symbols and symbols into word phrases
- Solve addition, subtraction, multiplication, and division equations involving rational numbers
- Evaluate polynomial and rational expressions

VOCABULARY
word problem

Problem Solving Strategy: Write an Equation

Presenting the Lesson

Introduce the Strategy Tell students they will write equations to solve problems.

Model the Four-Step Problem Solving Process Present the stamp collections problem described on page 266.

- **Understand:** Remind students that the process of asking oneself questions about the problem helps to establish basic relationships between numbers.
- **Decide:** Emphasize how important it is to decide exactly what your variable is to represent and write this information as part of your solution.
- **Solve:** Have students keep clearly in mind the process of using inverse operations.
- **Look back:** Point out that substituting your answer value for the variable in the original equation is a very effective form of looking back.

Check Understanding *Write an equation for this word problem and then solve: Dennis checked out 3 more books from the library than Mary did. Together they checked out 19 books. How many books did Dennis check out?* {$x + (x + 3) = 19$; $x =$ 8 books.}

Guided Practice
Have students do exercises 1 and 7 on page 267.

Independent Practice
Have students complete pages 266 and 267 independently.

Closing the Lesson *Describe the four steps used to solve word problems by writing an equation.* ((1) Choose a variable and organize the information given in the problem, (2) Write an equation based on the information, (3) Solve the equation, and (4) Check.)

LESSON 11
PAGES 269–270

OBJECTIVE
To solve simple inequalities over the rational numbers

PREREQUISITES
Concepts
- Understand inequalities and the symbols used in them
- Understand the addition property of equality

Skills
- Use the four-step process to solve equations involving rational numbers
- Add, subtract, multiply, and divide integers and rational numbers
- Follow the order of operations

VOCABULARY
addition property, multiplication property

MATERIALS
Copymasters
Reteach 76, 77, 78, pp.146–148

Solving Inequalities

Presenting the Lesson

Introduce the Skill Remind students of the addition property of equality and tell them the addition property can also be used with inequalities. Write on the board $x - 5 < 11$ and, with input from students, solve it by adding 5 to each side of the inequality. Ask a student to solve $x + 2 > {}^{-}10$, showing the steps. ($x > {}^{-}12$) Have students work through the exercises at the top of page 269. Develop the fact that when both sides of an inequality are multiplied or divided by a negative number, the inequality sign must be reversed. With input from the class, work through the examples on page 270. Make sure students understand when to reverse the inequality.

Check Understanding *When you add the same number to both sides of an inequality, is the resulting inequality still true?* (Yes.) *When you multiply both sides of an equation by a number n, is the resulting inequality still true?* (Yes if n is positive; no if n is ≤ 0.) *Solve this inequality:* $-\frac{9}{8}x > 2$. ($x < {}^{-}\frac{16}{9}$)

Guided Practice

Have students do exercises 4, 5, and 11 on pages 268 and 270.
Check that they reverse the inequality when appropriate.

Independent Practice

Have students complete pages 268–270 independently.

Closing the Lesson *Solve and show your steps:* $\frac{x + 2}{{}^{-}7} < 3$ *and* $14a - 5 > {}^{-}11$. ($x > {}^{-}23$ and $a > {}^{-}\frac{3}{7}$)

LESSON SUPPORT

UNIT 9 REVIEW

PAGES 271–273

Item Analysis

Items	Unit Obj.
1–24	9A
25–27	9B
28–37	9C
38–55	9D
56–61	9E
62–64	9F
65–67	9G

Answers to Unit 9 Review items can be found on pages 271–273 of the Teacher's Annotated Edition.

Administering the Review

This page reviews concepts and skills taught in this unit. Be sure students understand all direction lines. You may want to do the first example in each section cooperatively to ensure understanding.

Scoring Chart

Number Correct	67	66	65	64	63	62	61	60	59	58	57	56	55	54	53
Score	100	99	97	96	94	93	91	90	89	87	85	84	82	81	79

Number Correct	52	51	50	49	48	47	46	45	44	43	42	41	40	39	38
Score	78	76	75	73	72	70	69	67	66	64	63	61	60	58	57

Number Correct	37	36	35	34	33	32	31	30	29	28	27	26	25	24	23
Score	55	54	52	51	49	48	46	45	43	42	40	39	37	36	34

Number Correct	22	21	20	19	18	17	16	15	14	13	12	11	10	9	8
Score	33	31	30	28	27	25	24	22	21	19	18	16	15	13	12

Number Correct	7	6	5	4	3	2	1
Score	10	9	7	6	4	3	1

After the Review

- The Item Analysis chart on the left shows the Unit 9 objective(s) covered by each test item. This chart can help you determine which objectives need review or extra practice.
- For additional assessment, use the Posttest for Unit 9, Copymaster Book, pp. 40–42.
- To provide extension opportunities, use Copymaster Book, p. 185.

UNIT 9 CUMULATIVE REVIEW

PAGE 274

Item Analysis

Items	Unit Obj.
1	9D
2	9B
3	1C
4	4C
5	7D
6	8D
7	2C
8	8E

Answers to Cumulative Review items can be found on page 274 of the Teacher's Annotated Edition.

Administering the Review

This page reviews concepts and skills from earlier units, as well as providing practice with standardized test formats. Students may circle their answers, or you may prefer to duplicate and distribute the answer sheet, Copymaster Book, p. 191. This page may be assigned as homework or as classwork.

Test-Taking Tip Make sure the result you get after working backward matches the information in the problem.

Scoring Chart

Number Correct	8	7	6	5	4	3	2	1
Score	100	84	72	60	48	36	24	12

After the Review

- The Item Analysis chart on the left shows the unit objective covered by each test item. This chart can help you determine which objectives need review or extra practice.

Using Formulas in Geometry

Vocabulary

area A measure of a region or a surface

circumference The distance around a circle. It is about 3.14 times the diameter.

cylinder A space figure with two congruent circular bases joined by a single curved surface

hypotenuse The side of a right triangle that is opposite the right angle

perimeter The distance around a polygon. It is found by adding the lengths of all the sides.

pi The ratio of the circumference to the diameter of a circle. Its value is about 3.14.

prism A polyhedron that has two congruent, parallel bases that are joined by parallelograms.

Pythagorean Property The square of the length of the hypotenuse of a right triangle is equal to the sum of the squares of the lengths of the other two sides.

surface area The total area of all the faces or surfaces of a space figure

volume A measure of the space within a closed figure in space

Unit Objectives

10A Use formulas to find the areas of circles, trapezoids, regular polygons, and complex plane figures

10B Visualize space figures using nets

10C Use formulas to find the surface area and volume of prisms, cylinders, and composite space figures

10D Use the Pythagorean Property

10E Explore how linear changes in plane and space figures affect changes in area and volume

10F Use a diagram to solve multi-step problems; use Find a Simpler Problem and other strategies to solve problems

About This Unit

The support pages that follow provide more information on prerequisite skills, methods for teaching skills and concepts, daily routines, tips on classroom management and materials, and useful dialogue techniques.

Prerequisite Skills and Concepts

Students should be able to

- find the perimeter of a polygon.
- find the circumference of a circle.

If not, use prerequisite Reteach Worksheets 79, 80, pp. 149–150.

Assessments

Use Beginning of the Year Inventory for entry-level assessment.

Ongoing Evaluation Quick Checks, Reteach Worksheets, the Skills Tutorial Inventories, and the Midyear Test help ensure that students are progressing adequately to meet the standards.

Summative Evaluation Use Test Preps, Unit Review (p. T160), Cumulative Review (p. T161), Reteach Worksheets, and the Computation Skills Tutorial to assure that students have achieved the standards for the unit.

Diagnosing Errors The Quick Checks highlight common errors and provide remediation. See also the **Teaching Strategies Handbook** pp. T148–T151, where short discussions labeled Common Misconceptions appear as needed with the strategies for key concepts.

Homework and Family Involvement

Home Note In the Student Book, the Dear Family home note provides objectives, vocabulary, and a sample skill discussion for family participation. (**Teaching Strategies Handbook** pages also provide homework and family involvement tips.)

Education Place Refer families to Houghton Mifflin's EduPlace Web site at **http://www.eduplace.com**; for resources and activities for students at **http://www.eduplace.com/math**; and additional resources and activities at **http://www.eduplace.com/parents**.

Lessons	Student Pages	Teacher Pages	Resources	State or Local Objectives	State or Local Assessment
10.1 Circumference and Area of Circles	277–279	**T152**	Unit 10 Pretest		
10.2 Complex Plane Figures	280–282	**T152**			
10.3 Area of a Trapezoid	283–284	**T153**	Reteach 81, 82, 83		
10.4 Algebra: Area of Regular Polygons	285–286	**T153**			
10.5 Area of Irregular Plane Figures on a Grid	287–288	**T154**			
10.6 Problem Solving Strategy: Solve a Simpler Problem	289–290	**T154**			
10.7 Spatial Visualization with Nets	291–292	**T155**	Reteach 84, 85, 86		
10.8 Surface Area of Prisms	293–295	**T155**	Extension 10		
10.9 Surface Area of Cylinders	296–297	**T156**			
10.10 Volume of Prisms	298–299	**T156**	Reteach 87, 88, 89		
10.11 Volume of Composite Space Figures	300–301	**T157**			
10.12 Algebra: Relating Length, Area, and Volume	302–303	**T157**	Reteach 90, 91		
10.13 Volume of Cylinders	304–305	**T158**			
10.14 Problem Solving Application: Use a Diagram	306–307	**T158**			
10.15 Algebra: Pythagorean Property of Right Triangles	308–310	**T159**	Reteach 92, 93; Unit 10 Posttest		

Teaching Strategies

Math Background — Using Formulas in Geometry

This unit is built around understanding and interpreting geometric formulas. Although students at this level have used some of the formulas presented in this unit before, they are now challenged to understand how to build new formulas from known formulas. They use what they know about finding the area of a parallelogram to find the area of a trapezoid. They examine how values of area and volume are affected when one of the values for the formula is changed. The problem solving strategy of using a diagram is emphasized because it is essential in solving geometric problems.

When Students Ask, Why Learn This?
Geometric formulas play a key role in the creative endeavors of many professions such as architectural design, bridge construction, and landscaping. Students can learn to appreciate the role geometric formulas play in their own lives, too, as they explore the relationship between area and volume. Expose them to problems like this: *How would you determine how much paint you need to repaint the walls of a room in your home?* A clear understanding of geometric formulas will simplify solving these problems.

A Positive Start
It might be fun to take on a classroom project that involves geometric formulas. Suppose you plan to paint the walls, obtain new curtains, and carpet the floor of your classroom. In addition, you are going to order four new computer stations to install in the classroom. Work together to determine geometric considerations, finding possibilities and limitations suggested by geometric formulas.

Linking Past and Future Learning

Examine the following chart of a three-year outlook on topics surrounding geometric formulas. It helps delineate the subtle progression through some very challenging concepts for students.

Concept/Skills	Last Year	This Year	Next Year
Area of a Trapezoid	Find areas of parallelograms; classify quadrilaterals	Develop formula for area of trapezoid and find areas of trapezoids	Find areas of irregular shapes by breaking down into known shapes
Volume of Cylinders	Find volumes of cylinders	Find volume of cylinders; explore how volume changes when linear measures change	Understand the formulation of the formula for volume of various solids
The Pythagorean Theorem	Classify triangles	Learn and use the Pythagorean Property	Understand the formulation of the Pythagorean Property

Methods and Management

Understanding and applying geometric formulas can be fun and interesting for students. The following strategies show how illustrating solution processes in organized steps is helpful when working with geometric formulas.

Teaching Strategy: Area of a Trapezoid

Students are generally not as familiar with trapezoids as they are with other quadrilaterals. Show them the relationship between a trapezoid and a quadrilateral they are more familiar with, the parallelogram.

▶ ***Show This:***

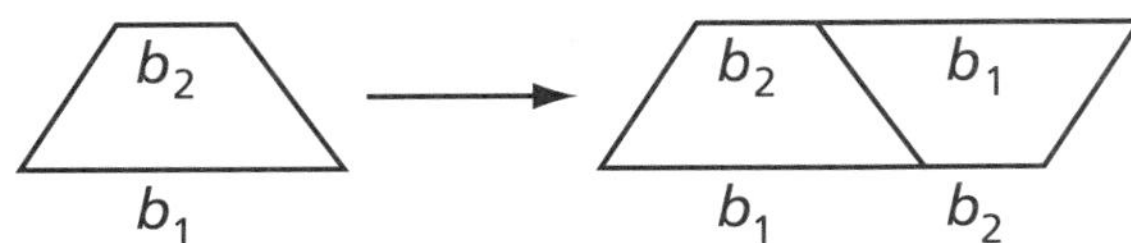

▶ ***Ask:*** *If I copy a trapezoid and flip it upside down, when I put the two trapezoids together, I form a parallelogram. How much larger is the parallelogram than the trapezoid?*
Students should be able to explain that because the parallelogram is made of two congruent trapezoids, it is two times as large as the trapezoid.

- Point out that the formula for finding the area of a parallelogram is Area = base times height or, in the parallelogram above, $A = (b_1 + b_2)h$. Ask, Because the trapezoid is half the size of the parallelogram, how could you express the area of the trapezoid? Students should determine that $A = \frac{1}{2}(b_1 + b_2)h$.

▶ ***Vocabulary Development*** Make sure that students use the words *base* and *height,* not *length* and *width,* when referring to the dimensions of parallelograms and trapezoids. Help them remember that the height is the distance from base to base.

Teaching Strategy: Volume of Cylinders

Provide students with a clear image of why the formula for finding the volume of a cylinder makes sense.

▶ ***Show This:***

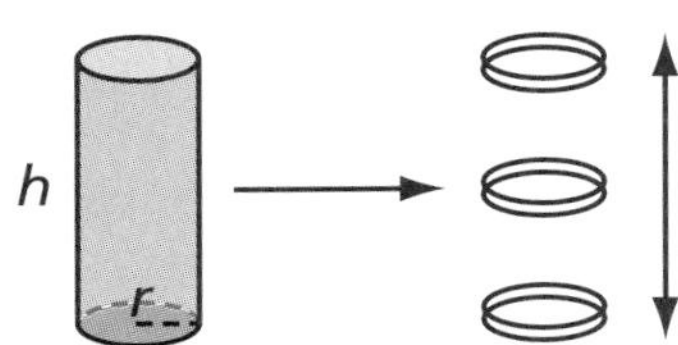

▶ ***Ask:*** *When you stack h circles on one another, you can see the volume of the cylinder filled in by circles. If the circular base of the cylinder has radius r, how would you express the area of the circular base?*
Students should know that the area is πr^2. Ask students how they would express the volume of the cylinder. They should see the volume as h times the area of the circular base or $V = \pi r^2 h$.

Teacher Tips

Management Working with formulas is greatly facilitated by using a calculator. However, students frequently make calculator errors. To minimize this problem, have pairs of students work together on problems, letting one student solve the problem using a calculator while the other checks the solution.

Showing, Describing It is important to relate formulas to geometric drawings. Encourage students to label their drawings of geometric figures with appropriate labels, such as *r* for radius.

Help from Home Have students bring various items from home that are shaped like cylinders. Students can make and test predictions about which cylinders have greater volumes.

Grouping When exploring the formula for the volume of a cylinder, have groups work together to develop a written explanation for why the formula makes sense. Groups can share their explanations with the rest of the class.

Visual Aids When exploring the Pythagorean Property, right triangles should be prominently displayed so that students learn to associate the theorem with this special group of triangles. Too often students come to falsely believe that the Pythagorean Property holds true for any triangle.

Teacher Tips

Materials Calculators are invaluable tools for working with the Pythagorean Property. They help students quickly and accurately find the necessary squares and square roots.

Memory Trigger Students often have trouble remembering the Pythagorean Property. A picture of a right triangle with squares connected off each side of the triangle builds a powerful image of the notion that the sum of the squares of two sides of the triangle is equal to the square of the third side.

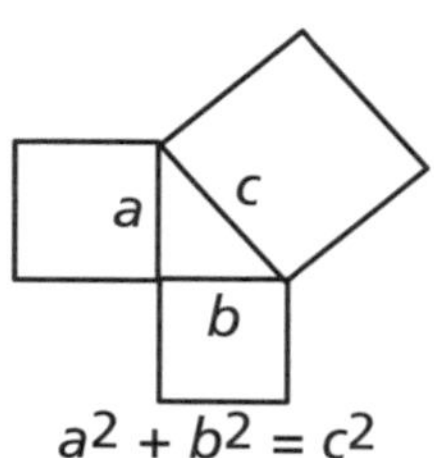

$a^2 + b^2 = c^2$

▶ ***Common Misconceptions*** Students often confuse the formula for the area of a circle with the formula for the circumference of a circle. Help students remember the difference by relating the idea that area is measured in square units and the formula for the area of the circle has a squared term in it, r^2.

Teaching Strategy: The Pythagorean Property

The Pythagorean Property contains several squared terms. Students need to have mastered finding a square root to be able to solve for one side of a right triangle.

▶ ***Show This:***

Pythagorean Property: $a^2 + b^2 = c^2$

$a = 3$, $c = 5$, $b = 4$

Students should substitute values for the variables, then check to determine if $3^2 + 4^2 = 5^2$. They will find that the left side of the equation equals $9 + 16$, or 25, and so does the right side. Therefore, the triangle above is a right triangle.

Opportunities to Assess

Observation

It is difficult to observe students' use of geometric formulas unless they are asked to write out the steps they follow to find the solution. Encourage students to show the values they substitute in formulas so that you can help determine at what stage they may have some misconceptions.

Homework

In this unit, students should be given homework problems that require them to use geometric formulas to find the area, surface area, and volume of geometric figures and solids in their home.

Family Involvement

Ask families to write brief descriptions of when they have used geometric formulas to solve a remodeling or other problem around the house. These descriptions can be shared and incorporated into lesson discussions throughout the unit.

Teacher/Student Dialogue

How to Help Students Find Errors

When using geometric formulas, students will sometimes make minor errors. They have trouble figuring out why they didn't get the correct answer when they feel that they really understand the process.

Teacher: Who has found the volume of the cylinder with radius 2 inches and height 4 inches?
Student: *I got 25.12 cubic inches.*

Teacher: Dia, I like the way you provided the correct label of cubic inches. However, I think the volume is greater than that.
Student: *But I used the right formula: $V = 2\pi rh$, and I used 2 for r, 4 for h, and 3.14 for π.*

Teacher: Did you write out your problem in steps?
Student: *I didn't write anything out, I just multiplied 2 times 4 times 3.14 and got 25.12.*

Teacher: Why don't you try writing out the formula on the board and then rewrite it underneath using the numbers you substituted for the variables.
Student: (Writes these steps on the board) *Oh, I see. I forgot to multiply by the other 2. That would make the volume 50.24 cubic inches.*

Teacher: That's right. Class, writing the steps out might be helpful for all of you. Tucker, did you write out the steps?
Student: *Yes. I can't see what I do wrong unless I write it all out.*

Questioning Techniques

It is tempting to tell students correct answers and to tell them where they made their mistakes. However, when students are prompted to locate their own errors, they are less likely to repeat the same sort of error. Use guiding questions, or suggestions like writing out steps, to help students develop a means by which they can check their work, correcting any errors along the way.

What to do

When

Sometimes lessons move along more quickly than planned. When you find yourself with extra time at the end of a lesson, it might be a good change of pace to have students reflect about what new concepts they learned that day or about the key concepts they learned in this unit. Then, have them write their ideas down for you. Sometimes a quiet moment of reflection helps students clarify what they know or still do not understand about a lesson. And it can be a great way for them to communicate to you privately about what they have learned.

What to do

Every Day

There are many great stories about the history of mathematics and the mathematicians who developed important mathematical formulas. There are particularly rich sources of stories about discoveries in geometry. Take the time each day to have a student research then relate a brief story about a famous mathematician or geometric discovery. These stories will add a human touch to a topic that sometimes feels very disconnected to students.

TEACHER SUPPORT

Unit 10 Using Formulas in Geometry

LESSON 1
PAGES 277–279

OBJECTIVE
To use formulas to find the circumference and area of a circle

PREREQUISITES
Concepts
- Understand area and perimeter and the geometry of a circle

Skills
- Perform computations using rational numbers
- Be able to find areas and perimeters of polygons

VOCABULARY
circle, center, radius, diameter, chord, circumference, pi

MATERIALS
Scissors and a circle divided evenly into 20 sections

Copymasters
Teaching Resource 10 (circle)

Circumference and Area of Circles

Presenting the Lesson

Introduce the Skill Review the various parts of a circle, including its circumference. Discuss the common approximations of 3.14 and $\frac{22}{7}$ for π. Show the class the circle on page 278 that has been evenly divided into 20 sections. Now, let a couple of students cut up each of the 20 sections and tape them to the board in a rectangular-like figure. Ask the class what the figure looks like. (parallelogram) *What is the length of the parallelogram?* (half the circumference, or $\frac{1}{2} \times 2\pi r$) *What is the height of the parallelogram?* (the radius of the circle) If this figure were a parallelogram, it would have an area $A = (\frac{1}{2} \times 2\pi r)(r)$ or $A = \pi r^2$.

Check Understanding *If a circle had a radius of 3.2 m, what would its circumference be to the nearest tenth of a meter?* (20.1 m) *What would its area be to the nearest tenth of a square meter?* (32 m^2)

Guided Practice

Have students do the first exercise in rows 1, 4, and 9 on pages 277–279.

Independent Practice

Have students complete pages 277–279 independently.

Closing the Lesson *If the radius of a circle is doubled, what happens to its circumference?* (It is doubled.) *If the radius of a circle is doubled, what happens to its area?* (It is quadrupled.)

LESSON 2
PAGES 280–282

OBJECTIVE
To use subdivision and formulas to compute the areas of complex plane figures

PREREQUISITES
Concepts
- Understand area and simple geometric figures

Skills
- Be able to find the area of simple geometric figures
- Perform computations using rational numbers

VOCABULARY
complex figure

Complex Plane Figures

Presenting the Lesson

Introduce the Skill On the board draw an incomplete rectangle with a semicircle at one of the short ends. Ask students to copy the figure and find a total area. They will probably say they need to know certain lengths and that they need to break the figure up into pieces and add the areas of the pieces. Label the rectangle 11.5 cm long and 6 cm wide, and have them find the area. Have a volunteer come to the board and explain how he/she did it. Do two other examples like this.

Check Understanding *A rectangle, which is 14 cm long and 8 cm wide, has a semicircle on each short side. What is the area of the total figure rounded to the nearest tenth?* (Multiply 14 times 8, and add 16 times 3.14 to get 162.2 cm^2.)

Guided Practice

Have students do exercises 1 and 7 on pages 280 and 281. Be sure that they divide the figure in exercise 7 correctly.

Independent Practice

Have students complete pages 280–282 independently.

Closing the Lesson *Who can summarize what the strategy for finding the area of complex plane figures is?* (Possible answer: You divide the figure up into smaller simpler figures whose area can easily be found. You then add all the areas together.)

LESSON 3

PAGES 283–284

OBJECTIVE

To use a formula to compute the area of a trapezoid

PREREQUISITES

Concepts

- Understand area and basic geometric figures

Skills

- Be able to find the area of common geometric figures and complex plane figures
- Perform computations with rational numbers

MATERIALS

Copymasters

Reteach 81, 82, 83, pp.151–153

Area of a Trapezoid

Presenting the Lesson

Introduce the Skill Draw a picture of a trapezoid on the board and ask the class what it is. Ask them to find the area of the trapezoid if it has the following dimensions: the lower base is 15 dm, the upper base is 9 dm, and the distance between the two bases is 3 dm. Have volunteers come to the board to explain how they did the problem. One may say they found the area of two triangles and a rectangle, another may have found the area of two triangles by drawing a diagonal. Use the second method to explain how to derive a formula for the area of a trapezoid.

Check Understanding *In order to find the area of a trapezoid, what information do you need?* (You need to know the lengths of the two parallel sides and the perpendicular distance between these sides.)

Guided Practice

Have students do exercises 1 and 11 on pages 283 and 284. Check to see that the students recognize that exercise 11 is the sum of two trapezoids.

Independent Practice

Have students complete pages 283 and 284 independently.

Closing the Lesson *What is the formula for the area of a trapezoid?* ($A = \frac{1}{2}(b_1 + b_2)h$)

LESSON 4

PAGES 285–286

OBJECTIVE

To use subdivision and the triangle area formula to compute the areas of regular polygons

PREREQUISITES

Concepts

- Understand area, perimeter, and basic geometric figures

Skills

- Be able to find the area of common geometric figures and complex plane figures
- Perform computations with rational numbers

VOCABULARY

regular polygon

Area of Regular Polygons

Presenting the Lesson

Introduce the Skill Draw a regular hexagon on the board and ask the students how they could find the area of the polygon. Mention that one way that works for all regular polygons is to draw isosceles triangles in the figure by finding the center of the regular polygon, and then connecting it to each vertex in the regular polygon. (Do this on the figure drawn.) Thus, they would create 6 isosceles triangles in a hexagon. If they found the area of one of the triangles and multiplied by the number of triangles, they would obtain the area of the regular polygon. The only thing they would need to know is the length of a side of the regular polygon (b) and the height (h) of one of the triangles. Tell them that in the regular hexagon, the side is 10 m and the perpendicular to a side is about 8.6 m. Put the formula on the board ($A = n \cdot \frac{bh}{2}$). Have them find the area of the regular hexagon. (258 m^2)

Check Understanding *How could you use this lesson to find the area of a square with a 2-in. side?* (Divide it into 4 triangles; each has an area of $\frac{1}{2} \times 2 \times 1 = 1$ in.^{2}; the area of all four triangles is 4 in.^{2}.)

Guided Practice

Have students do exercises 1 and 9 on pages 285 and 286.

Independent Practice

Have students complete pages 285 and 286 independently.

Closing the Lesson *How do you find the area of a regular polygon?* (Possible answer: Find the length of a side of the regular polygon, find the height of one of its triangles, compute the area of one of the triangles, and multiply that by the number of sides.)

LESSON 5
PAGES 287–288

OBJECTIVE
To use a grid to estimate the areas of irregular plane figures

PREREQUISITES
- Understand area and basic geometric figures

Skills
- Be able to find the area of common geometric figures
- Perform computations with rational numbers

MATERIALS
Grid paper, and an overhead transparency of grid paper

Copymasters
Teaching Resource 6 (centimeter squared paper)

Estimating Area of Irregular Plane Figures on a Grid

Presenting the Lesson

Introduce the Skill Mention that one way to estimate the area of an irregular figure is to superimpose a grid over the figure. Draw an outline of your hand on the grid paper. Have the students do this at their desks with their own grid paper. Explain how to count all the squares totally within the figure first. Then, put parts of squares together to make whole squares and add the sum of these parts to the ones obtained earlier. This new total is an estimate of the area.

Check Understanding *Why don't we usually find the area of a parallelogram this way?* (Possible answer: Formulas are usually more accurate.)

Guided Practice
Have students do exercise 1 on page 287.

Independent Practice
Have students complete pages 287 and 288 independently.

Closing the Lesson *How do you estimate area using a grid?* (Possible answer: You count all the squares and pieces of squares.)

LESSON 6
PAGES 289–290

OBJECTIVE
To apply the Use a Simpler Problem strategy to find how a change in side length affects the area of a plane figure

PREREQUISITES

Concepts
- Understand the four-step problem solving process

Skills
- Perform computations using rational numbers

MATERIALS
grid paper

Copymasters
Teaching Resource 5 (quarter-inch squared paper)

Problem Solving Strategy: Solve a Simpler Problem

Presenting the Lesson

Introduce the Strategy Point out that in this lesson students will use the strategy of solving a simpler problem to help solve the main problem.

Model the Four-Step Problem Solving Process Present the photo enlargement problem described on page 289.

- **Understand:** Asking oneself questions about the problem in this case pinpoints the absence of specific dimensions.
- **Decide:** Emphasize how important it is to generalize from simple cases.
- **Solve:** Have students keep clearly in mind how a variable can be introduced in order to arrive at a generalization of the pattern.
- **Look back:** Mention that the solution may be a decimal rather than an integer.

Check Understanding *What kind of problems would lend themselves to using this method?* (Possible answer: ones that involve large numbers or complex ideas)

Guided Practice
Have students do exercise 1 on page 290 using grid paper.

Independent Practice
Have students complete pages 289 and 290 independently.

Closing the Lesson *What does the strategy of solving a simpler problem mean?* (Possible answer: By looking at a simpler problem, you may be able to see a pattern and generalize.)

LESSON 7
PAGES 291–292

OBJECTIVE
To construct space figures from nets

PREREQUISITES
Concepts
- Understand basic two- and three-dimensional geometric figures

Skills
- Be able to visualize figures from different perspectives

VOCABULARY
net

MATERIALS
Scissors and grid paper

Copymasters
Teaching Resource 5 (squared paper), 12–19 (nets)
Reteach 84, 85, 86, pp. 154–156

Spatial Visualization with Nets

Presenting the Lesson

Introduce the Skill Have the class draw these nets on their grid paper.

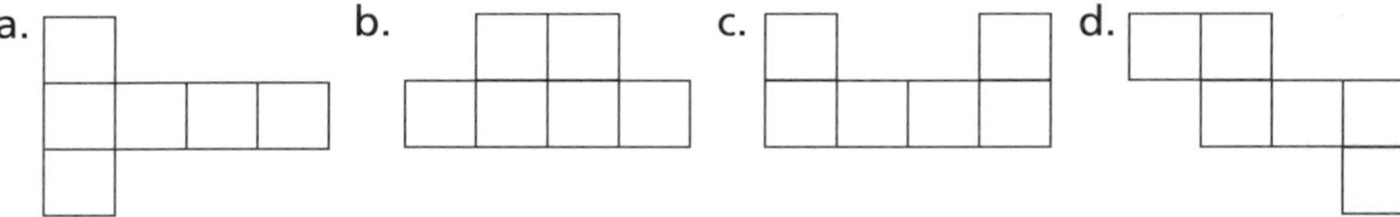

Ask them which ones they think could be folded up to make a cube. (a and d) After they have made their guesses, have them cut out the figures and try to fold them to verify their conjectures.

Check Understanding *In what situations is the use of nets important?* (Possible answer: in the design of packages and scale models)

Guided Practice

Have students do exercise 1 and create one net for a cube in exercise 6 on pages 291 and 292.

Independent Practice

Have students complete pages 291 and 292 independently.

Closing the Lesson *How many polygons make up the net for a pentagonal pyramid?* (six)

LESSON 8
PAGES 293–295

OBJECTIVE
To use a formula to compute the surface areas of prisms

PREREQUISITES
Concepts
- Understand area and formulas for finding the area of common plane figures

Skills
- Be able to find the areas of common plane figures
- Perform computations with rational numbers

VOCABULARY
surface area

MATERIALS
Models of prisms and a ruler

Copymasters
Extension 10, p. 186

Surface Area of Prisms

Presenting the Lesson

Introduce the Skill Draw a picture of a rectangular prism on the board with a base of length l, width w, and height h, and write the formula $A = 2lw + 2lh + 2wh$ or $A = 2(lw + lh + wh)$. Now, measure the sides and write the dimensions on the figure on the board, and have the class find the surface area. Show the class a triangular prism and ask them what information they will need in order to find its surface area. (The height of the triangle to a particular base of the triangle, and the lengths and widths of the three rectangles.) Write those lengths on a diagram on the board, and have the class find the surface area of the triangular prism.

Check Understanding *What is the simple formula for the surface area of a cube?* ($A = 6s^2$) *What does s stand for in this formula?* (the length of the edge of a cube)

Guided Practice

Have students do exercises 1 and 8 and the first exercises in rows 14 and 19 on pages 294–295.

Independent Practice

Have students complete pages 294–295 independently.

Closing the Lesson *What is the surface area of a space figure?* (Possible answer: It is the total area of all the surfaces making up the space figure.)

LESSON SUPPORT

LESSON 9
PAGES 296–297

OBJECTIVE
To use a formula to compute the surface areas of cylinders

PREREQUISITES
Concepts
- Understand area and formulas for finding the area of common plane figures
- Understand surface area

Skills
- Be able to find the areas of common plane figures and the surface area of prisms
- Perform computations with rational numbers

MATERIALS
Model of a cylinder and a ruler

Surface Area of Cylinders

Presenting the Lesson

Introduce the Skill Hold up a cylinder and ask the class how they could find the surface area of the cylinder. (Find the area of one of the circles and double it. Then, find the area of the rectangle that makes up the lateral surface of the cylinder.) You may need to remind them that the net for a cylinder consists of two circles and a rectangle. Ask the class what measurements they will need to find the surface area. (The radius and the height of the cylinder) Have a student find those measurements for the cylinder up front and draw a diagram on the board that includes those measurements. Then, ask the class to find the surface area of the cylinder. Ask a volunteer to show how he/she did the problem. Discuss the formula $A = 2(\pi r^2) + 2\pi rh$. Show where each part of the formula comes from.

Check Understanding *What two measurements do you need in order to find the surface area of a cylinder?* (the radius of the base and the height of the cylinder)

Guided Practice
Have students do exercises 1 and 8 on pages 296 and 297.

Independent Practice
Have students complete pages 296 and 297 independently.

Closing the Lesson *What similarities exist between finding the surface area of a cylinder and finding the surface area of a prism?* (Possible answer: In both cases, you find the areas of all the plane figures that make up the net for the space figure.)

LESSON 10
PAGES 298–299

OBJECTIVE
To use a formula to compute the volumes of prisms

PREREQUISITES
Concepts
- Understand area and formulas for finding the area of common plane figures

Skills
- Be able to find the areas of common plane figures
- Perform computations with rational numbers

Copymasters
Reteach 87, 88, 89, pp. 157–159

Volume of Prisms

Presenting the Lesson

Introduce the Skill Ask the class if they could create a formula for the volume of a rectangular prism knowing the lengths of the three sides. ($V = l \times w \times h$) Mention that the $l \times w$ is the area of the base, and so a formula that works for all prisms is $V = Bh$, where B equals the area of the base of the prism. Have them find the volume of a rectangular prism whose base is 6 cm by 8 cm and whose height is 5 cm. (240 cm^3) Have them find the volume of a triangular prism with a base whose side is 6 in., whose altitude to that side is 8 in., and whose height is 4 in. (96 $in.^3$)

Check Understanding *If the height of a prism is doubled, what happens to its volume?* (It is doubled.)

Guided Practice
Have students do exercises 1, 4, and 7 on pages 298 and 299.

Independent Practice
Have students complete pages 298 and 299 independently.

Closing the Lesson *When would you need to find the volume of a prism?* (Possible answer: When manufacturers ship objects like cereal boxes or candy bars in larger cartons, they need to find the optimum volume for the cartons.)

LESSON 11
PAGES 300–301

OBJECTIVE
To use subdivision and formulas to compute the volume of composite space figures

PREREQUISITES
Concepts
- Understand area and volume formulas for finding the area of common plane figures and volumes of prisms

Skills
- Be able to find the volumes of prisms
- Perform computations with rational numbers

MATERIALS
Centimeter or inch cubes

Volume of Composite Space Figures

Presenting the Lesson

Introduce the Skill Show the class a figure you have made up of centimeter or inch cubes. Ask the class how they might find the volume of the figure. (Find the volumes of the various prisms in the figure and add them together.) Do that with the class and check your answer by counting all the cubes in the figure, even those that may be hidden. Discuss how this process is similar to the process they used when finding the area of complex plane figures. Have them find the volume of the house below. Draw it on the board with the dimensions given. (6,210 cubic feet)

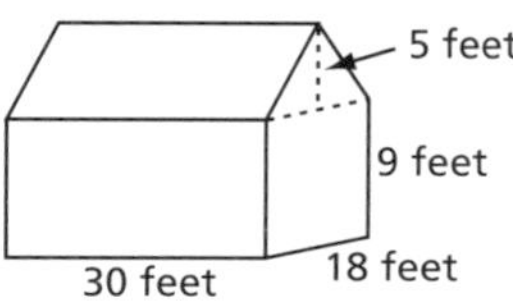

Check Understanding *How do you find the volume of a composite space figure?* (Break the figure down into figures such as prisms.)

Guided Practice
Have students do the first exercises in rows 1 and 3 on pages 300 and 301.

Independent Practice
Have students complete pages 300 and 301 independently.

Closing the Lesson *Why would you ever need to know how to find the volume of composite space figures?* (Possible answer: Most houses and buildings are not simple prisms but are made up of two or more prisms.)

LESSON 12
PAGES 302–303

OBJECTIVE
To understand how the surface area and volume of a space figure change when a linear dimension changes

PREREQUISITES
Concepts
- Understand area and volume formulas for finding the area of common plane figures and volumes of prisms

Skills
- Be able to find the surface areas and volumes of prisms
- Perform computations with rational numbers

VOCABULARY
scale factor

MATERIALS
Copymasters
Reteach 90, 91, pp. 160–161

Relating Length, Area, and Volume

Presenting the Lesson

Introduce the Skill Draw a picture of a cube and then another cube whose edges are twice as long. Now ask students questions like, *What happens to the area of a face if the edges of a cube are doubled?* (The area of the face is 4 times greater, or quadrupled.) *What happens to the surface area of a cube if its edges are doubled?* (The new cube's surface area is 4 times greater, or quadrupled.) *What happens to the volume of a cube if its edges are doubled?* (The new cube's volume is 8 times greater.) Tell students that when the length of an edge is changed to form a new figure, the ratio of the new length to the old length is called the scale factor.

Check Understanding *If the volume of a cube is 27 cm^3, what is the volume of a new cube that is formed by multiplying each edge by a scale factor of 4?* ($27 \times 64 = 1{,}728$ cm^3)

Guided Practice
Have students do exercises 1 and 7 on pages 302 and 303.

Independent Practice
Have students complete pages 302 and 303 independently.

Closing the Lesson *If the scale factor in the enlargement of a cube is 3, how does the surface area for the new cube compare to that of the old cube?* (It is 9 times the surface area of the original cube.) *How do the volumes compare?* (The new cube has a volume equal to 27 times that of the original cube.)

LESSON 13
PAGES 304–305

OBJECTIVE
To use a formula to compute the volume of cylinders

PREREQUISITES
Concepts
- Understand formulas for finding the area of circles and volumes of prisms

Skills
- Be able to find the volumes of prisms
- Perform computations with rational numbers

Volume of Cylinders
Presenting the Lesson

Introduce the Skill Draw a picture of a cylinder on the board and tell students that the formula for finding the volume of cylinder is $V = \pi r^2 \cdot h$. Have them find the volumes for the following cylinders using 3.14 for π and put their work into a chart similar to the one below. Note that the base is a circle, so the formula for volume of a cylinder includes the formula for area of a circle.

Radius	Height	Volume
6 cm	7 cm	(791.28 cm^3)
6 cm	3.5 cm	(395.64 cm^3)
3 cm	7 cm	(197.82 cm^3)

Now, have the students look at the chart and explain what happened to the volume when the height was halved (The volume was halved.) and when the radius was halved (The volume was reduced by a factor of four.).

Check Understanding *If one cylinder has a radius of 2 inches and a height of 5 inches and another has a radius of 4 inches and a height of 5 inches, how would their volumes compare?* (The first cylinder would be four times smaller than the second.)

Guided Practice
Have students do the first exercise in rows 2 and 5 on page 305.

Independent Practice
Have students complete pages 304 and 305 independently.

Closing the Lesson *If the radius and height are multiplied by the same scale factor to form two different cylinders, why does the cylinder whose radius changed have more of an effect on the volume than the cylinder whose height changed?* (Possible answer: Changing the height only changes one dimension, but changing the radius changes the area of the base, which is a two-dimensional change.)

LESSON 14
PAGES 306–307

OBJECTIVE
To use a diagram to model and solve problems

PREREQUISITES
Concepts
- Understand area concepts and the four-step process of problem solving

Skills
- Be able to compute the area of common figures and complex plane figures
- Perform computations with rational numbers

Problem Solving Application: Use a Diagram
Presenting the Lesson

Introduce the Focus of the Lesson Explain to students that in this lesson they will need to use or interpret a diagram in order to solve the problem.

Model the Four-Step Problem Solving Process Work through the problem of the circle area on page 306 with your students.

Discuss the Problem Solving Tips Point out to students that the four Problem Solving Process steps—Understand, Decide, Solve, and Look back—are listed in the box on page 306. Make sure students understand that each step is distinct from the others.

Check Understanding *Why does drawing a diagram help you solve a problem?* (It helps you see relationships and may help you generalize.)

Guided Practice
Have students do problems 1 and 5 on pages 306 and 307.

Independent Practice
Have students complete pages 306 and 307 independently.

Closing the Lesson *In what kinds of problems would you use the strategy of using a diagram?* (Possible answer: ones in which the diagram might help me see relationships)

LESSON 15

PAGES 308–310

OBJECTIVE

To understand and apply the Pythagorean Property of right triangles and verify it by direct measurement

PREREQUISITES

Concepts

- Understand right triangles and rectangles

Skills

- Perform computations with rational numbers
- Be able to solve simple equations

VOCABULARY

Pythagorean Property, hypotenuse, Pythagorean triple

MATERIALS

Grid paper and scissors

Copymasters

Teaching Resource 5 (quarter-inch squared paper)
Reteach 92, 93, pp. 162–163

Pythagorean Property of Right Triangles

Presenting the Lesson

Introduce the Skill Have students draw a right triangle on their piece of grid paper with one leg 3 units long and the other 4 units long. Have them draw the squares on the grid paper that fit on the two legs of the triangle. Now, have them cut those squares out and combine them to see if they can make a square to fit onto the hypotenuse of the triangle. (They can. Cut the 4 × 4 square into two pieces, each 4 × 2. Now, cut each 4 × 2 piece into a 3 × 2 piece and a 1 × 2 piece. You can build these four pieces onto the 3 × 3 square to get a 5 × 5 square.) Tell them that this works in all right triangles, not just this special case. Write down the Pythagorean Property and its inverse, and tell them that together these will be called the Pythagorean Property and that it is very useful. (Pythagorean Property: In a right triangle, the square of the hypotenuse equals the sum of the squares of the legs. Inverse: If the sum of the squares of two sides of a triangle equals the square of the third side, then the triangle is a right triangle.) Have them use the inverse to check to see which of the following are right triangles: (1) 5 cm, 12 cm, and 13 cm (Yes); (2) 4 in., 6 in., and 8 in. (No); and (3) 6 ft., 8 ft., and 10 ft. (Yes)

Have them use the Pythagorean Property to solve for the diagonals of the following rectangles: 15 m by 8 m (17 m) and 10 ft. by 12 ft. (about 15.6 ft.) Discuss how, as in the last example, the hypotenuse may not be a rational number. However, you can use a calculator to find an approximation to it, just as we approximate the area of circles by using 3.14 and $\frac{22}{7}$ for π.

Check Understanding *If a triangle has sides that measure 9 cm, 12 cm, and 15 cm, is it a right triangle? How do you know?* (Yes. Square the two small sides and add them together and see if you get the square of the largest side. In this case you do, so it is a right triangle.)

Guided Practice

Have students do the first exercise in row 1 on page 308, and row 11 on page 310. Check to see that they add the squares of both sides in exercise 11 to get the square of the diagonal.

Independent Practice

Have students complete pages 308–310 independently.

Closing the Lesson *Who can state the two parts to the Pythagorean Property?* (In a right triangle, the square of the hypotenuse equals the sum of the squares of the two legs. If a triangle is such that the sum of the squares of two sides is equal to the square of the third side, then it is a right triangle.)

UNIT 10 REVIEW

PAGES 311–313

Item Analysis

Items	Unit Obj.
1–6	10A
7–10	10B
11–16	10C
17–19	10E
20–23	10D
24–25	10A, 10F

Answers to Unit 10 Review items can be found on pages 311–313 of the Teacher's Annotated Edition.

Administering the Review

This page reviews concepts and skills taught in this unit. Be sure students understand all direction lines. You may want to do the first example in each section cooperatively to ensure understanding.

Scoring Chart

Number Correct	25	24	23	22	21	20	19	18	17	16	15	14	13	12	11
Score	100	96	92	88	84	80	76	72	68	64	60	56	52	48	44

Number Correct	10	9	8	7	6	5	4	3	2	1
Score	40	36	32	28	24	20	16	12	8	4

After the Review

- The Item Analysis chart on the left shows the Unit 10 objective(s) covered by each test item. This chart can help you determine which objectives need review or extra practice.
- For additional assessment, use the Posttest for Unit 10, Copymaster Book, pp. 45–47.
- To provide extension opportunities, use Copymaster Book, p. 186.

UNIT 10 CUMULATIVE REVIEW

PAGE 314

Item Analysis

Items	Unit Obj.
1	10A
2	10B
3	9A
4	8D
5	1E
6	2A
7	9A
8	9F

Answers to Cumulative Review items can be found on page 274 of the Teacher's Annotated Edition.

Administering the Review

This page reviews concepts and skills from earlier units, as well as providing practice with standardized test formats. Students may circle their answers, or you may prefer to duplicate and distribute the answer sheet, Copymaster Book, p. 191. This page may be assigned as homework or as classwork.

Test-Taking Tip Make a plan for solving multi-step problems. Decide what steps are needed to solve the problem before you begin to work.

Scoring Chart

Number Correct	8	7	6	5	4	3	2	1
Score	100	88	75	62	50	38	25	13

After the Review

- The Item Analysis chart on the left shows the unit objective covered by each test item. This chart can help you determine which objectives need review or extra practice.

The Coordinate Plane: Graphs and Transformations

Vocabulary

coefficient (of an expression) The numerical factor in each term containing a variable

direct variation A linear function of the form $y = kx$. k, a nonzero number, is called the constant of variation.

linear function A function whose ordered pair solutions lie on the same line.

monomial An expression consisting of a number, a variable, or the product of a number and one or more variables

nonlinear function A function whose ordered pair solutions do not lie on a straight line

polynomial An expression that is itself a monomial or is the sum or product of monomials

reflection A transformation that changes the position of a figure by flipping it about a line to form its mirror image

terms (of a polynomial) Each monomial that is part of a polynomial

translation A transformation that changes the position of a figure by sliding it in the same plane

Unit Objectives

11A Use tables of values to graph first, second, and third order polynomials

11B Identify symmetric figures on the plane and find a rule relating to their coordinates

11C Identify congruent and similar figures on the plane

11D Find the image of a polygon on the plane after a translation or a reflection

11E Graph linear functions that represent direct variation and understand slope as a rate of change

11F Graph nonlinear functions associated with changes in area and volume

11G Identify a two-variable equation that represents a problem situation; use Write an Equation and other strategies to solve problems

About This Unit

The support pages that follow provide more information on prerequisite skills, methods for teaching skills and concepts, daily routines, tips on classroom management and materials, and useful dialogue techniques.

Prerequisite Skills and Concepts

Students should be able to

- plot points on a coordinate grid.

If not, use prerequisite Reteach Worksheet 94, p. 164.

Assessments

Use Beginning of the Year Inventory for entry-level assessment.

Ongoing Evaluation Quick Checks, Reteach Worksheets, the Skills Tutorial Inventories, and the Midyear Test help ensure that students are progressing adequately to meet the standards.

Summative Evaluation Use Test Preps, Unit Review (p. T174), Cumulative Review (p. T175), Reteach Worksheets, and the Computation Skills Tutorial to assure that students have achieved the standards for the unit.

Diagnosing Errors The Quick Checks highlight common errors and provide remediation. See also the **Teaching Strategies Handbook** pp. T164–T167, where short discussions labeled Common Misconceptions appear as needed with the strategies for key concepts.

Homework and Family Involvement

Home Note In the Student Book, the Dear Family home note provides objectives, vocabulary, and a sample skill discussion for family participation. (**Teaching Strategies Handbook** pages also provide homework and family involvement tips.)

Education Place Refer families to Houghton Mifflin's EduPlace Web site at http://www.eduplace.com; for resources and activities for students at http://www.eduplace.com/math; and additional resources and activities at http://www.eduplace.com/parents.

Lessons	Student Pages	Teacher Pages	Resources	State or Local Objectives	State or Local Assessment
11.1 Algebra: Graphing Polynomials	317–319	**T168**	Unit 11 Pretest		
11.2 Symmetry in the Coordinate Plane	320–322	**T168**			
11.3 Congruence and Similarity	323–325	**T169**	Reteach 95, 96, 97		
11.4 Translations and Reflections	326–328	**T169**			
11.5 Algebra:Equations with Two Variables	329–331	**T170**			
11.6 Problem Solving Application: Choose an Equation	332–333	**T170**			
11.7 Algebra: Graphing Linear Functions	334–335	**T171**	Reteach 98, 99, 100; Extension 11		
11.8 Algebra: Slope of a Line	336–337	**T171**			
11.9 Algebra: Direct Variation	338–339	**T172**			
11.10 Problem Solving Strategy: Write an Equation	340–341	**T172**			
11.11 Algebra: Nonlinear Functions	342–344	**T173**	Reteach 101, 102, 103; Unit 11 Posttest		

Teaching Strategies

Math Background — Coordinate Plane: Graphs and Transformations

Graphing equations and illustrating transformation of graphs in the coordinate plane are activities that provide connections between algebraic and geometric concepts. Students at this level progress from graphing coordinate pairs to graphing equations of lines through understanding slope and points on a line. They begin to observe relationships between symmetric figures in the plane and their coordinate points.

In the unit, students also begin to see what happens as you take a given graph of an equation and manipulate it by reflecting it across a line or translating it up or down. As they see how these manipulations affect the graph of an equation, they will also gain some insights into how to formulate the equation of the new graph formed through translations and reflections.

When Students Ask, Why Learn This?
A good sense of coordinate graphing helps students develop spatial sense. It also helps students gain intuition about such tasks as reading and interpreting maps. The algebraic components of developing and graphing equations lay the foundation for all future mathematical topics they will study in high school and beyond.

A Positive Start
It is important for students to see how the study of equations and graphing in the coordinate plane are useful in the real world. Invite practicing geographers, surveyors, geologists, or astronomers into the classroom so that they can provide students with a look at how they use these skills in their careers. Students may also be encouraged to study such activities through research in the library or on the Internet.

Linking Past and Future Learning

The concepts of graphing in the coordinate plane progress nicely across Levels 6, 7, and 8. The following chart provides some insights as to how topics move forward.

Concept/Skills	Last Year	This Year	Next Year
Symmetry in the Coordinate Plane	Identify a figure that has a vertical line of symmetry	Draw lines of symmetry for figures in the coordinate plane and determine the lines' equation	Test whether graphs of equations are symmetric in the plane
Translations and Reflections	Reflect a figure across a vertical line of symmetry	Find the image of a polygon on a plane after a translation or reflection	Develop a new equation that represents a translation or reflection of a given equation
Graphing Linear Functions	Graph ordered pairs in four quadrants; generate input and output values to graph	Graph linear functions with direct variation; understand slope as the rate of change	Verify that a point lies on a line given by an equation

Methods and Management

This unit ends the year. As you plan, look for opportunities to incorporate skills from previous units—to enhance the material and to check student comprehension.

Teaching Strategy: Symmetry

Students should be able to identify lines of symmetry. When they work in the coordinate plane, students will ultimately be able to not only draw lines of symmetry but also determine the equation of the line of symmetry.

▶ ***Show This:***

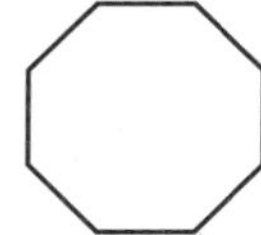

▶ ***Ask:*** *How many lines of symmetry can you find in the regular octagon above?* Show the eight lines of symmetry; four through the midpoints of opposite sides and four through opposite vertices.

▶ ***Common Misconceptions*** Make sure that students feel comfortable with the idea of a figure being symmetric within itself. This will help them when they reflect figures across given lines. Some students confuse these lines with the lines of reflection found within a given figure.

Teaching Strategy: Translations and Reflections

Reflections are very pleasing to the eye. Suggest that students create a design in the coordinate plane, impose a line of symmetry, and reflect the design across the line.

▶ ***Show This:***

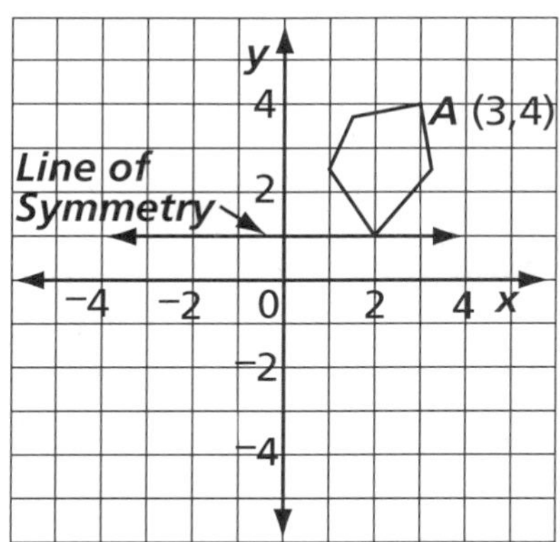

▶ ***Ask:*** *How many ways can you reflect this figure across the given line of symmetry?* (one way) *What will the coordinates of point A be when the figure is reflected across the line of symmetry?*
Students can count and find that the new coordinates will be (3, ⁻2).

▶ ***Common Misconceptions*** Students tend to have difficulty with this sort of activity when the line of symmetry actually "goes through" the original graph. Be careful to avoid these at the beginning and gradually work your way up to them.

Teacher Tips

Visual Aids Post pictures of symmetry in nature around the room. Pictures can range from plants of the rain forest to the human body.

Pacing Students will be actively engaged in sketching and discussing many graphs in this unit. Make sure that you set boundaries for how much time you allow for each exercise so that you keep your lessons moving at the desired pace.

Materials Students will benefit from folding and flipping plane figures. Cut out many figures that have lines of symmetry and some that don't so students gain experience in recognizing symmetric figures.

Help from Home Ask family members to be creative and locate items around the house that are symmetric. Students can record and report what they find.

Vocabulary Students will relate well to a definition of a symmetric figure as a plane figure that can be folded in half so that the two halves match. Students may need to actually fold many figures before this definition makes sense.

Class Book Have students choose their best illustration of translations and reflections and write an explanation of how they developed their graphs. You can then compile these graphs into a class book to be shared with families.

More Materials Students will be working on a lot of grid paper when learning about reflections and translations. To save on materials, have students divide the grid paper in sections so that they can fit four or more graphs on each side.

Quick Tip Examining reflections is quite insightful when you can use mirrors to reflect across a line of symmetry. If you don't have access to enough mirrors, use sheets of foil to serve as reflectors.

Grouping Divide the class into groups and then give each group a linear equation to graph. Make sure each of the equations differ only by a constant and have groups compare their graphs. They can then develop a generalization about linear graphs and translations.

Words of Experience Students are already familiar with plotting points to determine the graph of a line. Be on the watch for students to revert to this same strategy when they are asked to graph a line based on the slope and the y-intercept.

Rise over Run Slope is generally defined as the slant of a line. Students often learn to talk about and compute slope as "rise over run." Help students see how "rise over run" makes sense when describing slope.

Teaching Strategy: Graphing Linear Functions

Students need to develop their sense of slopes of lines, and determine the approximate slant of the graph of a line based on the given slope alone.

▶ ***Show This:***

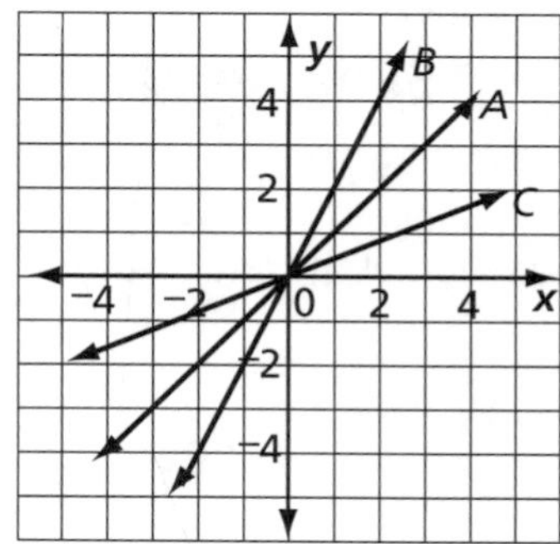

Point out that slope of line A is 1. Any line "flatter" than line A, such as line C, has a slope less than 1. Similarly, any line "steeper" than line A, such as line B, has a slope greater than one.

▶ ***Ask:*** *What would you approximate the slopes of lines B and C to be? Why?*

The slope of B is approximately a slope of 2 and the slope of C is about $\frac{1}{2}$.

▶ ***Common Misconceptions*** Probably the biggest difficulty students have in developing a sense of slope is working with negative slopes. In particular, students will have trouble seeing a slope of $^-1$ as being greater than a slope of $^-2$. On a number line, they can conceptually come to understand that $^-1$ is greater than $^-2$, but when viewing lines, a line with slope $^-2$ is steeper than a line with slope $^-1$. Work with students to understand this very difficult concept by equating "more steep" with "more negative."

Opportunities to Assess

Observation

Students need a lot of practice in graphing equations. As students engage in this type of activity, you will have plenty of opportunity to observe areas of difficulty as well as areas that seem simple for students.

Homework

Accurate graphing requires time and careful concentration. Provide students with the opportunity to practice these skills at home where they may have fewer time constraints than at school.

Family Involvement

Invite family members who use tools of coordinate graphing in their daily lives to come to class and share their experiences. Students may be surprised at the many ways coordinate graphing is useful.

Teacher/Student Dialogue

Providing "Wait Time" During Discussions

Sometimes you will find yourself asking a question that no one seems to respond to. The temptation is to answer the question yourself, but this may send a signal to the class that if they remain silent, you will always end up providing the answers. Instead, try to find ways to get students to respond, allowing sufficient wait time for them to come up with the answer or a clarifying question.

Teacher: What do you think the coordinate of point *A* will be when we translate the rectangle two units to the left and four units down?

Students: *(No response)*

Teacher: *(Waits at least fifteen seconds)*

Students: *(No response)*

Teacher: Try thinking about moving in one direction first and how that might affect the coordinate. Then, think about how moving in the other direction might affect things. Gabriel?

Student: *I'm not sure.*

Teacher: I'd like you all to turn to the person next to you and quickly exchange ideas about what you think the answer would be. *(Waits as students engage in quiet discussion)* Now, who thinks they have some idea of how to get started on finding the new coordinate? Grace, you and Douglas?

Student: *We think that you should subtract 2 from the original x-coordinate and subtract 4 from the original y-coordinate.*

Teacher: Nice job. I agree.

Questioning Techniques

Students are often unsure of how to respond to a given question or feel uncomfortable speaking out in class. Rather than provide answers to questions immediately, you can try several ways of urging students to respond. First, you might offer a hint at how to find the answer, again allowing sufficient wait time. If students are still reluctant, having them talk to their neighbor is a good next step. Talking to one person is less threatening than talking to the whole class. Plus, students feel more confident in finding a solution when they have someone to bounce their ideas off of.

What to do

When

Families are often worried that a student is falling behind in mathematics, especially when the student finds some of the algebraic and coordinate graphing concepts difficult. They may ask you for suggestions on what they can do to help. Suggest that they have the student explain the steps they are following on some of their homework problems. They may want to obtain some related activity books from a local library or educational materials store, or arrange for the student to work with another student after school.

LESSON SUPPORT

Unit 11 The Coordinate Plane: Graphs and Transformations

LESSON 1
PAGES 317–319

OBJECTIVE
To use tables of values to compute ordered pairs for a variety of expressions

PREREQUISITES
Concepts
- Understand linear graphs and tables of values

Skills
- Be able to graph in the coordinate plane
- Perform computations with rational numbers

VOCABULARY
x-axis, *y*-axis, quadrant, graph of a polynomial, parabola

MATERIALS
Coordinate grid paper and straightedge

COPYMASTERS
Teaching Resource 19 (coordinate plane)

Graphing Polynomials

Presenting the Lesson

Introduce the Skill Write the rule $2x + 3 = y$ on the board and tell students you would like to create a table of values that satisfy this rule. Ask students how they could find what value corresponds to $x = 2$. Have students find six ordered pairs, at least one of which has a negative x value, that satisfy the given rule. Now, draw a set of axes on the board and label the x-axis and y-axis, and have a volunteer graph their values for the rule. Also, discuss how the points graphed seem to lie in a straight line. Have the students find a set of values for $y = x^2 - 4$ and $y = 2x^2 + 1$. Discuss how these are not straight lines.

Check Understanding *If $3x - 4 = y$, what y value would correspond to $x = {}^-1$?* ($^-7$) *What y value would correspond to $x = 5$?* (11)

Guided Practice

Have students do the first exercise in rows 1, 3, and 4 on pages 317–319.

Independent Practice

Have students complete pages 317–319 independently.

Closing the Lesson *What shape is the graph of $x^2 + 5 = y$?* (a parabola) *What can you tell me about points in the second quadrant?* (The x values are negative and the y values are positive.)

LESSON 2
PAGES 320–322

OBJECTIVE
To identify symmetric figures in the coordinate plane and find a rule related to their coordinates

PREREQUISITES
Concepts
- Understand basic geometric figures

Skills
- Be able to graph ordered pairs

VOCABULARY
line of symmetry

MATERIALS
Coordinate grid paper

COPYMASTERS
Teaching Resource 19 (coordinate plane)

Symmetry in the Coordinate Plane

Presenting the Lesson

Introduce the Skill Have students create a coordinate plane and graph the hexagon whose vertices are at ($^-2$, 0), (2, 0), ($^-3$, 2), (3, 2), ($^-2$, 4), and (2, 4). Have them fold the figure about the y-axis. Ask them what they noticed. (One half folds on top of the other half.) Tell them that the y-axis is a line of symmetry for the hexagon. Ask, *What do you notice about the vertices of the hexagon?* (Each y value has two x values that are opposite in sign.)

Check Understanding *Is the figure with vertices (2, 1), (3, 2), (2, $^-1$), and (3, $^-2$) symmetric about either of the axes?* (Yes. It is symmetric about the x-axis)

Guided Practice

Have students do the first exercise in rows 1, 2, and 7 on pages 320 and 321. Check to see that students are able to find the matching points in exercises 2 and 7.

Independent Practice

Have students complete pages 320–322 independently.

Closing the Lesson *When is a figure symmetric about both the x- and y-axis?* (Possible answer: For every ordered pair (a, b), the figure would also have to have (^-a, b), (a, ^-b), and (^-a, ^-b). Students may use a specific point to illustrate this idea.)

LESSON 3
PAGES 323–325

OBJECTIVE
To identify congruent and similar figures in the coordinate plane

PREREQUISITES
Concepts
- Understand congruent segments, angles, and polygons
- Understand graphing on a coordinate grid

Skills
- Be able to graph points on a grid
- Perform computations with rational numbers

VOCABULARY
congruent polygons, similar polygons corresponding sides, corresponding angles

MATERIALS
Coordinate grid paper

COPYMASTERS
Teaching Resource 19 (coordinate plane)
Reteach 95, 96, 97, pp. 165–167

Congruence and Similarity

Presenting the Lesson

Introduce the Skill Draw two congruent quadrilaterals on an overhead transparency of grid paper, and ask the class what they need to know in order to say whether the figures are congruent. (Corresponding sides and angles would have to be congruent.)

Show them two figures that are similar but not congruent. Explain the conditions needed for figures said to be similar. Draw a triangle on the overhead grid transparency with one vertex at the origin, and ask them to draw a triangle congruent to it on the grid paper. Now, ask them to draw another triangle where the sides are twice as long as those of the original.

Check Understanding *If two triangles are congruent, are they similar? Explain.* (Yes. Congruent figures have congruent angles and sides that have a ratio of 1 to 1.) *If two triangles are similar, are they congruent?* (Not necessarily. The corresponding angles are congruent, but the corresponding sides may not be congruent.)

Guided Practice

Have students draw the polygons in exercises 1 and 3 on pages 323 and 324. Check to see that the corresponding sides in triangle three are twice as long as the original sides.

Independent Practice

Have students complete pages 323–325 independently.

Closing the Lesson *Where would you use the idea of similar figures?* (Possible answer: reducing or enlarging photographs)

LESSON 4
PAGES 326–328

OBJECTIVE
To find the image of a polygon in the coordinate plane after a translation or a reflection

PREREQUISITES
Concepts
- Understand the congruence relation and graphing on the coordinate plane

Skills
- Be able to graph points on the coordinate plane

VOCABULARY
geometric transformations, reflection, translation (or slide)

MATERIALS
Coordinate grid paper

COPYMASTERS
Teaching Resource 19 (coordinate plane)

Translations and Reflections

Presenting the Lesson

Introduce the Skill Have students draw the quadrilateral with vertices (2, 1), (6, 6), (9, 1), and (5, 2) on their grid papers. Have them fold their papers about the x-axis, mark where the vertices land, and sketch in the new quadrilateral. Have them label all of the vertices and ask, *What happened to the points when you reflected or flipped them about the* x*-axis?* (The x values stayed the same, but the y values became the opposite of the given y values.) Have students draw a triangle with vertices at (3, $^-3$), ($^-1$, 4), and ($^-5$, $^-4$). Now, have them add 3 to each x-coordinate and $^-1$ to each y-coordinate, obtaining the coordinates (6, $^-4$), (2, 3), and ($^-2$, $^-5$). Have them draw the triangle with those vertices. Ask, *How do the two triangles compare?* (They are congruent.)

Check Understanding *If the point ($^-4$, 6) is translated 4 units left and 2 units up, what are its new coordinates?* ($^-8$, 8)

Guided Practice

Have students do the first exercise in rows 1 and 8 on pages 326 and 328 and exercise 3 on page 327.

Independent Practice

Have students complete pages 326–328 independently.

Closing the Lesson *If a point in the third quadrant is reflected about the x-axis, what quadrant is it in? Explain.* (It is in the second quadrant, since the y-coordinate changes signs and the x-coordinate remains the same.)

LESSON 5
PAGES 329–331

OBJECTIVE
To find some solutions for two-variable linear equations with a trial-and-error method and with a table of values

PREREQUISITES
Concepts
- Understand simple linear equations in one variable

Skills
- Be able to solve simple linear equations in one variable
- Perform computations with rational numbers

VOCABULARY
dependent and independent variables

Equations with Two Variables

Presenting the Lesson

Introduce the Skill Put the following equations on the board and ask for a volunteer to solve them: $2p = 6$ and $y - 4 = 7$. Now, write $y = 3x + 2$ and ask for a volunteer to solve it. Explain that there are many solutions to this equation and it would be impossible to find them all. What we do is make a table listing *some* of the points that satisfy the equation. Do this for $x = 0, 2,$ and 21. Have the students find three more solutions for the equation. Have the students find five solutions to the equation $y = 2x - 3$.

Check Understanding *If $y = \frac{x}{2} + 3$, what does y equal if x equals 4?* (5) *What does y equal if x equals zero?* (3) *What does y equal if $x = {}^{-}6$?* (0)

Guided Practice

Have students do the first exercise in rows 1 and 2 and exercise 5 on pages 329–331.

Independent Practice

Have students complete pages 329–331 independently.

Closing the Lesson *How do you find solutions for an equation in two variables?* (Possible answer: You pick a value for one of the variables and substitute it into the equation and solve for the other variable.)

LESSON 6
PAGES 332–333

OBJECTIVE
To choose the correct equation to solve problems

PREREQUISITES
Concepts
- Understand linear equations in two variables

Skills
- Be able to verify if an ordered pair satisfies an equation in two variables
- Perform computations with rational numbers

Problem Solving Application: Choose an Equation

Presenting the Lesson

Introduce the Focus of the Lesson Explain to students that in this lesson they will need to choose an equation in order to solve the problem.

Model the Four-Step Problem Solving Process Work through the problem of the spring extensions on page 332 with your students.

Discuss the Problem Solving Tips Point out to students that the four Problem Solving Process steps—Understand, Decide, Solve, and Look back—are listed in the box on page 332. Make sure students understand that each step is distinct from the others.

Check Understanding *If a person worked 4 hours, he/she would earn \$28. How could you use that information to verify which of these formulas is correct: $P = 7 + h$; $P = 7h$?* (Substitute 28 for P and 4 for h and see if the statement is true.)

Guided Practice

Have students do the first problem on page 332. Check to see that students correctly substitute into the equations before choosing the equation.

Independent Practice

Have students complete pages 332 and 333 independently.

Closing the Lesson *What is the process you could use to find out which equation correctly represents the data in a table?* (Substitute some of the ordered pairs from the table into the equations and see if they make true statements.)

LESSON 7
PAGES 334–335

OBJECTIVE
To graph linear functions

PREREQUISITES
Concepts
- Understand graphing on the coordinate plane

Skills
- Be able to graph a table of values with two variables

VOCABULARY
function, linear function, "exactly one"

MATERIALS
Coordinate grid paper

Copymasters
Teaching Resource 19 (coordinate plane)
Reteach 98, 99, 100, pp. 168–170
Extension 11, p. 187

Graphing Linear Functions

Presenting the Lesson

Introduce the Skill Write the equation $y = 2x - 3$ on the board and ask the students to find six ordered pairs that satisfy the equation. Make a similar list on the board from some pairs suggested by students. Be sure to include at least one with a negative x value. Have the students graph those points and ask them, *What do you notice about all the points?* (They lie on a straight line.) Ask, *How many values did you get for y once you put in a value for x?* (Just one) Explain to them that the equation $y = 2x - 3$ is a function because for each value of x you get exactly one value for y. It is a linear function because it is a function whose graph is a straight line. Have them graph $y = \frac{x}{2} + 3$ and $y = x^2 - 2$. Discuss the fact that the first is another linear function, but the second is not because its graph is not a straight line.

Check Understanding *If an equation is a linear function, what can you tell me about it?* (Possible answers: For every x value, there is exactly one y value; Its graph is a straight line.)

Guided Practice

Have students do the first exercise in rows 3 and 4 on pages 334 and 335. Check to see that the graph in exercise 3 is a line bisecting the first and third quadrants.

Independent Practice

Have students complete pages 334 and 335 independently.

Closing the Lesson *Do you know any formulas that are linear functions?* (Possible answers: $C = 2\pi r$; $S = (n - 2)180$ for the sum of the angles of a polygon; $P = 4s$ for the perimeter P of a square of side s)

LESSON 8
PAGES 336–337

OBJECTIVE
To understand that the slope of a line is the ratio of the vertical change per unit horizontal change

PREREQUISITES
Concepts
- Understand and interpret graphs of lines

Skills
- Be able to plot a linear equation given a table of values

VOCABULARY
slope of a line, rise, run

Slope of a Line

Presenting the Lesson

Introduce the Skill On an overhead transparency of grid paper, graph the line $y = 2x - 3$. Discuss the steepness of the line and how mathematicians refer to the slope of the line. Define the slope as the change in y values divided by the change in x values for any two points on the line, and explain that this is often referred to as "rise over run." Pick two points out on the line such as $(1, {}^{-}1)$ and $(4, 5)$ and show them how to find the slope (2). Have them pick two other points on the line and verify that it doesn't matter which two points you use.

Check Understanding *If a line goes through the points* $(3, {}^{-}1)$ *and* $({}^{-}5, 3)$, *what is the slope of that line?* $({}^{-}\frac{1}{2})$

Guided Practice

Have students do the first exercise in rows 1 and 4 on pages 336 and 337.

Independent Practice

Have students complete pages 336 and 337 independently.

Closing the Lesson *What does it mean if a line has a slope of* ${}^{-}2$? (Possible answer: It means that from any point on the line, a step one unit to the right and two units down arrives at another point on the line.)

LESSON 9
PAGES 338–339

OBJECTIVE
To understand how direct variation problems can be solved using linear graphs

PREREQUISITES
Concepts
- Understand linear equations and the slope of a line

Skills
- Be able to find the slope of a line given its equation in the form "$y =$"

VOCABULARY
direct variation, constant of variation

Direct Variation

Presenting the Lesson

Introduce the Skill Discuss with the class the fact that it is customary to leave a 15% tip when you dine out. Build a table like the one found on page 338 in which, if your meal cost \$1.00, you would leave a tip of \$.15, if it cost \$2.00 you'd leave a tip of \$.30, etc. Tell students that this pattern is an example of direct variation. If x is the cost of the meal and y is the amount of the tip, then $y = 0.15x$. Ask them to examine the table and ask them to find how much the tip goes up every time the cost of the meal goes up \$1.00. (\$.15) Explain that this is what is called the constant of variation for this example, and that it is the coefficient of the x term if the equation is written as "$y =$." Explain how to find the constant of variation by substituting for x and y in the equation $y = mx$.

Check Understanding *If 2.3 is the constant of variation between two variables x and y, what would be the equation for the direct variation? ($y = 2.3x$)*

Guided Practice

Have students do the first exercises in rows 1, 3, and 5 on pages 338 and 339. In exercise 3, check to see that they divide y by x, not vice versa.

Independent Practice

Have students complete pages 338 and 339 independently.

Closing the Lesson *Can you think of some everyday examples of direct variation?* (Possible answers: sales taxes; the perimeter of a square versus the length of a side)

LESSON 10
PAGES 340–341

OBJECTIVE
To write an equation for verbal descriptions that represent linear functions

PREREQUISITES
Concepts
- Understand the four-step process for solving problems
- Understand, analyze, and interpret graphs and understand direct variation

Skills
- Perform computations with rational numbers

Problem Solving Strategy: Write an Equation

Presenting the Lesson

Introduce the Strategy Point out that in this lesson students will use the strategy of writing an equation to help solve problems.

Model the Four-Step Problem Solving Process Present the problem of Jayne's earnings described on page 340.

- **Understand:** Discuss how this is a case of direct variation.
- **Decide:** Knowing that this is direct variation, you can write the equation $y = mx$.
- **Solve:** You can substitute x and y values in your equation.
- **Look back:** Ask, Did the graph have 80 on the "lawn" axis? (No.)

Check Understanding *If a fair costs \$5.00 to enter and \$.65 a ride, write an equation for what you spent (y) if you went on x rides.* ($y = 5 + 0.65x$)

Guided Practice

Have students do problem 1 on page 341. Check to see that the equation they used was $s = 18m$.

Independent Practice

Have students complete pages 340 and 341 independently.

Closing the Lesson *How does writing an equation help you solve a problem?* (Possible answer: It helps you generalize from particular cases.)

LESSON 11
PAGES 342–344

OBJECTIVE
To graph functions of the form $y = nx^2$ and $y = nx^3$ in the context of changes of area and volume

PREREQUISITES
Concepts
- Understand linear functions and their graphs

Skills
- Be able to graph linear functions

MATERIALS
Coordinate grid paper

Copymasters
Teaching Resource 19 (coordinate plane)
Reteach 101, 102, 103, pp. 171–173

Non-Linear Functions

Presenting the Lesson

Introduce the Skill Ask the class what the formula is for finding the area of a square. ($A = s^2$) Have students find six ordered pairs that satisfy the equation. Point out that for each *s* value there is only one *A* value, so the relation is a function. However, point out that it is a non-linear function. Have students graph the ordered pairs and see that it is not a straight line. Have someone draw it on the overhead transparency grid paper. Have him/her graph five values where *x* is negative. Discuss why these new points don't apply to this particular situation.

Check Understanding *Which of the following are non-linear functions?* $y = x^2 + 1$, $y = 2x - 5$, $y = 3 - x^2$. (The first and third equations are non-linear functions.)

Guided Practice

Have students do exercise 1 on page 345. Check to see that they recognize that it is non-linear because the *x* values are squared.

Independent Practice

Have students complete pages 345–347 independently.

Closing the Lesson *What is a non-linear function?* (Possible answer: It is a function whose graph is not a straight line.)

LESSON SUPPORT

UNIT 11 REVIEW
PAGES 345–347

Item Analysis

Items	Unit Obj.
1–4	11D
5–9	11A
10–11	11B
12–20	11E
21	11C
22–23	11E
24–25	11F
26–28	11G

Answers to Unit 11 Review items can be found on pages 345–347 of the Teacher's Annotated Edition.

Administering the Review

This page reviews concepts and skills taught in this unit. Be sure students understand all direction lines. You may want to do the first example in each section cooperatively to ensure understanding.

Scoring Chart

Number Correct	28	27	26	25	24	23	22	21	20	19	18	17	16	15	14
Score	100	97	94	90	86	83	79	76	72	68	65	61	58	54	50

Number Correct	13	12	11	10	9	8	7	6	5	4	3	2	1
Score	47	43	40	36	32	29	25	22	18	14	11	7	4

After the Review

- The Item Analysis chart on the left shows the Unit 11 objective(s) covered by each test item. This chart can help you determine which objectives need review or extra practice.
- For additional assessment, use the Posttest for Unit 11, Copymaster Book, pp. 52–54.
- To provide extension opportunities, use Copymaster Book, p. 187.

UNIT 11 CUMULATIVE REVIEW

PAGE 348

Item Analysis

Items	Unit Obj.
1	11E
2	11D
3	9C
4	8A, 8B, 8C
5	9E
6	10D
7	10E
8	4G

Answers to Cumulative Review items can be found on page 348 of the Teacher's Annotated Edition.

Administering the Review

This page reviews concepts and skills from earlier units, as well as providing practice with standardized test formats. Students may circle their answers, or you may prefer to duplicate and distribute the answer sheet, Copymaster Book, p. 173. This page may be assigned as homework or as classwork.

Test-Taking Tip Take time to visualize a problem. Use each bit of information to add to your mental picture.

Scoring Chart

Number Correct	8	7	6	5	4	3	2	1
Score	100	88	75	63	50	38	25	13

After the Review

- The Item Analysis chart on the left shows the unit objective covered by each test item. This chart can help you determine which objectives need review or extra practice.

Teacher Notes

Contents

UNIT 1 • TABLE OF CONTENTS

Introduction to Algebraic Thinking

We will be using this vocabulary:

mean the average of a set of data

median the middle point of the data set when they are arranged from least to greatest

mode the number(s) that occur most often in a set of data

variable a letter that is used to represent one or more numbers

order of operations the rules that define the established order in which the operations in an expression are to be evaluated

solve an equation find the value of the variable that makes the equation a true statement

exponent a number that tells how many times a base is used as a factor

evaluate an expression find the value of the expression

Dear Family,

During the next few weeks, our math class will be studying some ideas from algebra. You can expect to see homework that provides practice with these skills. Here is a sample you may want to keep handy to give help if needed.

Evaluating Expressions

To find the value of the expression $7(8 - 5)^2 + 9$, you apply the order of operations. First perform operations inside parentheses, then simplify exponents, then multiply and divide in order from left to right, and finally, add and subtract in order from left to right.

$7(8 - 5)^2 + 9 = 7(3)^2 + 9$	First subtract inside the ( ).
$= 7(9) + 9$	Then square the result.
$= 63 + 9$	Multiply to simplify.
$= 72$	Finally, add.

To find the value of $a \div b + 7 \cdot c$ when $a = 42$, $b = 6$, and $c = 3$, substitute for the variables in the expression. Then use the order of operations to evaluate the expression.

$a \div b + 7 \cdot c = 42 \div 6 + 7 \cdot 3$	Substitute for the variables.
$= 7 + 21$	Then divide and multiply.
$= 28$	Finally, add.

During this unit, students will continue to learn new techniques related to the study of algebra.

Sincerely,

Name ______________________________

Whole Numbers and Data

Guided Practice Ex. 1; Row 2, p. 3
Independent Practice Complete pp. 3 & 4

The **line plot** shows the number of hours that **32** students in Johnson Middle School spent reading last weekend. Which measure—range, mean, median, or mode—best represents the number of hours the typical student read?

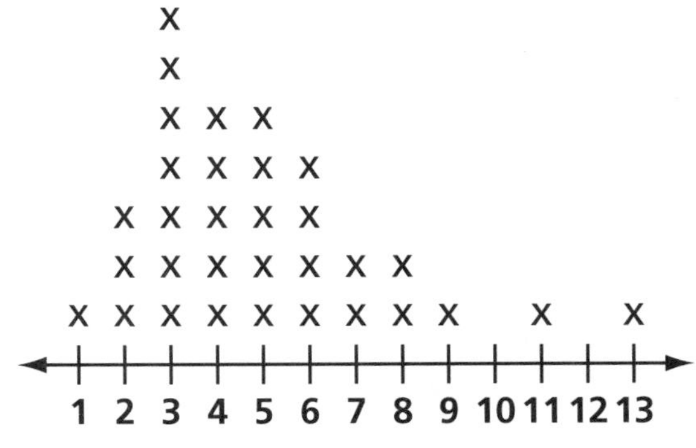

- The **range,** or spread, of the data is the difference between the least and greatest values.

The range is **13 − 1 = 12.**

- The **mean**, or average, is the most commonly used *typical* value.

To find the mean, find the sum of the data items divided by the number of pieces of data. There are **32** items of data.

$$\frac{1 + (3 \cdot 2) + (7 \cdot 3) + (5 \cdot 4) + (5 \cdot 5) + (4 \cdot 6) + (2 \cdot 7) + (2 \cdot 8) + 9 + 11 + 13}{32} = \frac{160}{32} \text{ or } 5$$

The mean is **5.**

- The **median**, or the middle number, is the most typical measure when there are gaps and a few values (called *outliers*) that are much higher or lower than most data.

When there are an odd number of data items, the median is the middle item. Since the number of data items is even, the median is the average of the two middle items, **4** and **5.**

The median is **4.5.**

- The **mode**, or the number that occurs most often, is the most typical measure in data sets when several data points cluster around it.

The tallest column is above the **3**. The mode is **3**.

You can see in the line plot that the majority of data points cluster around the mode. You can say that the mode best represents the number of hours the typical student spent reading last weekend.

Use the data at the right to complete.

1. Make a line plot of the data in the table.

40 45 50 55 60

Miles Driven Each Day in October											
47	49	40	46	45	49	44	56	45	60	41	59
48	60	41	55	49	46	50	59	45	55	56	46
56	44	45	47	48	40	48					

2. Find the mean, median, mode, and range for the data.

mean: 49 median: 48 mode: 45 range: 20

Check Understanding *At Lincoln Middle School students were asked which sport was their favorite, and the responses were: baseball 108 votes, soccer 79 votes, football 37 votes, basketball 257 votes, and swimming 42 votes. Would you display this data using a line plot, bar graph, or line graph? Explain.* (Bar graph, since the categories are not numerical.)

Graphs are also used to display the relationships among the data. A bar graph is a good choice when you want to compare data that can be counted. Use the bar graph to answer the questions.

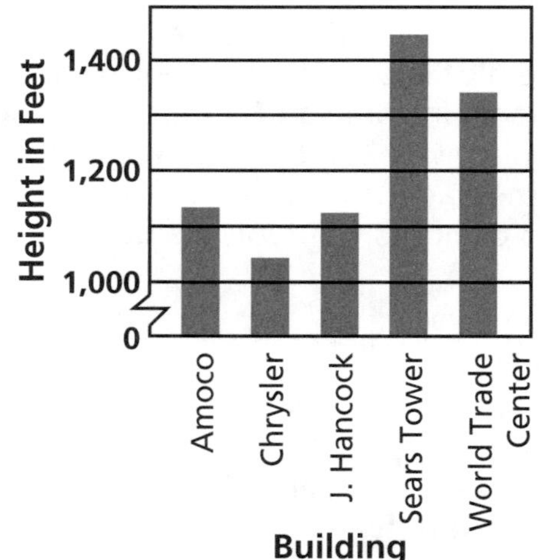

3. Each mark on the vertical axis represents how many feet? 100 ft

4. Which two buildings are about the same height? Amoco and J. Hancock

5. Is it true that the Sears Tower is about **4** times taller than the Chrysler Building? Explain.

No; The lengths of the bars are not proportional to the buildings' heights because the 0 to 1,000 mark does not represent 100 ft.

A line graph is more appropriate when you want to compare changes or trends over time. Use the line graph shown to answer the questions below.

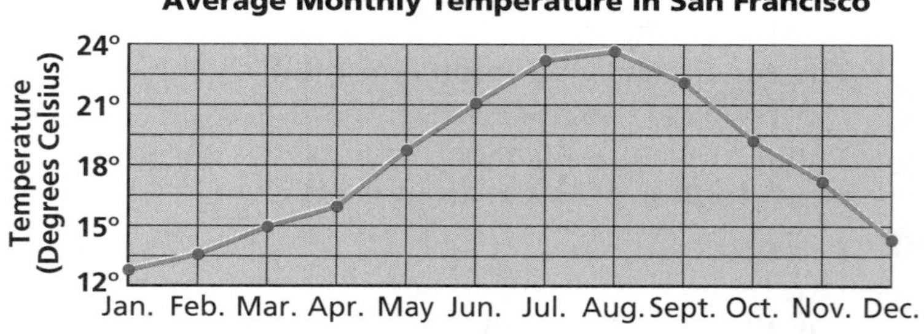

6. Name the three warmest months.

July, August, September

7. Find the temperature range.

11°C

8. In what months is the average temperature below **18**°C?

January, February, March, April, November, December

Problem Solving Reasoning

Which measure would best describe the data? Explain.

Answers may vary.

9. Price of a family home in the United States

median; wide range of data

10. Number of raisins in a box

The number most likely will be the mode or close to it.

11. Points scored per game during the season

mean; probably are few outliers

Test Prep ★ Mixed Review

12 **Which is an equivalent fraction for $4\frac{1}{3}$?** C; Level 6 objective

A $\frac{8}{3}$ B $\frac{12}{3}$ C $\frac{13}{3}$ D $\frac{41}{3}$

13 **73,165 − 1,000 =** G; Level 6 objective

F 63,165 H 73,065

G 72,165 J 73,155

Closing the Lesson *What kind of graph might you construct if you recorded the temperature every hour for the next 48 hours and wanted to display your data?* (A line graph, so you could see what happens to the temperature over time.)

Name ______________________

Expressions

Guided Practice Row 1, p. 5; First ex. in rows 3 & 6, p. 5, & Row 7, p. 6
Independent Practice Complete pp. 5–6

A **variable** is a letter, such as *n* or *x*, that represents one or more numbers.

An **expression** is a combination of numbers, letters, and symbols of operation (+, −, ×, and ÷) or grouping (parentheses or brackets). There are two types of expressions.

Numerical expressions contain only numbers and symbols.

3 + (12 − 8)

Variable expressions contain numbers, symbols, and variables.

3 + (12 − *n*)

To **evaluate** or find the value of a variable expression, you can substitute numbers for the variables. Then, simplify the numerical expression.

Evaluate **3 + (12 − *n*)** for the given values of *n*.

Value of *n*	1. Substitute for the variable.	2. Evaluate the numerical expression.
***n* = 3**	**3 + (12 − 3)**	**3 + 9 = 12**
***n* = 5**	**3 + (12 − 5)**	**3 + 7 = 10**
***n* = 8**	**3 + (12 − 8)**	**3 + 4 = 7**

Remember: Perform operations inside grouping symbols first.

Simplify.

1. 7 + (13 − 9) 11   8 × (19 − 4) 120   8 ÷ 4 + 10 12

2. 5 × 7 + 12 47   (37 − 28) × 4 36   17 − (42 ÷ 7) 11

Evaluate the expression for *x* = 2, *y* = 6, and *z* = 8.

3. 10 − *y* 4   *z* ÷ 4 2   3 · *z* + 2 26

4. (*x* + 5) − *y* 1   22 − (*y* + *z*) 8   *x* + *y* + *z* 16

5. (*x* + *y*) × 10 80   *z* ÷ (*y* ÷ 3) 4   (48 ÷ *z*) + 12 18

Complete the table by evaluating the expression for each given value of the variable.

6.

a	3 × *a* + 2
0	2
3	11
6	20

t	4 + (*t* − 3)
5	6
7	8
9	10

m	(*m* + 9) − 4
3	8
5	10
7	12

Check Understanding *To evaluate the expression 16 + 4(9 − 3), what would you do first? Explain.* (You would evaluate what is grouped with parentheses first (9 − 3 = 6); then you would multiply 4 × 6 (24) and add 16 to get 40.)

There are several ways to indicate the multiplication expression "**7** times ***n***."

$7 \times n$ $\quad$ $7 \cdot n$ $\quad$ $7(n)$ $\quad$ $7n$

When variables are involved, the last method is used most often.

Evaluate **5*n* + 7** for ***n* = 3**.

$$5n + 7 = 5(3) + 7 = 15 + 7 = 22$$

Evaluate **2(*x* + 9)** for ***x* = 4**.

$$2(x + 9) = 2(4 + 9) = 2(13) = 26$$

Evaluate **3*t* − 12** for ***t* = 10**.

$$3t - 12 = 3(10) - 12 = 30 - 12 = 18$$

Evaluate the expression for $x = 8$, $y = 3$, and $z = 4$.

7. $5x + 2$ 42 $\qquad$ $4(y + 9)$ 48 $\qquad$ $5x + x$ 48

8. $\frac{(z + 12)}{4}$ 4 $\qquad$ $\frac{16}{x} + 11$ 13 $\qquad$ $24y - 8y$ 48

9. $12y \div (z + 5)$ 4 $\qquad$ $2x - 4$ 12 $\qquad$ $(3 \cdot 5) + 2x$ 31

Problem Solving Reasoning

Algebraic expressions are used to represent word phrases. Write an algebraic expression for the word phrase.

10. the number *g* increased by itself $g + g$

11. the value of **9** decreased by the product of a number *m* and **3** $9 - 3m$

12. one more than **2** times a number *d* $2d + 1$

13. How many different ways can you write the expressions in exercise **12**? Explain.

$2 \times d + 1$, $2 \cdot d + 1$, $2(d) + 1$, $1 + 2d$, $1 + 2 \times d$, $1 + 2 \cdot d$, $1 + 2(d)$; There are several ways to indicate multiplication; also, you can add numbers in any order.

Test Prep ★ Mixed Review

14 $1{,}000{,}000 + 30{,}000 + 2{,}000 + 70 =$

A 1,327,000 $\qquad$ C 1,302,070

B 1,320,700 $\qquad$ D 1,032,070 $\quad$ D; Level 6

15 If $\frac{7}{9} + n = \frac{7}{9}$, then what does n equal?

F 0 $\quad$ F; Level 6 $\qquad$ H 1

G $\frac{7}{9}$ $\qquad$ J $\frac{9}{7}$

Closing the Lesson *If m = 6 and p = 7, how would you evaluate 3(m + p)?* (Substitute 6 for *m* and 7 for *p*, add them together, since they are in parentheses, and then multiply by 3 obtaining 39.)

Name ______________________________

Order of Operations

Guided Practice First ex. in rows 2, 12, 14, & 16, pp. 7–8
Independent Practice Complete pp. 7–8

An expression that has two or more different operation symbols can be evaluated in different ways, depending on the order in which you do the operations. To make sure that you get the correct value, you need to follow the rules for the **order of operations**.

Order of Operations

1. Perform all operations inside grouping symbols first.
2. Multiply and divide from left to right.
3. Add and subtract from left to right.

Simplify.

1. Divide first.
2. Then multiply.

$20 \div 5 \times 4$
4×4
16

Simplify.

1. Subtract inside parentheses first.
2. Divide.
3. Then add.

$48 \div (8 - 2) + 10$
$48 \div 6 + 10$
$8 + 10$
18

Other Examples

Remember the **left to right rule** for addition and subtraction and for multiplication and division.

+ and − in same expression

$10 - 4 + 6$
$6 + 6$
12

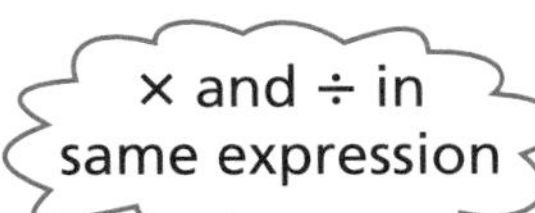

$12 \div 3 \times 2$
4×2
8

Simplify. Follow the order of operations.

1. $8 + 12 - 4$ 16 $8 + (12 - 4)$ 16 $23 - 8 + 7$ 22

2. $8 \cdot (6 - 4)$ 16 $18 \div 6 + 4$ 7 $24 \div 6 \div 2$ 2

3. $29 - (19 + 7)$ 3 $29 - 19 + 7$ 17 $24 \div (6 \div 2)$ 8

4. $(7 + 8) \times (9 - 6)$ 45 $(42 - 27) \div 3$ 5 $6 - 4 - 2$ 0

5. $5 \cdot 5 + 1 \cdot 8$ 33 $16 - 4 \cdot 4 + 3$ 3 $8 \div 4 \times 2$ 4

6. $4 \times 3 - 8 \div 2 \div 2 \times 5 + 1$ 3   **7.** $6 \times 8 - 4 \times 8 - 8 - 8$ 0

8. $2 + 10 + 5 \times 6 \div 3 - 2 \times 3$ 16   **9.** $16 - 2(12 \div 3 + 1)$ 6

10. $3 + 2 \times 3 + 2 \times 3 + 2$ 17   **11.** $12(16 - 2 - 2) - 40$ 104

Write true or false.

12. $6 + 3 \times 2 = 18$ false $18 - (4 \cdot 4) = 2$ true $3(8 - 4) = 20$ false

13. $16 \div 8 \times 2 = 1$ false $(36 - 18) \times 2 = 36$ true $6 \times 4 + 2 \times 4 = 32$ true

Check Understanding *Who can evaluate 12 ÷ 4 × 3?* (12 ÷ 4 = 3 and 3 × 3 = 9) *Why didn't you multiply first and then divide?* (The left to right rule states you do multiplication and division as they appear left to right.) *How do you evaluate the expression 16 − 4 × 2 + 3?* (4 × 2 = 8, and 16 − 8 = 8 and 8 + 3 = 11)

An algebraic expression is also evaluated using the order of operations.

Evaluate **4x + 7** for **x = 11**.

	$4x + 7$
1. Substitute **11** for *x*.	$4(11) + 7$
2. Multiply.	$44 + 7$
3. Then add.	51

Evaluate **36 − (t + 12)** for **t = 19**.

	$36 - (t + 12)$
1. Substitute **19** for *t*.	$36 - (19 + 12)$
2. Add.	$36 - 31$
3. Then subtract.	5

Evaluate for $a = 5$, $b = 7$, and $c = 12$.

14. $c - a + b$ 14 $5b - 7a$ 0 $a + b - c$ 0

15. $3a + 2b$ 29 $c - (b - a)$ 10 $4c \div (a + 3)$ 6

Write parentheses to make a true number sentence.

16. $(18 - 15) \div 3 = 1$ $6 \times (5 + 4) = 54$ $(20 + 5) \times 4 = 100$

17. $4 \times (9 + 3) \div 2 = 24$ $(17 - 13) \times (20 \div 5) = 16$ $(8 + 16) \div (2 \times 2) = 6$

Problem Solving Reasoning Solve.

18. Gene said that **4 + 6 × 2** is equal to **48**. Sharon said that it is equal to **16**. Who is correct? Explain. Sharon; 4 + 6 × 2 is evaluated as 4 + (6 × 2).

19. Use each of the numbers **2, 3, 4,** and **5** exactly once to write an expression whose value is **9**. Possible answer: (5 + 4) × (3 − 2)

Quick Check

Use the line plot to answer the question.

20. Find the median. 11

21. Find the mean. $10\frac{1}{4}$

22. Find the mode. 7

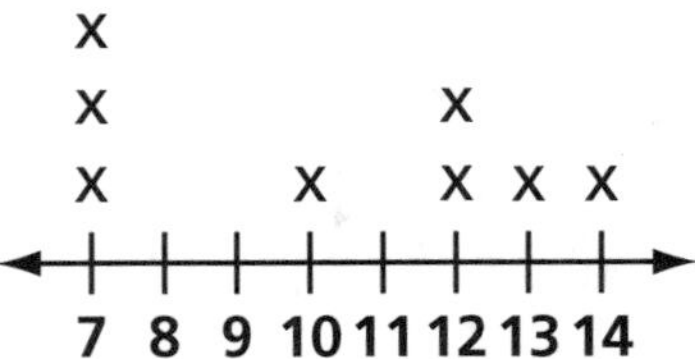

Evaluate the expression for $a = 9$, $b = 6$, and $c = 18$.

23. $a \cdot c - b$ 156 **24.** $\frac{c}{a} + b$ 8 **25.** $5a + c$ 63

Simplify. Be sure to follow the order of operations.

26. $(75 + 25) \div 10$ 10 **27.** $(24 + 8) \div 4 + 4$ 12

28. $32 \div 4 + 3 \cdot 10$ 38

Closing the Lesson *What does the left to right rule mean?* (Possible answer: You do multiplication and division as they appear going left to right, and do addition and subtraction as they appear going left to right.

Work Space.

Item	Error Analysis
20–22	**Common Error** Watch for students who confuse mean, median, and mode. **Reteaching** Reteach 2
23–25	**Common Error** Watch for students who cannot substitute for variables correctly. **Reteaching** Reteach 3
26–28	**Common Error** Watch for students who do not follow the left to right rule. **Reteaching** Reteach 4

Name ______________________________

Solving Addition and Subtraction Equations

When you solve an equation, you use inverse operations to get the variable alone on one side of the equation. The questions below can be solved by writing an equation.

Guided Practice Rows 1, 5 & 9, pp. 9–11
Independent Practice Complete pp. 9–11

- What number can be added to **18** to get **47**?
- What number can be subtracted from **29** to get **12**?

Open equations contain a variable. To **solve an equation** means to find the value of the variable that makes the open equation true. Such a value is called a **solution.**

You can check your solution by substituting it into the original equation.

Solving an Addition Equation

Addition and subtraction are inverse operations. When you solve an equation, you use inverse operations to get the variable alone on one side of the equation. So to solve an addition equation, subtract the same number from both sides of the equation.

Solve. $n + 28 = 42$

1. Subtract **28** from each side. $n + 28 - 28 = 42 - 28$
2. Simplify each side. $n + 0 = 14$; $n = 14$

✔Check: $14 + 28 = 42$

Solve. $37 = m + 12$

1. Subtract **12** from each side. $37 - 12 = m + 12 - 12$
2. Simplify each side. $25 = m + 0$; $25 = m$

✔Check: $37 = 25 + 12$

Solve for the variable. Check your solution.

1. $y + 12 = 45$ — $y = 33$, Check: $33 + 12 = 45$

$h + 29 = 42$ — $h = 13$, Check: $13 + 29 = 42$

$c + 64 = 108$ — $c = 44$, Check: $44 + 64 = 108$

2. $74 = x + 25$ — $x = 49$, Check: $74 = 49 + 25$

$17 = b + 9$ — $b = 8$, Check: $17 = 8 + 9$

$67 = r + 65$ — $r = 2$, Check: $67 = 2 + 65$

3. $23 + h = 47$ — $h = 24$, Check: $23 + 24 = 47$

$83 = 75 + w$ — $w = 8$, Check: $83 = 75 + 8$

$72 = t + 15$ — $t = 57$, Check: $72 = 57 + 15$

4. $22 = a + 19$ — $a = 3$, Check: $22 = 3 + 19$

$61 = t + 48$ — $t = 13$, Check: $61 = 13 + 48$

$18 + k = 35$ — $k = 17$, Check: $18 + 17 = 35$

Check Understanding *If you wanted to solve the equation $x - 3 = 5$, what would you do, and why would you do it?* (Add 3 to both sides of the equation, because adding 3 undoes the operation of subtracting 3.)

Subtraction equations are solved in a similar way.

Solving a Subtraction Equation

To solve a subtraction equation, add the same number to both sides of the equation.

Solve.
1. Add **15** to both sides.
2. Simplify.

$$\begin{aligned} a - 15 &= 22 \\ a - 15 + 15 &= 22 + 15 \\ a + 0 &= 37 \\ a &= 37 \end{aligned}$$

✔**Check:** $37 - 15 = 22$

Solve.
1. Add **23** to both sides.
2. Simplify.

$$\begin{aligned} 19 &= t - 23 \\ 19 + 23 &= t - 23 + 23 \\ 42 &= t - 0 \\ 42 &= t \end{aligned}$$

✔**Check:** $19 = 42 - 23$

When the variable is being subtracted, add the variable to both sides of the equation. Study these examples.

Solve.
1. Add x to both sides.
2. Simplify.
3. Subtract.
4. Simplify.

$$\begin{aligned} 28 - x &= 12 \\ 28 - x + x &= 12 + x \\ 28 &= 12 + x \\ 28 - 12 &= 12 - 12 + x \\ 16 &= x \end{aligned}$$

✔**Check:** $28 - 16 = 12$

Solve.
1. Add n to both sides.
2. Simplify.
3. Subtract.
4. Simplify.

$$\begin{aligned} 15 &= 42 - n \\ 15 + n &= 42 - n + n \\ 15 + n &= 42 \\ 15 - 15 + n &= 42 - 15 \\ n &= 27 \end{aligned}$$

✔**Check:** $15 = 42 - 27$

Solve. Remember to check your answer.

5. $k - 14 = 15$

$k = 29$, Check: $29 - 14 = 15$

$n - 9 = 17$

$n = 26$, Check: $26 - 9 = 17$

$d - 38 = 48$

$d = 86$, Check: $86 - 38 = 48$

6. $44 = x - 18$

$x = 62$, Check: $44 = 62 - 18$

$11 = c - 18$

$c = 29$, Check: $11 = 29 - 18$

$31 = t - 8$

$t = 39$, Check: $31 = 39 - 8$

7. $13 - y = 8$

$y = 5$, Check: $13 - 5 = 8$

$23 = 35 - z$

$z = 12$, Check: $23 = 35 - 12$

$12 = m - 11$

$m = 23$, Check: $12 = 23 - 11$

8. $32 = a - 14$

$a = 46$, Check: $32 = 46 - 14$

$21 = t - 21$

$t = 42$, Check: $21 = 42 - 21$

$28 - d = 15$

$d = 13$, Check: $28 - 13 = 15$

Name ______________________________

Equations can be solved in **vertical format** instead of **horizontal format.**

Solve.

1. Subtract **24** from each side.
2. Simplify.

$$\begin{array}{rcr} x + 24 & = & 73 \\ -\ 24 & & -\ 24 \\ \hline x & = & 49 \end{array}$$

✔Check: 49 + 24 = 73

Solve.

1. Add **17** to each side.
2. Simplify.

$$\begin{array}{rcr} x - 17 & = & 42 \\ +\ 17 & & +\ 17 \\ \hline x & = & 59 \end{array}$$

✔Check: 59 − 17 = 42

Solve using the vertical format. Check your answer by substitution.

9. $m + 32 = 57$

$m = 25$, Check: $25 + 32 = 57$

$43 = y - 8$

$y = 51$, Check: $43 = 51 - 8$

$g - 17 = 18$

$g = 35$, Check: $35 - 17 = 18$

10. $x + 72 = 81$

$x = 9$, Check: $9 + 72 = 81$

$54 = v - 17$

$v = 71$, Check: $54 = 71 - 17$

$48 = 22 + b$

$b = 26$, Check: $48 = 22 + 26$

11. $n + 4 = 4$

$n = 0$, Check: $0 + 4 = 4$

$x - 23 = 23$

$x = 46$, Check: $46 - 23 = 23$

$t - 15 = 15$

$t = 30$, Check: $30 - 15 = 15$

Problem Solving Reasoning

Decide whether Equation A or Equation B should be used to solve the problem. Then solve.

Equation A: $n + 15 = 32$ Equation B: $n - 15 = 32$

12. The difference between a number and **15** is **32**. What is the number? B; 47

13. The sum of a number and **15** is **32**. What is the number? A; 17

14. How are the equations in exercises **12** and **13** alike? How are they different?

They both contain the same numbers, but the operations are different.

Test Prep ★ Mixed Review

15 **What is the value of 4 in 9.546?**

C; Level 6 objective

A four
B four tenths
C four hundredths
D four thousandths

16 **What is the product of 9 and 0.5?**

H; Level 6 objective

F 0.045
G 0.45
H 4.5
J 45

Closing the Lesson *What do you do to solve an addition equation?* (Answers will vary: You subtract the number that was added to the variable from each side of the equation.)

Name ______________________________

Solving Multiplication and Division Equations

Guided Practice First ex. in Rows 1, 4, 5 & 7, pp. 12–13
Independent Practice Complete pp. 12–13

You have solved addition and subtraction equations. Multiplication and division equations can be solved in a similar way.

Solving Multiplication and Division Equations

Multiplication and division are inverse operations.

- To solve a **multiplication** equation, **divide** both sides of the equation by the same non-zero number.
- To solve a **division** equation, **multiply** both sides of the equation by the same non-zero number.

Remember, to write the product of **5** and ***x***, you can write **5*x***.
Similarly, to write ***x*** divided by **5**, you write $\frac{x}{5}$.

Solve. $7n = 42$

1. Divide each side by 7. $\frac{7n}{7} = \frac{42}{7}$
2. Simplify each side. $n = 6$

✔Check: 7(6) = 42

Solve. $8 = \frac{d}{4}$

1. Multiply each side by **4**. $4 \cdot 8 = 4 \cdot \frac{d}{4}$
2. Simplify each side. $32 = d$

✔Check: 8 = 32 ÷ 4

Solve for the variable. Check your solution.

1. $5c = 85$ — $c = 17$, Check: $5 \cdot 17 = 85$

$12x = 156$ — $x = 13$, Check: $12 \cdot 13 = 156$

$84 = 3t$ — $t = 28$, Check: $84 = 3 \cdot 28$

2. $\frac{w}{7} = 12$ — $w = 84$, Check: $\frac{84}{7} = 12$

$\frac{p}{3} = 9$ — $p = 27$, Check: $\frac{27}{3} = 9$

$8 = \frac{m}{4}$ — $m = 32$, Check: $8 = \frac{32}{4}$

3. $8h = 96$ — $h = 12$, Check: $8 \cdot 12 = 96$

$35r = 245$ — $r = 7$, Check: $35 \cdot 7 = 245$

$88a = 792$ — $a = 9$, Check: $88 \cdot 9 = 792$

4. $\frac{a}{20} = 40$ — $a = 800$, Check: $\frac{800}{20} = 40$

$\frac{f}{56} = 4$ — $f = 224$, Check: $\frac{224}{56} = 4$

$3 = \frac{x}{13}$ — $x = 39$, Check: $3 = \frac{39}{13}$

Check Understanding *What would you do to solve the equation $\frac{b}{4} = 8$?* (Multiply both sides by 4, getting $b = 32$.)

Name ______________________________

Solve for the variable. Check your solution.

5. $k + 21 = 49$ — $k = 28$, Check: $28 + 21 = 49$

$21d = 126$ — $d = 6$, Check: $21 \cdot 6 = 126$

$83 = 96 - p$ — $p = 13$, Check: $83 = 96 - 13$

6. $210 = 7g$ — $g = 30$, Check: $210 = 7 \cdot 30$

$\frac{n}{12} = 36$ — $n = 432$, Check: $\frac{432}{12} = 36$

$12 = \frac{m}{36}$ — $m = 432$, Check: $12 = \frac{432}{36}$

7. $t - 14 = 14$ — $t = 28$, Check: $28 - 14 = 14$

$149 = c + 72$ — $c = 77$, Check: $149 = 77 + 72$

$15m = 180$ — $m = 12$, Check: $15 \cdot 12 = 180$

8. $\frac{r}{2} = 28$ — $r = 56$, Check: $\frac{56}{2} = 28$

$2x = 28$ — $x = 14$, Check: $2 \cdot 14 = 28$

$121 = j - 11$ — $j = 132$, Check: $121 = 132 - 11$

Problem Solving
Reasoning

Decide whether Equation A or Equation B should be used to solve the problem. Then solve.

Equation A: $8n = 32$ Equation B: $\frac{n}{8} = 32$

9. A number divided by **8** is **32**. What is the number? B; 256

10. The product of a number and **8** is **32**. What is the number? A; 4

11. How are the equations in exercises **9** and **10** alike? How are they different?

They use the same numbers, but different operations.

Test Prep ★ Mixed Review

12 There were 85 rows with 36 seats in each row. How many seats were there?

A 306 C 3,030
B 2,960 D 3,060 D; Level 6

13 $\frac{2}{3} \times \frac{3}{5} =$

F $\frac{1}{3}$ H $\frac{5}{8}$
G $\frac{2}{5}$ G; Level 6 J 2

Closing the Lesson *What would you do to solve* $\frac{m}{3} = 7$ *and why would you do that?* (Multiply both sides by 3, because multiplying by 3 is the inverse of dividing by 3.) *What is the inverse operation of subtraction?* (Addition)

Name ____________________

Guided Practice Problems 1 & 2, p. 15
Independent Practice Complete p. 15

Problem Solving Strategy: Write an Equation

Sometimes you can write an equation to solve a problem.

Reread the problem and look for the facts you know and what you are trying to find, the variable, or unknown.

Problem

The pet store owner received a shipment of 6 dozen goldfish. She has 4 display tanks. If she wants to separate the shipment equally in all of the display tanks, how many fish should she put in each tank?

1 Understand

"Asking yourself questions will help you identify the variable."

As you reread, ask yourself questions.

- What information do you know?
  There are **6** dozen goldfish.
  There are **4** display tanks.
- What else do you already know?
  One dozen equals **12**.
- What do you need to find?
  how many goldfish to put in each tank

2 Decide

"Choose a variable. Then use it and the facts from the problem to write an equation."

Choose a method for solving.

Try the strategy Write an Equation.

- Let g = the number of fish in each tank.
- Verbal Model:

total number of goldfish ÷ number of tanks = number of goldfish in each tank

- Write the equation. $(6 \times 12) \div 4 = g$

3 Solve

"Is the answer to the equation the solution of the problem?"

Solve the equation.

Remember the order of operations.

$72 \div 4 = g$
$18 = g$

4 Look back

Look back at the original problem. Make sure you use the correct labels in the answers.

Check your answer. Then write your answer as a full sentence.

Did you answer the question?

Answer Yes; She should put 18 goldfish in each tank.

How did writing an equation help you solve the problem?
Answers will vary. Sample answer: It helped to organize the information and decide which operation to use.

Check Understanding *Write an equation to solve this problem. If Mary worked for 17 hours and got paid $102.00, how much did she make each hour?* ($17p = 102$)

Name ______________________

Use the Write an Equation strategy or any other strategy you have learned to solve.

1. You have **5** hours to drive from City A to City B, a distance of **360** miles. If the speed limit is **65** miles per hour, will you be able to make it without breaking the law? Explain.

Think: Are you finding a missing factor or a product? Which equation could you use to find the time *t*?

$65t = 360$ or $t = 65 \cdot 360$

missing factor; $65t = 360$

No; The maximum distance you can drive in 5 h is $65 \cdot 5$, or 325 mi. This is less than 360 mi.

2. You have a collection of **22** key chains. Your aunt gives you her collection of key chains, so now you have **51**. How many key chains did your aunt give you?

Think: Are you finding a missing addend or a sum? Which equation could you use to find the number of key chains *n*?

$22 + 51 = n$ or $22 + n = 51$

missing addend; $22 + n = 51$

29 key chains

3. You and **3** of your friends have lunch at the Pizza Palace. The bill, including tax and tip, is **$24**. If you share the cost equally, what will each of you pay?

$6

4. The Pizza Palace offers **3** types of crust, **3** sizes of pizza, and **2** different cheese toppings. How many different cheese pizzas are possible?

18 different pizzas

5. How could you arrange **10** coins so that you have **5** rows with **4** coins in each row? Draw your solution.

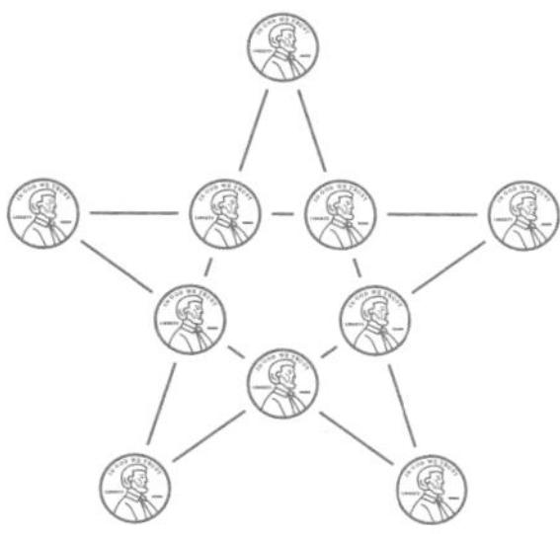

6. How many circles will be needed for figure **4**? 10 for figure **5**? 15

figure **1**

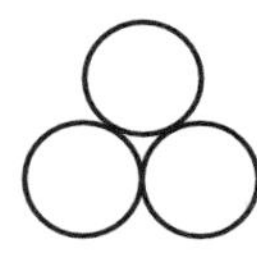

figure **2**

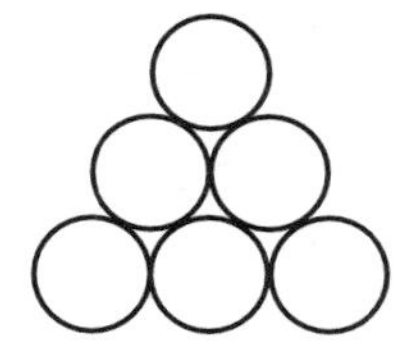

figure **3**

7. You are very excited that it will be your birthday in **24** days. Today is Tuesday. What day of the week is your birthday on?

Friday

8. Every member of the seventh grade class is allowed to bring a guest from another school to the dance. Every class member attends the dance and exactly half the students bring a guest. There are **108** students at the dance. How many are members of the seventh grade class?

72 students

Closing the Lesson *Write a problem that could be solved by this equation:* $\frac{m}{3} = 14$. (Solutions will vary: Maria divided her marbles into three groups of 14 each. How many marbles did Maria start with?)

Name ______________________________

Properties

In algebra and other math classes, you will find it helpful to use the number properties for addition and multiplication. Study the properties stated below.

Guided Practice First ex. in Rows 1, 8 & 19, pp. 16–17
Independent Practice Complete pp. 16–18

	Arithmetic	Algebra
Commutative Property of Addition: The order of the addends does not change the sum.	$8 + 12 = 12 + 8$	$a + b = b + a$
Commutative Property of Multiplication: The order of the factors does not change the product.	$8 \cdot 12 = 12 \cdot 8$	$a \cdot b = b \cdot a$
Associative Property of Addition: The grouping of the addends does not change the sum.	$(4 + 5) + 7 = 4 + (5 + 7)$	$(a + b) + c = a + (b + c)$
Associative Property of Multiplication: The grouping of the factors does not change the product.	$(4 \cdot 5) \cdot 7 = 4 \cdot (5 \cdot 7)$	$(a \cdot b) \cdot c = a \cdot (b \cdot c)$

Computations can be made simpler by combining the properties with mental-math strategies.

Simplify: **18 + (94 + 12)**

Look for combinations of multiples of **10** or **100**.

$18 + (94 + 12)$

1. Use the commutative property. $18 + (12 + 94)$
2. Use the associative property. $(18 + 12) + 94$
3. Simplify. $30 + 94$
   124

Simplify: **25 · (7 · 4)**

Look for multiples of **10** or **100**.

$25 \cdot (7 \cdot 4)$

1. Use the commutative property. $25 \cdot (4 \cdot 7)$
2. Use the associative property. $(25 \cdot 4) \cdot 7$
3. Simplify. $100 \cdot 7$
   700

Name the property.

1. $g + t = t + g$ commutative prop. of addition

$3 + (5 + 4) = 3 + (4 + 5)$ commutative prop. of addition

2. $5 \cdot (6 \cdot 9) = (5 \cdot 6) \cdot 9$ associative prop. of multiplication

$7 \cdot 15 = 15 \cdot 7$ commutative prop. of multiplication

3. $(7 + 3) + 4 = (3 + 7) + 4$ commutative prop. of addition

$(x + y) + z = x + (y + z)$ associative prop. of addition

Use the properties to complete the equation.

4. $8 + 22 =$ 22 $+ 8$

$3 \cdot$ 7 $= 7 \cdot 3$

5. $(7 \cdot 15) \cdot 12 = 7 \cdot ($ 15 $\cdot 12)$

$(m +$ r $) + t = m + (r + t)$

6. 25 $+ 17 = 17 + 25$

$($ 4 $\cdot 15) \cdot M = 4 \cdot (15 \cdot M)$

7. $($ 38 $+ 62) + 29 = (62 + 38) + 29$

$k \cdot 12 = 12 \cdot$ k

Check Understanding *What property is illustrated by (17 + 16) + 24 = 17 + (16 + 24)?* (associative) *What property is illustrated by this: 5 × (19 × 4) = 5 × (4 × 19)?* (commutative property of multiplication)

Name ______________________

Here are more properties to help you solve equations.

	Arithmetic	Algebra
Identity Property of Addition: Adding zero to any number equals that number.	$5 + 0 = 5$ $0 + 5 = 5$	$a + 0 = a$ $0 + a = a$
Identity Property of Multiplication: Multiplying one by any number equals that number.	$5 \cdot 1 = 5$ $1 \cdot 5 = 5$	$a \cdot 1 = a$ $1 \cdot a = a$
Zero Property of Multiplication: Multiplying zero by any number equals zero.	$5 \cdot 0 = 0$ $0 \cdot 5 = 0$	$a \cdot 0 = 0$ $0 \cdot a = 0$

Name the property.

8. $0 + t = t$ identity prop. of addition

$(2 + b) \cdot 0 = 0$ zero prop. of multiplication

9. $n \cdot 0 = 0$ zero prop. of multiplication

$1m = m$ identity prop. of multiplication

Solve. Name the property you used.

10. $893 \cdot n = 0$ 0; zero prop. of multiplication

$13 + a = 15 + 13$ 15; commutative prop. of addition

11. $17 \cdot 0 = q$ 0; zero prop. of multiplication

$s \cdot 1 = 17$ 17; identity prop. of multiplication

12. $17 + b = 17$ 0; identity prop. of addition

$17 + 0 = 0 + t$ 17; identity prop. of addition

13. $(17 + 0) + n = 17 + (0 + 1)$ 1; associative prop. of addition

$17 \cdot m = 1 \cdot 17$ 1; commutative prop. of multiplication

Use the properties to simplify.

14. $476 \cdot 252 \cdot 0 =$ 0

$22 + (25 + 18) =$ 65

$2 \cdot (327 \cdot 5) =$ 3,270

15. $(5 \cdot 27) \cdot 2 =$ 270

$345 \cdot 1 =$ 345

$30 + (45 + 70) =$ 145

16. $4 \cdot (15 \cdot 5) =$ 300

$(75 + 18) + 25 =$ 118

$251 + 0 =$ 251

17. $250 \cdot (7 \cdot 4) =$ 7,000

$1 \cdot 703 = 703 \cdot$ 1

$(50 \cdot 25) \cdot 2 =$ 2,500

18. $17 + (49 + 3) =$ 69

$(25 + 32) + 8 =$ 65

$1 \cdot 84 \cdot 16 \cdot 0 =$ 0

Use the properties to solve.

19. $(3x + 4) = (4 + 6)$ $x = 2$

$16(16 - x) = 16$ $x = 15$

20. $18y + 10 = 10$ $y = 0$

$\left(\frac{p}{2} \times 6\right) = (6 \times 4)$ $p = 8$

21. $7n - 7 = 0$ $n = 1$

$(4 \times 5) + 4 = 4 + 4p$ $p = 5$

22. $12(5 - x) = 0$ $x = 5$

$(3p + 8) + 12 = (8 + 12) + 1$ $p = \frac{1}{3}$

Do you think any of the properties of addition and multiplication are true for subtraction and division? Write true or false.

23. false $4 - 2 = 2 - 4$ | false $4 \div 2 = 2 \div 4$

24. false $5 - 0 = 0 - 5 = 5$ | false $(8 \div 4) \div 2 = 8 \div (4 \div 2)$

25. false $14 \div 2 = 2 \div 14$ | false $19 - 14 = 14 - 19$

26. true The term *order* is key when describing the commutative property.

27. true The term *grouping* is key when describing the associative property.

Problem Solving Reasoning Write an equation for the problem. Show how you would use a property to solve.

28. Beth bought **5** sheets of postage stamps. There were **3** rows of **20** stamps on each sheet. How many stamps did she buy?

Possible answer: $5 \times 3 \times 20 = (5 \times 20) \times 3$; 300 stamps

29. The table shows that the attendance at the games varied each week last month.

Week	1	2	3	4
Attendance	249	150	751	850

What was the total attendance last month? Possible answer: $249 + 150 + 751 + 850 = (249 + 751) + (150 + 850)$; 2,000 people

Quick Check

Solve for the variable. Be sure to check your solution.

30. $13 = q - 8$ $q = 21$

31. $n + 6 = 10$ $n = 4$

32. $15 = 20 - y$ $y = 5$

33. $5v = 45$ $v = 9$

34. $\frac{w}{16} = 3$ $w = 48$

35. $12 = \frac{n}{5}$ $n = 60$

Solve the equation. Name the property you used.

36. $(9 + 18) + 27 = 9 + (n + 27)$ $n = 18$; associative prop. of addition

37. $18t = 2 \cdot 18$ $t = 2$; associative prop. of multiplication

38. $y + 88 = 88$ $y = 0$; identity prop. of addition

Work Space.

Item	Error Analysis
30–32	**Common Error** Watch for students who do not rewrite a subtraction as an addition. **Reteaching** Reteach 5
33–35	**Common Error** Watch for students who do not multiply or divide on each side. **Reteaching** Reteach 6
36–38	**Common Error** Watch for students who do not recognize specific properties. **Reteaching** Reteach 7

Closing the Lesson *Why is it important to know and be able to use these properties?* (Answers will vary. They help you do computations quickly and easily, even in your head; they simplify the work you may need to do.)

Name ______________________________

Guided Practice First ex. in Rows 1, 7, 10, 13 & 17, pp. 23–25
Independent Practice Complete pp. 23–25

Using the Distributive Property

The **distributive property** combines two operations. You can think of it as distributing multiplication over addition.

$(3 \cdot 2) + (3 \cdot 5)$

2 5

3 { * * * * * * * } 3
* * * * * * *
* * * * * * *

6 + 15
21

$3 \cdot (2 + 5)$

2 + 5

* * * * * * *
* * * * * * * } 3
* * * * * * *

$3 \cdot (7)$
21

The models show that

$$(3 \cdot 2) + (3 \cdot 5) = 3 \cdot (2 + 5)$$

The distributive property holds for both addition and subtraction.

	Arithmetic	Algebra
Distributive Property of Multiplication Over Addition	$4(7 + 3) = 4 \cdot 7 + 4 \cdot 3$	$a(b + c) = a \cdot b + a \cdot c$
Distributive Property of Multiplication Over Subtraction	$4(7 - 3) = 4 \cdot 7 - 4 \cdot 3$	$a(b - c) = a \cdot b - a \cdot c$

Use the distributive property to complete the equation.

1. $5(7 + 6) = 5 \cdot \underline{\ 7\ } + 5 \cdot \underline{\ 6\ }$ $3(6 + 8) = \underline{\ 3\ } \cdot 6 + 3 \cdot \underline{\ 8\ }$

2. $8 \cdot 9 + 8 \cdot 5 = \underline{\ 8\ }(\underline{\ 9\ } + 5)$ $6 \cdot \underline{\ 2\ } + \underline{\ 6\ } \cdot 7 = \underline{\ 6\ }(2 + \underline{\ 7\ })$

3. $7(y + 10) = 7y + 7 \cdot \underline{\ 10\ }$ $6(a + b) = 6\ \underline{\ a\ } + 6\ \underline{\ b\ }$

4. $5(9 - 2) = \underline{\ 5\ } \cdot 9 - 5 \cdot \underline{\ 2\ }$ $6(8 - 3) = \underline{\ 6\ } \cdot \underline{\ 8\ } - \underline{\ 6\ } \cdot \underline{\ 3\ }$

5. $3 \cdot 12 - 3 \cdot 7 = \underline{\ 3\ }(\underline{\ 12\ } - 7)$ $10 \cdot \underline{\ 7\ } - \underline{\ 10\ } \cdot 4 = \underline{\ 10\ }(7 - \underline{\ 4\ })$

6. $a \cdot \underline{\ 9\ } - a \cdot 6 = a(9 - \underline{\ 6\ })$ $y(t - \underline{\ w\ }) = \underline{\ y\ } \cdot \underline{\ t\ } - \underline{\ y\ } \cdot w$

Write +, –, or · to complete the equation.

7. $3(2 + 3) = 3 \underline{\ \cdot\ } 5$ $4 \underline{\ \cdot\ } (8 - 5) = 32 - 20$ $64 + 8y = 8(8 \underline{\ +\ } y)$

8. $8(7 \underline{\ -\ } 4) = 56 - 32$ $5(28 - 27) = 5 \underline{\ \cdot\ } 1$ $36 - 4a = 4(9 \underline{\ -\ } a)$

9. $7(9 - y) = 63 \underline{\ -\ } 7y$ $4(t + 1) = 4t \underline{\ +\ } 4$ $a \underline{\ \cdot\ } (b + c) = a \cdot b \underline{\ +\ } a \cdot c$

Use the distributive property to rewrite the expression. Then simplify.

10. $(6 \cdot 8) + (4 \cdot 8)$ $\underline{8(6 + 4);\ 80}$ $(5 \cdot 10) - (5 \cdot 5)$ $\underline{5(10 - 5);\ 25}$

11. $(7 \cdot 11) + (6 \cdot 7)$ $\underline{7(11 + 6);\ 119}$ $(4 \cdot 4) + (4 \cdot 8)$ $\underline{4(4 + 8);\ 48}$

12. $(3 \cdot 9) + (4 \cdot 5) + (2 \cdot 5)$ $\underline{(3 \cdot 9) + 5(4 + 2);\ 57}$ $(6 \cdot 8) + (2 \cdot 11) - (4 \cdot 8)$ $\underline{(2 \cdot 11) + 8(6 - 4);\ 38}$

Check Understanding *How do you use the distributive property to simplify $6 \cdot 7 + 6 \cdot 93$?* [6(7 + 93); 600] *How would you simplify $3(t - 4) + 5$?* [(3 × t − 3 × 4)+ 5; 3t − 12 + 5; 3t − 7]

The distributive property can also be combined with mental math strategies.

Simplify: $(7 \cdot 14) + (7 \cdot 26)$

Combine the multiplications to get a multiple of **10**.

Think: $7(14 + 26) = 7 \cdot 40$ or **280**

Simplify: 8×37

Break apart the multiplication.

Think: $8(30 + 7) = 240 + 56$ or **296**

When the expression includes a variable, use the distributive property to simplify the expression, then substitute for the variable before you evaluate.

> Sometimes the distributive property is written as $(a + b)c = a \cdot c + b \cdot c$ and $(a - b)c = a \cdot c - b \cdot c$.

Evaluate: $12(n - 4)$ for $n = 6$

Think: $12(n - 4) = 12n - (12 \cdot 4)$

$$= 12(6) - 48$$
$$= 72 - 48$$
$$= 24$$

✔ **Check:** $12(6 - 4) \rightarrow 12(2) = 24$

Evaluate: $(x + 2)8$ for $x = 9$

Think: $(x + 2)8 = x(8) + (2 \cdot 8)$

$$= 9(8) + 16$$
$$= 72 + 16$$
$$= 88$$

✔ **Check:** $(9 + 2)8 \rightarrow 11(8) = 88$

In algebra, the distributive property is used to simplify **like** or **similar terms** in an expression.

Expression	Like or Similar Terms
$5x + x + 7$	$5x$ and x
$7m + 9 + 23$	9 and 23
$3a + 2b + 8a + 9b$	$3a$ and $8a$; $2b$ and $9b$

Remember x is really $1 \cdot x$.

Simplify: $5x + 9x$

$$5x + 9x = (5 + 9)x$$
$$= 14x$$

Simplify: $5x + 2(2x + y)$

$$5x + 2(2x + y) = 5x + 2 \cdot 2x + 2y$$
$$= 5x + 4x + 2y$$
$$= 9x + 2y$$

Use the distributive property to simplify.

13. $(9 \cdot 76) + (9 \cdot 24) =$ 900 $(16 \cdot 176) + (16 \cdot 24) =$ 3,200

14. $(545 \cdot 10) - (45 \cdot 10) =$ 5,000 $(128 \cdot 9) - (28 \cdot 9) =$ 900

15. $(27 \cdot 8) + (27 \cdot 2) =$ 270 $(42 \cdot 17) - (42 \cdot 7) =$ 420

16. $(214 \cdot 87) + (214 \cdot 13) =$ 21,400 $(13 \cdot 5) + (13 \cdot 5) =$ 130

Evaluate for the given value of the variable.

17. $4(6 + x)$ for $x = 3$ 36 $6(8 + k)$ for $k = 5$ 78 $12(c - 8)$ for $c = 11$ 36

18. $(a + 5)3$ for $a = 8$ 39 $t(7 - 4)$ for $t = 9$ 27 $5(y - 2)$ for $y = 15$ 65

19. $n(12 - 4)$ for $n = 10$ 80 $(4 + p)8$ for $p = 9$ 104 $(x - 9)5$ for $x = 16$ 35

Name ________________________________

Simplify by adding or subtracting like terms.

20. $4(6 + 2x)$ — $24 + 8x$

$2(8k - 4)$ — $16k - 8$

$3(3a + 7)$ — $9a + 21$

21. $5b + 7b + 9$ — $12b + 9$

$3x + 2y + 9x$ — $12x + 2y$

$6 - t + 9 + 4t$ — $15 + 3t$

22. $2m + 6(3m + n)$ — $20m + 6n$

$4(2a + 5c) - 7c$ — $8a + 13c$

$5(x + 4y) + 2(2x + y)$ — $9x + 22y$

Problem Solving Reasoning

Show how to use the distributive property to solve.

23. A store sold **64** video tapes on Thursday and **36** on Friday. Each video tape costs **$18**. What was the total video tape sales for both days?

$(64 \cdot 18) + (36 \cdot 18) = 18(64 + 36)$; $1,800

24. Cia worked **47** hours one week and **53** hours the next week. She earns **$9.00** an hour. How much did she earn in the two weeks?

$(47 \cdot 9) + (53 \cdot 9) = 9(47 + 53)$; $900

25. Joey, Henry, and Lena went to the bookstore. They each paid **$2** for the bus, **$7** for one book, and **$5** for a second book. How much did they spend altogether?

3($2) + 3($7) + 3($5) = 3($2 + $7 + $5); $42

26. Gina runs **8** laps at each practice session. She practiced **4** times last week and **5** times this week. How many laps has she run?

$(8 \times 4) + (8 \times 5) = 8(4 + 5)$; 72 laps

Test Prep ★ Mixed Review

27 What is the value of the expression $2x - 2$ when $x = 3$? B; Obj. 1B

A 8

B 4

C 3

D 1

28 If $\frac{x}{6} = 12$, $x = ?$ J; Obj. 1D

F 2

G 6

H 18

J 72

Closing the Lesson *What are like terms?* (Possible answer: Like terms have the same variables raised to the same power, such as *3t* and *5t*.) *Is division distributive over addition?* (Answers will vary. No, because $8 \div (4 + 2) \neq 8 \div 4 + 8 \div 2$.)

Name ________________________________

Expressions with Exponents

Guided Practice First ex. in Rows 1, 5, 8 & 10, pp. 22–23
Independent Practice Complete pp. 22–23

Exponents may be used when multiplying a number or a variable by itself.

An **exponent** tells how many times to use the **base** as a **factor**. The entire expression is called a **power**.

$\underbrace{4 \cdot 4 \cdot 4}_{\text{factors}} = 4^3$ (exponent: 3; base: 4; 4^3 is the power)

$x \cdot x = x^2$

Read as "**4** cubed" or "**4** to the third power"

Read as "*x* squared"

You can use exponents in evaluating and simplifying expressions.

Simplify 5^3.

$5^3 \rightarrow 5 \cdot 5 \cdot 5 = 125$

Simplify $3 \cdot 3 \cdot a \cdot a \cdot a \cdot b$ by using exponents.

$3 \cdot 3 \cdot \underbrace{a \cdot a \cdot a}\cdot b \rightarrow 3^2a^3b = 9a^3b$

Evaluate $2m^2$ for $m = 3$.

$2m^2 = 2 \cdot m \cdot m$

$= 2 \cdot 3 \cdot 3$

$= 18$

Simplify using exponents.

1. $6 \cdot 6 \cdot 6 \cdot 6$ 6^4 $4 \cdot 4$ 4^2 $7 \cdot 7 \cdot 7$ 7^3

2. $a \cdot a$ a^2 $x \cdot x \cdot x \cdot y$ x^3y $t \cdot t \cdot r \cdot r$ t^2r^2

3. $3 \cdot 3 \cdot x \cdot y \cdot y \cdot y$ $9xy^3$ $9 \cdot m \cdot m \cdot n \cdot n \cdot n$ $9m^2n^3$ $2 \cdot k \cdot k \cdot k \cdot k$ $2k^4$

4. $8 \cdot w \cdot 8 \cdot w \cdot 8 \cdot g$ $512w^2g$ $x \cdot y \cdot x \cdot y \cdot x \cdot x \cdot y$ x^4y^3 $a \cdot b \cdot a \cdot b \cdot c \cdot a$ a^3b^2c

Evaluate.

5. 3 squared 9 8^2 64 5 cubed 125

6. 10^1 10 4 to the third power 64 2 to the fifth power 32

7. 1^{10} 1 7 to the second power 49 10^4 10,000

Evaluate for $a = 3$, $b = 7$, $x = 2$.

8. a^2 9 x^3 8 $2b^2$ 98

9. $a^2 \cdot x^3$ 72 $b \cdot x^4$ 112 $5x^3$ 40

Check Understanding *How could you simplify $3 \cdot x \cdot x \cdot y \cdot x \cdot y$? ($3x^3y^2$) What does $2x^2$ equal if $x = 3$? (18)*

Name ______________________

You can now include powers in the rules for the Order of Operations.

Order of Operations

1. Perform all operations inside grouping symbols first.
2. **Evaluate powers.**
3. Multiply and divide from left to right.
4. Add and subtract from left to right.

Evaluate: $3 + 5^2$

$$3 + 5^2 = 3 + 25 = 28$$

Evaluate: $(9 - 7)^3 + 12$

$$(9 - 7)^3 + 12 = 2^3 + 12 = 8 + 12 = 20$$

Evaluate: $4(5^2 - 14)$

$$4(5^2 - 14) = 4(25 - 14) = 4(11) = 44$$

Evaluate for $a = 2$, $m = 3$, and $x = 5$.

10. $(1 + m)^2 =$ 16 | $5 + a^2 - 8 =$ 1 | $(x^2 + 1) \div 13 =$ 2

11. $4m - 2a =$ 8 | $3(a + x) =$ 21 | $4a^2 - 5 =$ 11

12. $7(4 - a) + 4x =$ 34 | $10a - 6m =$ 2 | $m^3 - x^2 =$ 2

13. $24 - (a + m + x) =$ 14 | $4m^2 \div (2a) =$ 9 | $x - m - a + 2 =$ 2

Problem Solving Reasoning Solve.

14. The eighth power of a number divided by the fifth power of that number is **27**. What is the number? Hint: Write **27** as a power.

3

15. A number squared and then multiplied by its cube is **32**. What is the number?

2

16. Look at exercises **14** and **15**. Do you see a shortcut for finding products and quotients of expressions with like bases? Try it with other bases. Does it still work?

Add the exponents to find products ($2^2 \cdot 2^3 = 2^5$); subtract the exponents to find quotients ($3^8 \div 3^5 = 3^3$).

Test Prep ★ Mixed Review

17 What is the median of the data 79, 64, 58, 60, 71? B; Obj. 1A

A 66.4 **C** 58

B 64 **D** 21

18 What is the range of the data 79, 64, 58, 60, 71? J; Obj. 1A

F 8 **H** 19

G 15 **J** 21

Closing the Lesson *How could you simplify y · y· 5· y· y?* ($5y^4$) *What does an exponent tell you?* (How many times the base is used as a factor.)

Name ______________________

Using Geometric Formulas

The distance around a polygon is called its **perimeter**. The distance around a circle is called the **circumference**. The table shows the **formulas**, or general rules, you can use to find the perimeter of some common geometric figures and the circumference of a circle.

Guided Practice First ex. in Rows 1, 4, 5 & 8, pp. 24–26
Independent Practice Complete pp. 24–26

Figure	Formula	Example
Rectangle w = width l = length	$P = 2l + 2w$	5 in., 2 in. $P = 2l + 2w$ $= 2(5) + 2(2)$ $= 10 + 4$ $= 14$ in.
Triangle s = side	$P = s_1 + s_2 + s_3$	7 cm, 3 cm, 6 cm $P = s_1 + s_2 + s_3$ $= 3 + 7 + 6$ $= 16$ cm
Circle d = diameter r = radius $d = 2r$	$C = \pi d$ or $2\pi r$ Read π as pi. $\pi \approx 3.14$ or $\frac{22}{7}$ $\approx$ is approximately equal to	5 cm $C = 2\pi r$ $\approx 2(3.14)(5)$ ≈ 31.4 cm

Find the perimeter or circumference. Use 3.14 for π. The dashed marks in the figures show the sides that are equal in length, or congruent to each other.

1. 1 ft, 2 ft $P =$ 6 ft   5 mm $P =$ 20 mm   12 cm, 2 cm $P =$ 28 cm

2. 2 in., 8 in. $P =$ 20 in.   3", 4", 5" $P =$ 12 in.   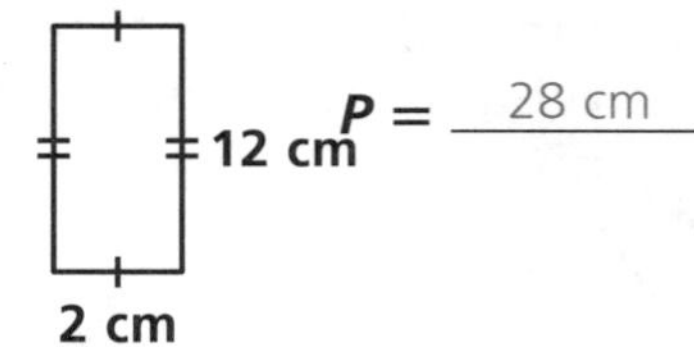 7 cm $P =$ 21 cm

3. 8 cm $C \approx$ 25.12 cm   7 cm $C \approx$ 43.96 cm   12 cm $C \approx$ 37.68 cm

Check Understanding *What is the perimeter of a figure?* (The distance around the figure.) *What is the perimeter of a square with sides equal to 6 cm?* (24 cm) *What is its area?* (36 cm^2)

Name ______________________

The measure of how much surface is covered by a figure is its **area**. Some common units for area are the square inch (in.^{2}) and the square centimeter (cm^2). The table shows the formulas you can use to find the area of some common geometric figures.

Figure	Formula	Example
Rectangle w = width l = length	$A = lw$	8 in., 4 in. $A = lw$ $= \mathbf{8 \cdot 4}$ $= \mathbf{32}$ in.^{2}
Triangle b = base h = height	$A = \frac{1}{2}bh$ or $\frac{bh}{2}$	8 in., 7 in. $A = \frac{bh}{2}$ $= \frac{7 \cdot 8}{2}$ or **28** in.^{2}
Circle d = diameter r = radius $d = 2r$	$A = \pi r^2$ $\pi \approx 3.14$ or $\frac{22}{7}$	4 cm $A = \pi r^2$ $\approx$ **(3.14)(4)(4)** $\approx$ **50.24** cm^2

Find the area of the figure. Use 3.14 for π.

4.

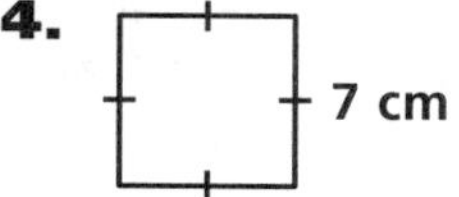

$A =$ 49 cm^2

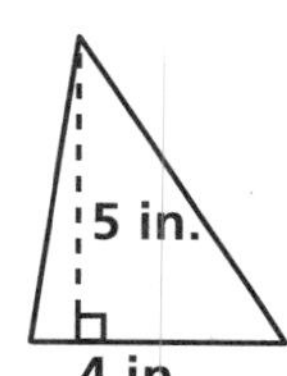

$A =$ 27 in.^{2}

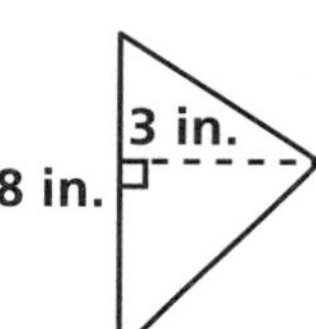

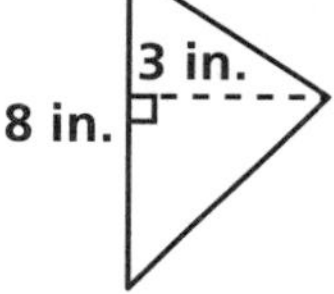

$A =$ 12 in.^{2}

5.

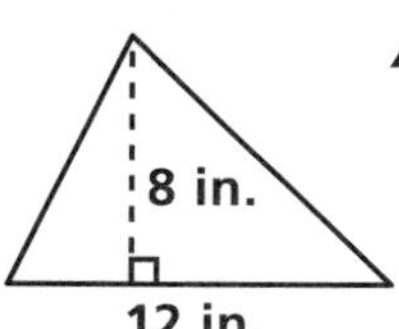

$A =$ 48 in.^{2}

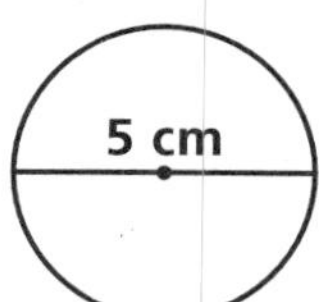

$A \approx$ 19.625 cm^2

3 ft
1 ft

$A =$ 3 ft^2

6.

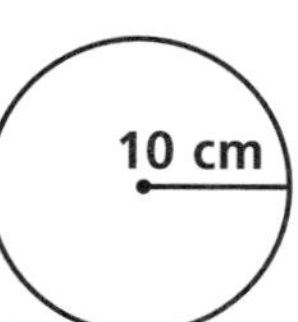

$A \approx$ 314 cm^2

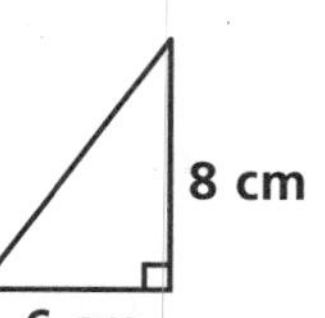

$A =$ 24 cm^2

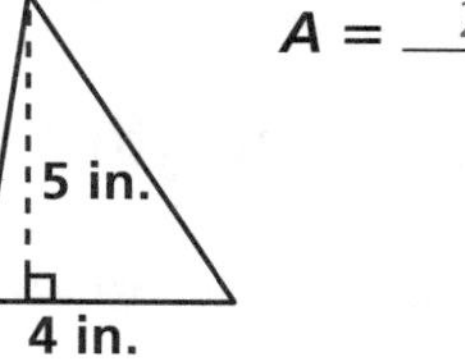

$A =$ 27 in.^{2}

7.

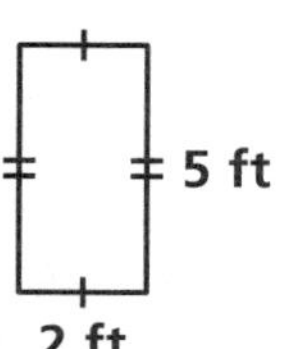

$A =$ 105 ft^2

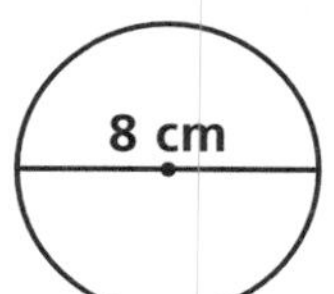

$A \approx$ 50.24 cm^2

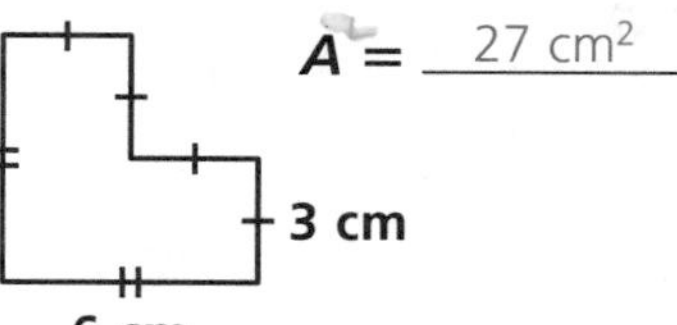

$A =$ 27 cm^2

Formulas are like any other equation in algebra. You can use them to find missing measures when the area or perimeter of a figure is known.

Find the length of the side of a square whose perimeter is **28** cm.

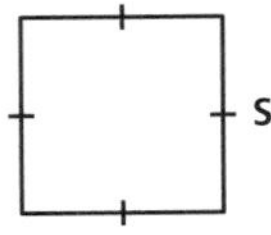

1. Write the formula. $P = 4s$
2. Substitute for P. $28 = 4s$
3. Solve the equation. $\frac{28}{4} = \frac{4}{4}s$

$7 = s$

The length of a side is **7** cm.

Two sides of a triangle are **12** cm and **19** cm. Find the length of the third side if its perimeter is **42** cm.

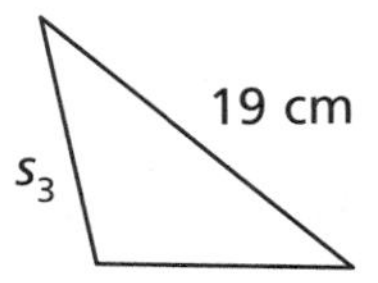

1. Write the formula. $P = s_1 + s_2 + s_3$
2. Substitute. $42 = 12 + 19 + s_3$
3. Solve. $42 = 31 + s_3$

$11 = s_3$

The missing side is **11** cm.

Write an equation to solve for the missing measure. Equations may vary.

8. 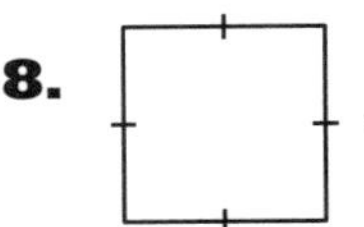

$P = 96$ cm

____

$s =$ 24 cm

12 cm

8 cm

x

$P = 50$ cm

____

$s =$ 22 cm

9. 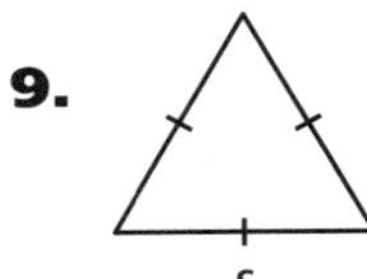

$P = 48$ ft

____

$s =$ 16 ft

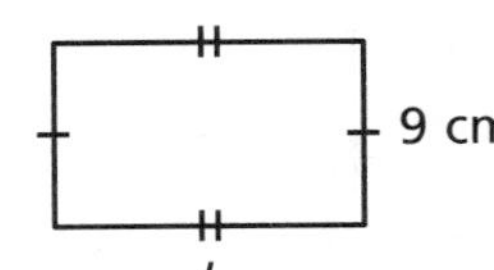

$A = 126$ in.^{2}

____

$l =$ 14 cm

Draw a diagram to illustrate the figure. Then solve and check. Check students' drawings.

10. A rectangle with length **11** in. and width **8** in. has a square with side of **3** in. shaded in one corner. What is the area of the unshaded part of the rectangle?

79 in.^{2}

11. A rectangle has dimensions **5** cm by **8** cm. Another rectangle has dimensions that are twice as long. Compare the perimeters of both rectangles. Compare the areas of both rectangles. What do you observe?

The perimeters double, but the areas increase 4 times.

Quick Check

Use the distributive property to evaluate.

12. $4(t + 3)$ for $t = 7$ 40

13. $z \cdot 3 - z \cdot 2$ for $z = 6$ 6

Write using exponents.

14. 7 to the fourth power 7^4

15. $4 \cdot 4 \cdot x \cdot x \cdot x \cdot x \cdot y \cdot y$ $4^2x^4y^2$

Find the perimeter or circumference and the area. Use 3.14 for π.

16. 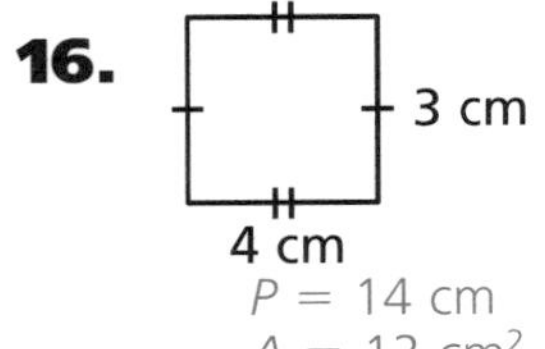

$P = 14$ cm
$A = 12$ cm^2

17. 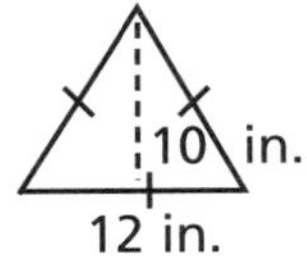

$P = 36$ in.
$A = 60$ in.^{2}

18. 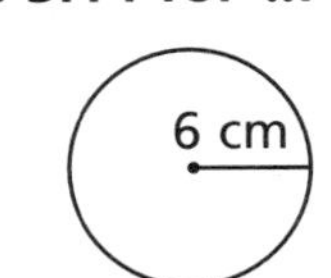

$C \approx 37.68$ cm
$A \approx 113.04$ cm^2

Work Space.

Item	Error Analysis
12–13	**Common Error** Students may not rewrite subtraction as addition. **Reteaching** Reteach 8
14–15	**Common Error** Students may not write powers correctly. **Reteaching** Reteach 9
16–18	**Common Error** Students may not use the correct units. **Reteaching** Reteach 10

Closing the Lesson *If an equilateral triangle has a perimeter of 36 cm, what is the length of one side?* (12 cm) *How did you get that?* (Since an equilateral triangle has 3 equal sides, I divided 36 by 3.)

Name ________________________________

Guided Practice Problems 1 & 2, p. 27
Independent Practice Complete pp. 27–28

Problem Solving Application: Use a Formula

The announcer said that when the ball left the pitcher's hand it was traveling at **90** miles per hour. You can use the formula below to determine how much time the batter had to swing the bat.

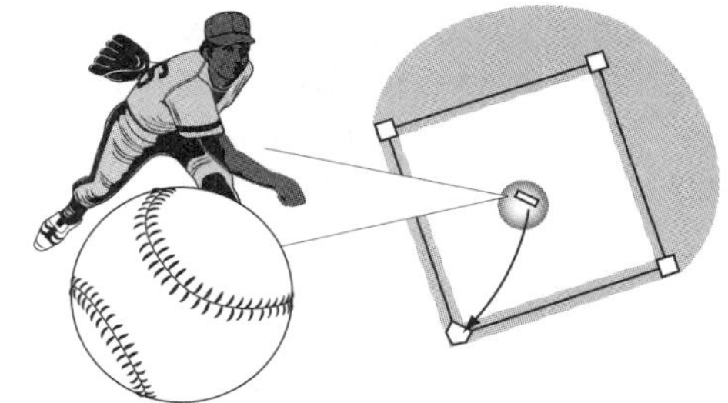

- The distance (d) that the ball travels is equal to the rate (r) multiplied by the time (t).

  Formula: $d = rt$

- It is a little over 60 feet from the pitcher's mound to home plate.

Notice that there are different units of measure in the statement of this problem: miles and feet.

Tips to Remember:

1. Understand 2. Decide 3. Solve 4. Look back

- Ask yourself whether you have solved a problem like this before. Think about the relationships between the units of measure. What facts do you know that will help you solve the problem?
- Think about the strategies you have learned and use them to help you solve a problem.

Solve.

1. How many feet per hour is the ball traveling? (Hint: Use unit rates.)

Think: There are **5,280** feet in 1 mile, so **90** miles equals how many feet?

$\frac{5{,}280 \text{ ft}}{1 \text{ mile}} \cdot \frac{90 \text{ miles}}{1 \text{ h}}$

Answer 475,200 feet per hour

2. Use your answer from exercise **1**. How many feet per second is this?

Think: There are **3,600** seconds in 1 hour, so use this fact to rewrite your answer to exercise **1**.

$\frac{475{,}200 \text{ ft}}{1 \text{ h}} \cdot \frac{1 \text{ h}}{3600 \text{ s}}$

Answer 132 feet per second

3. Use the formula $t = \frac{d}{r}$ to decide if the batter has more or less than **1** second to swing the bat. Explain your answer.

The batter has less than one second to swing the bat. The ball is traveling 132 ft per second and there are less than 132 feet between the pitcher's mound and the batter. $t = \frac{d}{r} = \frac{60}{130}$, or about 0.45 s.

Check Understanding *How would I find the time it took to travel a distance of 18 miles at a rate of 2 miles per hour?* (Use the formula $d = rt$, substitute for d, and r, and solve for t.)

Remember that a formula is another name for an equation. Write a formula or use any other strategy to solve.

4. Your school's football team scored **26** points last weekend. Use the information below to determine how many touchdowns were scored.

6-point touchdowns	?
1-point conversions	**2**
3-point field goals	**2**

$6(x) + 1(2) + 3(2) = 26$; 3 touchdowns

5. Dominique made **11** two-point baskets, **2** three-point baskets, and **5** one-point foul shots. Use the information to determine how many points Dominique scored.

$P = 11(2) + 2(3) + 5(1)$; 33 points

6. A car travels **2** hours at **65** miles per hour, **1** hour at **60** miles per hour, and **1** hour at **45** miles per hour. What is the total mileage?

$m = 2(65) + 1(60) + 1(45)$; 235 miles

7. The distance between two cities is **1,800** miles. If you drive at a constant **65** miles per hour, could you complete the trip in one day? Explain.

$t = 1{,}800 \div 65$; t is between 27 and 28 hours.

No; There are only 24 hours in a day.

8. A bag of fertilizer covers **60** square feet. How many bags would be needed to cover a lawn that measures **25** feet by **20** feet? Remember — you can't buy a portion of a bag!

$A = 25 \cdot 20 = 500 \text{ ft}^2$

$60 \cdot x = 500$; 9 bags

9. A rule of thumb for changing a Celsius temperature to a Fahrenheit temperature is "double the Celsius temperature and add **30°**." The radio announced it would be **26°C** today. Is this beach weather? Explain.

$F \approx 2C + 30$; 82°

Yes; 82°F is warm enough for the beach.

Extend Your Thinking

10. Consider the formula $d = rt$.

distance rate time

Use what you know about inverse operations and equations to write a formula to find a missing rate (r).

$r = \frac{d}{t}$

11. Look back at exercise **9**. Explain how to use the formula you wrote in exercise **9** to find an equivalent formula for changing a Fahrenheit temperature to a Celsius temperature.

$F = 2C + 30$, so $C = \frac{F - 30}{2}$

Closing the Lesson *In which step of the problem solving process does the use of a formula arise?* (In the second step when deciding on a strategy to solve the problem.) *How do you change a rate from distance per hour to distance per second?* (Multiply by $\frac{1}{3{,}600}$ or divide by 3,600, since there are 3,600 seconds in an hour.)

Name ______________________

Unit 1 Review

Use the line plot at the right. It shows how many sandwiches 15 seventh graders ate one week.

1. What is the mean? 6.7

2. What is the median? 7

3. What is the mode? 8

4. What is the range? 9

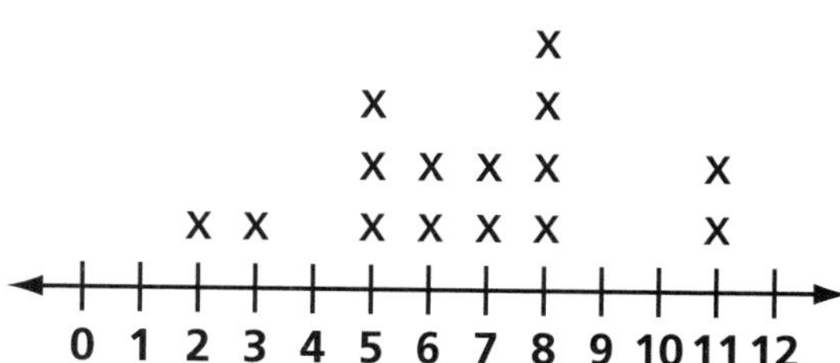

Evaluate the expression. If it contains variables, use these values: $x = 5$, $y = 4$.

5. $25 + x + y$ 34 **6.** $(x + y) - 7$ 2 **7.** $5y - 4x$ 0

8. $8 \cdot 9 - 7 \cdot 4$ 44 **9.** $4(5 + 2) - 8$ 20 **10.** $6(2 + 1)^2 - 28$ 26

Solve the equation. Name the property that you used.

11. $(23 + 48) + 52 = 23 + (48 + \underline{52})$ Property associative (addition)

12. $22 \cdot \underline{1} = \underline{1} \cdot 22 = 22$ Property identity (multiplication)

13. $18(\underline{39} - \underline{19}) = 18 \cdot 39 - 18 \cdot 19$ Property distributive (subtraction)

Solve the equation.

14. $n + 18 = 53$ 35 **15.** $8t = 216$ 27 **16.** $\frac{w}{6} = 18$ 108

Simplify the expression.

17. $5(x + 12)$ $5x + 60$ **18.** $6(2n - 4)$ $12n - 24$

19. $3x + 27 + 7x$ $10x + 27$ **20.** $12n - (6n + 3)$ $6n - 3$

Write the perimeter (*P*) and area (*A*) of the figure.

21. A rectangle, length **13** cm and width **4** cm

$P =$ 34 cm $A =$ 52 cm^2

22. A right triangle, sides **5** in., **12** in., and **13** in.

$P =$ 30 in. $A =$ 30 in.^{2}

Solve.

23. A builder has **40** yd² of outdoor carpeting. He is carpeting a rectangular patio that is **12** feet wide. How long can the patio be? $3\frac{1}{3}$ yd or 10 ft

Name ____________________

The line plot shows the ages of 14 soccer players.

Use the line plot for exercises **1** and **2**.

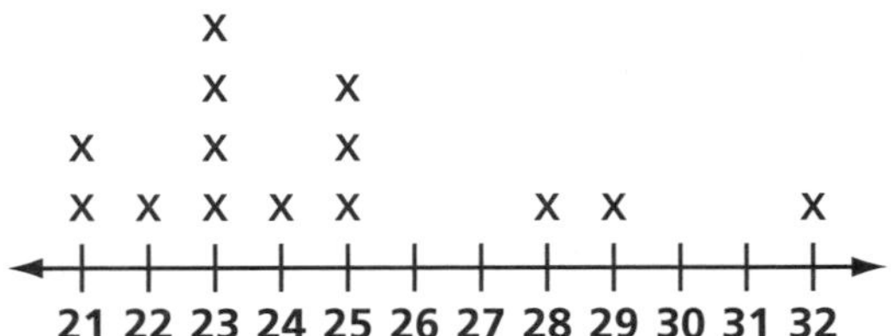

1 **What is the mean age of the players?**

C; Obj. 1A

A 23 **C** 24.6

B 23.5 **D** 26.5

2 **What is the median age of the players?**

G; Obj. 1A

F 23 **H** 24.6

G 23.5 **J** 26.5

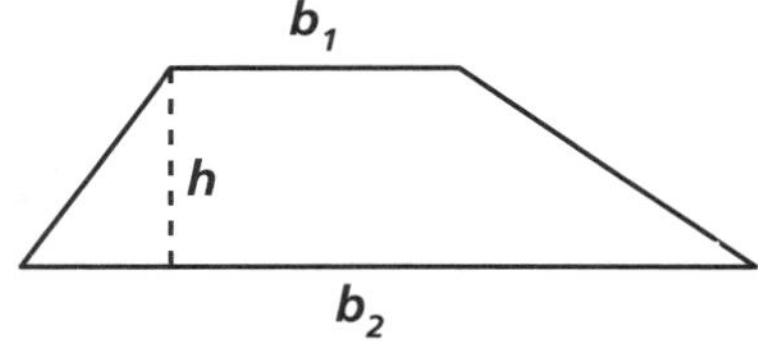

3 **An expression for the area of a trapezoid is $\frac{1}{2}h(b_1 + b_2)$. What is the area of a trapezoid whose height is 6 units and whose bases measure 5 units and 7 units?**

A 72 units^2 **C** 36 units^2 C; Obj. 1B and 1E

B 42 units^2 **D** 6 units^2

Use the advertisement for exercises **4** and **5**.

4 **If *c* represents the number of cubic yards of topsoil, which is a correct expression for the total cost (in dollars) of a delivery?**

F 96 J; Obj. 1B

G $96c$

H $75c + 21$

J $21c + 75$

5 **What is the total cost for a delivery of 3 cubic yards of topsoil?**

A $96 B; Obj. 1B and 1D

B $138

C $246

D $288

E Not here

6 **Write a simplified form of this expression: $10 + 2(n - 5) + 7n \cdot 3$.**

F $33n - 60$ H; Obj. 1C

G $23n + 5$

H $23n$

J $24n$

K Not here

UNIT 2 • TABLE OF CONTENTS

Number Theory, Decimals, and Fractions

We will be using this vocabulary:

numerator the top number in a fraction; names the number of parts being considered

denominator the bottom number in a fraction; names the number of equal parts in the whole

common denominator denominators of two or more fractions that are the same

common factor a number that divides two or more numbers evenly

simplest form a fraction whose numerator and denominator have only **1** as a common factor or a mixed number whose fraction is in simplest form

algebraic expression a group of numbers, variables, and addition, subtraction, multiplication, or division symbols

Dear Family,

During the next few weeks, our math class will be learning and practicing addition, subtraction, multiplication, and division of decimals and fractions. You can expect to see homework that provides practice with these skills. Here is a sample you may want to keep handy to give help if needed.

Multiplication of Mixed Numbers

To find the product $4\frac{2}{3} \times 1\frac{2}{7}$, you need to write each mixed number as a fraction. One way to do this is shown below.

$$4\frac{2}{3} = \frac{3 \times 4 + 2}{3} \rightarrow \frac{14}{3} \qquad 1\frac{2}{7} = \frac{7 \times 1 + 2}{7} \rightarrow \frac{9}{7}$$

Now it is possible to multiply. Before multiplying you can try to simplify by dividing a numerator and a denominator by a common factor.

$$\frac{14}{3} \times \frac{9}{7} = \frac{\overset{2}{\cancel{14}} \cdot \overset{3}{\cancel{9}}}{\underset{1}{\cancel{3}} \cdot \underset{1}{\cancel{7}}} \qquad \frac{2 \cdot 3}{1 \cdot 1} = \frac{6}{1} \rightarrow 6$$

During this unit, students will need to continue practicing all operations with both decimals and fractions.

Sincerely,

Name ______________________________

Guided Practice: First ex. in Rows 1, 4 & 10, pp. 33–34
Independent Practice: Complete pp. 33–34

Comparing and Ordering Decimals

Use place value to read and write decimals.

The decimal number **1.38** is read "one and thirty-eight hundredths."

PLACE VALUES

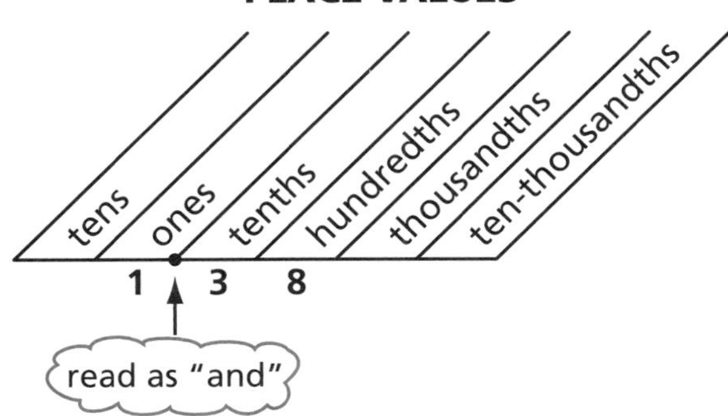

The place values extend in both directions.

You **compare** two decimals by comparing their place values from left to right. You may need to write zeros in one or more decimal places.

Compare 6.35 and 6.358.

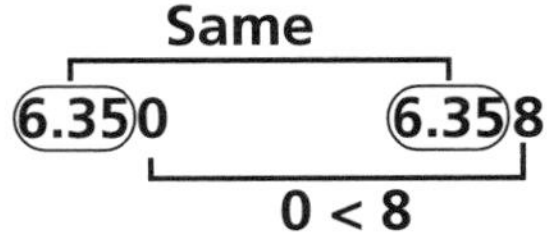

Since **0 < 8**, you know **6.35 < 6.358.**
6.35 is to the left of **6.358** on the number line.

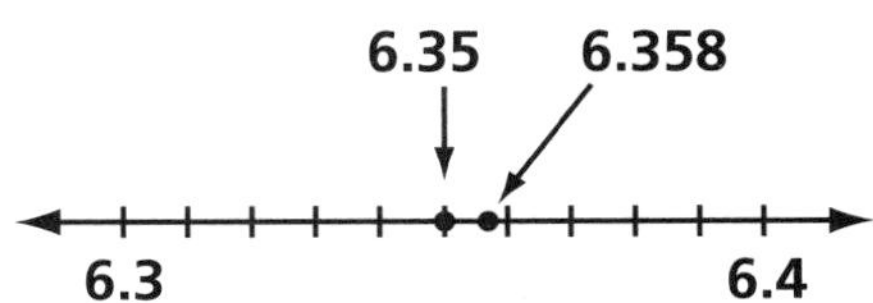

To order decimals, you can compare the digits in each place. You can also use a number line.

Order from least to greatest.
0.25, 0.5, 0.52, 0.2

Order: **0.2 < 0.25 < 0.5 < 0.52**

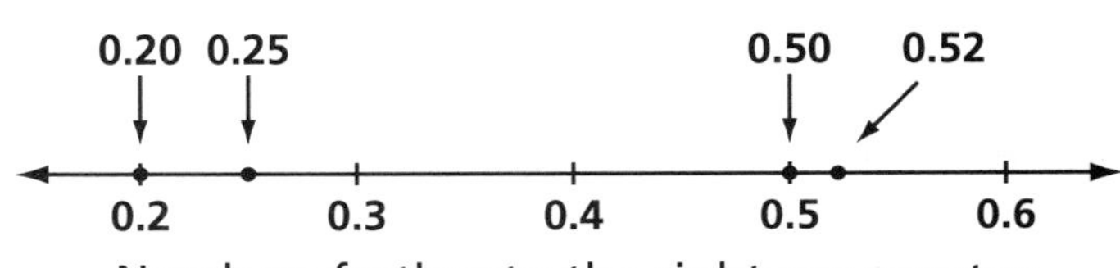

Numbers farther to the right are greater.

Write the decimal number.

1. six and three tenths 6.3   nineteen and sixteen hundredths 19.16

2. twelve and four hundredths 12.04   eighty and sixty-three thousandths 80.063

3. fifty-two thousandths 0.052   nine hundred three thousandths 0.903

Write the decimal in words.

4. **0.3** three tenths   **1.0005** one and five ten-thousandths

5. **15.08** fifteen and eight hundredths   **8.5022** eight and five thousand twenty-two ten-thousandths

6. **200.002** two hundred and two thousandths   **13.108** thirteen and one hundred eight thousandths

Check Understanding *Who can read these two decimals to me? 4.38 and 0.894* (four and thirty-eight hundredths and eight hundred ninety-four thousandths) *Which of them is greater and how do you know that?* (4.38 because 0.894 < 1)

Compare. Write <, >, or = between the pair of numbers to make a true sentence.

7.	0.3 __<__ 0.8	0.04 __<__ 0.2	0.1 __>__ 0.01	1.4 __<__ 1.5
8.	0.56 __<__ 0.65	2.43 __>__ 2.34	0.630 __=__ 0.63	2.06 __>__ 2.05
9.	0.05 __>__ 0.049	4.02 __=__ 4.020	4.002 __<__ 4.020	2.49 __>__ 2.43
10.	1.92 __>__ 1.29	0.83 __>__ 0.793	0.692 __>__ 0.594	17.1 __=__ 17.10

Write the decimals in order from least to greatest.

11. 0.42, 0.24, 0.4, 0.2 0.2 < 0.24 < 0.4 < 0.42

1.7, 0.71, 7.1, 1.07 0.71 < 1.07 < 1.7 < 7.1

12. 5.82, 5.28, 5.8, 5.028 5.028 < 5.28 < 5.8 < 5.82

4.1, 4.05, 4.51, 4.15 4.05 < 4.1 < 4.15 < 4.51

13. 1.47, 1.204, 0.92, 4.1 0.92 < 1.204 < 1.47 < 4.1

3.4, 0.08, 6.01, 0.24 0.08 < 0.24 < 3.4 < 6.01

Problem Solving
Reasoning

Solve.

14. Use the digits **2, 0, 8,** and **5**. Make the greatest and least numbers possible.

greatest: 8 . 5 2 0

least: 0 . 2 5 8

15. Use the digits **9, 4, 3,** and **7**. Make the greatest and least numbers possible.

greatest: **0.** 9 7 4 3

least: **0.** 3 4 7 9

16. Ted's race time was **2** minutes **37.01** seconds. Juan's race time was **2** minutes **36.07** seconds. Who won the race? Explain.

Juan

17. Stacey crossed the finish line at **6.3** minutes, Jillian crossed at **6.4** minutes, and Jenn finished between Stacey and Jillian. Write a possible finish time for Jenn.

Sample answer: 6.301 minutes

Test Prep ★ Mixed Review

18 What is the mean of this data set?

79, 64, 58, 60, 71

B; Obj. 1A

A 66.4 **C** 58

B 64 **D** 21

19 What is the value of this expression?
$11 + 5 \times 3 - 2 \times 8$

G; Obj. 1C

F 32 **H** 128

G 10 **J** 192

Closing the Lesson *What are some real-life uses for decimals?* (Answers will vary. Possible answers: money, measuring distances, measuring time, batting averages)

Name ______________________

Guided Practice: First ex. in each section, pp. 35–36
Independent Practice: Complete pp. 35–36

Rounding and Estimating Decimals

To **round** a number to a given decimal place, look at the digit in the place to its right.

- If the digit is **4** or less, drop all the digits after the given place.

Round to the nearest tenth:
3.4̲25 → 3.4

- If the digit is **5** or more, add **1** to the digit in the given place, and drop all digits after it.

Round to the nearest hundredth:
3.05̲56 → 3.06

Other Example

Eric scored 41 hits in 165 times at bat. What is Eric's batting average?

batting average = $\frac{\text{number of hits}}{\text{times at bat}}$

1. Write the ratio of hits to times at bat as a decimal.

$$\frac{41}{165} = 0.24848$$

2. Round the decimal. Batting averages are usually rounded to the nearest thousandth.

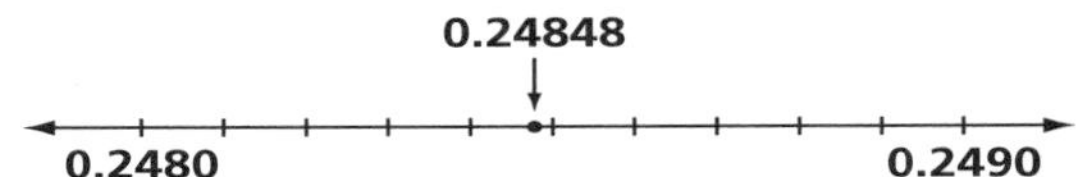

Since Eric's batting average is closer to **0.248** than **0.249**, his average rounds to **0.248.**

Round to the nearest tenth.

1.	**0.64** 0.6	**1.43** 1.4	**7.92** 7.9	**25.07** 25.1
2.	**0.152** 0.2	**2.52** 2.5	**0.79** 0.8	**0.315** 0.3
3.	**19.96** 20.0	**26.08** 26.1	**17.98** 18.0	**1.46** 1.5

Round to the nearest hundredth.

4.	**6.543** 6.54	**14.328** 14.33	**29.2635** 29.26	**19.4709** 19.47
5.	**29.151** 29.15	**3.849** 3.85	**0.7969** 0.80	**2.38604** 2.39
6.	**32.096** 32.10	**30.014** 30.01	**24.652** 24.65	**19.898** 19.90

Round to the nearest thousandth.

7.	**20.0507** 20.051	**65.93945** 65.939	**10.1065** 10.107	**24.2873** 24.287
8.	**36.5821** 36.582	**0.89703** 0.897	**64.0518** 64.052	**0.199878** 0.200
9.	**16.5701** 16.570	**4.22814** 4.228	**19.5056** 19.506	**18.64845** 18.648

Check Understanding *If I round 2.483 to 2.5, to what place would I have rounded?* (tenths) *If a number has been rounded to 7.62, what could the original number have been?* (any number ≥ 7.615 and < 7.6325)

You use decimals to write money amounts. To **estimate** with money, you can round to the nearest cent or the nearest dollar.

Amount	Nearest Cent	Nearest Dollar
$5.248	$5.25	$5
$94.6432	$94.64	$95

Round to the nearest cent.

10. $.298 $.30 $1.649 $1.65 $.484 $.48 $8.357 $8.36

11. $.336 $.34 $2.944 $2.94 $7.135 $7.14 $6.524 $6.52

12. $5.109 $5.11 $6.802 $6.80 $0.005 $.01 $3.152 $3.15

Round to the nearest dollar.

13. $6.29 $6 $10.89 $11 $3.49 $3 $7.45 $7

14. $18.95 $19 $28.25 $28 $39.99 $40 $45.49 $45

15. $5.84 $6 $36.39 $36 $7.05 $7 $9.69 $10

Problem Solving
Reasoning

Solve.

16. The nurse estimated Jerry's temperature to be **101°F**. If the thermometer reads in tenths, give a number that his temperature could have been.

Sample answer: 100.7°F

17. Carla is **138.7** cm tall and Brad is **139.4** cm tall. Are they both "about **139** cm tall?" Explain.

Yes; Each height rounded to the nearest centimeter is 139 cm.

Test Prep ★ Mixed Review

18 What is the value of this expression?
$4 \times (7 + 14) - 2$ A; Obj. 1C

A 82
B 76
C 40
D 23

19 What is the area of a triangle of height 6 units and base 7 units? H; Obj. 1E

F 42 $units^2$
G 36 $units^2$
H 21 $units^2$
J 13 $units^2$

Closing the Lesson *Can you think of some times when you might need to round decimals?* (Answers will vary: When calculating averages like batting averages and field goal averages, when dividing two numbers that do not have a simple quotient, or when estimating distances to the nearest tenth of a meter.)

Name ____________________

Guided Practice: First ex. in Rows 1, 3, 5 & 8, pp. 37–38
Independent Practice: Complete pp. 37–38

Adding and Subtracting Decimals

You add decimals as you do whole numbers. Remember to **line up** the decimal points when you write the problem in **vertical form.**

Find **2.7 + 5.21.**

1. Estimate: **2.7 + 5.21**

Round to the nearest whole number.

2.7 rounds to → 3
+ 5.21 rounds to → + 5
estimate → 8

2. Add: **2.7 + 5.21**

Decimal points and all place values line up.

2.70
+ 5.21
7.91

2.7 and 2.70 are equivalent decimals.

Other Example

Add: **6.78 + 2.4 + 12**

6.78
2.40
12.00
21.18

Estimating first helps you to check that your answer is reasonable.

You subtract decimals as you do whole numbers. Remember to line up the decimal points. Be sure to estimate first.

Subtract: 5.6 − 2.05
Estimate: **6 − 2 = 4**

5 . 6 10 (6 crossed out, regrouped to 5 and 10)
− 2 . 0 5
3 . 5 5

Write a zero and regroup.

Subtract: 48 − 3.74
Estimate: **48 − 4 = 44**

4 8 . 10 10 (8 crossed out, regrouped to 7; 10 crossed out, regrouped to 9 and 10)
− 3 . 7 4
4 4 . 2 6

Write two zeros and regroup.

Subtract: 623.457 − 54.6
Estimate: **620 − 50 = 570**

6 2 3 . 4 5 7
− 5 4 . 6 0 0
5 6 8 . 8 5 7

You may want to write two zeros.

Round to the nearest whole number. Estimate the sum.

1. 8.42 + 1.1 9   11.92 + 5 17   4.87 + 12.059 17

2. 26.85 + 33.935 61 $45.37 + $37.42 $82   0.045 + 0.84 1

Round to the nearest whole number. Estimate the difference.

3. 5.05 − 0.505 4   62 − 58.76 3   24.01 − 2.1 22

4. 41.73 − 9.765 32   5.1724 − 0.388 5   23 − 8.046 15

Add. Check that your answer is reasonable.

5. 5.9 + 6.8 = 12.7   16.008 + 0.029 = 16.037   1.72 + 4.8 = 6.52   15.77 + 3.2171 = 18.9871

6. 3.47 + 0.092 3.562   12.05 + 42.671 54.721   108 + 45.04 + 3.042 156.082

7. $15.65 + $6.92 $22.57   1.557 + 4 + 0.004 5.561   6.00002 + 0.065 6.06502

Check Understanding *How do you add 5.47 to 3.8?* (Check that students write a zero in the empty column and can explain why.) *Write the difference between 7.23 and 2.579.* (4.651) *What do you need to do in order to subtract decimals?* (Line up the decimal points.)

Subtract. Check that your answer is reasonable.

8.

7.5	24.062	5.86	22.26
− 2.4	− 0.059	− 3.5	− 9.667
5.1	24.003	2.36	12.593

9. 23.05 − 16.77 6.28   68 − 35.27 32.73   241.782 − 67.594 174.188

10. $692 − $49.95 $642.05   3.542 − 0.715 2.827   3.97 − 2 1.97

11. $39.12 − $6.75 $32.37   65.02 − 4.554 60.466   0.12 − 0.005 0.115

Problem Solving Reasoning Solve.

12. Does it cost more for a pencil and notebook, or for a pen, eraser, and binder?

binder **$1.95**
eraser **$0.45**
notebook **$2.29**
pen **$0.98**
pencil **$0.15**

pen, eraser, and binder

13. You buy a card for **$2.85** and a gift. You give the cashier **$20** and receive **$1.22** in change. How much is the gift?

$15.93

Quick Check

Write the decimals in order from least to greatest.

14. 0.556, 0.566, 0.56, 0.656

0.556, 0.56, 0.566, 0.656

15. 1.771, 1.117, 0.117, 1.17

0.117, 1.117, 1.17, 1.771

Round the decimal to the nearest hundredth and to the nearest thousandth.

16. 0.8911 — 0.89; 0.891

17. 4.0559 — 4.06; 4.056

18. 1.9989 — 2.00; 1.999

Write the sum or difference.

19. 9.635 + 0.078 — 9.713

20. 63.95 + 1.393 + 5.2 — 70.543

21. 12.35 + 9.996 — 22.346

22. 6.913 − 2.58 — 4.333

23. 8.4 − 6.533 — 1.867

24. 0.908 − 0.52 — 0.388

Work Space.

Item	Error Analysis
14–15	**Common Error:** Incorrect ordering of decimals places. **Reteaching** Reteach 11
16–18	**Common Error:** Do not regroup to the left. **Skills Tutorial** Strand 8: Skill 2, Practice 1–4
19–24	**Common Error:** Watch for students who do not line up the decimal points when they add or subtract. **Skills Tutorial** Strand 8: Skill 10

Closing the Lesson *Why is estimating first a good idea?* (It gives you a way to check if your answer is reasonable.) *When in real life would you add or subtract two decimals?* (Answers will vary: When you are working with money and you need to add or subtract, as with a check book, or when computing distances using the odometer of a car.)

Name ______________________

Multiplying Decimals and Powers of Ten

Guided Practice: First ex. in each section, pp. 39–41
Independent Practice: Complete pp. 39–41

You multiply decimals as you do whole numbers, but you need to know where to place the decimal point in the product.

Find the product of **0.4** and **3.52**.

1. Multiply the numbers.

$$\begin{array}{r} 3.52 \\ \times\ 0.4 \\ \hline 1408 \end{array}$$

2. Count the number of decimal places in each factor. The total is the number of decimal places in the product. Count the places from the right.

3.52	← 2 decimal places
× 0.4	← 1 decimal place
1.408	← 3 decimal places

decimal point is located **3** places from the right

Find the product of **0.5** and **1.2**.

1.2	← 1 decimal place
× 0.5	← 1 decimal place
0.60	← 2 decimal places

0.60 = 0.6

What pattern do you see?

10 × 0.6 = 6	$\mathbf{10^1 \times 0.56 = 5.6}$	**10 × 0.325 = 3.25**
100 × 0.6 = 60	$\mathbf{10^2 \times 0.56 = 56}$	**100 × 0.325 = 32.5**
1,000 × 0.6 = 600	$\mathbf{10^3 \times 0.56 = 560}$	**1,000 × 0.325 = 325**

When multiplying by a positive power of **10**, move the decimal point to the right the same number of places as the exponent for **10**. This is also the number of zeros in the standard form of the power.

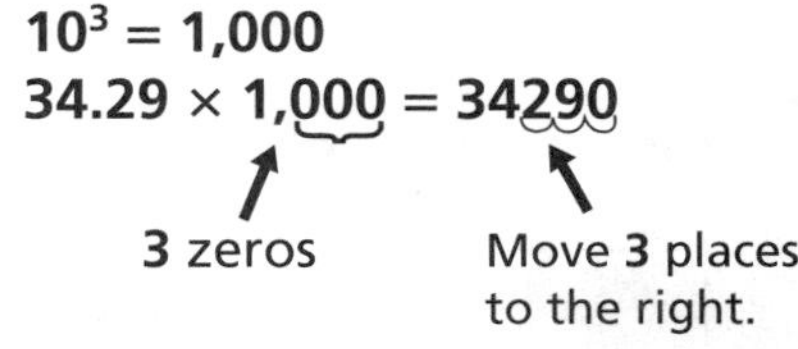

A caret (‸) can be used to show where the decimal point will be after a number is multiplied by a power of ten.

For example: **6.20‸** is **620**.

Write *how many* decimal places the product will have.

1.	0.08 × 0.02 4	0.05 × 0.003 5	0.8 × 0.2 2	3 × 0.02 2
2.	0.1 × 0.1 2	0.08 × 0.0004 6	0.07 × 0.006 5	9 × 0.9 1

Write a caret where the decimal point would be after multiplying by the power of 10 shown. Write zeros if necessary.

3. by 10^1:	68.5‸	9.8‸2	2.0‸04	18.9‸867	27.9‸
4. by 10^3:	7.860‸	0.067‸	9.380‸	0.155‸	0.095‸
5. by 10^2:	25.70‸	0.04‸6	34.65‸	0.00‸67	45.90‸

Check Understanding *Who can explain how to multiply 5.8 by 0.43?* (Have a student come to the board and explain.)

Multiply.

6. $0.3 \times 0.8 =$ 0.24 $0.06 \times 0.07 =$ 0.0042 $0.04 \times 0.06 =$ 0.0024 $0.006 \times 0.9 =$ 0.0054

7.

$$\begin{array}{r} 32.4 \\ \times\ 0.03 \\ \hline 0.972 \end{array} \qquad \begin{array}{r} 9.12 \\ \times\ 4 \\ \hline 36.48 \end{array} \qquad \begin{array}{r} 1.6 \\ \times\ 0.8 \\ \hline 1.28 \end{array} \qquad \begin{array}{r} 7.5 \\ \times\ 0.005 \\ \hline 0.0375 \end{array}$$

8.

$$\begin{array}{r} 15.004 \\ \times\ 0.02 \\ \hline 0.30008 \end{array} \qquad \begin{array}{r} 7.05 \\ \times\ 0.003 \\ \hline 0.02115 \end{array} \qquad \begin{array}{r} 26.1 \\ \times\ 3.4 \\ \hline 88.74 \end{array} \qquad \begin{array}{r} 8.45 \\ \times\ 0.092 \\ \hline 0.7774 \end{array}$$

Multiply. Use mental math.

9. $24 \times 10^1 =$ 240 $0.9632 \times 10^4 =$ 9,632 $60.25 \times 10^3 =$ 60,250

10. $863 \times 10^2 =$ 86,300 $0.00895 \times 10^5 =$ 895 $0.934 \times 10^4 =$ 9,340

11. $84.5 \times 10^1 =$ 845 $0.0034 \times 10^3 =$ 3.4 $0.63 \times 10^3 =$ 630

Write the area of the rectangle.

12.

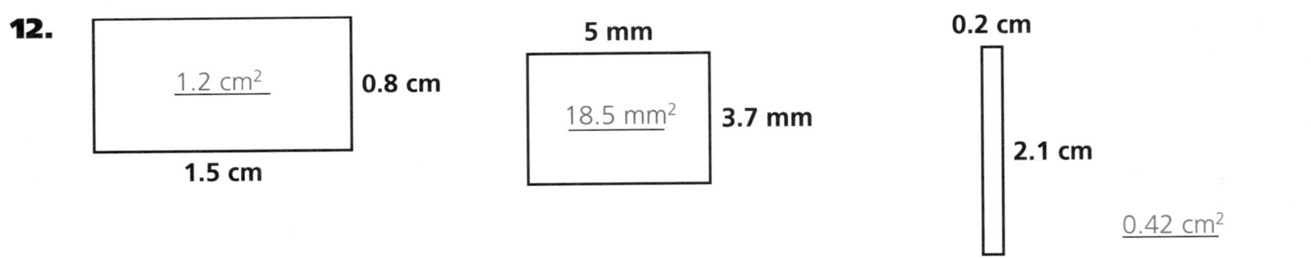

13.

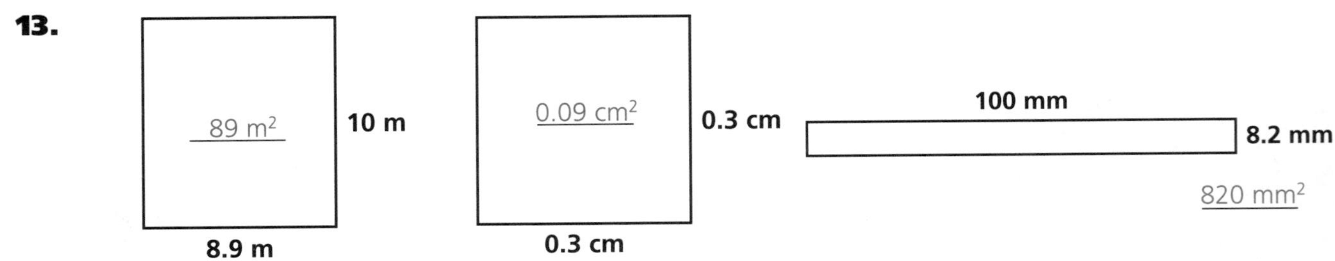

Name ______________________

Multiply.

14. 0.8 × 0.1 = 0.08 | 18.6 × 0.047 = 0.8742 | 75.63 × 0.008 = 0.60504 | 8.05 × 0.97 = 7.8085

15. 0.467 × 0.64 = 0.29888 | 64.87 × 0.8 = 51.896 | 12.3 × 8.21 = 100.983 | 9.82 × 0.03 = 0.2946

16. 30.4 × 5.08 = 154.432 | 0.076 × 9.7 = 0.7372 | 4.12 × 5.75 = 23.69 | 65.5 × 0.063 = 4.1265

Problem Solving
Reasoning

Solve.

17. A jet traveled at an average speed of **345.6** mph. What distance did it cover in **4.5** hours?

1,555.2 mi

18. Each book is **2.9** cm thick. Will **45** of these books fit on a bookstore shelf that is **130** cm long? Explain.

No; 2.9 × 45 = 130.5, which is greater than 130.

19. A tile costs **$0.69**. How much would a box of **100** tiles cost? How much would **10** of the boxes cost?

$69; $690

Test Prep ★ Mixed Review

20 **What is the volume of a rectangular prism that measures 4 units in length, 3 units in width, and 8 units in height?** D; 1E

A 15 units^3

B 96 units

C 96 units^2

D 96 units^3

21 **1.867 − 0.43 + 72.491 − 25.4 =** F; Obj. 2A

F 48.528

G 48.915

H 65.331

J 71.388

Closing the Lesson *How is multiplying decimals similar to multiplying whole numbers? How is it different?* (Possible answer: First, you multiply the numbers just like whole numbers, but then you must place the decimal point in the product.)

Name ____________________

Guided Practice: First ex. in each section, pp. 42–44
Independent Practice: Complete pp. 42–44

Dividing Decimals and Powers of Ten

You know how to divide a restaurant bill for **$10.00** among **4** people. Each will pay **$2.50.** You can use what you know about money to help you divide other decimal amounts by a whole number.

Find 2.056 ÷ 5.

1. Estimate first. Think of money.

$2.00 ÷ 5 = $.40

The answer should be close to **0.40.**

2. Divide as you would for whole numbers. Write extra zeros in the dividend if necessary.

```
   4112
5)2.0560
 -20
   05
   -5
    06
    -5
     10
    -10
      0
```

3. Place the decimal point directly above the decimal point in the dividend.

```
   .4112
5)2.0560
```

2.056 ÷ 5 = 0.4112

It is close to the estimate of **0.40.** The answer is reasonable.

Divide. Round the quotient to the nearest thousandth.
Check that your answer is reasonable.

1.	5)7.565 — 1.513	8)0.3472 — 0.043	9)556.02 — 61.78	6)0.0558 — 0.009
2.	12)0.8352 — 0.070	15)9.645 — 0.643	18)38.7 — 2.15	11)0.0726 — 0.007
3.	7)3.445 — 0.492	8)0.0026 — 0.000	13)562.011 — 43.232	16)0.528 — 0.033
4.	32)1.784 — 0.056	40)0.064 — 0.002	68)125.32 — 1.843	52)25.033 — 0.481

Find the average. Round to the nearest hundredth.

5. 2.5, 3.6, 9.4, and 8.1 ___5.9___ 0.95, 0.82, 0.44, 0.65, and 0.89 ___0.75___

6. 0.044, 0.035, 0.56, 0.32, 0.81 ___0.35___ 2.32, 5.27, 6.99, 4.41, 5.49, 10.67 ___5.86___

Check Understanding *If I divide 3.67 by 8, is my answer greater than one? Explain.* (Since 8 > 3.67, the quotient is less than one.)

Name ______________________________

Bananas are on sale at **$.68** per pound. To the nearest tenth, how many pounds of bananas can you buy for **$5.78**?

You can extend what you know about dividing whole numbers to divide by a decimal. Study the example below.

Multiplying both the divisor and the dividend by the same power of **10** does not change the quotient. So to divide a decimal by a decimal:

1. Write the divisor as a whole number.

2. Multiply the dividend by the same number, writing zeros if necessary.

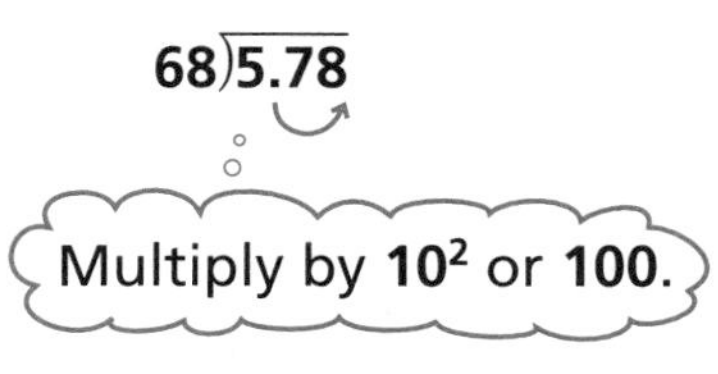

3. Divide as usual, writing zeros as necessary. Place the decimal point in the quotient.

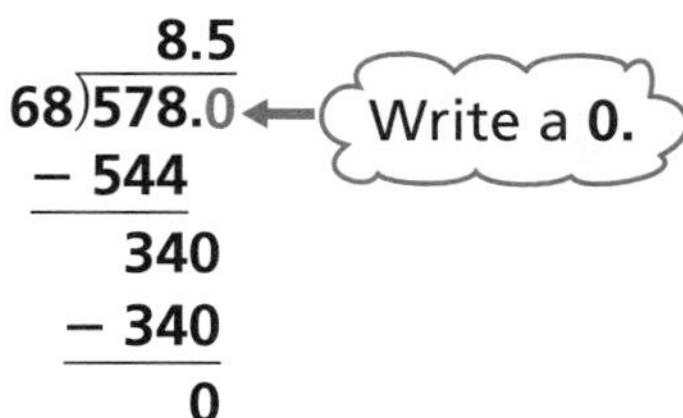

You can buy **8.5** pounds of bananas.

Find the quotient.

7.	0.3)15.6 → 52	0.8)27.2 → 34	0.9)2.16 → 2.4	0.4)0.96 → 2.4
8.	0.07)44.1 → 630	0.06)1.38 → 23	0.005)1.2 → 240	0.03)1.35 → 45
9.	0.21)5.46 → 26	3.5)17.5 → 5	0.11)63.8 → 580	0.14)5.32 → 38
10.	0.015)4.56 → 304	0.12)0.8448 → 7.04	0.036)7.344 → 204	0.28)0.168 → 0.6

What pattern do you see?

0.6 ÷ 10 = 0.06	56 ÷ 10^1 = 5.6	6.2 ÷ 10 = 0.62
0.6 ÷ 100 = 0.006	56 ÷ 10^2 = 0.56	6.2 ÷ 100 = 0.062
0.6 ÷ 1,000 = 0.0006	56 ÷ 10^3 = 0.056	6.2 ÷ 1,000 = 0.0062

The decimal point is moved one place to the left for each **0** in the multiple of ten, or equal to the exponent in the power of ten.

334.29 ÷ 1,000 = 0.03429 (3) 108.2 ÷ 10^2 = 1.082 (2)

A caret (‸) is used to show where the decimal point will be after it is divided by a power of ten.

For example: 6.20‸ is 620.

Write a caret where the decimal point would be after dividing by the power of 10 shown. Write zeros if necessary.

11. by 10: ‸7 ‸0.006 ‸0.9 75‸0 64‸.2

12. by 100: ‸83.1 ‸00.47 ‸06 ‸00.005 ‸00.80

13. by 10^3: ‸000.060 ‸085.3 ‸024 ‸00.75 ‸005

Divide. Use mental math.

14. 24 ÷ 10^1 = 2.4 0.9632 ÷ 10^4 = 0.00009632 60.25 ÷ 10^3 = 0.06025

15. 863 ÷ 10^2 = 8.63 89,500 ÷ 10^5 = 0.895 0.934 ÷ 10^4 = 0.0000934

Problem Solving Reasoning Solve.

16. Bill paid **$22.24** for **3.2** pounds of fish. What is the price per pound?

$6.95

17. A car used **19.5** gallons of gasoline to travel **354.9** miles. On the average, how many miles per gallon did the car get?

18.2 miles per gallon

18. A stack of **1,000** sheets of paper is **10.6** cm high. How thick is each sheet of paper?

0.0106 cm

Test Prep ★ Mixed Review

19 1.57 × 0.15 = C; Obj. 2A

A 2.355

B 23.55

C 0.2355

D 0.02355

20 Which shows these numbers ordered from least to greatest? J; Obj. 2F

29.1, 29.8, 29.09, 2.99

F 29.1, 29.8, 29.09, 2.99

G 2.99, 29.8, 29.09, 29.1

H 29.8, 29.1, 29.09, 2.99

J 2.99, 29.09, 29.1, 29.8

Closing the Lesson *When might you want to divide a decimal by a whole number or by a power of 10?* (Answers will vary: When you are doing conversions in the metric system or when doing unit pricing and comparative shopping.)

Name ___________________________

Guided Practice: First ex. in each section, pp. 45–46
Independent Practice: Complete pp. 45–46

Prime Factorization, Greatest Common Factor, and Least Common Multiple

A **prime number** is a whole number with exactly two factors, itself and **1**. For example, **2, 3, 5, 7, 11,** and **13** are prime numbers.

Composite numbers have more than two factors.

To write the **prime factorization** of a number means to write the number as the product of prime numbers.

Write the prime factorization of **36**.

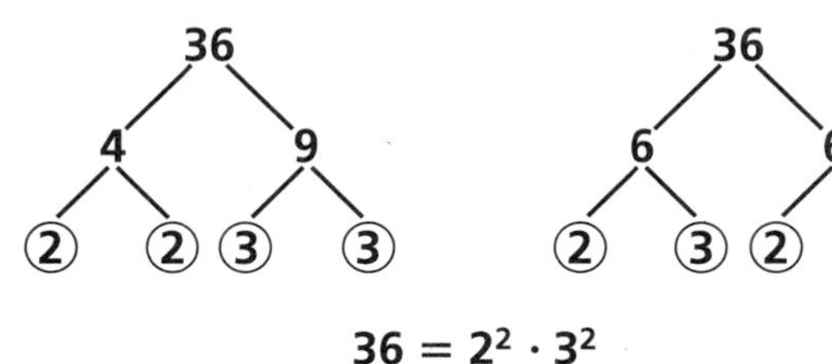

$36 = 2^2 \cdot 3^2$

Both **tree diagrams** give the same prime factorization. The circled numbers are all prime.

Write the prime factorization of **56**.

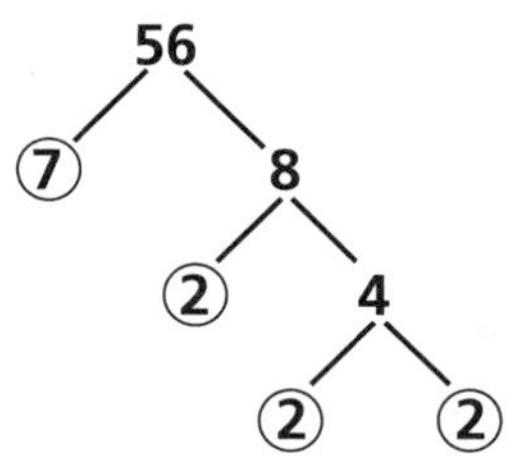

$56 = 2^3 \cdot 7$

Write the prime factorization of the number.

1. $16 = \underline{2^4}$ $\quad 10 = \underline{2 \cdot 5}$ $\quad 24 = \underline{2^3 \cdot 3}$

2. $54 = \underline{2 \cdot 3^3}$ $\quad 45 = \underline{3^2 \cdot 5}$ $\quad 62 = \underline{2 \cdot 31}$

3. $50 = \underline{2 \cdot 5^2}$ $\quad 18 = \underline{2 \cdot 3^2}$ $\quad 70 = \underline{2 \cdot 5 \cdot 7}$

4. $60 = \underline{2^2 \cdot 3 \cdot 5}$ $\quad 100 = \underline{2^2 \cdot 5^2}$ $\quad 144 = \underline{2^4 \cdot 3^2}$

Write the product of the prime factorization.

5. $2^3 \cdot 3 = \underline{24}$ $\quad 3^2 \cdot 7 = \underline{63}$ $\quad 2 \cdot 3 \cdot 7 = \underline{42}$

6. $2 \cdot 3^2 \cdot 5 = \underline{90}$ $\quad 3^2 \cdot 11 = \underline{99}$ $\quad 2^2 \cdot 5^2 \cdot 7 = \underline{700}$

Check Understanding *Who can tell us how to find the GCF of 40 and 24?* (Factor the two numbers into prime factors and then select all the factors in common.)

The **greatest common factor (GCF)** of two numbers is the greatest number that is a factor of both numbers.

Find the greatest common factor of **24** and **36**.

Method 1: List each number's factors.

24: 1, 2, 3, 4, 6, 8, **12,** 24

36: 1, 2, 3, 4, 6, 9, **12,** 18, 36

The common factors are **1, 2, 3, 4, 6,** and **12**. The *greatest* of these factors is **12**.

Method 2: Find the product of all **common** prime factors.

$24 = 2 \cdot 2 \cdot 2 \cdot 3$ $\quad 36 = 2 \cdot 2 \cdot 3 \cdot 3$

GCF is $\mathbf{2 \cdot 2 \cdot 3 = 2^2 \cdot 3}$, or **12**.

The **least common multiple (LCM)** of two numbers is the least number that is a multiple of both numbers.

Find the least common multiple of **20** and **24**.

Method 1: List each number's multiples.

20: 20, 40, 60, 80, 100, **120,** 140, . . .

24: 24, 48, 72, 96, **120,** 144, . . .

The least *common* multiple is **120**.

Method 2: Multiply the greatest power of each prime number that appears in either.

$20 = 2 \cdot 2 \cdot 5$ $\quad 24 = 2 \cdot 2 \cdot 2 \cdot 3$

LCM is $\mathbf{2 \cdot 2 \cdot 5 \cdot 2 \cdot 3 = 2^3 \cdot 3 \cdot 5}$, or **120**.

Find the greatest common factor.

7. **16 and 40** 8   **24 and 30** 6   **18 and 24** 6   **36 and 48** 12

8. **12 and 64** 4   **24 and 52** 4   **10 and 16** 2   **44 and 66** 22

9. **42 and 63** 21   **20 and 45** 5   **28 and 34** 2   **36 and 84** 12

Find the least common multiple.

10. **8 and 12** 24   **12 and 16** 48   **6 and 8** 24   **15 and 20** 60

11. **9 and 12** 36   **15 and 35** 105   **3 and 15** 15   **17 and 51** 51

12. **6 and 10** 30   **12 and 30** 60   **9 and 15** 45   **24 and 36** 72

Quick Check

Solve.

13. **7.2 × 0.09 =** 0.648   **14.** **0.021 × 0.63 =** 0.01323

15. $0.3\overline{)9.774}$ 32.58   **16.** $1.2\overline{)0.0054}$ 0.0045   **17.** $0.15\overline{)85.5}$ 570

18. Write the first five multiples of 16. 16, 32, 48, 64, 80

19. Write the prime factorization of 72. $2^3 \cdot 3^2$

20. What is the GCF of **12** and **16**? 4

21. What is the LCM of **12** and **16**? 48

Work Space.

Item	Error Analysis
13–17	**Common Error:** Students may not place the decimal point correctly. **Skills Tutorial** Strand 8, Skills 11, 12
18–21	**Common Error:** Students may find a product, not the LCM, or confuse LCM and GCF. **Skills Tutorial** Strand 5: Skill 5, 6,8,9

Closing the Lesson *When would you ever use the GCF or LCM of two numbers?* (Answers will vary. GCF: when simplifying fractions, and LCM: when finding a common denominator)

Name ______________________

Equivalent Fractions

Guided Practice: First ex. in each section, pp. 47–48
Independent Practice: Complete pp. 47–48

Fractions that represent the same number are **equivalent fractions**. You can multiply the numerator and the denominator of a fraction by the same non-zero number to find an equivalent fraction. This is because it is the same as multiplying by **1**.

$\frac{2}{3}$ is equivalent to $\frac{8}{12}$ because $\frac{2}{3} \rightarrow \frac{2 \cdot 4}{3 \cdot 4} = \frac{8}{12}$

$\frac{2}{3}$ is equivalent to many fractions.

$\frac{2}{3} \rightarrow \frac{2 \cdot 2}{3 \cdot 2} = \frac{4}{6}, \quad \frac{2}{3} \rightarrow \frac{2 \cdot 3}{3 \cdot 3} = \frac{6}{9}, \quad \frac{2}{3} \rightarrow \frac{2 \cdot 7}{3 \cdot 7} = \frac{14}{21}$

Both of these models show $\frac{2}{3}$.

The ratio of shaded parts to total parts is equivalent.

$\frac{2}{3}$

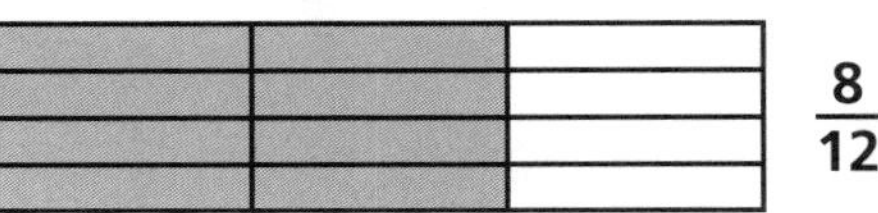
$\frac{8}{12}$

Name the fraction represented by the model. Then name an equivalent fraction.

Answers for equivalent fractions may vary; Sample answers are given.

1. 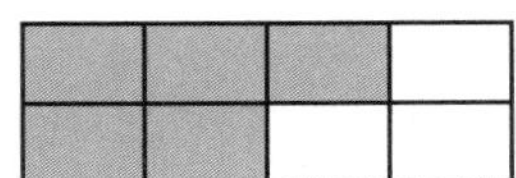 $\frac{5}{8}; \frac{10}{16}$ 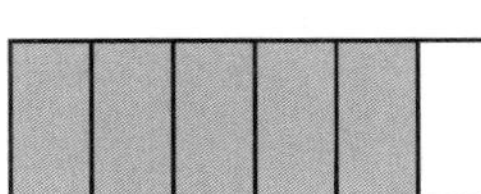 $\frac{5}{6}; \frac{10}{12}$ 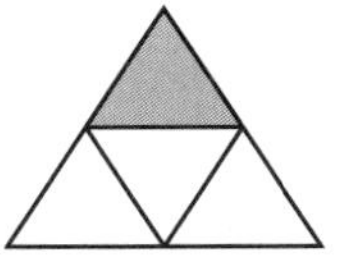 $\frac{1}{4}; \frac{2}{8}$

2. 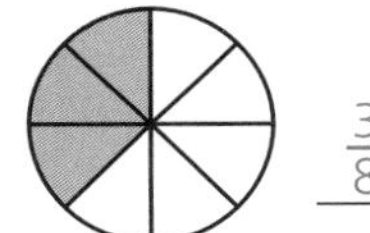 $\frac{3}{8}; \frac{6}{16}$ 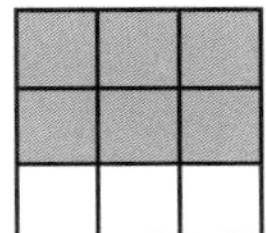 $\frac{6}{9}; \frac{2}{3}$ 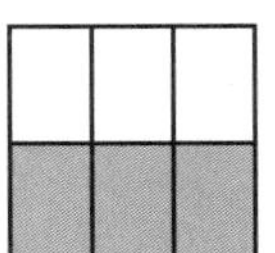 $\frac{3}{6}; \frac{2}{4}$

Find the missing numerator.

3. $\frac{4}{5} = \frac{12}{15}$ $\frac{5}{6} = \frac{35}{42}$ $\frac{2}{3} = \frac{34}{51}$ $\frac{11}{12} = \frac{55}{60}$

4. $\frac{6}{7} = \frac{12}{14}$ $\frac{3}{4} = \frac{30}{40}$ $\frac{1}{5} = \frac{10}{50}$ $\frac{4}{15} = \frac{12}{45}$

5. $\frac{1}{3} = \frac{7}{21}$ $\frac{3}{5} = \frac{27}{45}$ $\frac{7}{8} = \frac{28}{32}$ $\frac{2}{17} = \frac{6}{51}$

6. $\frac{7}{8} = \frac{56}{64}$ $\frac{7}{10} = \frac{14}{20}$ $\frac{4}{6} = \frac{48}{72}$ $\frac{7}{12} = \frac{28}{48}$

Name five equivalent fractions for the fraction. Answers may vary.

7. $\frac{3}{5}$ $\frac{6}{10}, \frac{9}{15}, \frac{12}{20}, \frac{15}{25}, \frac{18}{30}$ $\frac{4}{9}$ $\frac{8}{18}, \frac{12}{27}, \frac{16}{36}, \frac{20}{45}, \frac{24}{54}$

8. $\frac{1}{3}$ $\frac{2}{6}, \frac{3}{9}, \frac{4}{12}, \frac{5}{15}, \frac{6}{18}$ $\frac{5}{6}$ $\frac{10}{12}, \frac{15}{18}, \frac{20}{24}, \frac{25}{30}, \frac{30}{36}$

9. $\frac{2}{7}$ $\frac{4}{14}, \frac{6}{21}, \frac{8}{28}, \frac{10}{35}, \frac{12}{42}$ $\frac{2}{3}$ $\frac{4}{6}, \frac{6}{9}, \frac{8}{12}, \frac{10}{15}, \frac{12}{18}$

Check Understanding *Can someone name me a fraction equivalent to $\frac{3}{5}$?* $\left(\frac{12}{20}\right)$ *How did you get that?* (I multiplied the numerator and denominator by 4.) *Who could simplify $\frac{18}{30}$ for me?* $\left(\frac{3}{5}\right)$ *What did you do?* (I divided the numerator and denominator by the GCF of 18 and 30, namely 6.)

The fractions $\frac{1}{2}$ and $\frac{2}{4}$ are equivalent. Of these two, $\frac{1}{2}$ is said to be in **simplest form**. A fraction is in simplest form when the greatest common factor of the numerator and denominator is **1**.

To write a fraction in simplest form, divide the numerator and denominator by their greatest common factor.

$$\frac{8}{20} \rightarrow \frac{8 \div 4}{20 \div 4} = \frac{2}{5}$$

4 is the GCF of **8** and **20**.

$$\frac{12}{36} \rightarrow \frac{12 \div 12}{36 \div 12} = \frac{1}{3}$$

12 is the GCF of **12** and **36**.

Write the fraction in simplest form.

10. $\frac{9}{12} = \frac{3}{4}$ $\frac{9}{18} = \frac{1}{2}$ $\frac{12}{14} = \frac{6}{7}$ $\frac{18}{36} = \frac{1}{2}$

11. $\frac{6}{9} = \frac{2}{3}$ $\frac{15}{24} = \frac{5}{8}$ $\frac{4}{20} = \frac{1}{5}$ $\frac{15}{25} = \frac{3}{5}$

12. $\frac{18}{24} = \frac{3}{4}$ $\frac{12}{30} = \frac{2}{5}$ $\frac{14}{20} = \frac{7}{10}$ $\frac{3}{51} = \frac{1}{17}$

13. $\frac{98}{100} = \frac{49}{50}$ $\frac{14}{35} = \frac{2}{5}$ $\frac{75}{135} = \frac{5}{9}$ $\frac{16}{32} = \frac{1}{2}$

Problem Solving Reasoning **Write the next three fractions in the pattern.**

14. $\frac{2}{3}\ \frac{4}{6}\ \frac{6}{9}$ $\frac{8}{12}, \frac{10}{15}, \frac{12}{18}$ $\frac{1}{4}\ \frac{2}{8}\ \frac{3}{12}$ $\frac{4}{16}, \frac{5}{20}, \frac{6}{24}$ $\frac{3}{5}\ \frac{6}{10}\ \frac{9}{15}$ $\frac{12}{20}, \frac{15}{25}, \frac{18}{30}$

15. $\frac{3}{4}\ \frac{6}{8}\ \frac{12}{16}$ $\frac{24}{32}, \frac{48}{64}, \frac{96}{128}$ $\frac{5}{6}\ \frac{10}{12}\ \frac{20}{24}$ $\frac{40}{48}, \frac{80}{96}, \frac{160}{192}$ $\frac{3}{7}\ \frac{6}{14}\ \frac{12}{28}$ $\frac{24}{56}, \frac{48}{112}, \frac{96}{224}$

Test Prep ★ Mixed Review

16 35.91 ÷ 0.19 = A; Obj. 2A

A 189

B 1.89

C 0.189

D 0.0189

17 **What is the greatest common factor of 54 and 180?** J; Obj. 2B

F 2

G 6

H 9

J 18

Closing the Lesson *What are equivalent fractions?* (fractions that name the same value) *How do you find equivalent fractions?* (Multiply or divide the numerator and denominator by the same whole number.)

Name ______________________________

Guided Practice: First ex. in Rows 1, 4 & 7, pp. 49–50
Independent Practice: Complete pp. 49–50

Equivalent Fractions and Decimals

You can write one half as the fraction $\frac{1}{2}$ or as the decimal **0.5**. They are equivalent. You can find equivalent fractions and decimals using the steps below.

Writing Fractions as Decimals
To write a fraction as a decimal, divide.

$$\frac{5}{12} \rightarrow 12\overline{)5.0000} = 0.4166$$

$$\begin{array}{r} 0.4166 \\ 12\overline{)5.0000} \\ -4\,8 \\ \hline 20 \\ -12 \\ \hline 80 \\ -72 \\ \hline 80 \end{array}$$

Remainder starts to repeat.

The decimal **0.41666 . . .** is a **repeating** decimal. The three dots mean the pattern keeps repeating. You may write it **$0.41\overline{6}$**.

Other Example

$$\frac{3}{4} \rightarrow \begin{array}{r} 0.75 \\ 4\overline{)3.00} \\ -2\,8 \\ \hline 20 \\ -20 \\ \hline 0 \end{array}$$

Remainder is **0**.

The decimal **0.75** is a **terminating** decimal.

Writing Decimals as Fractions
To write a decimal as a fraction, use what you know about place value.

0.7 = seven tenths or $\frac{7}{10}$

Remember to simplify fractions when you can.

Other Examples

0.48 = **48** hundredths or $\frac{48}{100}$

0.325 = **325** thousandths or $\frac{325}{1,000}$

2.4 = **2** ones and **4** tenths or $2\frac{4}{10}$

Write the fraction as a decimal. Use bar notation to write repeating decimals.

1. $\frac{4}{5}$ = 0.8 $\frac{2}{3}$ = $0.\overline{6}$ $\frac{3}{8}$ = 0.375 $\frac{4}{9}$ = $0.\overline{4}$

2. $\frac{7}{10}$ = 0.7 $2\frac{4}{8}$ = 2.5 $\frac{1}{12}$ = $0.08\overline{3}$ $\frac{7}{20}$ = 0.35

3. $\frac{4}{11}$ = $0.\overline{36}$ $1\frac{1}{15}$ = $1.0\overline{6}$ $\frac{7}{30}$ = $0.2\overline{3}$ $2\frac{5}{18}$ = $2.2\overline{7}$

Write the decimal as a fraction or mixed number in simplest form.

4. 0.4 = $\frac{2}{5}$ 0.05 = $\frac{1}{20}$ 0.125 = $\frac{1}{8}$ 0.3 = $\frac{3}{10}$

5. 0.06 = $\frac{3}{50}$ 1.29 = $1\frac{29}{100}$ 0.086 = $\frac{43}{500}$ 0.72 = $\frac{18}{25}$

6. 1.15 = $\frac{23}{20}$ 2.5 = $\frac{5}{2}$ 1.85 = $\frac{37}{20}$ 3.1 = $\frac{31}{10}$

Check Understanding *What would 0.235 become when written as a fraction?* ($\frac{235}{1,000}$, which could be simplified as $\frac{47}{200}$) *Which is greater, 0.45 or $\frac{4}{9}$?* (0.45)

Compare. Write <, >, or = to make a true sentence.

7. $\frac{6}{11}$ < $0.\overline{5}$ $\frac{5}{8}$ = 0.625 $\frac{11}{16}$ < 0.7 $\frac{8}{9}$ > 0.8

8. $\frac{7}{8}$ > 0.7 $\frac{2}{15}$ = $0.1\overline{3}$ $\frac{4}{5}$ > 0.4 $\frac{40}{100}$ = 0.4

Problem Solving Reasoning Write each fraction as a decimal. Use a bar to write the repeating decimals. Describe the patterns you observe.

9. $\frac{1}{9}$ $\frac{2}{9}$ $\frac{3}{9}$ $\frac{4}{9}$ $\frac{5}{9}$

$0.\overline{1}$, $0.\overline{2}$, $0.\overline{3}$, $0.\overline{4}$, $0.\overline{5}$

The repeating pattern is the numerator.

10. $\frac{1}{11}$ $\frac{2}{11}$ $\frac{3}{11}$ $\frac{4}{11}$ $\frac{5}{11}$

$0.\overline{09}$, $0.\overline{18}$, $0.\overline{27}$, $0.\overline{36}$, $0.\overline{45}$

The repeating pattern is 9 times the numerator.

11. $\frac{1}{3}$ $\frac{4}{3}$ $\frac{7}{3}$ $\frac{10}{3}$ $\frac{13}{3}$

$0.\overline{3}$, $1.\overline{3}$, $2.\overline{3}$, $3.\overline{3}$, $4.\overline{3}$

Each decimal part is $0.\overline{3}$; the whole number parts increase by 1.

12. $\frac{1}{6}$ $\frac{2}{6}$ $\frac{3}{6}$ $\frac{4}{6}$ $\frac{5}{6}$

$0.1\overline{6}$, $0.\overline{3}$, 0.5, $0.\overline{6}$, $0.8\overline{3}$

The hundredths place repeats 6, then 3, then 0.

13. How is the pattern with multiples of $\frac{1}{6}$ different from the other three patterns?

Every third decimal terminates. Not all the decimals are repeating.

Test Prep ★ Mixed Review

14 What number is missing? $\frac{12}{15} = \frac{4}{x}$
B; Obj. 2C

A 3

B 5

C 12

D 15

15 What is the least common multiple of 24 and 30? H; Obj. 2B

F 6

G 54

H 120

J 240

Closing the Lesson *Why is it important to be able to change fractions to decimals and vice-versa?* (Answers will vary: Since fractions and decimals are names for the exact same number, you may need to change from one to the other to make sense of a problem or to help you solve a problem.)

Name ________________________________

Guided Practice: First ex. in Rows 1 & 6, pp. 51–52
Independent Practice: Complete pp. 51–52

Comparing and Ordering Fractions

You can compare fractions with like denominators by comparing their numerators.

Compare $\frac{5}{8}$ and $\frac{3}{8}$. Since **5 > 3**, $\frac{5}{8} > \frac{3}{8}$.

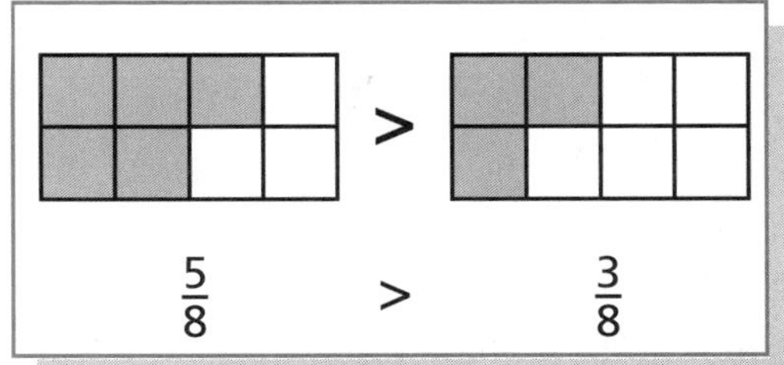

You can compare fractions with unlike denominators, too. Rewrite one or both fractions using a common denominator.

Compare $\frac{7}{12}$ and $\frac{5}{6}$.

Use **12** as the common denominator.

$\frac{7}{12}$ $\qquad$ $\frac{5}{6} = \frac{10}{12}$

7 < 10, so $\frac{7}{12} < \frac{10}{12}$, or $\frac{7}{12} < \frac{5}{6}$.

Compare $\frac{2}{3}$ and $\frac{3}{5}$.

Use **15** as the common denominator.

$\frac{2}{3} = \frac{10}{15}$ $\qquad$ $\frac{3}{5} = \frac{9}{15}$

10 > 9, so $\frac{10}{15} > \frac{9}{15}$, or $\frac{2}{3} > \frac{3}{5}$.

To order more than two fractions with different denominators, rewrite them using a common denominator.

Write the fractions $\frac{3}{4}$, $\frac{1}{2}$, and $\frac{2}{7}$ in order from least to greatest.

$\frac{3}{4} = \frac{21}{28}$ $\qquad$ $\frac{1}{2} = \frac{14}{28}$ $\qquad$ $\frac{2}{7} = \frac{8}{28}$

Think: LCM of **4, 2,** and **7** is **28.**

$\frac{8}{28} < \frac{14}{28} < \frac{21}{28}$ so $\frac{2}{7} < \frac{1}{2} < \frac{3}{4}$

Compare. Write <, >, or = to make a true sentence.

1.	$\frac{3}{4}$ = $\frac{21}{28}$	$\frac{12}{36}$ = $\frac{33}{99}$	$\frac{3}{4}$ > $\frac{1}{2}$	$\frac{3}{4}$ > $\frac{4}{9}$
2.	$\frac{3}{16}$ < $\frac{4}{15}$	$\frac{4}{7}$ > $\frac{4}{9}$	$\frac{16}{20}$ = $\frac{32}{40}$	$\frac{45}{54}$ = $\frac{5}{6}$
3.	$\frac{5}{6}$ > $\frac{13}{40}$	$\frac{3}{4}$ = $\frac{27}{36}$	$\frac{45}{54}$ > $\frac{3}{4}$	$\frac{9}{10}$ > $\frac{6}{7}$
4.	$\frac{14}{16}$ = $\frac{35}{40}$	$\frac{21}{27}$ = $\frac{56}{72}$	$\frac{7}{8}$ > $\frac{6}{7}$	$\frac{4}{3}$ > $\frac{6}{5}$

Write the name for fraction A and B. Compare the fractions using <.

5.

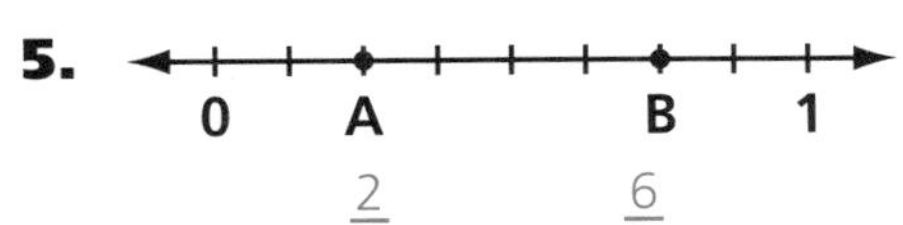

$\frac{2}{8}$ < $\frac{6}{8}$

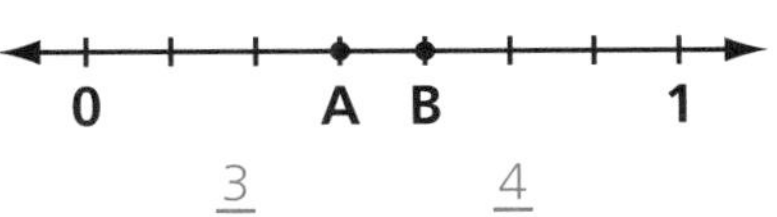

$\frac{3}{7}$ < $\frac{4}{7}$

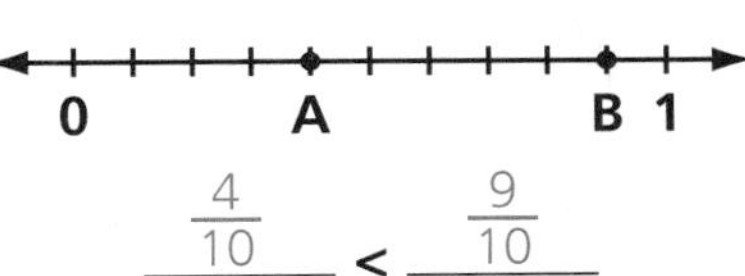

$\frac{4}{10}$ < $\frac{9}{10}$

Check Understanding *How could you find out which is greater, $\frac{2}{3}$ or $\frac{3}{5}$?* ($\frac{2}{3}$ is greater because when you use common denominators, $\frac{2}{3} = \frac{10}{15}$ and $\frac{3}{5} = \frac{9}{15}$.)

Write the fractions in order from least to greatest.
Answers may vary.

6. $\frac{2}{3}\ \frac{4}{5}\ \frac{1}{2}$ $\frac{1}{2}\ \frac{2}{3}\ \frac{4}{5}$ | $\frac{3}{4}\ \frac{5}{8}\ \frac{1}{2}$ $\frac{1}{2}\ \frac{5}{8}\ \frac{3}{4}$

7. $\frac{1}{3}\ \frac{5}{6}\ \frac{3}{12}$ $\frac{3}{12}\ \frac{1}{3}\ \frac{5}{6}$ | $\frac{3}{4}\ \frac{5}{6}\ \frac{3}{8}$ $\frac{3}{8}\ \frac{3}{4}\ \frac{5}{6}$

Problem Solving Reasoning **Use number sense to compare. Think about where the fractions would be on a number line. Write > or < to make a true sentence.**

8. $\frac{1}{2} > \frac{1}{3}$ $\frac{1}{5} < \frac{1}{4}$ $\frac{1}{12} > \frac{1}{15}$

9. $\frac{3}{5} > \frac{3}{6}$ $\frac{4}{8} < \frac{4}{5}$ $\frac{7}{8} > \frac{7}{10}$

10. Write a note to a friend describing how to compare different fractions that have the same numerators.

Sample answer: When two fractions have the same numerators, the greater fraction will have the lesser denominator.

Quick Check

Write three equivalent fractions for the given fraction.
Answers may vary.

11. $\frac{10}{12}$ $\frac{5}{6}, \frac{15}{18}, \frac{20}{24}$ **12.** $\frac{8}{9}$ $\frac{16}{18}, \frac{24}{27}, \frac{32}{36}$ **13.** $\frac{14}{21}$ $\frac{2}{3}, \frac{28}{42}, \frac{56}{84}$

Write the fraction or mixed number as a decimal. Use bar notation for repeating decimals.

14. $\frac{7}{8}$ 0.875 **15.** $\frac{17}{20}$ 0.85 **16.** $\frac{17}{12}$ $1.41\overline{6}$

Write the decimal as a fraction or mixed number in simplest form.

17. 0.56 $\frac{14}{25}$ **18.** 0.225 $\frac{9}{40}$ **19.** 3.448 $3\frac{56}{125}$

Write the fractions in order from least to greatest.

20. $\frac{5}{8}\ \frac{2}{3}\ \frac{3}{4}\ \frac{7}{12}$ $\frac{7}{12}\ \frac{5}{8}\ \frac{2}{3}\ \frac{3}{4}$ **21.** $\frac{1}{4}\ \frac{3}{16}\ \frac{5}{8}\ \frac{1}{3}$ $\frac{3}{16}\ \frac{1}{4}\ \frac{1}{3}\ \frac{5}{8}$

Work Space.

Item	Error Analysis
11–13	**Common Error:** Watch for students who add instead of multiplying. **Skills Tutorial** Strand 5: Skills 7, 10
14–16	**Common Error:** Some students may misplace the bar. **Skills Tutorial** Strand 8: Skills 3, 5
17–19	**Common Error:** Watch for incorrect place value in the denominator. **Skills Tutorial** Strand 8: Skills 4, 6
20–21	**Common Error:** Watch for students who do not find a common denominator. **Reteaching** Reteach 12

Closing the Lesson *Why are common denominators important?* (Answers will vary but might include the following: You need them to add and subtract fractions.)

Name ______________________

Guided Practice: First ex. in Rows 2 & 5, pp. 53–54
Independent Practice: Complete pp. 53–54

Adding Fractions and Mixed Numbers

A **mixed number** is greater than **1**. It has a whole-number part and a fractional part.

To add fractions or mixed numbers, they must have a common denominator. Use the least common multiple of the denominators as the common denominator.

You should write the sum in simplest form. A mixed number is in simplest form if its fractional part is in simplest form.

Adding Fractions: Find $\frac{3}{8}$ and $\frac{2}{3}$.

1. Rewrite with a common denominator.

$$\frac{3}{8} = \frac{9}{24}, \quad + \frac{2}{3} = \frac{16}{24}$$

2. Add.

$$\frac{3}{8} = \frac{9}{24}, \quad + \frac{2}{3} = \frac{16}{24}, \quad \frac{25}{24}$$

3. Simplify.

$$\frac{3}{8} = \frac{9}{24}, \quad + \frac{2}{3} = \frac{16}{24}, \quad \frac{25}{24} = 1\frac{1}{24}$$

Adding Mixed Numbers: Find $4\frac{3}{4}$ and $5\frac{2}{5}$.

1. Rewrite with a common denominator.

$$4\frac{3}{4} = 4\frac{15}{20}, \quad + 5\frac{2}{5} = 5\frac{8}{20}$$

2. Add the fractions, then add the whole numbers.

$$4\frac{3}{4} = 4\frac{15}{20}, \quad + 5\frac{2}{5} = 5\frac{8}{20}, \quad 9\frac{23}{20}$$

3. Simplify.

$$4\frac{3}{4} = 4\frac{15}{20}, \quad + 5\frac{2}{5} = 5\frac{8}{20}, \quad 9\frac{23}{20} = 10\frac{3}{20}$$

Write the sum in simplest form.

1. $\frac{3}{7} + \frac{2}{7} =$ $\frac{5}{7}$ $\qquad \frac{5}{12} + \frac{3}{12} =$ $\frac{2}{3}$ $\qquad \frac{4}{5} + \frac{3}{5} =$ $1\frac{2}{5}$ $\qquad \frac{8}{15} + \frac{2}{15} =$ $\frac{2}{3}$

2. $\frac{2}{3} = \frac{14}{21}$, $+\frac{5}{7} = \frac{15}{21}$, $1\frac{8}{21}$ $\qquad \frac{1}{4} + \frac{3}{8}$, $\frac{5}{8}$ $\qquad \frac{3}{8} + \frac{5}{16}$, $\frac{11}{16}$ $\qquad \frac{3}{5} + \frac{7}{12}$, $1\frac{11}{60}$

Check Understanding *What is the first step in adding $\frac{1}{3}$ and $\frac{3}{5}$?* (Find the LCD (15) and change $\frac{1}{3}$ to $\frac{5}{15}$ and $\frac{3}{5}$ to $\frac{9}{15}$.) *What do we do if the sum of the fractions is greater than one?* (Write it as a mixed number, reducing the fraction to simplest form.)

Write the sum in simplest form.

3. $\frac{3}{10} + \frac{4}{5}$ = $1\frac{1}{10}$ $\frac{5}{9} + \frac{2}{3}$ = $1\frac{2}{9}$ $\frac{2}{3} + \frac{5}{8}$ = $1\frac{7}{24}$ $\frac{6}{9} + \frac{5}{6}$ = $1\frac{1}{2}$

4. $2\frac{1}{5} + 3\frac{2}{5} =$ $5\frac{3}{5}$ $3\frac{2}{7} + 5\frac{3}{7} =$ $8\frac{5}{7}$ $10\frac{4}{9} + 6\frac{7}{9} =$ $17\frac{2}{9}$

5. $3\frac{1}{2} + 4\frac{3}{4}$ = $8\frac{1}{4}$ $5\frac{1}{9} + 8\frac{2}{3}$ = $13\frac{7}{9}$ $12\frac{2}{5} + 7\frac{1}{2}$ = $19\frac{9}{10}$ $18\frac{3}{7} + 7\frac{1}{3}$ = $25\frac{16}{21}$

6. $9\frac{3}{4} + 7\frac{2}{5}$ = $17\frac{3}{20}$ $3\frac{6}{13} + 2\frac{1}{2}$ = $5\frac{25}{26}$ $17\frac{5}{12} + 6\frac{2}{3}$ = $24\frac{1}{12}$ $20\frac{4}{11} + 7\frac{2}{3}$ = $28\frac{1}{33}$

Problem Solving Reasoning Solve.

7. Kinsley purchased **$3\frac{1}{4}$** yards of fabric. The two-piece outfit she is making needs **$1\frac{5}{8}$** yards for each piece. Does she have enough fabric? Explain.

Yes; She needs $1\frac{5}{8}$ yd + $1\frac{5}{8}$ yd = $3\frac{1}{4}$ yd, which she has.

8. Your younger brother grew **$1\frac{3}{4}$** inches last year. He was **$46\frac{1}{2}$** inches tall at the beginning of the year. Is he **4** feet tall yet? Explain.

Yes; He is $46\frac{1}{2}$ in. + $1\frac{3}{4}$ in. = $48\frac{1}{4}$ in., which is greater than 4 ft = 48 in.

Test Prep ★ Mixed Review

9 What number is missing? $\frac{?}{8} = \frac{24}{64}$

A 3 A; Obj. 2C
B 4
C 6
D 24

10 $\frac{3}{4} + \frac{1}{2} + \frac{1}{4} =$

F $\frac{1}{4}$ J; Obj. 2A
G $\frac{1}{2}$
H 1
J $1\frac{1}{2}$

Closing the Lesson *How do you add mixed numbers with different denominators?* (Find the LCD, write equivalent fractions with the LCD as denominator, add the fractions, add the whole numbers, and simplify if necessary.)

Name ____________________

Guided Practice: First ex. in Rows 2 & 5, pp. 55–56

Independent Practice: Complete pp. 55–56

Subtracting Fractions and Mixed Numbers

To subtract fractions or mixed numbers, you must have a common denominator. Use the least common multiple of the denominators as the common denominator.

Subtracting Fractions

Subtract $\frac{1}{4}$ from $\frac{5}{6}$.

1. Rewrite with a common denominator.

$$\frac{5}{6} = \frac{10}{12}$$
$$-\frac{1}{4} = \frac{3}{12}$$

2. Subtract.

$$\frac{5}{6} = \frac{10}{12}$$
$$-\frac{1}{4} = \frac{3}{12}$$
$$\frac{7}{12}$$

Subtracting Mixed Numbers

Subtract $1\frac{2}{3}$ from $6\frac{1}{4}$.

1. Rewrite with a common denominator.

$$6\frac{1}{4} = 6\frac{3}{12}$$
$$-1\frac{2}{3} = 1\frac{8}{12}$$

2. Subtract the fractions. Regroup if neccesary.

$$6\frac{1}{4} = 6\frac{3}{12} \rightarrow 5\frac{15}{12}$$
$$-1\frac{2}{3} = 1\frac{8}{12} \rightarrow -1\frac{8}{12}$$
$$\frac{7}{12}$$

3. Subtract the whole numbers.

$$6\frac{1}{4} = 6\frac{3}{12} \rightarrow 5\frac{15}{12}$$
$$-1\frac{2}{3} = 1\frac{8}{12} \rightarrow -1\frac{8}{12}$$
$$4\frac{7}{12}$$

Write the difference in simplest form.

1. $\frac{10}{12} = \frac{10}{12}$, $-\frac{2}{3} = \frac{8}{12}$; $\frac{1}{6}$

$\frac{3}{4} - \frac{3}{8}$; $\frac{3}{8}$

$\frac{7}{16} - \frac{1}{8}$; $\frac{5}{16}$

$\frac{9}{10} - \frac{2}{5}$; $\frac{1}{2}$

2. $\frac{6}{7} - \frac{1}{2}$; $\frac{5}{14}$

$\frac{7}{9} - \frac{1}{6}$; $\frac{11}{18}$

$\frac{6}{11} - \frac{1}{3}$; $\frac{7}{33}$

$\frac{9}{15} - \frac{1}{2}$; $\frac{1}{10}$

Check Understanding *How do you subtract $2\frac{3}{4}$ from $5\frac{1}{6}$?* (Rewrite $5\frac{1}{6}$ as $4\frac{14}{12}$, and $2\frac{3}{4}$ as $2\frac{9}{12}$. Then, subtract the fractions from one another and the whole numbers from one another.)

Write the difference in simplest form.

3. $8\frac{2}{3} - 4\frac{1}{3} =$ $4\frac{1}{3}$ ______ $12\frac{5}{9} - 6\frac{2}{9} =$ $6\frac{1}{3}$ ______ $18\frac{5}{8} - 5\frac{2}{8} =$ $13\frac{3}{8}$ ______

4. $8\frac{5}{8} - 3\frac{2}{8} = 5\frac{3}{8}$ $\quad$ $4\frac{1}{2} - 3\frac{3}{4} = \frac{3}{4}$ $\quad$ $10\frac{1}{3} - 6\frac{2}{5} = 3\frac{14}{15}$ $\quad$ $8\frac{1}{2} - 5\frac{5}{6} = 2\frac{2}{3}$

5. $12\frac{4}{9} - 6\frac{2}{3} = 5\frac{7}{9}$ $\quad$ $15\frac{4}{5} - 8 = 7\frac{4}{5}$ $\quad$ $16 - 3\frac{5}{6} = 12\frac{1}{6}$ $\quad$ $9\frac{5}{12} - 4\frac{3}{4} = 4\frac{2}{3}$

Problem Solving
Reasoning

Solve.

6. Shane cut a $12\frac{1}{2}$-foot board into two pieces. One piece is $4\frac{3}{4}$ feet long. How long is the other piece?

$7\frac{3}{4}$ feet

7. San Francisco had $6\frac{1}{3}$ inches of rain last month. Seattle had $8\frac{1}{4}$ inches. How much more rain did Seattle have than San Francisco?

$1\frac{11}{12}$ in.

Test Prep ★ Mixed Review

8 $\frac{1}{4} + \frac{5}{6} =$ B; Obj. 2A

A $\frac{6}{10}$

B $1\frac{1}{12}$

C $1\frac{6}{4}$

D $\frac{5}{4}$

9 **What is the value of $3(x^2 + 2)$ when $x = 4$?** H; Obj. 1C

F 18

G 21

H 54

J 64

Closing the Lesson *When might you need to subtract mixed numbers or fractions?* (Answers will vary: When you are finding the difference between two measures such as lengths, heights, or times.)

Name ______________________

Guided Practice: Problem 5, p. 58

Independent Practice: Complete pp. 57–58

Problem Solving Application: Use a Diagram

You can use a diagram that represents information visually. In this lesson, diagrams are used to help solve problems.

Tips to Remember:

1. Understand 2. Decide 3. Solve 4. Look back

- Ask yourself if you have solved a problem like this before.
- Think about the relationships shown in the diagram. What information is displayed or represented by the diagram?
- Think about the strategies you have learned. Use them to help you solve a problem.

Assume that four friends live on the same straight east-west street. The following information is also known.

- Kareem lives **3.7** km from Amal.

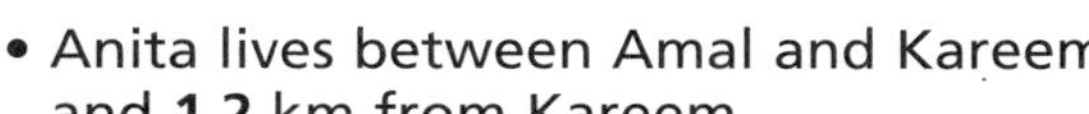

- Anita lives between Amal and Kareem, and **1.2** km from Kareem.

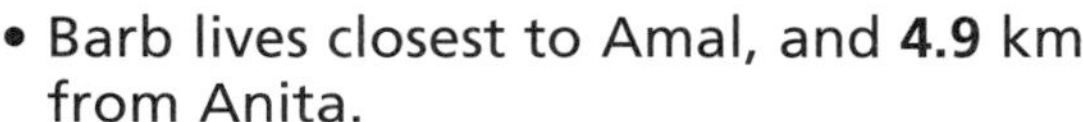

- Barb lives closest to Amal, and **4.9** km from Anita.

Where Do They Live?

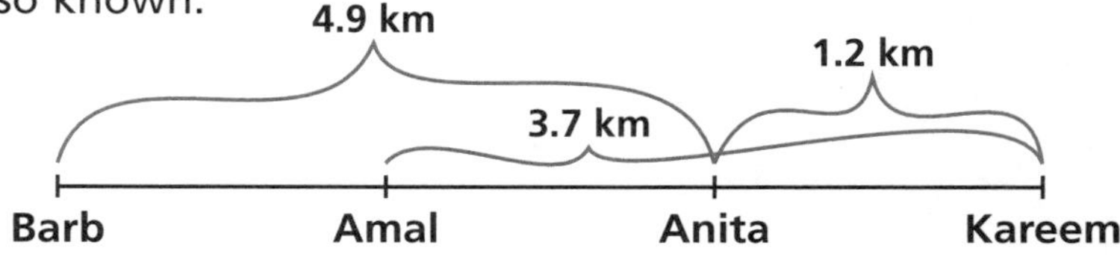

Think: How does the diagram show each piece of information?

Solve. Use the diagram above.

1. Which two friends live the closest to one another? Explain your reasoning.

Think: Do you have enough information to decide how far each friend lives from the other?

Yes; Barb and Kareem: 4.9 + 1.2 = 6.1 km; Barb and Amal: 6.1 − 3.7 = 2.4 km; Amal and Anita: 3.7 − 1.2 = 2.5 km

Answer Anita and Kareem; Because they are only 1.2 km apart.

2. Where does Emily live if she is the same distance to Barb as she is to Kareem? How far does she live from each?

Think: Is there only one place that Emily could live? How can you find her distance to Kareem?

Barb and Kareem live farthest apart, 6.1 km. Emily is half that distance from each.

Answer Emily is 3.05 km from both Barb and Kareem.

Check Understanding *Why is drawing a diagram a good strategy?* (Answers will vary: It helps you visualize what is given and what you need to find.)

Solve.

3. A student survey showed that science was more popular than language arts, but not as popular as math. Social studies was the least favorite subject. Draw a diagram to show the subjects from least to most favorite.

4. Among the **22** girls in seventh grade, **6** play only basketball, **8** play only softball, and **5** play neither sport. Draw a diagram to show how many girls play both.

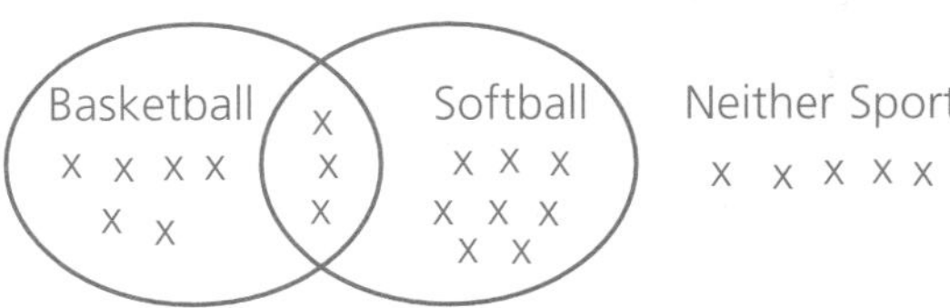

3 girls play both sports.

5. Joe goes a total of **2** blocks east and **2** blocks north to get from his house to the park. How many different routes can Joe take that are **4** blocks long? One route is shown.

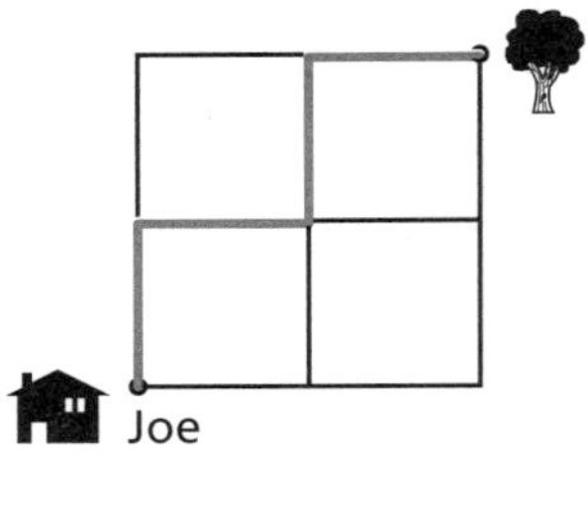

6 routes

6. Erin lives one block north of the park. How many different routes that are **5** blocks long can Carlos take to get to Erin's house? One route is shown.

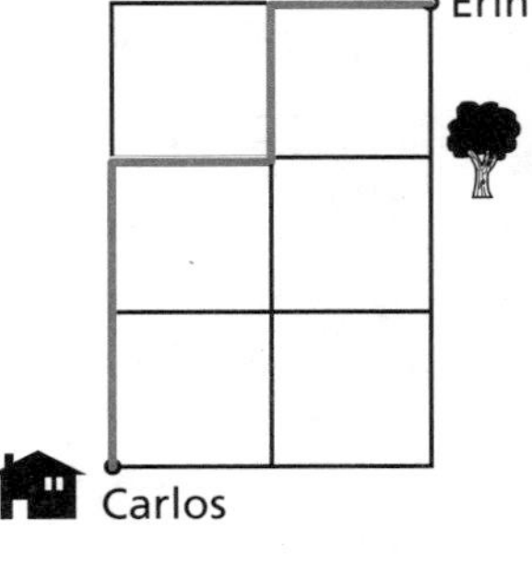

10 routes

7. A unit is divided in half. Then the half is divided in half. Suppose you continue to divide the smallest part in half. What would the next three fractional parts be called? $\frac{1}{16}$, $\frac{1}{32}$, $\frac{1}{64}$

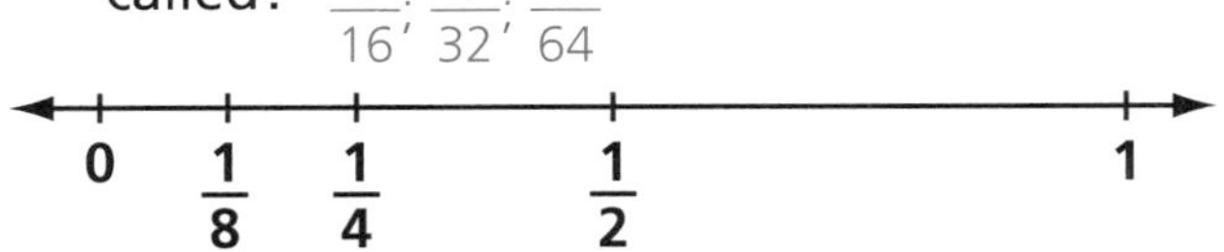

8. A unit is divided in thirds. Then one third is divided in thirds. Suppose you continue to divide the smallest part in thirds. What would the next three fractional parts be called? $\frac{1}{81}$, $\frac{1}{243}$, $\frac{1}{729}$

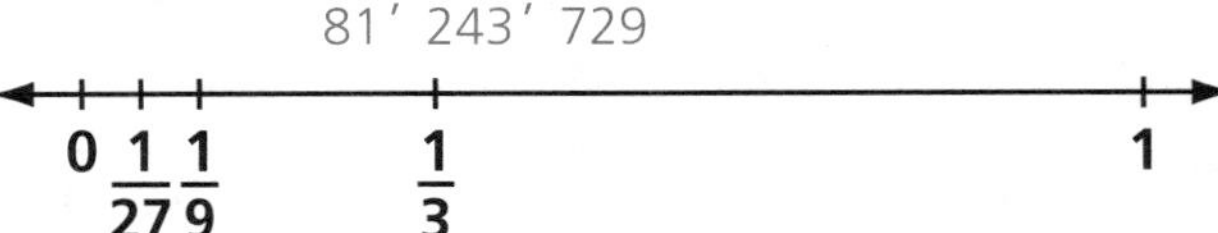

Extend Your Thinking

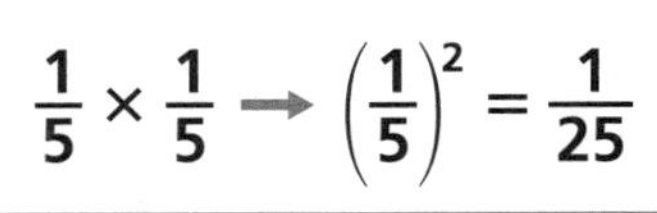

$$\frac{1}{5} \times \frac{1}{5} \rightarrow \left(\frac{1}{5}\right)^2 = \frac{1}{25}$$

9. Look at the fractions you listed in problem **7**. How could you write the fractions using exponents in the denominator? Describe the pattern.
$\frac{1}{2^4}$, $\frac{1}{2^5}$, $\frac{1}{2^6}$; The power of 2 in the denominator keeps increasing by 1.

10. Look at the fractions you listed in problem **8**. How could you write the fractions using exponents in the denominator? Describe the pattern.
$\frac{1}{3^4}$, $\frac{1}{3^5}$, $\frac{1}{3^6}$; The power of 3 in the denominator keeps increasing by 1.

Closing the Lesson *When do you think it would be a good time to use a diagram?* (Answers will vary: When a lot of information is given and you need to visualize it in order to solve the problem.)

Name ______________________

Guided Practice: First ex. in Rows 1 & 7, pp. 59–60
Independent Practice: Complete pp. 59–61

Multiplying Fractions and Mixed Numbers

To multiply fractions or mixed numbers, no common denominator is needed. Look at the pattern:

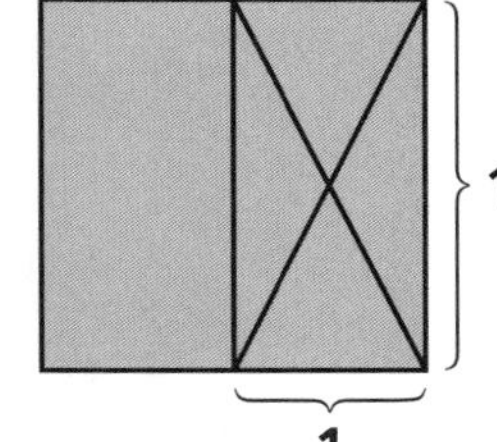

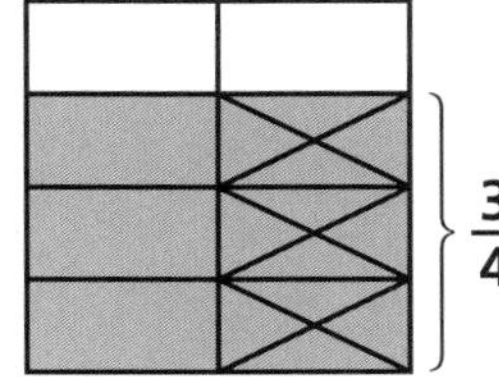

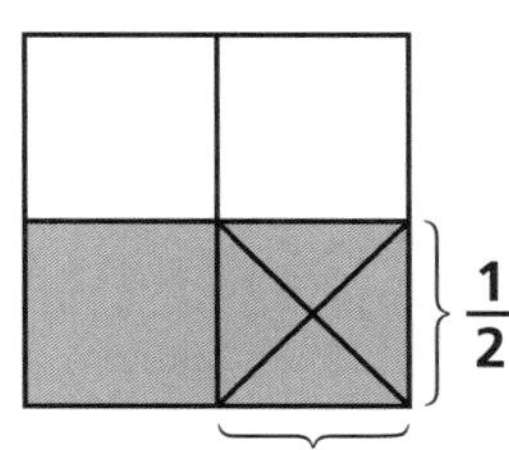

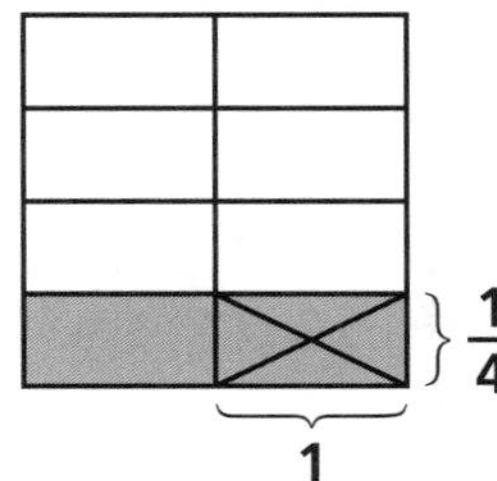

Think: $\frac{1}{2}$ of 1 — $\frac{1}{2} \times 1 = \frac{1}{2}$

Think: $\frac{1}{2}$ of $\frac{3}{4}$ — $\frac{1}{2} \times \frac{3}{4} = \frac{3}{8}$

Think: $\frac{1}{2}$ of $\frac{1}{2}$ — $\frac{1}{2} \times \frac{1}{2} = \frac{1}{4}$

Think: $\frac{1}{2}$ of $\frac{1}{4}$ — $\frac{1}{2} \times \frac{1}{4} = \frac{1}{8}$

Find $\frac{3}{7} \times \frac{4}{5}$.

1. Multiply the numerators.

$\frac{3}{7} \times \frac{4}{5} = \frac{3 \cdot 4}{7 \cdot 5} = \frac{12}{}$

2. Then, multiply the denominators.

$\frac{3}{7} \times \frac{4}{5} = \frac{3 \cdot 4}{7 \cdot 5} = \frac{12}{35}$

When each factor is less than **1**, the product is less than **1**.

Find **6** $\times \frac{3}{4}$.

1. If one factor is a whole number, write it as a fraction with a denominator of **1**.

$6 \times \frac{3}{4} = \frac{6}{1} \times \frac{3}{4}$

2. Multiply the numerators. Then, multiply the denominators.

$\frac{6}{1} \times \frac{3}{4} \rightarrow \frac{6 \cdot 3}{1 \cdot 4} = \frac{18}{4}$

3. Simplify if necessary.

$\frac{18}{4} = \frac{9}{2}$

$\frac{9}{2} = 4\frac{1}{2}$

When a whole number and a fraction less than 1 are multiplied, the product is less than the whole number.

Write the product in simplest form.

1.	$\frac{2}{3} \times \frac{5}{7} =$ $\frac{10}{21}$	$\frac{12}{13} \times \frac{1}{5} =$ $\frac{12}{65}$	$8 \times \frac{2}{5} =$ $3\frac{1}{5}$
2.	$\frac{7}{8} \times 5 =$ $4\frac{3}{8}$	$\frac{3}{4} \times \frac{8}{9} =$ $\frac{2}{3}$	$\frac{14}{15} \times 2 =$ $1\frac{13}{15}$
3.	$\frac{6}{10} \times \frac{4}{5} =$ $\frac{12}{25}$	$7 \times \frac{3}{5} =$ $4\frac{1}{5}$	$\frac{1}{2} \times \frac{1}{2} =$ $\frac{1}{4}$

Check Understanding *How can you simplify $\frac{2}{3} \times \frac{15}{22}$ before multiplying?* (Divide out 2 from 2 and 22. Divide out 3 from 3 and 15, leaving $\frac{1}{1} \times \frac{5}{11} = \frac{5}{11}$.)

Sometimes you can simplify before multiplying.

Find $\frac{3}{4} \times \frac{1}{9}$.

1. Divide a numerator and a denominator by a common factor before multiplying.

$\frac{\overset{1}{\cancel{3}}}{4} \times \frac{1}{\underset{3}{\cancel{9}}}$

Divide by **3**.

2. Multiply.

$\frac{1}{4} \times \frac{1}{3} = \frac{1}{12}$

Find $3\frac{7}{8} \times 3\frac{1}{5}$.

1. Round to the nearest whole number to estimate.

$3\frac{7}{8} \times 3\frac{1}{5}$

close to **4**

close to **3**

4×3

The product is close to **12**.

2. Rewrite mixed numbers as fractions.

$3\frac{7}{8} \times 3\frac{1}{5} = \frac{31}{8} \times \frac{16}{5}$

3. Divide a numerator and a denominator by a common factor. Then multiply.

$\frac{31}{\underset{1}{\cancel{8}}} \times \frac{\overset{2}{\cancel{16}}}{5} = \frac{62}{5}$

4. Simplify. Check that your answer is reasonable.

$\frac{62}{5} = 12\frac{2}{5}$

The actual product is close to the estimate. The answer is reasonable.

Round to the nearest whole number. Estimate the product.

4. $4\frac{1}{5} \times 5\frac{1}{3} =$ 20 $\qquad \frac{3}{8} \times 3\frac{4}{5} =$ 2 $\qquad \frac{5}{6} \times \frac{7}{8} =$ 1

Try to simplify before multiplying. Write the product in simplest form.

5. $\frac{1}{2} \times \frac{2}{5} = \frac{1}{5}$ $\qquad \frac{5}{6} \times \frac{3}{20} = \frac{1}{8}$ $\qquad \frac{5}{12} \times 108 =$ 45

6. $4\frac{1}{5} \times 5\frac{1}{3} = 22\frac{2}{5}$ $\qquad 10 \times 1\frac{3}{5} =$ 16 $\qquad 3\frac{1}{4} \times 2\frac{2}{3} = 8\frac{2}{3}$

7. $3\frac{3}{4} \times \frac{2}{7} = 1\frac{1}{14}$ $\qquad 5\frac{1}{5} \times \frac{4}{13} = 1\frac{3}{5}$ $\qquad \frac{3}{4} \cdot \frac{15}{18} \cdot \frac{16}{20} = \frac{1}{2}$

Write the product in simplest form.

8. $\frac{2}{3} \times \frac{9}{16} = \frac{3}{8}$ $2\frac{1}{2} \times 3\frac{1}{3} = 8\frac{1}{3}$ $7\frac{1}{2} \times 1\frac{3}{5} = 12$

9. $3\frac{1}{8} \times 4 = 12\frac{1}{2}$ $\frac{7}{8} \times 2 \times 1\frac{1}{4} = 2\frac{3}{16}$ $6 \times 4\frac{1}{3} = 26$

Problem Solving Reasoning Solve.

10. Try both problems. Would you rather multiply fractions or decimals? Explain.

$4\frac{1}{2} \times 2\frac{1}{4} = 10\frac{1}{8}$ $4.5 \times 2.25 = 10.125$

Sample explanation: When using paper and pencil, using fractions involves fewer computations. When using a calculator, decimals are easier to enter.

11. Explain to your friend why you do not multiply mixed numbers as shown.

$2\frac{4}{5} \times 6\frac{1}{3} = 12\frac{4}{15}$

You cannot expect a correct answer, because you have not multiplied $\frac{4}{5}$ and 6 or 2 and $\frac{1}{3}$. So your answer will be less than the actual answer.

Quick Check

Write the sum or difference in simplest form.

12. $1\frac{3}{8} + 2\frac{6}{8} = 4\frac{1}{8}$

13. $\frac{7}{12} + \frac{2}{3} = 1\frac{1}{4}$

14. $3\frac{5}{6} + 5\frac{7}{10} = 9\frac{8}{15}$

15. $4\frac{1}{5} - 3\frac{3}{5} = \frac{3}{5}$

16. $\frac{3}{4} - \frac{1}{3} = \frac{5}{12}$

17. $2\frac{2}{5} - 1\frac{1}{2} = \frac{9}{10}$

Write the product in simplest form.

18. $\frac{2}{3} \times \frac{7}{8} = \frac{7}{12}$ **19.** $4 \times \frac{5}{6} = 3\frac{1}{3}$ **20.** $3\frac{1}{3} \times 2\frac{2}{5} = 8$

Work Space.

Item	Error Analysis
12–14	**Common Error:** Watch for students who do not regroup fractions that are greater than 1. **Skills Tutorial** Strand 6A: Skills 1–5
15–17	**Common Error:** Watch for students who do not regroup before subtracting. **Skills Tutorial** Strand 6B: Skills 1–6
18–20	**Common Error:** Watch for students who factor two numerators or two denominators to simplify. **Skills Tutorial** Strand 7A: Skills 1–5

Closing the Lesson *Explain how to multiply two mixed numbers.* (Change the mixed numbers to fractions, simplify if possible, multiply the numerators, multiply the denominators, and simplify if needed.)

Name ______________________

Guided Practice: First ex. in Rows 1, 7 & 11, pp. 62–64
Independent Practice: Complete pp. 62–64

Dividing Fractions and Mixed Numbers

Reciprocals

Two numbers are **reciprocals** if their product is **1**.

$\frac{1}{4}$ and **4** are reciprocals because $\frac{1}{4} \times \frac{4}{1} = \frac{4}{4}$ **or 1.**

$\frac{2}{5}$ and $2\frac{1}{2}$ are reciprocals because $\frac{2}{5} \times \frac{5}{2} = \frac{10}{10}$ **or 1.**

$4\frac{1}{3}$ and $\frac{3}{13}$ are reciprocals because $\frac{13}{3} \times \frac{3}{13} = \frac{39}{39}$ **or 1.**

Dividing Fractions

To divide fractions, multiply the first fraction by the reciprocal of the second fraction.

Divide: $\frac{6}{8} \div \frac{3}{8}$

$\frac{6}{8} \div \frac{3}{8} \rightarrow \frac{\cancel{6}^{2}}{\cancel{8}_{1}} \times \frac{\cancel{8}^{1}}{\cancel{3}_{1}} = 2$

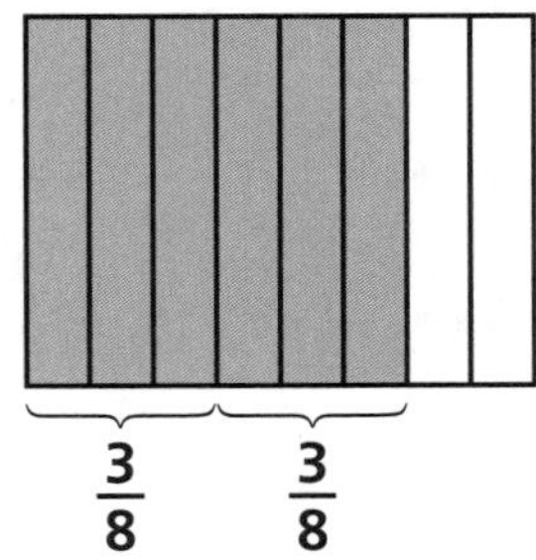

There are two groups of $\frac{3}{8}$ in $\frac{6}{8}$.

Divide: $\frac{5}{9} \div \frac{2}{3}$

$\frac{5}{9} \div \frac{2}{3} = \frac{5}{\cancel{9}_{3}} \times \frac{\cancel{3}^{1}}{2}$ or $\frac{5}{6}$

reciprocals

Divide: $\frac{4}{5} \div \frac{8}{15}$

$\frac{4}{5} \div \frac{8}{15} = \frac{\cancel{4}^{1}}{\cancel{5}_{1}} \times \frac{\cancel{15}^{3}}{\cancel{8}_{2}} \rightarrow \frac{3}{2} = 1\frac{1}{2}$

Write the quotient in simplest form.

1. $\frac{7}{9} \div \frac{2}{3} =$ $1\frac{1}{6}$ $\qquad$ $\frac{6}{7} \div \frac{4}{7} =$ $1\frac{1}{2}$ $\qquad$ $\frac{3}{7} \div \frac{21}{5} =$ $\frac{5}{49}$

2. $\frac{1}{5} \div \frac{1}{6} =$ $1\frac{1}{5}$ $\qquad$ $\frac{1}{2} \div \frac{1}{3} =$ $1\frac{1}{2}$ $\qquad$ $\frac{5}{7} \div \frac{10}{12} =$ $\frac{6}{7}$

3. $\frac{3}{4} \div \frac{3}{8} =$ 2 $\qquad$ $\frac{3}{8} \div \frac{3}{4} =$ $\frac{1}{2}$ $\qquad$ $\frac{2}{5} \div \frac{3}{10} =$ $1\frac{1}{3}$

4. $\frac{5}{6} \div \frac{5}{12} =$ 2 $\qquad$ $\frac{5}{12} \div \frac{5}{6} =$ $\frac{1}{2}$ $\qquad$ $\frac{1}{3} \div \frac{1}{4} =$ $1\frac{1}{3}$

Check Understanding *What is the meaning of 20 ÷ 5?* (How many 5's in 20. Answer: 4) *What is the meaning of* $\frac{3}{4} \div \frac{2}{5}$*?* (How many $\frac{2}{5}$'s in $\frac{3}{4}$. Answer: $1\frac{7}{8}$)

Dividing Mixed Numbers

To divide mixed numbers, rewrite each as a fraction first.

Divide: $2\frac{1}{3} \div 1\frac{2}{5}$

Round to the nearest whole number to estimate: $2 \div 1 = 2$

1. Rewrite as fractions.

   $2\frac{1}{3} \div 1\frac{2}{5} = \frac{7}{3} \div \frac{7}{5}$

2. Rewrite using multiplication and the reciprocal of the divisor.

   $\frac{7}{3} \div \frac{7}{5} = \frac{7}{3} \times \frac{5}{7}$

3. Multiply. Simplify first if you can.

   $\frac{\cancel{7}^{1}}{3} \times \frac{5}{\cancel{7}_{1}} = \frac{5}{3}$

4. Simplify.

   $\frac{5}{3} = 1\frac{2}{3}$

   So there are $1\frac{2}{3}$ groups of $1\frac{2}{5}$ in $2\frac{1}{3}$.

Other Example

Divide: $3\frac{1}{3} \div \frac{5}{9}$

Estimate: $3 \div \frac{1}{2} \rightarrow 3 \times 2 = 6$

$3\frac{1}{3} \div \frac{5}{9} \rightarrow \frac{10}{3} \div \frac{5}{9} \rightarrow \frac{\cancel{10}^{2}}{\cancel{3}_{1}} \times \frac{\cancel{9}^{3}}{\cancel{5}_{1}} = \frac{6}{1}$ or 6

So there are 6 groups of $\frac{5}{9}$ in $3\frac{1}{3}$.

Round to the nearest whole number. Estimate the quotient.

5. $4\frac{1}{3} \div 2\frac{1}{5}$ 2 $\qquad 4\frac{7}{8} \div 2\frac{1}{2}$ 2 $\qquad 10\frac{2}{3} \div 3\frac{1}{3}$ 3

6. $2\frac{1}{5} \div 4\frac{1}{3}$ $\frac{1}{2}$ $\qquad 5\frac{5}{6} \div 3$ 2 $\qquad 8\frac{5}{8} \div \frac{7}{8}$ 9

Write the quotient in simplest form. Check that your answer is reasonable.

7. $3\frac{1}{3} \div \frac{5}{9} =$ 6 $\qquad 2\frac{2}{5} \div 1\frac{2}{3} =$ $1\frac{11}{25}$ $\qquad 1\frac{1}{2} \div 2\frac{2}{5} =$ $\frac{5}{8}$

8. $2\frac{2}{3} \div \frac{8}{9} =$ 3 $\qquad 4\frac{1}{2} \div \frac{1}{4} =$ 18 $\qquad 1\frac{1}{4} \div 4\frac{1}{2} =$ $\frac{5}{18}$

9. $5\frac{1}{4} \div \frac{7}{16} =$ 12 $\qquad 2\frac{2}{3} \div 1\frac{6}{7} =$ $1\frac{17}{39}$ $\qquad \frac{1}{2} \div 1\frac{1}{6} =$ $\frac{3}{7}$

When you divide a whole number and a fraction, rewrite the whole number as a fraction with a denominator of 1. Divide as usual.

Divide: $10 \div \frac{5}{6}$

$$10 \div \frac{5}{6} \rightarrow \frac{10}{1} \div \frac{5}{6} \rightarrow \frac{\overset{2}{\cancel{10}}}{1} \times \frac{6}{\underset{1}{\cancel{5}}} \text{ or } \frac{12}{1} \text{ or } 12$$

Divide: $4\frac{2}{3} \div 8$

$$4\frac{2}{3} \div 8 \rightarrow \frac{14}{3} \div \frac{8}{1} \rightarrow \frac{\overset{7}{\cancel{14}}}{3} \times \frac{1}{\underset{4}{\cancel{8}}} = \frac{7}{12}$$

Write the quotient in simplest form.

10. $\frac{3}{5} \div 3 =$ $\frac{1}{5}$ $\qquad \frac{8}{11} \div 2 =$ $\frac{4}{11}$ $\qquad 6\frac{1}{3} \div 6 =$ $1\frac{1}{18}$

11. $7 \div 1\frac{3}{4} =$ 4 $\qquad 18 \div \frac{9}{10} =$ 20 $\qquad 5 \div \frac{1}{10} =$ 50

12. $4\frac{1}{2} \div 4 =$ $1\frac{1}{8}$ $\qquad 4 \div 4\frac{1}{2} =$ $\frac{8}{9}$ $\qquad \frac{1}{10} \div 5 =$ $\frac{1}{50}$

Problem Solving Reasoning Solve.

13. You live $\frac{3}{4}$ mile from school. Tiffany lives 3 miles from school. How many times as far from school does Tiffany live than you?

4 times as far

14. Todd has $12\frac{1}{2}$ feet of string. It takes $1\frac{1}{3}$ feet to make a key chain. How many can he make?

9 key chains

Test Prep ★ Mixed Review

15 $\frac{9}{10} + \frac{1}{6} =$ A; Obj. 2A

A $\frac{32}{30}$

B $\frac{10}{60}$

C $\frac{9}{16}$

D $\frac{10}{16}$

16 Which is the correct order from least to greatest? $\frac{3}{4}$, 0.35, 0.78, $\frac{3}{5}$ G; Obj. 2F

F $\frac{3}{4}$, $\frac{4}{5}$, 0.35, 0.78

G 0.35, $\frac{3}{5}$, $\frac{3}{4}$, 0.78

H 0.35, 0.78, $\frac{3}{4}$, $\frac{3}{5}$

J $\frac{3}{5}$, 0.35, $\frac{3}{4}$, 0.78

Closing the Lesson *How do you divide a mixed number by a mixed number?* (Write each mixed number as a fraction, and then write a multiplication sentence using the reciprocal of the divisor. Remember to simplify, if possible, before multiplying. Simplify the result also, if possible.)

Name ______________________________

Guided Practice: Problem 3, p. 65
Independent Practice: Complete pp. 65–66

Problem Solving Strategy: Draw a Diagram

To solve some problems, you may want to draw a diagram to help you think about the many possibilities.

You can draw a picture. Label information you know. Analyze the information.

Problem

Placing toothpicks end-to-end, how many different rectangles can you make using 12 toothpicks? A rectangle with a length of 1 and a width of 2 is the same rectangle as one with a length of 2 and a width of 1.

1 Understand

"Think about the units of measure we usually use. What is our unit of measure in this problem?"

As you reread, ask yourself questions.

- What do you know about the toothpicks?
  You have **12** toothpicks.
  The toothpicks will be placed end-to-end to form a rectangle.
  The perimeter of the rectangle will be **12** "toothpicks."
- What information do you already know?
  A rectangle has **4** sides.
- What do you need to find? How many different rectangles have a perimeter of 12 toothpicks.

2 Decide

"Why is it important to draw all the toothpicks the same length?"

Choose a method for solving.

Try the Draw a Diagram strategy.

- What will your first diagram be?
- How many toothpicks are used in this rectangle? 12

3 Solve

"How can you organize your drawings?"

Draw additional diagrams to solve the problem.

Organize your approach so that you do not miss any rectangles and that you don't draw the same rectangle more than once.

4 Look back

"Make sure you have used each rectangle just once."

Check that you have answered the question.

How many different rectangles did you draw? List the length and width of each.

Length	4	3	5
Width	2	3	1

How did drawing a picture help you solve the problem?

You can see that the shorter side can only have lengths of 1, 2, or 3.

Check Understanding *In the problem solving steps, what does the step "Decide" mean?* (Decide on a method you will use to solve the problem.)

Use the Draw a Diagram strategy or any other strategy you have learned to solve these problems.

1. What is the perimeter of each of the rectangles you drew on the previous page? What is the area of each rectangle?

Think: Do you have to compute the perimeter to complete the table?

No; The perimeter is always 12.

Length	Width	Perimeter	Area
5	1	12	5
4	2	12	8
3	3	12	9

2. The diagram below shows the first four square numbers. What are the next two square numbers? 25, 36

Think: Is there a pattern in the arrangement of dots and numbers?

The dots are arranged in squares; the numbers are the square numbers.

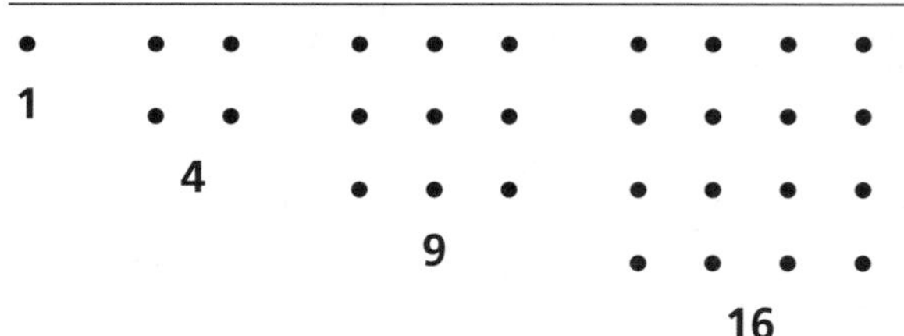

3. Before lunch there was $\frac{7}{8}$ gallon of milk in the refrigerator. After lunch there was $\frac{1}{4}$ gallon left. How much milk was drunk at lunch? $\frac{5}{8}$ gal

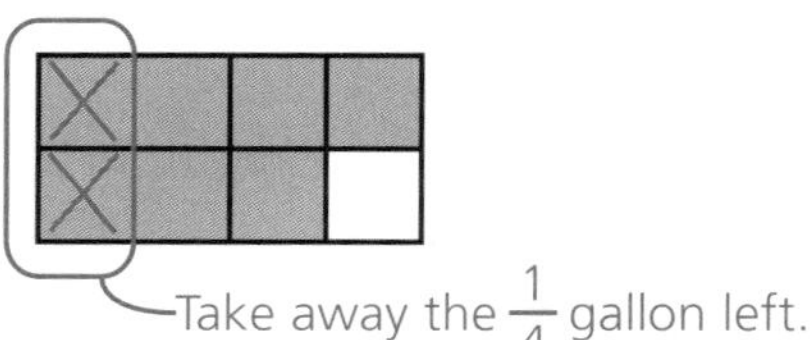

4. While helping to take inventory at the department store, Antonio worked $2\frac{1}{2}$ hours on Monday and $1\frac{3}{4}$ hours on Tuesday. How much longer did he work on Monday? $\frac{3}{4}$ h

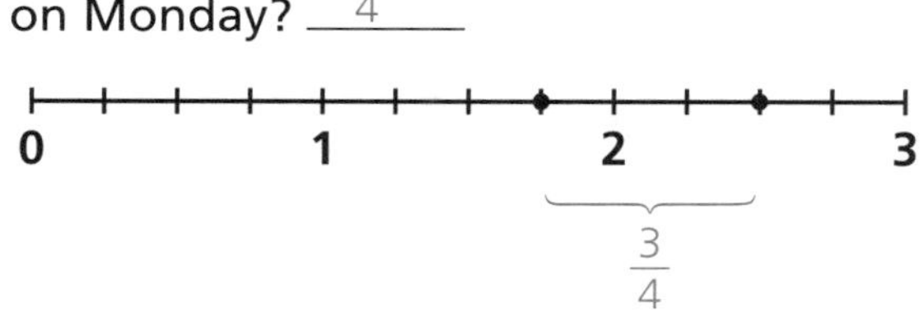

5. Your family buys a **3**-pound bag of Golden Delicious apples for **$2.29**. Your aunt bought a pound of Macintosh apples for **$.79** a pound. Which is the better buy? Explain.

The 3-lb bag, because $2.29 ÷ 3 = $.76 per pound, which is less than $.79

6. In January, you measured **108.3** cm and your brother was **97.8** cm. In December, you were **111.7** cm and your brother was **101.1** cm. Who grew more during the year? Explain.

You did. You grew 111.7 − 108.3 = 3.4 cm. Your brother grew 101.1 − 97.8 = 3.3 cm.

7. How many different squares are in this figure? (Hint: the squares can be different sizes.)

14 squares

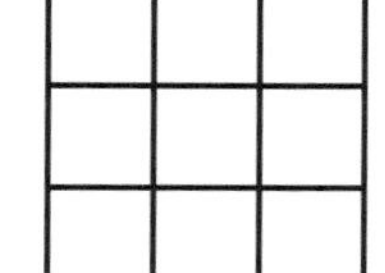

8. Is it possible to trace the figure shown without lifting your pencil from the paper, and without tracing over any line more than once?

Yes; One path is shown.

Closing the Lesson *When might you want to use this strategy?* (Answers will vary: When there are many possibilities and drawing a picture will help you organize those possibilities or when geometric figures or measurements are involved.)

Name ______________________

Guided Practice: First ex. in Rows 1 & 5, pp. 67–68
Independent Practice: Complete pp. 67–68

Expressions with Fractions and Decimals

You reviewed operations with fractions and decimals in this unit. You can simplify expressions with fractions and decimals just as you do expressions with whole numbers.

Order of Operations

1. Perform all operations within parentheses first.
2. Evaluate all powers.
3. Multiply and divide from left to right.
4. Finally, add and subtract from left to right.

Simplify: $\left(\frac{4}{5}\right)^2 - \frac{3}{10} \times \frac{2}{5}$

Original problem	$\left(\frac{4}{5}\right)^2 - \frac{3}{10} \times \frac{2}{5}$
Evaluate powers and multiply.	$\frac{16}{25} - \frac{3}{25}$
Subtract.	$\frac{16}{25} - \frac{3}{25} \rightarrow \frac{13}{25}$

Simplify: 3.4(8 + 2.04)

Original problem	**3.4(8 + 2.04)**
Add inside parentheses.	**3.4(10.04)**
Multiply.	**3.4 × 10.04 → 34.136**

Simplify. Write answers in simplest form.

1. $4.2^2 - 3.1^2$ 8.03 $3(12.05 - 8.9)$ 9.45 $14.8 + 2.1 \times 4$ 23.2

2. $\frac{3}{5} + 4 \times \frac{1}{8}$ $1\frac{1}{10}$ $6\frac{2}{3} - 2\frac{1}{2} + 3$ $7\frac{1}{6}$ $\frac{4}{9} + \left(\frac{2}{3}\right)^2$ $\frac{8}{9}$

3. $12.6 \div 0.2 \times 0.03$ 1.89 $(4 + 0.07)^2$ 16.5649 $(12 - 5.5) \times \frac{1}{2}$ 3.25

4. $3(3^2 - 2.2) \div \frac{2}{5}$ 51 $\frac{3}{4} \div 1\frac{1}{2} + \frac{3}{4} \times 1\frac{1}{2}$ $1\frac{5}{8}$ $(2 + 3 \times 4)^2 - 24$ 172

Check Understanding *What is the function of parentheses in an expression?* (Parentheses tell you to perform the operation within parentheses first.)

To evaluate algebraic expressions, substitute for the variable and simplify.

Evaluate: $3.1x + 2x$. Use $x = 1.5$.

Original problem	$3.1x + 2x$
Substitute $x = 1.5$.	$3.1(1.5) + 2(1.5)$
Multiply and add.	$4.65 + 3.0 \rightarrow 7.65$

Evaluate: $y^2 + 3y$. Use $y = \frac{3}{4}$.

Original problem	$y^2 + 3y$
Substitute $y = \frac{3}{4}$.	$\left(\frac{3}{4}\right)^2 + 3\left(\frac{3}{4}\right)$
Evaluate powers and multiply.	$\frac{9}{16} + \frac{9}{4}$
Add. Use the LCD of 16.	$\frac{9}{16} + \frac{36}{16} \rightarrow \frac{45}{16} \rightarrow 2\frac{13}{16}$

Evaluate. Let $a = 0.04$, $b = \frac{1}{3}$, and $c = 6$.

5. $\frac{c}{8} + 7$ $7\frac{3}{4}$ $\qquad$ $5b + 1$ $2\frac{2}{3}$ $\qquad$ $10a + 6.5$ 6.9

6. $a \div 8 \cdot c$ 0.03 $\qquad$ $3.2c + 1.5c$ 28.2 $\qquad$ $\frac{6}{5}b + \frac{3}{5}b$ $\frac{3}{5}$

7. $2(a + c)$ 12.08 $\qquad$ $b \cdot c + a$ 2.04 $\qquad$ $200a - c$ 2

Problem Solving Reasoning Solve.

8. Curtis simplified $0.8 \div 0.2 \times 0.04$ and got 10. Latoya simplified and got 1.6. Is either correct? Explain.

No; You need to work from left to right.

$\underbrace{0.8 \div 0.2}_{4} \times 0.04$

$4 \times 0.04 = 0.16$

9. When Max evaluated a^2 for $a = \frac{4}{5}$ he got $\frac{8}{10}$. Explain how Max went wrong.

He doubled both the numerator and denominator, instead of multiplying them by themselves.

Test Prep ★ Mixed Review

10 What is the greatest common factor of 20, 28, and 36? B; Obj. 2B

A 2

B 4

C 8

D 18

11 $5k + 7(k + 8) =$ H; Obj. 2D

F $12k + 8$

G 68

H $12k + 56$

J $68k$

Closing the Lesson *In what order are the operations to be done in an expression?* (Work in parentheses, simplify powers, multiply and divide in order from left to right, add and subtract in order from left to right.)

Name ____________________

Guided Practice: First ex. in Rows 1 & 5, pp. 69–70
Independent Practice: Complete pp. 69–70

Solving Equations with Fractions and Decimals

You have solved equations with whole numbers. You can solve equations with fractions and decimals as you do with whole numbers.

Properties of Equality

Equivalent equations can be formed by

- adding the same number to both sides of an equation.
- subtracting the same number from both sides of an equation.
- multiplying both sides of an equation by the same non-zero number.
- dividing both sides of an equation by the same non-zero number.

Solve: $n + \frac{2}{5} = \frac{3}{4}$

Original equation	$n + \frac{2}{5} = \frac{3}{4}$
Subtract $\frac{2}{5}$ from both sides.	$n + \frac{2}{5} - \frac{2}{5} = \frac{3}{4} - \frac{2}{5}$
Use an LCD of **20**. Simplify.	$n = \frac{7}{20}$

Solve: $a - 2.7 = 9.04$

Original equation	$a - 2.7 = 9.04$
Add **2.7** to both sides.	$a - 2.7 + 2.7 = 9.04 + 2.7$
Simplify.	$a = 11.74$

Solve. Write the answers in simplest form.

1. $x - \frac{2}{3} = \frac{1}{4}$ $x = \frac{11}{12}$ — $n + \frac{4}{5} = 2\frac{1}{2}$ $n = 1\frac{7}{10}$ — $w - 2\frac{1}{5} = 6$ $w = 8\frac{1}{5}$

2. $n + 3.8 = 10$ $n = 6.2$ — $x - 2.06 = 6.1$ $x = 8.16$ — $t + 0.4 = 8.1$ $t = 7.7$

3. $x + 10\frac{2}{3} = 15$ $x = 4\frac{1}{3}$ — $3.02 + h = 8$ $h = 4.98$ — $x - 4.02 = 9.8$ $x = 13.82$

4. $w - 5.2 = .003$ $w = 5.203$ — $m - 2\frac{2}{5} = 7\frac{1}{3}$ $m = 9\frac{11}{15}$ — $n - 4\frac{1}{2} = 8.5$ $n = 13$

Check Understanding *In the equation $x - 5.3 = 8.25$, what should I do to solve it?* (Add 5.3 to both sides and simplify.) *What should I do to solve the equation $(\frac{3}{4})p = 6$?* (Multiply both sides by $\frac{4}{3}$ and simplify.)

Some equations involve multiplication and division. Use what you know about reciprocals to solve them.

Solve: $\frac{4}{5}x = 8$

Original equation	$\frac{4}{5}x = 8$
Multiply by $\frac{5}{4}$.	$\frac{\cancel{5}^1}{\cancel{4}_1} \cdot \frac{\cancel{4}^1}{\cancel{5}_1}x = \frac{5}{4} \cdot 8$
Simplify.	$x = 10$

Solve: $\frac{n}{1.4} = 8.6$

Original equation	$\frac{n}{1.4} = 8.6$
Multiply by **1.4**.	$\frac{\cancel{1.4}^1}{1} \cdot \frac{n}{\cancel{1.4}_1} = (1.4)(8.6)$
Simplify.	$n = 12.04$

Solve.

5. $\frac{c}{8} = 7.5$ $c = 60$ $5.2b = 17.68$ $b = 3.4$ $10a = 17.02$ $a = 1.702$

6. $\frac{1}{4}a = 5$ $a = 20$ $3n = 6\frac{3}{4}$ $n = 2\frac{1}{4}$ $\frac{6}{5}b = \frac{12}{15}$ $b = \frac{2}{3}$

7. $0.04a = 1.08$ $a = 27$ $2\frac{1}{2}x = 8.75$ $x = 3.5$ $\frac{n}{0.01} = 0.5$ $n = 0.005$

Quick Check

Write the quotient in simplest form.

8. $\frac{3}{4} \div \frac{1}{2}$ $1\frac{1}{2}$ **9.** $10 \div \frac{5}{6}$ 12 **10.** $2\frac{3}{4} \div 1\frac{1}{3}$ $2\frac{1}{16}$

Evaluate the expression for $a = 1.2$ and $b = \frac{3}{4}$.

11. $2(a + 3b)$ 6.9 **12.** $1.5a - 0.1b$ 1.725 **13.** $\frac{b}{6} + \frac{5}{6}a$ 1.125

Solve the equation.

14. $4.06 + j = 9$ $j = 4.94$ **15.** $n - 1\frac{5}{8} = 3\frac{1}{6}$ $n = 4\frac{19}{24}$

16. $4k = 1\frac{2}{3}$ $k = \frac{5}{12}$ **17.** $0.2a = 0.98$ $a = 4.9$

Work Space.

Item	Error Analysis
8–10	**Common Error:** Watch for students who cannot write the reciprocal of a mixed number. **Skills Tutorial** Strand 7B: Skills 1–5
11–13	**Common Error:** Watch for students who do not use the order of operations correctly. **Reteaching** Reteach 13
14–17	**Common Error:** Watch for students who do not use the correct inverse operation. **Reteaching** Reteach 14

Closing the Lesson *What is the secret to solving one-step linear equations?* (Apply the inverse operation to both sides of the equation and simplify.)

Name ______________________

Write the sum or difference.

1. $3.6 + 0.98 + 3.004 =$ 7.584
2. $\frac{2}{3} + \frac{3}{4} =$ $1\frac{5}{12}$
3. $1\frac{1}{6} + 2\frac{3}{8} =$ $3\frac{13}{24}$
4. $9.5 - 6.622 =$ 2.878
5. $\frac{9}{10} - \frac{1}{6} =$ $\frac{11}{15}$
6. $4\frac{5}{9} - 1\frac{1}{3} =$ $3\frac{2}{9}$

Write the product or quotient.

7. $6.4 \times 0.08 =$ 0.512
8. $\frac{2}{3} \times \frac{5}{8} =$ $\frac{5}{12}$
9. $3\frac{3}{4} \times 1\frac{3}{5} =$ 6
10. $10.5 \div 0.15 =$ 70
11. $\frac{5}{6} \div \frac{1}{5} =$ $4\frac{1}{6}$
12. $2\frac{2}{3} \div 1\frac{3}{5} =$ $1\frac{2}{3}$

Write the greatest common factor (GCF) or the least common multiple (LCM) of the numbers.

13. 6 and 10; GCF 2
14. 6 and 18; LCM 18
15. 20, 24, and 36; GCF 4

Write three equivalent fractions for the fraction. Possible answers are given.

16. $\frac{5}{6}$ $\frac{10}{12}, \frac{15}{18}, \frac{20}{24}$
17. $\frac{3}{8}$ $\frac{6}{16}, \frac{9}{24}, \frac{12}{32}$
18. $\frac{12}{15}$ $\frac{4}{5}, \frac{8}{10}, \frac{24}{30}$

Evaluate the expression. Use $a = 0.4$, $b = \frac{3}{4}$, and $c = 8$.

19. $3(a + c)$ 25.2
20. $1.5a + 2.5c$ 20.6
21. $\frac{5}{6}b - \frac{1}{2}a$ 0.425 or $\frac{17}{40}$

Solve.

22. Four friends live on the same street, shown at the right. Yan lives **1.8** miles from Roberta, and Leon lives **2.3** miles from Ilse. The greatest distance between any two friends is **3.9** miles. Which two friends live nearest to each other? How far are they from each other?

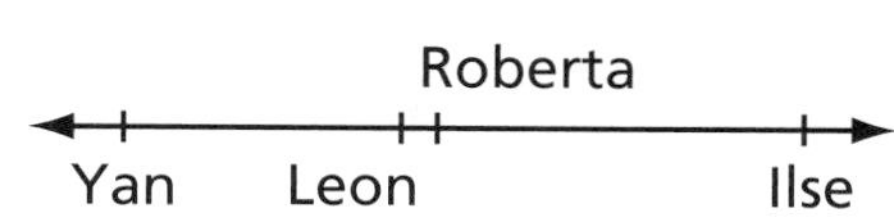

Leon and Roberta are closest. They are 0.2 miles apart.

Name ______________________________

Cumulative Review ★ Test Prep

1

"This winter, Middleton's December snowfall totaled $3\frac{3}{8}$ inches, and January's total of $12\frac{1}{4}$ inches was much worse."

"The average daily snowfall for the last 7 days of February was $2\frac{3}{4}$ inches."

How many more inches of snow did Middleton have in January than in December? C; Obj. 2A and 2F

A $9\frac{7}{8}$ inches C $8\frac{7}{8}$ inches

B $9\frac{5}{8}$ inches D $8\frac{5}{8}$ inches

2 What was the total snowfall in Middleton during the last seven days of February? G; Obj. 2A and 1A

F 23 inches H $9\frac{3}{4}$ inches

G $19\frac{1}{4}$ inches J $2\frac{3}{4}$ inches

3 The prime factorization of 90 is? B; Obj. 2B

A $2 \times 5 \times 9$

B $2 \times 3^2 \times 5$

C $2 \times 2^3 \times 5$

D 9×10

4 Lajoia scored 35 points on each of her vocabulary tests. She has a total of 385 points. Which equation could be used to find the number of vocabulary tests Lajoia has taken? J; Obj. 1F

F $385 \times 35 = n$

G $35 \div n = 385$

H $35 \times 385 = n$

J $385 \div 35 = n$

5 $n - 189 = 215$

What would be the first step you would use in finding the value of n? A; Obj. 1D

A Add 189 to both sides.

B Add 215 to both sides.

C Subtract 189 from both sides.

D Subtract 215 from both sides.

6 When Scott was asked how long he spent on his "fraction-math" project, he answered that he spent the reciprocal of $\frac{4}{7}$ hour. How long did he spend on the project? J; Obj. 2E

F $\frac{4}{7}$ hr H $1\frac{4}{7}$ hr

G $\frac{3}{4}$ hr J $1\frac{3}{4}$ hr

7 A cake is cut into 12 equal slices. Four slices have roses on them. What decimal shows the part of the cake that does not have roses? D; Obj. 2J

A 0.25 C 0.6 E Not here

B 0.3 D 0.67

UNIT 3 • TABLE OF CONTENTS

Measurement

We will be using this vocabulary:

meter a standard unit of length in the metric system (A meter is a little longer than a yard.)

liter a standard unit of capacity in the metric system (A liter is a little greater than a quart.)

gram a standard unit of mass in the metric system (The mass of a raisin is about a gram.)

Celsius scale a metric temperature scale in which the boiling temperature of water is **100**°C and the freezing temperature of water is **0**°C

Fahrenheit scale a customary temperature scale in which the boiling temperature of water is **212**°F and the freezing temperature of water is **32**°F

24-hour clock a clock scale that starts and ends at midnight; for example, **1430** means it is **14** hours and **30** minutes after midnight (**0000**), or **2:30** P.M.

Dear Family,

During the next few weeks, our math class will be studying units of measure in both the metric and customary systems of measure. This unit includes units of length, capacity, mass or weight, area, volume, time, and temperature. You can expect to see homework that provides practice with these skills. Here is a sample you may want to keep handy to give help if needed.

Finding Equivalent Measures

To change from a larger unit of measure to a smaller unit of measure, you need to multiply.

2.5 square feet = ___?___ square inches

2.5 × 144 = 360

Think: 1 square foot = 144 square inches. Since a square inch is smaller in area than a square foot, you need more of them.

2.5 square feet = 360 square inches

To change from a smaller unit of measure to a larger unit of measure, you need to divide.

436.5 cm = _?_ m

436.5 ÷ 100 = 4.365

Think: 1 m = 100 cm. Since a meter is longer than a centimeter, you need fewer of them.

436.5 cm = 4.365 m

During this unit, students will continue to learn new techniques related to problem solving and will continue to practice basic skills with fractions and decimals.

Sincerely,

Name ____________________

Metric Units of Length

Guided Practice: Ex.1, 5, 11, & 13, pp. 75–76
Independent Practice: Complete pp. 75–76

The basic, or standard, unit of length in the metric system is the **meter (m)**. Look at the chart. Notice how the prefix of each unit of measure tells you how that unit is related to the meter. Notice, also, that each unit is **10** times greater than the next lesser unit.

Measurement	Symbol	Meaning	Familiar Approximations
kilometer	km	**1,000** meters	**11** football fields end to end
hectometer	hm	**100** meters	little more than a football field
dekameter	dam	**10** meters	width of a two lane street
meter	m	**1** meter	height of a kitchen sink
decimeter	dm	**0.1** meter	length of a new piece of chalk
centimeter	cm	**0.01** meter	width of your index finger
millimeter	mm	**0.001** meter	thickness of a dime

What metric unit of length (km, m, cm, or mm) would you use to measure the item?

1. distance from home to school __km__ distance around your waist __cm__

2. thickness of a pencil eraser __mm__ distance run by a marathon runner __km__

3. width of the head of a nail __mm__ your height __cm__

4. length of the school hall __m__ thickness of this piece of paper __mm__

Circle the best estimate of the length of each item.

5. width of a textbook
2 cm **(20 cm)** **40 cm**

6. thickness of a nickel
(2 mm) **20 mm** **40 mm**

7. height of a doorknob
(1 m) **2 m** **3 m**

8. distance from New York to California
30 km **300 km** **(3,000 km)**

9. height of milk glass
2 cm **5 cm** **(15 cm)**

10. length of average car
1 m **(5 m)** **10 m**

Use the centimeter ruler to write equivalent measures.

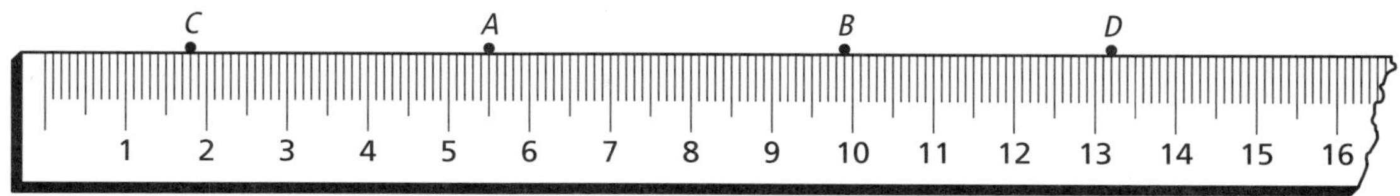

11. Point *A* = __5.5__ cm = __5__ cm __5__ mm Point *B* = __9.9__ cm = __9__ cm __9__ mm

12. Point *C* = __1.8__ cm = __1__ cm __8__ mm Point *D* = __13.2__ cm = __13__ cm __2__ mm

Check Understanding *A line segment measures 58 cm. How many millimeters is that?* (580) *About how thick is a dime?* (1 mm) *How many meters are there in a kilometer?* (1,000) *What portion of a meter is a centimeter?* (0.01)

Each metric unit of length is **10** times longer than the next shorter unit. To change from one metric unit of length to another, you multiply or divide by a power of **10**.

Larger to Smaller		**Smaller to Larger**
4 km = ___?___ m There are **1,000** m, or **10**^{3} m, in every kilometer, so multiply by **1,000.** Move the decimal point **3** places to the **right.** **4** km = **4,000** m longer unit smaller number 	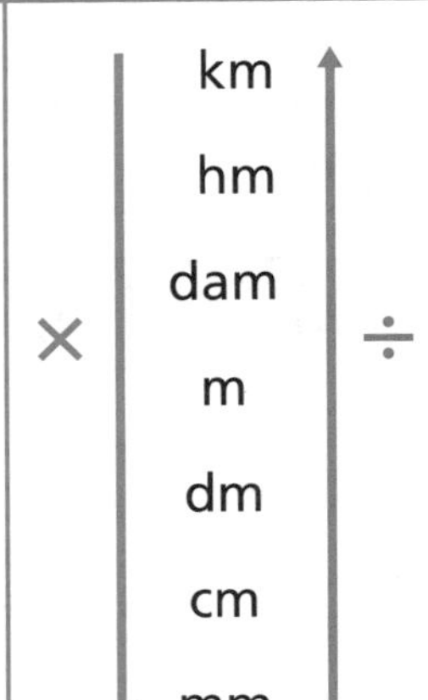 × km hm dam m dm cm mm ÷	**62** cm = ___?___ m There are **100** cm, or **10**^{2} cm, in every meter, so divide by **100.** Move the decimal point **2** places to the **left.** **62** cm = **0.62** m shorter unit larger number 

Complete.

13. **32** m = 3,200 cm | **162** mm = 16.2 cm | **500** cm = 5 m

14. **17** mm = 0.017 m | **42** km = 42,000 m | **7.3** cm = 73 mm

15. **8.2** m = 8,200 mm | **16** m = 160 dm | **3,500** cm = 35 m

16. **4.4** dm = 44 cm | **80** m = 0.08 km | **0.2** km = 200 m

17. **152** cm = 1.52 m | **8.3** m = 83 dm | **2.5** m = 250 cm

Problem Solving Reasoning Use what you know about units of length to solve.

18. Juanita used a meter stick to measure the width of her school desk. She recorded the width as **605** cm. Is this reasonable?

Explain. No; 605 cm = 6.05 m

19. Jacob walks **400** m around his block every morning. How many times would he need to walk around the block to walk **2** km?

5

Test Prep ★ Mixed Review

20 Every 5th person gets a pen. Every 7th person gets a pencil. Every 21st person gets a pad of paper. Which person is the first to get all three? C; Obj. 2B

A the 735th **C** the 105th

B the 210th **D** the 35th

21 What is the solution of the equation $a - 0.6 = 7.24$? F; Obj. 2E

F 7.84 **H** 7.18

G 7.30 **J** 6.64

Closing the Lesson *What would be an appropriate metric unit with which to measure the length of the school building?* (meters) *How many centimeters is 3.64 m?* (364 cm)

Name ______________________________

Metric Units of Capacity and Mass

Guided Practice: Ex. 1, 3, & 7, pp. 77–78
Independent Practice: Complete pp. 77–78

The standard unit of capacity in the metric system is the **liter (L).** The table below shows the most common metric units for capacity, or liquid measure. Notice how the prefix of each unit of measure tells you how that unit is related to the liter.

Remember: Capacity is the amount of liquid a container can hold.

Measurement	Symbol	Meaning	Familiar Approximations
kiloliter	kL	**1,000** liters	a wading pool
hectoliter	hL	**100** liters	a large rubbish barrel
dekaliter	daL	**10** liters	a bucket
liter	L	**1** liter	little more than a quart
deciliter	dL	**0.1** liter	capacity of a small juice glass
centiliter	cL	**0.01** liter	about **2** teaspoons
milliliter	mL	**0.001** liter	an eye dropper

Each metric unit of capacity is **10** times greater than the next lesser one. To change from one unit of capacity to another, you multiply or divide by a power of **10.**

Larger to Smaller (×)

5.2 L = __?__ mL

There are **1,000** mL, or 10^3 mL, in every liter, so multiply by **1,000.** Move the decimal point **3** places to the **right.**

5.2 L = **5,200** mL

larger unit
smaller number

Smaller to Larger (÷)

642 L = __?__ kL

There are **1,000** L, or 10^3 L, in every kiloliter, so divide by **1,000.** Move the decimal point **3** places to the **left.**

642 L = **0.642** kL

smaller unit
larger number

What metric unit (kL, L, or mL) would you use to measure the capacity?

1. gasoline in a car's tank __L__ water being held back by a dam __kL__

2. vanilla used in a recipe __mL__ oil carried on an ocean tanker __kL__

Complete.

3. **53** L = __0.053__ kL **1.62** L = __1,620__ mL **400** mL = __0.4__ L

4. **2.9** mL = __0.0029__ L **2.4** kL = __2,400__ L **8.1** cL = __81__ mL

5. **8.2** L = __8,200__ mL **160** L = __0.160__ kL **2,400** cL = __24__ L

6. **9.7** dL = __97__ cL **80** L = __80,000__ mL **0.7** kL = __700__ L

Check Understanding *If a fishtank holds 5 L of water, how many mL of water does it hold?* (5,000 mL) *If a metric ton is 1,000 kg, how many kilograms is 4.32 metric tons?* (4,320 kg)

The standard unit of mass in the metric system is the **gram (g)**. The table shows the most common metric units for measuring mass.

Measurement	Symbol	Meaning	Familiar Approximations
kilogram	kg	1,000 grams	a pair of sneakers
hectogram	hg	100 grams	little more than a pair of golf balls
dekagram	dag	10 grams	a coin
gram	g	1 gram	a raisin
decigram	dg	0.1 gram	a spider
centigram	cg	0.01 gram	a few grains of salt
milligram	mg	0.001 gram	less than a grain of salt

Each metric unit of mass is **10** times heavier than the next lighter one. To change from one unit of mass to another, you multiply or divide by a power of **10**.

- **Larger to Smaller**

  14 g = __?__ mg

  14 g = **14,000** mg

  Multiply by 10^3.

- **Smaller to Larger**

  154.6 g = __?__ kg

  154.6 g = **0.1546** kg

  Divide by 10^3.

Complete.

7. 52 g = 52,000 mg　　1.9 kg = 1,900 g　　800 mg = 0.8 g

8. 9 mg = 0.009 g　　622 g = 622,000 mg　　5.7 cg = 57 mg

9. 16.2 g = 16,200 mg　　0.3 g = 3 dg　　4,300 mg = 4.3 g

10. 150 dg = 15 g　　90 cg = 0.9 g　　0.08 kg = 80 g

Problem Solving Reasoning

Solve.

11. The capacity of a bottle of milk is **1** L. Can the milk be poured into a container with a capacity of **7** dl? Explain.

No; 7 dL < 1 L

12. A hardware store manager equally divided a **10** kg bag of nails into **500** g bags. How many bags of nails did she fill?

20

Test Prep ★ Mixed Review

13 Which expression is equivalent to $4(n + \frac{1}{2}) + \frac{1}{8} \times 2^3$? A; Obj. 2D

A $4n + 3$

B $4n + 2\frac{1}{4}$

C $4n + 1$

D 3

14 In solving $\frac{m}{3} = 0.6$ using inverse operations, what would you do first? H; Obj. 2E

F Multiply both sides by 0.6.

G Divide both sides by 0.6.

H Multiply both sides by 3.

J Divide both sides by 3.

Closing the Lesson *A container has a capacity of n liters. How many kL is that?* ($\frac{n}{1,000}$ kL) *An object has a mass of n milligrams. How many cg is that?* ($\frac{n}{10}$ cg)

Name ________________________________

Metric Units of Area and Volume

Guided Practice: First ex. in Rows 1, 3, 6 & 9, pp. 78–80
Independent Practice: Complete pp. 79–80

You know that **1** m = **100** cm, so the two squares at the right have the same area.

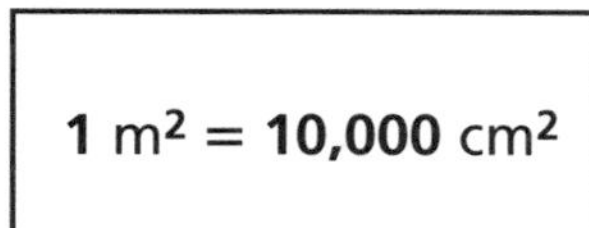

1 m^2 = **10,000** cm^2

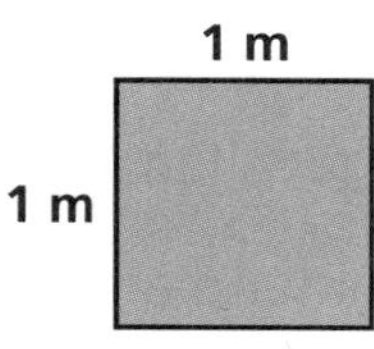

Area = **1** m^2

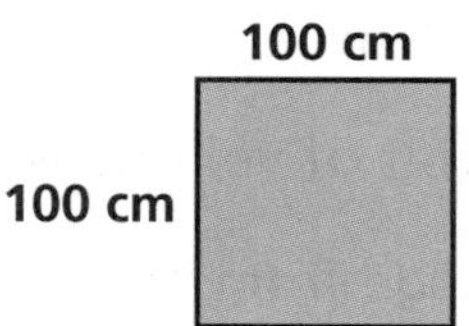

Area = **10,000** cm^2

Each metric unit of area is **100** times larger than the next smaller unit.

To change from one metric unit of area to another, you multiply or divide by a power of **100** (10^2).

Larger to Smaller

2.1 km^2 = __?__ m^2

In the chart, km^2 is **3** units above m^2. So to change from km^2 to m^2, multiply by 100^3 or **1,000,000.** Move the decimal point **6** places to the **right**.

2.1 km^2 = **2,100,000** m^2

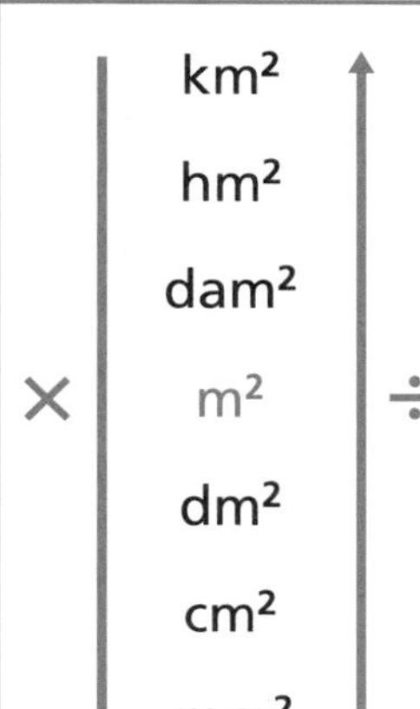

Smaller to Larger

700 cm^2 = __?__ m^2

In the chart, cm^2 is **2** units below m^2. So to change from cm^2 to m^2, divide by 100^2 or **10,000.** Move the decimal point **4** places to the **left**.

0.0700.

700 cm^2 = **0.07** m^2

What metric unit of area (km^2, m^2, cm^2, mm^2) would you use to measure the area of the item?

1. living room floor __m^2__ your state __km^2__ sheet of paper __cm^2__

2. a postage stamp __cm^2__ (or mm^2) school playground __m^2__ head of a nail __mm^2__

Complete.

3. 75 m^2 = __750,000__ cm^2 0.75 m^2 = __7,500__ cm^2 62 cm^2 = __6,200__ mm^2

4. 35 cm^2 = __0.0035__ m^2 400 mm^2 = __4__ cm^2 1.5 cm^2 = __150__ mm^2

5. 78 m^2 = __0.000078__ km^2 0.5 km^2 = __500,000__ m^2 16 mm^2 = __0.16__ cm^2

Circle the equivalent area.

6. 45 m^2 450 cm^2 4,500 cm^2 (450,000 cm^2) 45,000 cm^2

7. 5,000 mm^2 500 cm^2 (50 cm^2) 0.5 cm^2 0.05 cm^2

8. 6 km^2 6,000 m^2 600,000 m^2 (6,000,000 m^2) 60,000 m^2

Check Understanding *A floor has an area of 14 m^2. How many square centimeters is that?* (140,000 cm^2) *A refrigerator has a volume of 1,800 dm^3. How many cubic meters is that?* (1.8 m^3)

You know that **1** m = **100** cm, so the two cubes shown at the right have the same volume.

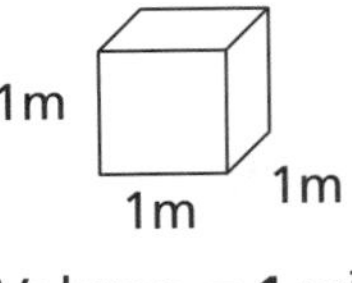

Volume = **1** m^3

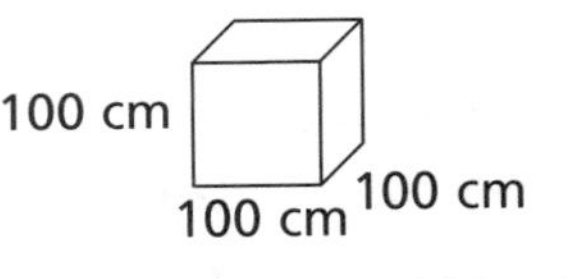

Volume = **1,000,000** cm^3

1 m^3 = **1,000,000** cm^3

Each unit of volume is **1,000** times larger than the next smaller unit.

To change from one metric unit of volume to another, you multiply or divide by a power of **1,000** (10^3).

Larger to Smaller		Smaller to Larger
0.004 km^3 = ___?___ m^3 To change from km^3 to m^3, multiply by **1,000**^{3} or **1,000,000,000**. Move the decimal point **9** places to the **right**. **0.004** km^3 = **4,000,000** m^3	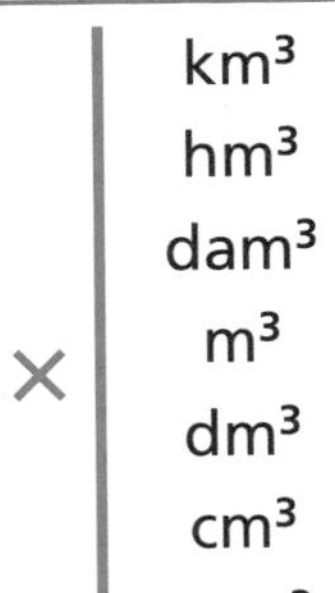 × km^3 hm^3 dam^3 m^3 dm^3 cm^3 mm^3 ÷	**2,000** cm^3 = ___?___ m^3 To change from cm^3 to m^3, divide by **1,000**^{2} or **1,000,000**. Move the decimal point **6** places to the **left**. **2,000** cm^3 = **0.002** m^3

Complete.

9. **75** cm^3 = 75,000 mm^3 **8** m^3 = 8,000,000 cm^3 **600** cm^3 = 0.6 dm^3

10. **10,000** dm^3 = 10 m^3 **1,000** m^3 = 1,000,000 dm^3 **9.7** cm^3 = 9,700 mm^3

11. **5** dm^3 = 5,000 cm^3 **0.11** m^3 = 110 dm^3 **920** mm^3 = 0.92 cm^3

Solve.

12. The volume of a box of sand is **1** dm^3. Will there be any sand left over after filling a container that has a volume of **800** cm^3? Explain.

Yes; 1 dm^3 = 1,000 cm^3

✓ Quick Check

13. **4,263** m = 4,263,000 mm

14. **5** dm **8** cm = 58 cm

15. **3** km **18** m = 3,018 m

16. **20** L = 0.02 kL

17. **2.3** mg = 0.0023 g

18. **0.15** kL = 150,000 mL

19. **92** cm^2 = 9,200 mm^2

20. **150** mm^3 = 0.15 cm^3

21. **0.4** km^3 = 400,000,000 m^3

Work Space.

Item	Error Analysis
13–15	**Common Error** Students may not multiply by the correct power of 10. **Reteaching** Reteach 17
16–21	**Common Error** Students may choose to multiply or divide incorrectly. **Reteaching** Reteach 18, 19

Closing the Lesson *Why do we multiply by 100 when changing from a larger unit of area to the next smaller unit of area?* (It takes 100 of the smaller area unit to make the next larger area unit.) *A cubic meter has how many cubic centimeters in it?* (1,000,000)

Name ____________________

Guided Practice: Problems 1 & 2, p. 81
Independent Practice: Complete p. 82

Problem Solving Application: Too Much or Too Little Information

Some problems give more facts than you may need. In a problem with many facts, it helps to identify which information is necessary for solving.

- Jan has **32** bean bag animals.
- Jan has spent **$220** for the bean bag animals.

Which facts are extra?

She keeps the bean bag animals on a 2-foot shelf.

She keeps art supplies on a 3-foot shelf.

Problem

In Jan's store, there are 32 bean bag animals on a 2-foot shelf. She keeps art supplies on a 3-foot shelf. Jan has spent a total of $220 on the bean bag animals. About what was the average cost of each bean bag animal?

Check Understanding *Can you solve the following problem, and if not, why not? "A 16-ounce bag of candy costs $2.49, and a smaller bag of candy costs only $1.79. Which bag is the better buy?"* (You need to know how many ounces the second bag contains before you can determine the better buy.)

In this lesson, you may also need to identify a missing fact that is necessary for solving.

Tips to Remember:

1. Understand	2. Decide	3. Solve	4. Look back

- Ask yourself: What do I know? What do I need to find?
- Organize facts in a list. Decide which facts are extra. Recheck your list as you solve. Is information missing?
- Think about the strategies you have learned and use them to help you solve a problem.

Cross out the extra information and then solve the problem. If the problem has information missing, list the fact or facts needed.

1. About what was the average cost to Jan for each bean-bag animal?

Think: How many animals did she buy for **$220**?

She bought 32 animals.

Answer

about $6.88

2. Mrs. Jaynes bought **3.4** pounds of chicken for **$6.28** and beef for **$4.93**. Which was the better buy?

Think: What do you need to compare?

unit price for 1 pound of each item

Answer

need to know how much beef was bought

Cross out the extra information and then solve the problem. If the problem has information missing, list the fact or facts you need.

3. A can of peas usually costs **$0.49**. How much do you save on each ~~15 oz~~ can of peas if you buy one dozen for **$5.52**?

$0.03

4. Pedro wants to buy a watch that costs **$140.** He works in the library after school. He earns **$15** per day, **$3.50** of which he saves toward the cost of the watch. How many workdays will it take for him to save **$140**?

40

5. Sarah worked 5 days for her mom. She was paid **$77.50** for working **5** days. How much was she paid per hour?

need to know how many hours she worked

6. ~~Forrest is 6 ft 4 in.~~ and just bought a new pair of ~~size 11 sneakers~~. He gave the clerk four **$20** bills to pay for the **$68** sneakers. His change was **$7.92.** How much was the sales tax on the sneakers?

$4.08

7. On Tuesday Eric picked up a prescription for **6** mL of medicine ~~that cost $12.30~~. By Saturday he had finished the bottle. If he took the same amount of medicine each day, how many mL did he take each day?

1.2 mL

8. A warehouse charged a store **$48** for 2 cartons. The first carton contained eight **12**-ounce packages, while the other contained six **1** pound packages. All cartons with the same total weight have an equal cost. How much would the store pay for a carton that has **6**-ounce packages in it?

need to know how many 6 ounce packages there are

Extend Your Thinking

9. Choose a problem in which a fact is missing. Suggest a reasonable amount for the misssing fact and then solve the problem.

Answers will vary. Possible answer: Ex. 8, there are sixteen 6-ounce packages, the cost of the carton is $24.00.

10. Explain your method for solving problem **6.** Is there more than one way to solve the problem?

Answers will vary. Possible answer:

$4 \times \$20 = \$68 + 7.92 + t$

Closing the Lesson *How can you know if a problem has too much or too little information?* (Read the problem very carefully.)

Name ____________________

Customary Units of Length

Guided Practice: First ex. in rows 1, 3, 6 & 9, pp. 83–84
Independent Practice: Complete pp. 83–84

This ruler measures to the nearest $\frac{1}{16}$-inch. Recall that sixteenths can be simplified to eighths, fourths, or halves.

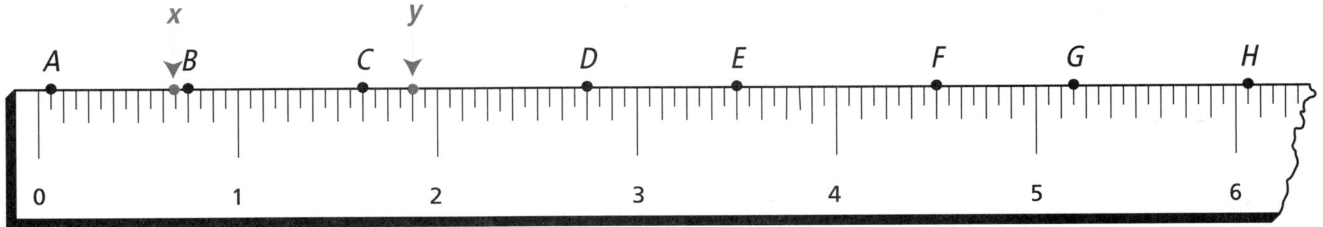

Every mark represents $\frac{1}{16}$ inch. So the distance from the zero point of the ruler to ***x*** is $\frac{11}{16}$ in. and to ***y*** *is* $1\frac{14}{16}$ in., or $1\frac{7}{8}$ in.
You may need to regroup to add or subtract units of length.

Add: **3** ft **6** in. + **2** ft **9** in.

- Add inches first. Regroup. Add feet.

6 in. + 9 in. = 15 in.

$$\begin{array}{r} {}^{1}\\ 3 \text{ ft } 6 \text{ in.} \\ + 2 \text{ ft } 9 \text{ in.} \\ \hline 6 \text{ ft } 3 \text{ in., or } 6\frac{1}{4} \text{ ft} \end{array}$$

Subtract: $9\frac{1}{4}$ ft − **6** ft **7** in.

- Regroup feet as inches. Subtract inches, then feet.

$9\frac{1}{4}$ ft = 9 ft 3 in.

$$\begin{array}{r} {}^{8}\quad\ {}^{15}\\ \not{9} \text{ ft } \not{3} \text{ in.} \\ + 6 \text{ ft } 7 \text{ in.} \\ \hline 2 \text{ ft } 8 \text{ in., or } 2\frac{2}{3} \text{ ft} \end{array}$$

Write the distance from zero to the given point in simplest form.

1. A $\frac{1}{16}$ in. B $\frac{3}{4}$ in. C $1\frac{5}{8}$ in. D $2\frac{3}{4}$ in.

2. E $3\frac{1}{2}$ in. F $4\frac{1}{2}$ in. G $5\frac{3}{16}$ in. H $6\frac{1}{16}$ in.

Write the sum or difference.

3. 7 ft 5 in. − 3 ft 2 in. = 4 ft 3 in. 5 ft 4 in. + 6 ft 5 in. = 11 ft 9 in.

4. 12 ft 9 in. + 4 ft 6 in. = 17 ft 3 in. 8 ft 5 in. − 2 ft 7 in. = 5 ft 10 in.

5. $2\frac{1}{2}$ ft − 1 ft 4 in. = 1 ft 2 in. $5\frac{1}{3}$ ft + 6 ft 9 in. = 12 ft 1 in.

Write the sum or difference. Express inches as part of a foot.

6. 3 ft + 7 ft 6 in. = $10\frac{1}{2}$ ft 4 ft 8 in. − 3 ft 2 in. = $1\frac{1}{2}$ ft

7. $5\frac{1}{4}$ ft + 3 ft 6 in. = $8\frac{3}{4}$ ft 9 ft − $2\frac{3}{4}$ ft = $6\frac{1}{4}$ ft

8. 6 ft 10 in. − 4 ft 1 in. = $2\frac{3}{4}$ ft 3 ft 8 in. + 5 ft 8 in. = $9\frac{1}{3}$ ft

Check Understanding *Into how many equal parts is each inch divided on your ruler? (16) How many $\frac{1}{16}$-inch parts are in $\frac{1}{4}$ inch? (4) How many feet are in 4 yards? (12 feet)*

To write a length using a different unit of measure, you need to know equivalent lengths.

Equivalent Lengths

12 inches = 1 foot
36 inches = 1 yard
3 feet = 1 yard
5,280 feet = 1 mile
1,760 yards = 1 mile

Larger to Smaller

$5\frac{1}{2}$ ft = ___?___ in.

1 ft = 12 in., so **multiply.**

$5\frac{1}{2} \times 12 = \frac{11}{2} \times 12$ or 66

Then, $5\frac{1}{2}$ ft = 66 in.

Smaller to Larger

38 ft = ___?___ yd

3 ft = 1 yd, so **divide.**

$$\begin{array}{r} 12\frac{2}{3} \\ 3\overline{)38} \\ \underline{36} \\ 2 \end{array}$$

Then, 38 ft = $12\frac{2}{3}$ yd.

Complete.

9. 6 ft = 72 in. $5\frac{1}{3}$ yd = 16 ft 6160 yd = $3\frac{1}{2}$ mi

10. 18 in. = $\frac{1}{2}$ yd 48 in. = 4 ft $2\frac{1}{2}$ mi = 13,200 ft

11. 2.4 mi = 12,672 ft 10.5 yd = 378 in. $1\frac{1}{4}$ mi = 2,200 yd

12. 81 ft = 27 yd $12\frac{3}{4}$ ft = 153 in. 0.2 mi = 1,056 ft

Problem Solving Reasoning Solve.

13. Last year Becca's height was 4 ft 5 in. This year her height is 57 in. How much did she grow?

4 in.

14. Jason needs 7 yd 2 ft of molding. It sells for $.68 per foot. How much will the molding cost?

$15.64

Test Prep ★ Mixed Review

15 What is the solution to the equation $3k = 2.04$? D; Obj. 2E

A 6.12
B 6.8
C 6.012
D 0.68

16 What is the volume of a small box that is 5 cm in width, 6 cm in length, and 4 cm in height? F; Obj. 3A

F 120 cm^3
G 120 cm^2
H 120 cm
J 15 cm

Closing the Lesson *From a board measuring 9 ft 3 in., you need to cut off a piece 2 ft 8 in. long and another that is 4 ft 10 in. How much of the original board will be left?* (1 ft 9 in.)

Name ________________________

Guided Practice: Row 1, ex 5–8; first ex. in rows 16 & 18, pp. 85–86
Independent Practice: Complete pp. 85–86

Customary Units of Capacity and Weight

Customary units of capacity or liquid measure are fluid ounce (fl oz), cup (c), pint (pt), quart (qt), and gallon (gal). Unlike the metric system, these units are not related by powers of **10**.

Equivalent Measures

- **8** fluid ounces = **1** cup
- **16** fluid ounces = **1** pint
- **2** cups = **1** pint
- **2** pints = **1** quart
- **4** quarts = **1** gallon
- **32** fluid ounces = **1** quart

Larger to Smaller

5 qt = __?__ fl oz

1 qt = **32** fl oz, so **multiply.**

5 × 32 = 160

Then, **5** qt = **160** fl oz.

Smaller to Larger

44 fl oz = __?__ c

8 fl oz = **1** c, so **divide.**

$$\begin{array}{r} 5\frac{4}{8} \\ 8\overline{)44} \\ \underline{40} \\ 4 \end{array}$$

Simplify. $5\frac{4}{8} = 5\frac{1}{2}$

Then, **44** fl oz = $5\frac{1}{2}$ c.

Complete.

1. **7** pt = $3\frac{1}{2}$ qt — **24** fl oz = 3 c — **3** qt = $\frac{3}{4}$ gal
2. $\frac{1}{2}$ c = $\frac{1}{4}$ pt — $\frac{1}{2}$ c = 4 fl oz — **5** gal = 40 pt
3. **48** fl oz = $1\frac{1}{2}$ qt — **3** qt = 12 c — **5** pt = 80 fl oz
4. $2\frac{1}{2}$ gal = 10 qt — $3\frac{3}{4}$ gal = 30 pt — **14** c = $3\frac{1}{2}$ qt

Write the sum or difference of the measures.

5. $2\frac{1}{2}$ c + $3\frac{1}{2}$ c + $\frac{3}{4}$ c = $6\frac{3}{4}$ c
6. **20** fl oz + **32** fl oz = $6\frac{1}{2}$ c
7. **64** fl oz + **32** fl oz = 3 qt
8. **3** qt − **1** pt = 80 fl oz
9. **3** gal **2** qt + **4** gal **1** qt = 7 gal 3 qt
10. **6** gal **1** qt − **2** gal **3** qt = 3 gal 2 qt
11. **5** qt **1** pt + **4** qt **1** pt = 10 qt 0 pt
12. **11** qt − **3** qt **1** pt = 7 qt 1 pt

Write true or false.

13. false — A gallon of maple syrup equals **64** fluid ounces.
14. true — Pouring **8** cups of milk is the same as pouring a half gallon of milk.
15. true — Taking **2** fluid ounces of cough syrup **4** times a day for **4** days is equal to a quart.

Check Understanding *Which is greater, 10 quarts or 2 gallons?* (10 quarts, because it equals $2\frac{1}{2}$ gallons) *If a truck weighed $4\frac{1}{4}$ tons, how many pounds would it weigh?* (8,500 pounds)

Customary units of weight are ounce (oz), pound (lb), and ton.

Equivalent Measures

16 ounces = 1 pound

2,000 pounds = 1 ton

Larger to Smaller

$3\frac{1}{2}$ lb = __?__ oz

1 lb = 16 oz, so **multiply.**

$3\frac{1}{2} \times 16 = \frac{7}{2} \times 16$ or 56

Then, $3\frac{1}{2}$ lb = 56 oz.

Smaller to Larger

56 oz = __?__ lb

Fact: 16 oz = 1 lb, so **divide.**

$$16\overline{)56} = 3\frac{8}{16}$$

$$\begin{array}{r} 48 \\ \hline 8 \end{array}$$

Simplify. $3\frac{8}{16} = 3\frac{1}{2}$

Then, 56 oz = $3\frac{1}{2}$ lb.

Complete.

16. 6,000 lb = __3__ tons 18 oz = __$1\frac{1}{8}$__ lb 4,500 lb = __$2\frac{1}{4}$__ tons

17. $\frac{1}{2}$ ton = __1,000__ lb $2\frac{1}{2}$ lb = __40__ oz $\frac{1}{4}$ ton = __8,000__ oz

Write the sum or difference of the measures.

18. 5 lb 6 oz + 12 lb 4 oz = __17__ lb __10__ oz 8 lb 6 oz − 4 lb 8 oz = __3__ lb __14__ oz

19. $2\frac{1}{2}$ lb + $3\frac{1}{4}$ lb = __5__ lb __12__ oz 5 lb 12 oz − 3 lb 8 oz = __$2\frac{1}{4}$__ lb

Problem Solving Reasoning Solve.

20. A bottling plant fills one hundred 20-fl oz bottles with spring water each minute. How many gallons of water are needed each hour?

__937.5 gal__

21. The combined weight of 45 crates, each with the same weight, is $3\frac{1}{2}$ tons. How many pounds does each crate weigh to the nearest pound?

__156 lb__

Test Prep ★ Mixed Review

22 What is the volume of water in a tank measuring 6 feet by 3 feet by 2 feet?

C; Obj. 3A

A 11 ft **C** 36 ft^3

B 18 ft^2 **D** 36 ft^2

23 The area of a tabletop is 4 square feet. What is the area in square inches?

G; Obj. 3B

F 576 in. **H** 48 in.

G 576 $in.^2$ **J** 48 $in.^2$

Closing the Lesson *How many cups are in a gallon?* (16) *If a gallon of a certain fluid weighed 24 pounds, how much would one pint of that fluid weigh?* (Since there are 8 pints in a gallon, then 1 pint would weigh $\frac{24}{8} = 3$ lb.)

Name ____________________

Guided Practice: First ex. in Rows 1, 3, 6 & 9, pp. 87–88
Independent Practice: Complete pp. 87–88

Customary Units of Area and Volume

In the Customary System, area is measured in square feet. A square foot, written "sq ft" or "ft^2," is a square whose sides are **1** foot long.

You know that **1** ft = **12** in., so the two squares at the right are the same size. Their areas are equal, so **1** ft^2 = **144** $in.^2$.

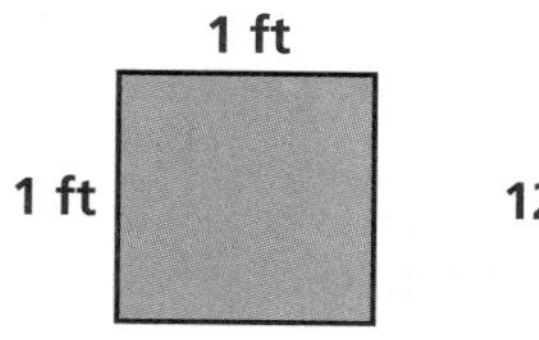

Area = **1** ft^2

12 in. / **12 in.**

Area = **144** $in.^2$

Equivalent Measures	
144 $in.^2$ =	**1** ft^2
9 ft^2 =	**1** yd^2
4,840 yd^2 =	**1** acre
640 acres =	**1** mi^2

Larger to Smaller

5 ft^2 = __?__ $in.^2$

1 ft^2 = **144** $in.^2$, so **multiply.**

5 × **144** = **720**

Then, **5** ft^2 = **720** $in.^2$.

Smaller to Larger

21 ft^2 = __?__ yd^2

9 ft^2 = **1** yd^2, so **divide.**

$$\begin{array}{r} 2\frac{3}{9} \\ 9\overline{)21} \\ \underline{18} \\ 3 \end{array}$$

Simplify. $2\frac{3}{9} = 2\frac{1}{3}$

Then, **21** ft^2 = $2\frac{1}{3}$ yd^2.

Which unit would you use to measure the item? Choose $in.^2$, ft^2, yd^2, acre, or mi^2.

1. classroom floor __ft^2__ your school grounds __acre__ store window __ft^2__

2. writing paper __$in.^2$__ your state __mi^2__ light switch cover __$in.^2$__

Complete.

3. 576 $in.^2$ = __4__ ft^2 0.75 acre = __3,630__ yd^2 35 yd^2 = __315__ ft^2

4. 5 yd^2 = __45__ ft^2 216 $in.^2$ = __1.5__ ft^2 18 ft^2 = __2__ yd^2

5. 3 acres = __14,520__ yd^2 0.5 mi^2 = __320__ acres 3 ft^2 = __432__ $in.^2$

Write true or false.

6. __false__ A field is **100** yd long by **60** yd wide, and its area is **18,000** ft^2.

7. __true__ The area of a **6**-inch square is $\frac{1}{4}$ ft^2.

8. __false__ Linoleum that costs **$3.50** per square foot will cost **$10.50** per square yard.

Check Understanding *If a refrigerator has a volume of 12 ft^3, is that more or less than the volume of a refrigerator with a volume of $1\frac{1}{2}$ yd^3? Explain.* (Since 1 yd^3 = 27 ft^3, then $1\frac{1}{2}$ yd^3 = 40.5 ft^3, so the second refrigerator is much larger.)

Volume is measured using cubic units. A cubic foot, written "cu ft " or "ft³," is a cube whose edges are **1** foot long.

You know that **1** ft = **12** in., so the two cubes at the right are the same size. The volumes are equal, so **1** ft^3 = **1,728** $in.^3$.

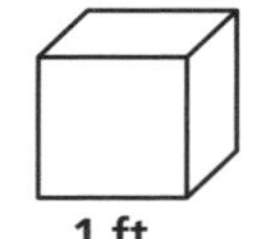
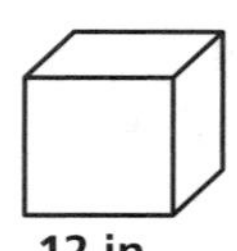

1 ft Volume = **1** ft^3

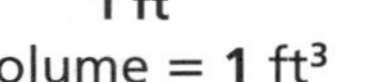

12 in. Volume = **1,728** ft^3

Equivalent Measures
1,728 $in.^3$ = **1** ft^3
27 ft^3 = **1** yd^3

Larger to Smaller

3 ft^3 = ___?___ $in.^3$

1 ft^3 = **1,728** $in.^3$, so **multiply.**

3 × 1,728 = 5,184

Then, **3** ft^3 = **5,128** $in.^3$.

Smaller to Larger

144 ft^3 = ___?___ yd^3

27 ft^3 = **1** yd^3, so **divide.**

$$\begin{array}{r} 5\frac{9}{27} \\ 27\overline{)144} \\ \underline{135} \\ 9 \end{array}$$

Simplify $5\frac{9}{27} = 5\frac{1}{3}$

Then, **144** ft^3 = **$5\frac{1}{3}$** yd^3.

Complete.

9. **2** ft^3 = ___3,456___ $in.^3$ **3** yd^3 = ___81___ ft^3 **72** ft^3 = ___$2\frac{2}{3}$___ yd^3

10. **432** $in.^3$ = ___$\frac{1}{4}$___ ft^3 **$4\frac{2}{3}$** yd^3 = ___126___ ft^3 **$\frac{1}{12}$** ft^3 = ___144___ $in.^3$

Solve.

11. A dump truck holds **10** yd^3 of sand. How many loads will it take to fill a hole that is **30** ft by **60** ft by **6** ft deep?

___40 loads___

12. A **5**-acre parcel is subdivided into parcels of **440** yd^2. How many parcels will there be?

___55 parcels___

✔ Quick Check

Complete.

13. **4** ft **9** in. + **7** ft **6** in. = ___12___ ft ___3___ in.

14. **$9\frac{1}{4}$** ft − **5** ft **8** in. = ___3___ ft ___7___ in.

15. **3** gal **2** qt + **6** gal **3** qt = ___10___ gal ___1___ qt

16. **$4\frac{3}{4}$** lb + **$1\frac{1}{2}$** lb = ___6___ lb ___4___ oz

17. **9.5** yd = ___28.5___ ft

18. **189** in. = ___$15\frac{3}{4}$___ ft

19. **1.4** mi = ___7,392___ ft

20. **156** fl oz = ___$9\frac{3}{4}$___ pt

21. **$5\frac{3}{8}$** lb = ___86___ oz

22. **$2\frac{1}{4}$** tons = ___4,500___ lb

23. **6** ft^2 = ___864___ $in.^2$

24. **30** ft^2 = ___$3\frac{1}{3}$___ yd^2

25. **10** yd^3 = ___270___ ft^3

Closing the Lesson *The price of linoleum at Dad's Floors is $1.30 per ft², and the price for the same linoleum at The Floor Store is $12.50 per yd². Which is the better buy? Explain.* (Dad's Floors: $1.30 per ft² x 9 ft² = $11.70 per yd²)

Work Space.

Item	Error Analysis
13–14, 17–19	**Common Error** Students may regroup 1 ft as 10 in. instead of 12. **Reteaching** Reteach 20
15–16, 20–22	**Common Error** Students may not know when to multiply or divide or may use incorrect units. **Reteaching** Reteach 21 and 22
23–25	**Common Error** Students may use linear units instead of square or cubic units. **Reteaching** Reteach 22

Name ______________________________

Guided Practice: Rows 1, 5, & 8, pp. 89–90
Independent Practice: Complete pp. 89–90

Temperature and Line Graphs

Two common temperature scales are the **Celsius (C)** and **Fahrenheit (F)** scales shown at the right.

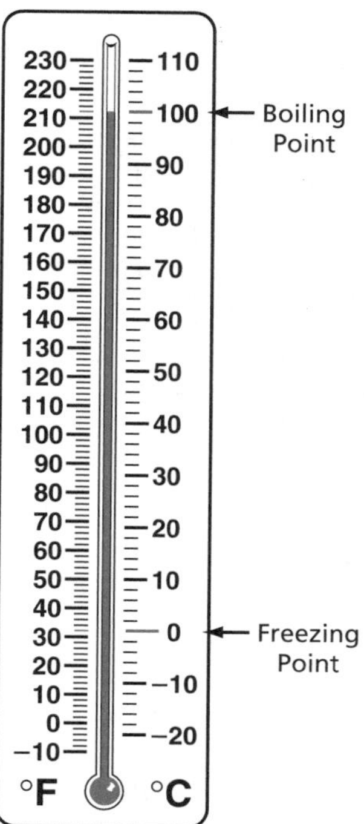

The boiling and freezing points on the Celsius scale are **100°** apart. These points are **180°** apart on the Fahrenheit scale. The temperatures *feel* the same, but the scale is different.

Celsius	Reference Points	Fahrenheit
100°	Boiling point	212°
37°	Body temperature	98.6°
32°	Hot summer day	90°
21°	A room in winter	70°
16°	Pleasant spring day	60°
0°	Freezing point	32°

The Celsius (C) and Fahrenheit (F) scales are both used in the United States. If you know the temperature in one scale, you can estimate what it will be in the other scale.

Celsius to Fahrenheit: Double, then add 30.

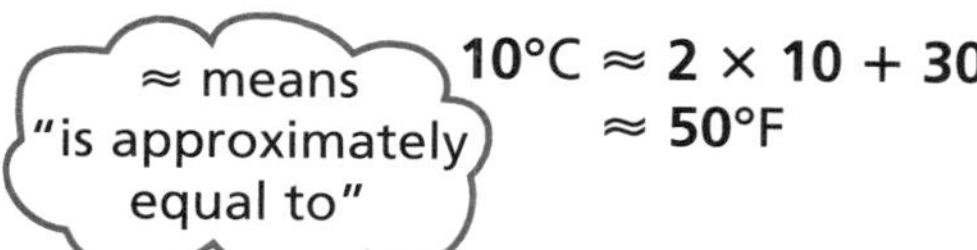

$10°C \approx 2 \times 10 + 30$
$\approx 50°F$

Fahrenheit to Celsius: Subtract 30, then divide by 2.

$70°F \approx (70 - 30) \div 2$
$\approx 20°C$

Write true or false. Use the temperature scales above to help you.

1. false **20°C** is colder than **20°F**. false You would swim at the beach at **35°F**.
2. false You need a sweater at **40°C**. true You would swim at the beach at **35°C**.
3. true You need a sweater at **40°F**. false **85°C** is normal in Honolulu.
4. true It snows at **10°F**. false **30°C** is normal winter weather in Chicago.

Complete. Estimate the Celsius or Fahrenheit temperature.

5. **80°F ≈** 25 °C **16°C ≈** 62 °F **72°F ≈** 21 °C
6. **22°C ≈** 74 °F **40°F ≈** 5 °C **28°C ≈** 86 °F
7. **90°F ≈** 30 °C **35°C ≈** 100 °F **66°F ≈** 18 °C

Check Understanding *The high temperature reported for Sydney today was 34°C. About how much is that in degrees Fahrenheit?* (98°) *If you were given a temperature in degrees Fahrenheit, what would you do to get an approximation in degrees Celsius?* (Subtract 30 and divide by 2.)

A **line graph** is best used to show trends, or changes in data over time. One or more sets of related data can be shown on the same graph.

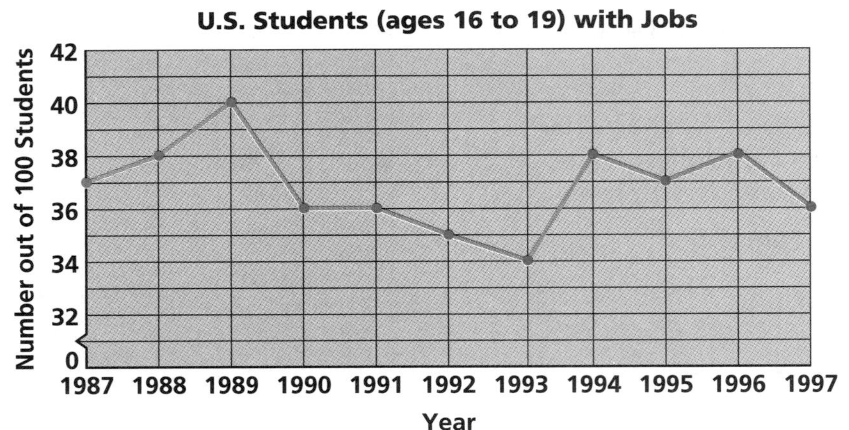

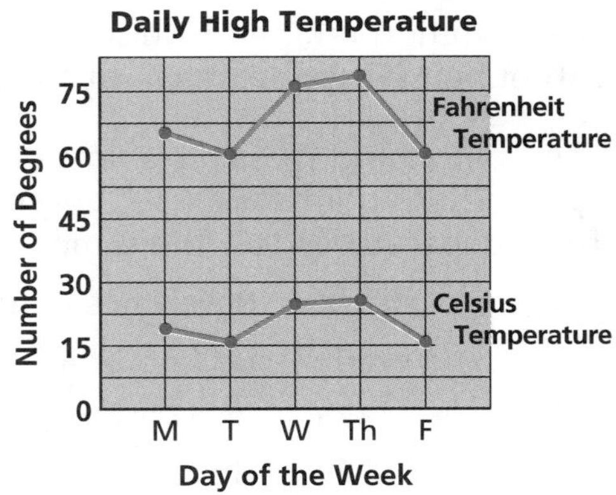

From the graph, you can see that in **1996**, **38** out of **100** students had jobs.

From the graph, you can see that on Wednesday the temperature was about **24**°C, or **76**°F.

Complete. Use the graphs above.

8. How many students out of **100** had jobs in **1990**? 36 In **1994**? 38

9. Between what two years was the decrease in students with jobs the greatest?

1989 and 1990 The increase greatest? 1993 and 1994

10. What was the approximate temperature on Tuesday? 60 °F and 16 °C

11. Which line graph shows the greatest change in the number of degrees,

Fahrenheit or Celsius? Fahrenheit

Problem Solving Reasoning

Solve.

12. Ben is traveling to New York City in July. Which of these is a reasonable temperature to expect: **10°F, 85°F,** or **113°F**?

85°F

13. Ashlea has a fever. Her body temperature is **2°** above normal. Which is more severe, **2°C** or **2°F**? Explain.

2°C. It is a greater change.

Test Prep ★ Mixed Review

14 **A container with a volume of 1 dm³ has a capacity of 1 L. What is the capacity in liters of a box that is 8 cm in width, 10 cm in length, and 5.5 cm in height?** B; Obj. 3A

A 4.4 L **C** 0.044 L

B 0.44 L **D** 0.08 L

15 **Two gallons of juice will fill how many cups?** H; Obj. 3B

F 8 **H** 32

G 16 **J** 64

Closing the Lesson *When is a line graph a good graph to use?* (Possible answer: when you want to show a trend over time)

Name ______________________________

Guided Practice: Rows 1 & 11; first ex. in rows 17 & 19, pp. 91–92
Independent Practice: Complete pp. 91–92

You can write equivalent units of time in the same way that you write equivalent lengths, capacities, areas, and volumes.

Equivalent Measures
60 seconds (s) = **1** minute (min)
60 minutes = **1** hour (h)
24 hours = **1** day
7 days = **1** week (wk)
52 weeks = **1** year (yr)
365 days = **1** year
366 days = **1** leap year
10 years = **1** decade
100 years = **1** century

Complete. Use the equivalent measures in the table at the right.

1. 180 s = ___3___ min 73 days = ___$\frac{1}{5}$___ yr

2. 32 h = ___$1\frac{1}{3}$___ days 60 days = ___1,440___ h

3. 8 days = ___192___ h 2,480 h = ___$103\frac{1}{3}$___ days

4. 60 wk = ___$1\frac{2}{13}$___ yr 8 decades = ___80___ yr

5. 3 wk = ___21___ days 22 min = ___1,320___ s

6. 24 h = ___1,440___ min 260 wk = ___$\frac{1}{2}$___ decade

7. 15 min = ___900___ s 2 yr = ___730___ days

8. 28 days = ___4___ wk 120 yr = ___12___ decades

9. 3 yr = ___156___ wk 150 yr = ___$1\frac{1}{2}$___ centuries

10. 10 min = ___$\frac{1}{6}$___ hr 6 h = ___$\frac{1}{4}$___ day

Time Zones

The continental United States (not including Alaska and Hawaii) has four time zones. Each zone is one hour later than the zone to its west.

If it is **5** P.M. in New York, then it is **4** P.M. in Illinois, **3** P.M. in Colorado, and **2** P.M. in California.

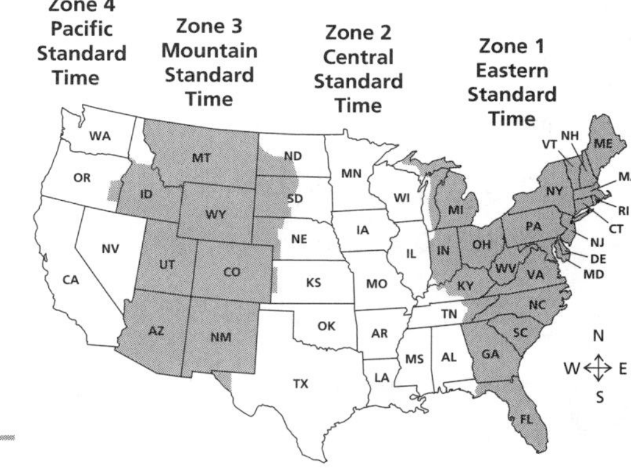

Complete.

11. It is noon in IL. What time is it in MD? ___1 P.M.___ In UT? ___11 A.M.___ In OR? ___10 A.M.___

12. A football game begins at **3** P.M. in NY.
What is the starting time on television in CA? ___noon___

13. It is midnight in NM. What time is it in NV? ___11 P.M.___ In OK? ___1 A.M.___ In FL? ___2 A.M.___

14. It is **9** A.M. in NY, where Joe lives. He wants to phone his aunt in eastern KS.

What time is it there? ___8 A.M.___

15. It is **2:30** P.M. in OH. What time is it in CO? ___12:30 P.M.___ In SC? ___2:30 P.M.___ In TX? ___1:30 P.M.___

16. How many hours time difference is there between MA and CA? ___3 hours___

Check Understanding *Using a 24-hour clock, what time is it if it is 4:30 P.M.?* (1630)

The U.S. armed forces use a **24**-hour clock. The time of day is written as a four-digit number from **0000** (midnight) to **1200** (noon) to **2400** (midnight).

Examples

3:00 A.M.	**0300**
7:30 A.M.	**0730**
1:15 P.M.	**1315**
8:45 P.M.	**2045**

In **24**-hour time, the first two digits tell the number of hours after midnight. The last two digits tell the number of minutes after the hour.

Write the 24-hour time as A.M. or P.M. time.

17. 2120 9:20 P.M. 1314 1:14 P.M. 1000 10:00 A.M. 1610 4:10 P.M.

18. 2215 10:15 P.M. 0710 7:10 A.M. 1255 12:55 P.M. 2321 11:21 P.M.

Write the A.M. or P.M. time as 24-hour time.

19. 9:20 A.M. 0920 3:40 P.M. 1540 5:18 A.M. 0518 11:00 P.M. 2300

20. 2:30 P.M. 1430 4:12 P.M. 1612 4:45 A.M. 0445 5:18 P.M. 1718

Solve.

21. Maria boarded a bus at **0930**. She traveled for $3\frac{1}{4}$ hours. What time did she arrive? Write your answer in both A.M. or P.M. time and **24**-hour time. 12:45 P.M., 1245

22. The Miscio family left Atlanta at **8:00** A.M. and arrived in Sacramento at **10:45** A.M. on a non stop flight. How long was the family in the air? 5 h 45 min

Quick Check

Complete. Estimate the Fahrenheit or Celsius temperature.

23. 60°F = 15 °C **24.** 80°C = 190 °F **25.** 35°F = 2 or 3 °C

Solve. Write the A.M. or P.M. time and the 24-hour time.

26. It is **2:30** P.M. in PA. What time is it in AZ, which is two time zones west of PA?

A.M. or P.M. time 12:30 P.M. **24**-hour time 1230

27. It is **1730** at an air force base in OR. What time is it in TN, which is three time zones to the east?

A.M. or P.M. time 8:30 P.M. **24**-hour time 2030

Work Space.

Item	Error Analysis
23–25	**Common Error** Watch for students who confuse the sequence of operations. **Reteaching** Reteach 23
26–27	**Common Error** Watch for students who think that 1000 is noon on the 24-hour clock. **Reteaching** Reteach 24

Closing the Lesson *How would you calculate how many minutes are in 3 weeks?* (3 weeks = 21 days = 504 h = 30,240 min)

Name ______________________

Guided Practice: Problem 1, p. 94
Independent Practice: Complete p. 94

Problem Solving Strategy: Make a Table

To solve some problems, making a table can help you to organize information and to plan a solution strategy.

When you make a table, think about how you will label the rows and columns.

Problem

One year the Buccaneers won 16, lost 4, and tied 3 games. The next year they won 17, lost 5, and tied 1. In the third year, they won 15, lost 2, and tied 6. What is the team's three-year record? Which was their best year?

1 Understand

"Asking yourself questions will help you identify the math ideas. Think about ways to compare records from one year to another."

As you reread the problem, ask yourself questions.

- What was the team's record each year?

First year: **16-4-3**
Second year: **17-5-1**
Third year: **15-2-6**

- What do you need to find? the team's three-year record and its best year

2 Decide

"A table will help you organize the information. It helps you think about how to solve the problem."

Choose a method for solving.

Try the strategy Make a Table.

- Set up a table with a row for each year. Use columns for wins, losses, and ties.

	Wins	Losses	Ties
Year **1**	16	4	3
Year **2**	17	5	1
Year **3**	15	2	6

- How will you decide which year the team had the best record?

3 Solve

"Is there more than one way to decide which year was the best record?"

Answer the two questions.

- Add a "Totals" row to the table. Find the total number of wins, losses, and ties for the three years.

wins: 48, losses: 11, ties: 10

	Wins	Losses	Ties
Year **1**	16	4	3
Year **2**	17	5	1
Year **3**	15	2	6
Totals	48	11	10

- Explain how you selected which year the team had the best record. Answers will vary.

calculated percent of wins in each year; Year 3 had the best record.

4 Look back

"Did everyone agree with the three-year totals? Did everyone select the same year as the best?"

Ask if your answers make sense.

- Did others agree with which year the team had their best record?

Answers will vary.

Check Understanding *What role does a table play in solving problems?* (Possible answer: It helps you organize the information so that you can see a pattern between the variables.)

Use the Make a Table strategy or any other strategy you have learned.

1. The table shows the annual per person consumption (in gallons) of milk and soda. If the trend continues, what will be the consumption of milk and soda in **2000**?

	1985	1990	1995
Milk	26.4	25.3	24.2
Soda	24.6	26.8	29.0

Think: What patterns do you see? How can you extend these patterns?

Milk decreased by 1.1 gal every 5 yrs; In 2000 milk will be 23.1 gal; soda 31.2; Soda increased by 2.2 gal; Extend the pattern by subtracting 1.1

Answer from 24.2 and adding 2.2 to 29.0.

2. Trent made **3** rectangles. The first was **3.2** cm by **4.6** cm. He doubled these dimensions to make the second rectangle and tripled them to make the third rectangle. Find the area and perimeter of each and describe any patterns.

Think: How can you organize your results? Use a table.

When the dimensions are doubled, the perimeter doubles, but the area increases 4 times; When the dimensions are tripled, the perimeter triples, but

Answer the area increases 9 times.

	Perimeter	Area
Rectangle 1	15.6 cm	14.72 cm^2
Rectangle 2	31.2 cm	58.88 cm^2
Rectangle 3	46.8 cm	132.48 cm^2

3. Describe the pattern and write the next three numbers in the pattern.

3, 7, 15, 31, 63, 127, 255

Double the number and add 1 to get the next one.

231, 23.1, 2.31, 0.231, 0.0231, 0.00231

Each number is 0.1 times the previous one.

4. A deli offers a choice of ham, turkey, or roast beef and a choice of provolone or Swiss cheese in their meat-and-cheese sandwiches. How many different sandwiches can you make?

6 different sandwiches

5. Find two consecutive numbers whose product is **240**.

15 and 16

6. Sarah is making a beaded necklace. She uses **2** red, **1** white, **3** blue and then starts over with the **2** red. If she continues this pattern, what color will the **28**th bead be?

blue

7. At **6:45** A.M. you begin an eight-mile hike. At **7:20** A.M. you have hiked one mile. If you hike at the same speed the entire day, when will you finish your hike?

11:25 A.M.

8. Ms. Bogardus is hanging mobiles in her classroom. Four of them will hang $2\frac{1}{2}$ feet from the ceiling. Three of them will hang down **18** inches. What is the shortest length of string (in yards) she will need?

$4\frac{5}{6}$ yd

Closing the Lesson *Can you think of places where tables are used to display information?* (Possible answer: Sports data often appear in tables.)

Name ______________________________

Unit 3 Review

Circle the best estimate of the measure.

1. **Capacity:** cup of cocoa

2.5 mL 25 mL (250 mL)

2. **Mass:** hamburger patty

(150 g) 1500 g 1.5 kg

3. **Temperature:** hot summer day

(30°C) 80°C 140°C

Complete.

4. 24 cm = 240 mm

5. 1.3 cm = 0.013 m

6. 55L = 0.055 kL

7. 2 L = 2,000 mL

8. 3.1 kg = 3,100 g

9. 5 mg = 0.005 g

10. 5.1 cm^2 = 0.00051 m^3

11. 0.2 cm^2 = 20 mm^2

12. 254 cm^2 = 0.000254 m^3

13. 254 cm^3 = 254,000 mm^3

14. $4\frac{1}{2}$ ft = 54 in.

15. 120 in. = $3\frac{1}{3}$ yd

16. 12 lb = 192 oz

17. 9 pt = $4\frac{1}{2}$ qt

18. $2\frac{1}{2}$ c = 20 fl oz

19. $\frac{1}{2}$ ton = 1,000 lb

20. What is the area of a rectangle with dimensions $1\frac{1}{2}$ ft by **6** in.?

Write your answer in square inches. 108 in.^{2}

Write the approximate Fahrenheit temperature.

21. 20°C = 70°F

22. 32°C = 94°F

Express the 24-hour clock time as a 12-hour clock time using A.M. and P.M.

23. 0745 7:45 A.M.

24. 1820 6:20 P.M.

25. 1223 12:23 A.M.

It is 2:15 P.M. in time zone 1. What time is it in the other time zones? (Use the map on page 91.)

26. Zone 2 1:15 P.M.

27. Zone 3 12:15 P.M.

28. Zone 4 11:15 A.M.

Problem Solving Reasoning

Solve.

29. The volume of a wheelbarrow is **3** cubic feet. A sandbox holds **3** cubic yards. How many trips will it take with the wheelbarrow to fill it? 27 trips

30. The standard workday is **8** hours. Steve worked **12** days in a row and was paid **$648.** How much did he make per hour?

$6.75

Use these boxes to answer questions 1 and 2.

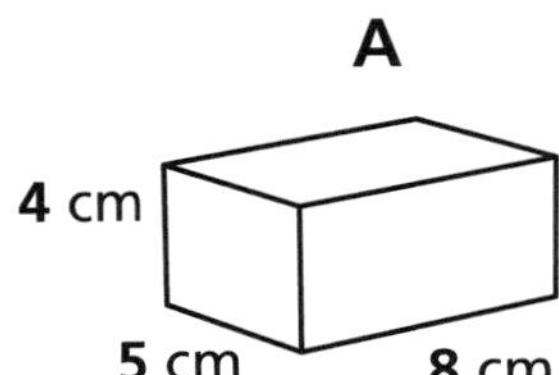

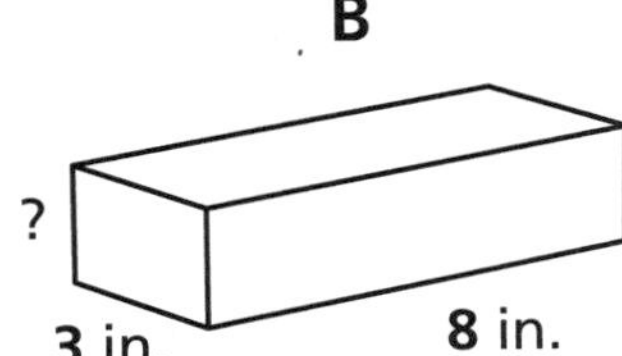

1 **What is the volume of box A?** C; Obj. 3A

A 160 cm C 160 cm^3

B 160 cm^2 D 17 cm

2 **The volume of box B is 48 $in.^3$. What is its height?** F; Obj. 3A

F 2 in. H 6 $in.^2$

G 2 $in.^2$ J 8 in.

Use these containers to answer questions 3 and 4.

3 **What is the mass of sand in grams?** B; Obj. 3B

A 5,200 g C 52 g

B 520 g D 5.2 g

4 **What is the volume of paint in pints?** H; Obj. 3B

F 40 pt H 160 pt

G 80 pt J 320 pt

5 **Which is the quotient of $1\frac{1}{8} \div \frac{2}{16}$?** A; Obj. 2A, 2B

A 9 C $\frac{1}{9}$

B $\frac{9}{64}$ D $\frac{1}{32}$

6 **The area formula for a triangle is $\frac{1}{2}bh$. What is the area of this triangle?** H; Obj. 1E

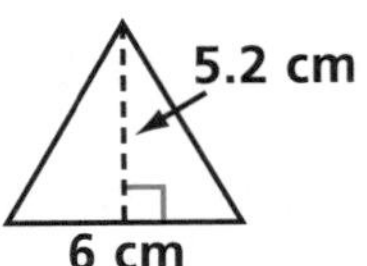

F 90.6 cm^2 H 15.6 cm^2

G 15.6 cm J 9.6 cm

7 **These are the number of coins some students counted in their backpacks.** D; Obj. 1A

9, 7, 3, 8, 4, 5, 23, 7, 16

What is the mode of the coin data set?

A 20 C 6.5 E Not here

B 9.1 D 7

8 **Evaluate for $a = 0.2$ and $b = \frac{3}{4}$.** J; Obj. 2E

$$2.8b + 3(a + b)$$

F 3.31 H 4.51 K Not here

G 3.41 J 4.95

9 **Which shows the value of $\frac{2}{3} \times 1\frac{1}{5} + 7^2$?** A; Obj. 2E

A $49\frac{4}{5}$ C $7\frac{4}{5}$

B $33\frac{7}{15}$ D $\frac{4}{5}$

UNIT 4 • TABLE OF CONTENTS

Ratios, Proportions, and Percents

We will be using this vocabulary:

ratio a comparison by division of two quantities with like units, such as cups of flour and cups of sugar

rate a comparison of two quantities with unlike units, such as words per minute

unit rate a rate that compares a quantity to **1** such as **45** miles per **1** hour

proportion an equation that states that two ratios are equal

direct proportion a relationship between two quantities such that both increase simultaneously

inverse proportion a relationship between two quantities such that one quantity increases as the other decreases

scale drawing a picture or drawing that is an enlargement or reduction of another

percent a ratio that compares a number with **100**

Dear Family,

During the next few weeks, our math class will be studying ratios, proportions, and percents. This includes setting up and solving proportions and using ratios and rates to solve problems. You can expect to see homework that provides practice with these skills. Here is a sample you may want to keep handy to give help if needed.

Solving a Proportion

One way to solve a proportion is to use the Cross Products Property. In a proportion, if $\frac{a}{b} = \frac{c}{d}$, then $a \cdot d = b \cdot c$.

"·" means "multiply"

Example $\frac{9}{36} = \frac{5}{n}$

$5 \cdot 36 = 9 \cdot n$ Apply the Cross Products Property.

$\frac{180}{9} = \frac{9 \cdot n}{9}$ Divide each side by **9**.

$20 = n$ Simplify.

Using Percents

To find values such as **8.5%** of a number, students need to be able to write a percent as a fraction and as a decimal.

Example $8.5\% \rightarrow \frac{8.5}{100} = \frac{85}{1{,}000} \rightarrow 0.085$

During this unit, students will continue to learn new techniques related to problem solving and will continue to practice basic skills with fractions and decimals.

Sincerely,

Name ______________________

Rates and Ratios

Guided Practice: First ex. in Rows 1, 3, 7 & 10, pp. 99–100
Independent Practice: Complete pp. 99–100

A **ratio** is a comparison by division of two like quantities.

Example:
Use *2 cups* of flour *to 1 cup* of sugar.
There are *2 girls to* every *3 boys* in the class.

Either of the two numbers in a ratio is called its **terms**.

Writing Ratios
A ratio is a comparison of **like** quantities. A ratio is usually written without units.

The ratio **2** girls to every **3** boys can be written in three forms:

2 to **3** or **2 : 3** or $\frac{2}{3}$

Ratios are not written as mixed numbers.

Other Example: The ratio **64** points to **56** points is written:

64 to **56** or **64 : 56** or $\frac{64}{56}$

A **rate** is a comparison of two unlike quantities.

Example:
She is driving ***45** miles per hour.*
The sale price is ***3** boxes for **$10**.*

We bought ***2** pizzas for **5** people.*

Writing Rates
A rate is a comparison of **unlike** quantities. A rate is always written with units.

The rate **2** pizzas for **6** people is written:

$\frac{\text{2 pizzas}}{\text{6 people}}$ *or* $\frac{2}{6}$ pizza per person

Rates are usually written in per unit form.

Other Example: The rate **6** classes each day is written:

$\frac{\text{6 classes}}{\text{1 day}}$ or **6** classes per day

Identify the comparison as a rate or ratio.

1. **3** inches per day rate
   22 students to **3** adults ratio
2. **15** rose bushes to **8** lily plants ratio
   6 pounds seed to **100** square feet rate
3. **4** computers for each classroom rate
   5 gal lemonade to **2** gal soda pop ratio

Write each comparison as a rate. Forms of answers may vary.

4. **32** oz box for **$2.24** $\frac{\text{32 oz}}{\text{\$2.24}}$
   68 miles per **2** gallons of gas $\frac{\text{68 mi}}{\text{2 gal}}$
5. **82** points for **4** games $\frac{\text{82 points}}{\text{4 games}}$
   30 points on each assignment 30 points per assignment
6. **$35** for **2** hours $\frac{\text{\$35}}{\text{2 h}}$
   8 campers in a cabin 8 campers per cabin

Write each comparison as a ratio in two ways. Forms of answers may vary.

7. **4** infielders to **3** outfielders 4:3 or $\frac{4}{3}$
   16 girls to **14** boys $\frac{16}{14}$ or 16:14
8. **2** cardinals to **3** robins $\frac{2}{3}$ or 2:3
   3 blue cars for every **10** cars 3:10 or $\frac{3}{10}$
9. **6** cups flour to **2** cups sugar $\frac{6}{2}$ or 6:2
   $5 to **$30** $\frac{5}{30}$ or 5:30

Check Understanding *What are two other ways to write the ratio $\frac{2}{5}$?* (2 to 5 and 2:5)

Like fractions, ratios can be simplified using multiplication and division. Before you simplify a ratio, you should always be sure that terms of the ratio are in the same unit.

Write the ratio of hours spent biking to hours spent studying in simplest form.

biking → **14** hours
studying → **6** hours

$$\frac{14 \text{ hours}}{6 \text{ hours}} = \frac{14}{6} \rightarrow \frac{7}{3}$$

Write the ratio of width to length in simplest form.

2 ft
4 in.

It is usually easier to change the greater unit to the lesser unit.

1 ft = 12 in.

$$\frac{4 \text{ inches}}{2 \text{ feet}} = \frac{4 \text{ inches}}{24 \text{ inches}} \rightarrow \frac{4}{24} \rightarrow \frac{1}{6}$$

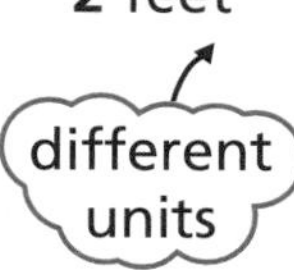

Write the ratio in its simplest form.

10. 3 days to **1** week $\frac{3}{7}$ — **45** pounds to **70** pounds $\frac{9}{14}$ — **1** hour to **1** day $\frac{1}{24}$

11. **1** pound to **32** ounces $\frac{1}{2}$ — **3** months to **2** years $\frac{1}{8}$ — **2** ft to **10** in. $\frac{12}{5}$

12. **5** feet to **5** yards $\frac{1}{3}$ — **4** dimes to **5** dollars $\frac{2}{25}$ — **4** cups to **1** pint $\frac{2}{1}$

13. **3** dollars to **5** dollars $\frac{3}{5}$ — **40** min to **1** h $\frac{2}{3}$ — **2** g to **50** mg $\frac{40}{1}$

14. **25** cm to **1** m $\frac{1}{4}$ — **8** hours to **3** days $\frac{1}{9}$ — **3** yards to **2** feet $\frac{9}{2}$

Problem Solving Reasoning

Solve.

15. Tonya traveled a distance of **150** miles in **3** hours. Melba traveled a distance of **98** miles in **2** hours. Who was traveling at a greater rate of speed? Explain.

Tonya; 50 miles per hour > 49 miles per hour

16. Lou typed **96** words in **2** minutes. Tara typed **126** words in **4** minutes. Rob typed **140** words in **5** minutes. Who is the fastest typist? Explain.

Lou; Lou (48 words per minute) vs Tara (31.5 words per minute) and Rob (28 words per minute)

Test Prep ★ Mixed Review

17 **The area of a lawn is 15 square yards. How many square feet is that?** D; Obj. 3B

A 5
B 45
C 90
D 135

18 **For the following data, what does the value 10.5 represent?** H; Obj. 1A

13, 7, 8, 17, 10, 8

F mode
G median
H mean
J range

Closing the Lesson *Can ratios be simplified?* (Possible answer: Ratios can be simplified because they can be written as fractions.) *Name three things you do that involve rates.* (Possible answers: buying food or goods at a store; getting paid for work, etc.)

Name ___________________________________

Unit Rates

Guided Practice: First ex. in Rows 1, 4 & 9, pp. 101–102
Independent Practice: Complete pp. 101–102

If you can make **20** paper stars in **5** minutes, then you can make **4** paper stars in **1** minute.

$$\frac{\textbf{20 stars}}{\textbf{5 minutes}} = \frac{\textbf{4 stars}}{\textbf{1 minute}}$$

Rates are simplified by writing them as **unit rates,** that is, rates whose second term is a single unit. To find a unit rate, you need to divide to find an equivalent rate with a denominator of **1** unit.

You were paid **$28** for **4** hours of work. Write the hourly wage as a rate. Then, find the unit rate.

$$\frac{\text{amount paid}}{\text{time}} \rightarrow \frac{\$28}{4\text{ h}} = \frac{\$28 \div 4}{4\text{ h} \div 4} \rightarrow \frac{\$7}{1\text{ h}}$$

The hourly wage is **$7.00** per hour.

You washed **50** plates in **8** minutes. Write this information as a rate. Then, find a unit rate.

$$\frac{\text{plates washed}}{\text{time}} \rightarrow \frac{50\text{ plates}}{8\text{ min}} = \frac{50\text{ plates} \div 8}{8\text{ min} \div 8}$$

$$= \frac{6.25\text{ plates}}{1\text{ min}}$$

You washed about **6** plates per minute.

Write the unit rate.

1. $\frac{\text{360 words}}{\text{5 minutes}}$ $\frac{\text{72 words}}{\text{1 minute}}$ $\frac{\text{6 beanbags}}{\$4.00}$ $\frac{\text{1.5 beanbags}}{\text{1 dollar}}$ $\frac{\text{96 students}}{\text{3 classrooms}}$ $\frac{\text{32 students}}{\text{1 classroom}}$

2. $\frac{\text{2 cups}}{\text{4 minutes}}$ $\frac{\text{0.5 cups}}{\text{1 minute}}$ $\frac{\text{2 bags}}{\text{8 people}}$ $\frac{\text{0.25 bags}}{\text{1 person}}$ $\frac{\text{42 yards}}{\text{3 plays}}$ $\frac{\text{14 yards}}{\text{1 play}}$

3. $\frac{\text{22.5 miles}}{\text{4 hour}}$ $\frac{\text{5.625 miles}}{\text{1 hour}}$ $\frac{\text{4 tops}}{\$5.00}$ $\frac{\text{0.8 tops}}{\text{1 dollar}}$ $\frac{\text{138 pages}}{\text{12 minutes}}$ $\frac{\text{11.5 pages}}{\text{1 minute}}$

4. 6 books for every 3 students
$\frac{\text{6 books}}{\text{3 students}}$, $\frac{\text{2 books}}{\text{1 student}}$

9 bars of soap for 3 dollars
$\frac{\text{9 bars}}{\$3.00}$, $\frac{\text{3 bars}}{\$1.00}$

5. 3 rulers for 3 students
$\frac{\text{3 books}}{\text{3 students}}$, $\frac{\text{1 book}}{\text{1 student}}$

3 pounds for 12 people
$\frac{\text{3 pounds}}{\text{12 people}}$, $\frac{\text{0.25 pounds}}{\text{1 person}}$

6. $1.00 for 10 fish hooks
$\frac{\$1.00}{\text{10 fish hooks}}$, $\frac{\$\ .10}{\text{1 fish hook}}$

45 people in 9 cars
$\frac{\text{45 people}}{\text{9 cars}}$, $\frac{\text{5 people}}{\text{1 car}}$

7. 60 hours in 6 weeks
$\frac{\text{60 hours}}{\text{6 weeks}}$, $\frac{\text{10 hours}}{\text{1 week}}$

$21.35 for 7 feet
$\frac{\$21.35}{\text{7 feet}}$, $\frac{\$3.05}{\text{1 foot}}$

8. 18 pine cones for 3 wreaths
$\frac{\text{18 pine cones}}{\text{3 wreaths}}$, $\frac{\text{6 pine cones}}{\text{1 wreath}}$

72 holes for 4 golf courses
$\frac{\text{72 holes}}{\text{4 golf courses}}$, $\frac{\text{18 holes}}{\text{1 golf course}}$

Check Understanding *If someone types at a rate of 320 words in five minutes, how many words can they type in a minute?* (64 words)

A **unit price** is the cost per unit of an item or service. Comparing unit prices can help you decide what is the better buy.

One brand of corn flakes comes in two different-sized boxes. The **15** oz box costs **$2.79.** The larger, **18** oz box costs **$3.29.** Which is the better buy, that is, which box has the lower cost per ounce?

You want to find the cost **per** ounce, so divide the cost by the number of ounces.

$2.79 for a **15** oz box

$\frac{\$2.79}{15\text{ oz}} \rightarrow 15\overline{)2.790}$ = **.186**

The unit price is about **$.186,** or **18.6¢,** per ounce.

$3.29 for an **18** oz box

$\frac{\$3.29}{18\text{ oz}} \rightarrow 18\overline{)3.2900}$ = **.1827**

The unit price is about **$.183,** or **18.3¢,** per ounce.

The **18** oz box is the better buy.

Find the unit price to the nearest tenth of a cent. Circle the item that is a better buy.

9. Foil: (**$5.59** for **200** feet) 2.8¢ per foot
or **$2.39** for **75** feet 3.2¢ per foot

Hot dogs: (**8** for **$2.19**) 27.4¢ per hot dog
or **10** for **$2.79** 27.9¢ per hot dog

Frozen yogurt: **0.5** gal for **$2.25** $4.50 per gallon
or (**2** gal for **$8.00**) $4.00 per gallon

10. Potatoes: **10**-lb bag for **$1.99** 19.9¢ per pound
or a (**25**-lb bag for **$4.50**) 18.0¢ per pound

Cereal: **16**-oz box for **$3.49** 21.8¢ per oz
or (**20**-oz box for **$4.19**) 21.0¢ per oz

Apples: (**3** dozen for **$4.80**) 13.3¢ per apple
or **6** for **90¢** 15¢ per apple

Problem Solving
Reasoning

Solve.

11. John bought a quart of Mill's ice cream for **$2.99.** Amy bought a half-gallon of Mill's ice cream for **$4.69.** Who got the better buy? Explain.

Amy; She paid $2.35 per quart, whereas John paid $2.99 per quart.

12. Both you and your friend have weekend jobs. You were paid **$84** for **12** hours of work. Your friend was paid **$72** for **9** hours of work. Who has the higher hourly wage? Explain. your friend; Your hourly wage is $7 per hour, whereas your friend's hourly wage is $8.00 per hour.

Test Prep ★ Mixed Review

13 **What is the value of the expression 3 + 5 × 7 − 2 × 6?** A; Obj. 1C

A 26
B 44
C 240
D 324

14 **What is the greatest common factor of 72, 15, and 45?** J; Obj. 2B

F 15
G 9
H 5
J 3

Closing the Lesson *If 6 bananas cost $1.50, what would the cost be per banana?* (25 cents per banana) *At this rate, how many bananas could you buy for $1.00?* (4 bananas)

Name ______________________

Proportions

Guided Practice: First ex. in Rows 1, 4 & 8, pp. 103–104
Independent Practice: Complete pp. 103–104

A **proportion** is an equation that states that two ratios are equal. To solve a proportion, you find the value of the missing term, ***n***.

$\frac{8}{5} = \frac{n}{25}$ proportion

Read the proportion as:
"**8** is to **5** as ***n*** is to **25**"

Here are two examples that show how to use mental math to solve proportions.

Solve: $\frac{8}{5} = \frac{n}{25}$

If the missing term is in the numerator, write both ratios with the same denominator. A common denominator of **5** and **25** is **25,** so rewrite $\frac{8}{5}$.

Multiply the numerator and the denominator by **5.** $\frac{5 \cdot 8}{5 \cdot 5} = \frac{n}{25}$

Simplify. $\frac{40}{25} = \frac{n}{25}$

The denominators both equal **25,** so $n = 40$.

Solve: $\frac{48}{n} = \frac{6}{9}$

If the missing term is in the denominator, write both ratios with the same numerator. Since **48** is a multiple of **6,** rewrite $\frac{6}{9}$ with a numerator of **48.**

Multiply both the numerator and the denominator by **8.** $\frac{48}{n} = \frac{6 \cdot 8}{9 \cdot 8}$

Simplify. $\frac{48}{n} = \frac{48}{72}$

The numerators both equal **48,** so $n = 72$.

Write the proportion as an equation. Sometimes the terms in a ratio are not whole numbers.

1. 8 is to 12 as *x* is to 48 $\frac{8}{12} = \frac{x}{48}$

24 is to 26 as 2 is to *x* $\frac{24}{26} = \frac{2}{x}$

9 is to *n* as 3 is to 12 $\frac{9}{n} = \frac{3}{12}$

2. *m* is to 20 as 4 is to 5 $\frac{m}{20} = \frac{4}{5}$

18 is to *t* as 6 is to 7 $\frac{18}{t} = \frac{6}{7}$

2.4 is to 2.8 as *w* is to 3 $\frac{2.4}{2.8} = \frac{w}{3}$

3. *a* is to *b* as *c* is to *d* $\frac{a}{b} = \frac{c}{d}$

10 is to 15 as 100 is to *h* $\frac{10}{15} = \frac{100}{h}$

8 is to $\frac{1}{2}$ as $\frac{3}{4}$ is to *x* $\frac{8}{\frac{1}{2}} = \frac{\frac{3}{4}}{x}$

Solve the proportion, that is, find the missing term.

4. $\frac{5}{3} = \frac{x}{12}$ 20 $\frac{n}{24} = \frac{5}{8}$ 15 $\frac{x}{10} = \frac{3}{5}$ 6

5. $\frac{8}{13} = \frac{t}{26}$ 16 $\frac{8}{m} = \frac{4}{3}$ 6 $\frac{28}{p} = \frac{7}{11}$ 44

6. $\frac{k}{9} = \frac{5}{3}$ 15 $\frac{8}{3} = \frac{n}{18}$ 48 $\frac{12}{15} = \frac{36}{x}$ 45

7. $\frac{m}{49} = \frac{3}{7}$ 21 $\frac{24}{m} = \frac{6}{6}$ 24 $\frac{x}{30} = \frac{8}{10}$ 24

Check Understanding *Write as many different proportions as you can from the cross products $3 \times 6 = 9 \times 2$.*
($\frac{3}{9} = \frac{2}{6}$; $\frac{9}{3} = \frac{6}{2}$; $\frac{9}{6} = \frac{3}{2}$; $\frac{6}{9} = \frac{2}{3}$)

Another way to solve proportions is to use **cross products** to write a related multiplication equation.

Cross Products Property

In a proportion, if $\frac{a}{b} = \frac{c}{d}$ then $a \cdot d = b \cdot c$

$\frac{7}{12} = \frac{m}{90}$

Cross multiply. $7 \cdot 90 = 12 \cdot m$

Divide each side by **12**. $\frac{630}{12} = \frac{12 \cdot m}{12}$

Simplify each side. $52.5 = m$

Solve the proportion. Use the Cross Products Property.

8. $\frac{1}{3} = \frac{15}{n}$ 45 $\qquad$ $\frac{5}{8} = \frac{x}{12}$ 7.5 $\qquad$ $\frac{5}{6} = \frac{15}{t}$ 18 $\qquad$ $\frac{n}{8} = \frac{108}{9}$ 96

9. $\frac{39}{13} = \frac{a}{24}$ 72 $\qquad$ $\frac{16}{24} = \frac{18}{m}$ 27 $\qquad$ $\frac{5}{6} = \frac{x}{432}$ 360 $\qquad$ $\frac{105}{h} = \frac{5}{8}$ 168

Problem Solving Reasoning Solve.

10. Maria bought **2** pairs of socks for **$5.50.** Could she buy a **dozen** pairs for less than **$35.00?** Explain. Yes; A dozen pairs would cost $33.00.

Quick Check

Identify each comparison as a ratio or a rate. Then, write a simplified ratio or rate.

11. **14 miles in 5 hours** rate, 14 mi:5 h or 2.8 miles per hour

12. **24 feet to 16 yards** ratio, 1:2

13. **$85 to $40** ratio, 17:8

Write the unit rate.

14. **1,000 words in 80 lines** 12.5 words per line

15. **3 notebooks for 8 students** $\frac{3}{8}$ notebook per student

16. **$6.38 for 24 oz** $.27 per oz

Solve the proportions.

17. $\frac{3}{8} = \frac{n}{40}$ 15 $\qquad$ **18.** $\frac{6}{n} = \frac{23}{16}$ 4.17 $\qquad$ **19.** $\frac{5}{12} = \frac{8}{n}$ 19.2

Work Space.

Item	Error Analysis
11–13	**Common Error:** Students may not write in lowest terms **Skills Tutorial** Strand 9, Skill 1
14–16	**Common Error:** Students may not round correctly. **Skills Tutorial** Strand 9, Skill 6
17–19	**Common Error:** Students may not solve the related multiplication equation. **Skills Tutorial** Strand 9, Skill 3

Closing the Lesson *When you use the Cross-Products Property, what are you really doing?* (Possible answer: multiplying both sides of the equation by the product of the two denominators)

Name ______________________________

Direct Proportion

Guided Practice: Ex. 1 & 4, pp. 105–106
Independent Practice: Complete pp. 105–106

Proportions are helpful in solving problems where both quantities increase simultaneously. There are different ways to set up the pairs of numbers in a problem as a proportion.

Lee is driving at **60** miles per hour. At this rate, how long will it take to go **150** miles?

Solution

You want to know *how long,* so the missing term is time.

$\frac{\text{distance}}{\text{time}} \rightarrow \frac{60}{1} = \frac{150}{x} \leftarrow \frac{\text{distance}}{\text{time}}$

Compare the distance in miles to the time it takes in hours to drive that distance.

Cross multiply. $60 \cdot x = 150$

Let x = hours needed to drive **150** miles at **60** mph.

Divide each side by **60**. $\frac{60 \cdot x}{60} = \frac{150}{60}$

Simplify. $x = 2.5$

It would take **2.5** hours to drive **150** miles.

Here is another example of setting up and solving a proportion.

If you work out on a stair climber for **5** minutes, you will use about **60** calories. How long will you need to exercise on the stair climber to use **420** calories?

Solution

Set up the proportion in greater to lesser order:

$\frac{\text{calories used}}{\text{minutes exercised}}$

$\frac{60}{5} = \frac{420}{n}$

Let n = number of minutes needed to use **420** calories.

Cross multiply. $60 \cdot n = 5 \cdot 420$

Divide each side by **60**. $\frac{60 \cdot n}{60} = \frac{2{,}100}{60}$

Simplify each side. $n = 35$

You would need to exercise for **35** minutes to use **420** calories.

Set up a proportion for each problem. Then, solve the problem.

1. A student got a job during school vacation. He earned **$82.50** for the first **3** days of work. If he continues to work at the same daily rate, how much will he earn after **5** days? $\frac{\$82.50}{3\text{ days}} = \frac{\$n}{5\text{ days}}$; $137.50

2. How far can a train travel in **45** minutes if it is traveling at **68** miles per hour? $\frac{68\text{ mi}}{60\text{ min}} = \frac{n\text{ mi}}{45\text{ min}}$; 51 miles

3. How many gallons would a car use on a trip of **171** miles if it used **7** gallons on a trip of **133** miles? $\frac{7\text{ gal}}{133\text{ mi}} = \frac{n\text{ gal}}{171\text{ mi}}$; 9 gal

Check Understanding *If 50 is to n as 4 is to 18, what can you tell me about n?*
(Possible answer: $n \neq 18$ since $4 \neq 50$.)

In **direct proportion** problems, as one term increases, so does the other. When solving direct proportion problems, you can write more than one proportion.

Take another look at the problem. Another way to solve it is to set up the proportion to compare quantities with similar units, that is, calories to calories and time to time.

Solution

- Set up the proportion in lesser to greater order.

  Let n = number of minutes on the stair climber to use **420** calories.

- Notice that in each case, the resulting multiplication equation after cross multiplying is the same except for the order of the factors.

$$\frac{\text{fewer calories}}{\text{more calories}} \quad \frac{60 \text{ cal}}{420 \text{ cal}} = \frac{5 \text{ min}}{n \text{ min}} \quad \frac{\text{less time}}{\text{more time}}$$

Cross multiply. $60 \cdot n = 420 \cdot 5$

Divide each side by **60**. $\frac{60 \cdot n}{60} = \frac{2{,}100}{60}$

Simplify each side. $n = 35$

Write and solve a proportion for each problem. Remember there is more than one way to set up the proportion.

4. A jet flies **102.5** miles in **25** minutes. At that rate, how far will it go in **1.5** hours? $\frac{25 \text{ min}}{90 \text{ min}} = \frac{102.5 \text{ mi}}{n \text{ mi}}$; 369 mi

5. If $4\frac{1}{4}$ yards of cloth cost **$25.50,** then how much will **8** yards cost? $\frac{4.25 \text{ yd}}{\$25.50} = \frac{8 \text{ yd}}{\$x}$; $48.00

6. Mario can buy a dozen pencils for **$1.20.** How much will he pay for **100** pencils? $\frac{12 \text{ pencils}}{100 \text{ pencils}} = \frac{\$1.20}{\$n}$; $10.00

Problem Solving Reasoning **Solve.**

7. Raj charges **$8** for a half hour of computer instruction. How many hours of instruction can you get for **$100**?

$6\frac{1}{4}$ h

8. Maddie puts aside **$3** for every **$5** she earns. How much will she need to earn in order to save **$200?**

$333.33

Test Prep ★ Mixed Review

9 **Nita runs 9 miles in the same time it takes Winnie to run 12 miles. What is the simplest form of the ratio 9:12?** C; Obj. 4A

A 1:15 **C** 3:4

B 1:33 **D** 3:8

10 **What value of n makes $\frac{1}{5} = \frac{n}{45}$ a true proportion?** G; Obj. 4B

F 40 **H** 5

G 9 **J** 1

Closing the Lesson *Can you think of any formulas which are direct proportions?* (Possible answer: The circumference of a circle and its radius are directly proportional ($C = 2\pi r$).)

Name ____________________

Inverse Proportion

Guided Practice: Problem 1, p. 107
Independent Practice: Complete pp. 107–108

Sometimes the relationship between two quantities is in **inverse proportion.** That is, as one term increases, the other decreases. For example, as the *speed* of a car *increases*, the *time* it takes to get to a destination *decreases*.

A car traveling on a straight road at the rate of **30** miles per hour takes **12** minutes to go a certain distance. How long will it take a car traveling at **40** miles per hour to go the same distance on the same road?

Solution

- Identify the variable for the missing term.

Let x = time in minutes it takes the car traveling at **40** mph to go the same distance.

- Set up a ratio using the term in the situation that has the same unit of measure.

Both x and **12** represent minutes, so write $\frac{x}{12}$.

- Set up both ratios of the proportion in the same order. Then solve.

Decide: Which represents the lesser time, x or **12**? x should be less than **12** since it takes less time driving faster.

$$\frac{x \text{ min}}{12 \text{ min}} = \frac{30 \text{ mph}}{40 \text{ mph}}$$

$$\frac{\text{less time}}{\text{more time}} = \frac{\text{slower rate}}{\text{faster rate}}$$

$$40x = 360$$

$$x = 9$$

It will take the car driving **40** mph **9** minutes to go the same distance as the car going **30** mph.

Write a proportion for each situation. Then solve the problem.

1. The scoutmaster thought he had enough food to feed **24** scouts at camp for **8** days. How long would the food last if **32** scouts arrived at the camp?

$\frac{24 \text{ scouts}}{32 \text{ scouts}} = \frac{x \text{ days}}{8 \text{ days}}$; 6 days

2. Working together, it takes Al and Marvin **3** hours to shell **20** quarts of peas. How long might it take to shell the peas if **3** more people joined them?

$\frac{2 \text{ people}}{5 \text{ people}} = \frac{n \text{ hours}}{3 \text{ hours}}$; 1.2 hours

3. A committee of **7** students took **5** days of after-school time to decorate the auditorium for a school program. How many days would it have taken **10** students to do the same work?

$\frac{t \text{ days}}{5 \text{ days}} = \frac{7 \text{ students}}{10 \text{ students}}$; 3.5 days

4. At an average speed of **46** miles per hour, it takes about **7** hours for a truck driver to go from one end of a turnpike to the other. How long should it take the driver to travel the turnpike at an average speed of **60** miles per hour?

$\frac{x \text{ hours}}{7 \text{ hours}} = \frac{46 \text{ mph}}{60 \text{ mph}}$; $5\frac{11}{30}$ hours

Check Understanding *In an inverse proportion, what happens between the variables involved?* (Possible answer: As one variable increases, the other one decreases.)

Decide whether these are direct or inverse proportion problems. Then solve.

5. It takes Robin **2** hours to deliver about **50** newspapers. How long might it take her to deliver **75** papers?

direct proportion; 3 hours

6. It took **20** workers $2\frac{1}{2}$ days to repair a street.

How long might the job have taken if only **15** workers had been working?

inverse proportion; $3\frac{1}{3}$ days

7. In Ohio the maximum speed limit was lowered from **70** miles per hour to **55** miles per hour. At one time, you could drive from Cleveland, OH to Columbus, OH in only **3** hours. How much time should you allow for this trip now?

inverse proportion; 3.8 hours

8. A airplane traveling at **550** miles per hour took **4** hours to go **2,200** miles. With a tailwind, the speed of the plane increased to **560** miles per hour. How far would the plane travel in **4** hours at the greater speed?

direct proportion; 2,240 miles

9. Five parent volunteers spent **14** evenings helping paint the classrooms in the school building. About how many volunteers could have completed the same job in only **10** evenings?

inverse proportion; 7 volunteers

Problem Solving Reasoning **Solve.**

10. Suppose you are baking **12** dozen cookies for a party. It takes **8** minutes to roll, cut, and place a **dozen** cookies on a small cookie sheet. How much total time could you save if you cut, roll, and place **18** cookies on a larger sheet in the same amount of time?

32 min

11. A candidate hired **15** people to make calls to registered voters before an election. In **4** days, the callers reached about **1,000** voters. At the same rate, about how many more voters could they have reached working for **6** days?

500 voters

Test Prep ★ Mixed Review

12 **What is the value of *n* in the proportion $\frac{3}{17} = \frac{n}{51}$?** B; Obj. 4B

A 3 **C** 17

B 9 **D** 37

13 **It cost a company $260 to rent 4 meeting rooms at a hotel. What is the average cost per room?** H; Obj. 4C

F $1,040 **H** $65

G $260 **J** $4

Closing the Lesson *Is this an example of an inverse proportion? Explain. Stephanie's Health Store usually buys 480 health bars, which come in 12 boxes. This month she only bought 9 boxes. How many health bars did she get?* (No, this is a direct proportion. Since the number of boxes is decreasing, so will the number of health bars.)

Name ______________________________

Guided Practice: Problem 2, p. 109
Independent Practice: Complete pp. 109–110

Problem Solving Application: Is the Answer Reasonable?

In order to look back to know if your answer is reasonable, you need to know some basic relationships between the common units of measure. If you know the number of seconds in a minute, you can decide whether this answer is reasonable or not by using dimensional analysis. **Dimensional analysis** is a procedure for applying unit rates in rewriting units of measure.

Lucine walks at a rate of 240 feet per minute. She says that she is walking at a rate of 40 feet per second. Is this answer reasonable?

In this lesson, you may also need to set up and solve proportions.

Tips to Remember:

1. Understand 2. Decide 3. Solve 4. Look back

- Ask yourself: What do I know? What do I need to find?
- When you can, make a prediction about the answer. When you finish solving, ask "Is the answer reasonable?"
- Think about the strategies you have learned and use them to help you solve a problem.

Use dimensional analysis to solve. Check to see that your answer is reasonable.

1. How fast is Lucine walking in feet per second? Is she walking **40** feet per second?

Think: **1** minute = **60** seconds, so

$$\frac{\textbf{240 feet}}{\textbf{1 minute}} \times \frac{\textbf{1 minute}}{\textbf{60 seconds}} = \frac{4\ \text{feet}}{1\ \text{second}}$$

Answer No; She is walking 4 feet per second.

2. Mrs. Dodge plans to travel **200** miles at **60** miles per hour. Is **4** hours a reasonable time to allow? Explain.

Think: $\textbf{200 miles} \times \frac{\textbf{1 hour}}{\textbf{60 miles}} = 3\frac{1}{3}$ hours

Answer Yes; 4 hours will give her a little extra time.

3. Paul has a yearly salary of **$34,000** and is paid weekly. He says that this works out at more than **$650** per week. Is his statement reasonable?

Think: **1** year = **52** weeks

Answer Yes; He makes about $654 per week.

4. Sally cycled a distance of **5** mi in **30** min and Hal cycled **8** km in **25** min. Sally claimed that her time was faster. Was her claim reasonable?

Think: **1** mi = **1.6** km

Answer No; Sally's rate is 10 miles per hour; Hal's rate is equivalent to 12 miles per hour.

Check Understanding *To change miles to feet, what unit ratio would you use?* $\left(\frac{5{,}280\ \text{ft}}{1\ \text{mi}}\right)$ *Why?*
(So the miles unit in the denominator of the unit rate cancels the miles you are rewriting.)

Solve. Use dimensional analysis where appropriate. Is the answer provided reasonable?

5. Mr. Field checked the price of an **18** ounce box of corn flakes and found it was **$3.99.** A tag on the shelf said the unit price was **2¢** per ounce. Is this reasonable? Explain.

No; The unit price is 22¢ per ounce.

6. The exchange rate from United States dollars to Canadian dollars is **$1.00** to **$1.45.** Is it reasonable to expect more than **250** Canadian dollars for **150** U.S. dollars? Explain.

No; 150 U. S. dollars is 217.5 Canadian dollars.

7. The area of a room that needs to be carpeted is **15** square yards. Is it reasonable to purchase **45** square feet of carpet to do the room? Explain.

No; 1 yd^2 = 9 ft^2; 15 yd^2 = 135 ft^2.

8. A car is traveling at **60** miles per hour. Is this faster than **50** feet per second? Explain.

Yes; 60 miles per hour is equivalent to 88 feet per second.

9. Can you earn **$500** in the next **3** weeks if you make **$5.25** per hour and work **6** hours per day, **5** days per week? Explain.

No; You will only earn $472.50.

10. A recipe calls for $1\frac{1}{4}$ cup of milk. If you only have **one** quart of milk, is it reasonable to try to **triple** the recipe? Explain.

Yes; 1 quart = 4 cups; $3\frac{3}{4}$ cups < 4 cups

Extend Your Thinking

11. If the exchange rate were **1.45** U.S. dollars to **1** Canadian dollar, how much would you get for **150** U.S. dollars?

103.45 Canadian dollars

12. Explain your method for solving problem **8.** Is there more than one way to solve the problem?

Explanations will vary; Students might try to write equivalent rates in feet per minute to compare rates.

$\frac{60 \text{ mi}}{1\text{h}} \cdot \frac{1 \text{ h}}{60 \text{ min}} \cdot \frac{1 \text{ min}}{60} \cdot \frac{5{,}280 \text{ ft}}{1 \text{ mi}} = \frac{88 \text{ ft}}{1 \text{ s}}$

Closing the Lesson *If you change from feet per hour to feet per minute, should you expect more or fewer feet than you have?* (Fewer, since time is shorter.)

Name ________________________________

Guided Practice: Ex. 1 & 7, pp. 111–112
Independent Practice: Complete pp. 111–113

A **scale drawing** is a picture or drawing in which the dimensions are proportional to the actual dimensions of an object. A scale drawing could be larger (an enlargement) or smaller (a reduction) than the actual object. Maps and blueprints are common examples of scale drawings.

The ratio of the measurements in the scale drawing to the actual measurements is called the **scale factor.** To find the actual size of an object, you can use the scale factor to write a proportion.

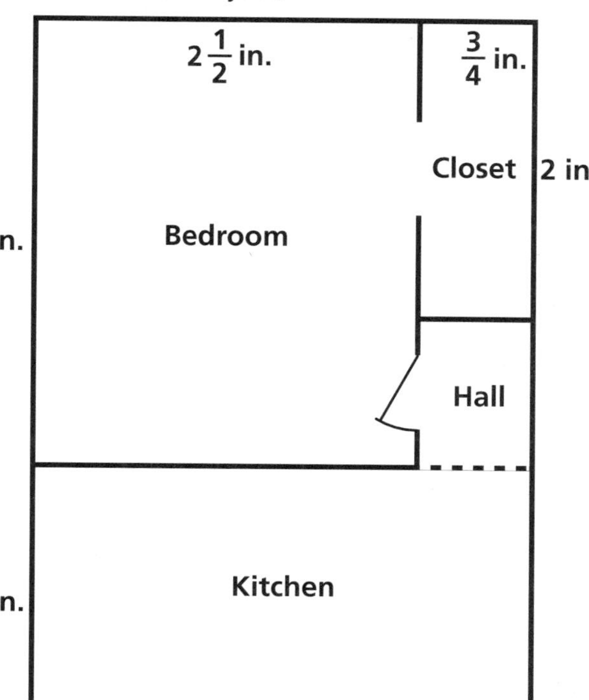

The blueprint has a scale factor of $\frac{1}{4}$ in. to **1** ft. What is the actual width of the bedroom?

Solution: Let x = width of the room in feet. Set up a proportion and simplify the fractions.

$2\frac{1}{2} = \frac{5}{2}$

feet ↓ inches ↓

$$\frac{1}{x} = \frac{\frac{1}{4}}{\frac{5}{2}}$$

Think: $\frac{1}{4} \times \frac{2}{5} = \frac{1}{10}$

$$\frac{1}{x} = \frac{1}{10}$$

$$x = 10$$

The bedroom is **10** feet wide.

Use the blueprint to complete the table.

	Room	Blueprint Length	Actual Length	Blueprint Width	Actual Width
1.	Bedroom	3 in.	12 ft	$2\frac{1}{2}$ in.	10 ft
2.	Kitchen	$1\frac{3}{4}$ in.	7 ft	$3\frac{1}{4}$ in.	13 ft
3.	Closet	2 in.	8 ft	$\frac{3}{4}$ in.	3 ft
4.	Hall	1 in.	4 ft	$\frac{3}{4}$ in.	3 ft

Use a scale factor of $\frac{1}{8}$ in. to 1 ft to find the actual length.

5. scale of $2\frac{1}{4}$ in. = actual length of 18 ft   scale of $1\frac{1}{2}$ in. = actual length of 12 ft

6. scale of $1\frac{3}{4}$ in. = actual length of 14 ft   scale of $2\frac{5}{8}$ in. = actual length of 21 ft

Check Understanding *If a map had a scale factor of 2 cm to 5 mi, what would that mean?* (Possible answer: Every 2 cm on the map corresponds to an actual distance of 5 mi.)

If you know the scale of a map, you can use proportions to estimate the actual distance.

On the trail map, the distance from Benson's Cabin to Roaring Falls is **3.8** cm. What is the actual distance between the two places?

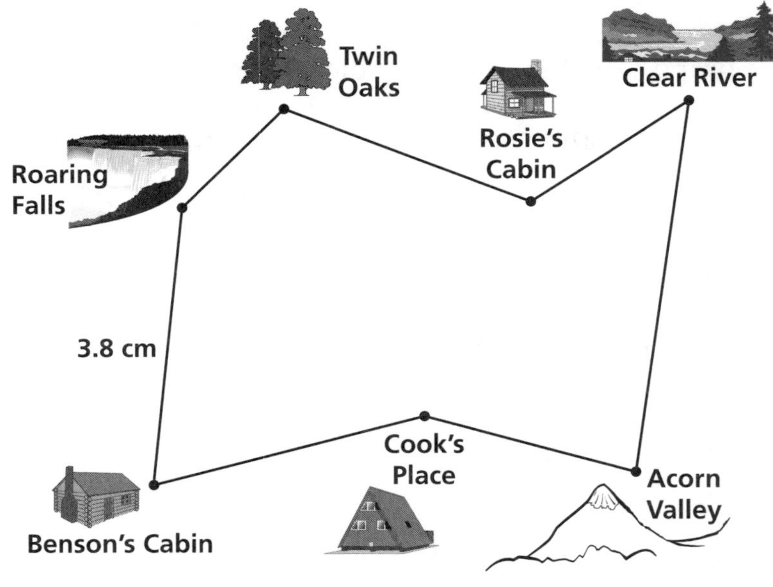

Solution:

Let x = actual distance in km

The map has been drawn using a **scale** of **2** cm : **3** km. Use the scale to set up the proportion:

$$\frac{2\text{ cm}}{3\text{ km}} = \frac{3.8\text{ cm}}{x}$$

$$2x = 3 \cdot 3.8$$

$$\frac{2x}{2} = \frac{11.4}{2}$$

$$x = 5.7$$

The actual distance from Benson's Cabin to Roaring Falls is **5.7** km.

Use a metric ruler to measure each trail to the nearest tenth of a centimeter. Then, find the actual distance. Measures may vary slightly.

7. Benson's Cabin to Roaring Falls scale 3.8 cm actual 5.7 km

8. Roaring Falls to Twin Oaks scale 1.9 cm actual 2.85 km

9. Twin Oaks to Rosie's Cabin scale 3.5 cm actual 5.25 km

10. Rosie's Cabin to Clear River scale 2.5 cm actual 3.75 km

11. Clear River to Acorn Valley scale 5.2 cm actual 7.8 km

12. Acorn Valley to Cook's Place scale 2.9 cm actual 4.35 km

13. Cook's Place to Benson's Cabin scale 3.7 cm actual 5.55 km

14. What is the actual roundtrip distance? 35.25 km

15. If you hike at a rate of **5** kilometers per hour, approximately how long will the roundtrip take? about 7 hours

Name ______________________________

Use a metric ruler to construct a scale drawing on the grid.

16. Measure the dimensions of the figure below in centimeters. Enlarge the figure by a scale factor of **3:1**; that is, draw all dimensions three times longer.

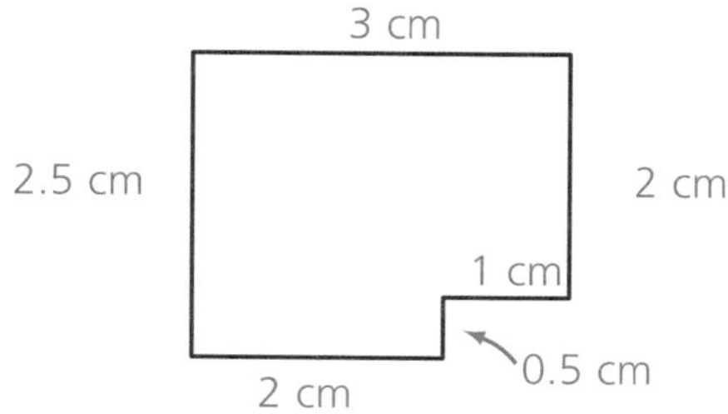

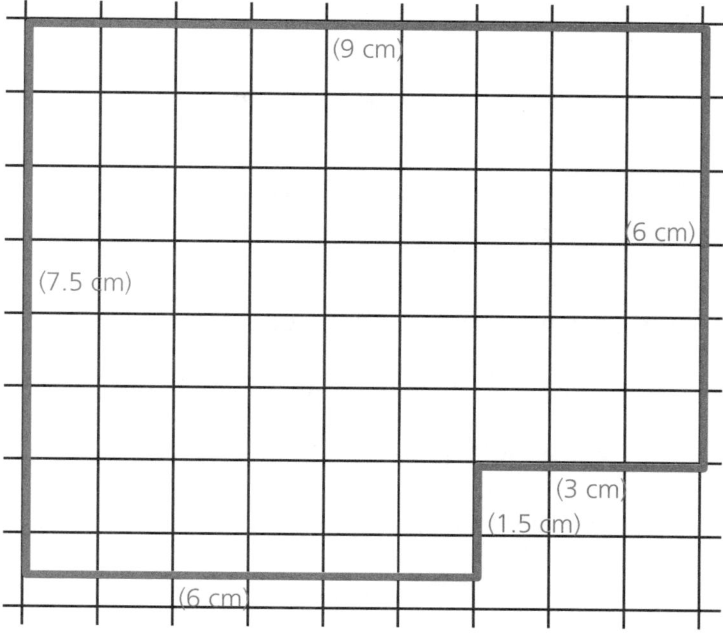

Use the figures in exercise 16 to complete.

17. What is the ratio of the perimeters of the enlarged and original figures? How is this ratio related to the scale factor?

Ratio of the perimeters is the same as the scale factor, 3 : 1.

18. What is the ratio of the areas of the enlarged and original figures? How is this ratio related to the scale factor?

Ratio of the areas is the square of the scale factor, or 9 : 1.

Quick Check

Decide whether the situation is a direct or inverse proportion. Then solve.

19. On the highway, a sports car averages **32** miles on a gallon of gas. The car went **512** miles on a tank of gas. About how much does the gas tank hold? direct; 16 gallons

20. Working together, it takes **2** students about **3** hours to set up the cafeteria for a party. How long would it have taken if **3** more students had offered to help? inverse; $1\frac{1}{5}$ h

The scale on a map is $\frac{1}{4}$ in. = 3 mi. Complete the statement.

21. 6 in. on the map represents 72 mi.

22. $1\frac{1}{4}$ in. represents **15** mi.

Work Space.

Item	Error Analysis
19–20	**Common Error** Watch for students who set up the terms in the wrong order. **Reteaching** Reteach 25, 26
21–22	**Common Error** Watch for students who cannot interpret scale factors correctly. **Reteaching** Reteach 27

Closing the Lesson *If the scale factor is $\frac{2}{3}$, what would be the length of a side in a scale drawing if the original side is 9 cm?* (6 cm)

Name ____________________

Guided Practice: Ex. 1, 13, 16, 19 & 22, pp. 114–116

Independent Practice: Complete pp. 114–116

Percents, Decimals, and Fractions

A **percent** is a ratio with a denominator of **100**. The symbol % means *per one hundred*. The square at the right contains **100** small squares. Each small square is **1%** of the whole square.

24 of the **100** little squares are shaded. So **24%** of the large square is shaded.

76 of the **100** little squares are unshaded. So **76%** of the large square is unshaded.

Complete. Do not use the same square more than once.

(gray)	X	X	X	O	R	R	B	Y	P
(gray)	X	X	X	O	R	R	B	Y	P
(gray)	X	X	X	O	R	R	B	Y	P
(gray)	X	X	X	O	R	R	B	Y	P
(gray)	X	X	X	O	R	R	B	Y	P
(gray)	X	X	O	O	R	R	B	P	P
(gray)	X	X	O	O	R	R	B	P	P
(gray)	X	X	O	O	R	R	B	P	P
(gray)	X	X	O	O	R	R	G	P	P
(gray)	X	X	O	O	R	R	G	P	P

Sample answers shown.

1. Shade **10%** of the squares gray. What percent of the grid is unshaded? 90%
2. Put X's in **25%** of the squares. What percent of the grid remains blank? 65%
3. Put O's in **15%** of the squares. What percent of the grid remains blank? 50%
4. Using different colors, show **20%; 8%; 2%; 5%; 15%**
   R B G Y P
5. What percent of the grid remains blank? 0%
6. Is the entire region marked or shaded? Yes.

Write the percent.

7. Mary's sweater is **80%** cotton. What percent is not cotton? 20%
8. Jamal said his team won **80%** of their games. What percent did they lose? 20%
9. If **93%** of your class has perfect attendance, what percent have been absent? 7%
10. If **70%** of Earth's surface is water, what percent is not water? 30%
11. So far, Mr. Quinn has planted **48%** of his farm in corn and **23%** in oats. What percent of the farm is not planted? 29%
12. A survey showed that **45%** of the class likes peas, **32%** likes carrots, and **38%** like neither. What percent of the class like both peas and carrots? 15%

Check Understanding *If a hundredths squared grid has 63 squares shaded, what percent is shaded? Not shaded?* (63%; 37%) *How do you change 62% to a decimal?* (62% $= \frac{62}{100}$ and $\frac{62}{100} = 0.62$)

Name ______________________________

Percents can be written in more than one form.

Percent Form	Fraction Form	Decimal Form
50%	$\frac{50}{100}$	**0.50**

Study these examples of how to use the meaning of percent to change between percent and decimal form.

Writing a Percent as a Decimal

To change from a percent to a decimal, remove the % symbol and multiply by **0.01.** This is the same as moving the decimal point two places to the left.

Write the percent as an equivalent fraction in hundredths first.

Write **58%** as a decimal.

$$58\% \rightarrow \frac{58}{100} \rightarrow 0.58$$

Write **7.5%** as a decimal.

$$7.5\% \rightarrow \frac{7.5}{100} \rightarrow 0.075$$

Writing a Decimal as a Percent

To change from a decimal to a percent, multiply the decimal by **100** and write a % symbol. This is the same as moving the decimal point two places to the right.

Write the decimal as an equivalent fraction in hundredths first.

Write **0.42** as a percent.

$$0.42 \rightarrow \frac{42}{100} \rightarrow 42\%$$

Write **0.2** as a percent.

$$0.2 \rightarrow \frac{20}{100} \rightarrow 20\%$$

Write the percent as a decimal.

13. 15% = 0.15   65% = 0.65   7% = 0.07   90% = 0.9 or 0.90

14. 60% = 0.6 or 0.60   7.5% = 0.075   20% = 0.2 or 0.20   73% = 0.73

15. 11% = 0.11   1.2% = 0.012   12.5% = 0.125   8.75% = 0.0875

Write the decimal as a percent.

16. 0.28 = 28 %   0.13 = 13 %   0.065 = 6.5 %   0.80 = 80 %

17. 0.92 = 92 %   0.43 = 43 %   0.5 = 50 %   0.3 = 30 %

18. 0.05 = 5 %   0.64 = 64 %   0.01 = 1 %   0.4 = 40 %

Study these examples of how to change between percent and fraction form.

Writing a Percent as a Fraction

Write the percent as an equivalent fraction in hundredths first. Then simplify.

Write **64%** as a fraction.

$$64\% \rightarrow \frac{64}{100} = \frac{16}{25}$$

Write **5%** as a fraction.

$$5\% \rightarrow \frac{5}{100} = \frac{1}{20}$$

Writing a Fraction as a Percent

Write the fraction as an equivalent fraction in hundredths first.

Write $\frac{3}{4}$ as a percent.

$$\frac{3}{4} \rightarrow \frac{75}{100} = 75\%$$

Other Example
Sometimes you may need to write the fraction as an equivalent fraction in thousandths first.

Write $\frac{3}{8}$ as a percent.

$$\frac{3}{8} \rightarrow \frac{375}{1{,}000} \rightarrow \frac{37.5}{100} = 37.5\%$$

Write the percent as a fraction.

19. 24% = $\frac{6}{25}$　　60% = $\frac{3}{5}$　　15% = $\frac{3}{20}$　　45% = $\frac{9}{20}$

20. 18% = $\frac{9}{50}$　　95% = $\frac{19}{20}$　　80% = $\frac{4}{5}$　　4% = $\frac{1}{25}$

Write the fraction as a percent.

21. $\frac{65}{100}$ = 65%　　$\frac{19}{50}$ = 38%　　$\frac{1}{8}$ = 12.5%　　$\frac{3}{25}$ = 12%

22. $\frac{3}{10}$ = 30%　　$\frac{6}{10}$ = 60%　　$\frac{1}{20}$ = 5%　　$\frac{11}{20}$ = 55%

Problem Solving Reasoning　**Solve.**

23. On Monday, **4** students were absent from a class of **25** students. What percent of the students in the class were present on Monday? 84%

24. Kayla got some money for her birthday. She spent **0.65** of her money on school supplies. What percent of her money is left? 35%

Test Prep ★ Mixed Review

25 **The scale on a map is 1 cm:500 m. What is the actual distance between towns that are 10.5 cm apart on the map?** C; Obj. 4D

A 47.6 m　　**C** 5,250 m

B 5,250 km　　**D** 5,250 cm

26 **A car went 84 miles in $3\frac{1}{2}$ hours? How can you express this rate as a unit rate?** J; Obj. 4C

F 294 miles per hour　　**H** $3\frac{1}{2}$ hours

G 84 miles　　**J** 24 miles per hour

Closing the Lesson *How do you change $\frac{1}{5}$ to a percent?* (Possible answer: Rewrite $\frac{1}{5}$ as $\frac{20}{100}$ and $\frac{20}{100}$ = 20%.) *What does percent mean?* (division by 100)

Name ______________________

Guided Practice: First ex. in Rows 1 & 5, pp. 117–118
Independent Practice: Complete pp. 117–118

Fractional and Decimal Percents

Sometimes you need to use fractions or decimals to write a percent as an equivalent fraction in hundredths or thousandths.

Writing a Percent as a Decimal

To write a percent as a decimal, remove the % symbol and multiply by **0.01.**

Write $\frac{1}{3}$% as a decimal. $\frac{1}{3} = 0.\overline{3}$

$\frac{1}{3}\% \rightarrow 0.\overline{3}\% \rightarrow 0.33\overline{3} \cdot 0.01 = 0.0033\overline{3}$ or $0.00\overline{3}$

Writing a Decimal as a Percent

To write a decimal as a percent, multiply the decimal by **100** and write a % symbol.

Write **0.00825** as a percent.

$0.00825 \cdot 100 = 0.825\%$

Writing a Percent as a Fraction

To write a percent as a fraction, remove the % symbol, and multiply by $\frac{1}{100}$.

Write $7\frac{1}{4}$% as a fraction.

$7\frac{1}{4}\% \rightarrow \frac{29}{4}\% \rightarrow \frac{29}{4} \cdot \frac{1}{100} = \frac{29}{400}$

Writing a Fraction as a Percent

To write a fraction as a percent, multiply by **100,** and write a % symbol.

Write $\frac{2}{3}$ as a percent.

$\frac{2}{3} \cdot 100 \rightarrow \frac{200}{3} = 66\frac{2}{3}\%$

Write the percent as a decimal and a fraction.

1. 18.5% = $0.185 = \frac{37}{200}$ 1.25% = $0.0125 = \frac{1}{80}$ 20% = $0.2 = \frac{1}{5}$ $22\frac{1}{2}\%$ = $0.225 = \frac{9}{40}$

2. $8\frac{3}{4}\%$ = $0.0875 = \frac{7}{80}$ 1.02% = $0.0102 = \frac{51}{5{,}000}$ $6\frac{1}{2}\%$ = $0.065 = \frac{13}{200}$ $8\frac{1}{6}\%$ = $0.081\overline{6} = \frac{49}{600}$

3. 62.4% = $0.624 = \frac{78}{125}$ 0.1% = $0.001 = \frac{1}{1{,}000}$ 0.5% = $0.005 = \frac{1}{200}$ $\frac{3}{4}\%$ = $0.0075 = \frac{3}{400}$

4. 21.5% = $0.215 = \frac{43}{200}$ $19\frac{3}{4}\%$ = $0.1975 = \frac{79}{400}$ 99% = $0.99 = \frac{99}{100}$ 0.99% = $0.0099 = \frac{99}{10{,}000}$

Write the decimal or fraction as a percent.

5. 0.544 = 54.4 % $\frac{5}{12}$ = $41.\overline{6}$ % $\frac{1}{3}$ = $33\frac{1}{3}$ % $\frac{3}{5}$ = 60 %

6. 0.0125 = 1.25 % 0.008 = 0.8 % 0.955 = 95.5 % $\frac{7}{40}$ = 17.5 %

7. $\frac{7}{20}$ = 35 % $\frac{7}{1000}$ = 0.7 % $\frac{5}{6}$ = $83\frac{1}{3}$ % 0.111 = 11.1 %

8. 0.625 = 62.5 % $\frac{1}{7}$ = $14.\overline{285714}$ % $\frac{4}{9}$ = $44.\overline{4}$ % 2.5 = 250 %

Check Understanding *What does $\frac{2}{9}$ equal when written as a percent?* ($22\frac{2}{9}$%)
Write $\frac{2}{3}$ as a decimal and as a percent. ($0.66\frac{2}{3}$ or $0.\overline{6}$, $66\frac{2}{3}$%)

Certain percents are used more often than others. Complete the following table of *benchmark* percents.

9.	**Percent**	50%	$33\frac{1}{3}\%$	25%	10%	1%	20%	5%	75%	15%	$66\frac{2}{3}\%$
10.	**Fraction**	$\frac{1}{2}$	$\frac{1}{3}$	$\frac{1}{4}$	$\frac{1}{10}$	$\frac{1}{100}$	$\frac{1}{5}$	$\frac{1}{20}$	$\frac{3}{4}$	$\frac{3}{20}$	$\frac{2}{3}$
11.	**Decimal**	0.5	$0.\overline{3}$	0.25	0.1	0.01	0.2	0.05	0.75	0.15	$0.\overline{6}$

Problem Solving
Reasoning

Solve.

12. A baked potato has **25** units of Vitamin A. Nutritionists suggest that the average daily amount should be **5,000** units of Vitamin A. What percent of the daily recommended amount does a baked potato have? 0.5%

13. You read in a newspaper that the bank offered an interest rate of $8\frac{5}{8}\%$ on a personal loan. What is the decimal form of this interest rate?

0.08625

14. Write $\frac{1}{8}, \frac{2}{8}, \frac{3}{8}, \ldots, \frac{8}{8}$ as percents. Describe the pattern that you observe.

12.5%, 25%, 37.5%, . . . , 100%; Each term is a consecutive multiple of 12.5%.

15. A sign painter ran out of paint. What percent of the sign still needs to be painted? 75%

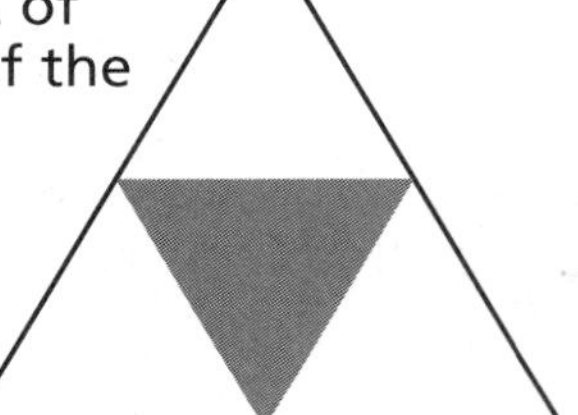

Quick Check

Write the percent as a decimal and a fraction.

16. 60%
$0.6 = \frac{3}{5}$

17. 8%
$0.08 = \frac{2}{25}$

18. 5.9%
$0.059 = \frac{59}{1,000}$

19. 0.2%
$0.002 = \frac{1}{500}$

20. 8.5%
$0.085 = \frac{17}{200}$

21. $66\frac{2}{3}\%$
$0.\overline{6} = \frac{2}{3}$

Write the decimal or fraction as a percent.

22. $\frac{3}{4}$
75%

23. 0.7
70%

24. $\frac{19}{25}$
76%

25. $\frac{9}{40}$
22.5%

26. 0.0175
1.75%

27. $\frac{1}{200}$
0.5%

Work Space.

Item	Error Analysis
16–21	**Common Error** Watch for students who do not write equivalent fractions or decimals in thousands. **Reteaching** Strand 10, Skill 6, Practice 1, Skill 7, Practice 1–2, 4–5
22–27	**Common Error** Watch for students who multiply by 100 instead of 0.01. **Skill Lab** Strand 10, Skill 3, Practice 1–4, Skill 4, Practice 1–4

Closing the Lesson *How do you change a fractional percent to a decimal?* (Remove the % symbol, write the fraction as a decimal, and multiply this decimal by 0.01.) *How do you write a decimal as a percent?* (Multiply the decimal by 100 and add the % symbol.)

Name ______________________

Percents Greater than 100%

Guided Practice: First ex. in Rows 1, 3 & 4, pp. 119–120
Independent Practice: Complete pp. 119–120

Percents greater than **100%** represent more than the whole. You may have scored more than **100%** on a test because of extra credit. You may have heard someone say, "I feel **200%** better!" The price of certain goods may have increased **350%**.

These are all examples of percents greater than **100%.** They are greater than **1,** and they may be written in decimal and fraction form.

Writing a Percent as a Decimal

To write a percent as a decimal, remove the % symbol and multiply by **0.01.**

Write **150%** as a decimal.

$150\% = 150 \cdot 0.01 \rightarrow 1.5$

Writing a Decimal as a Percent

To write a decimal as a percent, multiply the decimal by **100** and write a % symbol.

Write **3** as a percent.

$3 \cdot 100 = 300\%$

Writing a Percent as a Fraction

To write a percent as a fraction, remove the % symbol and multiply by $\frac{1}{100}$.

Write **225%** as a fraction or mixed number in simplest form.

$$225\% = 225 \cdot \frac{1}{100} = \frac{225}{100} = 2\frac{25}{100} \rightarrow 2\frac{1}{4}$$

simplest form

Writing a Fraction as a Percent

To write a fraction as a percent, multiply by **100**, and write a % symbol.

Write $\frac{5}{4}$ as a percent.

$\frac{5}{4} \cdot 100 \rightarrow \frac{500}{4} \rightarrow 125\%$

Write the percent as a decimal and a fraction or mixed number in simplest form.

1. $185\% = 1.85 = 1\frac{17}{20}$ $125\% = 1.25 = 1\frac{1}{4}$ $240\% = 2.4 = 2\frac{2}{5}$ $225\frac{1}{2}\% = 2.255 = 2\frac{51}{200}$

2. $181\% = 1.81 = 1\frac{81}{100}$ $1{,}000\% = 10 = \frac{10}{1}$ $6\frac{1}{2}\% = 0.065 = \frac{13}{200}$ $380\% = 3.8 = 3\frac{4}{5}$

3. $625\% = 6.25 = 6\frac{1}{4}$ $190\% = 1.9 = 1\frac{9}{10}$ $500\% = 5 = \frac{5}{1}$ $415\% = 4.15 = 4\frac{3}{20}$

Write the decimal or fraction as a percent.

4. $5.4 = 540\%$ $\frac{15}{12} = 125\%$ $\frac{4}{3} = 133\frac{1}{3}\%$ $\frac{6}{5} = 120\%$

5. $\frac{8}{5} = 160\%$ $3.25 = 325\%$ $1.18 = 118\%$ $\frac{7}{6} = 116\frac{2}{3}\%$

6. $1.05 = 105\%$ $\frac{7}{3} = 233\frac{1}{3}\%$ $222 = 22{,}200\%$ $4 = 400\%$

Check Understanding *Write 175% as a fraction or mixed number in simplest form and as a decimal.* ($1\frac{3}{4}$, 1.75)

Complete the following table of some *benchmark* percents.

7.	**Percent**	100%	150%	500%	225%	1000%	175%	400%	125%	200%	$133\frac{1}{3}$%
8.	**Fraction**	1	$\frac{3}{2}$	5	$2\frac{1}{4}$	10	$1\frac{3}{4}$	4	$\frac{5}{4}$	2	$\frac{4}{3}$
9.	**Decimal**	1	1.5	5	2.25	10	1.75	4	1.25	2	$1.\overline{3}$

Complete. Write your answer as a fraction in simplest form, a decimal, or a percent.

10. Kate earned **$400**. She needed **$250** for a new CD player. What percent of the money needed is the money raised? 62.5%

11. A bus will hold **60** people. There are **80** students who decided to go on the field trip. What percent of the bus capacity is the number of students wishing to go? $133\frac{1}{3}$%

12. Kymea bought a pager two years ago for **$90.** Her sister just paid **30%** more for one. What fraction of Kymea's price was her sister's price? $\frac{13}{10}$

13. A vitamin capsule provides **3** times the daily requirement of Vitamin C. What percent of the daily requirement is that? 300%

Problem Solving Reasoning Solve.

14. "Satisfaction guaranteed or double your money back." What percent of the cost of the item will you receive if you are not satisfied?

200%

15. Write $\frac{4}{4}, \frac{5}{4}, \frac{6}{4}, \ldots, \frac{10}{4}$ as percents.

Describe the pattern that you observe.

100%, 125%, 150%, . . . , 250%; Each percent is 25% more than the preceding one.

Test Prep ★ Mixed Review

16 Mia has 79¢. What percent of a dollar is that? A; Obj. 4E

A 79%
B 7.9%
C 0.79%
D 0.079%

17 The scale on a map is 1 in.: 5 mi. How far apart on the map are towns whose actual distance from each other is $27\frac{1}{2}$ miles? F; Obj. 4D

F $5\frac{1}{2}$ in.
G $22\frac{1}{2}$ in.
H $137\frac{1}{2}$ in.
J $5\frac{1}{2}$ mi

Closing the Lesson *How would you write 110% as a decimal?* (First, remove the % symbol → 110. Then, multiply by 0.01 (or divide by 100) → 1.10.)

Name ______________________

Guided Practice: First ex. in Rows 1, 4, 7 & 10, pp. 121–122
Independent Practice: Complete pp. 121–122

Estimating with Fractions, Decimals, and Percents

Two numbers that form a basic division fact are **compatible numbers**. For example, **6** and **30** are compatible numbers because **30 ÷ 6 = 5.** You can use compatible numbers to estimate with percents.

Estimate $\frac{11}{16}$ of **389.**

1. Think: $\frac{11}{16}$ is close to $\frac{12}{16} = \frac{3}{4}$.
2. **389** is close to **400,** which is a compatible number with **4.**
3. $\frac{11}{16}$ of 389 $\approx \frac{3}{4}$ of 400 $\rightarrow \frac{3}{4} \times 400 \rightarrow 300$

So $\frac{11}{16}$ of **389** is about **300.**

Estimate **42%** of **209.**

1. Think: **42%** is close to **40%** $= \frac{2}{5}$
2. **209** is close to **200,** which is a compatible number with **5.**
3. 42% of 209 $\approx \frac{2}{5}$ of 200 $\rightarrow \frac{2}{5} \times 200 \rightarrow 80$

So **42%** of **209** is about **80.**

Circle the correct answer.

1. 78% is closer to $\frac{1}{2}$ or $\frac{3}{4}$ (circled)? 87% is closer to $\frac{1}{2}$ or $\frac{3}{4}$ (circled)? 33% is closer to $\frac{1}{3}$ (circled) or $\frac{3}{10}$?

2. 61% is closer to $\frac{1}{2}$ or $\frac{2}{3}$ (circled)? 21% is closer to $\frac{1}{4}$ or $\frac{1}{5}$ (circled)? 72% is closer to $\frac{2}{3}$ or $\frac{3}{4}$ (circled)?

3. 27% is closer to $\frac{1}{4}$ (circled) or $\frac{1}{3}$? 45% is closer to $\frac{2}{5}$ (circled) or $\frac{3}{5}$? 38% is closer to $\frac{1}{2}$ or $\frac{1}{3}$ (circled)?

Find compatible numbers. Answers may vary.

4. $\frac{3}{5}$ of 127 5 and 125 $\frac{2}{3}$ of 797 3 and 750 $\frac{1}{4}$ of 156 4 and 160

5. $\frac{7}{16}$ of 45 16 and 48 $\frac{27}{50}$ of 8,900 50 and 9,000 $\frac{2}{7}$ of 342 7 and 350

6. $\frac{1}{8}$ of 620 8 and 640 $\frac{13}{16}$ of 902 20 and 1,000 $\frac{8}{9}$ of 27 9 and 27

Estimate. Record your method and your solution. Estimates may vary.

7. $\frac{3}{7}$ of 50 $\frac{1}{2}$ of 50 = 25 $\frac{11}{34}$ of 62 $\frac{1}{3}$ of 60 = 20 $\frac{2}{11}$ of 311 $\frac{1}{6}$ of 300 = 50

8. $\frac{7}{12}$ of 53 $\frac{1}{2}$ of 50 = 25 $\frac{2}{9}$ of 478 $\frac{1}{5}$ of 500 = 100 $\frac{13}{16}$ of 212 $\frac{3}{4}$ of 200 = 150

9. 0.55 of 515 $\frac{1}{2}$ of 500 = 250 0.78 of 419 $\frac{3}{4}$ of 400 = 300 0.62 of 41 $\frac{3}{5}$ of 40 = 24

Check Understanding *How would you estimate 7% of 123?* (Think: 10% of 120 is 12, 7% is a little more than half that, so 8 would be a good estimate.)

You can also use rounding to estimate answers. Remember that dividing a number by **10**, or finding $\frac{1}{10}$ of a number, is the same as moving the decimal point one place to the left.

Estimate **15%** of **$48.92.**

15% of **$48.92** is close to **15%** of **$50.**

10% of $50 = $5.00
+ 5% of $50 = $2.50
15% of $50 = $7.50

15% of **$48.92** is about **$7.50.**

Estimate **30%** of **$81.99.**

30% of **$81.99** is close to **30%** of **$80.**

10% of $80 = $8
10% of $80 = $8
+ 10% of $80 = $8
30% of $80 = $24

30% of **$81.99** is about **$24.**

Estimate. Estimates may vary.

10. 10% of 42 4.2 | 10% of $834.75 $83.48 | 11% of 83 8.8

11. 15% of 38 6 | 15% of $139 $21 | 14% of 29 4.5

12. 20% of $81.95 $16 | 20% of 72 14 | 22% of $91.62 $18.18

13. 30% of $158.62 $48 | 50% of $482.99 $240 | 5% of 182 9

Problem Solving Reasoning **Solve.**

14. Mr. Johnson's restaurant bill was **$87.89.** He wants to leave a **15%** tip. Explain how to estimate the tip. Methods may vary.
10% of $90 = $9.00
5% of 90 = $4.50; total: $13.50

15. A video game that sells for **$38.99** is on sale at **20%** off. Explain how you would estimate the amount you would save.
20% = $\frac{1}{5}$; $38.99 ≈ $40.00; $8.00

Quick Check

Write the percent as a decimal and a fraction.

16. 60% 0.6 = $\frac{3}{5}$

17. 400% 4 = $\frac{4}{1}$

18. 350% 3.5 = $\frac{7}{2}$

Write the decimal or fraction as a percent.

19. 18 1,800%

20. $\frac{9}{6}$ 150%

21. 1.09 109%

Estimate. Estimates may vary slightly.

22. 9% of 38 4

23. 36% of 92 30

24. 22% of 41 8

Work Space.

Item	Error Analysis
16–18	**Common Error** Watch for students who move the decimal in the wrong direction. **Skill Lab** Strand 10, Skills 4, 7
19–21	**Common Error** Watch for students who cannot write whole numbers as percents. **Skill Lab** Strand 10, Skills 3, 5
22–24	**Common Error** Watch for students who cannot find compatible numbers. **Reteaching** Reteach 28

Closing the Lesson *Explain what the general strategy is in estimating fractions, decimals, and percents.* (Possible answer: Round the fractions, decimals, and percents to ones easy to use, round the whole number to a compatible number, and multiply.)

Name ____________________

Guided Practice: Ex. 1, p. 123
Independent Practice: Complete pp. 123–124

Problem Solving Strategy: Work Backward

To solve problems, you may need to work backward, using inverse operations to "undo" the operations that have been done.

Problem

You use your birthday money to go to a concert. You spend half of your money on the ticket, half of what you have left on a T-shirt, $3.00 on a program, and you have $8.00 left. How much money did you receive for your birthday?

1 Understand

"Asking yourself questions will help you identify the math ideas."

As you reread, ask yourself questions.

- How much money did you have at the end?

  You had **$8.00** at the end.

- How much did you have just before your last purchase?

  You spent **$3.00** on a program, so you must have had **$11.00.**

- What do you need to find? how much you got for your birthday

2 Decide

"Writing out the steps in the problem helps you think about how to solve the problem."

Choose a method for solving.

Try the strategy Draw a Diagram.

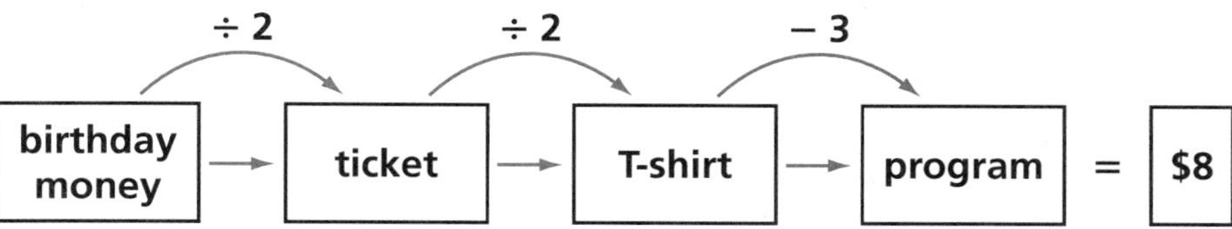

- How will you find how much money you began with?

3 Solve

"Doing the opposite, or using inverse operations, brings you back to the beginning."

Start at the ending amount and work backward.

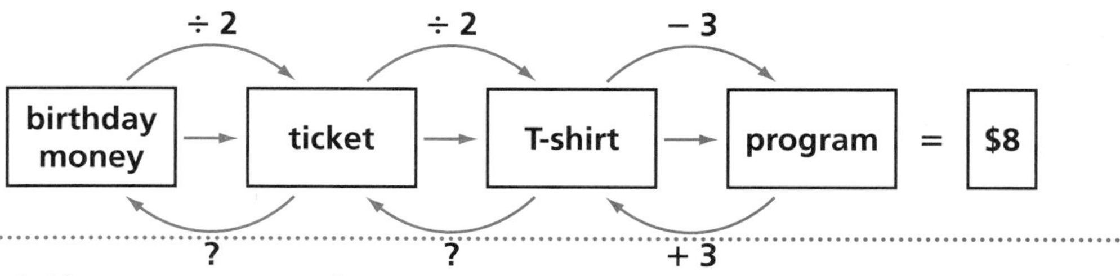

4 Look back

"Check your answer by performing the calculations in the problem. Did you end up with $8?"

Ask if your answer makes sense.

- Check your answer.
- How did working backward help you solve the problem?

  By using the ending amount and inverse operations, the solution was found.

Check Understanding *When is it a good idea to try to use the method of working backward?* (When you have an end result but do not know what you started out with.)

Use the Work Backward strategy or any other strategy you have learned to solve these problems.

1. Your friend likes number puzzles and says, "I'm thinking of a number. If you add **3** to my number, then multiply by **5**, and then subtract **4**, you will get **26**." What is your friend's number?

Think: Start with **26** and work backward using inverse operations. What is the first operation you need to undo?

undo -4 by $+4$

Answer 3

2. You go to the movies and spend half your money on the admission. You spend **$6.00** for popcorn and large soda. You give your last **$3.00** to your friend. How much money did you have when you arrived?

Think: Start with the **$3.00** and work backward using inverse operations. What is the first step you need to undo?

undo spending $6 by adding $6

Answer $18

3. The concert you attended was part of a **42** week tour that included **5** concerts per week. The concert promoter paid **$9,660,000** in expenses for shipping, insurance, and facility rental. What was the average expense per concert?

$46,000.00

4. Concert promoters use ticket agencies to help sell their tickets. One agency has **2000** each of tickets at three different prices—**$18.50**, **$26**, and **$35**. If the agency adds a **$2.50** service charge to each ticket and sells all the tickets, how much money will the agency collect?

$174,000.00

5. What will be the next figure in this pattern? Explain your reasoning.

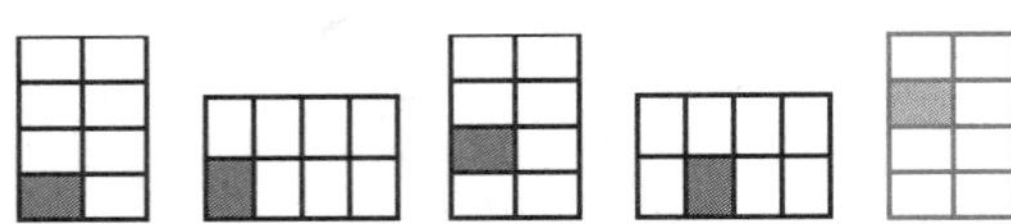

As the figure changes vertically, you shade the next one on the left.

6. With **one** straight cut, you can cut a circle into **two** pieces. Shown are the results of using **one**, **two**, and **three** straight cuts. What is the greatest number of pieces you can make using **five** straight cuts?

2 **4** **7**

16 pieces

7. The sum of two consecutive numbers is **55**. The product of the same two consecutive numbers is **756**. What are the numbers?

27 and 28

8. You are scheduling a chess tournament for **6** members of the chess club. Each member must play a game against each of the other members. How many games will you schedule?

15 games

Closing the Lesson *How is solving the equation $\frac{x}{3} = 12$ similar to working backward?* (Possible answer: You reverse what was done to the variable.)

Name ______________________

Unit 4 Review

Write the comparison as a ratio in simplest form.

1. 18 girls to 16 boys 9:8

2. 6 cups flour to 2 cups sugar 3 to 1

3. 4 feet to 4 yards $\frac{1}{3}$

4. 2 days to 6 hours $\frac{8}{1}$

Write the rate as a unit rate.

5. 84 minutes for 6 pages 14 minutes per page

6. 371 miles for 14 gallons of gas 26.5 miles per gallon

7. Determine the better buy: 6 apples for $1.25 or 8 apples for $1.50? 8 apples for $1.50

Solve.

8. $\frac{n}{36} = \frac{4}{9}$ 16

9. $\frac{3}{10} = \frac{x}{40}$ 12

10. $\frac{16}{18} = \frac{24}{m}$ 27

11. $\frac{8}{n} = \frac{2}{9}$ 36

12. You can purchase a **dozen** juices for **$7.20**. At that rate, what will **30** juices cost you?

$18.00

13. Estimate what a **15%** tip for a restaurant bill of **$58.62** would be.

$9.00

14. Using a scale factor of $\frac{1}{4}$ inch = **1** foot, what would the actual dimensions be for a scale measurement of $3\frac{1}{2}$ inches?

14 ft

15. It would take Nigel **2** hours to paint **12** mailboxes. How long should it take if **2** friends help him paint the **12** mailboxes?

40 minutes

Write the percent as a decimal and a fraction in simplest form.

16. 80% $0.8 = \frac{4}{5}$

17. 42% $0.42 = \frac{21}{50}$

18. 250% $2.50 = 2\frac{1}{2}$

19. 65% $0.65 = \frac{13}{20}$

20. 20% $0.2 = \frac{1}{5}$

21. 120% $1.20 = 1\frac{1}{5}$

Write the decimal or fraction as a percent.

22. 0.15 15%

23. 0.205 $20\frac{1}{2}\%$

24. 0.005 0.5%

25. $\frac{3}{5}$ 60%

26. $\frac{3}{25}$ 12%

27. $\frac{7}{8}$ $87\frac{1}{2}\%$ or 87.5%

Solve.

28. The speed limit on a highway is **55** mph. A speed sensor showed that a car went **900** ft in **8** s. Is the car traveling over the speed limit? Explain.

Yes; 55 miles per hour is about 81 feet per second. The car was traveling about 112 feet per second.

29. In the morning, **20%** of the jars of salsa in a store were sold. In the afternoon, $\frac{7}{8}$ of what was left was sold. There are **14** jars left. How many jars were there at the start? How many jars were sold in the morning? In the afternoon?

140; 28 and 98

Name ______________________________

Use this picture for exercises 1 and 2.

1 **The smaller figure above is a scale drawing of the larger figure. What is the value of x?** B; Obj. 4D

A 2.1 units

B 4.2 units

C 6.3 units

D 9.45 units

2 **What is the value of y?** F; Obj. 4D

F 4.5 units

G 3 units

H 2 units

J 1.5 units

3 **What is the unit price of a CD in the special offer?** B; Obj. 4C

A $7.50

B $8.50

C $9.00

D $10.00

4 **The ratio of boys to girls in the glee club is 15 to 9. If there are 24 girls, then how many boys are there?** F; Obj. 4B

F 40

G 35

H 30

J 15

5 **Simplify: $4x - 2x \div x$** C; Obj. 1C

A 2

B $\frac{2}{x}$

C $4x - 2$

D $4 - 2x$

6 **Which should you do first to solve the equation?** G; Obj. 1D

$$8x + 4 = 8$$

F Add 4 to both sides.

G Subtract 4 from both sides.

H Divide both sides by 8.

J Multiply both sides by 8.

K Divide both sides by x.

7 **The ratio of girls to boys at Hill City High School is 7:6. There are 504 boys. How many girls are there?** D; Obj. 4G

A 432

B 505

C 517

D 588

E Not here

8 **The advertisement for a medicine claimed there was a $\frac{9}{10}$ of a 1% chance that there would be any side effects. What is the decimal equivalent of $\frac{9}{10}$ of 1%?** F; Obj. 4E

F 0.009

G 0.09

H 0.9

J 9.0

K Not here

UNIT 5 • TABLE OF CONTENTS

Applications of Percent

Lesson		Page

We will be using this vocabulary:

percent equation $r\%$ of b is p

rate usually written as a percent, but can be a decimal or fraction

base the whole or entire amount; **100%** of the original number

percentage a part of the base expressed in the same units of measure as the base

percent change the ratio of the amount of change to the original amount

discount a percent of the list price of an item that the buyer does not pay

net price the price of an item after any discount to the list price, or original

commission a part of the selling price that is paid to the seller

simple interest
interest = principal · rate · time

compound interest interest paid on interest that has been added to the principal

Dear Family,

During the next few weeks, our math class will be studying the applications of percents. This will include solving percent equations, which will help to prepare for algebra. You can expect to see homework that provides practice with these skills. Here is a sample you may want to keep handy to give help if needed.

Solving a Percent Equation

A percent equation has three quantities. Knowing two of the three allows you to solve for the third.

Percent equation: $n\%$ of b = p

↑ ↑ ↑

rate × base = percentage

A **$58** sweater is discounted **15%**. Find the discount and selling price.

The discount is **15%** of **$58**. Let d = discount.

d is 15% of \$58	Write the percent equation.
$d = 0.15 \cdot 58$	Write **15%** as a decimal.
$d = 8.70$	Simplify.

The discount is **$8.70** and the selling price is **$58.00 − $8.70 = $49.30**

During this unit, students will continue to learn new techniques related to problem solving and will continue to practice basic skills with fractions and decimals.

Sincerely,

Name ____________________

Guided Practice: First ex. in Rows 1, 4 & 9, pp. 129–130
Independent Practice: Complete pp. 129–130

The Percent Equation: Solving for the Percentage

There is a wide variety of applications for percents. You can solve problems involving percents using the **percent equation.**

For example, to find how much you will save on a sweater on sale for **20%** off the regular price, you can use the equation at right. In this problem you are solving for the **percentage.**

Rate × Base = Percentage
20% of **\$40** is ***n***

Rate:	usually written as a percent, but can be a decimal or fraction	**Base:**	the whole or entire amount—**100%** of the original number	**Percentage:**	a part of the base expressed in the same units as the base

Find: 20% of \$40

1. Write the percent equation. **20% of \$40 = n**

2. Write **20%** as a decimal. **$0.2 \cdot 40 = n$**

3. Simplify. **$8 = n$**

So **20%** of **\$40** is **\$8.00.**

Find: $8\frac{1}{4}$% of 140

1. Write the percent equation. **$8\frac{1}{4}$% of 140 = n**

2. Write **$8\frac{1}{4}$%** as a decimal. **$0.0825 \cdot 140 = n$**

3. Simplify. **$11.55 = n$**

So **$8\frac{1}{4}$%** of **140** is **11.55.**

You can also use a proportion. Find **35%** of **\$75.**

1. Write the percent as a fraction.

35% → $\frac{35}{100}$

2. Write the proportion and solve.

$$\frac{35}{100} = \frac{n}{\$75}$$

$\$75 \cdot 35 = 100n$ So $n = \frac{\$75 \cdot 35}{100}$ or **\$26.25.**

Write the percent as a decimal and as a fraction.

1. 12% = $0.12, \frac{12}{100}$ 6% = $0.06, \frac{6}{100}$ 30% = $0.3, \frac{3}{100}$ or $\frac{3}{10}$

2. 4.5% = $0.045, \frac{45}{100}$ 25.5% = $0.255, \frac{25.5}{100}$ 9.7% = $0.097, \frac{9.7}{100}$

3. $15\frac{1}{4}$% = $0.1525, \frac{15.25}{100}$ $5\frac{1}{2}$% = $0.055, \frac{5.5}{100}$ $33\frac{1}{3}$% = $0.\overline{3}, \frac{33\frac{1}{3}}{100}$ or $\frac{33.\overline{3}}{100}$

Solve for the percentage.

4. 75% of 800 is 600 15% of 176 is 26.4 50% of 135 is 67.5

5. 40% of \$82.50 is \$33 90% of 946 is 851.4 17% of 68 is 11.56

6. 8% of 484 is 38.72 25% of \$68.50 is \$17.13 45% of \$315 is \$141.75

7. $9\frac{1}{4}$% of 200 is 18.5 $12\frac{1}{2}$% of 176 is 22 $52\frac{1}{4}$% of 20 is 10.45

8. $3\frac{1}{3}$% of 3 is 0.1 $4\frac{1}{2}$% of 1 is 0.045 $1\frac{1}{3}$% of 2 is $0.02\overline{6}$

Check Understanding *What is the formula for the percentage? (r × b = p) What is the difference between a percent and a percentage? (A percent is a rate, and a percentage is some amount of the base.)*

A percent can be written as a decimal or fraction. In most percent equations, the percent is written as a decimal to make multiplying easier. However, if the rate has a repeating decimal equivalent such as $33\frac{1}{3}$%, it is easier to write the percent as a fraction.

Find **$33\frac{1}{3}$% of 78**.

1. Write the percent equation. $\mathbf{33\frac{1}{3}\% \text{ of } 78 = n}$
2. Write $33\frac{1}{3}$% as a fraction. $\mathbf{\frac{1}{3} \cdot 78 = n}$
3. Simplify. $\mathbf{26 = n}$

So **$33\frac{1}{3}$% of 78** is **26**.

Writing a Percent as a Fraction

$$8\frac{1}{3}\% = \frac{25}{3} \cdot \frac{1}{100} = \frac{25}{300} = \frac{1}{12}$$

Solve for the percentage.

9. $33\frac{1}{3}$% of **1,266** is 422 — $8\frac{1}{3}$% of **180** is 15 — $15\frac{1}{3}$% of **240** is 36.8

10. $16\frac{2}{3}$% of **360** is 60 — $12\frac{2}{3}$% of **300** is 38 — $66\frac{2}{3}$% of **1,500** is 1,000

11. $22\frac{2}{9}$% of **81** is 18 — $6\frac{1}{9}$% of **270** is 16.5 — $30\frac{1}{9}$% of **840** is $252.9\overline{3}$

12. $8\frac{1}{6}$% of **300** is 24.5 — $7\frac{1}{7}$% of **70** is 5 — $3\frac{1}{6}$% of **36** is 1.14

13. $2\frac{2}{9}$% of **90** is 2 — $9\frac{1}{6}$% of **60** is 5.5 — $4\frac{1}{7}$% of **28** is 1.16

Problem Solving
Reasoning

14. Jericho answered **90%** of the questions correctly on the current events quiz. The quiz had **40** questions. How many did he miss?

4

15. The ABC cereal company claims that one serving of their new cereal provides **two-thirds** of the daily requirement of vitamin A. The daily requirement is **42** mg. How many mg will you get by eating one serving of the new cereal?

28 mg

Test Prep ★ Mixed Review

16 **What is the value of n in the proportion $\frac{5}{42} = \frac{n}{126}$?** B; Obj. 4B

A 5
B 15
C 42
D 89

17 **You drive 175 miles in $3\frac{1}{2}$ hours. What is your unit rate?** H; Obj. 4C

F 1 hour
G 50 miles
H 50 miles per hour
J 58 miles per hour

Closing the Lesson *What would you do to find 18% of 240?* (Change the 18% to a decimal, 0.18, and multiply by 240 obtaining 43.2.)

Name ______________________

Guided Practice: First ex. in Rows 1 & 10, pp. 131–132
Independent Practice: Complete pp. 131–132

The Percent Equation: Solving for the Base

In the last lesson you used multiplication to solve for the percentage in the percent equation. To solve for the **base**, you need to divide.

Rate × Base = Percentage
8% of *n* is 20

Suppose there are **20** people in the front row of a theater. This represents **8%** of the total audience. What is the total number of people in the audience?

Find: **8%** of what number is **20**?

1. Write the percent equation. **8% of n = 20**

2. Write **8%** as a decimal. $0.08 \cdot n = 20$

3. Divide each side by **0.08**. $\frac{0.08 \cdot n}{0.08} = \frac{20}{0.08}$

4. Simplify. $n = 250$

So, there are **250** people in the audience.
Is the answer reasonable? Think: **10%** of **250** is **25,** so **8%** is reasonable.

Find: $12\frac{1}{2}$% of what number is **10.5**?

1. Write the percent equation. $12\frac{1}{2}\%$ of $n = 10.5$

2. Write the $12\frac{1}{2}$% as a decimal. $0.125 \cdot n = 10.5$

3. Divide each side by **0.125**. $\frac{0.125 \cdot n}{0.125} = \frac{10.5}{0.125}$

4. Simplify. $n = 84$

So, **10.5** is $12\frac{1}{2}$ % of **84**.

Check: $12\frac{1}{2}\% \cdot 84$ and $0.125 \cdot 84 = 10.5$

Solve for the base.

1. **10%** of what number is **22**? 220 | **15%** of what number is **9**? 60

2. **25%** of what number is **38**? 152 | **30%** of what number is **36**? 120

3. $6\frac{1}{2}$% of what number is **5.2**? 80 | $10\frac{1}{4}$% of what number is **41**? 400

4. **8.5%** of what number is **3.4**? 40 | **30.2%** of what number is **151**? 500

5. **40** is **50%** of what number? 80 | **60** is **75%** of what number? 80

6. **72** is **60%** of what number? 120 | **5** is **20%** of what number? 25

7. **135** is **45%** of what number? 300 | **65** is **25%** of what number? 260

8. **35%** of what number is **70**? 200 | **12%** of what number is **48**? 400

9. **2.5%** of what number is **5**? 200 | **3** is **4%** of what number? 75

Check Understanding *How could I solve the following equation: If $16\frac{2}{3}$% of a number is 12, what is the number?* (Change $16\frac{2}{3}$% to a fraction and substitute into the percent equation, obtaining $(\frac{1}{6})b = 12$. Now divide both sides by $\frac{1}{6}$, obtaining 72.)

You know that a rate such as $33\frac{1}{3}\%$ has this repeating decimal equivalent: $0.\overline{3}$. Instead of using the decimal, write the equivalent fraction in the percent equation and divide to solve for the base.

Recall that when you divide by a fraction you find its reciprocal and multiply.

Find: $33\frac{1}{3}\%$ of what number is **24**?

1. Write the percent equation. $33\frac{1}{3}\%$ of $n = 24$
2. Write the percentage as a fraction. $\frac{1}{3} \cdot n = 24$
3. Divide each side by $\frac{1}{3}$. $\frac{\frac{1}{3} \cdot n}{\frac{1}{3}} = \frac{24}{\frac{1}{3}}$
4. Simplify. $n = 72$

So **24** is $33\frac{1}{3}\%$ of **72**.

> Dividing by the fraction form of the percent is also useful when the percent is a common fraction such as $10\% = \frac{1}{10}$, $25\% = \frac{1}{4}$, or $50\% = \frac{1}{2}$. **Think:** Dividing by the fraction $\frac{1}{10}$ is the same as multiplying by **10**.

Solve for the base.

10. $33\frac{1}{3}\%$ of what number is **45**? 135

$33\frac{1}{3}\%$ of what number is **120**? 360

11. $66\frac{2}{3}\%$ of what number is **36**? 54

$66\frac{2}{3}\%$ of what number is **80**? 120

12. **10%** of what number is **17**? 170

25% of what number is **29**? 116

13. **300** is **50%** of what number? 600

7 is **20%** of what number? 35

Problem Solving Reasoning

14. There were **18** people at the rehearsal, which is **90%** of the cast. How many people are in the cast?

20

15. The sign said everything was **25%** off. Tori saved **$8** on her purchase. What was the original price of the item?

$32

Test Prep ★ Mixed Review

16 The scale on a map is 1 cm:50 m. How far apart on the map are buildings whose actual distance from each other is 0.85 km? A; Obj. 4D

A 17 cm **C** 850 cm

B 85 cm **D** 17 m

17 What is the percent equivalent of $\frac{9}{25}$? J; Obj. 4E

F 9% **H** 25%

G 11% **J** 36%

Closing the Lesson *If you use the form r × b = p and r is written as a decimal, what do you do once you have substituted into the equation in order to solve for b?* (Divide by *r*.)

Name ____________________

Guided Practice: First ex. in Rows 1, 5 & 8, pp. 133–134
Independent Practice: Complete pp. 133–134

The Percent Equation: Solving for the Percent

Rate × Base = Percentage
n% of 15 is 3

You have used division to solve for the base in the percent equation. To solve for the **rate** or **percent**, you also need to divide.

Suppose that last Monday, **3** of **15** math club members were chosen as finalists in a competition. What percent of the club were finalists?

Find: What percent of **15** is **3**?

1. Write the percent equation. $n\%$ of $\mathbf{15} = \mathbf{3}$
2. Divide each side by **15**. $\frac{n\% \cdot 15}{15} = \frac{3}{15}$
3. Simplify. $n\% = 0.2$
4. Write as a percent. $n = 20$

So **3** is **20%** of **15**.

You may have recognized that $\frac{3}{15} = \frac{1}{5}$ and $\frac{1}{5} = 20\%$.

When you know the fraction form of the percent, you do not need to rewrite it as a decimal.

Find: What percent of **328** is **41**?

1. Write the percent equation. $n\%$ of $\mathbf{328} = \mathbf{41}$
2. Divide each side by **328**. $\frac{n\% \cdot 328}{328} = \frac{41}{328}$
3. Simplify. $n\% = 0.125$
4. Write the decimal as a percent. $n = 12.5$

So **41** is **12.5%** of **328**.

Is the answer reasonable?

Think, **10%** of **328** = **32.8**. Since **12.5%** is close to **10%**, the answer is reasonable.

When you solve the equation for the percent, the result is a decimal. Write the decimal as a percent.

Solve for the percent.

1. What percent of **40** is **32**? 80%   What percent of **810** is **540**? $66\frac{2}{3}\%$
2. What percent of **75** is **7.5**? 10%   What percent of **24** is **16**? $66\frac{2}{3}\%$
3. What percent of **64** is **8**? 12.5%   What percent of **1,200** is **1,050**? 87.5%
4. What percent of **68** is **10.2**? 15%   What percent of **144** is **43.2**? 30%
5. **320** is what percent of **960**? $33\frac{1}{3}\%$ **15.5** is what percent of **124**? 12.5%
6. **8.1** is what percent of **90**? 9%   **297** is what percent of **300**? 99%
7. **10** is what percent of **25**? 40%   **128** is what percent of **1,024**? 12.5%

Check Understanding *If the percentage is greater than the base, what can you tell me about the rate?* (It is greater than 100%.)

Recall that percents can be greater than **100%**.

For example, suppose you need to save **$380** for a new CD player, and you actually save **$456**. Then you have more than **100%** of what you need.

Think: 456 is more than **100%** of **380**.

Write: 456 is what percent of **380**?

Find: **456** is what percent of **380**?

1. Write the percent equation. $456 = n\% \text{ of } 380$
2. Divide each side by **380**. $\frac{456}{380} = \frac{n\% \cdot 380}{380}$
3. Simplify. $1.2 = n\%$
4. Write the decimal as a percent. $120 = n$

So **456** is **120%** of **380**.

Solve for the percent.

8. What percent of **200** is **400**? 200%

9. What percent of **60** is **72**? 120%

10. **86** is what percent of **43**? 200%

11. **80** is what percent of **60**? $133\frac{1}{3}\%$

What percent of **44** is **55**? 125%

What percent of **80** is **104**? 130%

135 is what percent of **45**? 300%

7 is what percent of **5**? 140%

Problem Solving Reasoning Solve.

12. On Friday, **27** of the **30** students attended band practice. What percent of the students were present?

90%

13. Suppose today is day **54** out of the **180**-day school year. What percent of the school year do you have remaining?

70%

Quick Check

Solve for the base, rate, or percentage.

14. What is **6%** of **180**? 10.8

15. What is **$83\frac{1}{3}$%** of **108**? 90

16. What is **105%** of **70**? 73.5

17. **72** is **25%** of what number? 288

18. **24** is **80%** of what number? 30

19. **69** is **$37\frac{1}{2}$%** of what number? 184

20. What percent of **36** is **24**? $66\frac{2}{3}\%$

21. What percent of **150** is **84**? 56%

Closing the Lesson *If we use the percent equation $r \times b = p$, what do we do to solve for the rate?* (Possible answer: Substitute the base and percentage into the equation, and divide both sides by the base. The rate is given as a decimal, so we need to change the decimal to a percent.)

Work Space.

Item	Error Analysis
14–16	**Common Error:** Students may not write the percent as a decimal or fraction correctly. **Skills Tutorial** Strand 10: Skill 8
17–19	**Common Error:** Students may confuse the dividend and divisor when finding the base. **Skills Tutorial** Strand 10: Skill 10
20–21	**Common Error:** Students may write the percent equation incorrectly. **Skills Tutorial** Strand 10: Skill 8

Name ______________________________

Guided Practice: Problem 1, p. 136
Independent Practice: Complete pp. 135–136

Problem Solving Strategy: Conjecture and Verify

To solve problems, you may need to begin by making a *guess,* or **conjecture.** Then you need to *check,* or **verify,** your conjecture. Sometimes you may need to revise the conjecture and try again.

Problem

Your friend's mom offered to buy lunch for you and your friends at a baseball game. Hot dogs were $1.25 and sodas were $1.00. She spent $19.50. When you asked her how many of each she bought she would only say, "3 more hot dogs than sodas." How many of each did she buy?

1 Understand

"Asking yourself questions will help you identify the math ideas."

As you reread, ask yourself questions.

- How much money did she spend?
  She spent **$19.50.**
- How much did the hot dogs and sodas cost?
  Hot dogs cost **$1.25** and sodas cost **$1.00.**
- What do you need to find? number of hot dogs and number of sodas

2 Decide

"What is a reasonable first conjecture for this problem? Would 15 hot dogs be reasonable?"

Choose a method for solving.
Try the strategy Conjecture and Verify. Revise if necessary.

- Make a conjecture and verify it.

  Try **9** hot dogs and **6** sodas.
  9 × $1.25 + 6 × $1.00 = $17.25

- A conjecture of 9 hot dogs gives a total cost that is too small.

3 Solve

"Since the first conjecture wasn't too far off, try a little larger number."

Revise your first conjecture.

- Make a new conjecture. Then verify it.

  Try **10** hot dogs and **7** sodas.

  10 × $1.25 + 7 × $1.00 = $19.50

  Were **3** more hot dogs than sodas purchased? yes

4 Look back

"Check your answer to see that all of the conditions were met."

Ask if your answer makes sense.

- How many of each item did your friend's mom buy?
  10 hot dogs, 7 sodas
- Is your answer reasonable? Explain.
  Yes; If hot dogs cost $1, the total would be $17.
- How did the Conjecture and Verify strategy help you solve the problem?
  Making a conjecture gave me a place to start and verifying it made me know I was right.

Check Understanding *What is another way of saying conjecture and verify?* (guess and check)

Use the Conjecture and Verify strategy or any other strategy you have learned.

1. You have scored **87**, **79**, and **80** on your math tests. The B-range is **84%–91%**. What is the lowest score you can earn on your fourth test and still have a B average?

Think: If my first conjecture gives an average of **85%**, am I finished? Why or why not?

No; Because it might not be the lowest score.

Answer 90

2. The length of a garden is twice its width. The perimeter is **90** feet. What are the dimensions of the garden?

Think: Could the longer dimension of the garden be more than **50** ft? Why?

No; Because the perimeter would be more than 90 feet.

Answer 30 ft by 15 ft.

3. Find the digits that represent letters in the sum. Use the digits: **1, 2, 4, 5, 6,** and **9.**

TWO	456
+ TWO	+ 456
SIX	912

4. Fill in the circles with **1**, **2**, **5**, and **8** so that the three numbers on all four sides add to **13**.

5. At the supermarket, canned peaches have been stacked in a pyramid shape, with **1** can on the top, **2** in the second row, **3** in the third row, and so on. There are **12** rows of cans. How many cans of peaches are displayed?

78 cans

6. Find the product of the nine fractions.

$$\frac{1}{2} \cdot \frac{2}{3} \cdot \frac{3}{4} \cdot \frac{4}{5} \cdot \frac{5}{6} \cdot \frac{6}{7} \cdot \frac{7}{8} \cdot \frac{8}{9} \cdot \frac{9}{10}$$

$\frac{1}{10}$

7. A weather balloon is launched at **10:30** A.M. It rises at a rate of **3.5** km every **30** minutes. What will be the altitude, or height, of the balloon at **2** P.M.?

24.5 km

8. You purchased a **$120** jacket that was on sale for **$80**. Your friend bought a **$100** jacket that was on sale for **$60**. Did you both receive the same rate of discount? If not, who received the better discount?

No. My friend received a 40% discount and mine was only $33\frac{1}{3}$%.

Closing the Lesson *When is the strategy of conjecture and verify good to use?* (Possible answer: When you can do a quick calculation to see if the numbers you guessed are consistent with the data or not.)

Name ________________________________

Guided Practice: Ex. 1 & 12, pp. 137–138
Independent Practice: Complete pp. 137–138

Percent of Increase or Decrease

Percents can be used to measure how much a quantity changes.

For example, suppose you paid **$12** for a CD two years ago. Now it sells for **$15**. The difference of **$3** is an increase of **25%**.

> The **percent of increase** or **percent of decrease** from one amount to another is the ratio of the amount of change compared to the original amount.
>
> **Percent Change** $= \dfrac{\text{amount of change}}{\text{original amount}}$
>
> Percent increase: new amount > original amount
>
> Percent decrease: new amount < original amount

Find the Percent of Increase:

Original price of CD: **$12**
New price of CD: **$15**

Percent Increase $= \dfrac{15 - 12}{12}$

$= \dfrac{3}{12}$

$= \dfrac{1}{4}$ or **25%**

The CD has increased **25%** in price.

Find the Percent of Decrease:

Original price of computer: **$1,250**
New price of computer: **$875**

Percent Decrease: $= \dfrac{1250 - 875}{1250}$

$= \dfrac{375}{1250}$

$= \dfrac{3}{10}$ or **30%**

The computer has decreased **30%** in price.

Find the amount of change and the percent change and write whether it is an increase or decrease.

	Original Amount	New Amount	Amount of Change	Percent Change	Increase or Decrease
1.	$72	$80	$8	$11\frac{1}{9}$%	Increase
2.	40	60	20	50%	Increase
3.	36	30	6	$16\frac{2}{3}$%	Decrease
4.	$15	$10.50	$4.50	30%	Decrease
5.	15	33	18	120%	Increase
6.	$35	$28	$7	20%	Decrease
7.	270	391.5	121.5	45%	Increase
8.	80	100	20	25%	Increase
9.	100	80	20	20%	Decrease
10.	35	105	70	200%	Increase
11.	$28\frac{1}{3}$	$11\frac{1}{3}$	17	60%	Decrease

Check Understanding *If the price of a mountain bike went from $280 in 1998 to $322 in 1999, how would I find the percent of increase?* (Subtract $280 from $322, obtaining $42 as the increase in the price. Now divide that by $280 to get 0.15. So the percent of increase was 15%.)

Problem Solving Reasoning Solve.

12. Julia increased her reading rate from **200** words per minute to **250** words per minute. By what percent did she increase her rate?

25%

13. In September, **30** students attended special art classes on Saturday. By November this number had increased by **200%**. What was the total attendance in the classes by November?

90 students

14. A pet shop had **300** canaries. This number decreased $\mathbf{83\frac{1}{3}\%}$ due to sales. How many canaries were sold?

50 canaries

15. The train from Chicago to Los Angeles increased its speed from **140** to **180** kilometers per hour. By what percent was the speed increased?

$28\frac{4}{7}\%$

16. Joan sold **80** magazines last year, but only **75** magazines this year. What was the percent of decrease?

$6\frac{1}{4}\%$

17. Last year Troop No. **113** sold **100** dozen cookies. How many will they have to sell this year to have a **20%** increase in sales?

120 dozen cookies

18. In a furniture store the price of a sofa was marked down from **$225** to **$200**. What was the percent of decrease?

$11\frac{1}{9}\%$

19. A football was marked down from **$28.00** to **$24.50**. By what percent was its price reduced?

$12\frac{1}{2}\%$

Test Prep ★ Mixed Review

20 **What number is 7% of 86?** A; Obj. 5A

A 6.02

B 8.14

C 12.28

D 60.2

21 **162 is 24% of what number?** H; Obj. 5A

F 38.9

G 188

H 675

J 3,888

Closing the Lesson *What is the general process you use to find percent of change?* (Possible answer: You need to find the amount of increase or decrease first, then divide that by the original amount.)

Name ____________________

Discount

Guided Practice: First ex. in Rows 1 & 7; Problem 13, pp. 139–140
Independent Practice: Complete pp. 139–140

You can use a percent to describe the savings you will receive on items that are sale priced.

For example, a store may advertise "25% off all items." You save **25%** of the cost of what you purchase. If you purchase a **$40** item, you will save **$10** on the item.

You can use the percent equation to find discounts. Become familiar with the different vocabulary used for describing discounts.

Rate: the percent of the ***list price*** that the buyer ***does not*** pay, or the **percent of discount**

Base: the price the store usually charges for an item; it is called the **list**, **marked**, **regular**, or original price

Percentage: the part of the list price that the buyer does not pay; it is called the **amount of discount**

Find the Amount of Discount:

You want to purchase a pair of sneakers that list for **$82.00**. They are marked **15%** off. How much will you save?

You will save **15%** of the original cost of **$82.**

1. Write the percent equation. **15% of $82 =** n
2. Write **15%** as a decimal. $0.15 \cdot 82 = n$
3. Simplify. $12.30 = n$

The sneakers have been discounted **$12.30**, which is the amount you save.

Find the Discount Rate:

A **$38** sweatshirt is on sale. A sign on the sale rack says, "Save **$9.50.**" What percent discount is this?

What percent of **$38** is **$9.50**?

1. Write the percent equation. $n\% \cdot 38 = 9.50$
2. Divide each side by **$38**. $\frac{n\% \cdot 38}{38} = \frac{9.50}{38}$
3. Simplify. $n\% = 0.25$
4. Write as a percent. $n = 25$

The discount was **25%.**

Complete the table.

	List Price	Discount Rate	Amount of Discount
1.	$45	10%	$4.50
2.	$240	15%	$36
3.	$250	6%	$15
4.	$24	10%	$2.40
5.	$6	12.5%	$.75
6.	$24.90	20%	$4.98

	List Price	Discount Rate	Amount of Discount
7.	$69	20%	$13.80
8.	$648	$33\frac{1}{3}$%	$215.78
9.	$840	4.5%	$37.80
10.	$19.95	20%	$3.99
11.	$15	30%	$4.50
12.	$6.95	40%	$2.78

Check Understanding *How do you calculate a rate of discount?* (Divide the discount by the original price.)

Problem Solving
Reasoning

Solve. Round to the nearest cent if necessary.

13. Holiday cards are on sale at **25%** off. What will you save on **3** boxes that have a list price of **$7.50** each?

$5.63

14. Rick offers to sell his collection of baseball cards to Pete for **$112**. He originally spent **$280** for the cards. What rate of discount is he offering?

40%

15. All books and CD's are usually **$33\frac{1}{3}$%** off. How much would you save on the purchase of four CD's that sell for **$15.95** each and two books that sell for **$7.95** each? $26.57

16. The gas station offers a **3%** discount for using cash. Your bill is **$15.50**. How much will you save?

$.47

17. The fuel oil company offers a **10%** discount for paying your bill within **10** days. Your fuel oil bill is **$124**. How much could you save by paying within **10** days?

$12.40

18. Espie received a scratch card in the mail that said save **10%**, **25%**, or **40%** off any purchase. Espie finds a **$145** jacket that she likes. The cashier scratches the card to reveal the discount rate. What is the greatest amount of money Espie could save? The least?

$58; $14.50

19. If you saved **$31.98** on a **$79.95** backpack, what was the discount rate?

40%

20. Which amount of money is greater, a **10%** discount on **$42** or a **42%** discount on **$10**? Explain.

Neither; They are equal, because $\$42 \times 0.1 = \$10 \times 0.42$.

Test Prep ★ Mixed Review

21 **What percent of 4,500 is 9?** A; Obj. 5A

A 0.2% **C** 20%

B 2% **D** 500%

22 **A store changed the price of a printer from $340 to $360. To the nearest tenth, what is the percent increase?** G; Obj. 5B

F 5.6% **H** 20%

G 5.9% **J** $20

Closing the Lesson *If you know the original price of an item and the discount rate, how do you find the discounted amount?* (Possible answer: Change the percent into a decimal or fraction and multiply by the original price.)

Name ____________________

List Price and Net Price

Guided Practice: Problems 1 & 15, pp. 141–142
Independent Practice: Complete pp. 141–142

In the last lesson you found the amount of discount on an item. Subtracting the amount of discount from the list price gives you the amount you need to pay. The amount that you pay for the item is called the **net price.**

Find the Net Price:

Carlos purchased a **$385** snowboard that is marked **15%** off. How much did he save? What was the net price?

Carlos saved **15%** of the original cost of **$385**.

1. Write the percent equation. $15\% \text{ of } \$385 = n$

2. Write **2%** as a decimal. $0.15 \cdot 385 = n$

3. Simplify. $57.75 = n$

4. Subtract.

$385.00	← List price
−$ 57.75	← Amount of discount
$327.25	← Net price

When you save **15%** off the list price of an item, you pay **85%** of the cost of the item.

Find the Discount Rate:

A **$450** season ski ticket is discounted when it is purchased before December 10. Anne paid **$360** for the pass. What percent was it discounted?

What percent of the **$450** did Anne pay?

What percent of **$450** is **$360**?

1. Write the percent equation. $n\% \cdot \$450 = \$360$

2. Divide each side by **$450**. $\frac{n\% \cdot 450}{450} = \frac{360}{450}$

3. Simplify. $n\% = \frac{4}{5}$

4. Write $\frac{4}{5}$ as a percent. $n = 80$

Anne paid **80%** of the cost and saved **20%**.

Complete the table.

	List Price	Percent Discount	Amount of Discount	Net Price
1.	**$20**	**10%**	$2	$18
2.	**$18**	**$33\frac{1}{3}\%$**	$6	$12
3.	**$600**	**4%**	$24	$576
4.	**$7.80**	20%	**$1.56**	$6.24
5.	**$7.50**	20%	**$1.50**	$6
6.	**$2,400**	25%	$600	**$1,800**
7.	$26	25%	**$6.50**	**$19.50**
8.	$30	**40%**	**$12**	$18
9.	$10	7.5%	**$0.75**	**$9.25**
10.	$250	**12.5%**	**$31.25**	$218.75
11.	**$18.95**	60%	**$11.37**	$7.58
12.	**$210**	**$33\frac{1}{3}\%$**	$70	$140

Check Understanding *How would you find the discount rate if you knew the original price and the net price?* (Divide the net price by the original price to find what percent of the original price you paid for the item. Now subtract that percent from 100%.)

Problem Solving Reasoning

Solve. Round to the nearest cent if necessary.

13. You are buying a birthday gift for your friend. The original price of the gift you choose is **$18.95** and is marked **15%** off. You have **$15** with you. Do you have enough money to buy the gift? Explain.

No; You need to pay 85% of $18.95, which is $16.10.

14. Mr. Lux is buying a used car marked **$1,000**. He can buy it for **$800**. What rate of discount is he getting? 20%

15. Eileen paid **$31.50** for a coat marked **$36**. What percent of discount did she receive? 12.5%

16. A sports store has reduced every item by $33\frac{1}{3}$%. What is the net price for a basketball that lists at **$42**? $28

17. A bargain store increases the discount rate the longer the item remains in the store. You save **10%** during the first **10** days, **20%** from day **11** to day **30**, and **50%** off after **30** days. A pair of pants that lists for **$48** has been at the store **28** days. What is the net price today? What would be the net price if you wait **3** days?

$38.40; $24

18. Lani saved **$20** on a **$120** jacket. Andre saved **$20** on a **$80** jacket. Who saved the most? Who received the better rate of discount? Explain.

They both saved $20; but Andre received a better rate, because $\frac{20}{80} > \frac{20}{120}$.

Quick Check

Write the percent of change. Identify whether it is a percent of increase or percent of decrease.

19. Originally: **$85**
Now: **$95**
$11\frac{3}{7}$%; increase

20. Originally: **$140**
Now: **$125**
$10\frac{5}{7}$%; decrease

21. Originally: **$5.50**
Now: **$4.95**
10%; decrease

22. A coat regularly sells for **$95**. It is discounted **15%**. What is the sale price? $80.75

23. A **$599** sofa is selling for **$525**. What is the percent of discount?

about 12.4%

24. A drug store buys cosmetics from its supplier at a 40% discount from the list price. How much does the store pay for a shipment that will sell for **$1,200**? $720

25. You buy a baby grand piano that lists for **$3,600**. You pay **$3,300**. What is the rate of discount? $8\frac{1}{3}$%

Work Space.

Item	Error Analysis
19–21	**Common Error:** Watch for students who do not use the original price as the base. **Reteaching** Reteach 30
22–23	**Common Error:** Watch for students who confuse base and percentage when writing the percent equation. **Reteaching** Reteach 31
24–25	**Common Error:** Watch for students who do not find the amount of discount before they write the percent equation. **Reteaching** Reteach 32

Closing the Lesson *How can you find the net price given the discount rate and the original price?* (Possible answer: Find the amount of discount by multiplying the discount rate by the original price. Subtract this amount from the original price to determine the net price, or, subtract the discount rate from 100% and multiply the result by the original price.)

Name ______________________________

Commission

Guided Practice: Ex. 1 & 10, pp. 143–144
Independent Practice: Complete pp. 143–144

People who work in sales often have part or all of their salary based on a **commission.** Commission is a percent of the total amount of the sale that is paid to the sales person.

For example, newspaper delivery people are paid a percentage of each newspaper they sell. They might keep **2.5¢** for each **50¢** newspaper they sell. The publisher would receive **47.5¢**.

The **commission** on a sale is found using the percent equation.

Rate: the percent of the amount of sales that is paid to the salesperson
Base: the total cost of the product, called the *amount of sales*
Percentage: the part of the amount of the sales that is paid to the salesperson, called the *commission*

The **net proceeds** is the difference between the amount of the sale and the commission.

Find the Amount of Commission:

You work in a department store where you earn a **2%** commission on all sales. One day you have **$164** in sales. What will your commission be?

You will earn **2%** of the **$164**.

1. Write the percent equation. $2\% \text{ of } 164 = n$
2. Write **2%** as a decimal. $0.02 \cdot 164 = n$
3. Simplify. $3.28 = n$

The commission that you earn is **$3.28**. The net proceeds for the store is **$164 – $3.28** or **$160.72**.

Find the Commission Rate:

You earn a commission of **$12** on a sale of **$240**. What is the commission rate?

What percent of **$240** is **$12**?

1. Write the percent equation. $n\% \cdot 240 = 12$
2. Divide each side by **$240**. $\frac{n\% \cdot 240}{240} = \frac{12}{240}$
3. Simplify. $n\% = 0.05$
4. Write **0.05** as a percent. $n = 5$

The commission rate is **5%**.

Complete the table.

	Amount of Sales	Commission Rate	Amount of Commission	Net Proceeds
1.	**$60**	**5%**	$3	$57
2.	**$800**	**3.5%**	$28	$772
3.	**$4,200**	**4.25%**	$178.50	$4,021.50
4.	**$750**	20%	**$150**	$600
5.	**$1,500**	5%	**$75**	$1,425
6.	$875	2%	**$17.50**	**$857.50**
7.	$500,000	**5%**	**$25,000**	$475,000
8.	$20,000	12%	**$2,400**	**$17,600**
9.	**$350**	7%	**$24.50**	$325.50

Check Understanding *In the percent equation b × r = p, what quantity represents the commission?* (It is *p,* the percentage.)

Problem Solving Reasoning Solve. Round to the nearest cent if necessary.

10. Martha sold magazines and received a commission of $6\frac{1}{4}$%. Her sales totaled **$240**. How much did she earn in commissions? What were the net proceeds? $15; $225

11. A real estate agent receives a **6%** commission for selling an **$8,000** piece of land. How much did she earn? How much was given to the owner of the land?

$480; $7,520

12. Find the amount of commission earned on a sale of **$200** at a rate of $6\frac{1}{2}$%. How much was given to the company?

$13; $187

13. Ted earned a commission of **$2.50** for each **$25** corsage he made for Mother's Day. How much commission would he receive for making **15** corsages? What is the commission rate?

$37.50; 10%

14. An insurance salesperson collected **$200** commission for selling policies worth **$1,600**. What is the commission rate?

12.5%

15. Mr. Finn collects rents for a real estate management company. He is paid $2\frac{1}{2}$% in commission. How much commission does he receive for collecting **$960** in rents? What are the net proceeds to the company?

$24; $936

16. A lumber company is purchasing **$9,000** worth of lumber through an agent whose commission is $8\frac{1}{3}$% of the sales. What are the net proceeds to the firm? $8,250

17. A ticket agent receives a **2.5%** commission on all concert tickets sold. The total sales were **$28,500**. How much commission did the agent earn?

$712.50

Test Prep ★ Mixed Review

18 Chuck buys a $65 pair of shoes on sale at 15% off. How much money does he save?

A; Obj. 5C

A $9.75 **C** $50

B $15 **D** $55.25

19 A car battery regularly priced at $67 is on sale for 5% off. What is the sale price?

J; Obj. 5C

F $3.35 **H** $62

G $33.50 **J** $63.65

Closing the Lesson *If you know the commission and the commission rate, how could you find the sales price?* (Substitute the commission for the percentage and the commission rate for the rate in the percent equation and solve for the base, which corresponds to the sales price.)

Name ______________________________

Guided Practice: Problems 1 & 9, pp. 145–146
Independent Practice: Complete pp. 145–146

Simple and Compound Interest

Another important application of percents is *interest*.

When you borrow money from a bank, you are charged a fee called interest. When you "invest" money in a savings account, you are paid interest.

A person who takes out a loan at the bank is a borrower. The borrower agrees to pay **interest** (a fee) for using the bank's money.

The simple interest formula is: Interest = principal × rate × time
$I = p \cdot r \cdot t$

p = **principal**, the amount borrowed
r = interest **rate** per year, expressed as a decimal
t = **time**, expressed in years

The **amount due** is what you pay back to the bank ($I + p$).

Find the Interest and Amount Due:

You borrow **$2,000** at **8%** interest for **6** months. How much interest will you pay? What is the amount due to the bank?

Think: 6 mo = $\frac{1}{2}$ yr or **0.5** yr

p = $2,000, r = 8%, t = 0.5 years

1. Write the interest formula. $I = p \cdot r \cdot t$
2. Substitute. $I = 2{,}000 \cdot 0.08 \cdot 0.5$
3. Simplify. $I = 80$
4. Add.
   $2,000 ← Principal
   + $80 ← Interest
   $2,080 ← Amount due

You pay **$80** interest and owe a total of **$2,080**.

Find the Interest and Amount Due:

You borrow **$12,000** at **6.5%** interest for **30** months. How much interest will you pay? What is the amount due to the bank?

Think: 30 mo = $2\frac{1}{2}$ yr or **2.5** yr

p = $12,000, r = 6.5%, t = 2.5 years

1. Write the interest formula. $I = p \cdot r \cdot t$
2. Substitute. $I = 12{,}000 \cdot 0.065 \cdot 2.5$
3. Simplify. $I = 1{,}950$
4. Add.
   $12,000 ← Principal
   + $ 1,950 ← Interest
   $13,950 ← Amount due

You pay **$1,950** interest and owe a total of **$13,950**.

Complete the table. Round to the nearest cent if necessary.

	Principal	Rate (per year)	Time	Interest	Amount Due
1.	$400	13%	3 months	$13	$413
2.	$900	12%	6 months	$54	$954
3.	$6,000	8%	18 months	$720	$6,720
4.	$2,500	6.5%	1 year	$162.50	$2,662.50
5.	$4,500	6.25%	1 year	$281.25	$4,781.25
6.	$8,400	9.25%	2 years	$1,554	$9,954
7.	$75,000	10.95%	20 years	$164,250	$239,250
8.	$37,525	17.99%	3 years	$20,252.24	$57,777.24

Check Understanding *If you borrowed $2,500.00 at 8% simple interest for one year, what would be the interest due at the end of the year?* (Substitute into the formula $I = p \cdot r \cdot t$ for the principal = $2,500.00, the rate = 0.08 and the time = 1 and compute the interest. I = $200.)

The simple interest formula finds interest just once.

With **compound interest**, the interest earned is added to the principal at regular intervals. The amount of principal changes. You calculate the new amount of interest using the new principal.

Compounded quarterly means that interest is paid at the end of every **3** months.

Compound interest is common when money is invested in a savings account.

You invest **$500** at **6%** interest compounded quarterly. What is your principal after **6** months?

1. Write the simple interest formula. $I = p \cdot r \cdot t$
2. Substitute. $I = 500 \cdot 0.06 \cdot \frac{1}{4}$
3. Simplify. $I = 7.50$
4. Add interest to principal. **$500 + $7.50 = $507.50**
5. Find the interest on the new principal. $I = 507.50 \cdot 0.06 \cdot \frac{1}{4}$
6. Simplify. $I = 7.61$

After **6** months you have a total of **$7.61 + $507.50, or $515.11**.

Complete the chart for the $1,200 investment at 6% compounded quarterly. Round to the nearest cent if necessary.

	Principal	Rate (per year)	Time	Interest
9.	**$1,200**	6%	3 months	$18.00
10.	$1,218	6%	3 months	$18.27
11.	$1,236.27	6%	3 months	$18.54
12.	$1,254.81	6%	3 months	$18.82

Problem Solving Reasoning Solve.

13. At the end of one year, what is the total amount of principal in the bank for **$1,200** at **6%** compounded quarterly? $1,273.63

Quick Check

Calculate the amount of commission and the net proceeds.

14. 6% commission on sales of **$15,500** $930; $14,570

15. 4.5% commission on sales of **565** $25.43; $539.57

16. Calculate the rate of commission if you earn **$18** on sales of **$225**. 8%

Calculate the interest on the loan

17. 8% interest on **$560** for **2** years $89.60

18. 4.5% interest on **$1,200** for **1** year $54

19. 6% interest on **$450** for **6** months $13.50

Work Space.

Item	Error Analysis
14–16	**Common Error:** Watch for students who do not understand the term *net proceeds*. **Reteaching** Reteach 33
17–19	**Common Error:** Watch for students who don't consistently write the time in years. **Reteaching** Reteach 34

Closing the Lesson *What is the difference between simple interest and compound interest?* (Possible answer: With simple interest you only earn interest on the principal, but with compound interest, you earn interest on the principal plus previous interest.)

Name ______________________

Guided Practice: Ex. 1, p. 147
Independent Practice: Complete pp. 147–148

Problem Solving Application: Use a Table

Most employed taxpayers in the United States have their income taxes withheld by their employer. The Internal Revenue Service provides employers with tables that show the amount of tax that must be withheld. A portion of the table for *not married* employees is shown.

In this lesson you will use the table to find the amount of tax to be withheld from an employee. The amount of the tax is based on the weekly salary and the number of exemptions claimed.

Federal Income Tax Withholding

Not Married			
Weekly salary		Number of exemptions	
At least	But less than	0	1
230	240	41.40	36.40
240	250	44.00	39.00
250	260	46.60	41.60
260	270	49.20	44.20
270	280	51.80	46.80
280	290	54.80	49.40
290	300	57.80	52.10

Tips to Remember:

1. Understand 2. Decide 3. Solve 4. Look back

- Ask yourself: What do I know? What do I need to find?
- Read the headings of the table carefully. Make sure you select the correct row and column in the table.
- Think about whether the table entry makes sense. Is it reasonable?

Use the federal income tax withholding table shown above.

1. Ms. Simoz earns **$280** a week and claims one exemption for herself. How much will be withheld from her paycheck?

Think: Which row of the table should I use? Which column?

Use the second-to-last row and the last column.

Answer $49.40

2. Ms. Simoz also has withheld from her pay **$20.30** for Social Security Tax (FICA) and **$25.83** for health insurance. What is her weekly take-home pay?

Think: How can you find what is left after the items have been withheld?

I need to subtract all the deductions from the $280 that she earned.

Answer $184.47

Check Understanding *If a married person with three exemptions pays a tax of $28.60, then how much might he or she earn per week?* (an amount between $270 and $280)

Use the federal income tax withholding table for married people.

Federal Income Tax Withholding

Married						
Weekly salary		**Number of exemptions**				
At least	**But less than**	**0**	**1**	**2**	**3**	**4**
230	240	32.30	28.30	24.60	21.20	17.70
240	250	34.40	30.40	26.40	23.00	19.50
250	260	36.50	32.50	28.50	24.80	21.30
260	270	38.60	34.60	30.60	26.60	23.10
270	280	40.70	36.70	32.70	28.60	24.90
280	290	42.80	38.80	34.80	30.70	26.70
290	300	45.10	40.90	36.90	32.80	28.80

3. Mr. Scheer earns **$291** a week. He claims **4** exemptions for himself, his wife, and their **2** children. How much will be withheld from his paycheck?

$28.80

4. Mr. Scheer pays a local tax of **$17.40** per week and his social security deduction is **$19.47** per week. What is his weekly take-home pay?

$225.33

5. How much more does a married person with two exemptions have withheld if they make **$270** versus **$269**?

$2.10

6. How much more does a married person making **$284** have withheld if they have one exemption rather than three exemptions?

$8.10

7. Brian needs to make **$220** a week after federal taxes are withheld. He is not married and has no exemptions. What weekly salary does he need?

$269.20

8. Suppose a person is married and has no exemptions. About what percent of her or his salary will be withheld for federal taxes?

about 14% or 15%, if her salary is in the range covered by the table

Extend Your Thinking

9. Who has more withheld, the married person with one exemption or the single person with one exemption? Both earn **$268**.

single person with one exemption

10. Use your answer to problem **4** to compute Mr. Scheer's take-home pay for the year.

$11,717.16

Closing the Lesson *Do you know any other tables in which information is given?* (Possible answer: bus schedules)

Name ______________________

Unit 5 Review

Solve for the percentage, base, or rate.

1. 60% of **492** is 295.2.

2. 33 $\frac{1}{3}$% of 843 is 281.

3. 15% of **$29.40** is $4.41.

4. 30% of what number is **27**? 90

5. 66 $\frac{2}{3}$% of what number is **30**? 45

6. What percent of **400** is **350**? 87$\frac{1}{2}$%

7. **28** is what percent of **35**? 80%

Find the percent of change.

8. Original amount: **40**
New amount: **32**

Percent of change 20%

Increase or decrease? decrease

9. Last year: **72** students tried out for the team.
This year: **60** students tried out for the team.

Percent of change 16 $\frac{2}{3}$%

Increase or decrease? decrease

Solve.

10. The list price of a hair dryer is **$28**. The selling price is **$19.60**.

What is the rate of discount? 30%

11. The list price of a reclining chair is **$210**. The discount rate is **20%**.

What is the amount of the discount? $42

12. The list price of an art book is **$89**. The discount rate is **25%**. What is the net price? $66.75

13. A broker sells **$580** in goods and receives a **7%** commission. What is the amount of the commission and the net proceeds?

commission: $40.60; net proceeds: $539.40

14. A sales clerk sold **$4,200** in clothing and received a commission of **$126**. What is the commission rate? 3%

15. Calculate the interest owed when you borrow **$850** at **6.5%** for **1** year. $55.25

16. You borrow **$3,800** at **9%** for **30** months. What will you pay in interest? What will you owe the bank? $855; $4,655

17. Your aunt bought movie tickets for your family. Children's tickets were **$4** and adult tickets were **$7**. She bought four more children's tickets than adult tickets, and the total cost was **$71**. How many of each type of ticket did she buy? adult: 5; children: 9

Name ______________________________

Cumulative Review
★ Test Prep

1

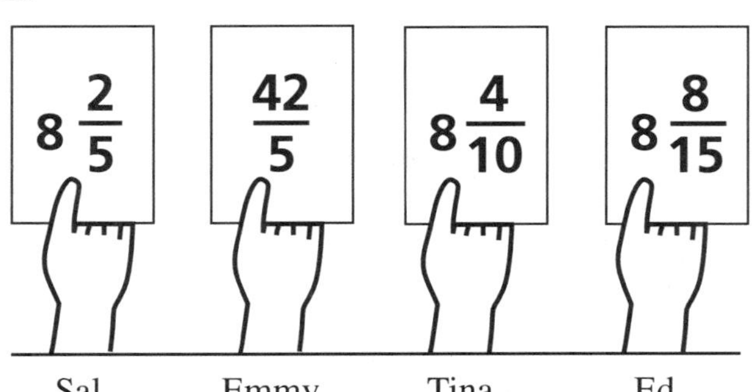

Four students were asked to write equivalent versions of the same fraction. Whose fraction is not equivalent to the others? C; Obj. 2C

A Tina

B Sal

C Ed

D Emmy

2 **One hundred seventy-one guests attended the class reunion at Hillside High, and the organizers said that this was a 90% attendance. How many were invited?** H; Obj. 5A

F 154

G 181

H 190

J 261

3 **Which best represents the percent of the figure that is shaded?** D; Obj. 5A

A $\frac{3}{32}$

B 0.94

C 3

D 9.4

4 **A bicycle regularly priced at $165 is on sale for 5% off. What is the sale price?** H; Obj. 5C

F $8.25

G $82.50

H $156.75

J $160

5 **What is the solution of the equation:**

$x - 2\frac{4}{5} = 1\frac{2}{5}$ A; Obj. 2E

A $4\frac{1}{5}$

B $1\frac{2}{5}$

C $3\frac{6}{5}$

D $3\frac{8}{5}$

E Not here

6 **A doctor bought a 5-foot-by-6-foot rectangular rug for her office. What is the area of the rug in square yards?** H; Obj. 3B

F 30

G 10

H $3\frac{1}{3}$

J $1\frac{1}{9}$

7 **A pattern for a quilt is made up of 36 squares. In the pattern, 20 of the squares have shades of blue in them. If the whole quilt has 144 squares, then what simplest form ratio represents the part of the quilt that is blue?** B; Obj. 4A

A $\frac{1}{4}$

B $\frac{5}{9}$

C $\frac{9}{5}$

D 4

UNIT 6 • TABLE OF CONTENTS

Data, Statistics, and Probability

We will be using this vocabulary:

mean the average of a set of data

median the middle number when a data set is arranged from least to greatest

mode the number(s) that occur(s) most often in a data set

frequency table a table that tallies the number of pieces of data in different intervals

outlier a piece of data that differs significantly from the rest of the data

quartile one of three items of data that separate the sorted data into roughly four quarters

permutation an arrangement or listing of objects in which order matters

probability a measure of how likely it is that an event will happen

independent events two or more events each of whose outcomes has no effect on the outcome of the other(s)

Dear Family,

During the next few weeks, our math class will be studying data, statistics, and probability. This includes work with reading and constructing graphs, which will help students prepare for algebra.

You can expect to see homework that provides practice with these skills. Here is a sample you may want to keep handy to give help if needed.

Finding the First, Second, and Third Quartiles, and the Range

4, 5, 5, **6**, 8, 9, 9, **10**, 11, 13, **15**, 15, 15, 18, 29

The first quartile is **6**.
The second quartile or median is **10**.
The third quartile is **15**.

The extremes are **4** and **29**.
The range is **29 − 4 = 25**.
29 is an outlier.

Determining the Probability of an Experiment

If an experiment involves two events, the probability of both of them occurring is found by multiplying their individual probabilities.

Example: You pick a letter from *a* to *j* and roll a number cube. What is the probability of picking a vowel (*a, e, i*) and rolling an even number?

$P(\text{Vowel and even number}) = P(\text{Vowel}) \cdot P(\text{even number})$

$$= \frac{3}{10} \cdot \frac{3}{6} = \frac{9}{60} \text{ or } \frac{3}{20}$$

During this unit, students will continue to learn new techniques related to problem solving and will continue to practice basic skills with fractions, decimals, and percents.

Sincerely,

Name ____________________

Line Plots and Histograms

Guided Practice: Ex. 1; First row of table in Ex. 6, p. 154
Independent Practice: Complete pp. 153–154

In Unit **1**, you learned to make a **line plot** and use the measures of central tendency—**mean, median,** and **mode**—to describe the data.

The data at the right shows the age at inauguration of the first 12 presidents of the United States.

President	Age	President	Age
Washington	57	Jackson	61
Adams, J.	61	Van Buren	54
Jefferson	57	Harrison	69
Madison	57	Tyler	51
Monroe	58	Polk	49
Adams, J.Q.	57	Taylor	64

This data is displayed below in a line plot.

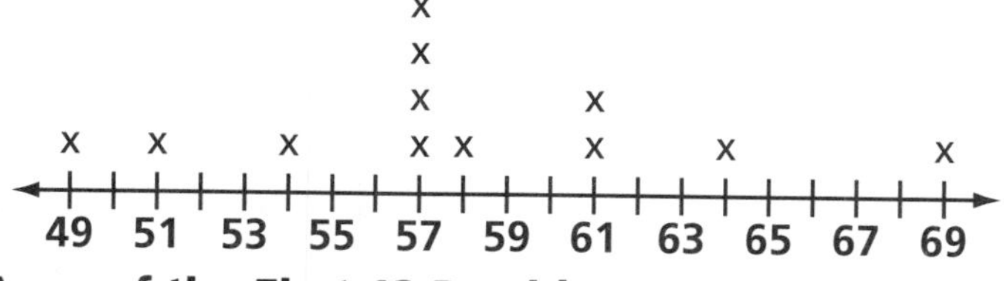

Ages of the First 12 Presidents at Inauguration

mean = $\frac{695}{12}$ or about **57.9**
median = **57**
mode = **57**
range = 69 − 49 or **20**

The mean, median, and mode are all about **57.** The typical age of a president at inauguration was **57.**

Use the data to answer the questions.

Ages of 20th-Century Presidents			
President	**Age**	**President**	**Age**
Clinton	46	Truman	60
Bush	64	F. Roosevelt	51
Reagan	69	Hoover	54
Carter	52	Coolidge	51
Ford	61	Harding	55
Nixon	56	Wilson	56
Johnson	55	Taft	51
Kennedy	43	T. Roosevelt	42
Eisenhower	62	McKinley	54

1. Make a line plot for the data in the table.

40 45 50 55 60 65 70

2. From your line plot, what conclusions can you make about the age of 20th-century presidents?

Possible answer: Nearly half were in their mid-fifties.

3. Find these measures.

Mean ≈ 54.56 Median 54.5 Mode 51 Range 27

4. Which measure best describes the data? Explain.

Possible answer: The mean, median, and mode are all very close together, so all of them describe the data well.

5. Compare the graphs and measures of central tendency for both sets of data on this page.

Possible answer: The mean, median, and mode for the earlier presidents was 3 to 7 years older; The later presidents had a greater range of ages.

Check Understanding *What is an internal frequency table?* (It is a table that tallies the data in intervals.) *Can you tell what each score is from an interval frequency table?* (No, but you can tell how many scores there are in any given interval.)

A **frequency table** tallies the number of pieces of data in different intervals. The intervals used must cover the **range** of the data. The frequency table below shows that for the interval 41–45 there were two presidents inaugurated in that age group.

A **histogram** is a special bar graph that represents data from a frequency table. Each bar represents the data for one interval of the frequency table. There are no spaces between the bars because there are no gaps between intervals. Where one interval ends, the next begins.

Interval	Tally	Frequency
41–45	||	2
46–50	|	1
51–55	𝍸 |||	8
56–60	|||	3
61–65	|||	3
66–70	|	1

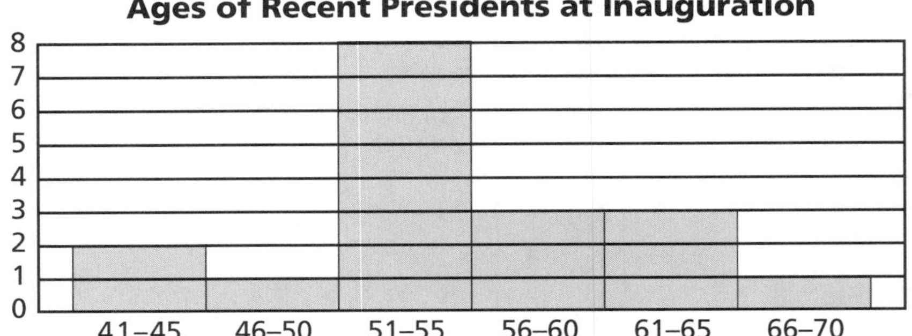

Solve.

6. Make a frequency table of the data. Use an interval of **10** points.

Test Scores for Period 4					
88	86	78	75	84	88
97	62	96	65	98	82
61	84	75	81	87	86
95	92	92	84	73	83
77	85	79	89	94	83

Interval	Tally	Frequency
60–69	|||	3
70–79	𝍸 |	6
80–89	𝍸 𝍸 ||||	14
90–99	𝍸 ||	7

Problem Solving Reasoning

Solve.

7. Draw a histogram of the data.

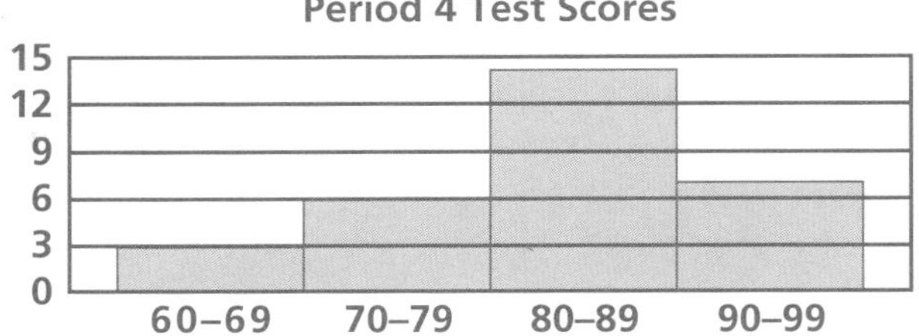

8. Write a description of the data based upon the graph. Include information about the range and comparison of number of students scoring A's **(90–100)**, B's **(80–89)**, C's **(70–79)**, and D's **(60–69)**.

Possible answer: The scores ranged from 61 to 98 and nearly half the class received a B. There were only 3 D's and the remaining scores were divided nearly equally between C's and A's.

Test Prep ★ Mixed Review

9 **What percent of 120 is 90?** C; Obj. 5A

A 100% **C** 75%

B 90% **D** 7.5%

10 **Jay is charged $46.75 for a pair of sneakers that had been marked down from $55. What was the discount rate?** F; Obj. 5C

F 15% **H** 85%

G about 17% **J** 117%

Closing the Lesson *If you used intervals to construct your histogram, what does the height of the bar in the histogram indicate?* (It tells you how many scores are in that interval.)

Name ____________________

Stem-and-Leaf Plots

Guided Practice: Ex. 1, p. 155
Independent Practice: Complete pp. 155–156

A **stem-and-leaf plot** can be used to organize and display data. When the data items have **2** digits, the **stem** represents the tens digit and the **leaves** represent the ones digits.

Make a stem-and-leaf plot of the congressional data.

Congressional Representation Western States

AK	3	ID	4	OR	7
AZ	8	NE	5	UT	5
CA	54	NV	3	WA	11
CO	8	NM	5	WY	3
HI	4	MT	3		

Step 1
Make the stem. Write the tens digits for the data in order from least to greatest.

0	
1	
2	
3	
4	
5	

Step 2
Record the data for the leaves. Write the ones digit for each data item.

0	3 8 8 4 4 5 3 5 3 7 5 3
1	1
2	
3	
4	
5	4

Step 3
Sort the data for the leaves from least to greatest. Write a title and include a key.

Congressional Representation

0	3 3 3 3 4 4 5 5 5 7 8 8
1	1
2	
3	
4	
5	4

Key: 5|4 represents 54 members of Congress

You can see that the range is **54 − 3,** or **51.**
The median of the data is between the seventh and eighth number, or 5.
The mode is 3, because it occurs most often—4 times.

Use the data about the congressional representation of the southern states to answer the questions.

Congressional Representation: Southern States

AL	AR	FL	GA	KY	LA	MS	NC	OK	SC	TN	TX	VA
9	6	25	13	8	9	7	14	8	8	11	32	13

1. Make a stem-and-leaf plot for the data.

Congressional Representation

0	6 7 8 8 8 9 9
1	1 3 3 4
2	5
3	2

Key: 1|3 represents 13 members of Congress

2. a. Find the measures.

Mean 12.5 Median 9

Mode 8 Range 26

b. Which measure best describes the data? Explain. The mean, because most of the numbers cluster around, or are close to, 12.

3. Items of data that are significantly different from the rest are **outliers.** What item(s) of data might be considered outliers for this data set?

25 and 32

4. Outliers can have a great effect on the mean. Find the mean without using the outliers. Is it more representative of the data? The new mean is about 11; It is close to the mean calculated with outliers; The new mean is slightly more representative.

Check Understanding *Who can explain to me what a stem-and-leaf plot is for?* (It is a very easy way to organize and order data.)

A **back-to-back stem-and-leaf** plot uses the same stem for two sets of data.

The example at the right shows the heights of **16** students in a fourth–grade class and **19** students in a seventh–grade class.

The plot shows that:

- most fourth graders are between **44** in. and **54** in. tall with a median of **46.5** in. and a range of **17** in.
- most seventh graders are between **54** in. and **68** in. tall with a median of **61** in. and a range of **23** in.

Seventh graders are taller than fourth graders, by about **14** or **15** inches.

Height in Inches

Fourth Grade		Seventh Grade
9 7	3	
9 7 7 6 6 6 5 4 0	4	8 9
4 3 3 1 0	5	1 4 5 5 6 8 9
	6	1 2 2 3 3 3 7 7 8
	7	1

Key: 0 | 4 represents 40 inches and 4 | 8 represents 48 inches

Problem Solving Reasoning Use the data to answer the questions.

5. Make a back-to-back stem-and-leaf plot for the ages of first ladies and their husbands. Presidential data is found in the last lesson. Add Presidents Harrison (**56**) and Cleveland (**48**).

Presidents		First Ladies
	2	1
	3	1 9
2 3 6 8	4	4 5 7 8 9 9
1 1 1 2 4 4 5 5 6 6 6	5	0 2 4 6 6 6 6 9
0 1 2 4 9	6	0 0 3

Ages of First Ladies

First Lady	Age	First Lady	Age
H. Clinton	45	E. Roosevelt	48
B. Bush	63	L. Hoover	54
N. Reagan	59	G. Coolidge	44
R. Carter	49	F. Harding	60
E. Ford	56	E. Wilson	52
P. Nixon	56	H. Taft	47
C. Johnson	50	E. Roosevelt	39
J. Kennedy	31	I. McKinley	49
M. Eisenhower	56	C. Harrison	56
E. Truman	60	F. Cleveland	21

6. From your plot, what conclusions can you make about the ages of first ladies compared with the ages of presidents? Include the median and range in your summary.

Possible answer: The median age for the presidents was 54 years, and the first ladies had a median of 51 years. The first ladies were slightly younger, but had a greater range of ages (42 years vs. 27 for the presidents).

Test Prep ★ Mixed Review

7 **Beth saved $600 on a used car that was on sale at 15% off the list price. What was the list price of the car?** B; Obj. 5C

A $9,000 **C** $3,400

B $4,000 **D** $900

8 **After 6 months, how much interest does Sam receive on his $500 investment, if his bank pays 4% simple interest annually?** F; Obj. 5D

F $10 **H** $24

G $20 **J** $250

Closing the Lesson *What are some reasons for using a stem-and-leaf plot to display the data?* (Possible answer: The original data is not lost and the median, mode, and range are easy to find.)

Name ____________________

Guided Practice: Numbers 1 & 3, p. 157
Independent Practice: Complete pp. 157–158

Box-and-Whisker Plots

A **box-and-whisker** plot shows how data are distributed. Unlike a stem-and-leaf plot, each piece of data is not displayed. Instead, the data are represented in **quartiles.**

- You know that the median separates the data set into 2 halves.
- **Quartiles** separate a data set into 4 quarters.

Number of Beans Out of 20 that Sprouted in Each Pot
8 13 9 16 4 9 10 12 15 10 5 6 11

To draw a box-and-whisker plot of the data in the chart, you can use the steps below.

1. Arrange the data in order from least to greatest. Identify the **extremes,** or least and greatest numbers, and the median of the entire data set.

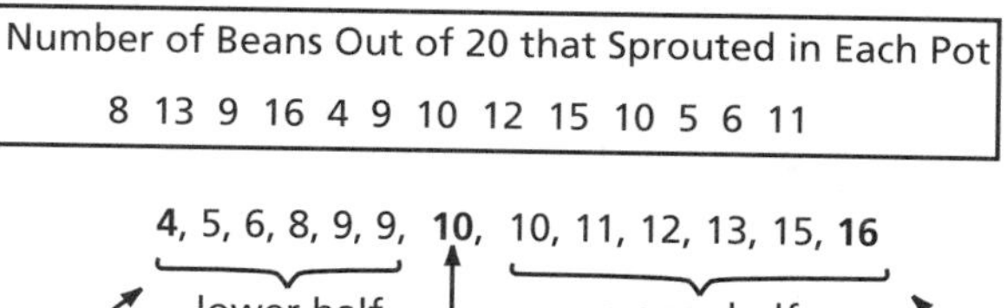

2. • Draw a number line. Below the line, draw a dot for each extreme and the median.
   - Draw a dot for the **first quartile.** It is the median of the lower half of the data set. Note that neither half of the data includes the median.
   - The **second quartile** is the median of the entire data set.
   - Draw a dot for the **third quartile.** It is the median of the upper half of the data set.

4 6 8 10 12 14 16

1st quartile $(6 + 8) \div 2 = 7$

2nd quartile

3rd quartile $(12 + 13) \div 2 = 12.5$

3. Draw a box-and-whisker plot. Draw a box as shown through the first and third quartiles. Draw a vertical line through the median. Show the whiskers by connecting the extremes to the first and third quartiles.

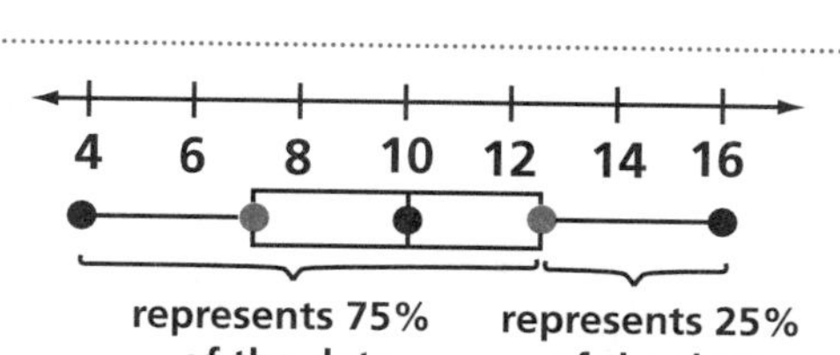

The box represents 50% of the data.

Answer the questions using the data set at the right.

Data:
33, 44, 63, 75, 52, 34, 15,
20, 68, 64, 41, 48, 67, 48

1. Sort the data from least to greatest.

15, 20, 33, 34, 41, 44, 48, 48, 52, 63, 64, 67, 68, 75

2. Find the items: Least 15 1st Quartile 34

2nd Quartile 48 3rd Quartile 64 Greatest 75

3. Draw a box-and-whisker plot.

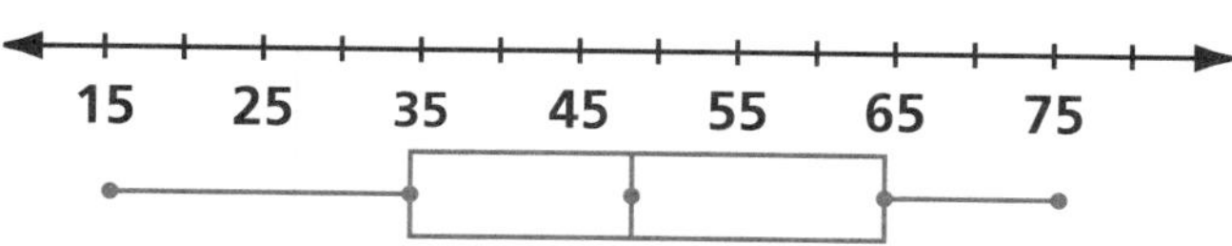

4. What percent of the data is greater than or equal to the median? 50%

5. What percent of the data is less than or equal to the first quartile? about 21%

Check Understanding *What does the third quartile represent?* (The score that has 75% of the scores below it and 25% above it.) *How do you find the third quartile?* (Arrange the data in ascending order. Divide the data set in half; then, find the median for the upper half of the data set.)

Multiple box-and-whisker plots can be drawn using the same axes. It is easy to visually compare the **5** items of data that were used to draw the plots.

Both families bought groceries for **52** weeks. The Rowes' greatest week equals the Mereks' median, so for half the weeks, the Mereks spent more than the Rowes' greatest week. For half the weeks, the Rowes spent less than what the Mereks spent a quarter of the weeks.

Weekly Grocery Bills for One Year

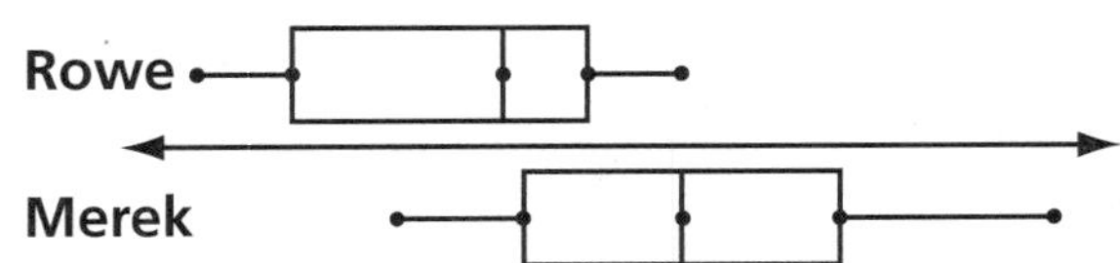

Use the data to answer the questions.

6. From the plots, would you agree that the average score of the top professional basketball players is going up each year? Explain. No; About half the scores for 1996–97 are the same as or greater than 1997–98.

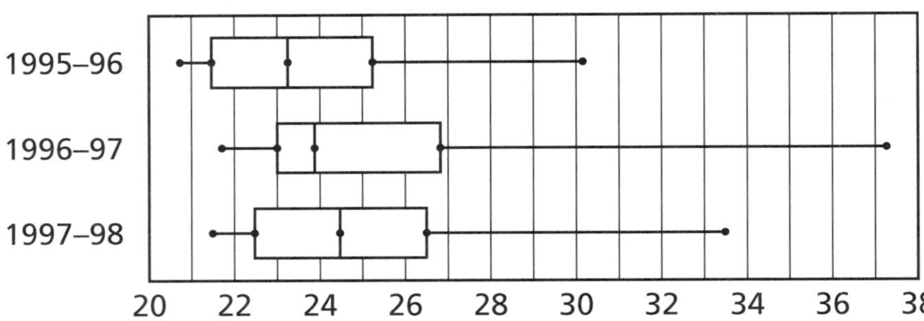

7. Compare the box-and-whisker plots for the last two seasons. Which season had the higher

a. greatest number? '96–'97 c. third quartile? '96–97 e. median? '97–'98

b. first quartile? '96–'97 d. least number? '96–'97

Quick Check

Use the plots below for exercises 8–10. Each shows the number of times a group of sixth graders rode the bus during one month.

Bus Rides (October)

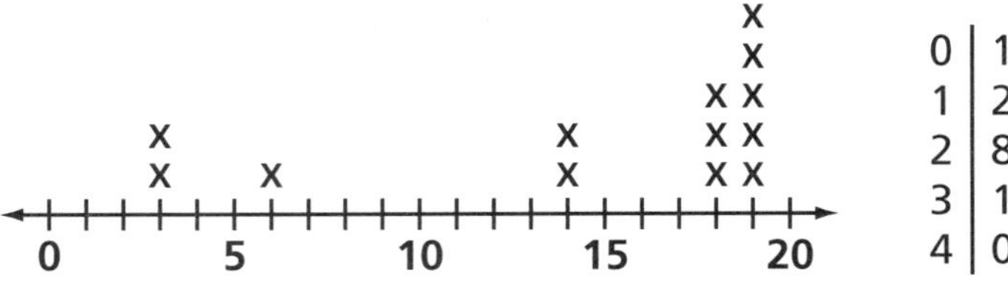

Bus Rides (January)

Stem	Leaf
0	1 3 3
1	2 6 8
2	8
3	1 5 6 6 7 8 8 9
4	0 0 0 1 1 2 2 2 2

8. What are the median and mode for the first set of data?

18 and 19

9. What are the median and mode of the second set of data?

37.5 and 42

10. What are the first and third quartiles for the first set of data?

10 and 19

Work Space.

Item	Error Analysis
8–9	**Common Error:** Students may confuse mode and median. **Reteaching** Reteach 36 and 37
10	**Common Error:** Students may include the median in either or both the upper or lower half of the data. **Skills Tutorial** Reteach 38

Closing the Lesson *If a score is in the box of a box-and-whisker plot, what can you tell me about that score?* (Possible answer: It is in the middle 50% of the scores.)

Name ______________________

Guided Practice: Ex. 1A & 1B; 3A, & 3B, p. 159
Independent Practice: Complete pp. 159–160

Two sets of related data can be graphed on a **scatter plot.** The chart below shows two sets of related data. Students were surveyed to find out the contents and weight of their bookbags.

Number of Books and Notebooks	2	3	2	1	4	5	4	3
Weight in Pounds	5	9	6	3	11	14	12	8

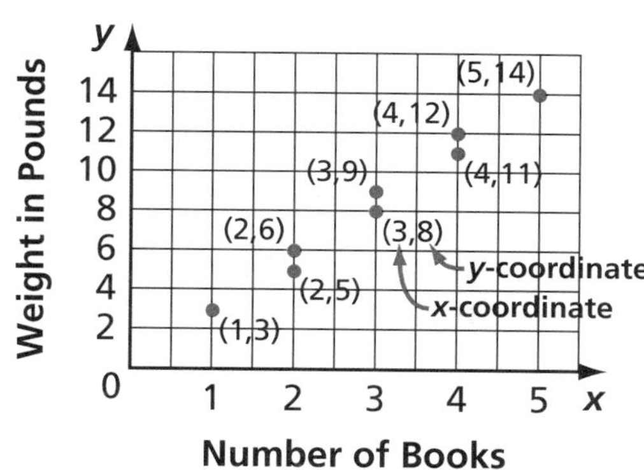

This data can be written as **ordered pairs (*x*, *y*);**
(2, 5), (3, 9), (2, 6), (1, 3), (4, 11), (5, 14), (4, 12), (3, 8).

The weight in pounds (*y*-coordinate) tends to increase as the number of books and notebooks (*x*-coordinate) increases. This is a **positive correlation.** For other data, the *y*-coordinate may tend to decrease as the *x*-coordinate increases. This is a **negative correlation.** If no pattern exists between the coordinates, then there is **no correlation.**

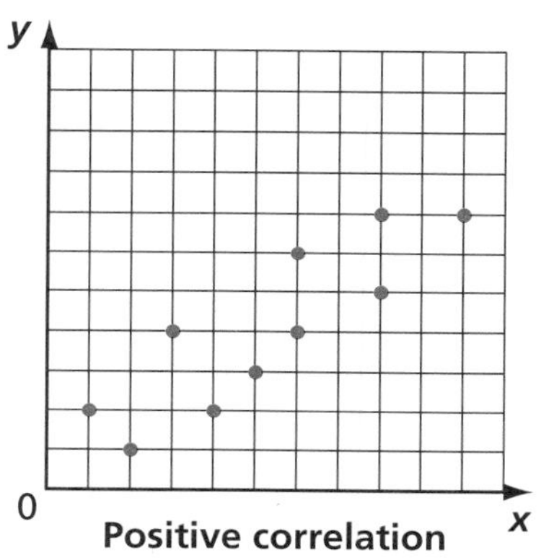

Positive correlation

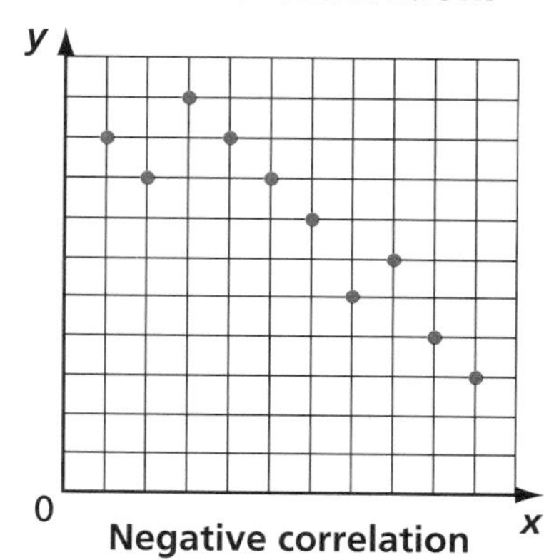

Negative correlation

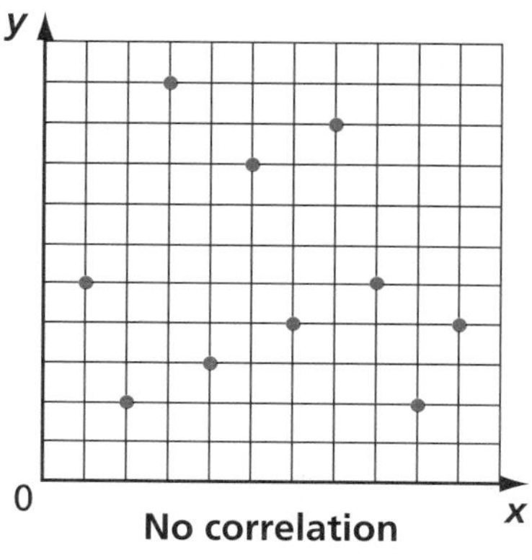

No correlation

Use the scatter plot to answer the questions.

1. Write the ordered pair represented by each letter.

A (6,1) *B* (8,4) *C* (2,4)

D (1,1) *E* (3,0) *F* (5,3)

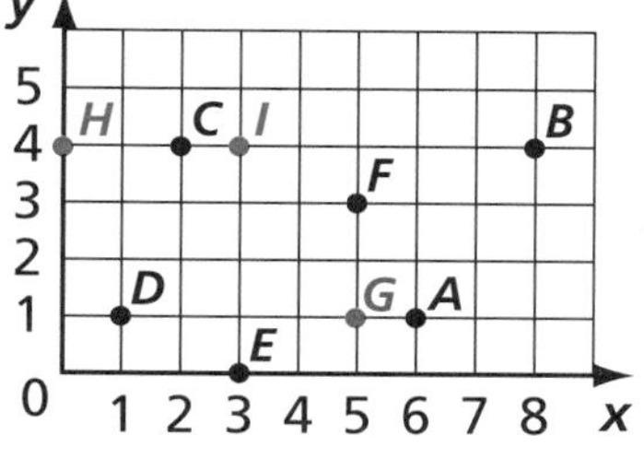

2. Plot the points on the scatter plot.

G(5, 1) *H*(0, 4) *I*(3, 4)

3. Draw a scatter plot for the ordered pairs below. Label each point with the correct letter.

A(8, 4.5), *B*(4, 2), *C*(6, 4), *D*(3, 1.5), *E*(7, 4)

F(2, 1), *G*(4, 3), *H*(5, 2.5), *I*(6, 3)

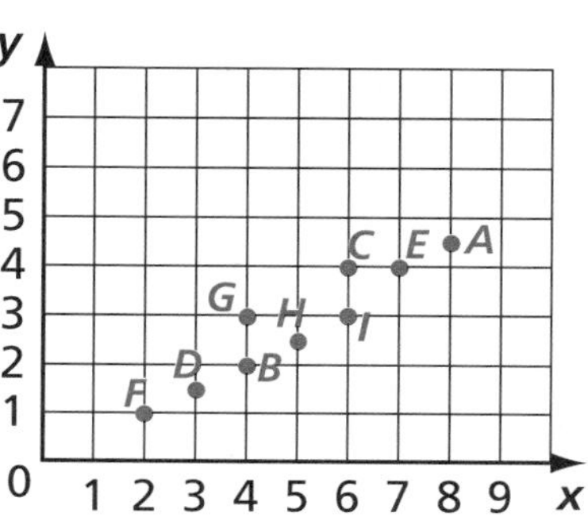

4. Describe the correlation.

positive correlation

Check Understanding *If you were to graph the height of a child versus age in years to age 15, what kind of correlation would you expect, and why?* (Positive, because the child will be growing during those years.)

5. Use the data in the table to draw a scatter plot.

Altitude (in 1,000's of feet)	0	5	10	15	20	25
Pressure (in pounds per sq in.)	14.7	12.3	10.2	8.4	6.8	5.4

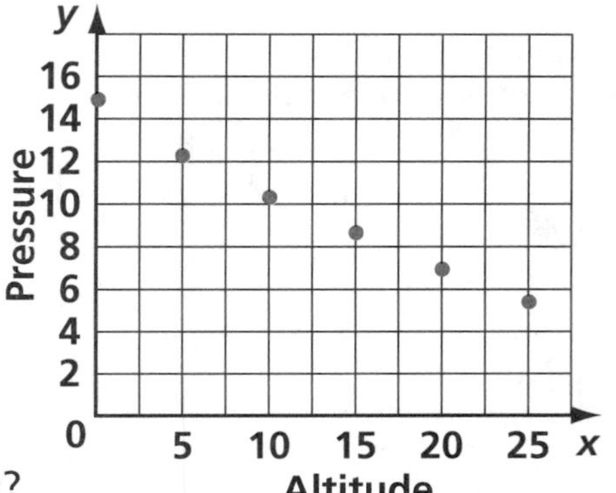

6. Describe the correlation.

negative correlation

7. What correlation would you expect for each of the following?

a. scatter plot showing number of children in a family and number of windows in a kitchen

no correlation

b. scatter plot of number of hours per day you are awake and the hours you are asleep

negative correlation

Problem Solving
Reasoning

Solve.

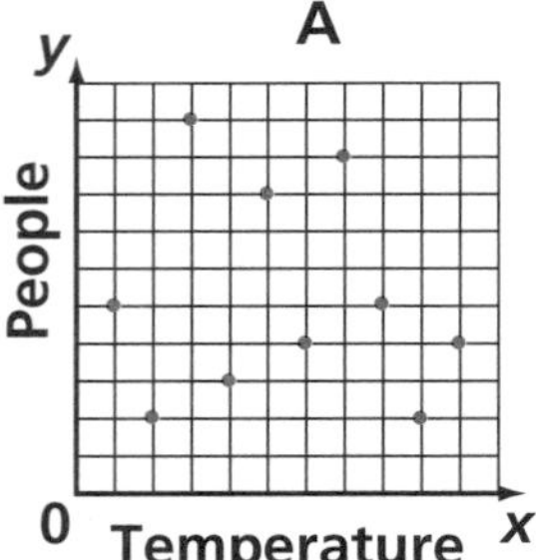

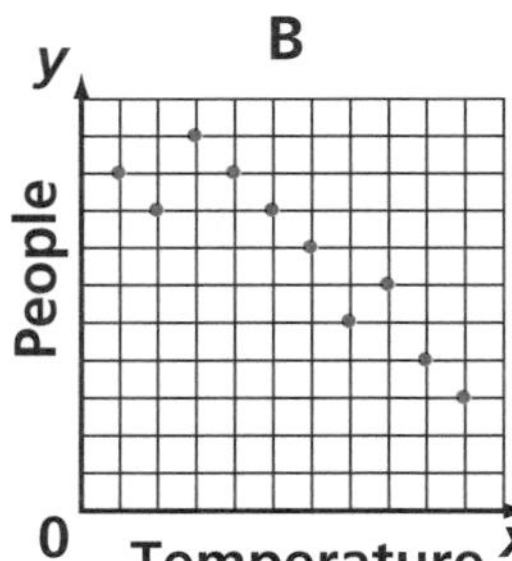

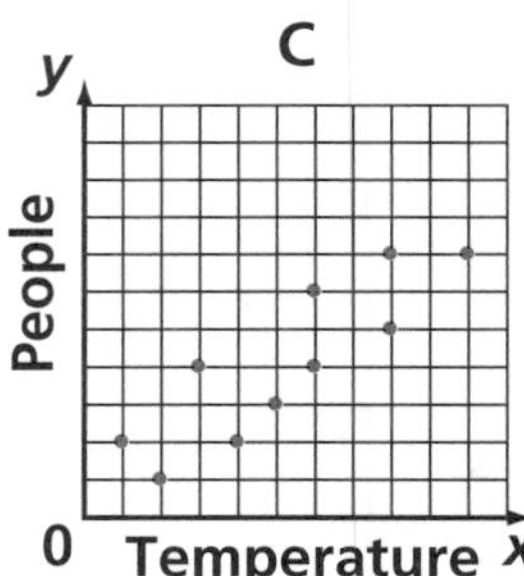

8. Which graph do you think represents daily temperature and number of people at the beach? Explain.

C; When the weather is warmer, more people go to the beach.

9. Which graph do you think represents daily temperature and people at the shopping mall? Explain.

Possible answer: A; People go shopping whether it is warm or cold outside.

Test Prep ★ Mixed Review

10 **The data show the number of cousins that 13 students have. What is the median value?**

D; Obj. 6A

Cousins

0	5 5 6 7
1	2 3 7 8
2	3 5 6 8 9

Key: 1 | 2 represents 12 cousins

A 5 **B** 7 **C** 16.2 **D** 17

11 **The ages of the eleven players on a parent-student soccer team are: 12, 50, 13, 48, 14, 41, 14, 52, 15, 56, 15. Which of these values does 50 represent?**

H; Obj. 6B

F range **H** upper quartile

G mean **J** median

Closing the Lesson *What would you expect for a correlation between number of hours of sleep and alertness in class the next day?* (positive)

Name ______________________

Misleading Graphs

Guided Practice: Ex. 1 & 2, p. 161
Independent Practice: Complete pp. 161–162

Look at the two graphs at the right. Both show the monthly sales for Pete's Restaurant, but they look very different.

Graph B could be misleading because the vertical scale does not start at zero. Monthly sales have tended to increase, but Graph B makes the increase look dramatic.

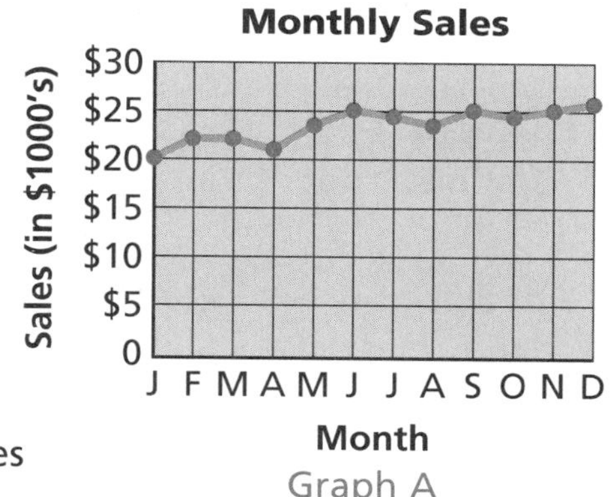

Graph A

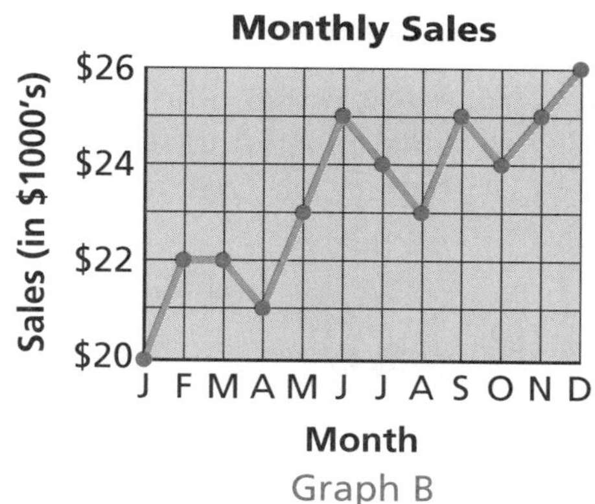

Graph B

Suppose Pete wants to attract new investors. Then, he would show Graph B. If sales had decreased, he might use a scale similar to Graph A. It would make the loss less apparent.

You may not want to include all the numbers from **0** to the top of the range in a graph's scale. Then, you can use jagged lines or a "broken scale" to show that part of the range has been omitted.

Use the graph to answer the questions.

You asked your friends to vote on their favorite ice cream flavor from the three choices shown.

1. Use just the lengths of the bars. Compare the number of people who chose vanilla with those who chose strawberry.

It appears that almost double chose vanilla.

2. Use the horizontal scale. Compare the number of people who chose vanilla with those who chose strawberry.

Only 4 more chose vanilla.

3. Graph the data so it is not misleading. Use a bar graph.

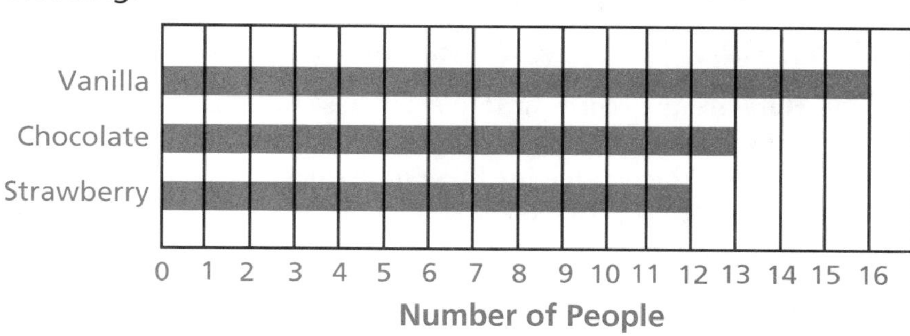

Check Understanding *Why would someone create a misleading graph?* (Possible answer: to support a particular viewpoint)

Another way that graphs can be misleading is when the widths of the bars vary. Both graphs show the number of Internet subscribers (in thousands) for two providers, but they look very different.

Graph A is misleading because the bars are not the same width and the height of the bars do not correspond to a vertical scale. Graph B is not misleading.

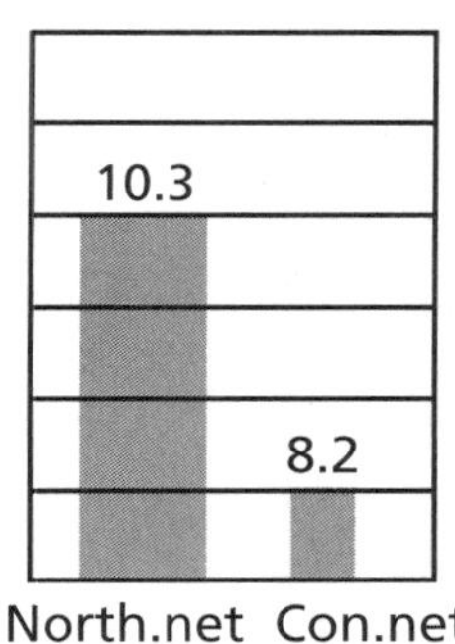

Graph A

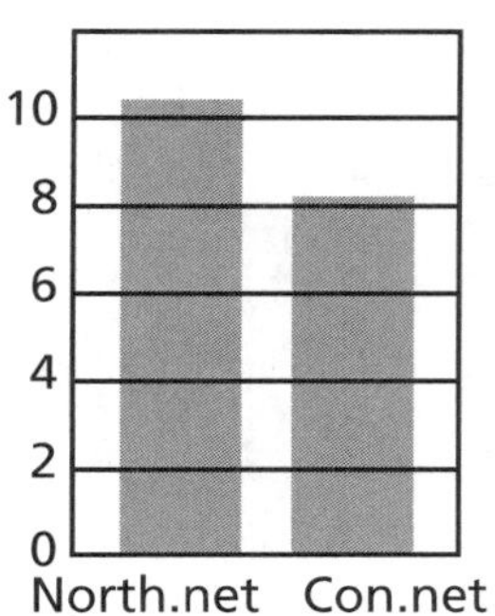

Graph B

Problem Solving
Reasoning

4. Draw two bar graphs–one that is misleading and one that is not. Use the data to the right.
Misleading graphs will vary.

Chocolate Sales for February **1–14**

Carbo's Chocolates: **328** pounds
Mrs. Sweet's Treats: **260** pounds
Yum Factory: **400** pounds

Misleading Graph
Chocolate Sales

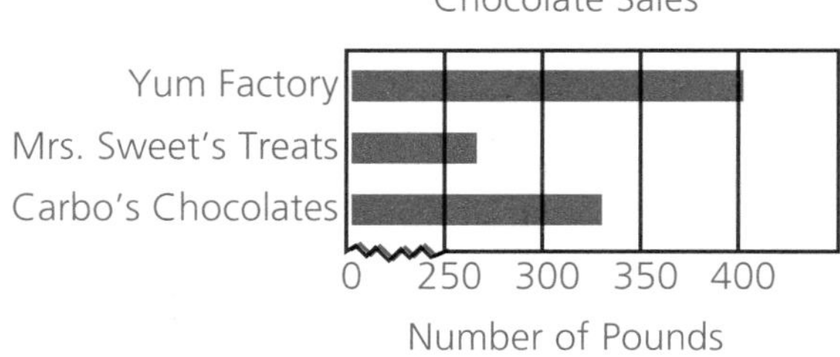

Number of Pounds

Accurate Graph
Chocolate Sales

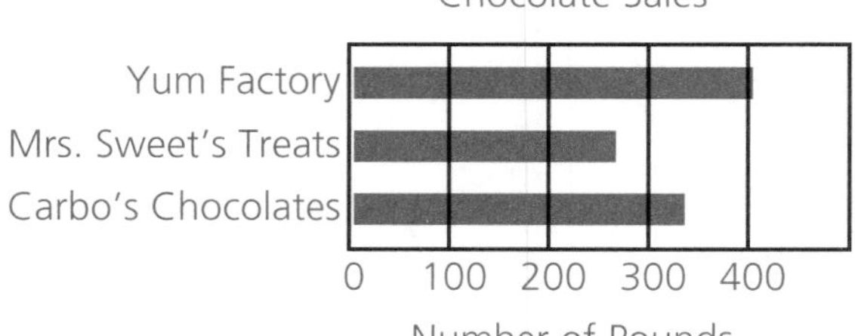

Number of Pounds

5. Draw two graphs–one that is misleading and one that is not. Use the data below.

Monthly High
Temperature (°F)

Jan.: **45°**
Feb.: **48°**
Mar.: **51°**
Apr.: **58°**
May: **72°**
June: **76°**

Misleading Graph
Temperatures

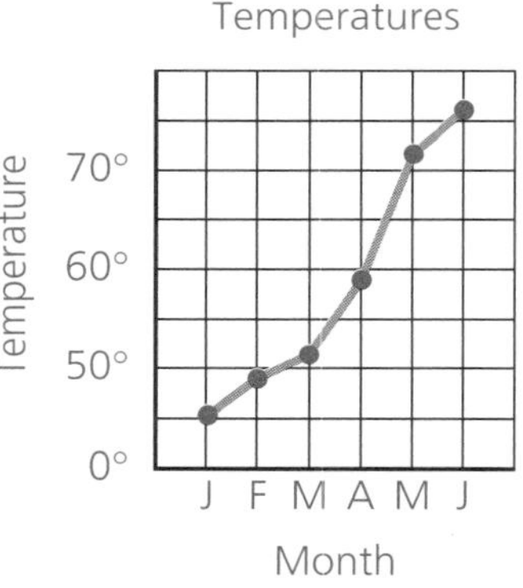

Accurate Graph
Temperatures

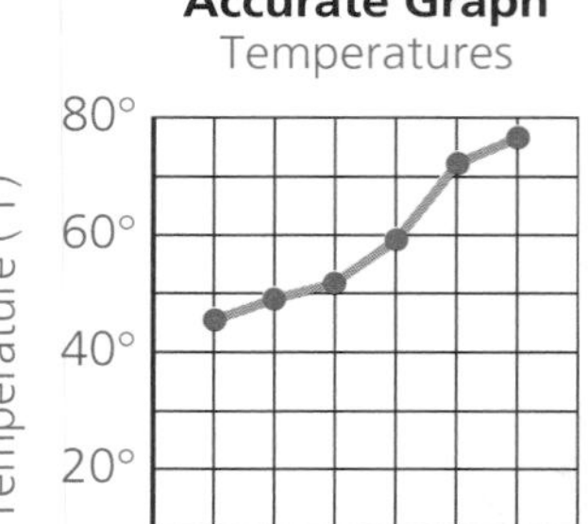

Test Prep ★ Mixed Review

6 **Here are the scores in Dan's art class for last Friday's test: 83, 76, 72, 69, 54, 85, 65, 88, 79, 75, 65. Which value for these data does 75 represent?** C; Obj. 6B

A range
B upper quartile
C median
D lower quartile

7 **Use the data in question 9. If you wanted to make a line plot of the data, which interval would be best to show on the number line?** H; Obj. 6A

F 45–100
G 55–100
H 65–90
J 75–80

Closing the Lesson *What might you do to make a misleading graph?* (Possible answer: Don't begin the vertical axes at zero; Don't show the trends over a sufficient amount of time; Make the size of the icons disproportionate to the actual data.)

Name ______________________________

Making Predictions from a Graph

Guided Practice: Ex. 1 & 3A, pp. 163
Independent Practice: Complete pp. 163–164

A scatter plot can be used to make predictions. Study the graphs below.

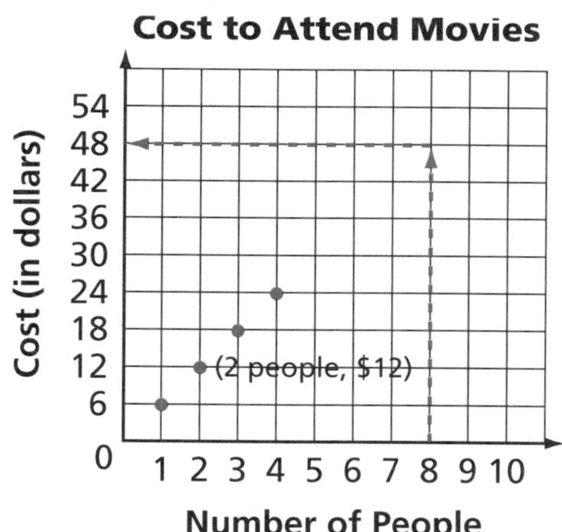

This graph shows the cost for certain numbers of people to go to the movies. The ordered pairs are (*number attending, total cost*). The ordered pairs are not connected, because you cannot have decimal parts of people.

You can use the graph to predict the cost for **8** people. Extend the pattern of points. Read up from the horizontal axis at **8**, and then read over to the left on the vertical axis. You could predict that the cost for **8** people would be a little less than **$50.**

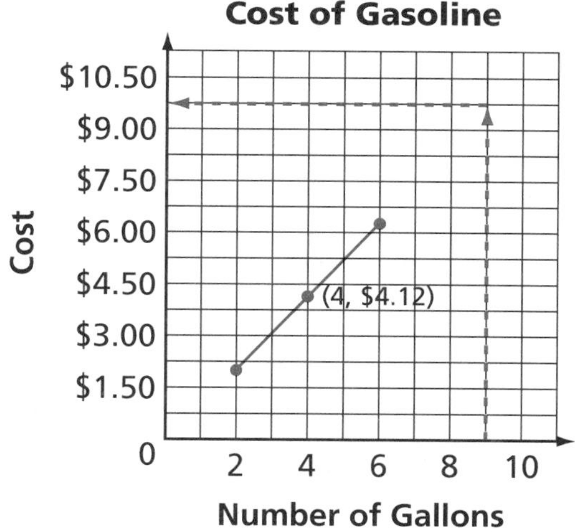

This graph shows the cost for certain numbers of gallons of gasoline. The ordered pairs are (*gallons of gas, cost*). The ordered pairs are connected, because you can buy decimal parts of a gallon of gas.

You can use the graph to predict the cost for **9** gallons. Use a straightedge to extend the line. Read up from the horizontal axis at **9;** then, read over to the left on the vertical axis. You could predict that **9** gallons would cost about **$9.**

Use the graphs to answer the question.

1. How much money did Derek start with? $65

2. How much did Derek have after **3** weeks? $80

3. If Derek continues to save at the same rate, predict the amount he will have after:

a. **5** weeks $90 b. **8** weeks $105

4. Estimate the cost of the following calls.

a. **2** minutes $.18 b. **3.5** minutes $.30

5. Extend the graph to predict the cost.

a. **6** minutes $.50 b. **7.5** minutes $.65

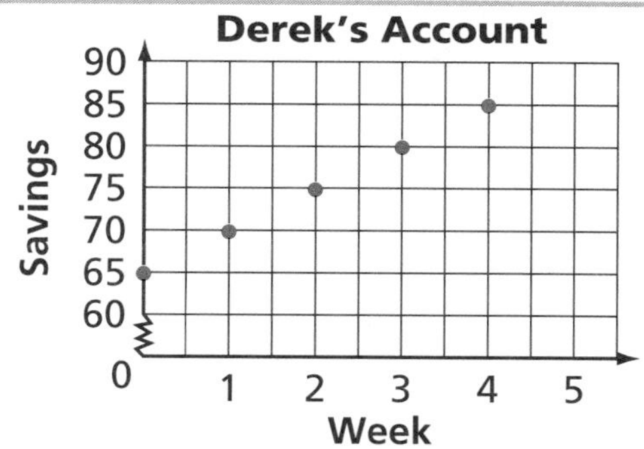

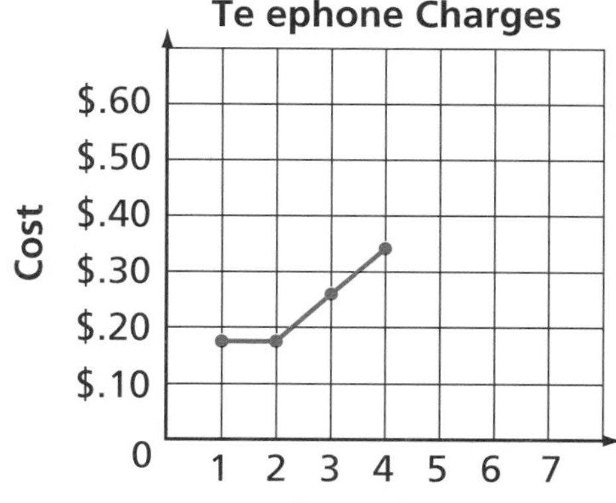

Check Understanding *Data from the Olympics indicate that the time needed to swim 50 meters has been decreasing at about 1.3 seconds every five years. Must this trend continue for the next 100 years?* (Possible answer: No. Swimmers will reach a limit and times will level off, or maybe minute amounts will decrease.)

Use the graphs to answer.

6. A fitness club began a membership drive. The graph shows the number of members at the end of each month for 6 months. How many members were there on January 1? 340

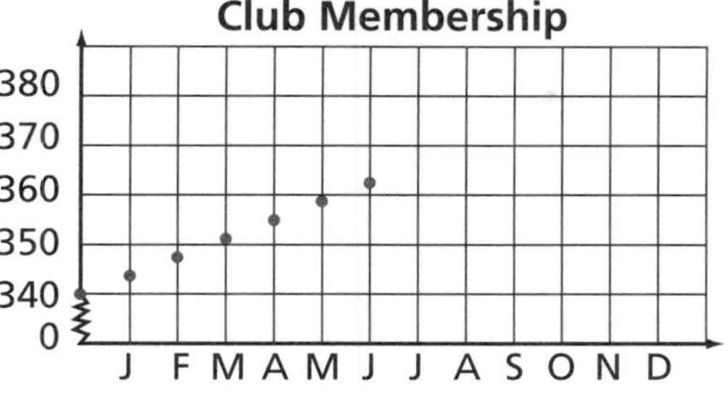

7. Estimate the number of members at the end of April. 355

8. If membership continues to increase at the same rate, predict the number of members at the end of:

a. September 372 b. December 388

Problem Solving Reasoning **Complete.**

9. Write the next three numbers.

8, 12, 16, 20, 24, 28, 32

10. Without writing each number, predict the 20th number in the sequence. 84

11. Write the next three numbers.

60, 57, 54, 51, 48, 45, 42

12. Without writing each number, predict the 20th number in the sequence. 3

Quick Check

A scatter plot is made of the two sets of data. Tell whether you would expect to see a positive correlation, a negative correlation, or no correlation.

13. The number of calories in snack foods and the number of grams of fat in the same snacks

positive correlation

14. The number of times people brush their teeth each day and the number of cavities they have

negative correlation

15. Why might the broken scale make the graph appear misleading?
Makes differences between data appear greater than they are.

16. What prediction about the attendance at game 10 would be reasonable?

about 500

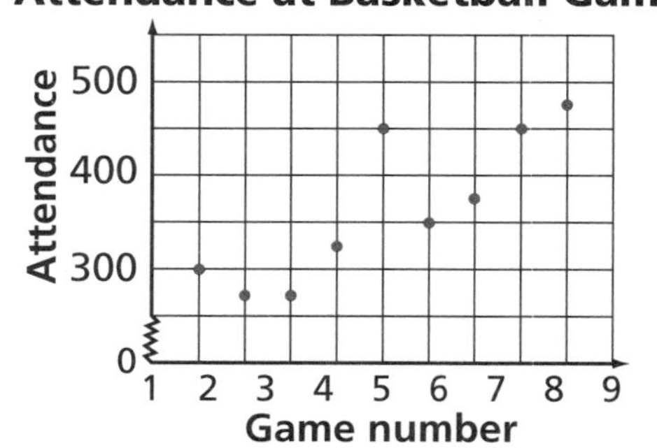

Work Space.

Item	Error Analysis
13–14	**Common Error** Students may confuse positive and negative correlation. **Reteaching** Reteach 39
15	**Common Error** Students may not recognize the significance of a broken scale. **Reteaching** Reteach 40
16	**Common Error** Students may not recognize the trend shown in the graph. **Skills Tutorial** Reteach 41

Closing the Lesson *What assumptions are you making when you make predictions based on graphs?* (Possible answer: You are assuming that the trend will continue in the same fashion and that the prediction makes sense in terms of a real-life situation.)

Name ________________________

Guided Practice: Problem 1, p. 166
Independent Practice: Complete pp. 165–166

Problem Solving Strategy: Make a List

To solve some problems, making a list may help you get started. A list may be a series of numbers, words, or symbols that are written horizontally or vertically.

Problem

Your friend just dropped three coins out of his pocket and they all landed heads up. Is it unusual for all three to be heads? How many ways could they have landed?

1 Understand

"Asking yourself questions will help you identify the math ideas."

As you reread, ask yourself questions.

- How many coins were dropped and how did they land?
  three coins; They all landed heads up.
- What else do you need to find? How many ways can they land?

2 Decide

"Could a tree diagram help to see the possible ways three coins can land?"

Choose a method for solving.

Try the strategy Make a List. Make a tree diagram to help you to see all the ways three coins can land.

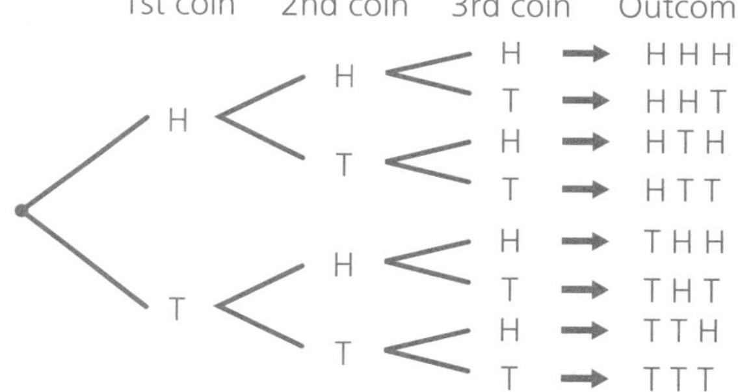

3 Solve

"Read to the end of each branch to make a list of the possible outcomes."

Answer the question.

- Make a list to find how many ways three coins can land.
  HHH, HHT, HTH, HTT, THH, THT, TTH, TTT 8 ways
- How often would you expect to get three heads?
  once in about every 8 tries

4 Look back

"Check your answer to see that all of the outcomes are different."

Ask if your answer makes sense.

- Toss three coins at once several times. Was three heads one of the outcomes? Answers will vary.
- How did making a list help you solve the problem?
  Possible answer: It helped me to see all the possible outcomes.

Check Understanding *When would it be a good idea to make a list in order to solve a problem?* (Possible answer: when it is important to consider all possible combinations or outcomes)

Use the Make a List strategy or any other strategy you have learned.

1. In your gym locker, you have a pair of shorts, wind pants, a tank top, a white T-shirt, and a blue T-shirt. How many different outfits could you wear?

Think: What tops can I wear with the shorts? With the pants?

any of 3: tank top, white T-shirt, blue T-shirt;

the same tops

Answer 6 outfits

2. The Ice Cream Shoppe sells a sundae that has two different flavors of ice cream. The choices are vanilla, chocolate, strawberry, mocha, and mint chocolate. How many different combinations of ice cream can you have in the sundae?

Think: Start with making a list of all the combinations that have vanilla.

V-C, V-S, V-M, V-MC

Answer 10 combinations for the sundae

3. You heard an advertisement for a company selling discount tapes. The first part of the telephone number, the exchange, contained the digits **6**, **3**, and **4**, but you don't remember the order. Make a list of all the possible telephone exchanges.

346 364 463

436 634 643

4. You've forgotten your three-digit password to log onto the school computer. You remember the first digit is **4**. How many different passwords would you have to check in order to log on?

100 passwords

5. The area of the large square is **16** square units.
a. What is the area of each small triangle?
b. How many triangles of all sizes are in the figure and what is the area of each size of triangle?

a. 2 square units
b. 16 triangles: 8 with area 2 square units; 4 with area 4 square units, and 4 with area 8 square units

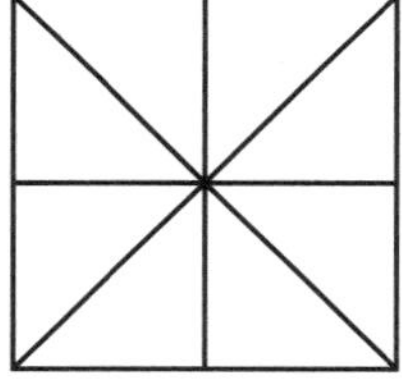

6. The area of the smallest triangle is **1** square unit.
a. What is the area of the largest triangle?
b. How many triangles of all sizes are in the figure and what is the area of each?

a. 16 square units
b. 27 triangles: 16 with 1 square unit, 7 with 4 square units, 3 with 9 square units, and 1 with 16 square units

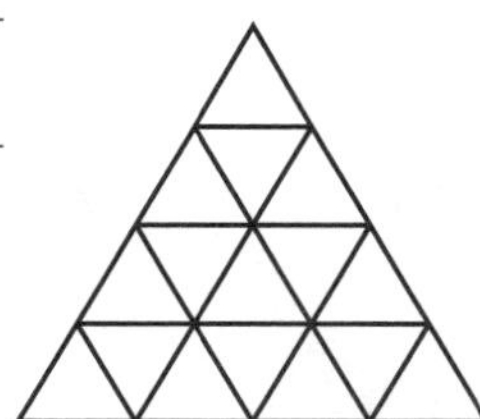

7. How many different combinations of **3** odd numbers have a sum of **15**? (Consider **3 + 3 + 9** to be the same as **3 + 9 + 3**.)

6 combinations

8. During the year you must read **3** books for English class. You can choose from a list of **6** books. How many different sets of **3** books can you choose?

20 sets of 3

Closing the Lesson *What does a list help you do?* (Anticipate all possible outcomes.)

Name ______________________

Guided Practice: Ex. 1 & 3, p. 167
Independent Practice: Complete pp. 167–168

Permutations and Combinations

Four players are still left in a tournament. In how many different ways can the four finish in the standings?

Call the players A, B, C, and D. Make a list of the different place finishes where ABCD means A finished first, B finished second, and so on.

Possible Place Finishes

ABCD	BACD	CABD	DABC
ABDC	BADC	CADB	DACB
ACBD	BCAD	CBAD	DBAC
ACDB	BCDA	CBDA	DBCA
ADBC	BDAC	CDAB	DCAB
ADCB	BDCA	CDBA	DCBA

A **permutation** is an arrangement or listing of objects in which *order is important*.

The number of permutations of n objects is $n \cdot (n-1) \cdot (n-2) \cdot \ldots \cdot 1$.
This number is represented by the expression $n!$.
It is read as "**n factorial.**"

The number of permutations of **4** players is

$$4! = 4 \cdot 3 \cdot 2 \cdot 1 \text{ or } 24$$

There are 24 ways in which they can finish in the standings. The *order* does matter.

How many ways can you arrange 6 students in the front row of the chorus?

$$\text{Number of permutations of } 6 \text{ students} = 6! = 6 \cdot 5 \cdot 4 \cdot 3 \cdot 2 \cdot 1 = 720$$

There are 720 arrangements. The order does matter.

Evaluate.

1. 2! 2 5! 120 3! 6

2. 7! 5,040 4! 24 6! 720

Solve.

3. List the permutations of the letters in the word BAN. How many of the permutations are words?

BAN, BNA, ABN, ANB, NAB, NBA; 2 are words.

4. How many different ways can you arrange five books on a shelf?

120 ways

5. How many different four-digit numbers can you make using the digits **3, 5, 1,** and **8?** No digit may repeat.

24 numbers

6. How many permutations are there for writing the names of the starting five players in the score book?

120 ways

Check Understanding *How many different ways could you select three people from a group of four?* (4)

A **combination** is a set of data in which order is *not* important. Making a list is one way to find the number of combinations of a set.

You order the daily special—a two-topping pizza. You can choose from five toppings. How many different two-topping pizzas could you order?

Possible Pizza Orders

PH	PO	PM	PG	HM
HO	HG	OM	OG	MG

To simplify the problem, label the toppings: P for pepperoni, H for hamburger, O for onions, M for mushrooms, and G for green peppers.

OM and MO are the same pizza, so order does not matter. There are **10** combinations. If order did matter, the permutations of **2** objects from a set of **5** would be $5 \cdot 4 = 20$, or twice as many.

Solve.

7. Count the number of combinations for choosing **2** people from a group of **4** people.

6 ways

8. How many ways can you select **3** pieces of fruit from a basket containing **5** pieces?

10 ways

9. A buffet has **5** appetizers. How many ways can you select **2** of them?

10 ways

10. A **5**-person team wants to select **3** co-captains. How many different combinations are there? Make a list.

ABC, ABD, ABE, BCD, BDE, CDE; 6 combinations

Problem Solving Reasoning **Solve.**

11. How many committees of 2 can be selected from a group of 6 students? (Hint: Label the students A, B, C, D, E, F.)

15 committees

12. How many committees of 2 can be selected from a group of 6 students if one is the speaker and one is the recorder?

30 committees

Test Prep ★ Mixed Review

13 **The number of miles 10 people jogged was recorded in this line plot. How many people jogged *at least* 3 miles?** A; Obj. 6A

Miles Jogged

A 6 **B** 5 **C** 4 **D** 3

14 **To find the range of a set of data from a box-and-whisker plot, what part(s) of the plot would you use?** J; Obj. 6A,6B

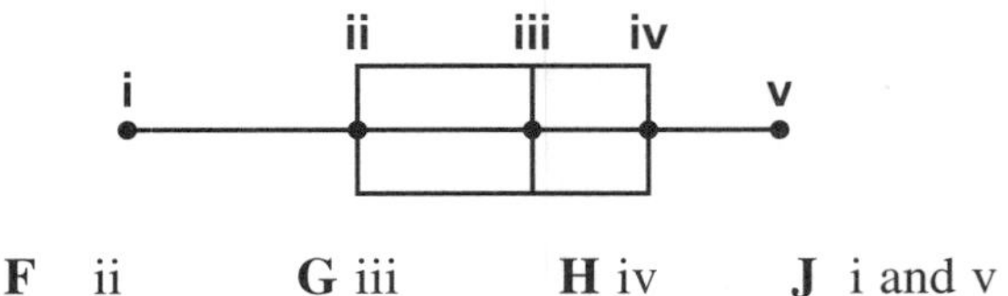

F ii **G** iii **H** iv **J** i and v

Closing the Lesson *What is the difference between a permutation and a combination?* (Possible answer: A permutation is an arrangement of elements in which the order is important, and a combination is an arrangement in which the order of elements is not important.)

Name ______________________________

Guided Practice: Ex. 1 & 8; First ex. in Row 6. pp. 169–170
Independent Practice: Complete pp. 169–170

Probability: Independent Events

The **probability of an event** tells you how likely it is that the event will happen. Probability is measured from **0** to **1**.

When the outcomes of an experiment are all equally likely, the probability (*P*) that an event (*E*) will occur is:

$$P(E) = \frac{\text{Number of favorable events}}{\text{Number of possible events}}$$

Experiment: Roll a Number Cube

Outcomes
1, 2
3, 4
5, 6

Probability of each outcome = $\frac{1}{6}$.

Experiment: Spin a Spinner

- Spin once. What is the probability of spinning a **5** or **6**?

2 *favorable* outcomes: **5** or **6**

8 possible outcomes

$P(\textbf{5 or 6}) = \frac{2}{8}$ or $\frac{1}{4}$

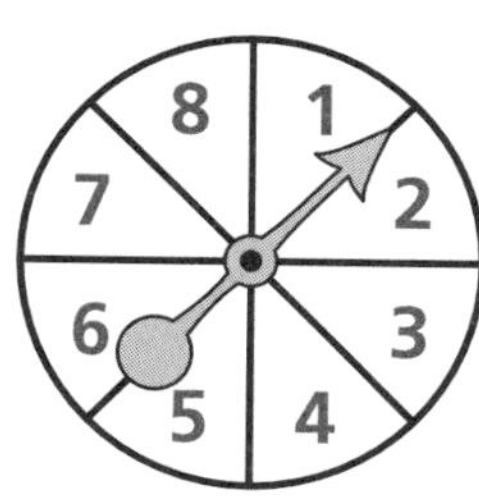

- Spin once. What is the probability of spinning an even number greater than **3**?

3 *favorable* outcomes: **4, 6, 8**

8 possible outcomes

$P(\text{even} > 3) = \frac{3}{8}$

Spin once. Write the probability of the event.

1. Probability of an odd number? $\frac{1}{2}$

2. Probability of an even number? $\frac{1}{2}$

3. Probability of an odd number or a number greater than **9**? $\frac{2}{3}$

4. Probability of a multiple of **3**? $\frac{1}{3}$

5. Probability of a factor of **36**? $\frac{7}{12}$

Write the probability of the event.

6. You toss two coins at the same time. What is the probability that

a. both land heads? $\frac{1}{4}$ b. both land tails? $\frac{1}{4}$ c. both coins are different? $\frac{1}{2}$

7. You write the letters of the word "coins" on **5** separate pieces of paper. You will select one piece of paper at random. What is the probability that you draw

a. a vowel? $\frac{2}{5}$ b. a consonant? $\frac{3}{5}$

Check Understanding A spinner is divided into 6 equal sections numbered 1–6. *What is the probability of landing on 1 or 2?* ($\frac{2}{6} = \frac{1}{3}$)

$P(\text{Red and } 4) = \frac{1}{16}$

Experiment: Spin Two Spinners

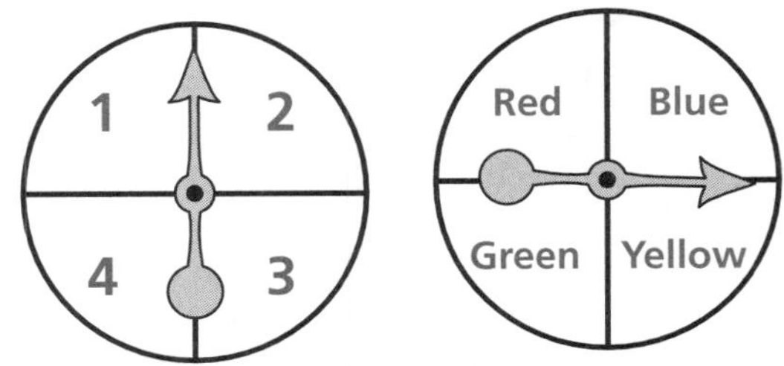

You spin the two spinners shown. What is the probability of spinning Red and **4?**

Method **1**: List all of the outcomes.

Outcomes			
Red, 1	Blue, 1	Green, 1	Yellow, 1
Red, 2	Blue, 2	Green, 2	Yellow, 2
Red, 3	Blue, 3	Green, 3	Yellow, 3
Red, 4	Blue, 4	Green, 4	Yellow, 4

1 *favorable* outcome: Red, 4
16 possible outcomes

$P(\text{Red and } 4) = \frac{1}{16}$

Method **2**: Multiply the probabilities of each event.

$P(\text{Red}) = \frac{1}{4}$, $P(4) = \frac{1}{4}$; $P(\text{Red and } 4) = \frac{1}{4} \cdot \frac{1}{4}$ or $\frac{1}{16}$

The result of the second spinner does not depend on the result of the first spinner. These events are **independent events.** The results for each spinner are independent of one another.

Spin each spinner once. Write the probability.

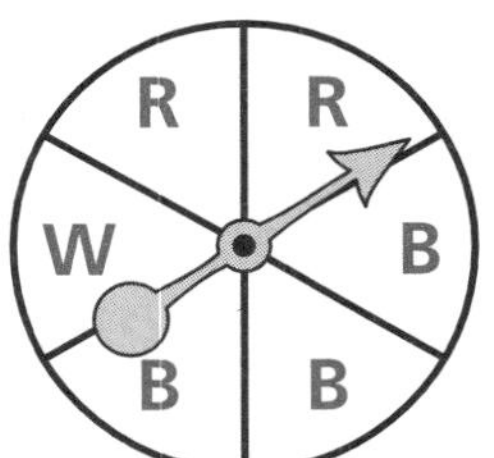

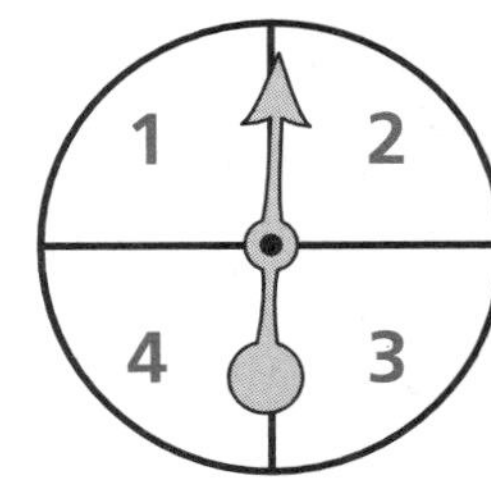

8. $P(\text{red and } 2) =$ $\frac{1}{12}$

9. $P(\text{red and even}) =$ $\frac{1}{6}$

10. $P(\text{not red and } 3) =$ $\frac{1}{6}$

11. $P(\text{blue and not } 2) =$ $\frac{3}{8}$

Problem Solving Reasoning Write the probability of the event.

12. You toss a coin and roll a number cube.

$P(\text{heads and } 4) =$ $\frac{1}{12}$ $P(\text{heads and even}) =$ $\frac{1}{4}$ $P(\text{tails and factor of } 6) =$ $\frac{1}{3}$

13. You select a letter at random from "ice" and a letter at random from "warm."

$P(\text{both are vowels}) =$ $\frac{1}{6}$ $P(\text{E and R}) =$ $\frac{1}{12}$ $P(\text{both are consonants}) =$ $\frac{1}{4}$

Test Prep ★ Mixed Review

14 To complete her basketball team, in how many ways can Fiona choose four other players from among her six friends? C; Obj. 6E

A 4 **C** 15

B 6 **D** 24

15 What number represents the median of the box-and-whisker plot? G; Obj. 6A

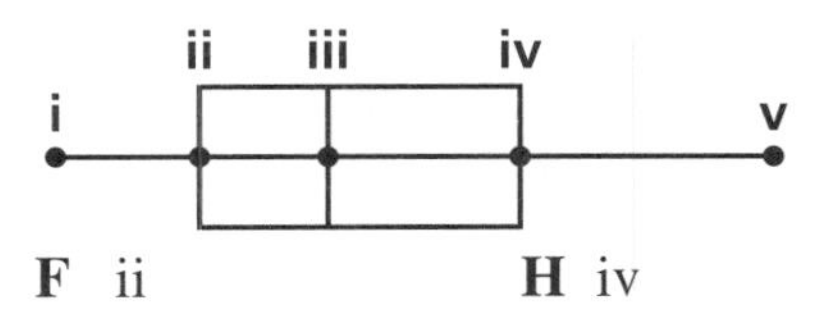

F ii **H** iv

G iii **J** i and v

Closing the Lesson *If all the outcomes are equally likely, how do you find the probability of an event?* (Possible answer: You divide the number of successful outcomes for the event by the total number of events possible.)

Name ______________________

Guided Practice: Ex: 1 & 2, p. 171
Independent Practice: Complete pp. 171–172

Probability: Dependent Events

When two or more events are combined, the result is a **compound event.** The probability of a compound event is related to the probabilities of the events that make it up.

Two events are independent if the outcome of one event has no effect on the outcome of the other. Two events are **dependent** if the outcome of the first event affects the outcome of a second event.

Probability of Independent Events (A and B)	Probability of Dependent Events (A and B)
$P(A$ and $B) = P(A) \cdot P(B)$	**$P(A$, then $B) = P(A) \cdot P(B$ after $A)$**

Independent Events

Draw a marble. Note the color. Replace it. Draw again. What is the probability that both marbles you draw are red?

$$P(\text{red and red}) = P(\text{red}) \cdot P(\text{red}) = \frac{4 \cdot 4}{10 \cdot 10} = \frac{16}{100} \text{ or } 0.16$$

Because the first red marble was replaced, the probability of drawing the second red marble was not affected.

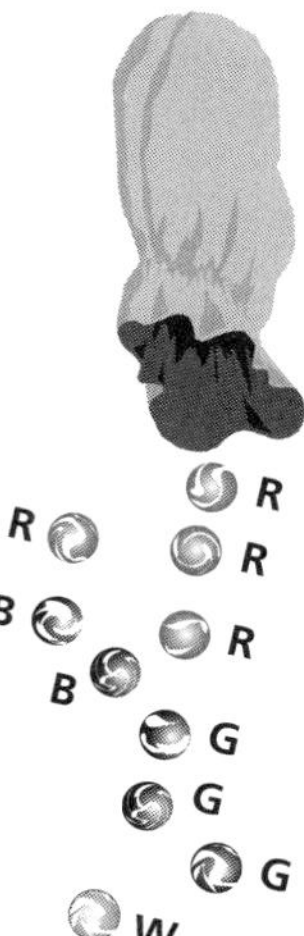

Dependent Events

Draw a marble. Note the color. Do not replace it. Draw again. What is the probability that both the marbles you draw are red?

$$P(\text{red, then red}) = P(\text{red}) \cdot P(\text{red after red}) = \frac{4}{10} \cdot \frac{3}{9} = \frac{12}{90} \text{ or about } 0.133$$

Without replacing the first red marble, the probability of drawing the second red marble was affected.

Write the probability of the compound event. Use the bag of marbles shown above. (R is red, G is green, B is blue, and W is white.)

1. With replacement, P**(blue and green)** = $\frac{3}{50}$

2. Without replacement, P**(blue and green)** = $\frac{1}{15}$

3. With replacement, P**(blue and red)** = $\frac{2}{25}$

4. Without replacement, P**(blue and red)** = $\frac{4}{45}$

5. With replacement, P**(white and white)** = $\frac{1}{100}$

6. Without replacement, P**(white and white)** = 0

Check Understanding *When are two events dependent events?* (when the outcome of one event affects the outcome of the other event)

You write the letters P-R-O-B-A-B-I-L-I-T-Y on separate pieces of paper and put them in a bag. You draw two letters without replacement. What is the probability of drawing two B's?

$$P(B, \text{ then } B) = P(B) \cdot P(B \text{ after } B)$$
$$= \frac{2}{11} \cdot \frac{1}{10}$$
$$= \frac{2}{110} \approx 0.018$$

This experiment is a dependent event. The result of the first event affected the probability of the second event.

Problem Solving Reasoning Write the probability of the compound event. Round to the nearest thousandth.

7. The letters M-I-S-S-I-S-S-I-P-P-I are placed in a bag. Without replacement, two letters are drawn.

P(both are S's) ≈ $0.1\overline{09}$ *P*(both are I's) ≈ $0.1\overline{09}$ *P*(both are P's) ≈ $0.0\overline{18}$

Quick Check

Solve. The Shutterbug Club has 7 members.

8. In how many ways can they stand in a line for a group photo? 5,040

9. How many combinations of **2** club officers are possible? 21

10. In how many ways can they elect one president and one vice president? 42

Find the probability. You either toss a coin (H or T) or roll a number cube (1, 2, 3, 4, 5, 6) or both.

11. *P*(4 or 5) $\frac{1}{3}$

12. *P*(T and not 4) $\frac{5}{12}$

13. *P*(number > **4** and H) $\frac{1}{6}$

A bag contains 16 cards, each with one of the letters M-A-T-H-E-M-A-T-I-C-S-I-S-A-O-K on it. Two draws are made without replacing the first card. Find the probability.

14. *P*(M, then M) $\frac{1}{120}$

15. *P*(M, then S) $\frac{1}{60}$

16. *P*(A, then K) $\frac{1}{80}$

Work Space.

Item	Error Analysis
8–10	**Common Error:** Watch for students who confuse ordered and unordered groups. **Reteaching** Reteach 42
11–13	**Common Error:** Watch for students who add the probabilities instead of multiplying them. **Reteaching** Reteach 43
14–16	**Common Error:** Watch for students who confuse independent and dependent events. **Reteaching** Reteach 44

Closing the Lesson *How do you find the probability of two dependent events?* (Possible answer: Find the probability of the first event; then, find the probability of the second event based upon the success of the first event having occurred. Now, multiply those two probabilities together.)

Name ______________________

Guided Practice: Problem 1, p. 173
Independent Practice: Complete pp. 173–174

Problem Solving Application: Use Graphs and Tables

This bar graph does not show numbers on the vertical scale. It is still useful for making comparisons.

In this lesson, you will use graphs and tables to compare, make estimates, or draw conclusions about the data in the graph.

Sales for Week 1 — XYZ Company

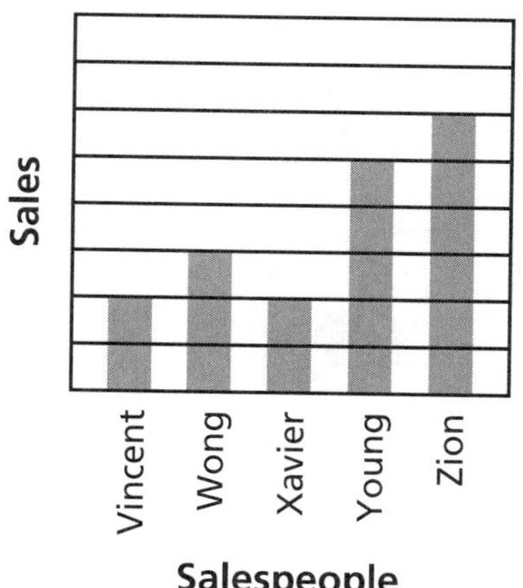

Tips to Remember:

1. Understand 2. Decide 3. Solve 4. Look back

- Ask yourself: What do I know? What do I need to find?
- When you can, make a prediction about the answer. Then, compare your answer and your prediction.
- Think about strategies you have learned and use them to help you solve a problem.

Use the bar graph shown above.

1. Who had sales that were three times what Vincent or Xavier had?

Think: If you triple the height of Vincent's bar, it would be the same height as whose bar?

Zion's

Answer Zion had 3 times as many sales as either Vincent or Xavier.

2. Who had sales that were the closest to the average for the company?

Think: What is the average for the company? Add the heights of all the bars. Each bar's height is the number of units or spaces tall it is. Divide that height by 5.

The average is $3\frac{3}{5}$ units.

Answer Wong's sales were closest to the average for the company.

3. About how many times Xavier's sales is Young's sales?

About 2 times as many

4. About what part of Zion's sales is Young's sales?

About $\frac{5}{6}$ of Zion's sales

Check Understanding *What are some of the reasons for using graphs instead of tables?* (Graphs will give you a quick picture of the total data set. It is easy to see trends, high points, low points, and make predictions or comparisons.) *What are some disadvantages of using graphs?* (Sometimes the exact data are lost; specific data are hard to distinguish.)

Use the table and graphs to answer problems 5–10.

Sales for Week 2 — XYZ Company

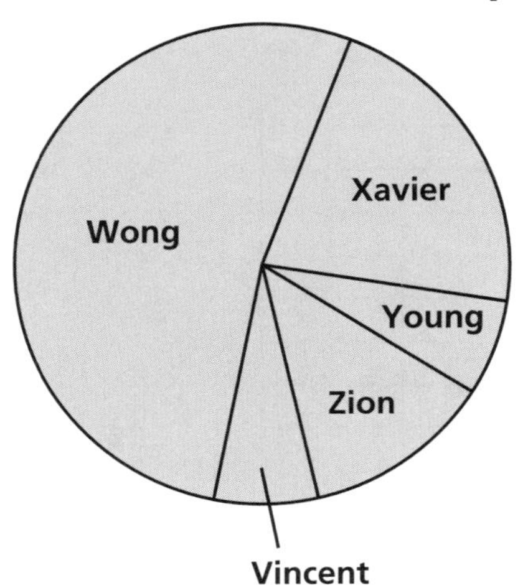

Sales ABC Company

Week	Sales
1	$1,799
2	$ 988
3	$3,040
4	$5,806
5	$4,109
6	$7,750
7	$9,032
8	$5,498

Sales ABC Company

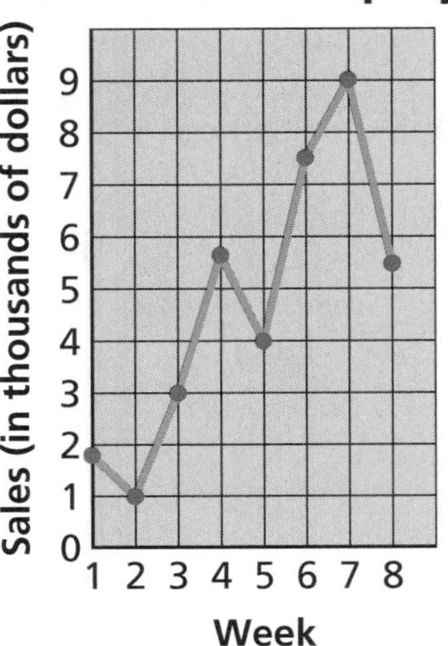

5. The circle graph shows the relationship of five parts (individual sales) to the whole (total company sales). Tell three things that the graph shows.

Possible answer: Wong had more than half the sales, Xavier had about one quarter of the sales, and the other three salespeople together had about a quarter of the sales.

6. In the XYZ Company sales for Week 2, about what percent of the total company sales were by Vincent, Zion, and Young together? Explain your reasoning.

About 25%; The circle graph represents their sales with an area about one quarter of the circle.

7. To find the difference in sales between the fifth and sixth weeks, would you use the table or the line graph? Explain why. What was the difference?

The table; Exact figures are difficult to read from the graph; $3,641.

8. To find the two weeks during which sales increased the most, would you use the table or the line graph? Explain why. Between which two weeks did the sales increase most?

Possible answer: The line graph, because it shows the differences more clearly; between weeks 5 and 6

Extend Your Thinking

9. Determine the mean, median, and range of sales for the ABC Company for the **8** weeks.

Mean: $4,752.75

Median: $4,803.50

Range: $8,044

10. In the XYZ Company sales for Week 2, about what was the ratio of Wong's sales to Young's sales? Explain.

About 6:1; Wong's sales were about one half of the total; Young's were about one third of one quarter, or one twelfth.

Closing the Lesson *What are some reasons for using tables over graphs?* (The representation of data is more precise and accurate. You can tell specific differences between various points, and you can find specific details you may be interested in.) *What are some disadvantages of using tables?* (Trends in the data may be harder to see; you need to scan all the data to find where high and low points may occur.)

Name ____________________

Use the line plot to complete exercises 1–3.

Student Heights

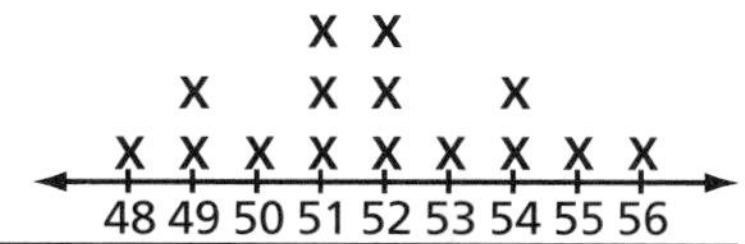

1. How many student heights are represented?

15

2. Range 8 Median 52

Mode 51

3. Suppose a new piece of data was plotted at **56**. Would the range, median, or mode change? Explain.

The range and mode would stay the same;

The mean and median would increase.

Use the histogram to complete exercises 4–6.

4. How many test scores are represented?

28

Test Scores

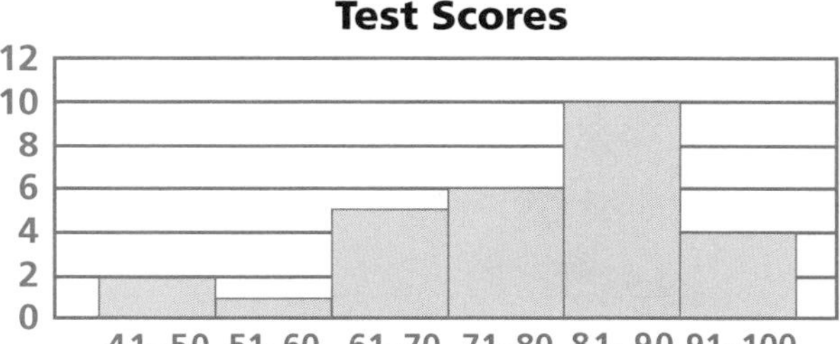

5. How many students scored above 70?

20

6. Write a description of the class results.

The median score was about 80, but there was a wide range of scores from 41 to 100.

Use the data below for exercises 7–10. It lists the ages of 18 moviegoers.

12, 15, 22, 36, 28, 18, 24, 32, 41, 18, 16, 25, 22, 34, 16, 26, 30, 18

7. Complete the stem-and-leaf plot of the data.

Ages of Moviegoers

Stem	Leaves
1	2 5 6 6 8 8 8
2	2 2 4 5 6 8
3	0 2 4 6
4	1

Key: 4 | 1 represents a moviegoer who is 41 years old.

8. Range 29 years Median 23 years

Mode 18 years

9. First quartile 18

Third quartile 30

10. Make a box-and-whisker plot for the data.

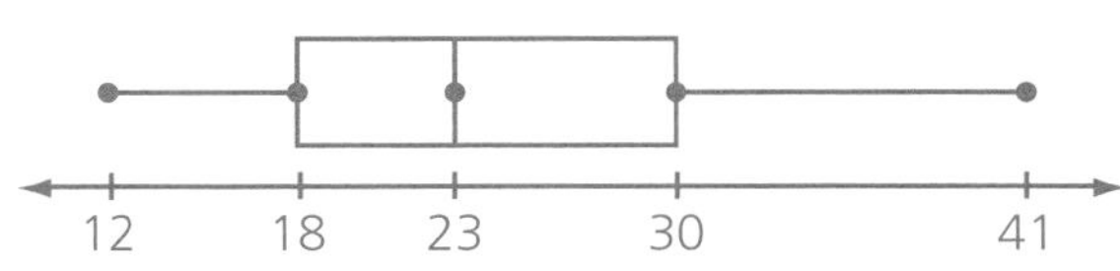

Use the graphs to complete.

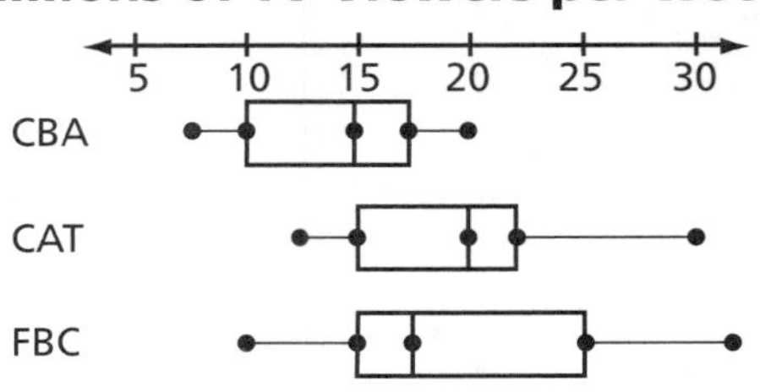

11. What was the median number of viewers (in millions) for each station?

CBA 15 CAT 20 FBC 17.5

12. What percent of the weekly averages are represented within the box? 50%

13. Which station do you believe had the best weekly averages? Explain. Possible answer: CAT, because over half the time, it had 20 million viewers or more.

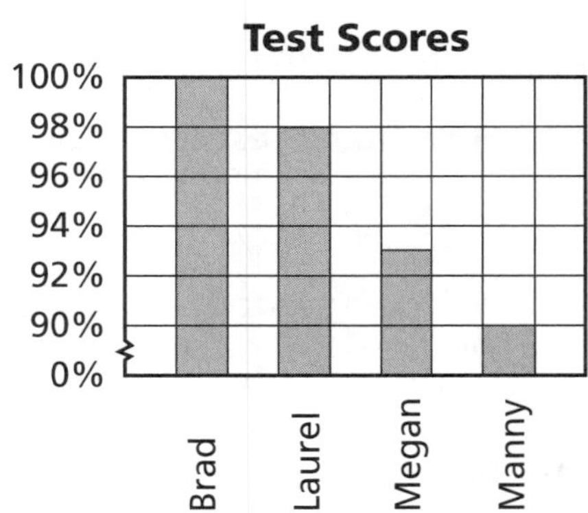

14. Did Laurel do twice as well on the test as Megan? Explain. Possible answer: The bars make it seem that way, but Laurel only scored 5 points (out of 100) more.

15. Is this a misleading graph? Explain.

Possible answer: Yes; It makes Manny's score of 90% look so insignificant.

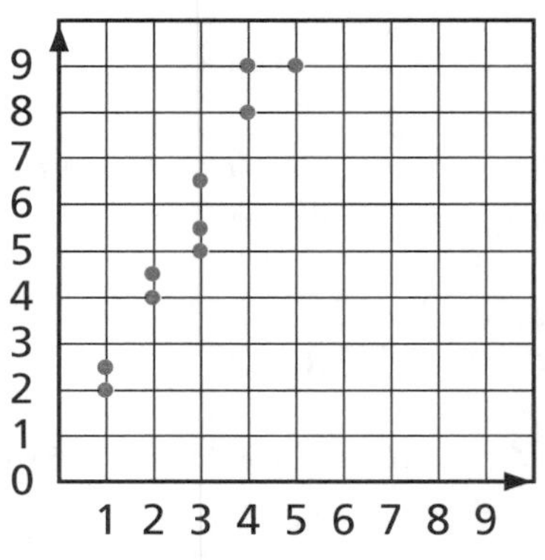

16. Complete the scatter plot for the ordered pairs below.

(3, 5), (1, 2), (4, 9), (3, 6.5), (2, 4)
(5, 9), (3, 5.5), (4, 8), (2, 4.5), (1, 2.5)

17. What type of correlation does the scatter plot show?

positive correlation

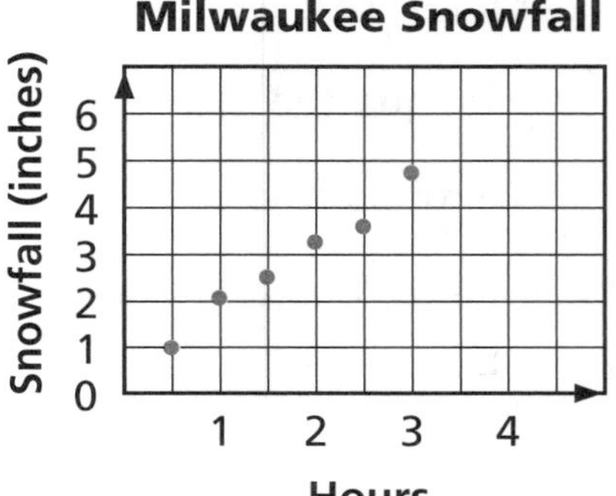

18. How much snow fell after **1** hour? 2 in.

19. How much snow fell after **2.5** hours? About $3\frac{1}{2}$ in.

20. The snow kept falling at the same rate. How much snow do you predict had fallen after **5** hours?

About 7.5 in.

Name ______________________________

Complete.

21. Calculate **5**! 120

22. How many permutations of the letters A, B, and C are there? six

23. In how many ways could you arrange **5** people in a line for a photograph?

120 ways

24. In how many ways could you select **2** people from a group of **5** people where order does not matter? 10 ways

25. List the different two-topping pizzas that you could order. The topping choices are onion, sausage, extra cheese, and green peppers. onion/sausage, onion/extra cheese, onion/green pepper, sausage/extra cheese, sausage/green pepper, and extra cheese/green pepper

26. What is the probability that a pizza selected at random from your list in exercise **25** contains onion?

$\frac{1}{2}$

27. You spin once. Write the probability.

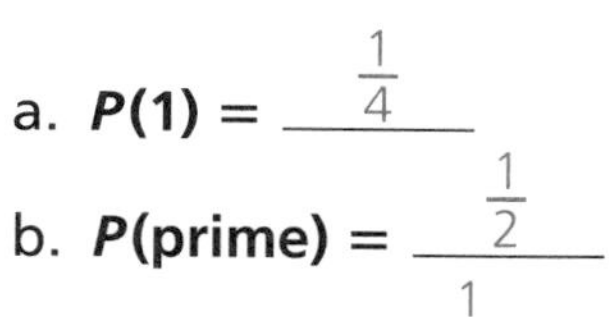

a. ***P*(1)** = $\frac{1}{4}$

b. ***P*(prime)** = $\frac{1}{2}$

c. ***P*(even)** = $\frac{1}{2}$

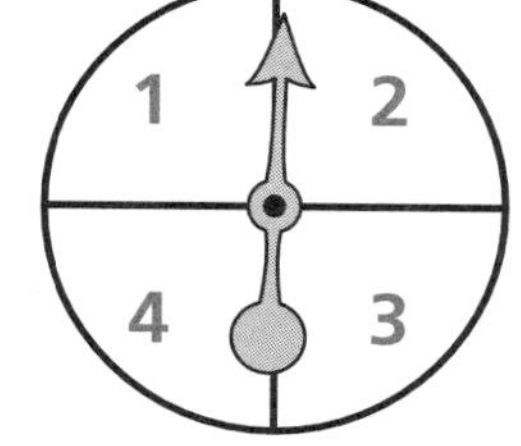

28. You select a card at random from a deck of 52 pattern block cards. The deck contains 4 hexagons, 6 trapezoids, 6 squares, 14 rhombuses, and 22 triangles. Write the probability.

a. ***P*(triangle)** = $\frac{11}{26}$

b. ***P*(hexagon)** = $\frac{1}{13}$

c. ***P*(rhombus)** = $\frac{7}{26}$

29. You toss a coin and roll a number cube numbered **1–6**. What is the probability that the outcome will be a head and a four?

$\frac{1}{12}$

30. Without replacement, you draw two number cards from the numbers 0–20 inclusive. What is the probability that you draw a prime number followed by a multiple of 4?

≈ 0.11

Name ___________________________

Cumulative Review
★ Test Prep

1 **Which scatter plot of the following sets of ordered pairs would tend to show a negative correlation?** D; Obj. 6A

A Linda's time spent studying and her test scores

B An athlete's age and her time for the 400 meters

C Pete's age and his height

D The age and resale value of a car

2 **Yumi needs to divide 0.5 L of liquid into laboratory samples that contain 0.02 L each. How many samples can she make?** G; Obj. 2B

F 2.5 H 250

G 25 J 2,500

3 **A class turned in pictures for an art exhibit. Only 36 pictures, or 75% of them, could be displayed. How many pictures were turned in?** B; Obj. 5A

A 40

B 48

C 54

D 60

4 **In a sample, 13 out of 25 seventh grade students said that they planned to go to the school play on Saturday. What percent of the students are going to the school play on Saturday?** F; Obj. 4E

F 52%

G 48%

H 45%

J 26%

5 **Sixteen students out of a sample of 50 seventh graders claimed they would vote for Jeff for class president. About how many students out of 135 students would you predict might vote for Jeff?** C; Obj. 4C

A 58 C 43

B 53 D 16

6 **Suppose it costs $41 in credit card interest to finance a $400 purchase over a year. How much could be saved by borrowing the money at a bank at 8.9% interest for a year?** G; Obj. 5D

F $6.40

G $5.40

H $.54

J $.06

7 **What value for n is the solution of the equation?** D; Obj. 2E

$$\frac{1}{2} + \frac{3}{4} + \frac{5}{8} = \frac{3}{4} + n + \frac{1}{2}$$

A $\frac{1}{2}$ C $\frac{5}{4}$

B $\frac{3}{4}$ D $\frac{5}{8}$

8 **Chris has 5 pounds of pennies. How many ounces is this?** G; Obj. 3B

F 16

G 80

H 160

J 530

K Not here

UNIT 7 • TABLE OF CONTENTS

Geometry

Dear Family,

During the next few weeks, our math class will be studying topics from geometry. We will work with plane figures such as parallel lines, triangles, polygons, and circle graphs and space figures such as prisms and pyramids.

You can expect to see homework that provides practice with these skills. Here is a sample you may want to keep handy to give help if needed.

We will be using this vocabulary:

segment part of a line that has two endpoints

ray part of a line that has one endpoint and continues indefinitely in the other direction

acute angle an angle whose measure is between 0° and 90°

right angle an angle whose measure is 90°

obtuse angle an angle whose measure is between 90° and 180°

complementary two angles whose measures total 90°

supplementary two angles whose measures total 180°

congruent same size and shape

isosceles triangle one with at least two sides congruent

polyhedron a closed figure in space whose faces are all polygons

circle graph a graph that represents data as part of a circle; the parts are often labeled using percents

Finding Measures of Angles

When two lines are parallel and crossed by a third line, called a transversal, corresponding angles are congruent. In the diagram, $\angle$**1** and $\angle$**2** are corresponding angles. If $\angle$**1** measures **40°**, $\angle$**2** would also measure **40°**.

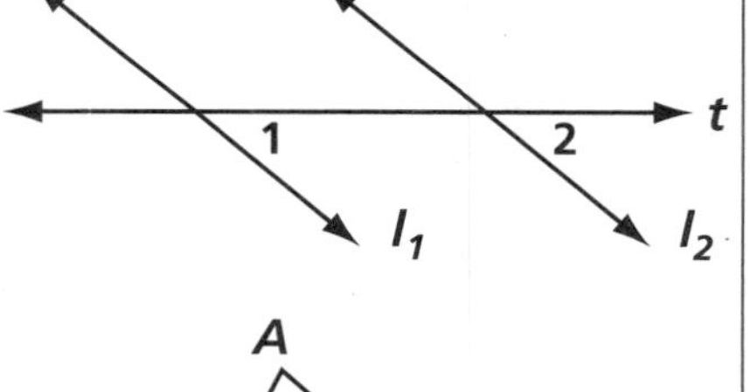

The sum of the angles of a triangle is **180°**. In the diagram, the measure of $\angle$**C** would be **180° − (42° + 75°) = 63°**.

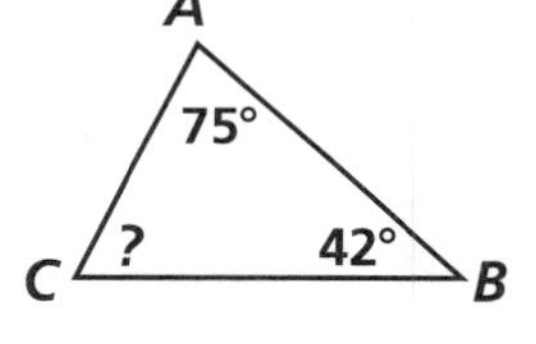

Reading Information from Circle Graphs

Region A in the circle graph represents **40%** of the **280** students surveyed. The number of students represented in this region is **40%** of **280 = 0.4 · 280** or **112** students.

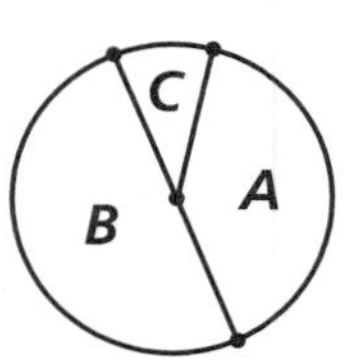

During this unit, students will continue to learn new techniques for problem solving and will continue to practice basic skills with fractions, decimals, and percents.

Sincerely,

Name ______________________

Points, Lines, and Angles

Guided Practice: Ex. 1 & 5, p. 181
Independent Practice: Complete pp. 181–182

Concept | **How to Name It**

A **point** locates a position in space. It has no length, width, or height. — Use a capital letter.

A **line** is a series of points that form a straight path. It has one dimension, length, although it can't be measured. — Use any two points on the line or a single letter. $\overleftrightarrow{BC}$ or $\overleftrightarrow{CB}$ or t

A **line segment** or **segment** is a part of a line. It has two endpoints. Its length can be measured. — Use the two endpoints. $\overline{DE}$ or $\overline{ED}$

A **ray** is a part of a line with one endpoint that continues indefinitely in the other direction. — Use the endpoint and any other point. $\overrightarrow{FG}$ or $\overrightarrow{FH}$

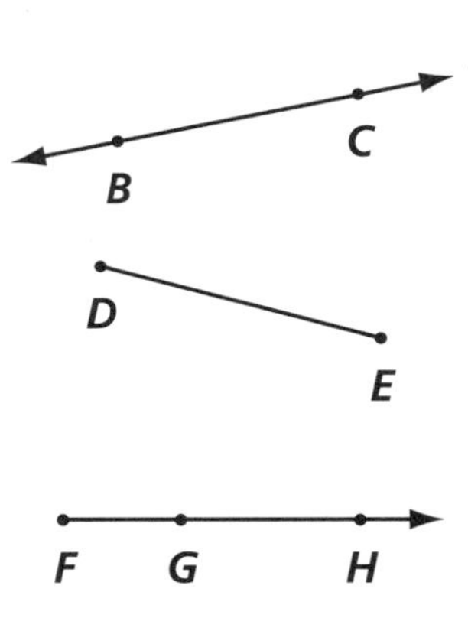

A line that is level with the horizon, left to right, is **horizontal.** A line that is straight up and down is **vertical.** Three or more points that lie on the same line, such as ***J, K,*** and ***L,*** are **collinear.**

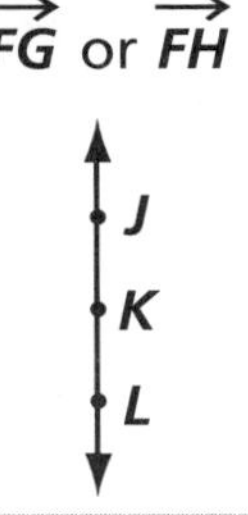

Use a straightedge when needed.

1. Draw a line. Label three points ***D, M, T*** on it. Write three different names for the line. Possible answers:

$\overleftrightarrow{DM}$, $\overleftrightarrow{DT}$, $\overleftrightarrow{MT}$

D M T

2. Draw a segment. Label the endpoints ***C*** and ***W***. Write two different names for the segment.

$\overline{CW}$, $\overline{WC}$

3. Draw a ray. Label the endpoint ***P***. Label two other points ***A*** and ***N*** on the ray. Write two different names for the ray.

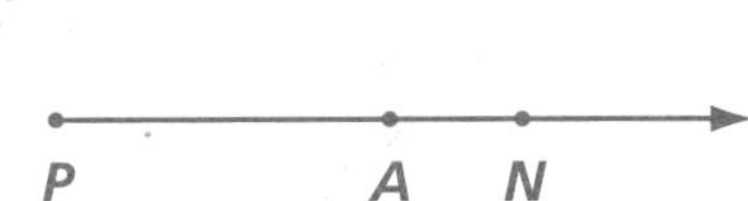

$\overrightarrow{PA}$, $\overrightarrow{PN}$

Answer the question.

4. How many lines can you draw through two points? only one

5. How many lines can you draw through one point? an infinite number

6. On $\overline{AB}$, what are points ***A*** and ***B*** called? endpoints

7. Which points are used to name a line? any two points on it

8. In exercises **1–3**, which set of points is collinear? *D, M,* and *T* or *P, A,* and *N*

Check Understanding Draw an angle on the board and label it *ABC*. Discuss the different ways to name the angle. *How could you name the rays containing the angle?* ($\overrightarrow{BA}$ and $\overrightarrow{BC}$)

An **angle** is formed by two rays that have the same endpoint.

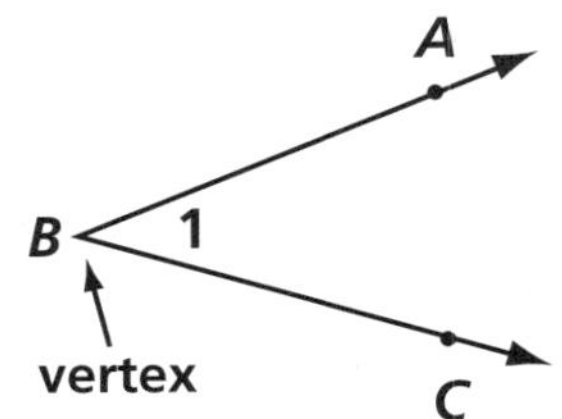

It is named using three points of the angle. The **vertex** is the middle point.

∠***ABC*** or ∠***CBA***

The angle could also be named ∠***B*** or ∠**1**.

You do not use ∠***P*** to refer to any of the angles at the right. It would not be clear which angle you were referring to. You may locate points on each ray. Then, use three points to name each angle.

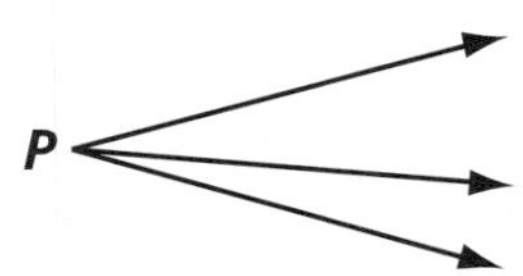

Name each angle in four ways.

9.

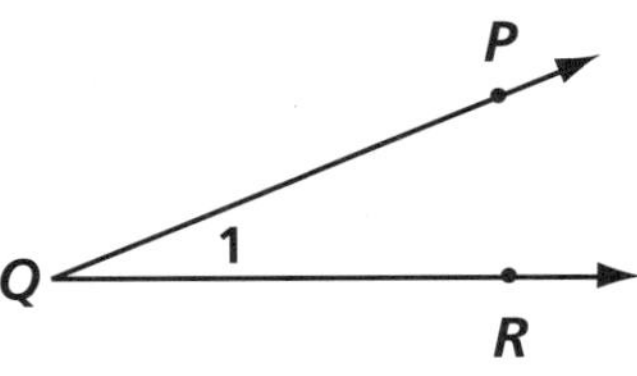

∠Q ∠PQR

∠RQP ∠1

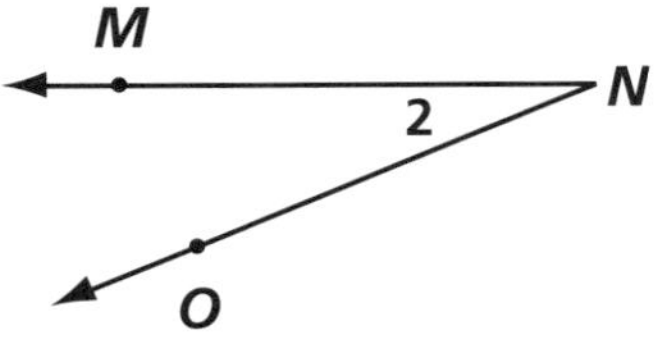

∠N ∠MNO

∠ONM ∠2

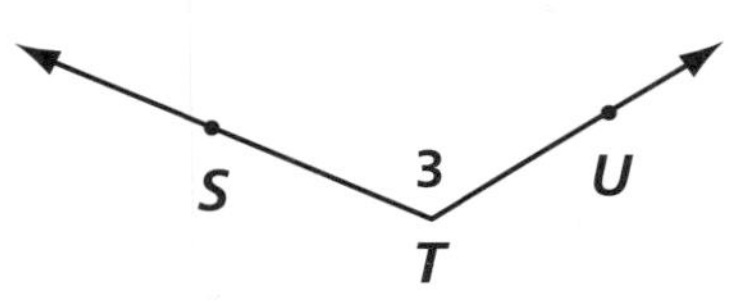

∠T ∠STU

∠UTS ∠3

Problem Solving Reasoning **Solve.**

10. How many different segments are shown? Name each one.

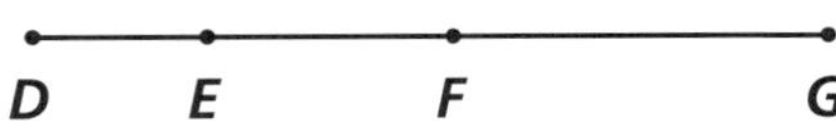

Six; $\overline{DE}$, $\overline{DF}$, $\overline{DG}$, $\overline{EF}$, $\overline{EG}$, $\overline{FG}$

11. How many different angles are shown? Name each one.

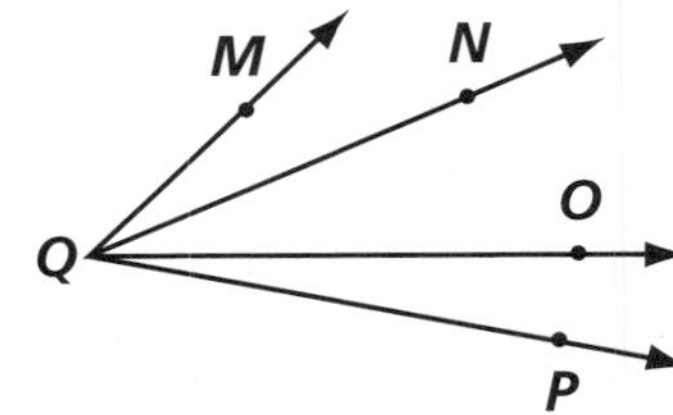

Six; ∠MQN, ∠MQO, ∠MQP, ∠NQO, ∠NQP, ∠OQP

Test Prep ★ Mixed Review

12 **What number is 9% of 360?** A; Obj. 5A

A 32.4 **C** 67.5

B 40 **D** 324

13 **Judy's bank gives her 4% interest on her $600 investment. The interest is compounded every quarter. Which amount best shows the value of her investment after one year?** G; Obj. 5D

F $624.00 **H** $701.91

G $624.36 **J** $6,243.60

Closing the Lesson *How does a segment differ from a line?* (A line is infinite in length and a segment has a finite length.)

Name ______________________

Planes

Guided Practice: Ex. 1 & 7, p. 183; Ex. 12, p. 184
Independent Practice: Complete pp. 183–184

A **plane** is a flat surface that extends indefinitely in all directions. It has two dimensions, length and width, although neither can be measured.

A plane is usually represented by a parallelogram.

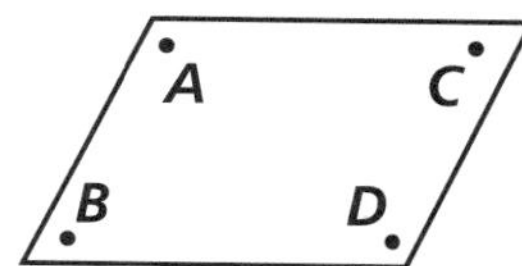

The plane indicated by the parallelogram is named using at least three points, such as ***ABC, BCD,*** or ***ABCD***.

Points, segments, or lines that are in the same plane are **coplanar.**
For example, in the plane at the right, $\overline{AB}$ and $\overrightarrow{CD}$ are coplanar.

$\overline{AB}$ and $\overleftrightarrow{EF}$ are not coplanar.

$\overrightarrow{CD}$ and $\overleftrightarrow{EF}$ are not coplanar.

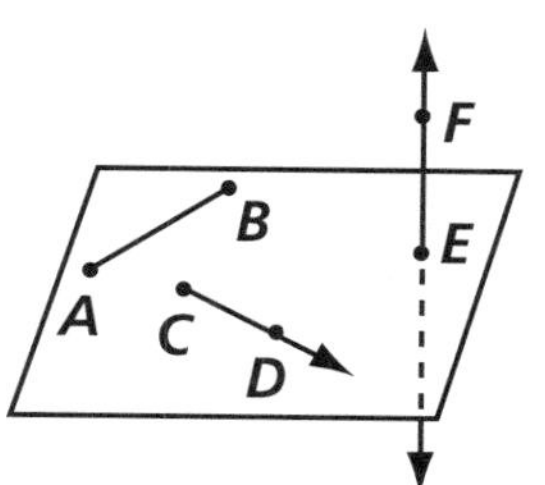

Planes are sketched by using parallelograms. A dashed line shows that a portion of a line is hidden by a plane.

Sketches of two planes:

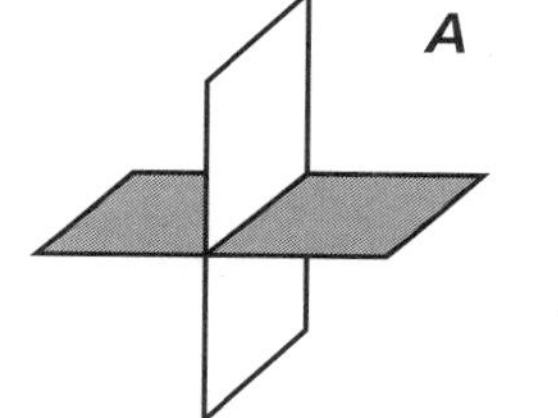

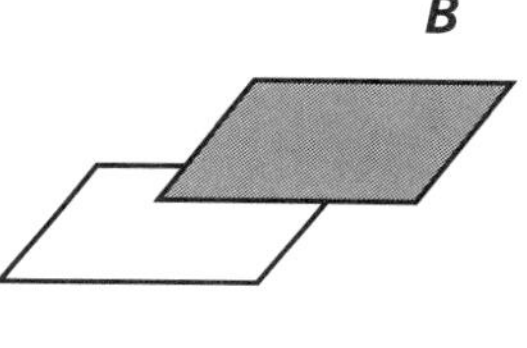

Sketches of three planes:

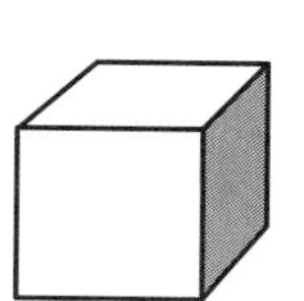

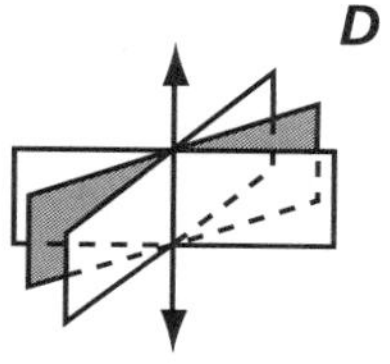

Use the sketches A–D above. Answer the question. Explain your reasoning.

1. Will any two planes always intersect? No; Sketch *B* shows planes that don't intersect.
2. Can the intersection of two planes be a single point? No; If you extend them infinitely, you get a line.
3. Can the intersection of two planes be a line? Yes; as in sketch *A*
4. Will any three planes intersect? No; You could put another plane above the two in sketch *B*.
5. Could the intersection of three planes be a single point? Yes; as in sketch *C*
6. Could the intersection of three planes be a line? Yes; as in sketch *D*

Use the diagram of a cube. Answer the question.

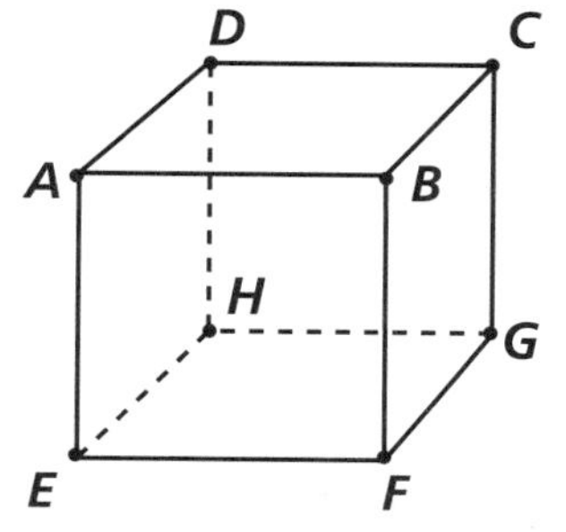

7. Name the intersection of planes ***ABCD*** and ***ABFE***. $\overleftrightarrow{AB}$
8. Name the intersection of planes ***ABCD*** and ***DCGH***. $\overleftrightarrow{CD}$
9. Name the planes that point ***B*** lies on. *ABCD, ABFE, BCGF*
10. Are $\overline{AB}$ and $\overline{EF}$ coplanar? Yes.
11. Are $\overline{AB}$ and $\overline{CG}$ coplanar? No.

Check Understanding *Can three planes intersect so that they have a line in common?* (Yes, as in a book, the binding is the line in which all the pages meet.)

You can sketch intersecting planes as shown below. Notice how the parallelograms help to give the sketch a three-dimensional look.

1. Sketch a horizontal plane.

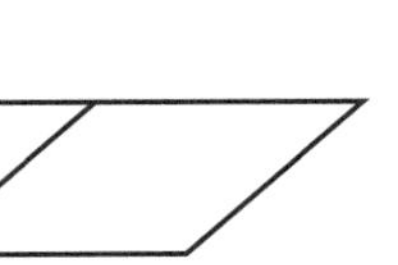

2. Sketch the vertical plane.

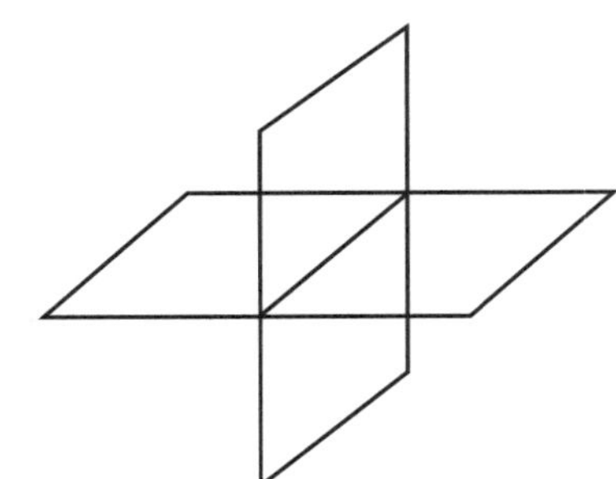

3. Erase hidden lines. Shade.

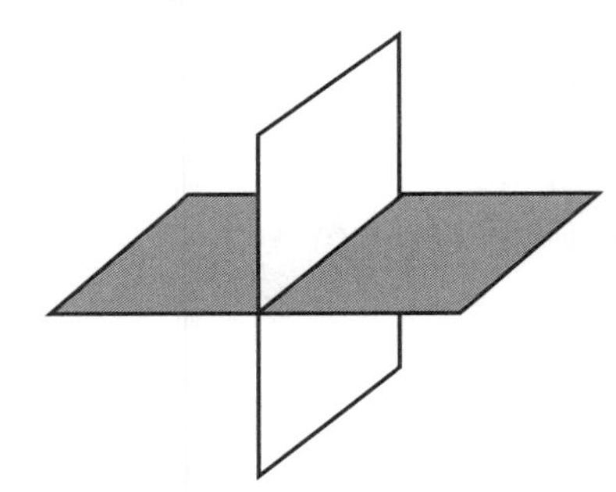

Sketch. Check students' sketches.

12. Two intersecting planes

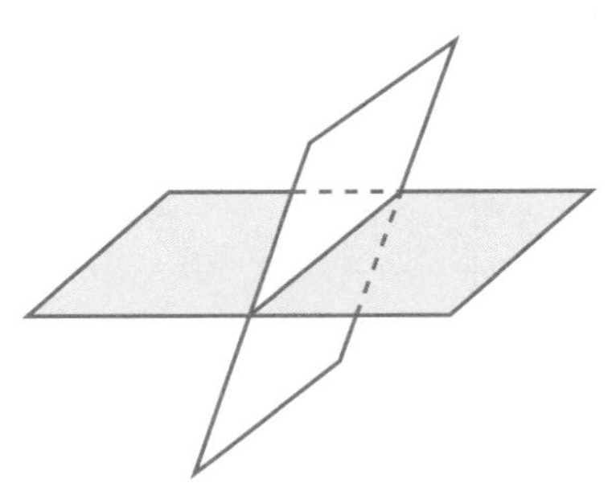

13. Three intersecting planes

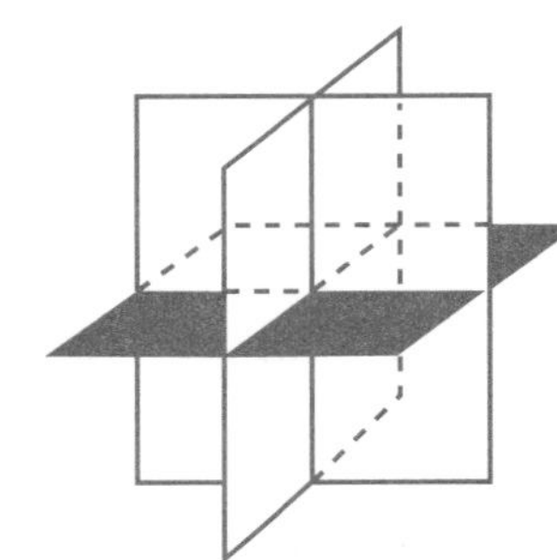

14. Two planes that do not intersect

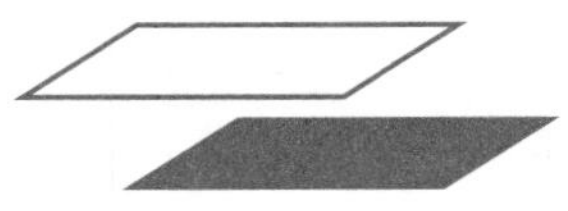

Solve.

15. How many planes are used to form the faces of this hat box?

8

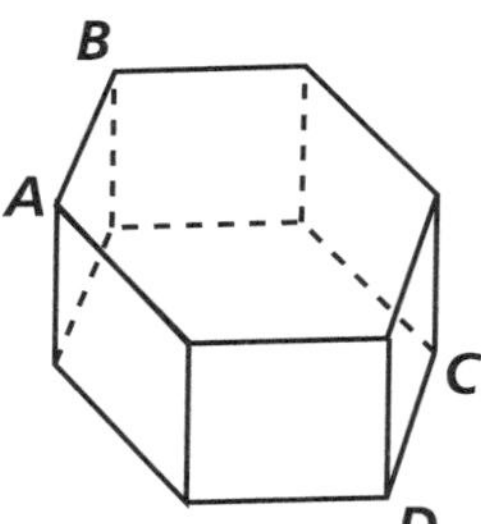

16. Sketch and shade the plane that $\overline{AB}$ and $\overline{CD}$ lie in.

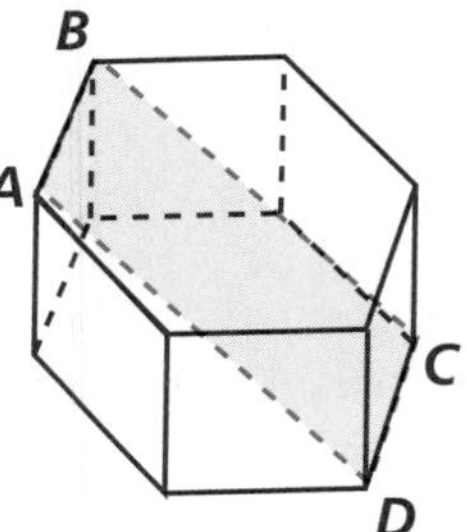

Test Prep ★ Mixed Review

17 **In the data represented in the stem-and-leaf plot, what is the mode?** A; Obj. 6A

0	2 5 6 7 8 9
1	2 4 4 7 9
2	1 2 3 6 8 9

Key: 2 | 9 represents 29

A 14 **C** 7

B 9 **D** 4

18 **The ages of the eleven players in Horseville's all-age soccer team were: 13, 51, 14, 47, 15, 42, 14, 53, 16, 57, 15. Which typical value does 16 represent?** J; Obj. 6B

F mean **H** range

G lower quartile **J** median

Closing the Lesson *If two different planes have two different points, A and B, in common, what can you tell me about the two planes?* (They intersect in line AB.)

Name ______________________________

Measuring Angles

Guided Practice: First ex. in Rows 1 & 4, pp. 185–186
Independent Practice: Complete pp. 185–186

A **protractor** can be used to approximate the measure of an angle. An angle is measured in units called **degrees**. Two angles are **congruent** if they have the same measure.

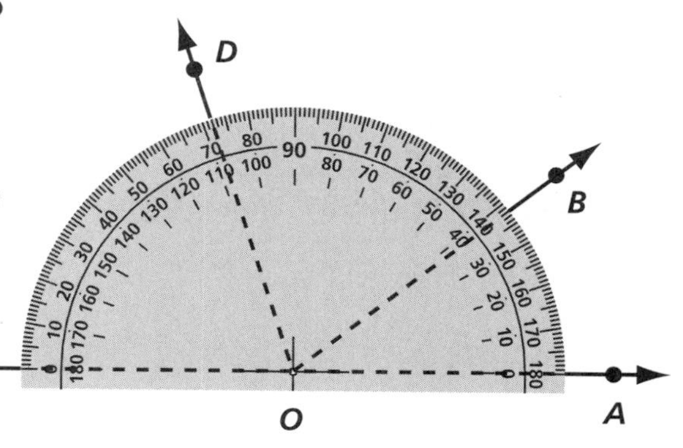

How to measure an angle:

1. Place the center of the protractor at the vertex of the angle.
2. Line up **0°** on the protractor with one ray of the angle.
3. Read the measure where the other ray crosses the protractor.

$\angle AOB = 38°$ $\angle COD = 72°$ $\angle AOD = 108°$

Be sure to read the correct scale (inside or outside). Ask yourself which scale starts at **0°** for your angle. Use that scale to read the angle measure.

Use a protractor to measure the angle. Write your answer on the answer line.

1. 62° 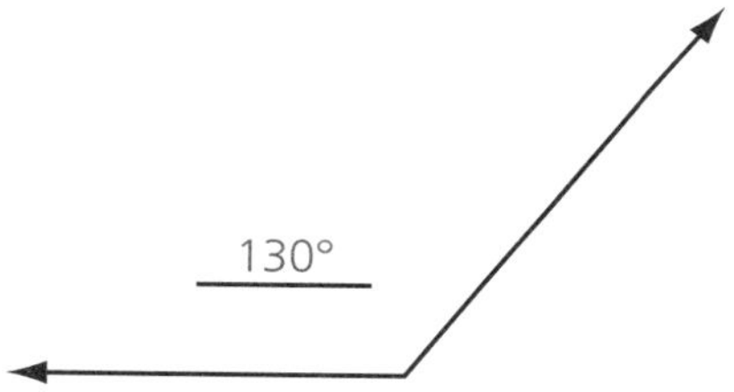 130° 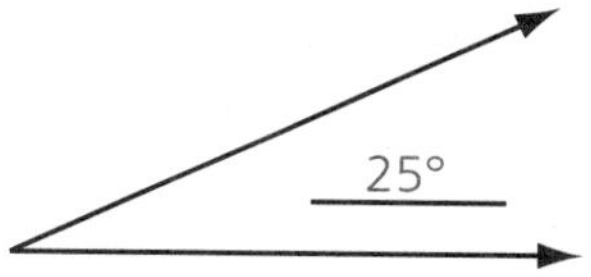 25°

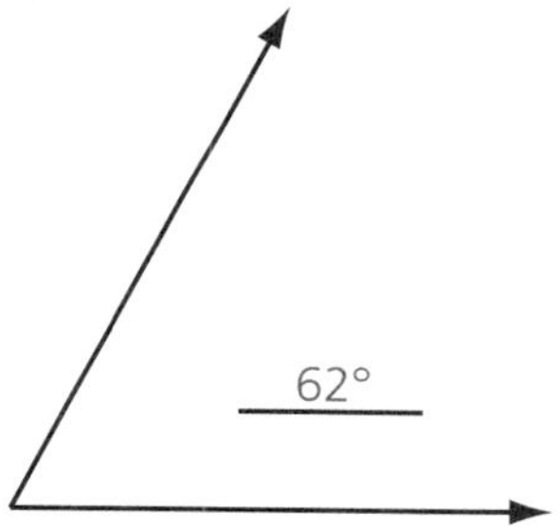

2. 40° 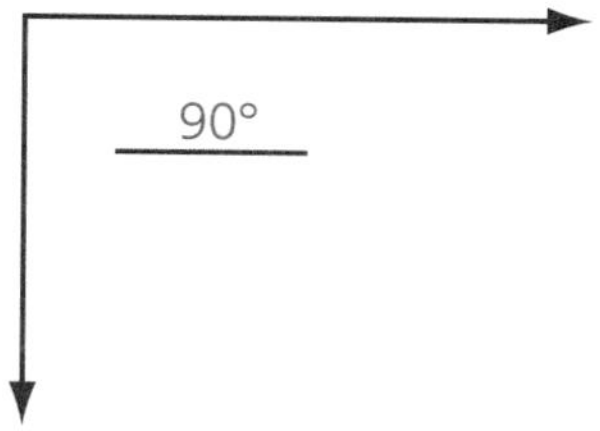 90° 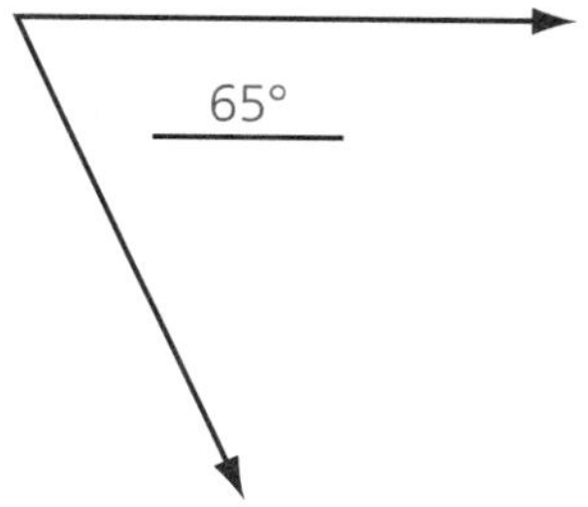 65°

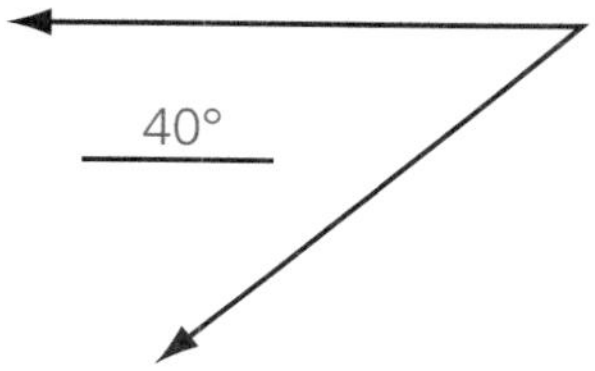

3. 120° 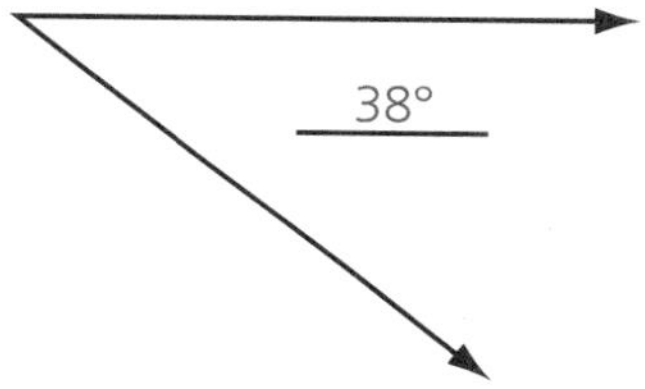 38° 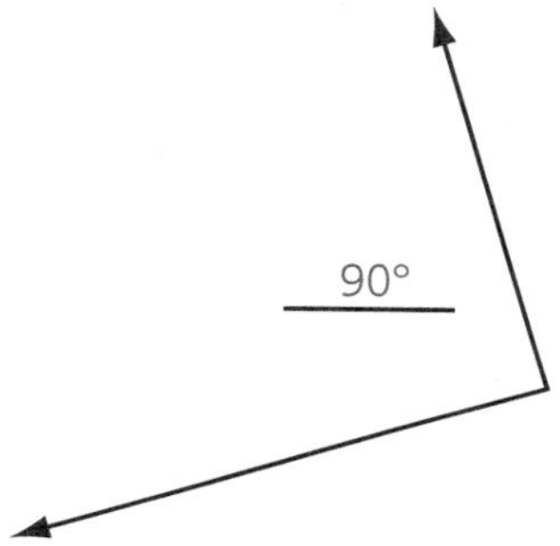 90°

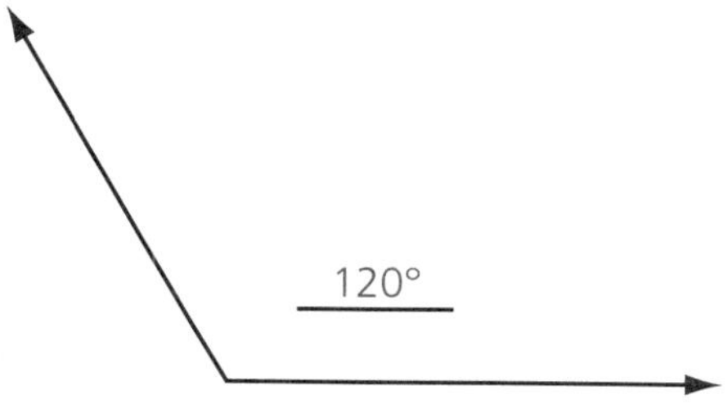

Check Understanding *What sort of angle is greater than a right angle and less than a straight angle?* (obtuse angle) *What can you tell me about two right angles?* (The sum of their measures is 180°; they are congruent.)

Angles are classified by their measures.

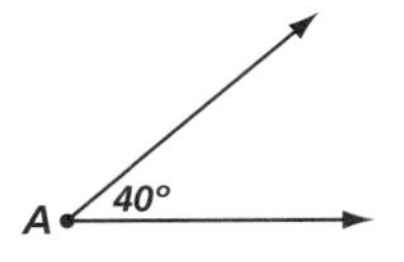

Acute angle
Its measure is between **0°** and **90°**.

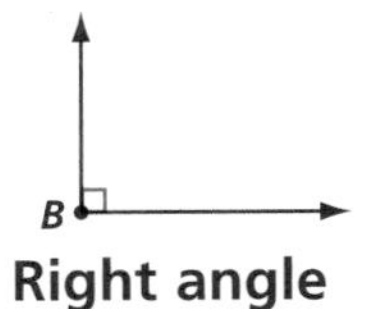

Right angle
Its measure is **90°**.

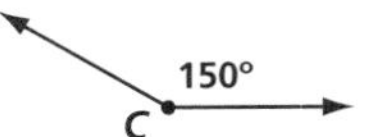

Obtuse angle
Its measure is between **90°** and **180°**.

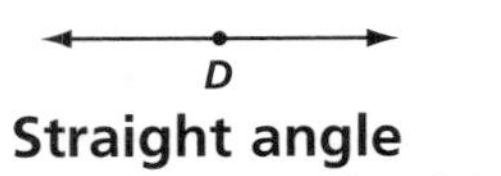

Straight angle
Its measure is **180°**.

Classify the angle as acute, right, obtuse, or straight.

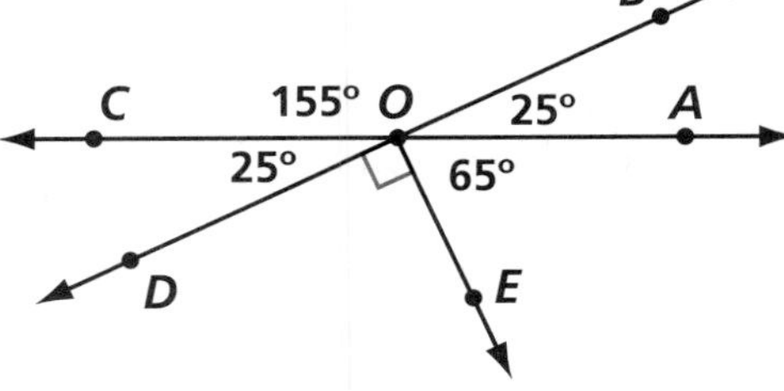

4. ∠*AOB* acute ∠*BOC* obtuse

5. ∠*COD* acute ∠*DOE* right

6. ∠*EOB* right ∠*AOC* straight

7. Name two pairs of congruent angles.
∠*AOB* and ∠*COD* ∠*COA* and ∠*AOD* or ∠*DOE* and ∠*BOE*

Problem Solving
Reasoning

Solve.

8. How many acute angles? Obtuse angles? 6; 6

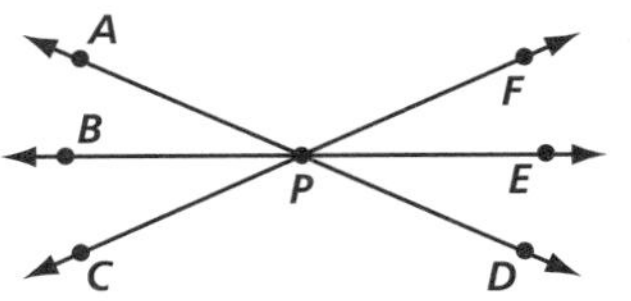

9. How many right angles? Straight angles? 4; 2

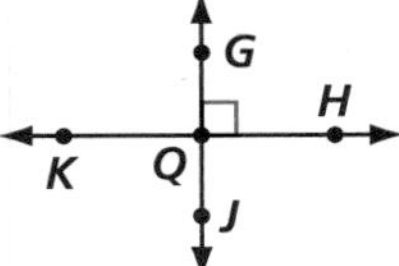

Quick Check

10. A line contains the points *P, Q,* and *R*. Write four ways to name this line. Possible answer: $\overleftrightarrow{PQ}$, $\overleftrightarrow{QP}$, $\overleftrightarrow{QR}$, $\overleftrightarrow{PR}$,

Use the angle below for exercises 11–13.

11. Write three ways to name the angle. ∠*LMN*, ∠*NML*, ∠*M*

12. Is the angle acute, obtuse, right, or straight? acute

13. Use your protractor. What is the measure of the angle? 40°

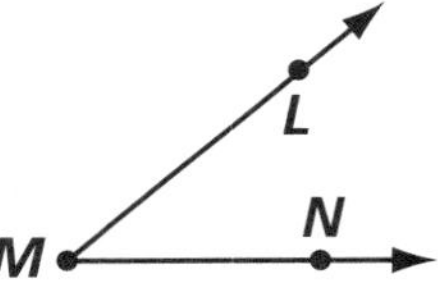

Use the cube at the right for exercises 14–15. Possible answers are given.

14. Name two lines that are coplanar with $\overleftrightarrow{AE}$. $\overleftrightarrow{DH}$ and $\overleftrightarrow{BF}$

15. Name a line that is not coplanar with $\overleftrightarrow{AE}$. $\overleftrightarrow{GH}$

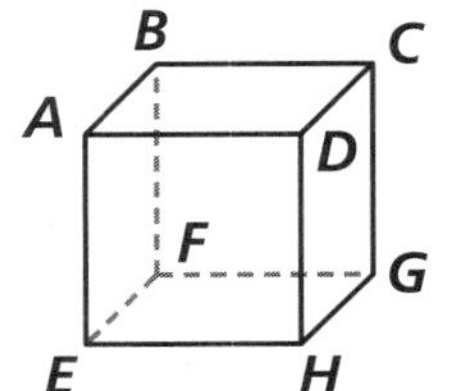

Work Space.

Item	Error Analysis
10–11	**Common Error:** Students may not write the vertex in the center position. **Reteaching** Reteach 46
12–13	**Common Error:** Students may use the incorrect scale to measure angles. **Reteaching** Reteach 47
14–15	**Common Error:** Students may think a plane must be part of a diagram for lines to be coplanar. **Reteaching** Reteach 48

Closing the Lesson *Why is it important to know how to measure angles?* (Possible answer: When surveying land or building a house, you need plans that accurately describe how things look.)

Name ____________________

Angle Relationships

Guided Practice: First ex. in Rows 1, 5 & 13, pp. 187–188
Independent Practice: Complete pp. 187–188

Pairs of angles may be related in several ways.

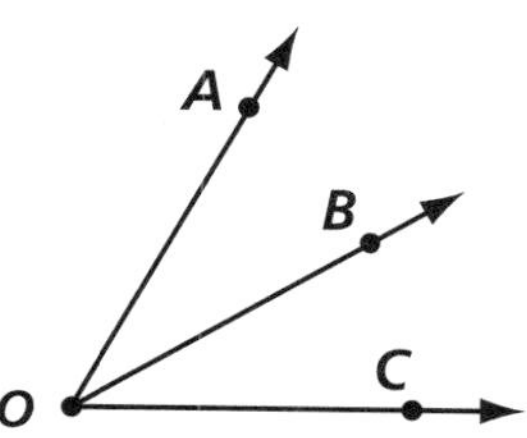

Adjacent angles
Two angles that share a common vertex and common side, but their interiors have no points in common

∠***AOB*** is adjacent to ∠***BOC***.

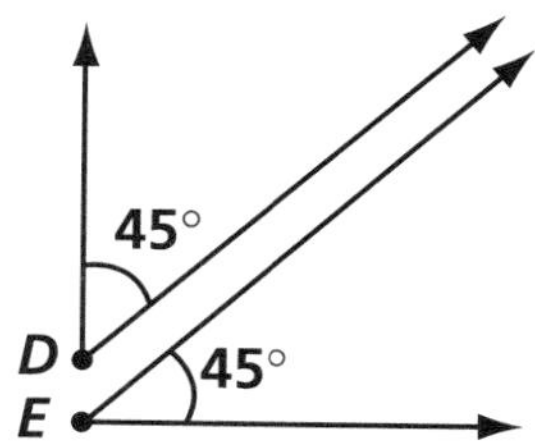

Complementary angles
Two angles whose measures total **90°**

Complementary angles may or may not be adjacent.

∠***D*** is complementary to ∠***E***.

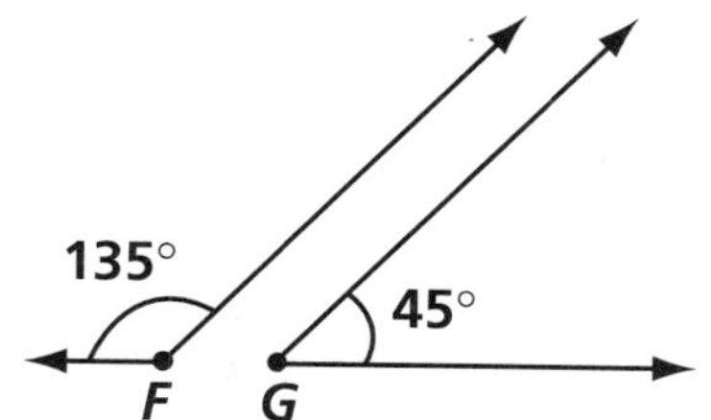

Supplementary angles
Two angles whose measures total **180°**

Supplementary angles may or may not be adjacent.

∠***F*** is supplementary to ∠***G***.

Suppose ∠***XYZ*** = **32°**. An angle complementary to ∠***XYZ*** would measure **90° − 32°**, or **58°**.
An angle supplementary to ∠***XYZ*** would measure **180° − 32°**, or **148°**.

Use the diagram to answer.

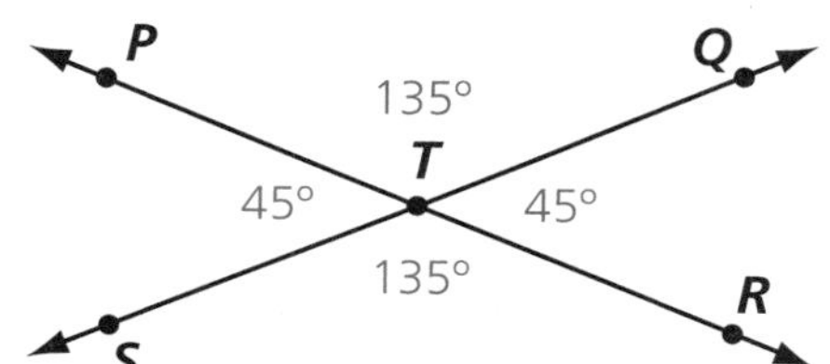

1. Name the adjacent angles in the diagram.

∠PTQ and ∠QTR, ∠PTQ and ∠PTS

∠PTS and ∠STR, ∠STR and ∠QTR

2. Measure the angles with a protractor. Write the measures on the diagram.

3. Name a pair of congruent angles. ∠PTS and ∠QTR

4. How many of the pairs of angles in exercise **1** are supplementary? all four pairs

---

Write the complement and supplement of the angle.

	Complement	Supplement
5. ∠***COB*** = **30°**	60°	150°
7. ∠***COB*** = **18°**	72°	162°
9. ∠***COB*** = **120°**		60°
11. ∠***COB*** = **2°**	88°	178°

	Complement	Supplement
6. ∠***COB*** = **72°**	18°	108°
8. ∠***COB*** = **90°**		90°
10. ∠***COB*** = **81°**	9°	99°
12. ∠***COB*** = **148°**		32°

Check Understanding *If two angles are supplementary what can you tell me about the sum of their measures?*
(They add up to 180°.)

Vertical angles are "opposite" angles that are formed when two lines intersect.

In the diagram, if $\angle \boldsymbol{AOC} = \mathbf{40°}$, then $\angle \boldsymbol{AOB} = \mathbf{140°}$ because the two angles are adjacent, and $\angle \boldsymbol{COB}$ is a straight angle.

Using the same reasoning, $\angle \boldsymbol{BOD} = \mathbf{40°}$. So vertical angles ***AOC*** and ***BOD*** have the same measure. They are congruent. By using the same reasoning, any two vertical angles are congruent.

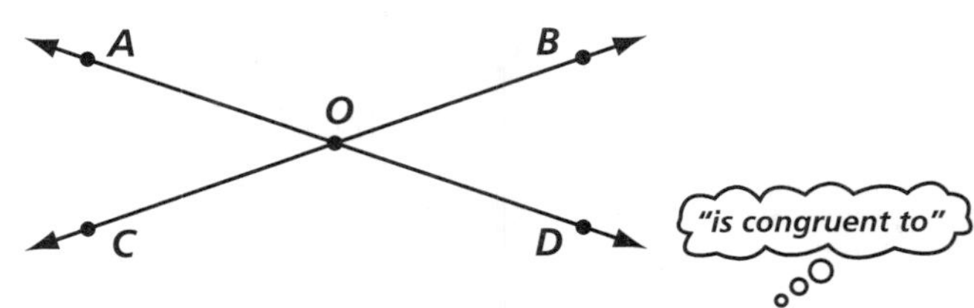

$\angle \boldsymbol{AOB}$ and $\angle \boldsymbol{COD}$ are vertical angles. $\angle \boldsymbol{AOB} \cong \angle \boldsymbol{COD}$

$\angle \boldsymbol{AOC}$ and $\angle \boldsymbol{BOD}$ are vertical angles. $\angle \boldsymbol{AOC} \cong \angle \boldsymbol{BOD}$

Find the missing measures of the angles. Use vertical, complementary, and supplementary angles.

13.

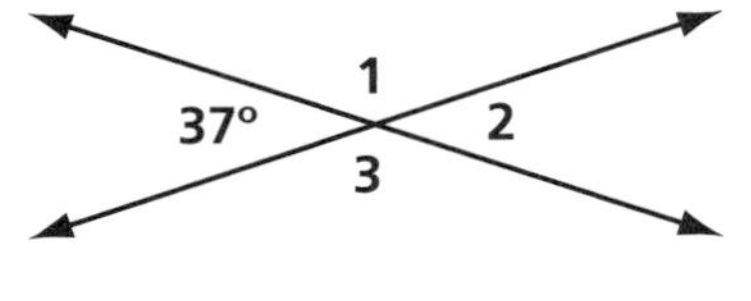

$\angle 1 =$ 143°, $\angle 2 =$ 37°

$\angle 3 =$ 143°

14.

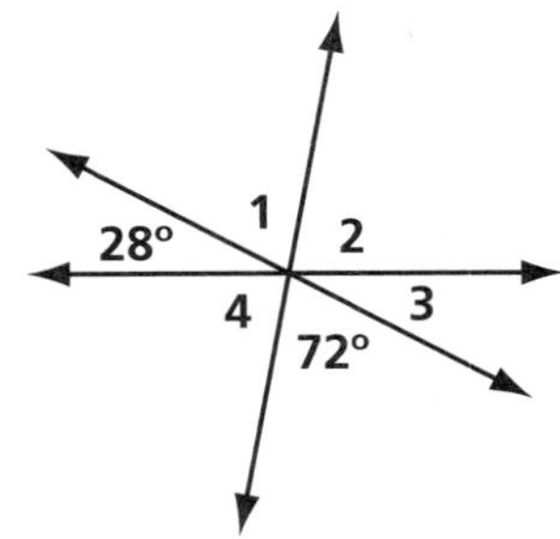

$\angle 1 =$ 72°, $\angle 2 =$ 80°

$\angle 3 =$ 28°, $\angle 4 =$ 80°

15.

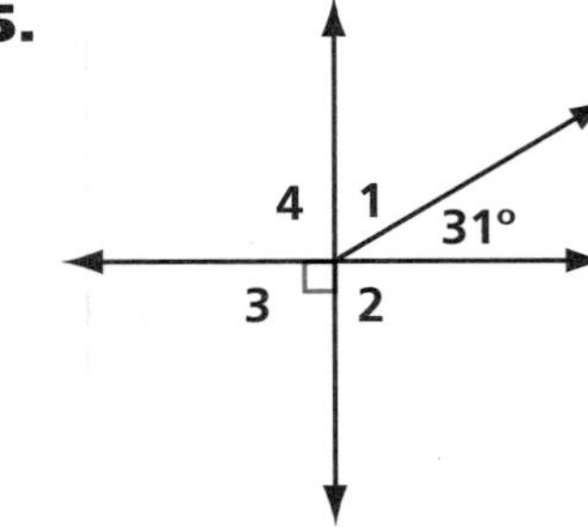

$\angle 1 =$ 59°, $\angle 2 =$ 90°

$\angle 3 =$ 90°, $\angle 4 =$ 90°

Problem Solving
Reasoning

Tell whether the statement is true or false. Explain your reasoning.

16. Every acute angle has a complement and supplement. True; Subtract the measure from either 180° or 90°.

17. Every obtuse angle has a complement and a supplement. False; No complement is possible since the angle is greater than 90°.

18. Vertical angles can be acute, obtuse, or right. True; examples in exercises 13–15

19. Vertical angles can be adjacent angles. No; Vertical angles do not have a common ray.

Test Prep ★ Mixed Review

20 **Which of the statements is false?** C; Obj. 7A

A *B* *C*

A *A* and *C* are collinear with *B*.

B $AB + BC = AC$

C $\overline{AC}$ represents a ray.

D $\overline{AC}$ represents the distance from *A* to *C*.

21 **Which of the statements is false?** G; Obj. 7A

F Two planes are shown intersecting at the line through points *A* and *B*.

G Points *A, B, C,* and *D,* are coplanar.

H Points *A, B,* and *C* are coplanar.

J Points *A, B,* and *D* are coplanar.

C *A* *D* *B*

Closing the Lesson *What can you tell me about vertical angles?* (Possible answers: They are the opposite angles or non-adjacent angles formed when two lines intersect; They are congruent to one another.)

Name ______________________

Guided Practice: Ex. 1, 4 & 7, pp. 189–190
Independent Practice: Complete pp. 189–190

Angle Relationships of Parallel Lines

A **transversal** is a line that intersects two other lines at two distinct points.

In the diagram, l_1 is a transversal to l_2 and l_3. If the lines are extended, you see that each line is a transversal of the other two.

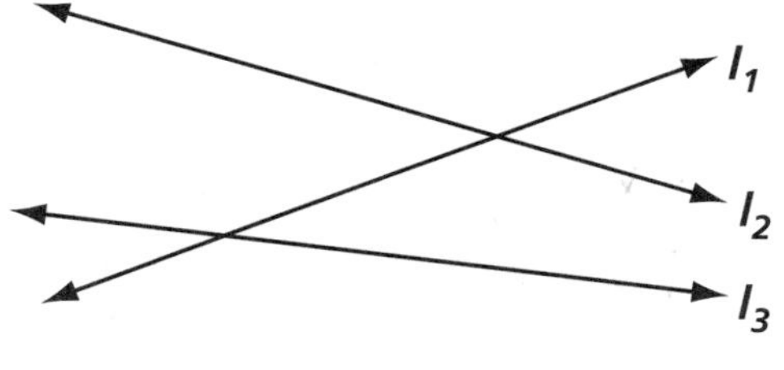

When a transversal intersects two lines, pairs of angles are formed that have special names.

Corresponding angles are on the same side of the transversal (*t*) and in a corresponding position with the lines, either both above or both below. The corresponding angles in the diagram at the right are:

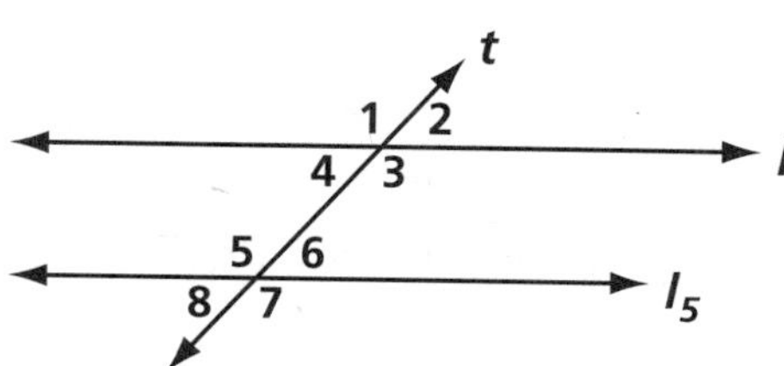

∠1 and ∠5, ∠2 and ∠6, ∠3 and ∠7, ∠4 and ∠8.

Lines in the same plane that do not intersect are **parallel.** Lines l_4 and l_5 are parallel.

Whenever lines l_4 and l_5 are parallel, corresponding angles will be congruent.

∠1 ≅ ∠5, ∠2 ≅ ∠6, ∠3 ≅ ∠7, ∠4 ≅ ∠8

Identify pairs of angles as vertical, supplementary, or corresponding.

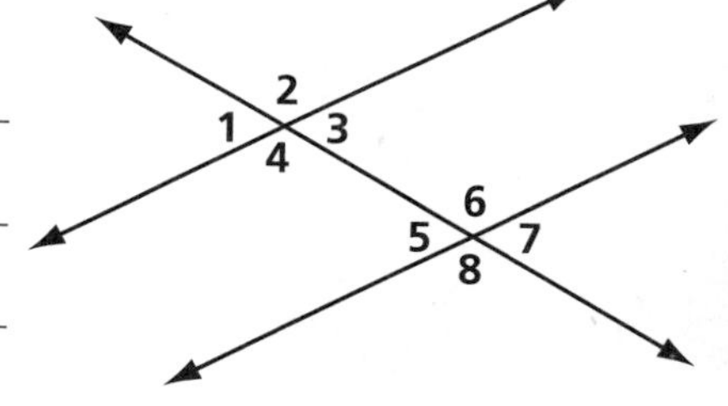

1. ∠1 and ∠4 supplementary ∠2 and ∠4 vertical

2. ∠1 and ∠5 corresponding ∠5 and ∠7 vertical

3. ∠6 and ∠7 supplementary ∠2 and ∠6 corresponding

Find the measure of the missing angles. Lines l_1 and l_2 are parallel.

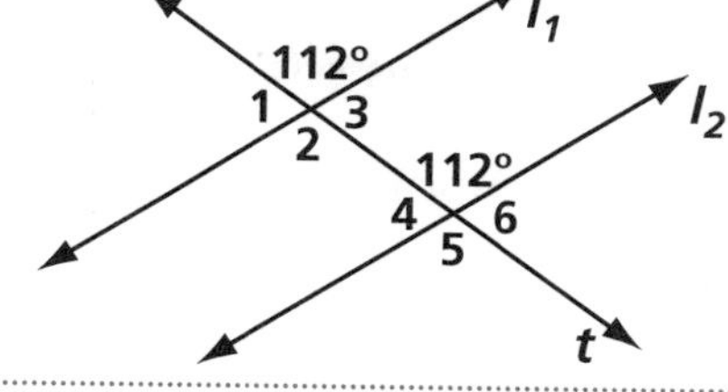

4. ∠1 = 68° ∠2 = 112° ∠3 = 68°

∠4 = 68° ∠5 = 112° ∠6 = 68°

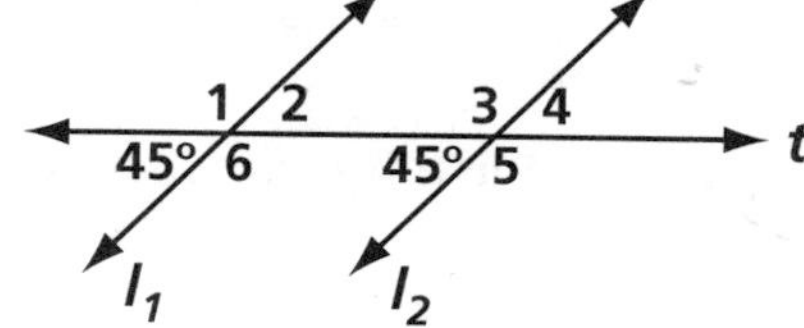

5. ∠1 = 135° ∠2 = 45° ∠3 = 135°

∠4 = 45° ∠5 = 135° ∠6 = 135°

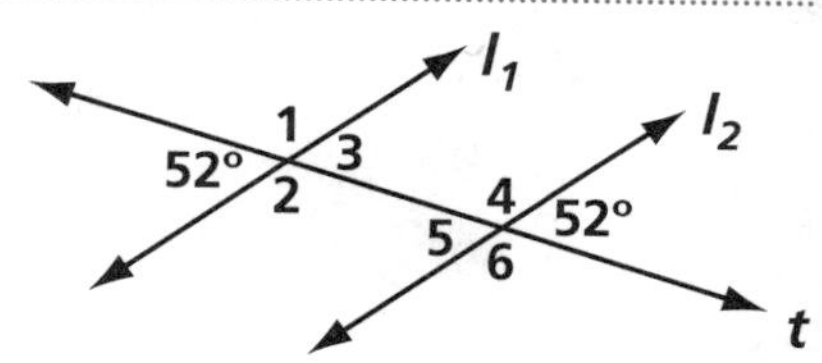

6. ∠1 = 128° ∠2 = 128° ∠3 = 52°

∠4 = 128° ∠5 = 52° ∠6 = 128°

Check Understanding *What are corresponding angles of parallel lines?* (angles on the same side of the transversal and in a corresponding position with the lines, either above the lines or below the lines)

Alternate interior angles are on opposite sides of the transversal (*t*) and interior (inside) to the two lines. In the diagram at the right, the alternate interior angles are:

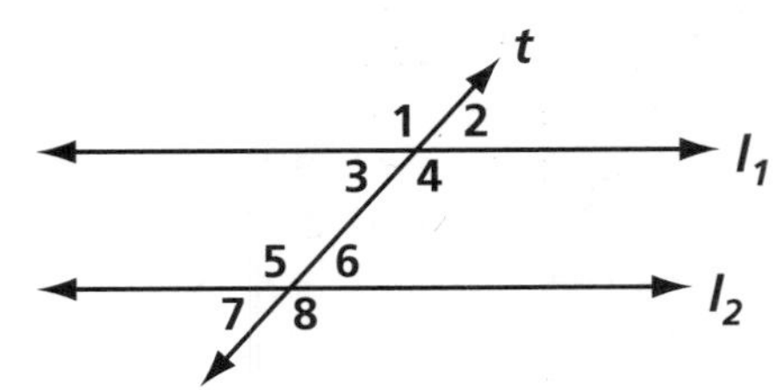

∠3 and **∠6**, **∠4** and **∠5**

For this figure there are:

- **4** pairs of vertical angles
- **8** pairs of supplementary angles
- **4** pairs of corresponding angles
- **2** pairs of alternate interior angles

Whenever lines l_1 and l_2 are parallel, alternate interior angles will be congruent.

∠3 ≅ ∠6, ∠4 ≅ ∠5

Find the measure of the angle. Justify your reasoning. Possible answers are given.

7. ∠2 = 73° because it is supplementary to ∠1.

8. ∠3 = 107° because it corresponds to ∠1.

9. ∠4 = 73° because it corresponds to ∠2.

10. ∠5 = 107° because it is a vertical angle to ∠3.

11. ∠6 = 73° because it is supplementary to ∠3.

12. ∠7 = 107° because it is a vertical angle to ∠1.

13. ∠8 = 73° because it is supplementary to ∠1.

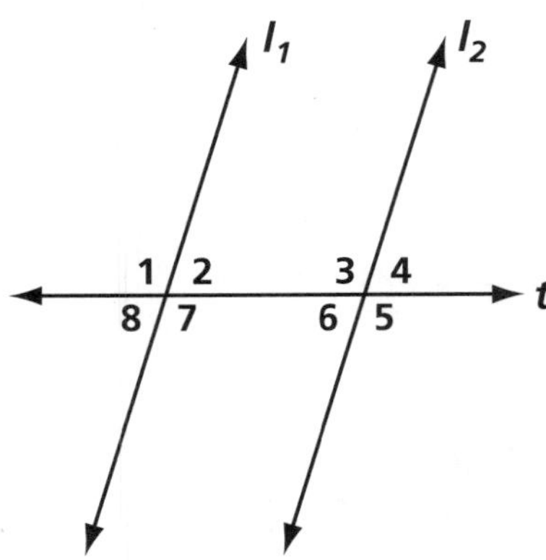

Given: l_1 and l_2 are parallel; ∠1 = 107°

Problem Solving Reasoning

Write true or false.

14. Corresponding angles are always congruent. False.

15. Vertical angles are always congruent. True.

16. Supplementary angles are always congruent. False.

17. Alternate interior angles are always congruent. False.

Test Prep ★ Mixed Review

18 **When the hands of a clock show exactly two o'clock, what is the angle between the hands?** D; Obj. 7B

A 10°

B 20°

C 30°

D 60°

19 **What other angle measures 40°?** J; Obj. 7C

F ∠*AOB*

G ∠*BOC*

H ∠*DOE*

J ∠*DOC*

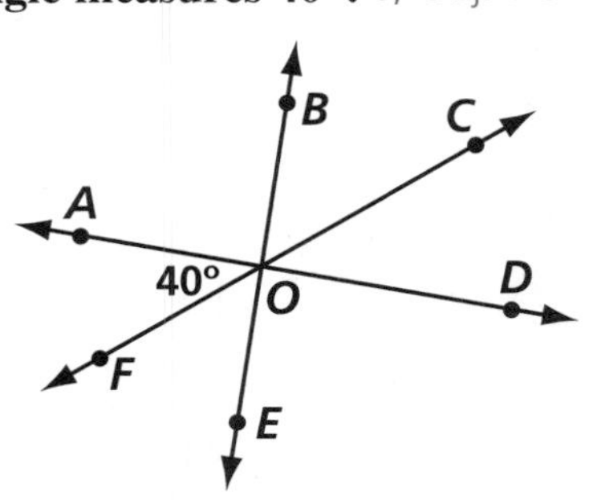

Closing the Lesson *What are alternate interior angles?* (angles on the opposite side of the transversal and interior to the two lines)

Name ______________________________

Triangles

Guided Practice: Ex. 1, 3 & 5, p. 191
Independent Practice: Complete pp. 191–192

You already know many things about triangles. In this lesson you will learn to classify them by their angles and by their sides. Note how two segments of equal length, **congruent segments,** are marked on the diagrams.

Classifying Triangles by their Angles

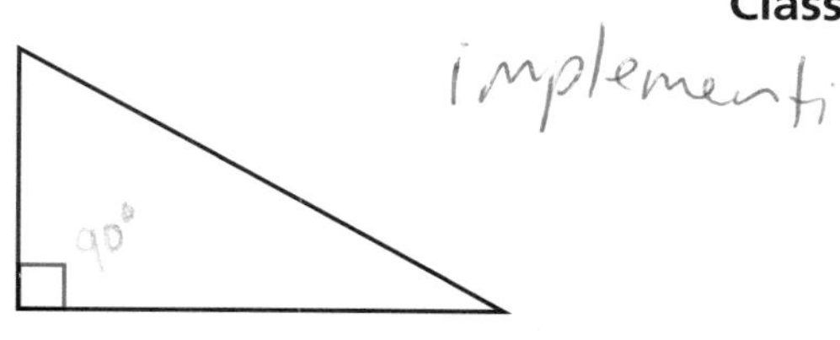

implementing

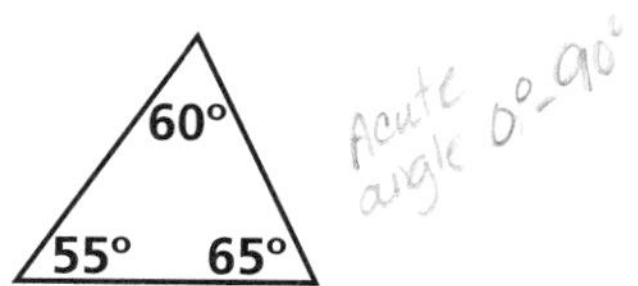

Acute angle 0°-90°

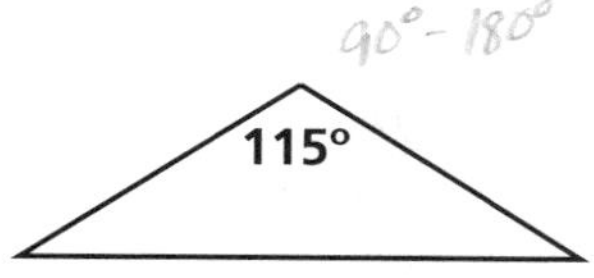

90°-180°

Right Triangle
A triangle with one right angle

Acute Triangle
A triangle with three acute angles

Obtuse Triangle
A triangle with one obtuse angle

Classifying Triangles by their Sides

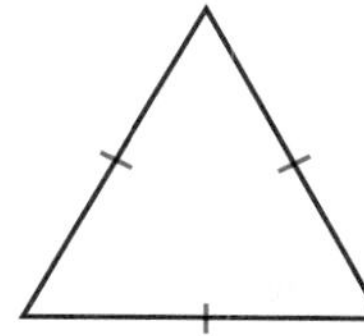

The marks show congruent sides.

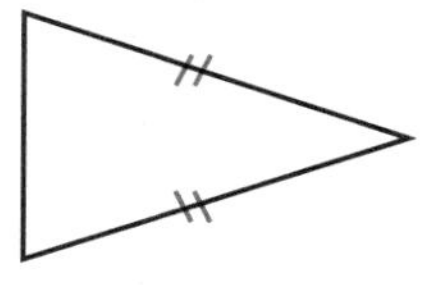

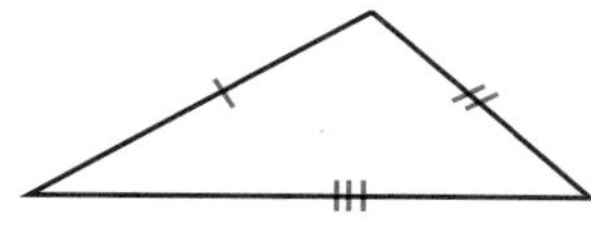

Equilateral Triangle
A triangle with all sides equal in measure, or congruent

Isosceles Triangle
A triangle with at least two sides equal in measure, or congruent

Scalene Triangle
A triangle with no sides equal in measure, or congruent

Classify the triangle by its sides and by its angles.

1. Sides isosceles
Angles right

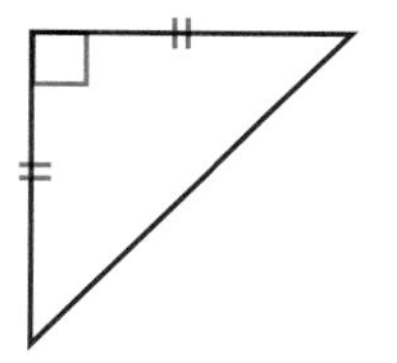

2. Sides isosceles
Angles acute

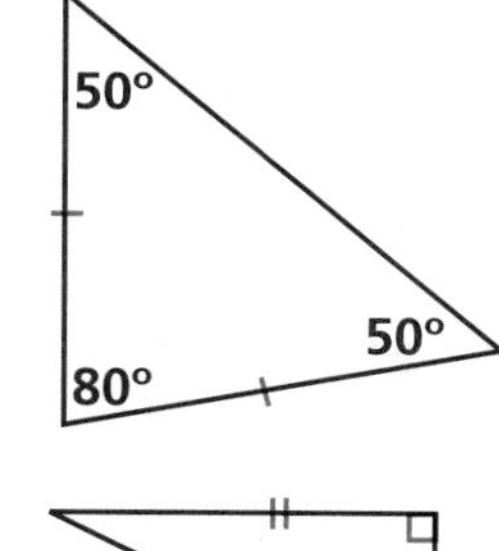

3. Sides scalene
Angles obtuse

4. Sides scalene
Angles right

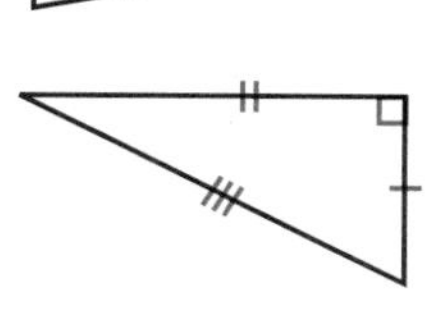

Make a sketch of the triangle, if possible. Possible answers are given.

5. An acute, isosceles triangle

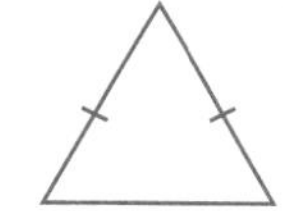

6. An obtuse, scalene triangle

7. An equilateral, obtuse triangle
no triangle possible

8. A right, isosceles triangle

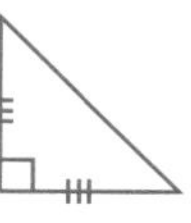

Check Understanding *Can a triangle be isosceles and right at the same time?* (Yes.) *Can a triangle be equilateral and a right triangle at the same time?* (No.) *Can a triangle have a right angle and an obtuse angle in it?* (No, because the sum of the angles would then be greater than 180°.)

Recall: The sum of the angle measures of a triangle is **180°**.

Example 1: Find $\angle B =$ ___?___

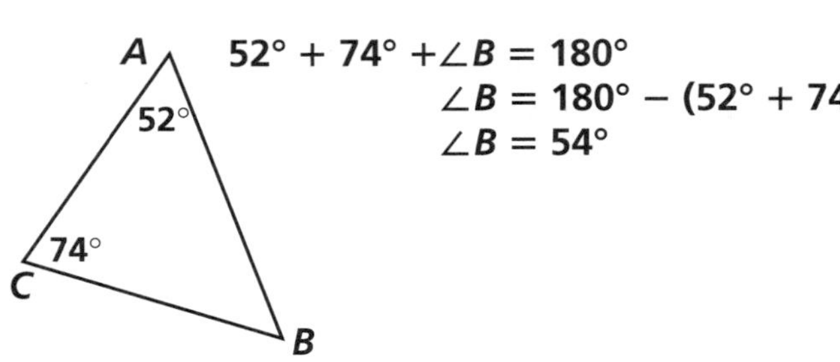

$52° + 74° + \angle B = 180°$
$\angle B = 180° - (52° + 74°)$
$\angle B = 54°$

Example 2: Find the measure of $\angle D$.

$\angle D \cong \angle E$

Let $x = \angle D = \angle E$.

$x + x + 54° = 180°$
$2x + 54° = 180°$
$2x = 126°$
$x = 63°$

So $\angle D = 63°$.

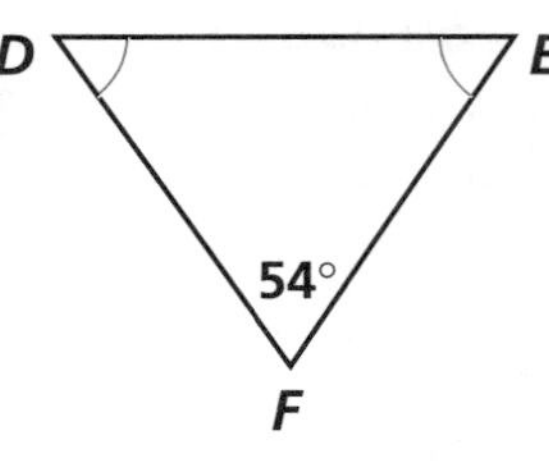

Find the measure of the angle.

9.

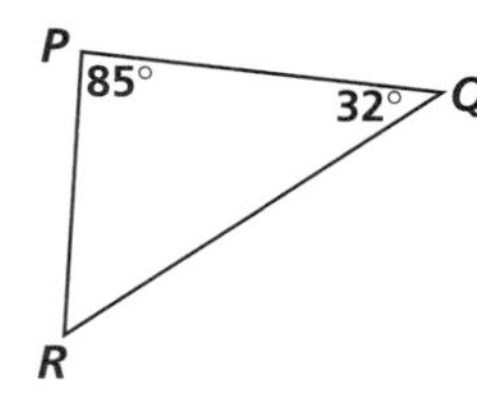

$\angle R =$ 63°

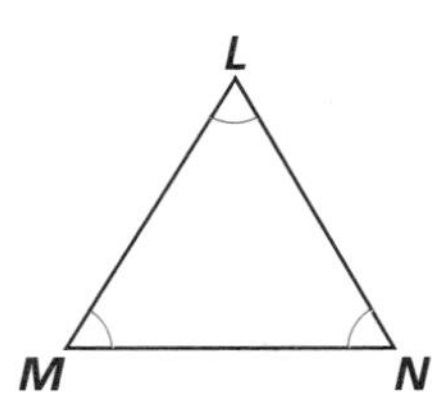

$\angle N =$ 60°

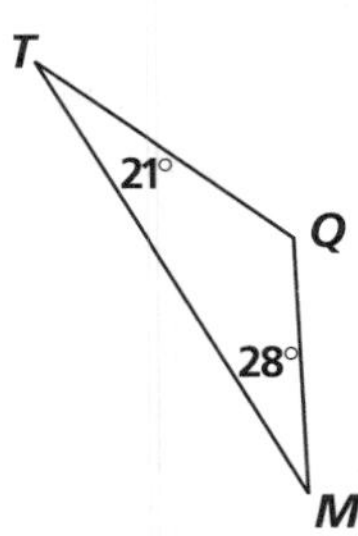

$\angle Q =$ 131°

10.

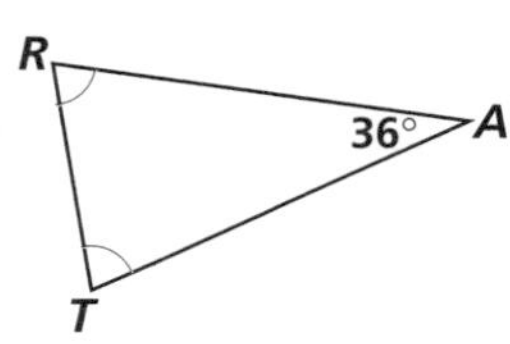

$\angle R =$ 72°

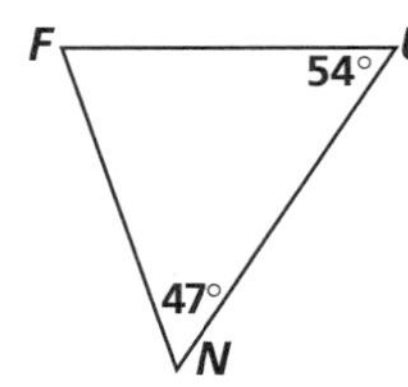

$\angle F =$ 79°

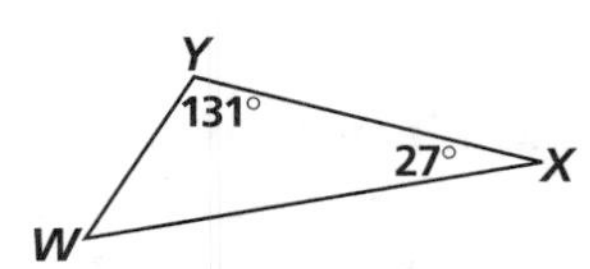

$\angle W =$ 22°

Quick Check

Use the diagram for exercises 11–14.
Possible answers are given for exercises 11–14.

11. Name a pair of vertical angles.

$\angle 1$ and $\angle 3$

12. Name a pair of supplementary angles.

$\angle 1$ and $\angle 2$

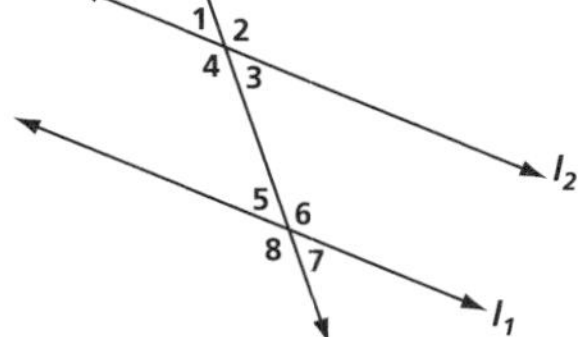

13. Name a pair of corresponding angles. $\angle 1$ and $\angle 5$

14. Name a pair of alternate interior angles. $\angle 3$ and $\angle 5$

Find the measure of the third angle of triangle *ABC*.

15. $\angle A = 18°, \angle B = 36°, \angle C =$ 126°

Work Space.

Item	Error Analysis
11–12, 15	**Common Error** They may confuse complementary and supplementary angles. **Reteaching** Reteach 49, 51
13–14	**Common Error** They may confuse corresponding and alternate interior angles. **Reteaching** Reteach 50

Closing the Lesson *There are seven possible ways of classifying a triangle. What are those seven ways?* (scalene right, scalene acute, scalene obtuse, isosceles right, isosceles acute, isosceles obtuse, equilateral acute)

Name ____________________________

Guided Practice: Ex. 1, p. 194
Independent Practice: Complete pp. 193–194

Problem Solving Strategy: Find a Pattern

To solve some problems, finding a pattern can help. The pattern may become clear by making a list, solving a simpler problem, or drawing a diagram. Once the pattern is observed, a generalization can be made.

Problem

Five friends have all met at a restaurant for a bit of a reunion. It has been two years since they've seen one another. If all friends shake hands with one another, how many handshakes are there?

1 Understand

"Asking yourself questions will help you identify the math ideas."

As you reread, ask yourself questions.

- How many people are there? 5
- Can a person shake his or her own hand? No.
- How many hands does each person shake? 4

2 Decide

"Could solving a simpler problem help? Is there a way to draw a diagram of the problem or make a table?"

Choose a method for solving.

- What if there were only one friend? Two friends? Three friends? Four friends?

1 person — **0** handshakes

2 people — **1** handshake

3 people — **3** handshakes

4 people — **6** handshakes

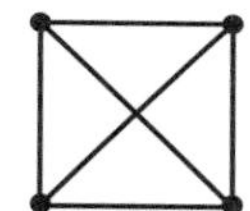

Number of people	1	2	3	4	5
Number of handshakes	0	1	3	6	? 10

3 Solve

"How can I organize the results to see a pattern? Is there more than one pattern?"

Describe the pattern. Solve the problem.

- What is the pattern you found? one pattern: add consecutive whole numbers to complete the list–$0 + 1 = 1$, $1 + 2 = 3$, $3 + 3 = 6$, $6 + 4 = 10$; another pattern: for n people, there are $\frac{n(n-1)}{2}$ handshakes: $\frac{5 \cdot 4}{2} = 10$
- Use your pattern to complete the chart.

4 Look back

"Check your answer to see that it makes sense."

Check your answer. Write your answer as a complete sentence.

Answer: There will be 10 handshakes.

Is there another pattern you could have used? Answers may vary.

Check Understanding *What was the basic idea of the strategy used?* (finding a pattern)

Use the Find a Pattern or any other strategy you have learned to solve these problems.

1. If ten people all greet one another with a handshake, how many handshakes will there be?

Think: How can you use the pattern from the previous page?

Extend the chart

Answer: 45

2. Remember you can use exponents to show repeated factors. For example:

$\mathbf{10^3 = 10 \cdot 10 \cdot 10}$, or **1,000**.

What is the ones digit of the number $\mathbf{3^{20}}$ written in standard form?

Think: Is there a pattern in the ones digits of $\mathbf{3^1}$, $\mathbf{3^2}$, $\mathbf{3^3}$, $\mathbf{3^4}$, and so on?

Yes; They repeat the pattern 3, 9, 7, 1, 3, 9, ...

Answer: 1

3. The circle below represents a pizza. Show how you could cut the pizza into eleven pieces using exactly four straight cuts.

lines are drawn in by student

4. To mark her property line along a **50**-foot road, a rancher needs to set down fence posts at the beginning and end and every **5** feet in between. If it takes **12** minutes to dig and set each post, how many hours will it take her to set the posts along the road?

11 posts, $2\frac{1}{5}$ hours

5. The first three *pentagonal numbers* are shown. What is the fifth pentagonal number?

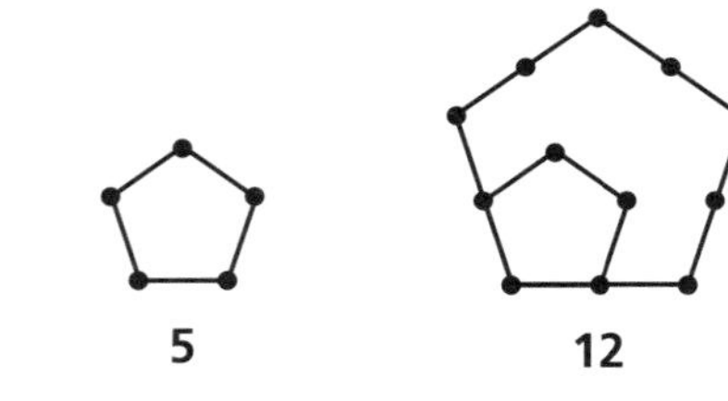

35

6. What is the sum of the first twenty odd numbers?

400

7. A segment that connects two vertices of a polygon and is not a side is called a **diagonal.** The diagonals of a rectangle are shown. How many diagonals does an **8**-sided polygon have?

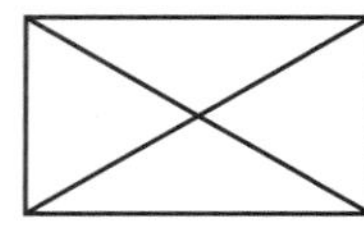

20

8. The first three figures in a pattern are shown. What will the area and the perimeter of the tenth figure be?

Figure 1

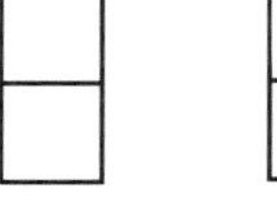
Figure 2

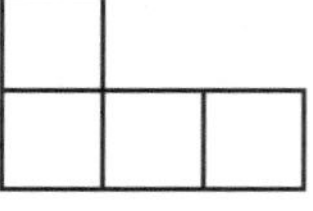
Figure 3

P: 24 units A: 11 square units

Check Understanding *What is the next number in this pattern?* 2, 5, 10, 17, . . .(26)

Name ______________________________

Guided Practice: Ex. 1, 4 & 9, pp. 195–196
Independent Practice: Complete pp. 195–196

Constructing Congruent Segments and Angles

The compass and straightedge are "construction tools." You can use them to make copies of geometric figures that are congruent to the original figure. You can construct congruent segments.

Constructing a Segment Congruent to $\overline{AB}$

1. Use a straightedge. Draw a segment that is longer than $\overline{AB}$. Label one endpoint *C*.

2. Set your compass to the length of $\overline{AB}$. Place the compass point at *C* and draw an arc. Label point *D*.

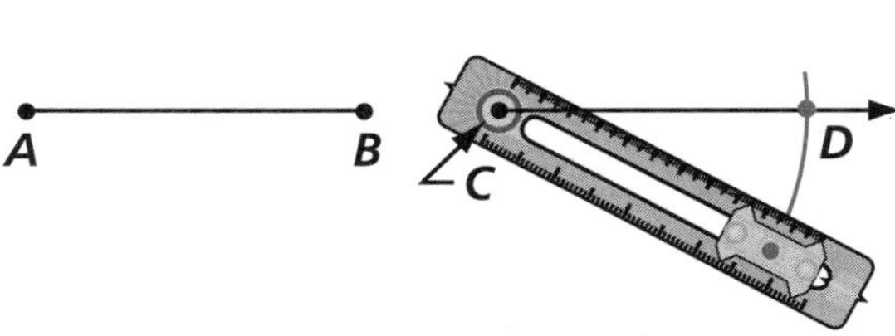

By construction, $\overline{AB} \cong \overline{CD}$.

You can also construct a segment that is twice as long as $\overline{AB}$. You simply repeat the construction again from endpoint *D*.

Use a straightedge and compass. Construct a line segment congruent to the given one.

1.

2.

3.

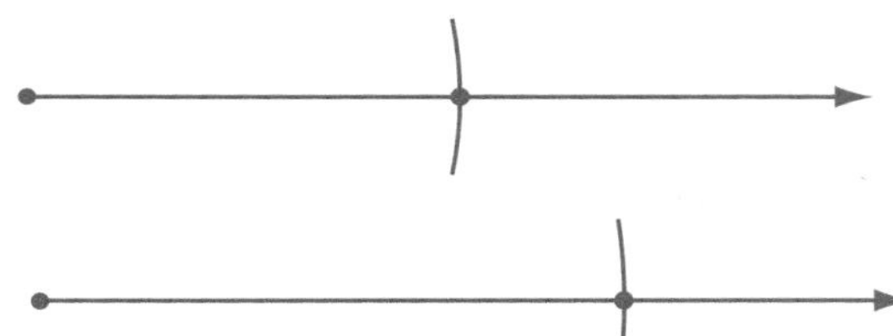

Use a straightedge, compass, and the lengths of $\overline{AB}$ and $\overline{CD}$ below. Construct a line segment of the given length.

A B C D

4. twice $\overline{AB}$

5. three times $\overline{AB}$

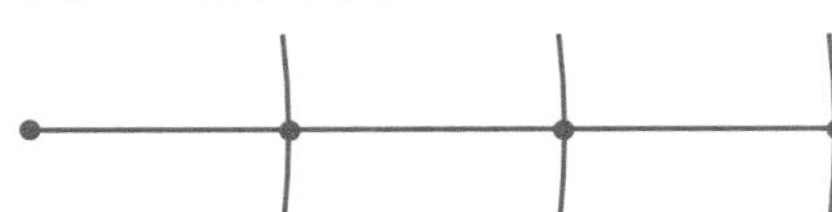

6. $\overline{AB} + \overline{CD}$

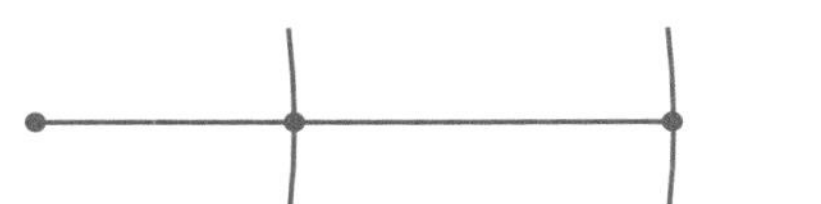

7. $\overline{CD} - \overline{AB}$

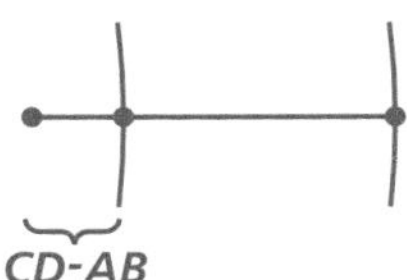

8. twice $(\overline{AB} + \overline{CD})$

Check Understanding *If you were going to construct a line segment three times as long as a given segment, what would you do?* (Construct a segment congruent to the original segment. Then, from the outer endpoint, construct another segment congruent to the original segment and repeat this step.)

Constructing an Angle Congruent to ∠A.

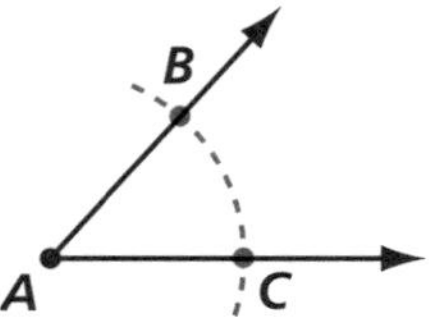

1. Draw a ray with endpoint ***D***. Place the compass point at ***A*** and draw an arc. Label points ***B*** and ***C***.

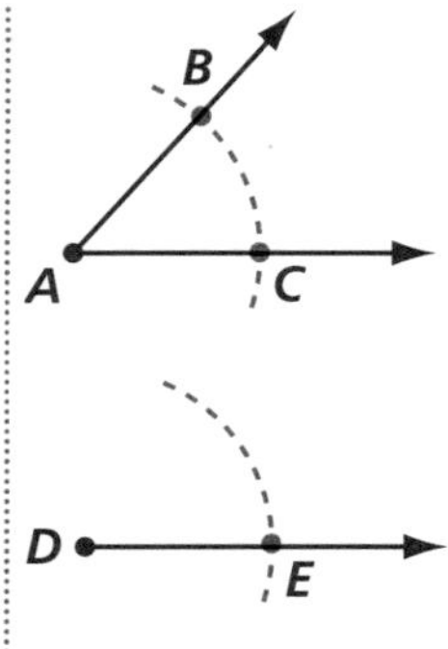

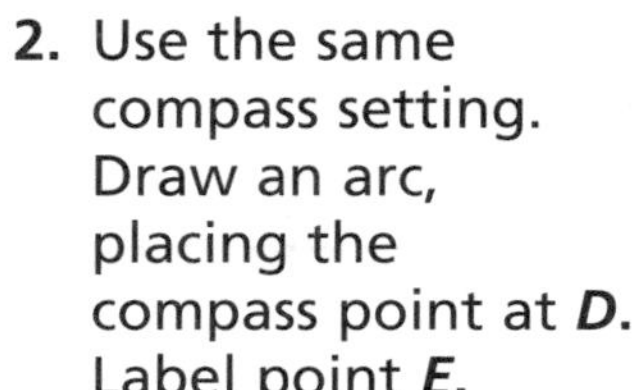

2. Use the same compass setting. Draw an arc, placing the compass point at ***D***. Label point ***E***.

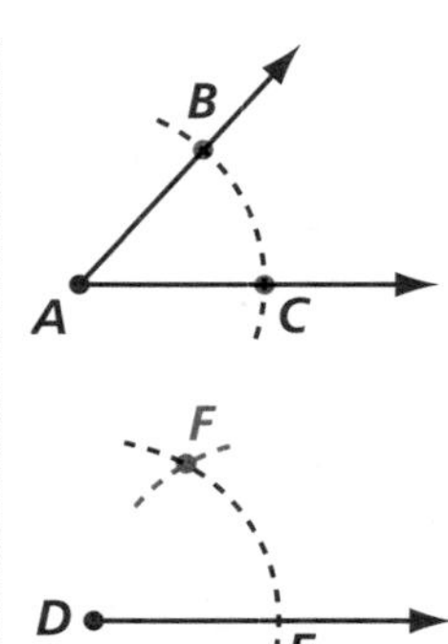

3. Set your compass to the length of $\overline{BC}$. Place the compass point at ***E***. Mark point ***F***.

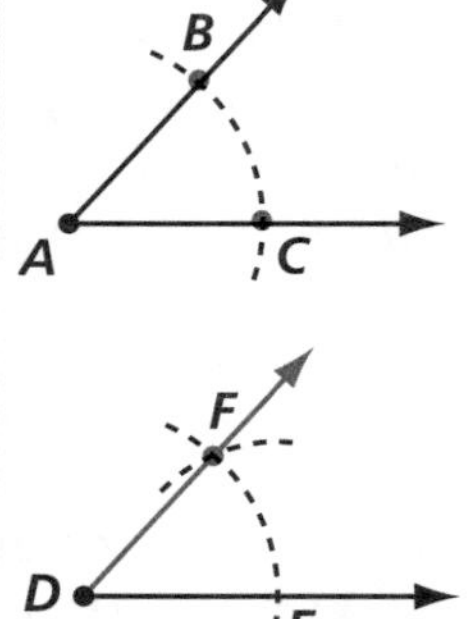

4. Draw a ray from ***D*** through ***F***.

By construction, ***∠BAC ≅ ∠FDE***.

Use a straightedge and compass. Construct a congruent angle below the angle.

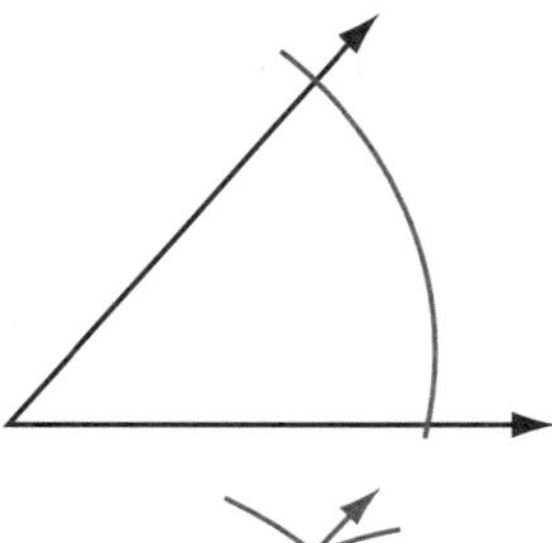

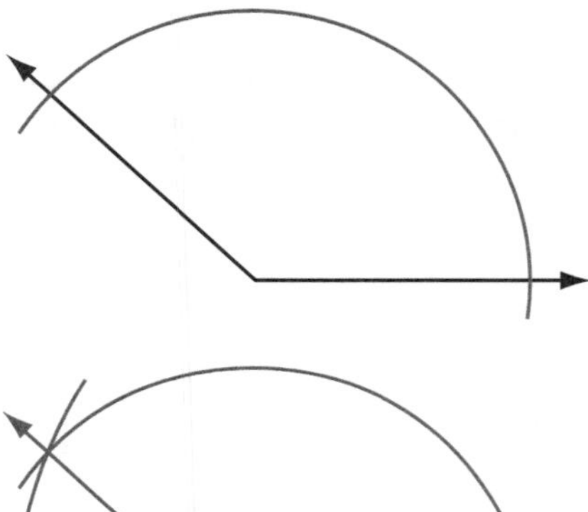

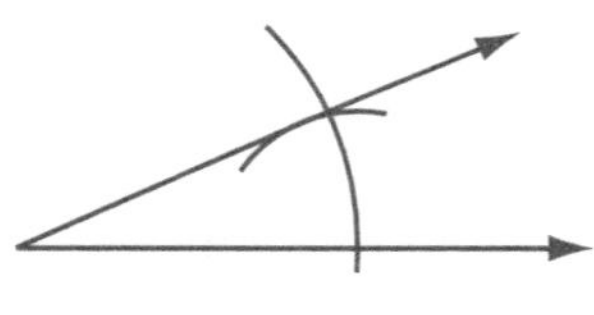

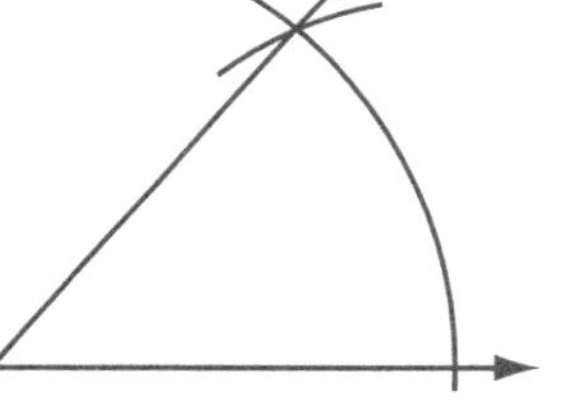

Test Prep ★ Mixed Review

10 **If lines *AB* and *CD* are parallel, how many angles altogether have a measure of 55°?** D; Obj. 7C

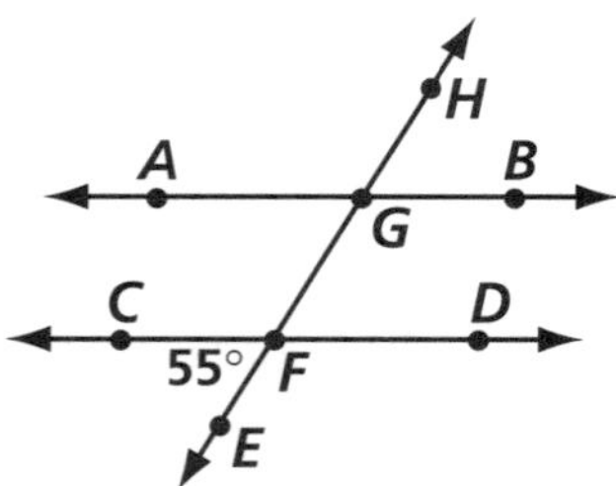

A one **C** three

B two **D** four

11 **How many triangles, of all sizes, are in the diagram?** H; Obj. 7D

F 25 **H** 48

G 40 **J** 56

Closing the Lesson *What is a geometric construction?* (a construction done using only compass and straightedge)

Name ____

Constructing Bisectors

Guided Practice: Construction 1, p. 197
Independent Practice: Complete pp. 197–198

A **bisector** divides a figure into two parts of equal measure. An angle bisector is a ray that divides the angle into two adjacent angles of equal measure. A segment bisector is a point, called a **midpoint,** that divides the segment into two segments of equal length.

Constructing an Angle Bisector

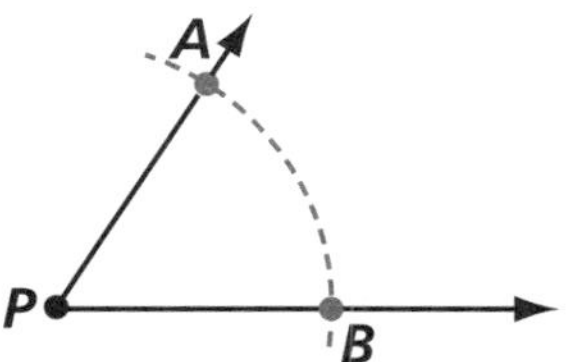

1. From point ***P,*** draw an arc that intersects both rays. Label the two points ***A*** and ***B.***

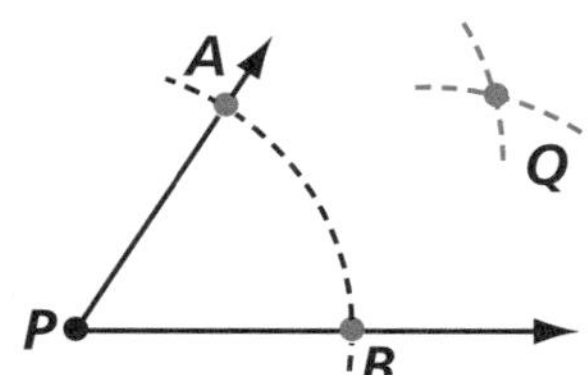

2. From point ***A*** and from point ***B,*** draw intersecting arcs. Label the point ***Q.***

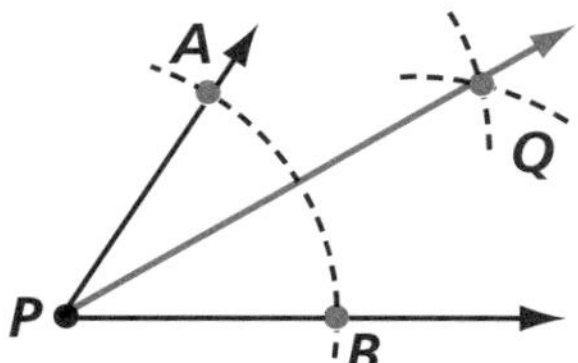

3. Draw ray ***PQ.*** Then, $\angle APQ \cong \angle BPQ$ by construction.

Constructing a Segment Bisector.

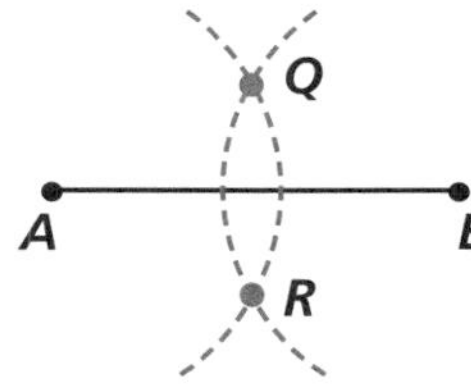

1. From point ***A*** and from point ***B,*** draw intersecting arcs above and below $\overline{AB}$. Label the points of intersection ***Q*** and ***R.*** Note: $\overline{AQ} \cong \overline{BQ}$ and $\overline{AR} \cong \overline{BR}$.

2. Draw a line through points ***R*** and ***Q.*** Label the point of intersection ***P.***

By construction, $\overline{AP} \cong \overline{BP}$.

Use a straightedge and compass. Bisect the angle or segment.

1.

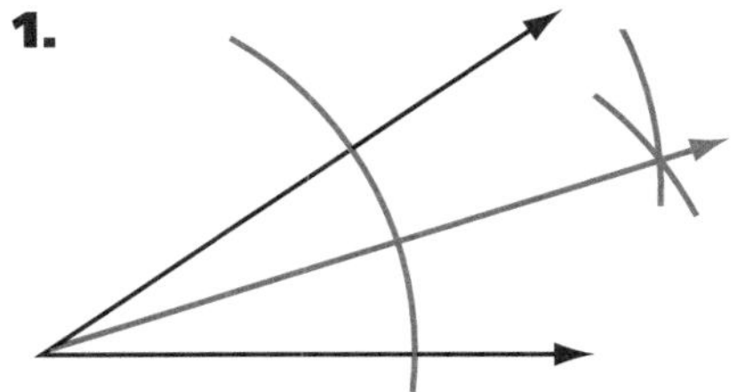

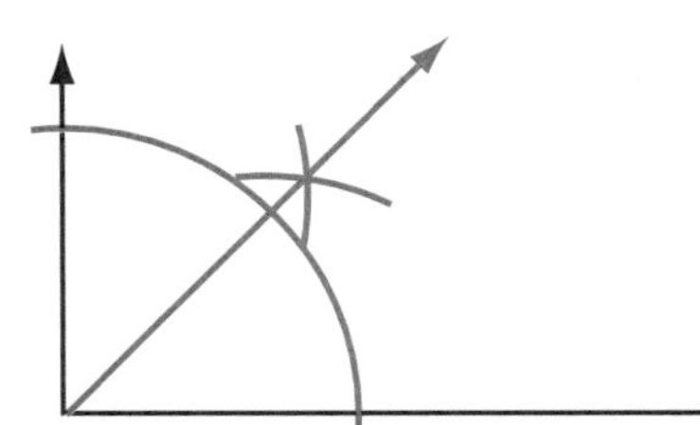

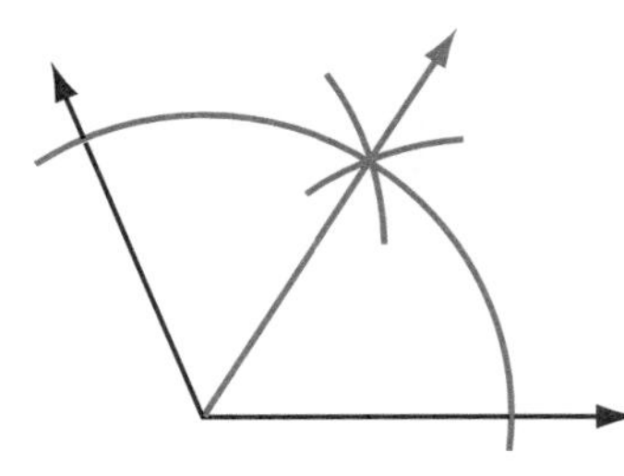

2.

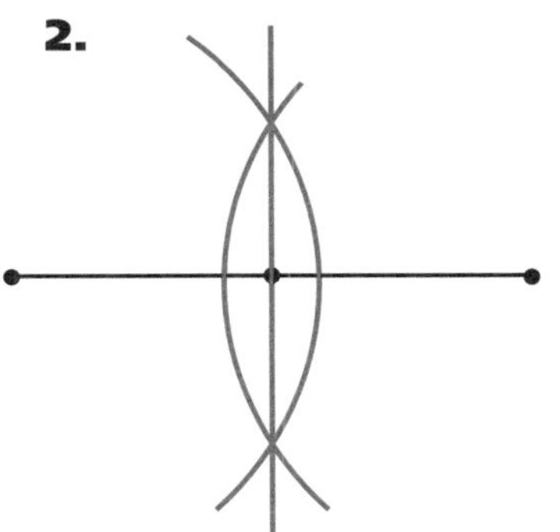

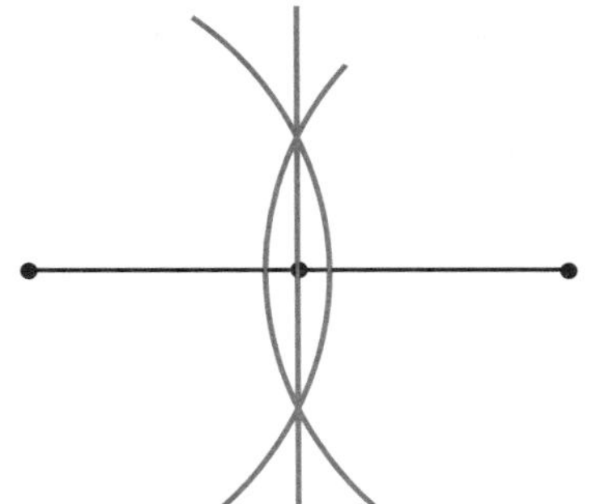

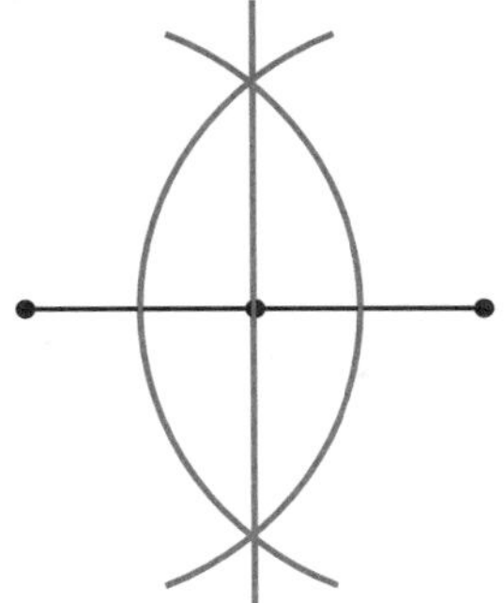

Check Understanding *When you bisect a segment, what other geometric figure do you construct?* (a line that is perpendicular to the segment)

Two lines that intersect to form four right angles are **perpendicular.**

Notice that in the second construction on page **197**, $\overleftrightarrow{QR}$ is perpendicular to $\overline{AB}$. You can use similar steps to construct perpendicular lines.

Constructing Perpendicular lines.

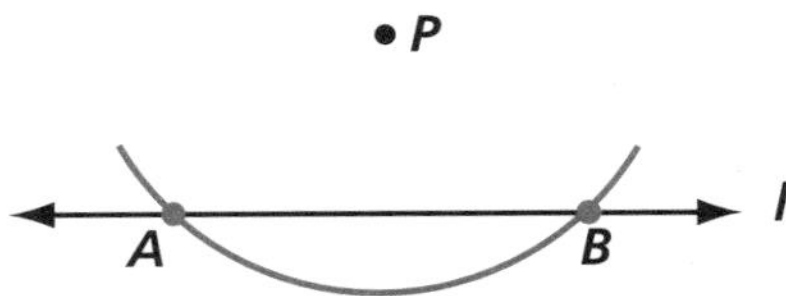

1. Draw an arc from ***P*** intersecting line ***l*** at two points. Label the points ***A*** and ***B***.

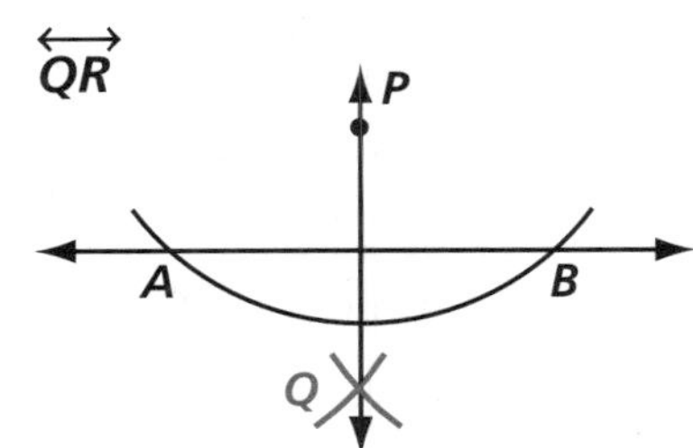

2. From ***A*** and from ***B***, draw intersecting arcs. Label the point of intersection ***Q***. Draw $\overleftrightarrow{PQ}$. By construction, $\overleftrightarrow{PQ}$ is perpendicular to $\overleftrightarrow{AB}$.

Use a straightedge and compass. Construct a line through *P* perpendicular to *l*.

3.

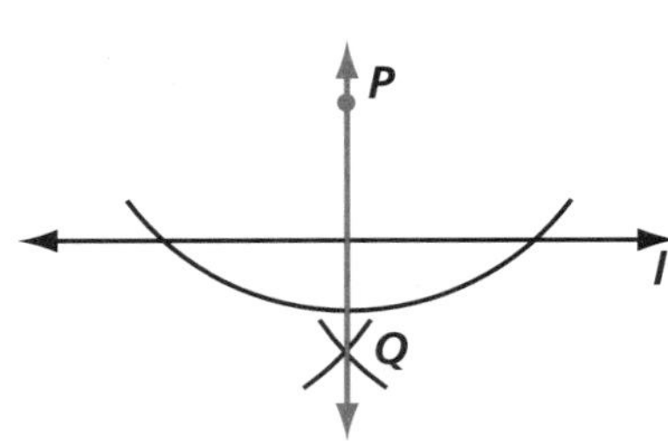

4.

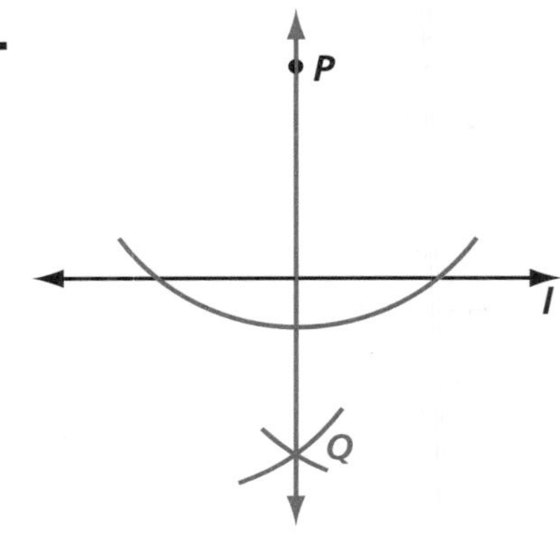

Problem Solving Reasoning Solve.

5. Suppose ***P*** is a point on line ***l***. Describe a method of constructing a line perpendicular to ***l***. (Hint: Start by finding two points on ***l*** that are the same distance from ***P***.)

Mark points *Q* and *R* so that $\overline{PQ} \cong \overline{PR}$.

Then, construct the bisector of $\overline{QR}$.

6. Describe a method for constructing a right triangle.

Draw two perpendicular lines intersecting at *P*.

Choose points *Q* and *R*, one on each line. Draw $\overline{QR}$ to form ΔPQR.

Test Prep ★ Mixed Review

7 **At what hour, on the hour, will the hands of a clock form a 150° angle?** B; Obj. 7B

A 5 o'clock only
B 5 and 7 o'clock
C 7 o'clock only
D 11 and 1 o'clock

8 **How many times, on the hour, will the hands of a clock form an acute angle during a 24-hour period?** J; Obj. 7B

F 2
G 4
H 6
J 8

Closing the Lesson *Can you think why it might be important to be able to bisect a segment?* (Possible answer: When you want to find the exact midpoint of the segment.)

Name ______________________________

Guided Practice: Ex. 1, 5, 7 & 12; First line in Ex. 11, pp. 199–201
Independent Practice: Complete pp. 199–201

Polygons and Congruent Figures

You have studied triangles and their properties. In this lesson you will learn about other polygons. **Polygons** are all closed figures made up of line segments joined at their endpoints.

A **quadrilateral** is a polygon that has four sides and four angles. It has two pairs of **opposite sides,** and two pairs of **opposite angles.** You use four letters to name quadrilaterals. Possible names for the figure at right are: quadrilateral ***ABCD,*** quadrilateral ***CBAD***.

Opposite sides: $\overline{AB}$ and $\overline{CD}$
$\overline{AD}$ and $\overline{BC}$

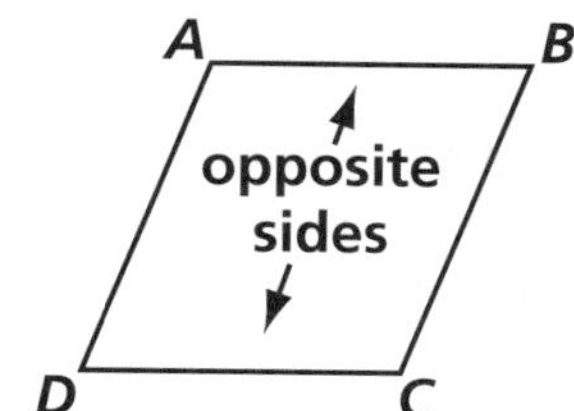

Opposite angles: $\angle A$ and $\angle C$
$\angle B$ and $\angle D$

Four quadrilaterals are shown. The arrowheads (< and <<) on the figures indicate parallel sides.

Parallelogram
A quadrilateral with both pairs of opposite sides parallel

Rhombus
A parallelogram with four congruent sides

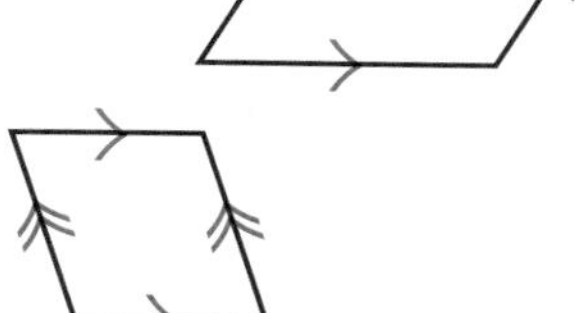

Rectangle
A parallelogram with four right angles

Square
A rectangle with four congruent sides

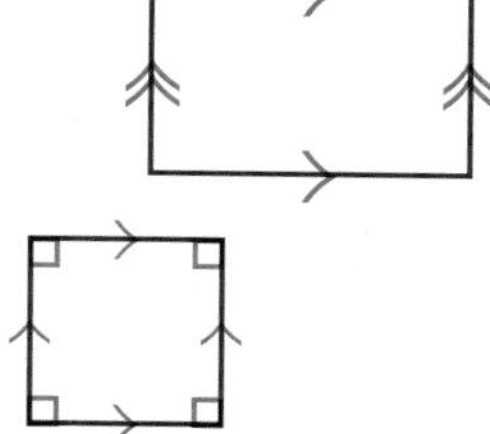

From the definitions, all four quadrilaterals are parallelograms. A square is both a rectangle and a rhombus.

Use the diagram to answer the following.

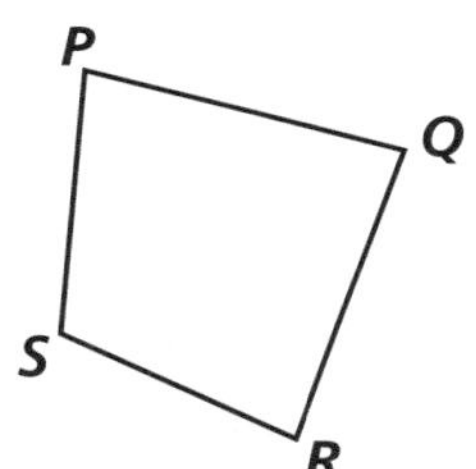

1. 3 different names for the quadrilateral *PQRS, QRSP, RSPQ*

2. Name the opposite sides $\overline{PQ}$ and $\overline{RS}$, $\overline{PS}$ and $\overline{QR}$

3. Name the opposite angles $\angle P$ and $\angle R$, $\angle S$ and $\angle Q$

Classify the figure. Use parallelogram (*P*), rectangle (*R*), rhombus (*Rh*), square (*S*), or none of these (*N*). Use all names that apply.

4.

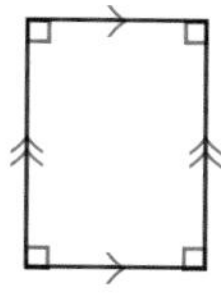

P, R

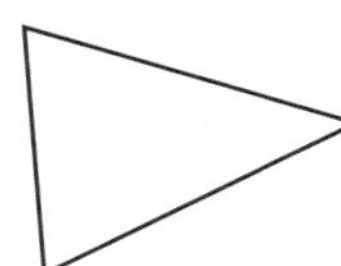

N

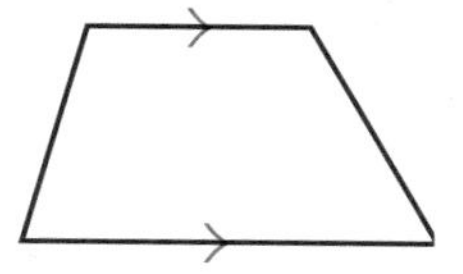

N

5.

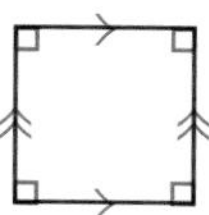

P, R, Rh, S

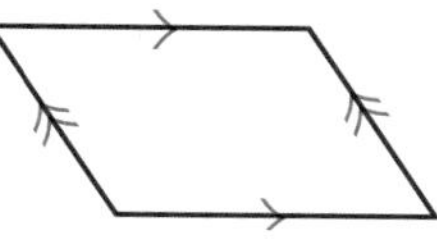

P

P, Rh

6.

N

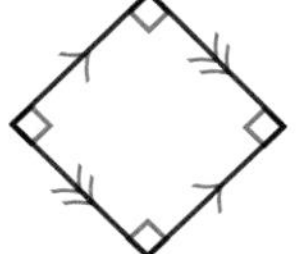

P, R, Rh, S

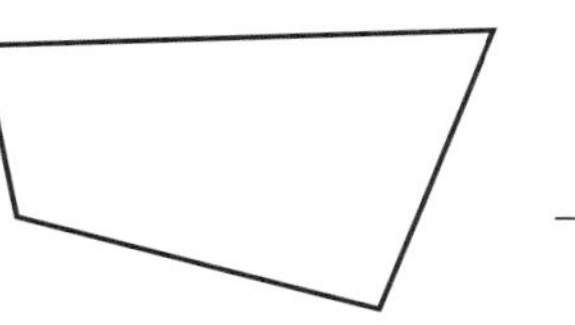

N

Check Understanding *If a polygon has all of its sides congruent is it a regular polygon?* (Not necessarily; a rhombus has all of its sides congruent, not all of its angles.)

Recall this list that names some other polygons and the number of sides and angles they have.

pentagon: **5** angles and sides hexagon: **6** angles and sides heptagon: **7** angles and sides

octagon: **8** angles and sides nonagon: **9** angles and sides decagon: **10** angles and sides

Two polygons are **congruent** if they are the same size and shape. This means that corresponding sides are congruent and their corresponding angles are congruent.

The two triangles at the right are congruent, so their corresponding sides are congruent and their corresponding angles are congruent.

Notice that the order in which the triangles are written does matter. Corresponding vertices are written in the same order. For example, if you know that $\triangle ABC \cong \triangle DEF$, then $\angle A \cong \angle D$ and $AB \cong DE$.

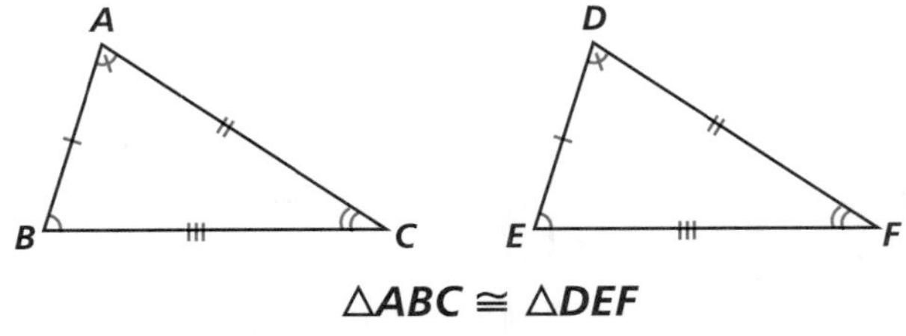

$\triangle ABC \cong \triangle DEF$

$\overline{AB} \cong \overline{DE}$	$\angle A \cong \angle D$
$\overline{BC} \cong \overline{EF}$	$\angle B \cong \angle E$
$\overline{AC} \cong \overline{DF}$	$\angle C \cong \angle F$

Complete.

7. If $\triangle DGE \cong \triangle LMN$, then $\overline{DG} \cong$ $\overline{LM}$, $\overline{GE} \cong$ $\overline{MN}$, $\overline{DE} \cong$ $\overline{LN}$, $\angle D \cong$ $\angle L$,

$\angle G \cong$ $\angle M$, $\angle E \cong$ $\angle N$.

8. If $\triangle TIL \cong \triangle ACP$, then $\overline{TI} \cong$ $\overline{AC}$, $\overline{IL} \cong$ $\overline{CP}$, $\overline{TL} \cong$ $\overline{AP}$, $\angle T \cong$ $\angle A$,

$\angle I \cong$ $\angle C$, $\angle L \cong$ $\angle P$.

9. If $\triangle XYZ \cong \triangle RST$, then $\overline{RS} \cong$ $\overline{XY}$, $\overline{ST} \cong$ $\overline{YZ}$, $\overline{RT} \cong$ $\overline{XZ}$, $\angle R \cong$ $\angle X$,

$\angle S \cong$ $\angle Y$, $\angle T \cong$ $\angle Z$.

10. If quadrilateral ***CARD*** $\cong$ quadrilateral ***MINE***, then

$\overline{CA} \cong$ $\overline{MI}$, $\overline{AR} \cong$ $\overline{IN}$, $\overline{RD} \cong$ $\overline{NE}$, $\overline{CD} \cong$ $\overline{ME}$,

$\angle C \cong$ $\angle M$, $\angle A \cong$ $\angle I$, $\angle R \cong$ $\angle N$, $\angle D \cong$ $\angle E$.

11. Complete to show that the triangles are congruent. Order may vary.

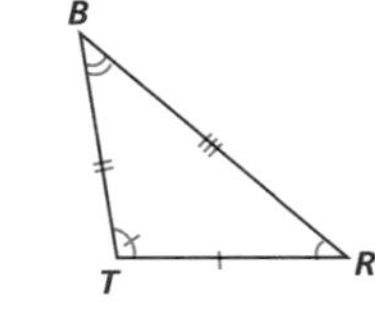

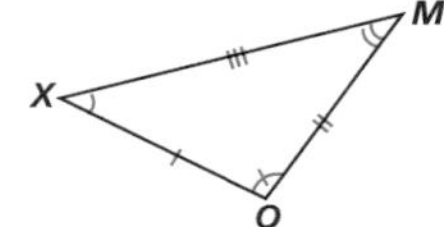

Corresponding Sides	Corresponding Angles
$\overline{BT} \cong \overline{MQ}$	$\angle R \cong \angle X$
$\overline{TR} \cong \overline{QX}$	$\angle T \cong \angle Q$
$\overline{BR} \cong \overline{MX}$	$\angle B \cong \angle M$

$\triangle$ BRT $\cong \triangle$ MXQ

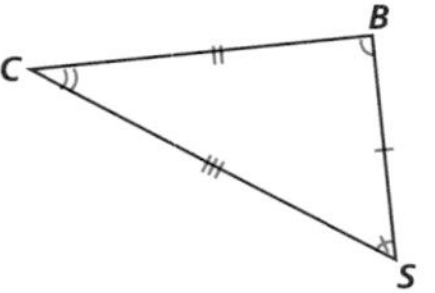

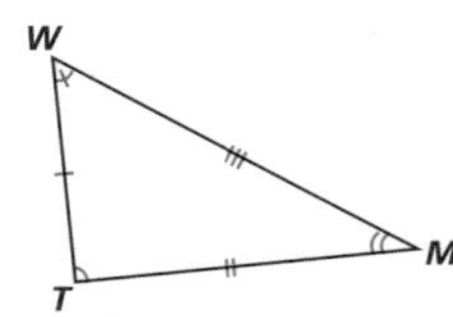

Corresponding Sides	Corresponding Angles
$\overline{BS} \cong \overline{TW}$	$\angle B \cong \angle T$
$\overline{BC} \cong \overline{TM}$	$\angle S \cong \angle W$
$\overline{CS} \cong \overline{MW}$	$\angle C \cong \angle M$

$\triangle$ BCS $\cong \triangle$ TMW

Name ____________________

Complete the sentence. Use the vocabulary and concepts from this lesson.

12. A parallelogram with four sides congruent and four right angles is a(n) ___square___.

13. In quadrilateral TERM, sides $\overline{TE}$ and $\overline{RM}$ are called ___opposite___ sides.

14. A quadrilateral with both pairs of opposite sides parallel is called a(n) ___parallelogram___.

15. A polygon with eight sides is called a(n) ___octagon___.

16. A decagon is a polygon with ___10___ sides and ___10___ angles.

17. If $\triangle TPQ \cong \triangle WIN$, then $\overline{TQ}$ corresponds to ___$\overline{WN}$___ and $\angle Q$ corresponds to ___$\angle N$___.

Problem Solving Reasoning

Solve. Polygons may vary. Check students' drawings.

18. Sketch two polygons whose corresponding sides are congruent, but corresponding angles are not congruent.

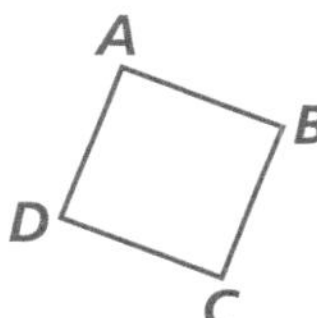

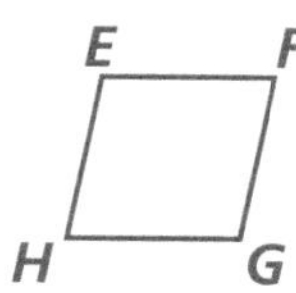

19. Sketch two polygons whose corresponding angles are congruent, but corresponding sides are not congruent.

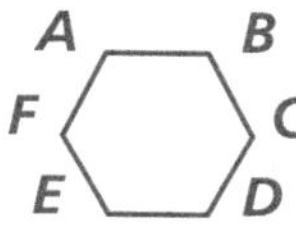

Quick Check

Construct a segment of the given length. Use the lengths below.

W ———— X   Y ———— Z

20. Twice WX

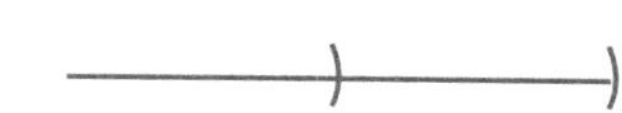

21. $WX + YZ$

Complete.

22. A ray that divides an angle into two congruent, adjacent angles is a(n) ___angle bisector___.

23. Two lines that meet at right angles are ___perpendicular___.

$\triangle DEF \cong \triangle JKL$. Name the corresponding parts.

24. $\angle D$ and ___$\angle J$___ **25.** $\overline{EF}$ and ___$\overline{KL}$___ **26.** $\overline{LJ}$ and ___$\overline{FD}$___

Work Space.

Item	Error Analysis
20–21	**Common Error:** They may not place segments end to end. **Reteaching** Reteach 52
22–26	**Common Error:** They may confuse angle bisectors and segment bisectors or use incorrect correspondence. **Reteaching** Reteach 53, 54

Closing the Lesson *Is every square a rhombus?* (Yes, because it is a parallelogram with four congruent sides.) *Are all rhombuses squares?* (No, because a rhombus need not have a right angle.)

Name ______________________

Circles and Central Angles

Guided Practice: Ex. 1, 8 & 11, pp. 202–203
Independent Practice: Complete pp. 202–203

A **circle** is the set of all points in a plane at a fixed distance, called the **radius,** from a fixed point called the **center.** A circle has no line segments for its sides, so it is not a polygon.

Circle Vocabulary

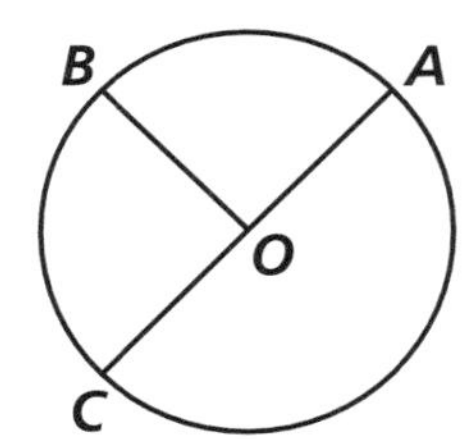

chord: a segment with its endpoints on a circle

diameter: a chord that passes through the center; $\overline{CA}$ is a diameter on this circle.

diameter = **2** · radius

central angle: an angle whose vertex is at the center of the circle; $\angle BOA$ is a central angle.

arc: a part of a circle; there are three types:
- semicircle, or half circle; $\overset{\frown}{CBA}$ is a semicircle
- minor arc; shorter than half a circle; $\overset{\frown}{AB}$ is a minor arc
- major arc; longer than half a circle; $\overset{\frown}{ACB}$ is a major arc

The measure of an arc equals the measure of the central angle that intersects its endpoints. You indicate an arc with this symbol: $\frown$

Central Angles and Arcs

Remember, there are **360°** in a circle.

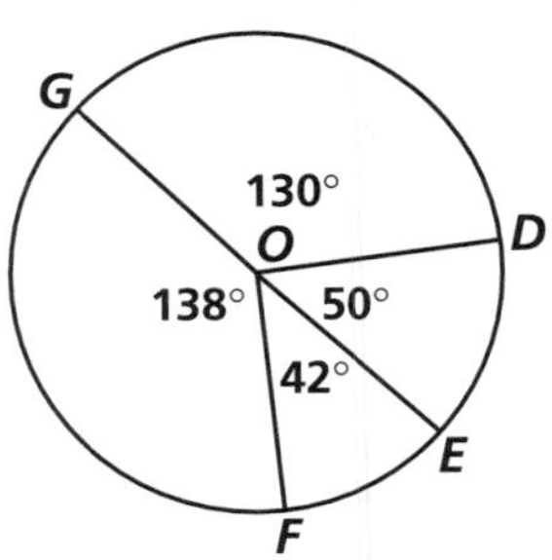

Center at *O*

$\angle DOE = 50°$, so $\overset{\frown}{DE} = 50°$

$\angle DOF = 92°$, so $\overset{\frown}{DF} = 92°$

$\angle GOE = 180°$, so $\overset{\frown}{GE} = 180°$

$\overset{\frown}{DE} = 50°$, so $\overset{\frown}{DGE} = 310°$

Identify the part of circle *O*. Use the vocabulary above.

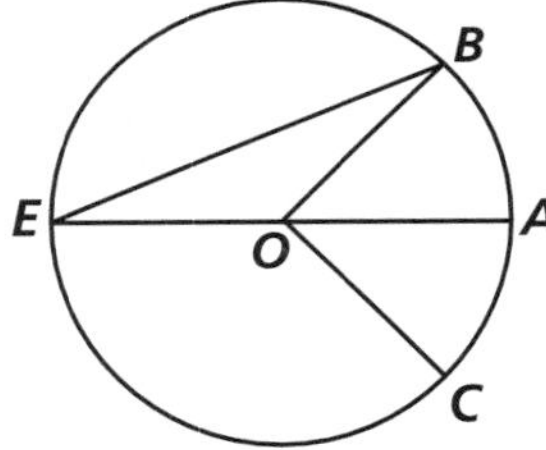

1. $\overline{AE}$: diameter

2. $\overline{OB}$: radius

3. $\overline{BE}$: chord

4. $\angle BOA$: central angle

5. $\overset{\frown}{EBA}$: semicircle

6. $\overset{\frown}{BC}$: minor arc

O: center

$\overset{\frown}{CEB}$: major arc

Write the measure of the arc or the angle.

7.

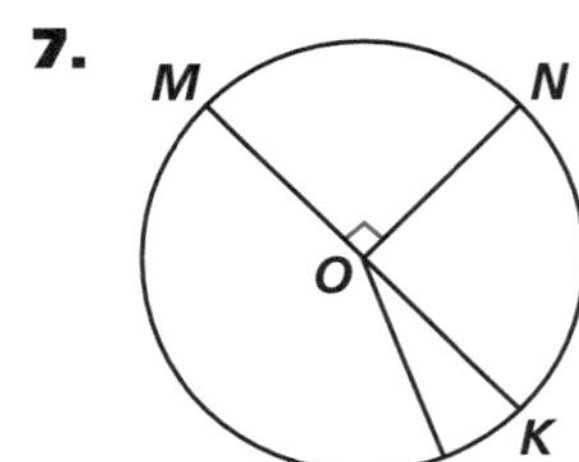

center at *O*
diameter $\overline{MK}$
$\angle LOK = 23°$
$\angle MON = 90°$

$\angle LOM =$ 157° $\overset{\frown}{LK} =$ 23°

$\overset{\frown}{LNM} =$ 203° $\overset{\frown}{MNK} =$ 180°

$\angle KON =$ 90° $\overset{\frown}{LM} =$ 157°

Check Understanding *If a central angle is 120°, what portion of the circle does it enclose?* ($\frac{1}{3}$)

Name ____________________

You know that a circle has **360°.** You can use this to find what fraction or percent of the whole circle each section represents when you know its central angle.

- What fraction of the circle does section AOB represent if $\angle AOB = 60°$?

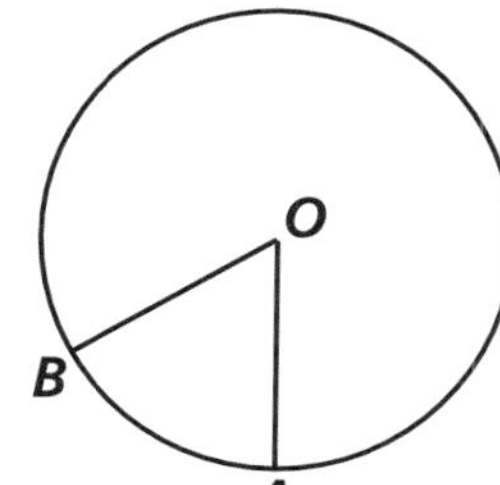

$\angle AOB = 60°$

$\frac{60}{360} = \frac{1}{6}$

So section AOB is $\frac{1}{6}$ of the circle.

- Find the measure of the central angle for the section that is $\frac{2}{5}$ of the circle.

$\frac{2}{5}$ of $360 = \frac{2}{5} \cdot \frac{360}{1}$

$= 144°$

- Find the measure of the central angle for the section that is **30%** of the circle.

30% of $360 = 0.30 \cdot 360$

$= 108°$

What part of a circle is the section with the given central angle?

8. 45° $\frac{1}{8}$ 135° $\frac{3}{8}$ 90° $\frac{1}{4}$

9. 20° $\frac{1}{18}$ 225° $\frac{5}{8}$ 15° $\frac{1}{24}$

10. 80° $\frac{2}{9}$ 200° $\frac{5}{9}$ 5° $\frac{1}{72}$

Write the measure of the central angle for the section that is the fractional part of a circle.

11. $\frac{1}{5}$ 72° $\frac{1}{12}$ 30° $\frac{3}{8}$ 135°

12. 25% 90°   10% 36°   40% 144°

13. $\frac{2}{3}$ 240°   60% 216°   75% 270°

Test Prep ★ Mixed Review

14 **How many diagonals are there in an octagon?** B; Obj. 7E

A 15   **C** 30

B 20   **D** 40

15 **Which description best refers to a pair of congruent polygons?** H; Obj. 7E

F They have three or more sides.

G Corresponding angles are congruent.

H Corresponding angles are congruent and corresponding sides are congruent.

J Corresponding sides are congruent.

Closing the Lesson *If a central angle of a section is 80°, what portion of the circle does it enclose?* ($\frac{80°}{360°} = \frac{2}{9}$)

Name ______________________

Circle Graphs

Guided Practice: Ex. 1 & 6, p. 204; Ex. 12, p. 206
Independent Practice: Complete pp. 204–206

The graph at the right is a **circle graph.** A circle graph can be used to represent parts of a whole. The parts of the circle graph are labeled as fractions, decimals, or percents. The entire circle represents **1** whole or **100%.**

Tran received **$300** for his birthday. The graph shows how he used his birthday money.

CD player:	**40%** of **$300** = **0.40 · $300,** or **$120**	
Savings:	**30%** of **$300** = **0.30 · $300,** or **$ 90**	
Sneakers:	**20%** of **$300** = **0.20 · $300,** or **$ 60**	
Sweater:	**10%** of **$300** = **0.10 · $300,** or **$ 30**	
Totals:	**100%**	**$300**

Use the circle graphs to answer the questions.

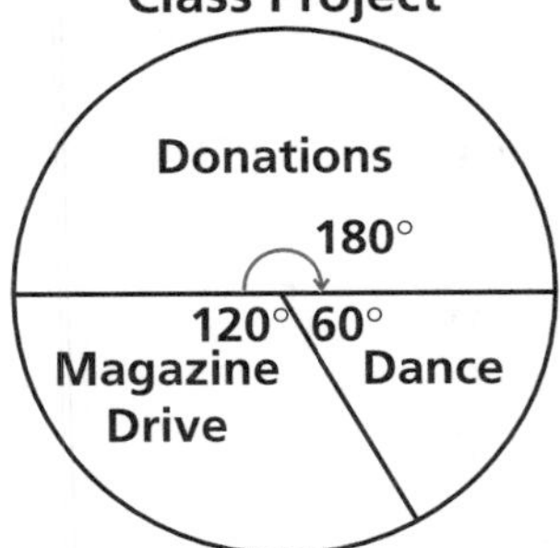

1. What percent of the money was raised by donations? 50% By the magazine drive? $33\frac{1}{3}\%$

By the school dance? $16\frac{2}{3}\%$

2. If the total money raised was **$900**, how much was raised by donations? $450 Magazine Drive? $300 Dance? $150

3. What category provided the least amount of money? Dance

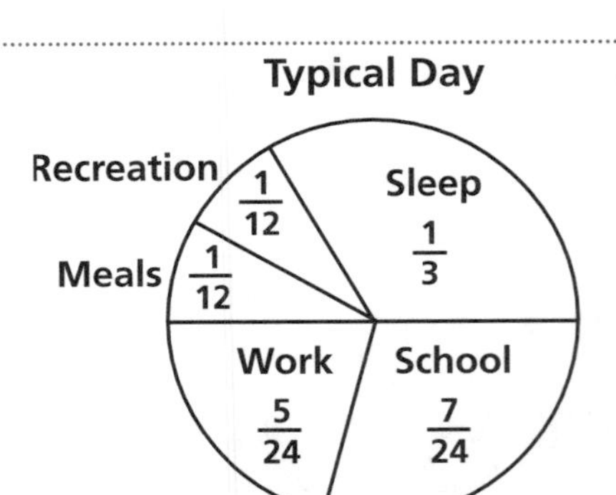

4. What category accounts for the greatest amount of time? Sleep

5. How many hours does each activity take?

Sleep 8 School 7 Work 5

Recreation 2 Meals 2

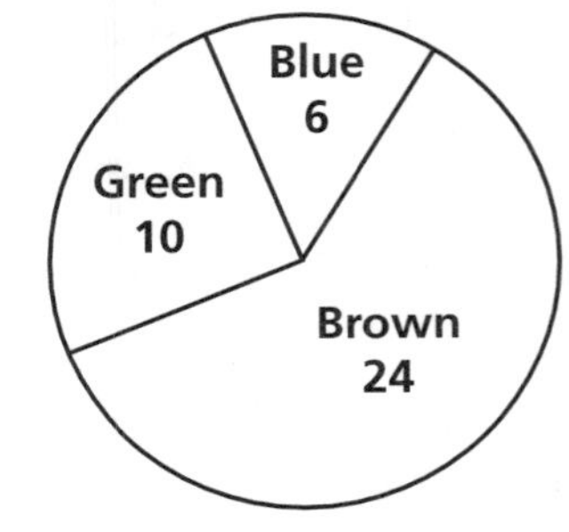

6. Which eye color is the most common? Brown

7. How many students were surveyed? 40

8. What percent have blue eyes? 15%

Check Understanding *If one portion of a circle graph is 15%, what is the size of the central angle? (54°) If a central angle is 120°, what fraction of the total circle does it enclose?* $(\frac{1}{3})$

Name ______________________________

To construct a circle graph, use what you know about central angles. You will need a protractor to draw angles accurately.

Complete the table and the circle graph. Use the central angle measures to construct each angle in the graph. Label each part with the correct category.

9. The family's income is **$48,000** a year. How much is spent in each category? What is the central angle for each category? Complete the circle graph.

Category	Percent	Expense	Central Angle
Food	25%	25% of $48,000 is $12,000.	25% of 360° is 90°.
Housing	25%	$12,000	90°
Insurance	15%	$7,200	54°
Recreation	10%	$4,800	36°
Savings	5%	$2,400	18°
Clothing	15%	$7,200	54°
Miscellaneous	5%	$2,400	18°

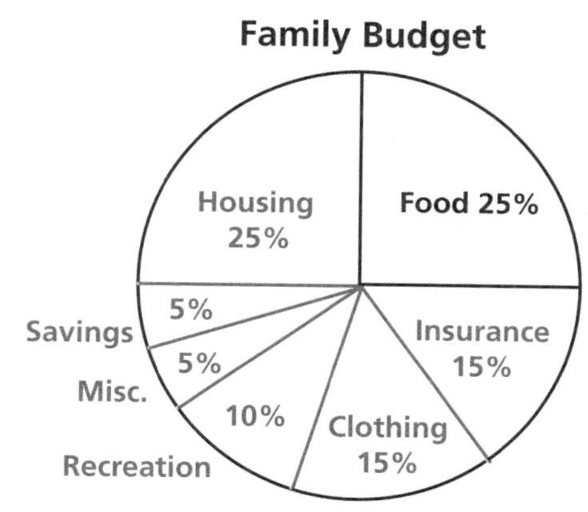

10. Find the sum of the following columns.

Percent 100% Expense $48,000 Central Angle 360°

11. The town of Middlefield has a budget of **$3,000,000.** It spends the money as shown in the table. What fraction of the budget was each category? What is the central angle for each category? Complete the circle graph.

Category	Amount	Fraction	Central Angle
Education	$1,000,000	$\frac{1,000,000}{3,000,000} = \frac{1}{3}$	$\frac{1}{3}$ of 360° = 120°
Highways	$750,000	$\frac{1}{4}$	90°
Health	$500,000	$\frac{1}{6}$	60°
Library Renovations	$375,000	$\frac{1}{8}$	45°
Miscellaneous	$375,000	$\frac{1}{8}$	45°

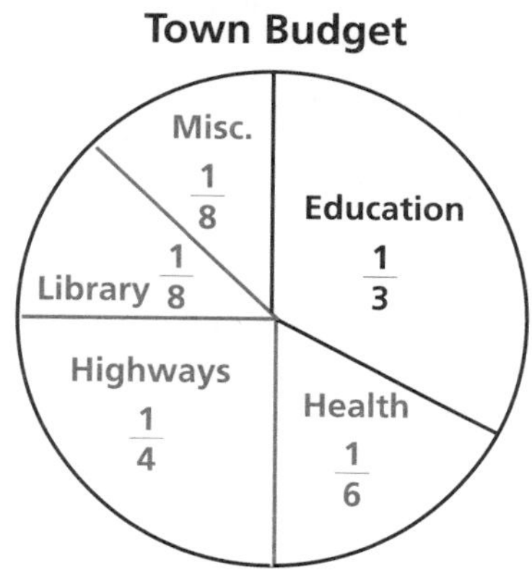

Use the circle graphs to answer the questions.

12. How many students selected pizza as their favorite meal? 80

13. How many students selected fish or hamburgers as their favorite meal? 58

14. What is the measure of the central angle for tacos?

100.8°

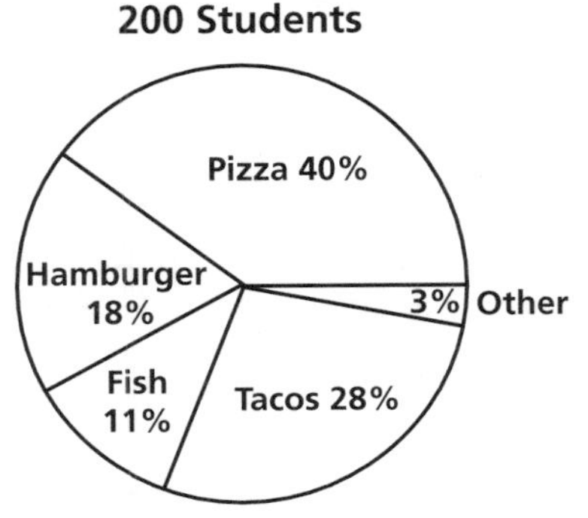

15. Approximate the number of students for each category.

no television 2 **0.5–2** hours 8

2.5–4 hours 10 more than **4** hours 30

16. What is the central angle for each category?

no television 14.4° **0.5–2** hours 57.6°

2.5–4 hours 72° more than **4** hours 216°

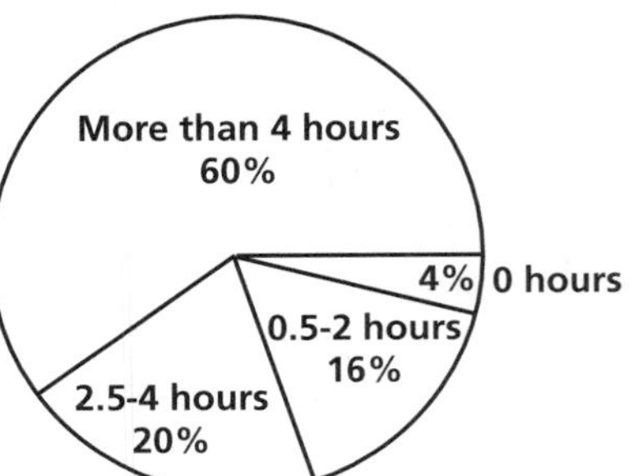

Problem Solving Reasoning Solve.

17. Which part of the circle corresponds to the results of **50** responses?

region D

300 people are surveyed.

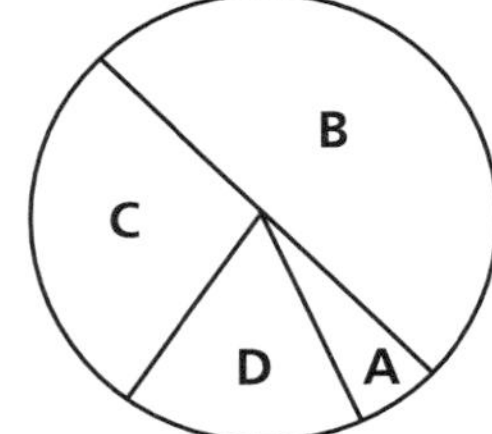

18. Part B represents approximately how many responses?

150 responses

Test Prep ★ Mixed Review

19 **What is the measure of ∠*AOB*?**
A; Obj. 7F

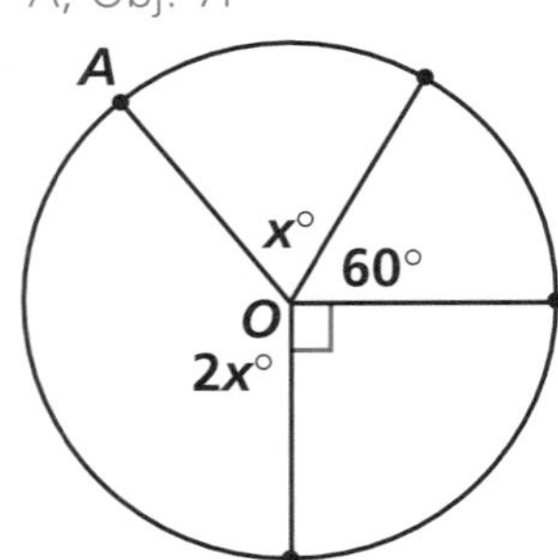

A 140°
B 120°
C 100°
D 70°

20 **Enid wants to represent 52% on her circle graph. Which number best represents the measure of the central angle she should make?** H; Obj. 7E

F 52°
G 104°
H 187°
J 308°

Closing the Lesson *If a central angle of a section is 108°, how would you find what percent of the circle is enclosed in that section?* (Possible answer: Divide 108° by 360°, obtaining 0.3. Now, change that to a percent by multiplying by 100 and writing the percent sign.)

Name ____________________________________

Guided Practice: Complete table for prism 1 (ex. 1) and pyramid 1 (ex. 2), pp. 207–208
Independent Practice: Complete pp. 207–208

The space figures shown have polygonal regions as sides. They are called **polyhedrons. Prisms** and **pyramids** are two types of polyhedrons.

- A prism has two parallel faces, called **bases.** The other faces are parallelograms.
- A pyramid has one base. The other faces are triangles. Prisms and pyramids are named for the shape of their bases.

The polygonal regions that are the sides of a polyhedron are its **faces.** The line segments where the faces meet are its **edges.** Each point where the edges meet is a **vertex.**

Prisms

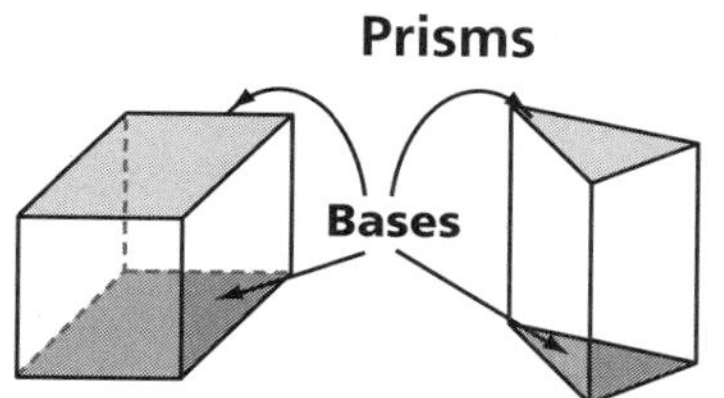

Pyramids

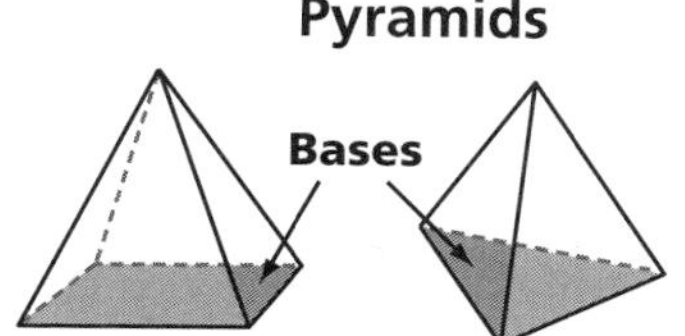

Other Polyhedrons

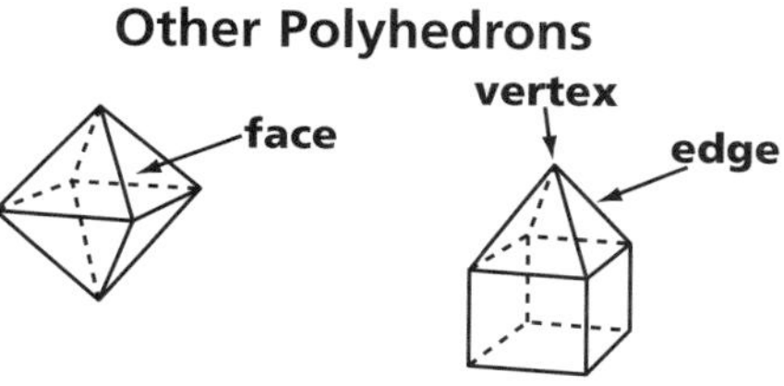

Complete the table. Count the number of faces, vertices, and edges.

1.

	Prism 1	Prism 2	Prism 3	Prism 4
				A prism whose base is an *n*-gon
Faces	6	5	8	$n + 2$
Vertices	8	6	12	$2n$
Edges	12	9	18	$3n$
Name	Rectangular Prism	Triangular Prism	Hexagonal Prism	

2.

	Pyramid 1	Pyramid 2	Pyramid 3	Pyramid 4
				A pyramid whose base is an *n*-gon
Faces	5	4	6	$n + 1$
Vertices	5	4	6	$n + 1$
Edges	8	6	10	$2n$
Name	Rectangular Pyramid	Triangular Pyramid	Pentagonal Pyramid	

Check Understanding *What is a polyhedron?* (a three dimensional figure whose sides are polygonal regions)

A cube is a prism that has six faces that are all congruent squares. You can use the lines formed by the edges of a cube to investigate relationships between two lines in space.

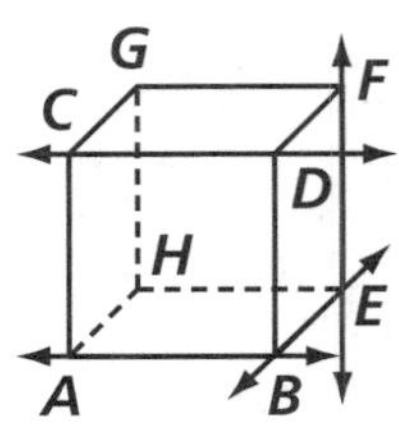

Skew lines are non-coplanar lines, which means they do not intersect.

You know that a polygon has diagonals. Some polyhedrons also have diagonals. It is a segment between two vertices that are not in the same face. For example, a cube has four diagonals.

Lines in space

$\overleftrightarrow{AB}$ and $\overleftrightarrow{CD}$ are parallel.

$\overleftrightarrow{AB}$ and $\overleftrightarrow{BE}$ are perpendicular.

$\overleftrightarrow{AB}$ and $\overleftrightarrow{FE}$ are skew.

Diagonals

$\overline{AF}$ $\overline{CE}$

$\overline{BG}$ $\overline{DH}$

Identify the relationship between the pair of lines.

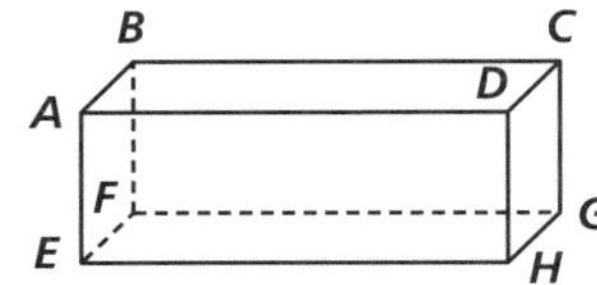

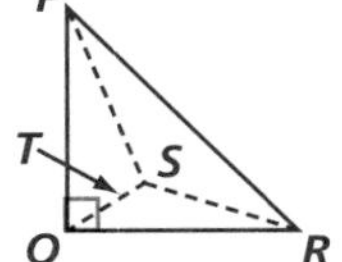

3. $\overleftrightarrow{BC}$ and $\overleftrightarrow{AB}$ perpendicular $\overleftrightarrow{BC}$ and $\overleftrightarrow{EH}$ parallel $\overleftrightarrow{BC}$ and $\overleftrightarrow{GH}$ skew

4. $\overleftrightarrow{PQ}$ and $\overleftrightarrow{QR}$ perpendicular $\overleftrightarrow{PQ}$ and $\overleftrightarrow{SR}$ skew $\overleftrightarrow{PQ}$ and $\overleftrightarrow{QS}$ perpendicular

5. Name two diagonals in the rectangular prism. Possible answer: $\overline{BH}$ and $\overline{AG}$

Problem Solving Reasoning Solve.

6. Compare the number of faces plus the number of vertices to the number of edges for each polyhedron in the tables for exercises 1 and 2. What pattern can you find?

vertices + faces = edges + 2

7. Show that the relationship you found in exercise 6 is true for any pyramid. (Hint: Use an *n*-gon as the base of the pyramid.)

$(n + 1) + (n + 1) = 2n + 2$ (edges + 2)

Quick Check

Use Circle *O* at the right. *O* is the center of the circle.

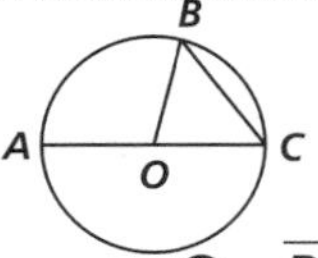

8. $\overline{OC}$ is a radius.

9. $\overline{BC}$ is a chord.

10. $\overset{\frown}{BC}$ is a minor arc.

11. $\angle BOC$ is a central angle.

You need to make a circle graph to show how people spend their time each day. You know that sleeping is 8 hours, school is 6 hours, and other activities is 10 hours. What is the measure of the central angle for each category?

12. Sleeping 120° **13.** School 90° **14.** Other 150°

Suppose you have a pentagonal prism. Find how many of each item it has.

15. Edges 15 **16.** Bases 2 **17.** Diagonals 10

Work Space.

Item	Error Analysis
8–14	**Common Error** Students may confuse radius and diameter and may write central angles as percents. **Reteaching** Reteach 55 and 56
15–17	**Common Error** Students may confuse prisms and pyramids. **Reteaching** Reteach 57

Closing the Lesson *What are some examples of where polyhedrons are used in everyday life?* (Possible answer: Most boxes are prisms.)

Name ______________________________

Guided Practice: 1 & 2, p. 209
Independent Practice: Complete p. 210

Problem Solving Application: Use a Diagram

You already know how to use proportions and measuring tools like rulers and protractors to interpret diagrams. You also know how to use construction tools to copy figures.

Sometimes you need to decide what kind of tool to use in drawing diagrams for problems.

Tips to Remember:

1. Understand 2. Decide 3. Solve 4. Look back

- Ask yourself: What do I know? What do I need to find?
- What kind of diagram can you use? Do you need to use a construction to solve a problem, or would an accurate drawing or rough sketch be sufficient?
- Think about strategies you have learned, and use them to help you solve a problem.

The scale drawing at the right shows a hexagonal frame and **3** pieces of cord.

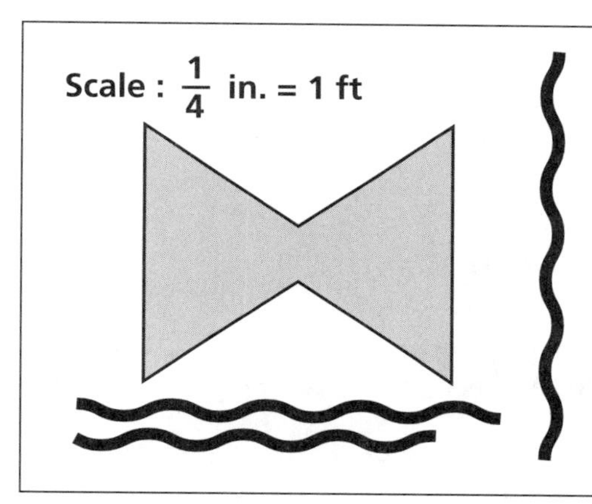

1. Does measuring the lengths answer the question "Is there enough cord to go around the outside of the frame?"

Think: What is the length of the perimeter? Of the cord?

about $5\frac{5}{8}$ in.; about $5\frac{1}{2}$ in.

Answer: The lengths are too close to be sure.

2. Draw two lines. Mark off lengths, end to end, of the sides of the polygon on one. Mark off lengths of the cord, end to end, on the other. Is there enough cord to go around the frame?

Think: What do the lengths of constructed segments represent?

The perimeter of the frame and the length of the cords.

Answer: No.

Check Understanding *What is the altitude or height of a triangle?* (It is a line drawn from the opposite vertex perpendicular to the side chosen as the base.) *How does the picture help you solve the problem?* (Possible answer: It helps you visualize relationships that you might not recognize without the picture.)

Use a diagram to help you solve each problem.

3. Sarah hiked **3** miles north, **5** miles east, **3** miles south, and **2** miles west. How far is she from her starting point? (Do you need to use measuring or construction tools? Is a sketch enough?)

3 miles

4. Matthew walked **2** miles north, turned right, walked **2** miles, turned right, walked **1** mile, turned right, walked **3** miles, turned right, walked **3** miles, turned right, and walked **1** mile. How far and in what direction is he from his starting point?

4 miles north

5. You want to tile a **4** foot by **6** foot region with one foot square tiles. How many tiles will you need?

24 tiles

6. You want to tile a **4** foot by **6** foot region with six inch square tiles. How many tiles will you need?

96 tiles

7. A transversal intersects three parallel lines. How many pairs of corresponding angles are formed?

12 pairs

8. Two streets meet at point *P*. One of the streets is shown. The streets meet at an angle of **135°**. How can you use just a compass and straightedge to draw the other street? Try it.

P

Construct perpendicular lines through point *P*.

Bisect one 90° angle. 90° + 45° = 135°

Extend Your Thinking

9. If you used two foot square tiles to cover a **4** foot by **6** foot rectangular region, how many tiles would you need? How is this answer related to the answer for problem **5**? Explain.

6 tiles; You need $\frac{1}{4}$ as many tiles; The tiles are double in length, but 4 times larger in area.

10. Explain your method for solving problem **6.** Did you need to draw all of the tiles, or could you use some other method?

Explanations will vary.

11. For which exercises did a sketch make a reasonably accurate diagram?

Possible answers: problems 3, 4, 5, and 7

12. Would the construction in problem 8 look the same for everyone in the class?

Possible answer: No; Some students' streets would go from NE to SW, whereas others would go from NW to SE.

Closing the Lesson *What kinds of diagrams and tools can you use to solve problems?* (Possible answers: construction tools (straightedge and compass), rulers, protractors, number lines, grid paper, lined paper)

Name ______________________

Unit 7 Review

Use the figure to complete the statement or answer the question.

1. Two lines that contain *E* are $\overleftrightarrow{DF}$, $\overleftrightarrow{EB}$

2. A pair of parallel lines are $\overleftrightarrow{AC}$ and $\overleftrightarrow{DF}$

3. A pair of perpendicular lines are $\overleftrightarrow{AC}$ (also $\overleftrightarrow{DF}$ and $\overleftrightarrow{BF}$), $\overleftrightarrow{BF}$

4. Name an acute angle. Possible answer: $\angle BEF$

5. Name an obtuse angle. $\angle DEB$

6. Name a right angle. $\angle BFE$

7. Name two rays with endpoint *F*. $\overrightarrow{FB}$, $\overrightarrow{FD}$

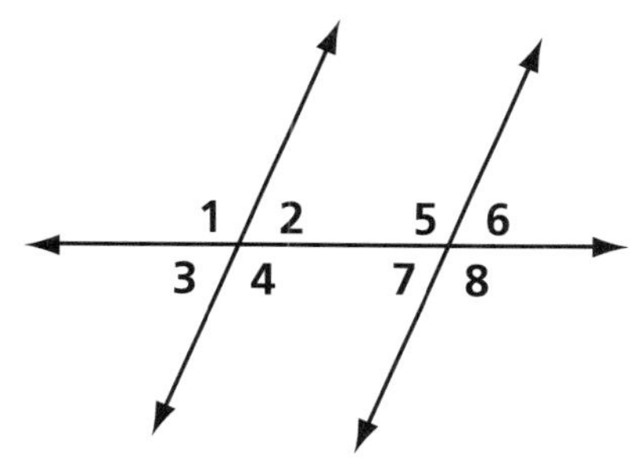

8. An angle vertical to $\angle 1$ is $\angle 4$.

9. An angle corresponding to $\angle 1$ is $\angle 5$.

10. An angle supplementary to $\angle 1$ is $\angle 2$ or $\angle 3$.

11. If $\angle 1 = 108°$, what other angle(s) measure $108°$?

$\angle 4$, $\angle 5$, and $\angle 8$

Write the measure of the angle if $\angle 1 = 108°$.

12. $\angle 3 =$ 72° **13.** $\angle 4 =$ 108° **14.** $\angle 5 =$ 108°

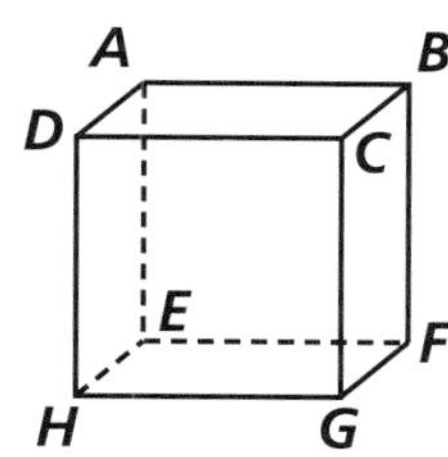

15. Name a line parallel to $\overleftrightarrow{AB}$. $\overleftrightarrow{DC}$, $\overleftrightarrow{GH}$, or $\overleftrightarrow{EF}$

16. Name a plane that contains $\overleftrightarrow{AB}$. *ABCD*, *ABFE*, or *ABGH*

17. Name a line perpendicular to $\overleftrightarrow{AB}$. $\overleftrightarrow{AD}$, $\overleftrightarrow{EA}$, $\overleftrightarrow{CB}$, or $\overleftrightarrow{FB}$

18. Name a line skew to $\overleftrightarrow{AB}$. $\overleftrightarrow{FG}$ or $\overleftrightarrow{EH}$

19. This polyhedron has 6 faces, 8 vertices, and 12 edges.

20. Name the four diagonals of the polyhedron.

$\overline{AG}$, $\overline{BH}$, $\overline{CE}$, and $\overline{DF}$

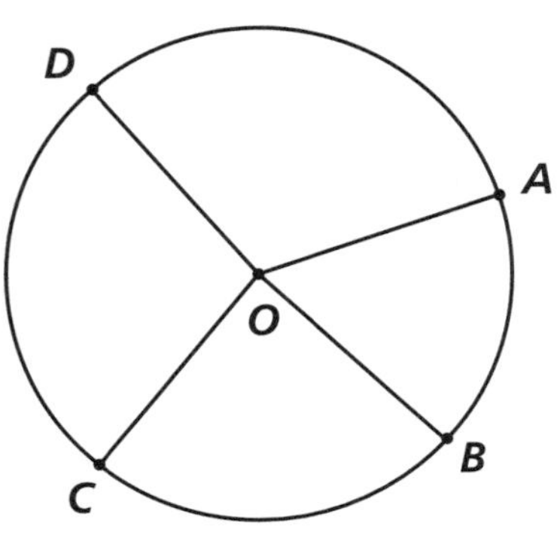

O is the center of the circle.

21. Name a radius. $\overline{AO}$, $\overline{BO}$, $\overline{CO}$, or $\overline{DO}$

22. Name a minor arc. $\overset{\frown}{AB}$, $\overset{\frown}{AC}$, $\overset{\frown}{DB}$, or $\overset{\frown}{DC}$

23. Name a major arc. Possible answer: $\overset{\frown}{ADC}$

24. Write the measure of the arc if $\angle AOB = 75°$.

$\overset{\frown}{AB}$ = 75° $\overset{\frown}{AD}$ = 105°

25. What fractional part of the circle does $\angle AOB$ represent? $\frac{5}{24}$

What percent is this? about 20%

Education of Teachers

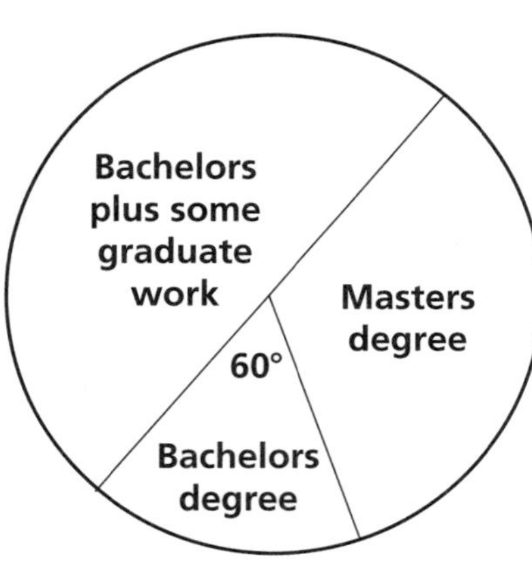

The circle graph shows the amount of education that the 300 teachers in one school district have.

26. How many teachers have a masters degree?

100 teachers

27. What percent of the teachers is this? $33\frac{1}{3}$

28. The number of teachers that have a bachelors degree plus some graduate work is **150.** What percent is this?

50%

29. What is the measure of the angle for the section "Bachelors degree plus some graduate work"?

180°

Write another name for the figure.

30. A parallelogram with four right angles square or rectangle

31. A quadrilateral with both pairs of opposite sides parallel parallelogram

32. A rectangular prism whose faces are congruent squares cube

Measure the angle to the nearest degree. Use a protractor.

33. 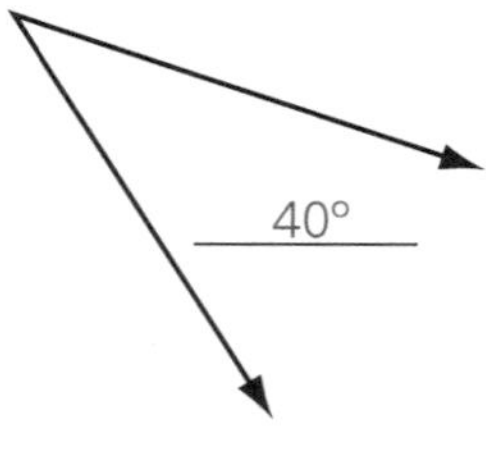 40°

34. 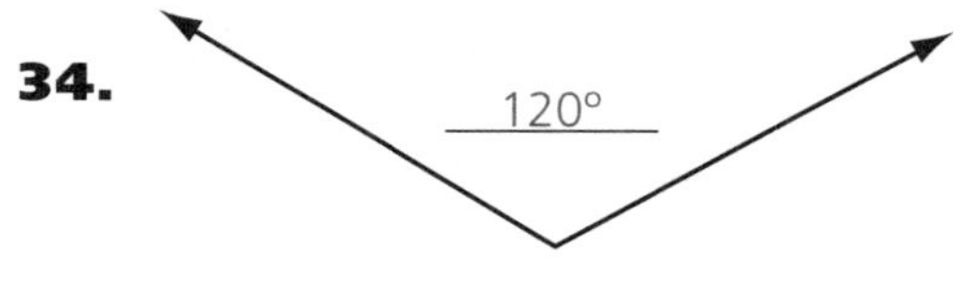 120°

35. 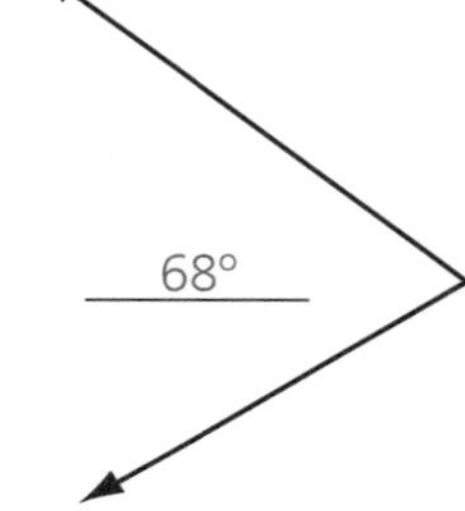 68°

Name ______________________

Answer the question. $\triangle ABC \cong \triangle PQR$.

36. Name the congruent sides and angles. $\overline{AB} \cong \overline{PQ}$, $\overline{BC} \cong \overline{QR}$, and $\overline{AC} \cong \overline{PR}$; $\angle A \cong \angle P$, $\angle B \cong \angle Q$, and $\angle C \cong \angle R$

Sketch the figure.

37. A right isosceles triangle

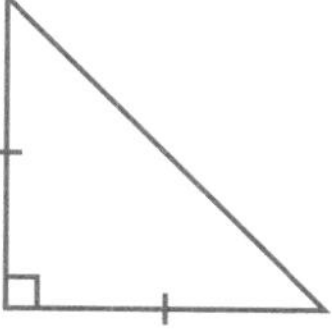

38. An obtuse scalene triangle

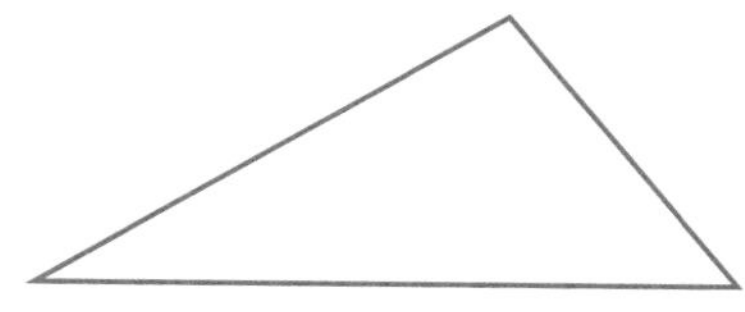

39. Two intersecting planes

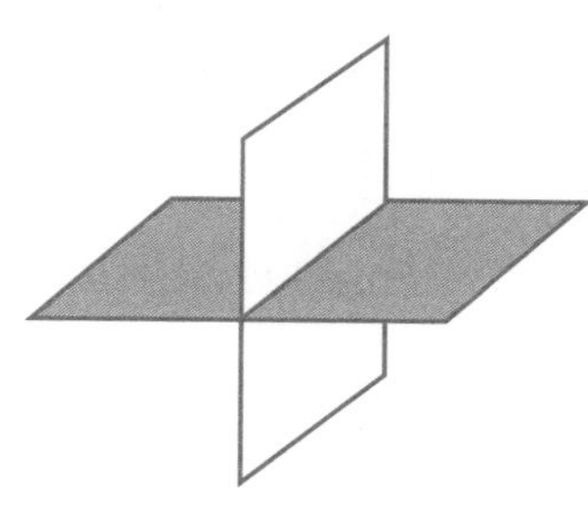

Write the measure of the angle.

40.

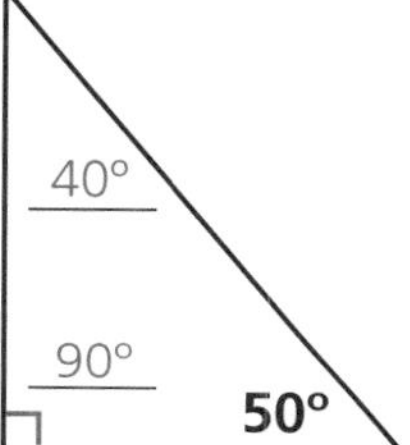

41.

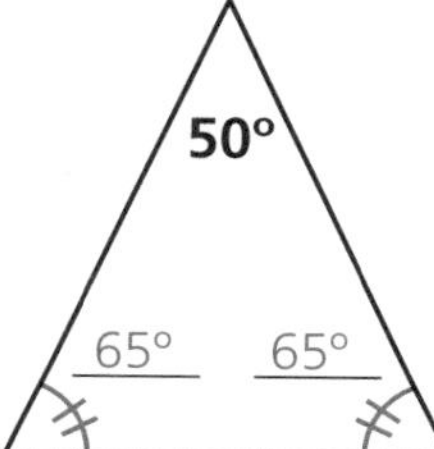

42. l_1 is parallel to l_2.

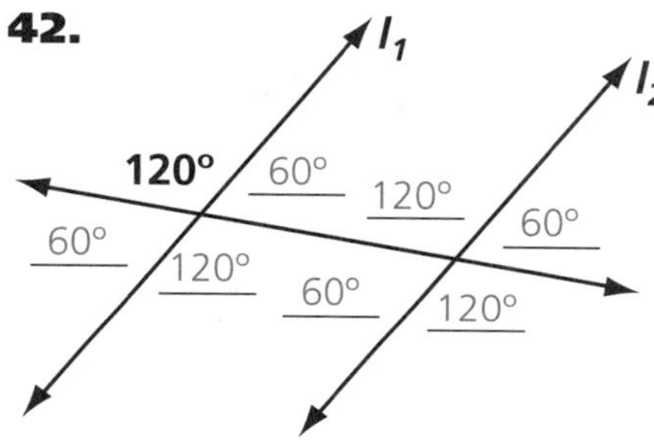

Construct the figure. Use a straightedge and compass.

43. An angle congruent to $\angle ABC$

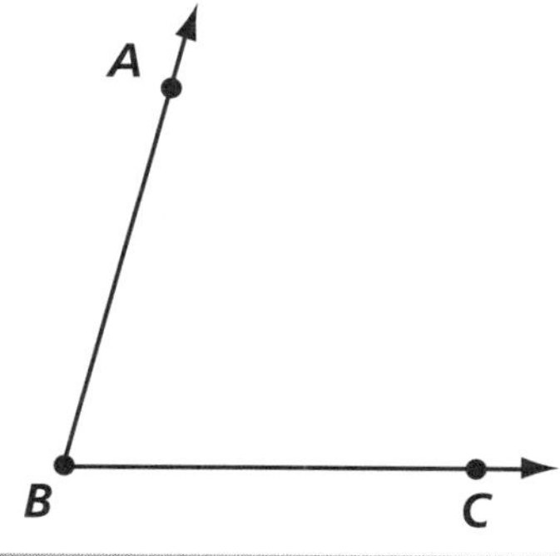

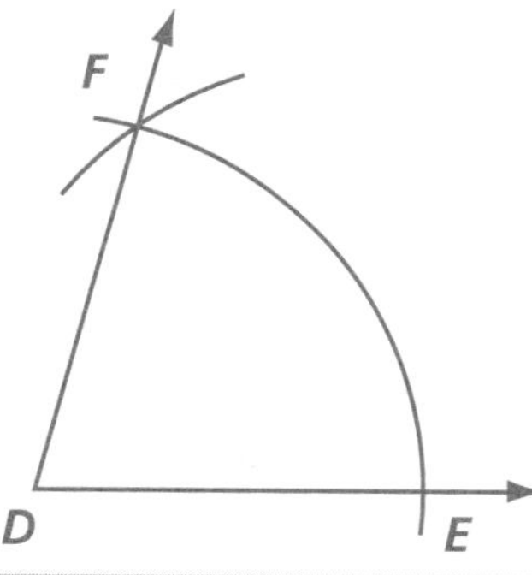

44. The midpoint of $\overline{DE}$

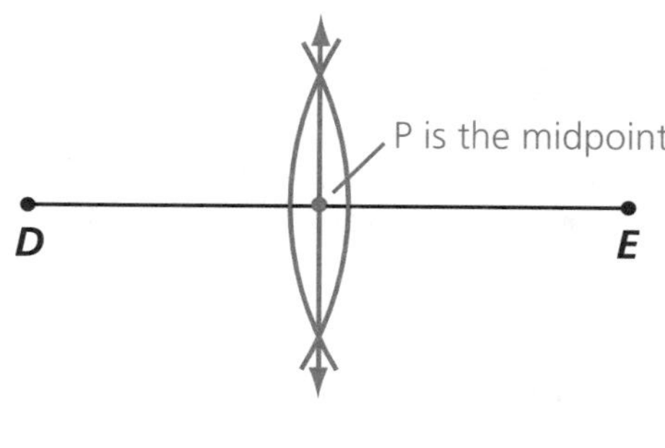

Solve.

45. What is the ones digit of 4^{15} when it is written in standard form? 4

46. From school, Rosita walks two blocks north, then **1** block west to her friend's house. Next, she walks with her friend **3** blocks east and **2** blocks north to the mall. They both walk back to her house, **4** blocks south and **2** blocks east of the mall. How many blocks and in which direction does Rosita walk each morning from her home to school? 4 blocks west

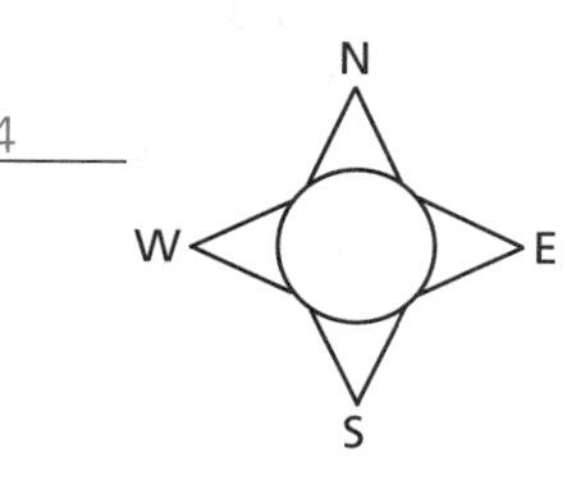

Name ____________________

Cumulative Review
★ Test Prep

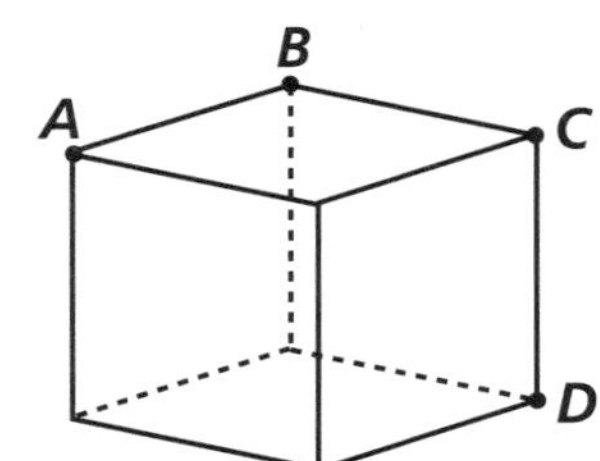

1 **Which of the statements is true?** D; Obj. 7A

A *A* and *C* are collinear with *B*.

B $AB + BC = AC$

C *A*, *B*, *C*, and *D* are coplanar.

D *CD* represents the distance from *C* to *D*.

2 **What other angle measures 30°?** H; Obj. 7C

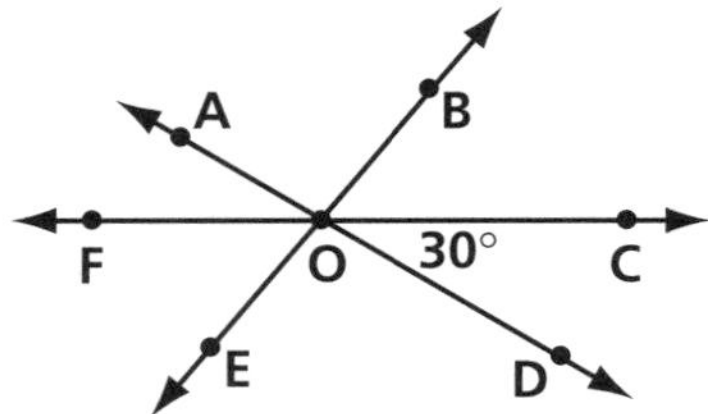

F $\angle BOC$ **H** $\angle AOF$

G $\angle EOF$ **J** $\angle EOD$

3 **Mark's bank gives him 3% interest on his $700 investment. The interest is compounded every quarter. After one year, what will be the value of his investment?** C; Obj. 5D

A $703.00 **C** $721.24

B $721.00 **D** $787.86

4 **A compact car uses 2.5 gallons of gas to go 90 miles. At that rate, about how many gallons of gas will be needed for a trip of 300 miles?** H; Obj. 4B

F less than 6 **H** between 8 and 9

G exactly 8 **J** more than 10

5 **If lines *AB* and *CD* are parallel, how many angles altogether in the diagram have a measure of 50°?** A; Obj. 7C

A four **C** two

B three **D** one

6 **If Annie buys a $73 pair of shoes that have been marked down 15%, how much cash does she save?** F; Obj. 5C

F $10.95 **H** $27

G $15 **J** $62.05

7 **Which speed is equivalent to 60 miles per hour?** A; Obj. 3B

A 5,280 feet per minute

B 1,760 feet per minute

C 88 feet per minute

D 30 feet per minute

8 **Of the 120 Grade 7 students in Wilson Middle School, 45% are boys. How many boys are in Grade 7?** G; Obj. 5A

F 45

G 54

H 55

J 66

UNIT 8 • TABLE OF CONTENTS

Integers and Rational Numbers

We will be using this vocabulary:

integer any number in the set . . . , $^-3$, $^-2$, $^-1$, 0, 1, 2, 3, . . .

positive integer an integer that is greater than **0**; for example **1, 2, 3,** . . .

negative integer an integer that is less than **0**; for example . . . , $^-3$, $^-2$, $^-1$

opposites two numbers whose sum is **0**; for example, $^-2$ and **2** are opposites since $^-2 + 2 = 0$

absolute value the distance of a number from **0** on the number line, regardless of direction; for example $|3| = 3$ and $|^-5| = 5$

rational number a number that can be expressed as the quotient of two integers; for example, $^-1.6 = \frac{^-16}{10}$ and $3 = \frac{^-3}{^-1}$

Dear Family,

During the next few weeks, our math class will be using addition, subtraction, multiplication, and division of positive and negative numbers to solve problems. This includes using the number line to locate, add, and subtract positive and negative numbers. You can expect to see homework that provides practice with these skills. Here is a sample you may want to keep handy to give help if needed.

Locating Integers and Rational Numbers

This number line shows some integers and rational numbers. Negative numbers are less than **0**. Positive numbers are greater than **0**. The number **0** is neither positive nor negative.

Negative Direction: numbers decrease

Positive Direction: numbers increase

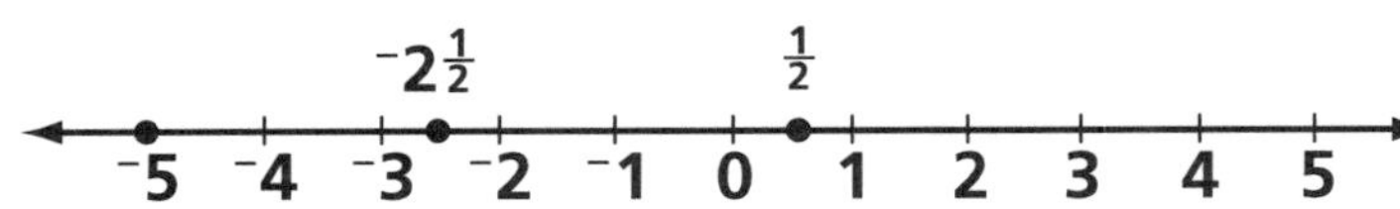

Read $^-$**5** as *negative* **5**.

Read $\frac{1}{2}$ as *positive one half*.

Notice that as you move right, you move in the positive direction. As you move left, you move in the negative direction.

During this unit, students will continue to learn new techniques related to problem solving and will continue to practice basic skills with fractions, decimals, and integers.

Sincerely,

Name ______________________________

Integers

Guided Practice: Ex. 1, 3, 8, 12, 16, 22 & 26, pp. 217–220
Independent Practice: Complete pp. 217–220

Integers are the set of numbers including positive whole numbers, negative whole numbers, and zero. The integers greater than **0** are called **positive integers.** They are sometimes written using a positive sign. For example, the number positive **5** is written as **⁺5** or **5.**

The integers less than **0** are called **negative integers.** They are always written with a negative sign. For example, the number negative **4** is written **⁻4.**

The integer **0** is neither positive nor negative. The number line below is labeled with integers.

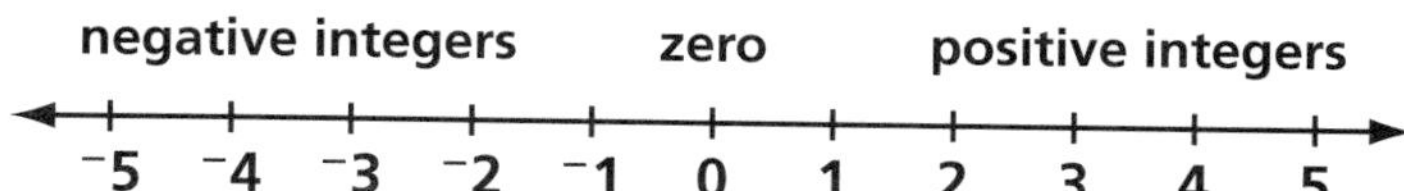

Pairs of integers that are the same distance from **0** on the number line are called **opposites.** The numbers **⁻3** and **3** are opposites because each integer is **3** units from **0.** The opposite of **6** is **⁻6.** The opposite of **⁻10** is **10.** The integer **0** is its own opposite.

Write the number in the set that is not an integer.

1. ⁻5, $\frac{1}{2}$, 8, ⁻2 $\frac{1}{2}$ 9, ⁻1, 0.25, 30 0.25

2. 0.175, ⁻12, 15, ⁻3, 0 0.175   ⁻4, 0, 17, $\frac{5}{8}$, ⁻12 $\frac{5}{8}$

Write the opposite of the integer.

3. 7 ⁻7   ⁻8 ⁺8 or 8   ⁻2 2   12 ⁻12

4. 0 0   23 ⁻23   ⁻67 67   45 ⁻45

Complete each statement by writing *positive* or *negative*.

5. The opposite of a negative number is positive.

6. The opposite of the opposite of a negative number is negative.

7. Two units to the right of **⁻3** is negative and **2** units to the left of the opposite of **⁻3** is positive.

Check Understanding *For what type of integer would its opposite be positive?* (The opposite of a negative integer is positive.) *For what type of integer would its absolute value be negative?* (None. The absolute value of an integer is always greater than or equal to zero.)

The **absolute value** of an integer is the distance it is from zero on the number line, regardless of whether the integer is to the left or to the right of **0.**

The absolute value of **4** (written as $|4|$) is **4,** since **4** is **4** units to the right of **0.**

4 units

$^-1$ 0 1 2 3 4

The absolute value of $^-3$ (written as $|^-3|$) is **3,** since $^-3$ is **3** units to the left of **0.**

3 units

$^-4$ $^-3$ $^-2$ $^-1$ 0 1

Opposite integers have the same absolute value, since both integers are the same distance from **0** but in opposite directions. For example, $^-5$ and $^+5$ both have an absolute value of **5.**

Write the absolute value of the integer.

8.	8 __8__	$^-11$ __11__	$^-27$ __27__	36 __36__
9.	$^-52$ __52__	0 __0__	73 __73__	$^-49$ __49__

Evaluate.

10.	$|^-5|$ __5__	$|12|$ __12__	$|^-86|$ __86__	$|94|$ __94__
11.	$|33|$ __33__	$|^-75|$ __75__	$|^-67|$ __67__	$|58|$ __58__

The number line shows how integers are ordered and helps you compare them.

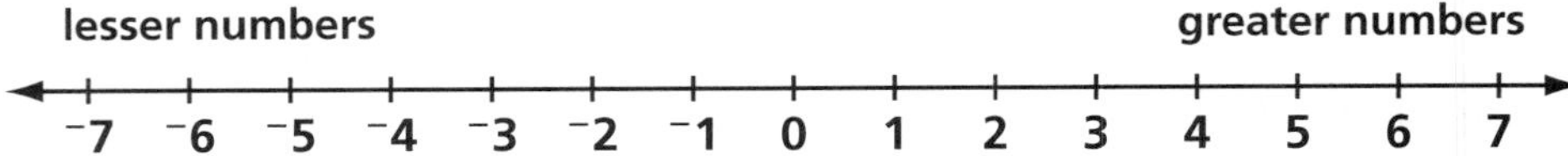

Notice that in a pair of numbers, the number that is farther to the left is the lesser number. The number that is farther to the right is the greater number.

$^-7 < {}^-2$ $5 > 2$

Compare. Write <, >, or =.

12.	$^-2$ (<) 2	$|^-3|$ (=) 3	7 (>) 5	4 (<) 6
13.	$|^-3|$ (>) $|2|$	$^-14$ (<) $^-12$	8 (>) 7	$^-12$ (<) 12
14.	3 (<) 5	$^-2$ (>) $^-3$	1 (>) 0	$|^-4|$ (<) $|^-5|$
15.	$|^-5|$ (=) $|5|$	0 (>) $^-5$	0 (<) 5	$|0|$ (<) $|5|$

Name ______________________________

On each number line, place a point for the integer or integers described.

16. the integers that have an absolute value of **4**

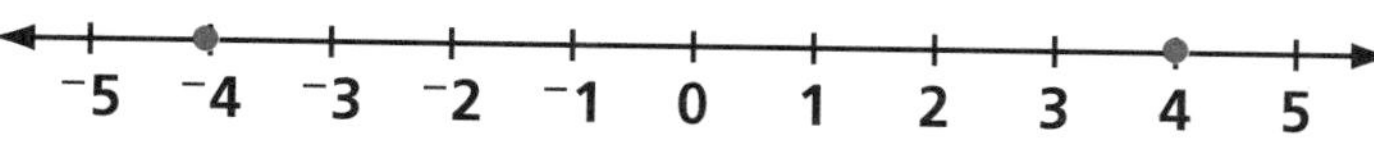

17. the integer that is **2** units to the right of $^-2$

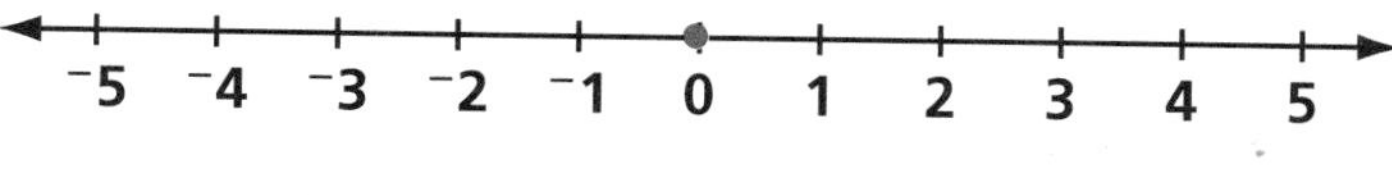

18. the integer that is the opposite of $^+3$

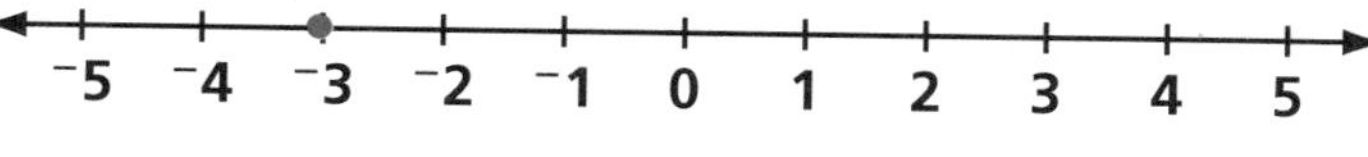

19. the integer that is **2** less than $^+1$

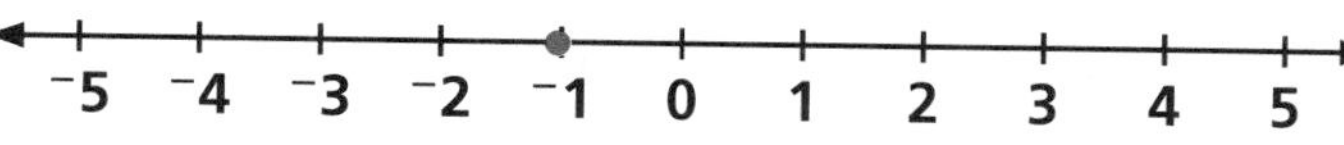

20. the integers that have an absolute value of **2**

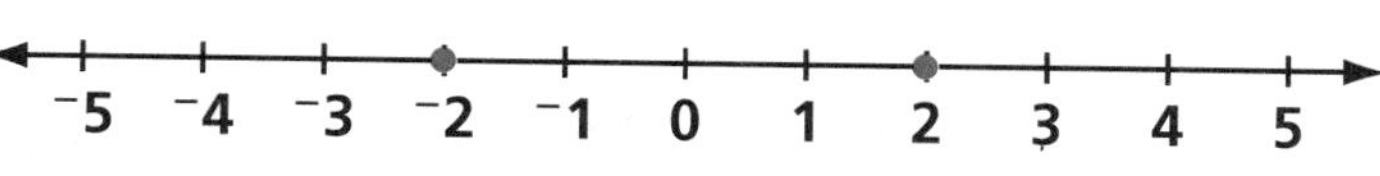

21. the integer that is **3** greater than $^-4$

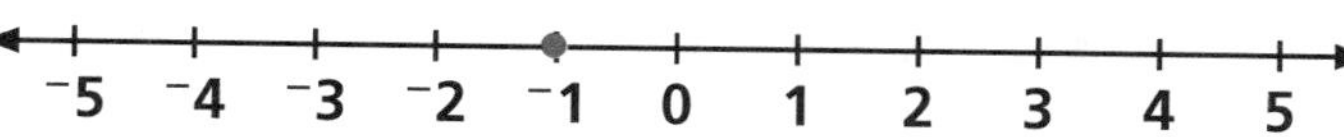

Look back at your answers to exercises **16** and **20**.

There are two integers that have an absolute value of **4**. Both $^-4$ and **4** are **4** units from **0**.

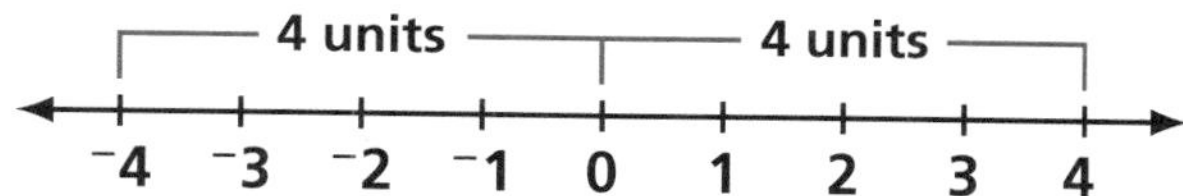

There are two integers that have an absolute value of **2**. Both $^-2$ and **2** are **2** units from **0**.

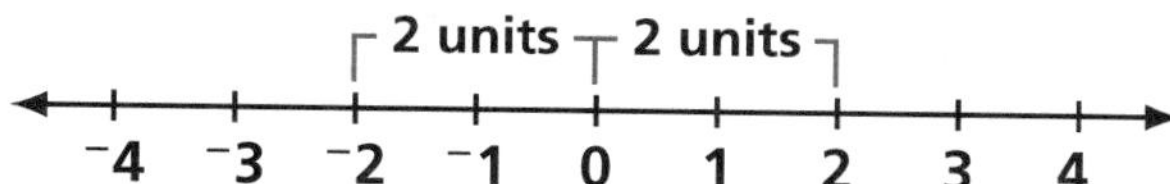

Another way to write these exercises is to use an equation.

$|n| = 4$

Think: What two integers are **4** units from **0**?

$n = {}^-4, n = 4$ (or $n = {}^+4$)

$|n| = 2$

Think: What two integers are **2** units from **0**?

$n = {}^-2, n = 2$

Complete.

22. What integers are **7** units from **0** on the number line? $^-7, 7$

23. What integers are **18** units from **0** on the number line? $^-18, 18$

24. What integers are **25** units from **0** on the number line? $^-25, 25$

Solve for *n*.

25. $|n| = 6$ $^-6, 6$ $|n| = 81$ $^-81, 81$ $|n| = 42$ $^-42, 42$

Integers have many applications.

Prices increase and decrease.

A **5** point increase in a stock price can be written as $^{+}$**\$5**.

During the winter, temperatures can fall below zero.

In January, the temperature was **10** degrees below **0**°F. The temperature was $^{-}$**10**°F.

Elevations can be described as above or below sea level.

A scuba diver is **20** m below sea level. The diver's position is $^{-}$**20** m.

Write an integer that represents the statement. Label the integer.

26. A running back for a football team lost **8** yards. $^{-}$8 yd

27. The Dow Jones average rose **2** points. 2 points

28. The temperature on a cold winter's day is **10** degrees below **0**°C. $^{-}$10°C

29. A person deposited **\$50** into a bank account. \$50

Problem Solving Reasoning **Solve.**

30. Uri took an elevator from the first floor up **5** floors to the cafeteria, down **2** floors to the mailroom, up **1** floor to visit a friend, and then down **2** floors to his workspace. Use integers to describe each activity. What floor did he end up on?

5, $^{-}$2, 1, $^{-}$2; third floor

31. Mount Everest is about **29,000** feet above sea level. The Marianas Trench in the ocean is about **36,200** feet below sea level. Mount McKinley is **20,320** feet above sea level. Death Valley is **282** feet below sea level. Use integers to describe each location. Then write the elevations in greatest to least order.

29,000 ft, $^{-}$36,200 ft, 20,320 ft, $^{-}$282 ft;
29,000 ft, 20,320 ft, $^{-}$282 ft, $^{-}$36,200 ft

Test Prep ★ Mixed Review

32 **A person bought a used sound system for \$160, then quickly sold it for \$224. What is the percent of increase from \$160 to \$224?**
C; Obj. 5B

A 4%
B 28%
C 40%
D 64%

33 **A money-market fund offers its customers $6\frac{1}{2}$% simple interest per year. What is the interest on a \$300 investment for 2 years?**
J; Obj. 5D

F \$13
G \$19.50
H \$36
J \$39

Closing the lesson *What is an integer?* (Any number in the set {... $^{-}$3, $^{-}$2, $^{-}$1, 0, 1, 2, 3...})

Name ______________________________

Guided Practice: Ex. 1, 2, 5 & 8, p. 221; Ex. 11, p. 222
Independent Practice: Complete pp. 221–222

You can add two integers by using a number line. When an addend is positive, move in the positive direction. When an addend is negative, move in the negative direction.

⁻**5** + **2** = ?

Find ⁻**5** + **2.**

Start at **0.** Move **5** units in the negative direction to ⁻**5.** Then, move **2** units in the positive direction.

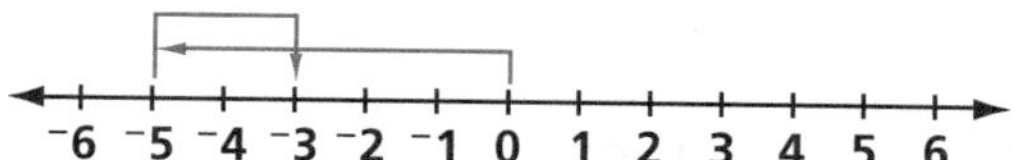

You stop at ⁻**3.**
The sum of ⁻**5** and **2** is ⁻**3.**

⁻**5** + **2** = ⁻**3**

Find **2** + ⁻**3.**

Start at **0.** Move **2** units in the positive direction to **2.** Then, move **3** units in the negative direction.

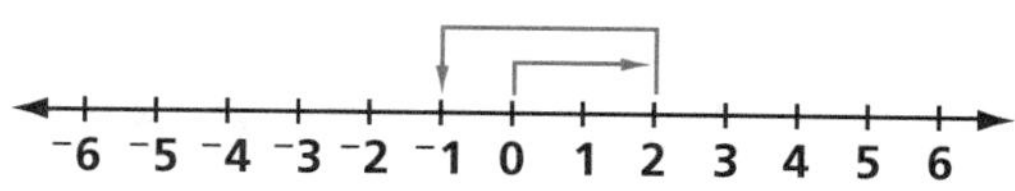

You stop at ⁻**1.**
The sum of **2** and ⁻**3** is ⁻**1.**

2 + ⁻**3** = ⁻**1**

Find the sum. Use the number line.

1. ⁻4 + 1 = ⁻3

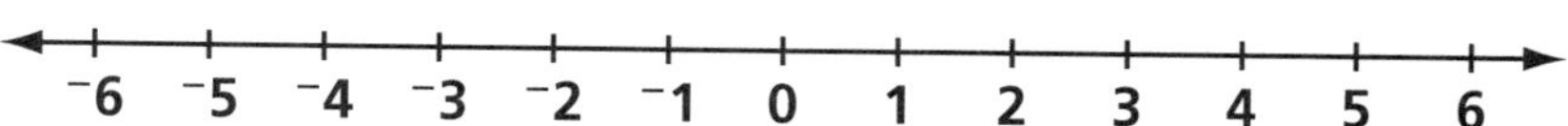

2. 5 + ⁻2 = 3

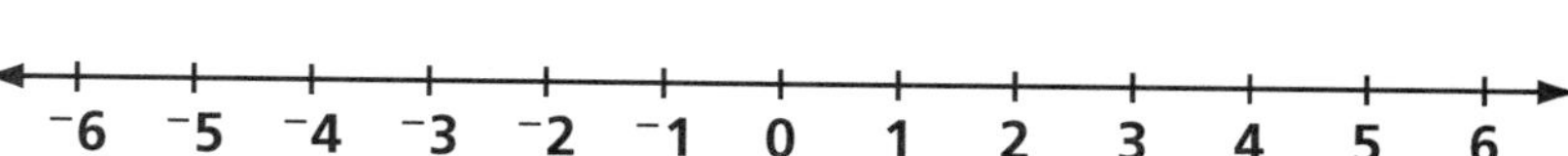

3. ⁻2 + ⁻3 = ⁻5

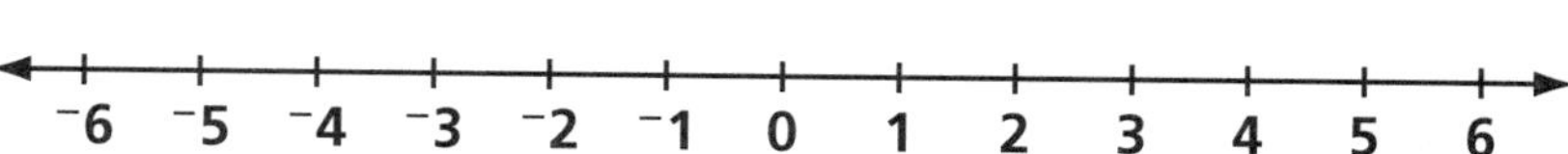

4. 4 + ⁻2 = 2

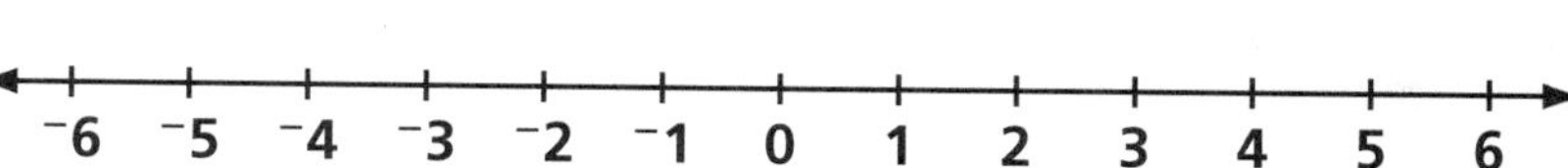

Add. Make your own number line to help you.

5.	⁻4 + 9 = 5	⁻5 + 7 = 2	⁻3 + 6 = 3
6.	⁻3 + 2 = ⁻1	⁻9 + 1 = ⁻8	⁻7 + 5 = ⁻2
7.	5 + ⁻4 = 1	6 + ⁻2 = 4	3 + ⁻8 = ⁻5
8.	2 + ⁻6 = ⁻4	9 + ⁻1 = 8	7 + ⁻3 = 4
9.	⁻7 + ⁻1 = ⁻8	⁻4 + 2 = ⁻2	⁻6 + 3 = ⁻3
10.	4 + ⁻5 = ⁻1	2 + ⁻1 = 1	⁻5 + ⁻1 = ⁻6

Check Understanding *How can you predict the sign of the sum of a positive integer and a negative integer?* (If the two integers have the same absolute value, the sum will be zero. Otherwise, the sum will have the same sign as that of the integer whose absolute value is larger.)

You do not need to draw a number line every time you add integers. Here are two methods you can use.

When both addends are positive, or both addends are negative, just add. Use the same sign as the addends to write the sum.	$^-4 + {}^-3 = {}^-7$ $2 + 8 = 10$

When one addend is positive and one addend is negative:

- find and compare the absolute values of the addends.
- subtract the lesser absolute value from the greater absolute value.
- use the same sign as the addend with the greater absolute value to write the sum.

$^-4 + 3 =$ ___?___
$|{}^-4| = 4$ and $|3| = 3$
$4 > 3$

The negative integer has a greater absolute value.

$4 - 3 = 1$, so
$^-4 + 3 = {}^-1$

$^-2 + 8 =$ ___?___
$|{}^-2| = 2$ and $|8| = 8$
$2 < 8$

The positive integer has a greater absolute value.

$8 - 2 = 6$, so
$^-2 + 8 = 6$

Write the sum.

11. $^-7 + 9 =$ __2__ $7 + {}^-4 =$ __3__ $^-18 + 18 =$ __0__

12. $^-37 + 4 =$ __$^-33$__ $12 + {}^-36 =$ __$^-24$__ $7 + {}^-14 =$ __$^-7$__

13. $4 + 18 =$ __22__ $16 + {}^-5 =$ __11__ $^-402 + 401 =$ __$^-1$__

Problem Solving
Reasoning

Solve.

14. In Chicago the temperature in the morning was $^-4$°F. It rose **15°** by early afternoon. What was the afternoon temperature? __11°F__

Closing the Lesson *Indicate the sign of each of these: the sum of two positive integers* (positive), *the sum of two negative integers* (negative), *the sum of a positive integer and a negative integer* (could be positive, negative, or zero; depends on the absolute values of the two integers being added).

Test Prep ★ Mixed Review

15 **In the set of data (42, 31, 60, 17, 22, 14, 35), what does 42 represent?** D; Obj. 6B

A median **C** lower quartile

B mean **D** upper quartile

16 **How many groups of 3 letters can you make with A, B, C, D, E?** H; Obj. 6E

F 3 **H** 10

G 5 **J** 20

Name ______________________________

Subtracting Integers

Guided Practice: Ex. 1, 3 & 6, p. 223; Ex. 7 & 11, p. 224
Independent Practice: Complete pp. 223–224

Addition and subtraction are inverse operations. To subtract an integer on the number line, you move in the *opposite* direction. When you subtract a *positive* integer, you move in the *negative* direction.

$2 - 5 = ?$

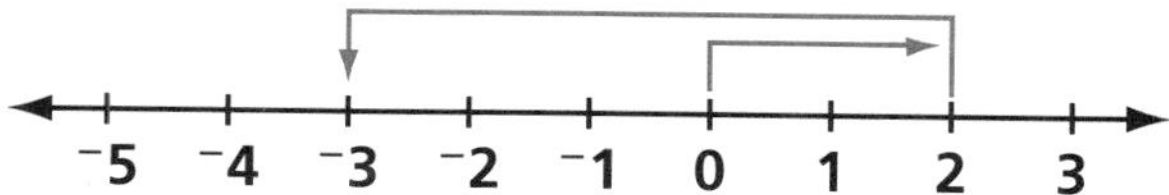

$2 - 5 = {}^{-}3$

When you subtract a *negative* integer, you move in the *positive* direction.

$2 - {}^{-}5 = ?$

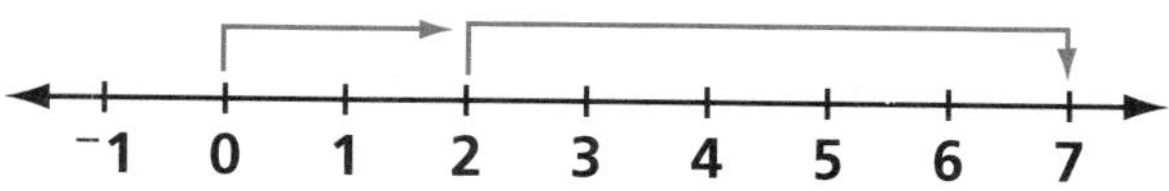

$2 - {}^{-}5 = 7$

Remember that addition and subtraction are related. Notice how each pair of subtraction-addition sentences are related.

Here is a rule for subtraction of integers.

$5 - 2 = 3$

$5 + {}^{-}2 = 3$

Subtracting **2** is the same as adding **$^{-}$2.**

$2 - 5 = {}^{-}3$

$2 + {}^{-}5 = {}^{-}3$

Subtracting **5** is the same as adding **$^{-}$5.**

$2 - {}^{-}5 = 7$

$2 + 5 = 7$

Subtracting **$^{-}$5** is the same as adding **5.**

> Subtracting an integer is the same as adding its opposite.

Write the difference as a sum. Then, find the sum.

1. $4 - 9$ $4 + {}^{-}9 = {}^{-}5$ $3 - 7$ $3 + {}^{-}7 = {}^{-}4$ ${}^{-}5 - {}^{-}9$ ${}^{-}5 + 9 = 4$

2. ${}^{-}3 - 2$ ${}^{-}3 + {}^{-}2 = {}^{-}5$ ${}^{-}4 - 3$ ${}^{-}4 + {}^{-}3 = {}^{-}7$ ${}^{-}6 - 1$ ${}^{-}6 + {}^{-}1 = {}^{-}7$

3. $6 - {}^{-}2$ $6 + 2 = 8$ ${}^{-}2 - {}^{-}6$ ${}^{-}2 + 6 = 4$ $7 - {}^{-}3$ $7 + 3 = 10$

Write the difference.

4. $3 - 8 = {}^{-}5$ $7 - 9 = {}^{-}2$ $6 - 4 = 2$

5. ${}^{-}4 - 1 = {}^{-}5$ ${}^{-}9 - 2 = {}^{-}11$ ${}^{-}8 - 6 = {}^{-}14$

6. ${}^{-}4 - 9 = {}^{-}13$ ${}^{-}7 - 9 = {}^{-}16$ ${}^{-}16 - {}^{-}4 = {}^{-}12$

Check Understanding *For each of these, find the difference: $^{-}8 - 3$ and $^{-}4 - {}^{-}6$. ($^{-}11$, 2)*

Remember that subtracting is the same as finding a missing addend.

$6 - {}^{-}8 =$ ___?___ is the same problem as ${}^{-}8 +$ ___?___ $= 6$

$6 - {}^{-}8 =$ <u>14</u>

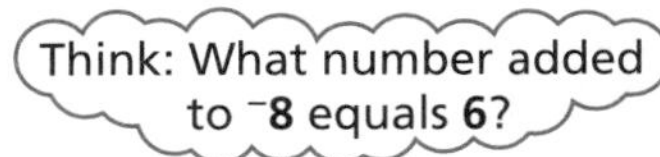

Write the missing addend.

7.	${}^{-}3 +$ <u>5</u> $= 2$	${}^{-}6 +$ <u>10</u> $= 4$	${}^{-}4 +$ <u>7</u> $= 3$
8.	${}^{-}6 +$ <u>3</u> $= {}^{-}3$	${}^{-}7 +$ <u>6</u> $= {}^{-}1$	${}^{-}5 +$ <u>3</u> $= {}^{-}2$
9.	$5 +$ <u>$^{-}4$</u> $= 1$	$8 +$ <u>$^{-}4$</u> $= 4$	$7 +$ <u>$^{-}4$</u> $= 3$
10.	$7 +$ <u>$^{-}8$</u> $= {}^{-}1$	$2 +$ <u>$^{-}7$</u> $= {}^{-}5$	$6 +$ <u>$^{-}12$</u> $= {}^{-}6$

Write the difference.

11.	$2 - {}^{-}9 =$ <u>11</u>	$6 - {}^{-}10 =$ <u>16</u>	$5 - {}^{-}3 =$ <u>8</u>
12.	${}^{-}3 - {}^{-}2 =$ <u>$^{-}1$</u>	${}^{-}8 - {}^{-}1 =$ <u>$^{-}7$</u>	${}^{-}7 - {}^{-}5 =$ <u>$^{-}2$</u>

Problem Solving Reasoning **Write true or false. Write an example to illustrate your answer.**

13. The difference of two positive numbers is always positive. <u>False; $2 - 7 = {}^{-}5$</u>

14. The sum of two negative integers is less than either addend.
<u>True; ${}^{-}2 + {}^{-}5 = {}^{-}7$; ${}^{-}7 < {}^{-}2$ and ${}^{-}7 < {}^{-}5$</u>

Quick Check

Write the absolute value of the integer.

15. ${}^{-}3$ <u>3</u> **16.** 0 <u>0</u> **17.** 4 <u>4</u>

Compare. Write <, >, or =.

18. $|{}^{-}4|$ (=) $|4|$ **19.** ${}^{-}9$ (>) ${}^{-}10$ **20.** $|{}^{-}3|$ (>) $|2|$

Find the sum.

21. $7 + {}^{-}3$ <u>$^{+}4$</u> **22.** ${}^{-}3 + {}^{-}9$ <u>$^{-}12$</u> **23.** $32 + {}^{-}32$ <u>0</u>

Write the difference as a sum. Then, find the sum.

24. ${}^{-}5 - {}^{-}3$ <u>${}^{-}5 + 3 = {}^{-}2$</u> **25.** $7 - 8$ <u>$7 + {}^{-}8 = {}^{-}1$</u>

26. ${}^{-}3 - 3$ <u>${}^{-}3 + {}^{-}3 = {}^{-}6$</u>

Work Space.

Item	Error Analysis
15–20	**Common Error** Some students may confuse opposites with absolute values. **Reteaching** Reteach 60
21–23	**Common Error** Some students may not write sums with the correct sign. **Reteaching** Reteach 61
24–26	**Common Error** Some students may change the signs of both numbers. **Reteaching** Reteach 62

Closing the Lesson *Why do we call ${}^{-}3$ and 3 additive inverses of each other?* (Because their sum equals zero, which is the additive identity element.)

Name ______________________________

Guided Practice: Ex. 3, p. 226
Independent Practice: Complete p. 226

Problem Solving Strategy: Draw a Diagram

You have used the Draw a Diagram strategy before. In this lesson you will find how it can help you solve problems with integers.

Number lines are diagrams that help to show the relationship of positive and negative numbers to each other.

Problem

A particle is in a magnetic field. It moves along a number line as the field changes. It starts at 0, and after each second, it moves to these locations: 1, ⁻2, 3, ⁻4. What is the total distance that the particle travels?

1 Understand

As you reread the problem, ask yourself questions.

"Asking yourself questions will help you identify the math ideas."

- What do you know about the position of the particle?
  It moves from **0** to **1** to **⁻2** to **3** to **⁻4** during the **4** seconds.
- What do you need to find? the total distance traveled

2 Decide

Choose a method for solving.

"A diagram will help you organize the information. It helps you think about how to solve the problem."

Try the Draw a Diagram strategy.

- How can you show the particle's positions on a number line?

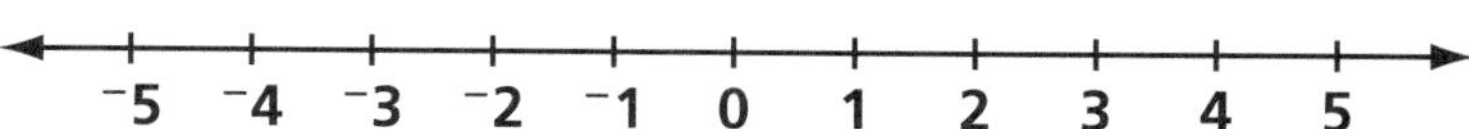

- How can you find the distance it moves during each second?

Count the length of each arrow.

3 Solve

Answer the question.

"Is there more than one way to find the sum of the distances?"

- List the distances that you need to total. 1, 3, 5, 7
- What is the total? 16 units

4 Look back

Check your answer. Write the answer as a full sentence.

"Make sure your answer matches what you were asked to find."

Answer The particle traveled 16 units.

How did your diagram help you to answer the question?

It helped to find the distance the particle moved each second.

Check Understanding *Have students work through problems 1 and 2 on page 226 and check their answers.*

Use the Draw a Diagram strategy or any other strategy you have learned.

1. Sue walked from her house **2** blocks east to Tammy's house. Together they walked **7** blocks west to the mall. After shopping they walked **6** blocks east to a restaurant. Then they walked back to Tammy's house for the evening. How many blocks did Sue walk?

Think: How can you use a number line to help you? Where will you place **0**?

You can make a move on the number line that goes with each part of problem; Put 0 in the middle of the line.

Answer 16 blocks

2. In the midwest, some days can have great temperature variations. One day in Detroit, the temperature was **45°F** at **6** A.M. At **9** A.M. it was **7°** warmer. From **9** A.M. until noon, the temperature fell **12°**. During the next three hours, the temperature increased by **16°**. What was the temperature at **3** P.M.?

Think: What would be a good way to organize this information?

You could make a vertical number line that would look like a thermometer.

Answer 56°F

3. Ramon has **$15** in his wallet. He spends **$8** for a CD. He earns **$5** for doing a chore. He spends **$3** for lunch. How much money does Ramon have left?

$9

4. The elevation of a level plot of land is **15** feet below sea level. A **32**-foot television antenna is erected on this site. How far above sea level is the antenna?

17 ft above sea level

5. A particle starts at $^{-}3$ on a number line. After **1** second it moves **5** units to the right; after **2** seconds it moves **10** units to the left; after **3** seconds it moves **15** units to the right. If this pattern continues, where is the particle after **5** seconds?

12

6. Four towns are located along a **24**-mile railroad line that runs from Northville to Southville. The town of Centerville is in the middle of the route. The town of Rockville is located **3** miles north of Centerville. How far is Rockville from Northville? How far is Rockville from Southville?

9 miles, 15 miles

7. According to the newspapers in Jane's town, the temperature there during the last **24** hours had plunged from **7°C** to $^{-}$**31°C**. What is the difference between these two temperatures?

38°C

8. On Joe's football team's next possession, they gained **10** yards on the first play, then lost **13** yards on the second play, and then managed to gain **7** yards on the third play. What was the team's total gain on these three plays?

4 yards

Closing the Lesson *Describe several problems for which it would be helpful to draw a diagram to solve the problem.* (Answers will vary.)

Name ______________________

Multiplying Integers

Guided Practice: Ex. 1 & 5, p. 227; Ex. 6 & 8, p. 228
Independent Practice: Complete pp. 227–228

Notice that in each pattern below, the first factor remains the same while the second factor decreases by **1.**

Pattern:

The product decreases by **4** each time.

Since **4 × 0 = 0,** then **4 × ⁻1** must be **4** less than **0,** or **⁻4.**

4 × 5 = 20
4 × 4 = 16
4 × 3 = 12
4 × 2 = 8
4 × 1 = 4
4 × 0 = 0
4 × ⁻1 = ?
4 × ⁻2 = ?
4 × ⁻3 = ?
4 × ⁻4 = ?
4 × ⁻5 = ?

4 × ⁻1 = ⁻4
4 × ⁻2 = ⁻8
4 × ⁻3 = ⁻12
4 × ⁻4 = ⁻16
4 × ⁻5 = ⁻20

5 × 5 = 25
5 × 4 = 20
5 × 3 = 15
5 × 2 = 10
5 × 1 = 5
5 × 0 = 0
5 × ⁻1 = ?
5 × ⁻2 = ?
5 × ⁻3 = ?
5 × ⁻4 = ?
5 × ⁻5 = ?

Pattern:

The product decreases by **5** each time.

Since **5 × 0 = 0,** then **5 × ⁻1** must be **5** less than **0,** or **⁻5.**

5 × ⁻1 = ⁻5
5 × ⁻2 = ⁻10
5 × ⁻3 = ⁻15
5 × ⁻4 = ⁻20
5 × ⁻5 = ⁻25

These examples show two patterns for multiplying integers.

> The product of a positive integer and a positive integer is positive.
> The product of a positive integer and a negative integer is negative.

The order in which factors are multiplied does not matter, so **4 × ⁻5** has the same product as **⁻5 × 4,** **3 × ⁻2** has the same product as **⁻2 × 3,** and so on.

> The product of a negative integer and a positive integer is negative.

Write the product.

1. 3 × ⁻6 = ⁻18   6 × ⁻7 = ⁻42   8 × 4 = 32   2 × ⁻9 = ⁻18

2. 5 × ⁻8 = ⁻40   9 × 6 = 54   7 × ⁻3 = ⁻21   3 × 3 = 9

3. ⁻3 × 8 = ⁻24   ⁻6 × 7 = ⁻42   ⁻3 × 2 = ⁻6   ⁻4 × 7 = ⁻28

4. ⁻2 × 4 = ⁻8   10 × ⁻5 = ⁻50   ⁻7 × 6 = ⁻42   3 × ⁻12 = ⁻36

5. ⁻11 × 3 = ⁻33   15 × ⁻2 = ⁻30   ⁻8 × 7 = ⁻56   16 × ⁻3 = ⁻48

Check Understanding *Find each of the following products: 7 × ⁻3, ⁻4 × ⁻5, ⁻4 × 6, ⁻1 × ⁻9, 4 × 8.*
(⁻21, 20, ⁻24, 9, 32)

How would you complete this pattern? Notice that the first factor remains the same while the second factor decreases by **1.**

$^-1 \times 4 = {}^-4$
$^-1 \times 3 = {}^-3$
$^-1 \times 2 = {}^-2$
$^-1 \times 1 = {}^-1$
$^-1 \times 0 = 0$
$^-1 \times {}^-1 = ?$
$^-1 \times {}^-2 = ?$
$^-1 \times {}^-3 = ?$
$^-1 \times {}^-4 = ?$

Pattern:
The product increases by **1** each time.

Since $^-1 \times 0 = 0$, then $^-1 \times {}^-1$ must be **1** greater than **0** or **1.**

$^-1 \times {}^-1 = 1$
$^-1 \times {}^-2 = 2$
$^-1 \times {}^-3 = 3$
$^-1 \times {}^-4 = 4$

The product of a negative integer and a negative integer is positive.

Write the product.

6. $8 \times 7 =$ 56 $\qquad 8 \times {}^-8 =$ $^-64$ $\qquad {}^-7 \times {}^-1 =$ 7

7. $^-3 \times 1 =$ $^-3$ $\qquad 7 \times 5 =$ 35 $\qquad 1 \times {}^-10 =$ $^-10$

8. $^-1 \times {}^-1 =$ 1 $\qquad 6 \times {}^-15 =$ $^-90$ $\qquad 10 \times 10 =$ 100

9. $0 \times 8 =$ 0 $\qquad {}^-4 \times {}^-5 =$ 20 $\qquad {}^-5 \times 4 =$ $^-20$

Problem Solving
Reasoning

Solve.

10. Hannah multiplied two numbers and got $^-$**4** as the product. She then added the two numbers and got **0** as the sum. What are the two numbers? $^-2$, 2

11. Jamal multiplied two numbers and got $^-$**4** as the product. He then subtracted the two numbers and got **5** as the difference. What are the two numbers?
1, $^-4$ (or 4, $^-1$)

Test Prep ★ Mixed Review

12 **What is the value of the expression $8 + {}^-12 + 12 - {}^-3$?** C; Obj. 8B

A 29 **C** 11

B 5 **D** $^-5$

Closing the Lesson *What can you say about the product of two integers?* (The product may be positive if both integers have the same sign, negative if one integer is positive and one integer is negative, or zero if at least one of the integers is zero.)

13 **From Tuesday through Friday, the class measured the temperatures in °C. Which list shows the temperatures in least to greatest order?** G; Obj. 8A

F $^-10$°C, 15°C, $^-20$°C, 25°C

G $^-20$°C, $^-10$°C, 15°C, 25°C

H $^-10$°C, $^-20$°C, 15°C, 25°C

J $^-10$°C, 15°C, 25°C, $^-20$°C

Name ____________________

Dividing Integers

Guided Practice: Ex. 1, 4 & 6, p. 229; Ex. 8 & 10, p. 230

Multiplication and division are inverse operations. You can use a related multiplication sentence to solve a division sentence.

$6 \times 4 = 24$ so $24 \div 4 = 6$

$^-8 \times 5 = {^-40}$ so $^-40 \div 5 = {^-8}$

$3 \times {^-2} = {^-6}$ so $^-6 \div {^-2} = 3$

$^-9 \times {^-3} = 27$ so $27 \div {^-3} = {^-9}$

These examples show the rules for dividing integers.

> The quotient of two positive integers or of two negative integers is positive.
>
> The quotient of a negative integer and a positive integer is negative.

Divide.

1. $^-36 \div {^-9} =$ 4 　 $^-24 \div 3 =$ $^-8$ 　 $28 \div {^-7} =$ $^-4$

2. $^-54 \div {^-6} =$ 9 　 $^-16 \div {^-4} =$ 4 　 $^-32 \div 8 =$ $^-4$

3. $^-81 \div 9 =$ $^-9$ 　 $^-42 \div {^-7} =$ 6 　 $36 \div {^-6} =$ $^-6$

Write the missing divisor.

4. $^-32 \div$ $^-8$ $= 4$ 　 $^-54 \div$ $^-6$ $= 9$ 　 $56 \div$ $^-14$ $= {^-4}$

5. $100 \div$ $^-4$ $= {^-25}$ 　 $35 \div$ $^-5$ $= {^-7}$ 　 $^-108 \div$ 9 $= {^-12}$

Write the missing dividend.

6. $^-12$ $\div 3 = {^-4}$ 　 100 $\div {^-5} = {^-20}$ 　 $^-60$ $\div {^-4} = 15$

7. $^-540$ $\div 6 = {^-90}$ 　 80 $\div 8 = 10$ 　 1,008 $\div {^-12} = {^-84}$

Check Understanding *Find each of the following quotients:* $^-20 \div {^-4}$, $15 \div {^-5}$, $8 \div 2$, $^-24 \div 4$. (5, $^-3$, 4, $^-6$)

Remember the rules for the order of operations to evaluate expressions with integers.

Order of Operations

1. Perform all operations inside parentheses first.
2. Multiply and divide from left to right.
3. Add and subtract from left to right.

Evaluate.

8. (2 × 3) − 2 4 | 2 × (3 − 2) 2 | 2 × 3 − 2 4

9. ⁻4 × ⁻2 × ⁻3 ⁻24 | ⁻4 × (⁻2 × ⁻3) ⁻24 | (⁻4 × ⁻2) × ⁻3 ⁻24

10. 1 × ⁻9 × ⁻6 54 | ⁻1 × 9 × ⁻6 54 | ⁻1 × ⁻9 × ⁻6 ⁻54

11. 24 ÷ 6 ÷ 2 2 | ⁻24 ÷ ⁻6 ÷ ⁻2 ⁻2 | (⁻24 ÷ ⁻6) ÷ ⁻2 ⁻2

12. (14 ÷ 2) + ⁻5 2 | 14 ÷ (2 + 5) 2 | (14 ÷ 2) + 5 12

13. (⁻16 − ⁻4) × 3 ⁻36 | (16 − 4) × ⁻3 ⁻36 | ⁻16 − ⁻4 × 3 ⁻4

14. 7 − ⁻3 × ⁻4 ⁻5 | 7 + ⁻3 × ⁻4 19 | (7 − ⁻3) × ⁻4 ⁻40

15. (6 × ⁻4) + ⁻5 − (18 ÷ ⁻3) ⁻23 | (⁻28 ÷ ⁻4) × (2 + ⁻5) − (⁻4 + 6) ⁻23

Problem Solving Reasoning Solve.

16. Kim played a video game. She started at **0,** gained **4** points, lost **6** points, gained **3** points, gained **2** more points, and finally lost **8** points. Where did she end up? What was her average score?

⁻5 points; ⁻1 point

17. The Dow Jones average on the stock market rose **3.8** points on Monday, rose **2.2** on Tuesday, fell **1.4** on Wednesday, rose **5.0** on Thursday, and rose **0.4** on Friday. What was the average daily change for the week?

2 point rise

Test Prep ★ Mixed Review

18 What is the value of ⁻9 × ⁻12 × ⁻6 × 2? A; Obj. 8C

A ⁻1,296 C 648

B ⁻648 D 1,296

19 What is the result when ⁻5 is multiplied by $(^{-}2)^3$? H; Obj. 8C

F ⁻45 H 40

G ⁻40 J 45

Closing the Lesson *Describe how to find the quotient of two integers, including how to determine whether the quotient will be positive, negative, or zero.* (It is similiar to finding the quotient of two whole numbers, except that with integers the quotient may be positive (if both integers have the same sign), negative (if one integer is positive and one integer is negative), or zero (if the dividend is zero).)

Name ____________________

Guided Practice: Ex. 1, p. 231; Ex. 4 & 6, p. 232
Independent Practice: Complete pp. 231–232

Rational Numbers on the Number Line

You know that positive integers (or whole numbers) have fractions and decimals between them on the number line. Negative integers also have numbers between them, such as $^{-}1\frac{1}{2}$ and $^{-}2.3$.

These numbers can be located on a number line. For example, $^{-}1\frac{1}{2}$ is between $^{-}1$ and $^{-}2$, and $^{-}2.3$ is between $^{-}2$ and $^{-}3$.

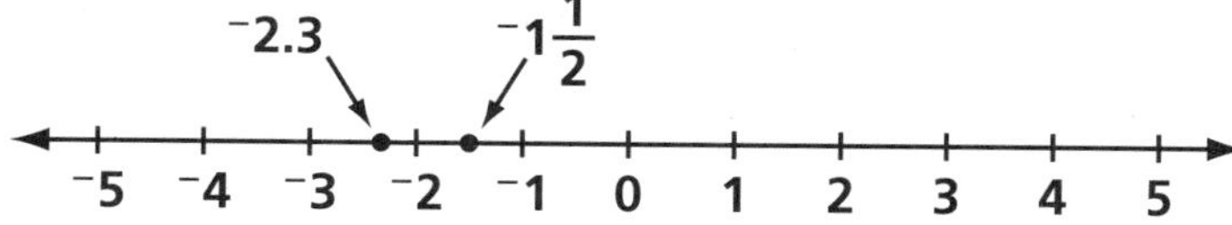

These numbers are called **rational numbers**, because they can be written as the *ratio* of two integers.

A negative rational number can be written in several ways. These represent the same number:

$\frac{^{-}3}{4}$ $\frac{3}{^{-}4}$ $^{-}\frac{3}{4}$

$^{-}1\frac{1}{2}$ can be written as $\frac{^{-}3}{2}$

$^{-}2.3$ can be written as $^{-}\frac{23}{10}$

0 can be written as $\frac{0}{1}$

A rational expression may contain more than one positive or negative sign. Follow these rules for simplifying negative rational numbers.

Rule	Rational Number	Simplify
The quotient of a negative integer and a positive integer is negative.	$\frac{^{-}4}{8}$	$^{-}\frac{1}{2}$
The quotient of a positive integer and a negative integer is negative.	$\frac{3}{^{-}9}$	$^{-}\frac{1}{3}$
If there is a negative integer in parentheses and there is a negative sign outside the parentheses, write the number's opposite.	$^{-}(\frac{2}{^{-}3})$ $^{-}(\frac{^{-}5}{7})$	$\frac{2}{3}$ $\frac{5}{7}$

Write the rational number as a ratio of two integers. Samples are given.

1. $^{-}7$ $\frac{^{-}7}{1}$ $2\frac{1}{2}$ $\frac{5}{2}$ $^{-}3.03$ $\frac{^{-}303}{100}$ 0.1708 $\frac{1,708}{10,000}$ or $\frac{427}{2,500}$ $^{-}6\frac{5}{6}$ $\frac{^{-}41}{6}$ $^{-}0.9$ $\frac{^{-}9}{10}$

2. 4.444 $\frac{4,444}{1,000}$ or $\frac{1,111}{250}$ $3\frac{7}{12}$ $\frac{43}{12}$ $^{-}1\frac{5}{8}$ $\frac{^{-}13}{8}$ $^{-}12.5$ $\frac{^{-}125}{10}$ or $\frac{^{-}25}{2}$ 0.1011 $\frac{1,011}{10,000}$ $^{-}15$ $\frac{^{-}15}{1}$

3. $^{-}2\frac{3}{12}$ $\frac{^{-}9}{4}$ $^{-}4.7$ $\frac{^{-}47}{10}$ $^{-}3\frac{1}{4}$ $\frac{^{-}13}{4}$ 1.03 $\frac{103}{100}$ 0.301 $\frac{301}{1,000}$ $^{-}0.79$ $\frac{^{-}79}{100}$

Check Understanding *Consider the following numbers:* $\frac{^{-}7}{^{-}6}$ *and* $^{-}(\frac{^{-}7}{3})$. *For each, name the closest two integers that the given number is between.* ($\frac{^{-}7}{^{-}6} = \frac{7}{6}$ and it is between 1 and 2; $^{-}(\frac{^{-}7}{3}) = \frac{7}{3}$ and it is between 2 and 3).

Place the rational numbers on the number line next to them.

4. $\frac{3}{4}$ $^{-}\frac{1}{2}$ $^{-}1\frac{1}{4}$ $2\frac{1}{2}$

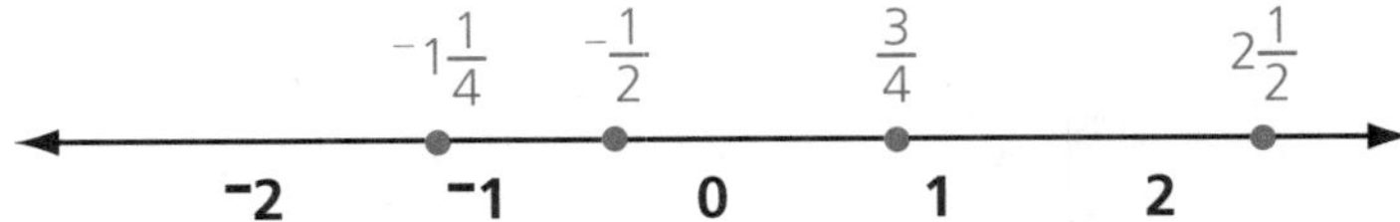

5. $^{-}1\frac{5}{8}$ $\frac{13}{8}$ $^{-}2\frac{7}{8}$ $2\frac{1}{8}$

$^{-}2\frac{7}{8}$ $^{-}1\frac{5}{8}$ $1\frac{5}{8}$ $2\frac{1}{8}$

−3 −2 −1 0 1 2 3

Simplify the expression.

6. $\frac{4}{^{-}8} = \underline{\ ^{-}\frac{1}{2}\ }$ $\frac{6}{12} = \underline{\ \frac{1}{2}\ }$ $^{-}(\frac{^{-}3}{^{-}6}) = \underline{\ ^{-}\frac{1}{2}\ }$ $\frac{^{-}3}{^{-}6} = \underline{\ \frac{1}{2}\ }$

7. $^{-}(\frac{4}{^{-}16}) = \underline{\ \frac{1}{4}\ }$ $^{-}(\frac{^{-}2}{4}) = \underline{\ \frac{1}{2}\ }$ $^{-}(\frac{3}{^{-}6}) = \underline{\ \frac{1}{2}\ }$ $\frac{^{-}8}{18} = \underline{\ \frac{^{-}4}{9}\ }$

Problem Solving
Reasoning

Solve.

8. The *density property* of rational numbers says that between two rational numbers is another rational number. Does the set of integers have the density property? Explain.

No, because there is no integer between 0 and ⁻1, for example.

Quick Check

Write the product or quotient.

9. 7 × (⁻8) = ⁻56

10. ⁻12 × 11 = ⁻132

11. ⁻14 × ⁻25 = 350

12. 156 ÷ ⁻12 = ⁻13

13. ⁻144 ÷ 16 = ⁻9

14. ⁻275 ÷ ⁻25 = 11

Write the rational number as a ratio of two integers.

15. ⁻17 $\frac{^{-}17}{1}$

16. $^{-}11\frac{3}{4}$ $\frac{^{-}47}{4}$

17. ⁻2.04 $\frac{^{-}204}{100}$ or $\frac{^{-}51}{25}$

Closing the Lesson *Given a rational number, how can you determine the closest two integers that the given number is between?* (Locate the number on the number line.)

Work Space.

Item	Error Analysis
9–11	**Common Error** Watch for students who use the incorrect sign for a product. **Reteaching** Reteach 63
12–14	**Common Error** Watch for students who use the incorrect sign for a quotient. **Reteaching** Reteach 64
15–17	**Common Error** Students may use fractions or decimals in the numerator, instead of integers. **Reteaching** Reteach 65

Name ______________________________

Guided Practice: Ex. 1, p. 233; Ex. 3, p. 234
Independent Practice: Complete p. 234

Adding and Subtracting Rational Numbers

To add or subtract rational numbers, use the same rules you used for integers.

Addition

- Both addends are positive or both are negative.

$^-\frac{3}{4} + {}^-\frac{1}{2}$	Add the absolute values.	$\frac{3}{4} + \frac{1}{2} = \frac{5}{4}$ or $1\frac{1}{4}$
	Use the same sign as the original addends ($^-$).	$^-1\frac{1}{4}$

- One addend is positive and one is negative.

$^-\frac{5}{6} + \frac{3}{4}$	Compare the absolute values.	$\frac{5}{6} > \frac{3}{4}$
	Find the difference of the absolute values.	$\frac{5}{6} - \frac{3}{4} = \frac{10}{12} - \frac{9}{12}$ or $\frac{1}{12}$
	Use the same sign as the greater value.	$^-\frac{1}{12}$

Subtraction

$^-\frac{4}{5} - {}^-\frac{2}{3}$	Rewrite as an addition expression.	$^-\frac{4}{5} + \frac{2}{3}$
	Compare the absolute values.	$\frac{4}{5} > \frac{2}{3}$
	Find the difference of the absolute values.	$\frac{4}{5} - \frac{2}{3} = \frac{12}{15} - \frac{10}{15}$ or $\frac{2}{15}$
	Use the same sign as the greater value.	$^-\frac{2}{15}$
4.3 − 6.55	Rewrite as an addition expression.	**4.3 − 6.55 = 4.3 + $^-$6.55**
	Compare the absolute values.	**6.55 > 4.3**
	Find the difference of the absolute values.	**6.55 − 4.3 = 2.25**
	Use the same sign as **$^-$6.55.**	**$^-$2.25**

Write the sum or difference. Write fractions in simplest form.

1. $\frac{2}{3} + {}^-\frac{5}{6}$ = $^-\frac{1}{6}$ $\qquad$ $^-\frac{7}{20} + \frac{1}{5}$ = $^-\frac{3}{20}$ $\qquad$ $\frac{2}{3} - {}^-\frac{1}{3}$ = 1 $\qquad$ $^-4 - 1\frac{2}{3}$ = $^-5\frac{2}{3}$

Check Understanding *Solve the following: $\frac{^-1}{6} + \frac{^-5}{9}$. Explain how you solved the problem.* (Find a common positive denominator and add: $\frac{^-1}{6} + \frac{^-5}{9} = \frac{^-3}{18} + \frac{^-10}{18} = \frac{^-13}{18}$.)

Find each sum or difference. Write fractions in simplest form.

2. $-\frac{9}{10} - -\frac{3}{5}$ = $-\frac{3}{10}$ $\qquad$ $-1\frac{1}{5} - -\frac{1}{5}$ = -1 $\qquad$ $-\frac{7}{12} + -\frac{3}{4}$ = $-1\frac{1}{3}$ $\qquad$ $2\frac{5}{6} + -\frac{5}{6}$ = 2

3. $19.6 + {}^-12.8$ = 6.8 $\qquad$ $22.3 - {}^-57.1$ = 79.4 $\qquad$ ${}^-14.7 - {}^-4.3$ = ${}^-10.4$ $\qquad$ ${}^-6.009 + 4.62$ = ${}^-1.389$

4. ${}^-6.82 + 7.09 + {}^-3.75$ = ${}^-3.48$ $\qquad$ $\frac{2}{3} + \frac{7}{8} + -\frac{5}{6}$ = $\frac{17}{24}$ $\qquad$ $-\frac{1}{7} + -\frac{3}{4} + \frac{19}{28}$ = $-\frac{3}{14}$ $\qquad$ $9.343 + {}^-10.47 + 5.72$ = 4.593

Problem Solving Reasoning

Complete. Let $a = 8$ and $b = -\frac{1}{2}$.

5. Find each sum or difference.

$a + b$ $7\frac{1}{2}$ $\qquad$ $|a + b|$ $7\frac{1}{2}$

$|a| - |b|$ $7\frac{1}{2}$ $\qquad$ $|b| - |a|$ ${}^-7\frac{1}{2}$

6. Find each sum or difference.

$a - b$ $8\frac{1}{2}$ $\qquad$ $b - a$ ${}^-8\frac{1}{2}$

$|a - b|$ $8\frac{1}{2}$ $\qquad$ $|a| + |b|$ $8\frac{1}{2}$

7. Write true or false. If $a > b$, then $|a + b| = |a| - |b|$. Explain.

False; only when *a* is positive and *b* is negative

8. Write true or false. If *a* is positive and *b* is negative, then $|a - b| = |a| + |b|$. Explain.

True; the opposite of *b* is positive

Test Prep ★ Mixed Review

9 Which expression is equivalent to $({}^-18 \times 5) \div {}^-(3^2)$? B; Obj. 8D

A $\frac{{}^-18 \times 5}{9}$ $\qquad$ C $\frac{{}^-18}{5 \times 9}$

B $\frac{{}^-18 \times 5}{{}^-9}$ $\qquad$ D $\frac{{}^-18}{5 \times 9}$

10 What is the value of $\frac{{}^-294 \div 7}{{}^-6}$? G; Obj. 8D

F 252 $\qquad$ H ${}^-7$

G 7 $\qquad$ J ${}^-252$

Closing the Lesson *Describe how to subtract one rational number from another.* (Change the subtraction problem to an addition problem. Instead of subtracting the number, add its opposite or additive inverse. Then, solve the resulting addition problem.)

Name ____________________

Guided Practice: Ex. 1, 4 & 7, pp. 235–236
Independent Practice: Complete pp. 235–236

Multiplying and Dividing Rational Numbers

You can multiply and divide rational numbers using the same rules that you used for integers.

Multiplication

$\frac{^-3}{4} \times \frac{^-2}{5} = \frac{6}{20}$, or $\frac{3}{10}$ — Both factors are negative, so the product is positive.

$\frac{^-4}{9} \times \frac{3}{8} = \frac{^-12}{72}$, or $\frac{^-1}{6}$ — One factor is positive and the other negative, so the product is negative.

Division

$\frac{^-1}{3} \div \frac{7}{8} = ^-\frac{1}{3} \times \frac{8}{7}$, or $\frac{^-8}{21}$ — The dividend is negative and the divisor is positive, so the quotient is negative.

2.49 ÷ ⁻0.3 = ⁻24.9 ÷ 3, or ⁻8.3 — The dividend is positive and the divisor is negative, so the quotient is negative.

Write the product or quotient in simplest form.

1. $\frac{3}{4} \times \frac{^-7}{9} = \underline{\frac{^-7}{12}}$ $\qquad ^-45 \times \frac{5}{12} = \underline{^-18\frac{3}{4}}$ $\qquad 2\frac{4}{5} \times \frac{^-5}{8} = \underline{^-1\frac{3}{4}}$

2. $36 \div \frac{^-3}{5} = \underline{^-60}$ $\qquad \frac{15}{16} \times \frac{^-2}{3} = \underline{\frac{^-5}{8}}$ $\qquad ^-\frac{4}{9} \times \frac{^-9}{10} = \underline{\frac{2}{5}}$

3. $\frac{^-7}{8} \div \frac{4}{5} = \underline{^-1\frac{3}{32}}$ $\qquad 0.32 \times {^-0.08} = \underline{^-0.0256}$ $\qquad \frac{1}{5} \times {^-2\frac{5}{7}} = \underline{\frac{^-19}{35}}$

4. $^-1\frac{1}{2} \times {^-1\frac{1}{5}} = \underline{1\frac{4}{5}}$ $\qquad ^-72 \div \frac{8}{9} = \underline{^-81}$ $\qquad 1.44 \div {^-12} = \underline{^-0.12}$

5. $\frac{4}{5} \times \frac{^-6}{7} = \underline{\frac{^-24}{35}}$ $\qquad 1\frac{1}{3} \div {^-2\frac{1}{6}} = \underline{\frac{^-8}{13}}$ $\qquad ^-36 \times \frac{^-7}{9} = \underline{28}$

6. $\frac{^-2}{5} \div \frac{^-11}{2} = \underline{\frac{4}{55}}$ $\qquad ^-0.72 \times {^-5} = \underline{3.6}$ $\qquad 15 \div \frac{^-5}{9} = \underline{^-27}$

Check Understanding *Find the value of each:* $\frac{^-1}{6} \times \frac{^-5}{2}$ $\left(\frac{5}{12}\right)$, $\frac{^-2}{3} \div \frac{^-5}{11}$ $\left(= \frac{^-2}{3} \times \frac{^-11}{5} = \frac{22}{15}\right)$.

When working with positive and negative variables, you must pay close attention to the signs.

When a negative sign is before a grouping symbol, distribute the negative sign to each addend in the group.

Evaluate $^-(a - b)$ for $a = \frac{1}{2}$ and $b = {}^-5$.

$$^-(a - b) = {}^-a - ({}^-b)$$
$$= {}^-a + b$$
$$= {}^-\frac{1}{2} + ({}^-5)$$
$$= {}^-5\frac{1}{2}$$

When a power has a negative sign, evaluate the power first, then find its opposite.

Evaluate $^-x^2$ and $(^-x)^2$ for $x = \frac{1}{6}$.

$$^-x^2 = {}^-(\tfrac{1}{6})^2 \qquad (^-x)^2 = ({}^-\tfrac{1}{6})^2$$
$$= {}^-\frac{1}{36} \qquad = \frac{1}{36}$$

Evaluate the expression when $x = {}^-\frac{1}{2}$, $y = \frac{2}{3}$, and $z = {}^-2$.

7. $x + y + z$ $\underline{{}^-1\frac{5}{6}}$ $-(x + y + z)$ $\underline{1\frac{5}{6}}$ $-(2x - y) + 3z$ $\underline{{}^-4\frac{1}{3}}$ $3x - (3y - z)$ $\underline{{}^-5\frac{1}{2}}$

8. $-z^2$ $\underline{{}^-4}$ $-(x^2 + y)$ $\underline{\frac{{}^-11}{12}}$ $x^3 + 9y^3$ $\underline{2\frac{13}{24}}$ $x^3 - z^3$ $\underline{7\frac{7}{8}}$

9. $-(x + 3y - z)$ $\underline{{}^-3\frac{1}{2}}$ $z + y - 4x^2$ $\underline{{}^-2\frac{1}{3}}$ $2xy$ $\underline{{}^-\frac{2}{3}}$ $3yz$ $\underline{{}^-4}$

Problem Solving
Reasoning

10. Use the relationship between multiplication and division to explain why you cannot divide an integer by 0.

Suppose $\frac{4}{0}$ has a quotient n; then $n \times 0 = 4$, but this is impossible because of the zero multiplication property.

11. For each of the equations below, use reasoning to deduce the value(s) of n.

$n = |10|$ $\underline{10}$ $|n| = 10$ $\underline{10, {}^-10}$ $|{}^-n| = 10$ $\underline{10, {}^-10}$

Quick Check

Write the sum or difference.

12. $\frac{3}{4} + ({}^-\frac{3}{8}) = \underline{\frac{3}{8}}$

13. ${}^-\frac{5}{6} + {}^-1\frac{1}{3} = \underline{{}^-2\frac{1}{6}}$

14. ${}^-2.4 - 2 = \underline{{}^-4.4}$

Write the product or quotient.

15. $2.3 \times {}^-4.5 = \underline{{}^-10.35}$

16. ${}^-2\frac{4}{5} \div \frac{1}{10} = \underline{{}^-28}$

17. ${}^-\frac{7}{8} \times {}^-1\frac{3}{5} = \underline{1\frac{2}{5}}$

Closing the Lesson *What can you say about the product of rational numbers?* (If the two numbers have the same sign, the product or quotient will be positive. If one of the numbers is positive and the other is negative, the product or quotient will be negative.)

Work Space.

Item	Error Analysis
12–14	**Common Error** Watch for students who do not write the correct sign for the sum or difference. **Reteaching** Reteach 66
15–17	**Common Error** Watch for students who do not write the correct sign for the product or quotient. **Reteaching** Reteach 67

Name ______________________________

Problem Solving Application: Use a Graph

Guided Practice: Ex. 1–4, p. 237
Independent Practice: Complete p. 238

The bar graph shows the favorite food of students at Lincoln Middle School.

You can use the graph to compare, make estimates, or draw conclusions about the data.

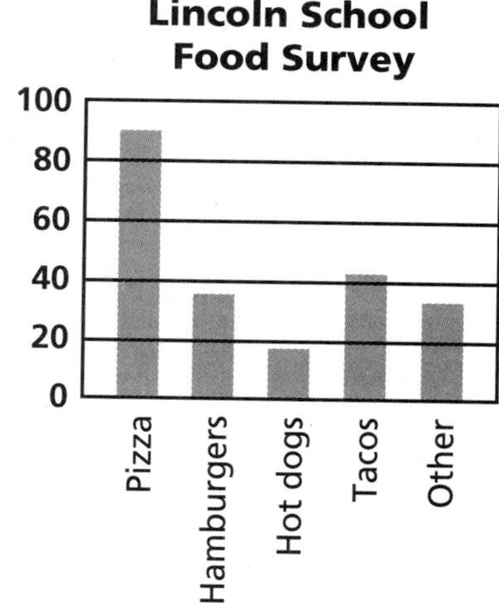

Tips to Remember

1. Understand 2. Decide 3. Solve 4. Look back

- Ask yourself whether you have solved other problems like this before.
- Try to estimate or predict your answer before solving. Use your estimate to check that your answer was reasonable.
- Think about strategies you have learned and use them to help you to solve the problem.

Solve.

1. Is it true that about $\frac{1}{5}$ of the students in the school listed pizza as their favorite food?

Think: Since "Pizza" represents $\frac{1}{5}$ of the bars, does this mean it represents $\frac{1}{5}$ of the responses?

No, because the bars are not all the same length.

Answer No, because 90 of the 220 students like pizza, and this is not $\frac{1}{5}$.

2. How many times as many students chose pizza as hot dogs?

Think: Should you think about subtraction or division to compare the two numbers?

You need to use division to compare.

Answer 5 times as many students like pizza.

3. About how many of the students did not choose pizza?

about 130

4. About what percent of the students chose tacos or hot dogs?

about 27%

Check Understanding *If a bar graph represents the results of a survey of automobile owners, how can you determine the number of people that participated in the survey?* (Determine the total number of people in each category by estimating the height of each bar. Add these category totals to determine the total number of people that participated in the survey.)

Use the line graph. It shows the average monthly 10 A.M. temperature at Lincoln School.

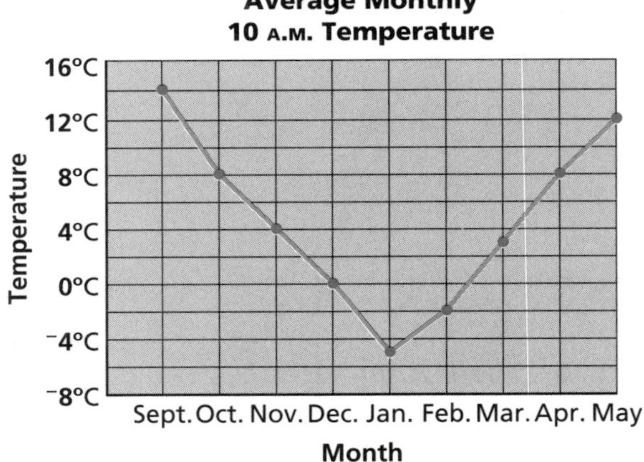

5. Is it reasonable to talk about the temperature in October being so many times greater than the January temperature? Explain your reasoning.

No; If you did you would have to say that 4°C is 2 times a temperature of 2°C, and that doesn't make sense.

6. Suppose the temperature was recorded on **20** school days in November and **16** days in December. Would the average temperature for the two months be halfway between **4°C** and **0°C**? Explain your reasoning.

No; You would add more 4°C days than 0°C, so the average would be closer to 4°C.

7. Between which two months did the average temperature increase the least? Explain how you can tell from the graph.

between January and February

8. Between which two months did the average temperature increase the most?

Between February and March and between March and April.

Extend Your Thinking

9. During one month of the following year, students collected the following data. Without calculating the monthly average, to which month in the graph will the average be closest? Then, calculate the average and write the answer below.

Temperatures in Degrees Celsius

⁻8	⁻4	1	0	3	⁻5	2	0	1	⁻1
4	6	3	0	⁻4	⁻6	⁻3	⁻1	1	⁻3

Answer The temperatures will average about 0°, so it will be closest to February or December. The average temperature is ⁻0.9°.

10. Look back at problem **8.** Explain the method you used to solve the problem. Tell what data you used from the graph. What operations did you use to find the answer?

I looked for the line segment that rose most steeply. Then, I subtracted the two values.

Closing the Lesson *Describe several situations in which you might use a graph to solve a problem.* (Answers will vary. Possible answer: information in newspapers and magazines, in scientific and business reports, and in other real-world settings)

Name ______________________

Unit 8 Review

Write the absolute value of the number.

1. $|{}^{-}6| =$ 6

2. $|22| =$ 22

3. $|{}^{-}4| =$ 4

4. $|2| =$ 2

5. $|0| =$ 0

6. $\left|\frac{-5}{8}\right| =$ $\frac{5}{8}$

Write the sum or difference.

7. $^{-}15 + 16 =$ 1

8. $18 + {}^{-}32 =$ $^{-}14$

9. $^{-}15 + {}^{-}8 =$ $^{-}23$

10. $^{-}15 - {}^{-}27 =$ 12

11. $27 - 32 =$ $^{-}5$

12. $8 - {}^{-}15 =$ 23

13. $^{-}5.8 + 9.03 =$ 3.23

14. $7.42 + {}^{-}4.66 =$ 2.76

15. $\frac{-4}{5} + \frac{3}{4} =$ $\frac{-1}{20}$

16. $\frac{2}{3} - \frac{-1}{4} =$ $\frac{11}{12}$

17. $^{-}1\frac{5}{8} - 3\frac{1}{3} =$ $^{-}4\frac{23}{24}$

18. $^{-}1.6 - {}^{-}2.9 =$ 1.3

Write the product or quotient.

19. $^{-}6 \times 3 =$ $^{-}18$

20. $^{-}12 \times {}^{-}7 =$ 84

21. $^{-}(8)^3 =$ $^{-}512$

22. $^{-}15 \div 3 =$ $^{-}5$

23. $^{-}65 \div {}^{-}5 =$ 13

24. $18 \div {}^{-}3 =$ $^{-}6$

25. $\frac{3}{5} \times \frac{-5}{9} =$ $\frac{-1}{3}$

26. $\frac{-4}{7} \times \frac{-3}{2} =$ $\frac{6}{7}$

27. $^{-}4.62 \times 3.4 =$ $^{-}15.708$

Solve.

28. A weight suspended from a string swings from left to right and back again. Each left-to-right or right-to-left swing is half as long as the previous one. The first swing was **4** m long. How far has the weight moved after **6** swings? $7\frac{7}{8}$ m

29. What is the average high temperature for the week if the daily high temperatures are **7**°F, **⁻4**°F, **⁻8**°F, **⁻10**°F, **⁻1**°F, **5**°F, and **4**°F?

$^{-}1$°F

The formula $t = g - 5.6k$ gives the temperature (t) in °C at a point in Earth's troposphere if you know the ground temperature (g) and the altitude of the point in kilometers (k). Use the formula to complete the table.

	Ground level temperature	Temperature at **4** km	Temperature at **6** km	Temperature at **8** km	Temperature at **10** km
30.	20°C	⁻2.4°C	⁻13.6°C	⁻24.8°C	⁻36°C
31.	⁻5°C	⁻27.4°C	⁻38.6°C	⁻49.8°C	⁻61°C

This week's cold spell!
(Daily lows in °F)
Monday .... $^-2$
Tuesday 3
Wednesday.. $^-5$
Thursday 15

1 **How would you order the temperatures from coldest to warmest?** B; Obj. 8A

A 2, 3, 5, 15

B $^-5, {}^-2, 3, 15$

C $^-2, {}^-5, 3, 15$

D $^-2, 3, {}^-5, 15$

2 **A storage building with an area of 2,000 ft^2 is to be partly converted at one end into an office with an area of 375 ft^2. By what percent will the storage area have been decreased?** F; Obj. 5B

F 81.2%

G 77%

H 23%

J 18.8%

Petty Cash Account 1/5/99
Lunch −\$2.85
Babysitting \$18.50
CD −\$12.35

3 **What is the final balance of the cash account?** C; Obj. 8D

A \$28.00

B \$9.00

C \$3.30

D $^-$\$3.30

4 **During a 24-hour period starting at 1 o'clock, how many times, on the hour, will the hands of a clock form an angle that is neither acute nor obtuse.** F; Obj. 7B

F 8 H 4

G 6 J 2

5 **Which equation has a solution that is equivalent to the equation $n - 12 = 18$?** B; Obj. 1D

A $2n = 27$

B $n - 5 = 25$

C $2n + 3 = 18$

D $\frac{45}{n} = 9$

6 **The formula for finding the temperature in degrees Fahrenheit (°F) given the temperature in degrees Celsius (°C) is $F = \frac{9}{5}C + 32$. The temperature on a spring day is 59°F. What is the equivalent temperature in degrees Celsius?** J; Obj. 1F

F 91°C

G 46°C

H 31°C

J 15°C

7 **Which operation do you perform first in simplifying the expression $3 \div 4.5 \times 1.8 + (1.2 + 3.8)^2$?** C; Obj. 2E

A $3 \div 45$

B 4.5×1.8

C $1.2 + 3.8$

D $(1.2 + 3.8)^2$

8 **How many diagonals are there in a heptagon?** H; Obj. 7E

F 7

G 10

H 14

J 28

UNIT 9 • TABLE OF CONTENTS

Algebra: Expressions and Equations

Dear Family,

During the next few weeks, our math class will be learning and practicing how to solve one-step and two-step equations involving whole numbers and rational numbers. Several new ideas leading up to this will also be included.

You can expect to see homework that provides practice with these skills. Here is a sample you may want to keep handy if help is needed.

We will be using this vocabulary:

exponent a number that tells how many times a base is to be used as a factor

power a number than can be expressed using a single base and exponent; 2^3 is **2** to the third power

square root a number such that its square is a given number. **5** and **⁻5** are square roots of **25**

irrational number a number that is not rational. The square root of **10** ($\sqrt{10}$) is an irrational number

monomial an expression consisting of a number, a variable, or the product of a number and one or more variables

polynomial an expression that is itself a monomial or is the sum or product of monomials

coefficient the numerical factor in a variable expression

constant the numerical term in a polynomial

scientific notation a notation for writing a number as a product of a number from **1** to **10** and a power of **10**

Solving Two-Step Equations

$3x + 5 = 29$	
$3x + (5 + {}^{-}5) = 29 + {}^{-}5$	Add the opposite (⁻5) to each side of the equation.
$3x + 0 = 24$	Simplify.
$\frac{3x}{3} = \frac{24}{3}$	Divide each side by 3.
$x = 8$	Simplify.

Check by substitution.

$3x + 5 = 29$	Original equation
$3(8) + 5 = 29$	Substitute 8 for the variable.
$24 + 5 = 29$	Add.

During this unit, students will need to continue practicing with opposites of numbers and all operations with rational numbers and decimals.

Sincerely,

Name ________________________

Expressions and Roots

Guided Practice: Ex. 1, 3, 7, 12 & 14, pp. 243–245
Independent Practice: Complete pp. 243–245

You have used powers with positive exponents to show repeated multiplication when you write, simplify, and evaluate expressions.

In the following examples you will see how the exponents in factors, products, and quotients are related to each other.

exponent

$\underbrace{5 \cdot 5 \cdot 5}_{\text{factors}} = 5^3$ (base: 5)

Read 5^3 as "5 cubed" or "5 to the third power."

Simplify: $5^2 \cdot 5^3$

Multiplying Powers When you multiply powers with the same base, add the exponents.

$$5^2 \cdot 5^3 = \underbrace{(5 \cdot 5)}_{\text{2 factors}} \cdot \underbrace{(5 \cdot 5 \cdot 5)}_{\text{3 factors}} = \underbrace{(5 \cdot 5 \cdot 5 \cdot 5 \cdot 5)}_{\text{2 factors + 3 factors}}$$
$$= 5^5 \rightarrow 3{,}125$$

Simplify: $\frac{5^5}{5^3}$

Dividing Powers When you divide powers with the same base, subtract the exponents.

$$\frac{5^5}{5^3} = \frac{\overbrace{5 \cdot 5 \cdot 5 \cdot 5 \cdot 5}^{\text{5 factors}}}{\underbrace{5 \cdot 5 \cdot 5}_{\text{3 factors}}} = \overbrace{5 \cdot 5}^{\text{5 factors − 3 factors}} \rightarrow 5^2 \rightarrow 25$$

Simplify: $\frac{5^3}{5^3}$

- You can simplify the expression using fractions.

$$\frac{5^3}{5^3} = \frac{5 \cdot 5 \cdot 5}{5 \cdot 5 \cdot 5} \rightarrow 1$$

- You can simplify the expression using exponents.

$$\frac{5^3}{5^3} = 5^{3-3} = 5^0 \rightarrow 1$$

You read 5^0 as "5 to the zero power."

Zero Exponents
If b is a nonzero number, then $b^0 = 1$.

Simplify: $\frac{5^3}{5^5}$

- You can simplify the expression using fractions.

$$\frac{5^3}{5^5} = \frac{5 \cdot 5 \cdot 5}{5 \cdot 5 \cdot 5 \cdot 5 \cdot 5} \rightarrow \frac{1}{5 \cdot 5} \rightarrow \frac{1}{25}$$

- You can simplify the expression using exponents.

$$\frac{5^3}{5^5} = 5^{3-5} \rightarrow 5^{-2} \rightarrow \frac{1}{5 \cdot 5} \rightarrow \frac{1}{5^2} \rightarrow \frac{1}{25}$$

You read 5^{-2} as "5 to the negative 2 power."

Negative Exponents
If b is a nonzero number and n is a positive integer, then $b^{-n} = \frac{1}{b^n}$.

Write the expressions using negative exponents.

1. $\frac{1}{4} =$ 2^{-2} $\quad\frac{1}{y} =$ y^{-1} $\quad\frac{1}{5 \cdot 5} =$ 5^{-2} $\quad\frac{1}{x \cdot x \cdot x \cdot x} =$ x^{-4}

2. $\frac{1}{2 \cdot 2 \cdot 2} =$ 2^{-3} $\quad\frac{1}{a^5} =$ a^{-5} $\quad\frac{1}{\left(\frac{1}{7}\right)^6} =$ $\left(\frac{1}{7}\right)^{-6}$ $\quad\frac{1}{\frac{b}{6}} =$ $\left(\frac{b}{6}\right)^{-1}$

Check Understanding *What is $(^-5)^{-11}(^-5)^9$ when simplified?* $(\frac{1}{25})$
Find $\sqrt{\frac{256}{25}}$. $(\frac{16}{5})$

Here are some other examples that show how to simplify both rational and variable expressions with negative exponents.

Simplify: $\left(\frac{3}{4}\right)^{-2}$ | Simplify: $\left(\frac{a}{4}\right)^{-2}$

1. Use the definition of negative exponents.

$\left(\frac{3}{4}\right)^{-2} = \frac{1}{\left(\frac{3}{4}\right)^2}$ | $\left(\frac{a}{4}\right)^{-2} = \frac{1}{\left(\frac{a}{4}\right)^2}$

2. Multiply.

$= \frac{1}{\frac{3}{4} \cdot \frac{3}{4}}$ | $= \frac{1}{\left(\frac{a}{4}\right)\left(\frac{a}{4}\right)}$

3. Write the reciprocal. Simplify.

$= \frac{1}{\frac{9}{16}} \rightarrow \frac{16}{9} \rightarrow 1\frac{7}{9}$ | $= \frac{1}{\frac{a^2}{16}} \rightarrow \frac{16}{a^2}$

Sometimes you need to use number properties to rewrite expressions before you can simplify them.

Use the associative and commutative properties to group numbers with the same base together.

Simplify: $(2^3 \cdot 3^5) \cdot (2^{-8} \cdot 3^2)$.
Write the result using positive exponents.

$$(2^3 \cdot 3^5) \cdot (2^{-8} \cdot 3^2) = (2^3 \cdot 2^{-8}) \cdot (3^5 \cdot 3^2)$$
$$= 2^{-5} \cdot 3^7$$
$$= \frac{3^7}{2^5}$$

$^-5$ is a negative exponent.

Simplify.

3. $(^-2)^{-5} = \frac{-1}{32}$ | $(^-x)^{-3} = \frac{-1}{x^3}$ | $(^-5)^{-4} = \frac{1}{625}$

4. $\left(\frac{3}{5}\right)^{-2} = \frac{25}{9}$ | $\left(\frac{1}{3}\right)^{-3} = 27$ | $\left(\frac{3}{7}\right)^{-2} = \frac{49}{9}$

5. $\left(\frac{4}{c}\right)^{-2} = \frac{c^2}{16}$ | $\left(\frac{1}{5}\right)^{-4} = 625$ | $\left(\frac{2}{11}\right)^{-2} = \frac{121}{4}$

6. $\left(\frac{-2}{b}\right)^{-1} = \frac{-b}{2}$ | $\left(\frac{-1}{3}\right)^{3} = \frac{-1}{27}$ | $\left(\frac{a}{7}\right)^{-3} = \frac{343}{a^3}$

Simplify. Write your result using positive exponents.

7. $5^{-9} \cdot 5^{-1} \cdot 5^6 = \frac{1}{5^4}$ | $x^{-3} \cdot x^6 = x^3$ | $a^{-5} \cdot a^3 \cdot a^{-8} = \frac{1}{a^{10}}$

8. $7^{-8} \div 7^{-3} = \frac{1}{7^5}$ | $y^{-4} \div y^5 = \frac{1}{y^9}$ | $2^6 \div 2^6 = 2^0$ or 1

9. $9^6 \div 9^{-9} = 9^{15}$ | $c^{-2} \div c = \frac{1}{c^3}$ | $(ab)^8 \div (ab)^{-2} = (ab)^{10}$

10. $(3^4 \cdot 5^5) \cdot (3^{-7} \cdot 5^3)$ $\frac{5^8}{3^3}$ | $(x^6 \cdot y^9) \cdot (x^{-6} \cdot y^{-5})$ y^4 | $(2^8 \cdot a^3) \cdot (2^{-3} \cdot a^{-2})$ 2^5a

11. $(5^2 \cdot 7^3) \div (5^{-3} \cdot 7^2)$ $5^5 \cdot 7^1$ | $(a^{-1} \cdot 4^2) \div (a^{-3} \cdot 4^7)$ $\frac{a^2}{4^5}$ | $(6^3 \cdot x^2) \div (6^{-4} \cdot x^{-2})$ $6^7 \cdot x^4$

Name ______________________________

You know that inverse operations "undo" each other. Raising a base to a power and finding a **root** or base are inverse operations, so they undo each other.

The square of any base is that number multiplied by itself. Since $(^-5)^2$ and $(5)^2$ equal **25**, both $^-5$ and **5** are called **square roots** of **25**.

$(^-5)^2 = (^-5)(^-5) \rightarrow 25$

$5^2 = (5)(5) \rightarrow 25$

The symbol for square root ($\sqrt{\ }$) is called a *radical sign*. The $\sqrt{\ }$ symbol represents the *principal*, or positive square root.

$\sqrt{25} = 5$ Think: $5 \times 5 = 25$ So $\sqrt{25}$ is 5.

$\sqrt{49} = 7$ Think: $7 \times 7 = 49$ So $\sqrt{49}$ is 7.

$\sqrt{\frac{36}{121}} = \frac{6}{11}$ Think: $\frac{6}{11} \times \frac{6}{11} = \frac{36}{121}$ So $\sqrt{\frac{36}{121}}$ is $\frac{6}{11}$.

When the square root of a number cannot be written as a fraction with integer terms, it is an **irrational number.**

You can estimate the square root of an irrational number between integer values.

Estimate. $\sqrt{17}$.

- $\sqrt{16} = 4$ and $\sqrt{25} = 5$, so $\sqrt{17}$ must be *between* **4** and **5.**
- $\sqrt{17}$ is closer to $\sqrt{16}$ than to $\sqrt{25}$, so $\sqrt{17}$ is closer to **4** than to **5.**

Find the square root.

12. $\sqrt{64}$ 8 $\sqrt{100}$ 10 $\sqrt{400}$ 20 $\sqrt{625}$ 25

13. $\sqrt{\frac{144}{169}}$ $\frac{12}{13}$ $\sqrt{\frac{4}{49}}$ $\frac{2}{7}$ $\sqrt{\frac{289}{676}}$ $\frac{17}{26}$ $\sqrt{\frac{1225}{529}}$ $\frac{35}{23}$

Tell whether the square root is rational or irrational. If it is rational, write the square root. If it is irrational, write which two integers the square root falls between.

14. $\sqrt{21}$ Irrational; 4 and 5 $\sqrt{31}$ Irrational; 5 and 6 $\sqrt{144}$ Rational; 12

15. $\sqrt{120}$ Irrational; 10 and 11 $\sqrt{225}$ Rational; 15 $\sqrt{150}$ Irrational; 12 and 13

Problem Solving Reasoning

You can find square roots of algebraic expressions with even powers. For example, $\sqrt{25x^2}$ is the same as $\sqrt{5x \cdot 5x}$ or $5x$, when x is positive. Find the square root. Assume $x > 0$.

16. $\sqrt{81x^4y^6}$ $9x^2y^3$

17. $\sqrt{\frac{x^2 \cdot 2^4}{y^6}}$ $x \cdot \frac{2^2}{y^3}$ or $\frac{2^2x}{y^3}$

Test Prep ★ Mixed Review

18 If two cubes, each numbered 1–6, are rolled, what is the probability that two fours appear?
D; Obj. 6F

A $\frac{1}{3}$ B $\frac{1}{6}$ C $\frac{1}{18}$ D $\frac{1}{36}$

19 Which of the following types of quadrilaterals has just one pair of parallel sides? F; Obj. 7E

F trapezoid H rectangle
G parallelogram J square

Closing the Lesson *Simplify $b^{-3}b^4 \div b^{-4}$. (b^5) Find $\sqrt{\frac{25}{64}}$. ($\frac{5}{8}$)*

Name ____________________

Guided Practice: Ex. 4, p. 246; Ex. 6, p. 247
Independent Practice: Complete pp. 246–247

Operations with Monomial Expressions

Algebraic expressions can be **monomials** or **polynomials.** A monomial is an expression that has a number, a variable, or has a product of a number and one or more variables. In a monomial, a numerical factor is called a **coefficient.**

A polynomial is an expression that is itself a monomial or is the sum or difference of monomials. In a polynomial, a numerical term is called a **constant.**

Monomials

8 is coefficient of x

$2, 8x,$ and $4a^2b^2$

4 is a coefficient of a^2b^2

Polynomials

constants

$8 + x, 8x + 5,$ and $4x - 3x^2 + 7y$

Monomials with the same variable base (or bases) and exponents have **like terms.**

- These monomials have like terms.

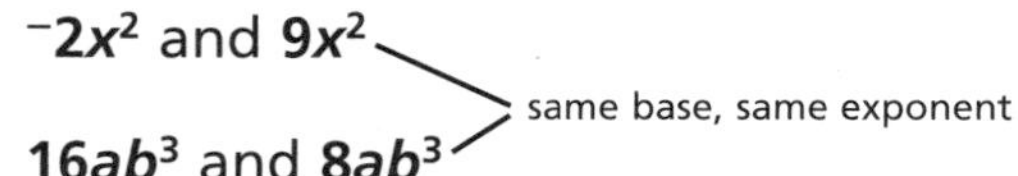

$^-2x^2$ and $9x^2$

$16ab^3$ and $8ab^3$

same base, same exponent

- These monomials have unlike terms.

$^-2a^3$ and $11b^3$

$3x^2y$ and $^-4xy^2$

different base, same exponents

When you multiply or divide monomials with like bases, you can use the rules of exponents to simplify factors.

Simplify: $3xy^7 \cdot 4x^2y^9$

To multiply powers, you add exponents.

$$3xy^7 \cdot 4x^2y^9 = (3 \cdot 4) \cdot (x \cdot x^2)(y^7 \cdot y^9)$$

$$= 12\,(x^{1+2})\,(y^{7+9}) \longrightarrow 12x^3y^{16}$$

Simplify: $\frac{6y^{14}}{2y^8}$

To divide powers, you subtract exponents.

$$\frac{6y^{14}}{2y^8} = \left(\frac{6}{2}\right)y^{14-8} \longrightarrow 3y^6$$

State whether the expression is a monomial or a polynomial.

1. $3x + 5y$ polynomial $\qquad 4x^2y^2$ monomial $\qquad 3$ monomial

2. $u^2 + 3u + 2$ polynomial $\qquad y^2 + (9 - 2)z^2$ polynomial $\qquad \frac{1}{2}z$ monomial

Write the coefficient of the variables.

3. $3x$ 3 $\qquad 5y$ 5 $\qquad 4x^2y^2$ 4 $\qquad y^2$ 1 $\qquad (9 - 2)z^2$ $9 - 2$ $\qquad \frac{1}{2}z$ $\frac{1}{2}$

Simplify.

4. $a^4b^9c^2 \cdot a^2b^5c^3$ $a^6b^{14}c^5$ $\qquad x^7 \cdot x^5$ x^{12} $\qquad 3g^4 \cdot 5g^6 \cdot 6g^2$ $90g^{12}$

5. $\frac{y^{13}}{y^8}$ y^5 $\qquad \frac{12b^{10}}{4b^2}$ $3b^8$ $\qquad 4z^5 \cdot \left(\frac{^-2z^7}{8z^3}\right)$ $^-2^9$

Check Understanding *Simplify:* $^-8xy - {}^-3xy$ *and* $\frac{(54c^5d)}{(9c^3)}$ (^-5xy and $6c^2d$)

Name ____________________

When you add or subtract monomials, you can use number properties to combine like terms.

Simplify: $^{-}5a^2b - 2a^2b$.

1. Rewrite it as an addition expression. $^{-}5a^2b - 2a^2b = {^{-}5a^2b} + {^{-}2a^2b}$

2. Use the distributive property. $= (^{-}5 + {^{-}2})a^2b$

3. Combine (add) the coefficients. $= {^{-}7a^2b}$

Simplify the expression.

6. $5x - 2x$ $\underline{3x}$ $7a - {^{-}4a}$ $\underline{11a}$ $2rs + {^{-}8rs}$ $\underline{^{-}6rs}$

7. $8a^2b^3 - {^{-}4a^2b^3}$ $\underline{12a^2b^3}$ $^{-}7x - {^{-}4x}$ $\underline{^{-}3x}$ $^{-}9x + 5x - {^{-}12x} + 2x$ $\underline{10x}$

8. $8m^2 - 2m^2 + 4m^2$ $\underline{10m^2}$ $3e - 7e + 6e + {^{-}2e}$ $\underline{0}$ $5a^5c^4 + 2a^5c^4 - 9a^5c^4$ $\underline{^{-}2a^5c^4}$

9. $^{-}6x^2 + 10x^2$ $\underline{4x^2}$ $a^3b^6c^9 - 5a^3b^6c^9$ $\underline{^{-}4a^3b^6c^9}$ $4x - {^{-}3x} + 8x + {^{-}6x} - 5x$ $\underline{4x}$

Problem Solving Reasoning Write and simplify an expression for the area of the figure.

10.

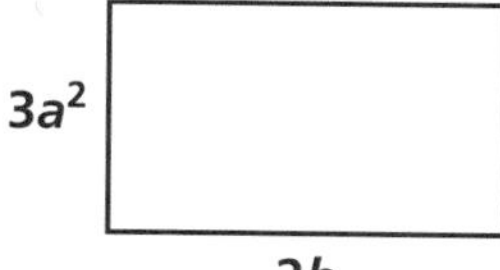

A: $\underline{6a^2b}$

11.

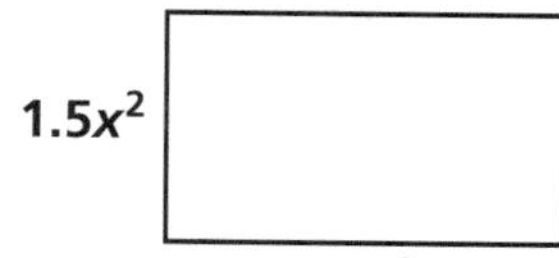

A: $\underline{3x^4}$

Test Prep ★ Mixed Review

12 Which expression has the value $^{-}19$?
C; Obj. 8A, 8B

A $9 + |{^{-}5}| + |{^{-}33}|$

B $9 - |{^{-}5}| - |{^{-}33}|$

C $9 + |{^{-}5}| - |{^{-}33}|$

D $^{-}9 + |{^{-}5}| - |{^{-}33}|$

13 What is the value of $^{-}9 \cdot {^{-}12} \div {^{-}6} \cdot 2$?
G; Obj. 8C

F $^{-}1296$

G $^{-}36$

H 36

J 1,296

Closing the Lesson *When can two monomials be added or subtracted?* (The monomials must have like terms.) *Can you simplify ($^{-}2ab^4$)($3a^2b^6$), even though the two factors do not have like terms?* (Yes, because this is multiplication, not addition or subtraction.)

Name ______________________

Guided Practice: Ex. 1 & 8, p. 248; Ex. 10 & 14, p. 249
Independent Practice: Complete pp. 248–249

Operations with Polynomial Expressions

You can also use the number properties to simplify polynomials.

To subtract integers, add the opposites.

Simplify: $8x - 7y - 6x + 4y$.

1. Rewrite the subtractions as additions.
2. Use the commutative and associative properties.
3. Use the distributive property to combine like terms.
4. Simplify.

$$
\begin{aligned}
8x - 7y - 6x + 4y &= 8x + {}^-7y + {}^-6x + 4y \\
&= 8x + {}^-6x + {}^-7y + 4y \\
&= (8 + {}^-6)x + ({}^-7 + 4)y \\
&= 2x + {}^-3y \text{ or } 2x - 3y
\end{aligned}
$$

Simplify by adding or subtracting like terms.

1. $2n + 3m + {}^-4n + 2m$ ____ ${}^-2n + 5m$ $\qquad$ $3x^2 + 2x + 4x^2 + {}^-3x$ ____ $7x^2 - x$
2. $4c + 5d + {}^-2c + {}^-3d$ ____ $2c + 2d$ $\qquad$ $a^2 + b^2 + 2a^2 + 2b^2$ ____ $3a^2 + 3b^2$
3. $6r + 5s + 7t + 5r + 2t$ ____ $11r + 5s + 9t$ $\qquad$ $3m + 4n + 2 + 2m + {}^-3n + 5$ ____ $5m + n + 7$
4. $5x^2 + 2x + 4 + 2x^2 + {}^-2x$ ____ $7x^2 + 4$ $\qquad$ $18y^2 + 8y + 5 + 9y^2 + 6y + {}^-7$ ____ $27y^2 + 14y^{-2}$
5. $(4x^2 + 3) - (x^2 + 2)$ ____ $3x^2 + 1$ $\qquad$ $(6r + 5) - (2r + 4)$ ____ $4r + 1$
6. $(6a^2 + 5b) - (2a^2 + 3b)$ ____ $4a^2 + 2b$ $\qquad$ $(6m + 2n) - (3m + n)$ ____ $3m + n$
7. $(7t^2 + 2y) - (6t^2 + 2y)$ ____ t^2 $\qquad$ $(8d + 6e) - (5d + 3e)$ ____ $3d + 3e$

You also use the distributive property when you multiply or divide a polynomial by a monomial.

Simplify: $3x(x^2 + {}^-4x + 5)$.

To multiply, use the distributive property to *multiply* each term.

$$
\begin{aligned}
3x(x^2 + {}^-4x + 5) &= 3x \cdot x^2 + (3x) \cdot ({}^-4x) + 3x \cdot 5 \\
&= 3x^3 + {}^-12x^2 + 15x \text{ or} \\
&\quad 3x^3 - 12x^2 + 15x
\end{aligned}
$$

Simplify: $\dfrac{6x^2 - 4x}{2x}$.

To divide, use the distributive property to *rewrite* the polynomial first.

$$
\frac{6x^2 - 4x}{2x} = \frac{2x(3x - 2)}{2x} = 3x - 2
$$

Multiply.

8. $3a(a + {}^-2)$ ____ $3a^2 + {}^-6a$ $\qquad$ $3a(a + 1)$ ____ $3a^2 + 3a$

9. $c(4c + d)$ ____ $4c^2 + cd$ $\qquad$ $2t(r + s)$ ____ $2rt + 2st$

Check Understanding *Simplify $(7x - 4y + 2z) - (3x + y - 8z)$ and ${}^-3c(c^2 + 5c - 1)$.* ($4x - 5y + 10z$ and ${}^-3c^3 - 15c^2 + 3c$)

Name ______________________

Simplify by multiplying.

10. $5x(3x + {}^-2)$ $15x^2 - 10x$ $\qquad$ $x({}^-3x + y)$ ${}^-3x^2 + xy$

11. $4(x^2 + 2x + {}^-2)$ $4x^2 + 8x + {}^-8$ $\qquad$ $6(y^2 + 3y + 2)$ $6y^2 + 18y + 12$

12. $2a(3a + 4b + c)$ $6a^2 + 8ab + 2ac$ $\qquad$ $2r(3r + 4s + {}^-3)$ $6r^2 + 8rs + {}^-6r$

13. ${}^-2a(3a + 4b + c)$ ${}^-6a^2 + {}^-8ab + {}^-2ac$ $\qquad$ ${}^-4x(2x + {}^-3y + 2z)$ ${}^-8x^2 + 12xy + {}^-8xz$

Simplify by dividing.

14. $\dfrac{9ab^2 + 3b}{3b}$ $3ab + 1$ $\qquad$ $\dfrac{6a^2b + {}^-4b}{2b}$ $3a^2 - 2$

15. $\dfrac{12n^2 + 10n + 6}{2}$ $6n^2 + 5n + 3$ $\qquad$ $\dfrac{16y^2 + {}^-8y + 12}{4}$ $4y^2 + {}^-2y + 3$

16. $\dfrac{20x^3 + 15x^2 + 10x}{5x}$ $4x^2 + 3x + 2$ $\qquad$ $\dfrac{12n^3 + 16n^2 + {}^-20n}{4n}$ $3n^2 + 4n - 5$

Problem Solving Reasoning Write an expression for the perimeter and area of the shaded figure.

17.

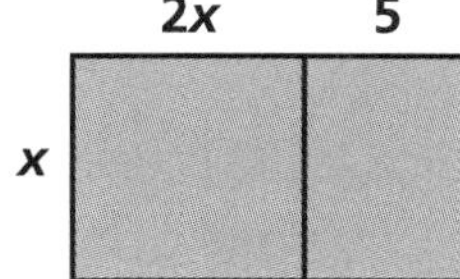

P: $6x + 10$

A: $2x^2 + 5x$

18.

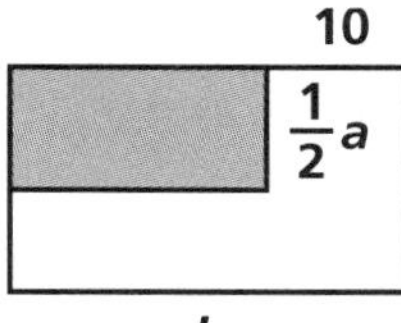

P: $a + 2b - 20$

A: $\frac{1}{2}ab - 5a$

Quick Check

Simplify.

19. 4^{-3} $\frac{1}{64}$ $\qquad$ **20.** $x^{-6} \div x^5$ $\frac{1}{x^{11}}$

21. $(2^3 \cdot y) \cdot (3^2 \cdot y^5)$ $72y^6$ $\qquad$ **22.** $\sqrt{64}$ 8

23. $8y^2 - {}^-2y^2$ $10y^2$ $\qquad$ **24.** $8y^2 \cdot {}^-2y^2$ ${}^-16y^4$

25. $\dfrac{8y^2}{{}^-2y^2}$ ${}^-4$ $\qquad$ **26.** $3x(3x^2 + 7)$ $9x^3 + 21x$

27. $6b^2 + 8b - (2b + 8b^2)$ ${}^-2b^2 + 6b$

Work Space.

Item	Error Analysis
19-22	**Common Error** Watch for students who interpret negative exponents incorrectly. **Reteaching** Reteach 69
23-25	**Common Error** Watch for students who forget to simplify the coefficients. **Reteaching** Reteach 70
26-27	**Common Error** Students may not recognize like terms. **Reteaching** Reteach 71

Closing the Lesson *Simplify* $xz^3(10x^2 - 3z) + {}^-4xz^4$. ($10x^3z^3 + {}^-7xz^4$) *How do you divide a polynomial by a monomial?* (Factor the numerator first, then divide.)

Name ______________________

Guided Practice: Ex. 1 & 2, p. 250; Ex. 9 & 10, p. 251

Independent Practice: Complete pp. 250–251

Evaluating Polynomial Expressions

Remember, to **evaluate** or find the value of a variable expression, you substitute numbers for the variables. Then, find the value of the numerical expression. The value of the expression depends on the values for the variable.

Evaluate **$3x + 4$** for **$x = 2$** and **$x = ^-2$**.

- Substitute **2** for **x**. Then evaluate.

$3x + 4$
$3(2) + 4$
$6 + 4$
10

- Substitute **$^-2$** for **x**. Then evaluate.

$3x + 4$
$3(^-2) + 4$
$^-6 + 4$
$^-2$

When you evaluate polynomials, you evaluate them in the same way.

Evaluate **$3x^2 - x - 4$** for **$x = 2$** and **$x = ^-2$**.

- Substitute **2** for **x** in each term. Then evaluate.

$3x^2 - x - 4$
$3(2)^2 - (2) - 4$
$3(4) - 2 - 4$
$12 - 2 - 4$
6

- Substitute **$^-2$** for **x** in each term. Then evaluate.

$3x^2 - x - 4$
$3(^-2)^2 - (^-2) - 4$
$3(4) + 2 - 4$
$12 + 2 - 4$
10

Evaluate the expressions.

1. $2x^2 - 3x + 1$ for $x = 2$

3

2. $3x^5 + 4x - 7$ for $x = 1$

0

3. $7x^3 - 2x^2 + 1x$ for $x = ^-1$

$^-10$

4. $^-2x^2 - x + 3$ for $x = ^-2$

$^-3$

5. $^-4x^2 + 5x - 2$ for $x = 3$

$^-23$

6. $6x^4 + 5x^2 + 12$ for $x = 0$

12

Evaluate the expressions to complete the tables below.

7.

x	$^-x^2$	2	$^-x^2 + 2$
$^-1$	$^-1$	2	1
0	0	2	2
1	$^-1$	2	1
2	$^-4$	2	$^-2$
3	$^-9$	2	$^-7$

8.

y	$2y^2$	y	$^-3$	$2y^2 + y - 3$
$^-1$	2	$^-1$	$^-3$	$^-2$
0	0	0	$^-3$	$^-3$
1	2	1	$^-3$	0
2	8	2	$^-3$	7
3	18	3	$^-3$	18

Check Understanding *Evaluate $x^4 - 3x^2 + 6x - 1$ for $x = 2$.* (15) *Do you get the same answer when you use $x = ^-2$?* (No. For $x = ^-2$, the answer is $^-9$.)

Name ______________________________

One way to evaluate polynomial expressions is to use an **electronic spreadsheet,** a computer program that organizes, uses, and stores numerical data. A spreadsheet looks like a table. As you change a value in one **cell** (box), the program automatically changes the values in all the other cells.

Study the spreadsheet below and determine the missing data.

On a computer X^2 means X^2.

	Evaluating a Polynomial Expression				
	X	X^2	5X	−2	X^2 + 5X − 2
9.	0	0	0	−2	−2
10.	1	1	5	−2	4
11.	2	4	10	−2	12
12.	3	9	15	−2	22
13.	4	16	20	−2	34
14.	5	25	25	−2	48
15.	6	36	30	−2	64
16.	7	49	35	−2	82
17.	8	64	40	−2	102

Problem Solving Reasoning

If you toss a ball up in the air at a rate of 20 meters per second, then the formula $h = {}^{-}5t^2 + 20t$ gives the height of the ball above the ground at time t seconds. Complete the spreadsheet. Then, answer the questions.

18.

T	−5T^2	20T	−5T^2 + 20T
1	−5	20	15
2	−20	40	20
3	−45	60	15
4	−80	80	0

Closing the Lesson *Given a polynomial expression, describe how to evaluate it for x = ⁻4.* (Evaluate each term of the expression by substituting ⁻4 for *x*. Then, combine these results by adding or subtracting to get the final answer.)

19. How long is the ball in the air before it hits the ground?

4 s

20. After how many seconds does the ball reach its highest height? What is its highest height?

2 s; 20 m

Test Prep ★ Mixed Review

Circle the letter of your choice.

21 **What is the simplest form of the expression $m^{-2} \cdot m^5 \cdot m^{-3}$?** D; Obj. 9A

A m^{30}

B m^{-30}

C $3m^{-30}$

D 1

22 **Which polynomial can be simplified to the expression $2xy + 3$?** H; Obj. 9A

F $\frac{14x^3y^3 + 21x^2y^2}{7xy}$

G $\frac{14x^3y^3 + 21x^2y^2}{7}$

H $\frac{14x^3y^3 + 21x^2y^2}{7x^2y^2}$

J $\frac{14x^3y^3 + 21x^2y^2}{7x^3y^3}$

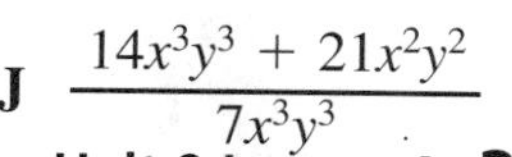

Name ______________________________

Guided Practice: Ex. 1 & 2, p. 252

Independent Practice: Complete p. 253

Problem Solving Application: Choose an Equation

In this lesson, equations are used to model problem situations. Clues in a problem can help you decide whether to choose an addition, subtraction, multiplication, or division equation. The following information is known.

- The yearly cost is **$1,800**
- There are **12** months in a year.

Understanding the relationship between the units in a problem will help you decide on the correct operation.

The yearly cost for renting a car from a dealer is **$1,800.** If n = *the cost per month*, then which equation below could be used to find the cost per month?

A $n + 12 = 1{,}800$ **C** $n \cdot 12 = 1{,}800$

B $n - 12 = 1{,}800$ **D** $\frac{n}{12} = 1{,}800$

Tips to Remember:

1. Understand 2. Decide 3. Solve 4. Look back

- Ask yourself whether you have solved a problem like this before.
- Think about the relationships between the units. Which operation do you use to relate the units or data in the problem? What unit will the solution have?
- Think about the strategies you have learned, and use them to help you solve a problem.

Solve.

1. In the problem above, which equation (A, B, C, or D) models the situation correctly?

Think: What operation do you use to write years as months? What expression do you use to write the monthly cost given the yearly cost?

multiply; $n \cdot 12$

Answer C

2. The quotient of **twice** a number x and **three** is **4**. Which equation, $\frac{2x}{3} = 4$ or $\frac{x + 2}{3} = 4$, models the situation correctly?

Think: Which operation do you use for "twice" a number? Which operation do you use to find a quotient?

multiply; divide

Answer $\frac{2x}{3} = 4$

Check Understanding *For "Three times a number increased by 4 is 8 times the number," choose an equation:* $3x + 4 = 8x$ *or* $3(x + 4) = 8x$. ($3x + 4 = 8x$)

Choose the appropriate equation. Do not solve.
Explain why you choose the equation. Explanations will vary.

3. If you divide Mara's age by **4,** then take away **2** more years, you get **10.** How old is Mara?

A $\frac{n}{4} + 2 = 10$ C $4n + 2 = 10$

B $\frac{n}{4} - 2 = 10$ D $4n - 2 = 10$

4. Mara takes **4** piano lessons per month. The total cost per month is **$60.** How much does each piano lesson cost?

F $n + 4 = 60$ H $4n = 60$

G $n - 4 = 60$ J $\frac{n}{4} = 60$

5. The rent for a basement apartment is **$20** less per month than for a first floor apartment. The rental fee for a basement apartment is **$750.** What is the rental fee for the first floor apartment?

A $n + 20 = 750$ C $20n = 750$

B $n - 20 = 750$ D $\frac{n}{20} = 750$

6. Dante wants to buy some used furniture for **$875.** He has saved **$650** toward the total cost. How much more does he need?

F $650 + n = 875$ H $650n = 875$

G $650 - n = 875$ J $\frac{n}{650} = 875$

7. A used typewriter costs about $\frac{1}{2}$ the price of a new one. If a used typewriter costs **$90,** how much did it cost new?

A $n + \frac{1}{2} = 90$ C $2n = 90$

B $n - \frac{1}{2} = 90$ D $\frac{n}{2} = 90$

8. The product of two and the sum of a number increased by three is the same as the number decreased by **4.**

F $2(n + 3) = n - 4$ H $2n + 3 = n - 4$

G $(2 + n) \cdot 3 = 4 - n$ J $n^2 + 3 = n - 4$

Extend Your Thinking

9. Choose a problem. Then, use the equation you picked to solve the problem. Check your answer in the original problem. Did you pick the correct equation?

Answers will vary.

10. Explain your method for choosing the correct equation in problem **8.** Which words or phrases helped you choose the operation?

Explanations will vary.

Closing the Lesson *Which operation does each of these phrases suggest? "more than"* (addition), *"increased by"* (addition), *"quotient"* (division), *"less than"* (subtraction), *"product"* (multiplication), *"decreased by"* (subtraction).

Name ______________________

Guided Practice: Ex. 1, 4, 7 & 12, pp. 254–255
Independent Practice: Complete pp. 254–255

A fast and accurate way to express numbers such as those to the right is to use **scientific notation.** In scientific notation, a number is written as the product of a factor between **1** and **10** and a power of ten.

For example:

- **4,000** can be written as: **4 × 1000** or **4×10^3.**
- **0.004** can be written as: **4 × 0.001** or **4×10^{-3}.**

A light year is about **9,460,000,000,000** kilometers.

The diameter of an electron is about **0.0000000000010** centimeters.

Use these steps to write greater or lesser numbers in scientific notation.

Greater Numbers

Write in scientific notation:
9,460,000,000,000

1. Move the decimal point to the left to get a number between **1** and **10.** Count the number of places you moved the decimal point. That number is the exponent of the power of **10.**

9.460,000,000,000.

12 places, so the exponent is **12** Exponents for greater numbers are positive.

2. Write the number in scientific notation.

9.46×10^{12}

a number between **1** and **10**

a positive power of **10**

Lesser Numbers

Write in scientific notation:
0.0000000000010

1. Move the decimal point to the right to get a number between **1** and **10.** Count the number of places you moved the decimal point. That number is the exponent of the power of **10.**

0.0000000000010

12 places, so the exponent is **12** Exponents for lesser numbers are negative.

2. Write the number in scientific notation.

1.0×10^{-12}

a number between **1** and **10**

a negative power of **10**

Express the number in scientific notation.

1. **300** 3×10^2 **40,000** 4×10^4 **700,000** 7×10^5

2. **264** 2.64×10^2 **92,400** 9.24×10^4 **58** 5.8×10^1

3. **6,100** 6.1×10^3 **8,400,000** 8.4×10^6 **6,429,500** 6.4295×10^6

Express the decimal in scientific notation.

4. **0.05** 5×10^{-2} **0.095** 9.5×10^{-2} **0.00000000001** 1×10^{-11}

5. **0.862** 8.62×10^{-1} **0.0000567** 5.67×10^{-5} **0.006** 6×10^{-3}

6. **0.00937** 9.37×10^{-3} **0.0695** 6.95×10^{-2} **0.01684** 1.684×10^{-2}

Check Understanding *Express 0.00251 in scientific notation.* (2.51×10^{-3}) *Is 0.64×10^{-1} in exact scientific notation?* (No. The first number must be between 1 and 10. The number is 6.4×10^{-2} in scientific notation.)

Name ______________________

You can write a number that is in scientific notation in standard form.

Write in standard form: **7.2×10^4**

A positive power of **10** represents a number greater than **1**.

Move the decimal point **4** places to the right. Write zeros as needed.

7.2×10^4

Write zeros to the right as needed.

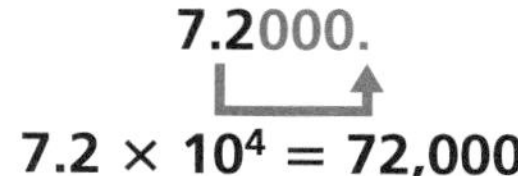

$7.2 \times 10^4 = 72{,}000$

Write in standard form: **8.4×10^{-7}**

A negative power of **10** represents a number between **0** and **1**.

Move the decimal point **7** places to the left. Write zeros as needed.

8.4×10^{-7}

Write zeros to the left as needed.

0.0000008.4

$8.4 \times 10^{-7} = 0.00000084$

Write these numbers in standard form.

7. 5.683×10^{-2} 0.05683 | 2.345×10^{-8} 0.00000002345

8. 1.834×10^{4} 18,340 | 4.1012×10^{-6} 0.0000041012

9. 9.36×10^{-5} 0.0000936 | 8.4368×10^{6} 8,436,800

10. 7.7519×10^{-9} 0.0000000077519 | 7.73192×10^{7} 77,319,200

11. 9.3×10^{12} 9,300,000,000,000 | 3.9768×10^{-7} 0.00000039768

Choose the standard form of the number given in scientific notation.

12. 7.3×10^4	0.00073	7.3	7,300	(73,000)
13. 9.1×10^{-2}	0.0091	(0.091)	0.00091	910
14. 8.65×10^2	(865)	8.65	0.0865	0.865
15. 6×10^{-3}	(0.006)	0.00006	0.6	6
16. 3.52×10^{-4}	352	0.0352	0.352	(0.000352)
17. 9.9×10^5	9,900	99,900	99,000	(990,000)
18. 1.92×10^{-1}	0.000192	(0.192)	192	0.0192

Sometimes a number may look as if it is written in scientific notation, but the first factor is not between **1** and **10.** In this case, to be in scientific notation, it must be rewritten in correct form.

$98 \times 10^4 = 9.8 \times 10^5$ $\quad 0.04 \times 10^{-5} = 4 \times 10^{-7}$ $\quad 0.53 \times 10^{-2} = 5.3 \times 10^{-3}$

Write these numbers in scientific notation.

19. 95×10^4 ___ 9.5×10^5 ___ $\quad 0.001 \times 10^{-10}$ ___ 1×10^{-13} ___

20. 75.7×10^{10} ___ 7.57×10^{11} ___ $\quad 56.29 \times 10^{-4}$ ___ 5.629×10^{-3} ___

21. 960×10^5 ___ 9.6×10^7 ___ $\quad 0.058 \times 10^{-3}$ ___ 5.8×10^{-5} ___

22. 855×10^7 ___ 8.55×10^9 ___ $\quad 75 \times 10^{-8}$ ___ 7.5×10^{-7} ___

23. 87.4×10^9 ___ 8.74×10^{10} ___ $\quad 984.3 \times 10^{-9}$ ___ 9.843×10^{-7} ___

24. Lightning strikes Earth about 864×10^4 times a year. ___ 8.64×10^6 ___

Problem Solving Reasoning Solve.

25. Write in standard form: An average size thundercloud holds about 610×10^{10} raindrops.

6,100,000,000,000

26. Write in standard form: The diameter of an atom is about 106×10^{-10} centimeters.

0.0000000106

27. Is 2.36×10^8 closer to **200** million or **1** billion? Explain.

236,000,000 is closer to 200 million.

28. Is 0.03×10^2 greater than **1** or between **0** and **1**?

3 is greater than 1.

Quick Check

Evaluate the expressions.

29. $x^2 - 3x + 2$ for $x = 2$ ___ 0 ___ **30.** $8 + 5x - 2x^3$ for $x = {}^{-}2$ ___ 14 ___

Write in scientific notation.

31. 0.00000678 ___ 6.78×10^{-6} ___

32. 3,050,000,000 ___ 3.05×10^9 ___

33. 17.9×10^{-2} ___ 1.79×10^{-1} ___

Write in standard form.

34. 2.3×10^{-4} ___ 0.00023 ___ **35.** 1.98×10^5 ___ 198,000 ___

Work Space.

Item	Error Analysis
29-30	**Common Error** Students may not evaluate each term. **Reteaching** Reteach 72
31-35	**Common Error** Students may not write the correct negative power of 10. **Reteaching** Reteach 73

Closing the Lesson *Given a decimal number between 0 and 1, describe a way to express it in scientific notation.* (Two steps: (1) "Move" the decimal point to the right so that there is one non-zero digit to its left. (2) Count the number of places that you moved the decimal point and use this as a negative exponent of the base 10.)

Name ______________________________

Guided Practice: Ex. 1, 3, 7 & 12, pp. 257–259
Independent Practice: Complete pp. 257–259

Solving Equations with Rational Numbers

You know how to solve equations using positive numbers. In this unit you will apply those same rules to solve equations with integers and rational numbers. Remember, addition and subtraction are inverse operations.

Solving Addition and Subtraction Equations

- To solve an addition equation, you subtract the same number from each side of the equation.
- To solve a subtraction equation, you add the same number to each side of the equation.

Solve: $x + 5 = 2$

1. Original equation $\quad x + 5 = 2$
2. Subtract **5** from each side. $\quad x + 5 - 5 = 2 - 5$
3. Simplify each side. $\quad x = {}^{-}3$

√ Check: $x + 5 = 2$

$^{-}3 + 5 = 2$

Solve: $x - \frac{3}{4} = 2$

1. Original equation $\quad x - \frac{3}{4} = 2$
2. Add $\frac{3}{4}$ to each side. $\quad x - \frac{3}{4} + \frac{3}{4} = 2 + \frac{3}{4}$
3. Simplify each side. $\quad x = 2 + \frac{3}{4}$
4. Write **2** as a fraction. $\quad x = \frac{8}{4} + \frac{3}{4}$

$x = \frac{11}{4}$ or $2\frac{3}{4}$

√ Check: $x - \frac{3}{4} = 2$

$2\frac{3}{4} - \frac{3}{4} = 2$

Solve these addition and subtraction equations. Check your answer by substitution.

1. $c + {}^{-}15 = 7$ $\underline{c = 22}$ $\quad 12 = b + 32$ $\underline{b = {}^{-}20}$ $\quad 16 + x = 25$ $\underline{x = 9}$

2. $b + 5.2 = 8.9$ $\underline{b = 3.7}$ $\quad 18 + x = {}^{-}15$ $\underline{x = {}^{-}33}$ $\quad 8.4 + x = 6.2$ $\underline{x = {}^{-}2.2}$

3. $12 - b = 17$ $\underline{b = {}^{-}5}$ $\quad 15 - x = 9$ $\underline{x = 6}$ $\quad y - 9 = 12$ $\underline{y = 21}$

4. $^{-}17 - a = 20$ $\underline{a = {}^{-}37}$ $\quad x - 11 = {}^{-}4$ $\underline{x = 7}$ $\quad a - 6 = {}^{-}12$ $\underline{a = {}^{-}6}$

Check Understanding *Solve and check* $^{-}9 = \frac{4}{x}$ *and* $n - 2 = {}^{-}7$. ($x = {}^{-}\frac{4}{9}$, *and* $n = {}^{-}5$)

Solve these addition and subtraction equations. Check your answer by substitution.

5. $a + 23 = 19$ $a = ^-4$ $104 = 92 + a$ $a = 12$ $b + 47 = ^-15$ $b = ^-62$

6. $^-86 + n = 100$ $n = 186$ $b + 3.6 = 5.2$ $b = 1.6$ $x + ^-78 = 33$ $x = 111$

7. $\frac{3}{4} + y = \frac{5}{4}$ $y = \frac{1}{2}$ $\frac{5}{8} + x = 1\frac{1}{8}$ $x = \frac{1}{2}$ $\frac{9}{11} - n = \frac{3}{11}$ $n = \frac{6}{11}$

8. $b - \frac{4}{7} = 1\frac{2}{7}$ $b = \frac{13}{7}$ or $1\frac{6}{7}$ $x + \frac{5}{9} = \frac{^-7}{9}$ $x = \frac{^-4}{3}$ or $^-1\frac{1}{3}$ $z + \frac{2}{3} = \frac{1}{12}$ $z = ^-\frac{7}{12}$

Remember, multiplication and division are inverse operations too.

Solving Multiplication and Division Equations

- To solve a multiplication equation, you divide each side of the equation by the same nonzero number.
- To solve a division equation, you multiply each side of the equation by the same nonzero number.

Solve: $6n = ^-30$

1. Original equation $6n = ^-30$

2. Divide each side by **6**. $\frac{6n}{6} = \frac{^-30}{6}$

3. Simplify each side. $1 \cdot n = ^-5$

$n = ^-5$

√ Check: $6n = ^-30$

$6(^-5) = ^-30$

Solve: $\frac{x}{3} = \frac{^-5}{6}$

1. Original equation $\frac{x}{3} = \frac{^-5}{6}$

2. Multiply each side by **3**. $3\left(\frac{x}{3}\right) = 3\left(\frac{^-5}{6}\right)$

3. Simplify each side. $x = \frac{^-5}{2}$

√ Check: $\frac{x}{3} = \frac{^-5}{6}$

$\frac{\frac{^-5}{2}}{3} = \left(\frac{^-5}{2}\right)\left(\frac{1}{3}\right)$

$= \frac{^-5}{6}$

Name ______________________

Solve the multiplication or division equation. Check your answer by substitution.

9. $7x = 28$ $x = 4$ | $4c = ^-36$ $c = ^-9$ | $2a = ^-144$ $a = ^-72$ | $9n = ^-81$ $n = ^-9$

10. $\frac{8}{9}x = 64$ $x = 72$ | $2.3x = 12.88$ $x = 5.6$ | $2a = ^-28$ $a = ^-14$ | $3b = 57$ $b = 19$

11. $2\frac{1}{4} = 7c$ $c = \frac{9}{28}$ | $^-228 = 4d$ $d = ^-57$ | $3\frac{5}{6}y = 46$ $y = 12$ | $\frac{2}{5} = \frac{3}{4}z$ $z = \frac{8}{15}$

12. $7 = \frac{n}{9}$ $n = 63$ | $\frac{^-12}{x} = 3$ $x = ^-4$ | $\frac{x}{2} = ^-32$ $x = ^-64$ | $\frac{1}{4} = \frac{4}{z}$ $z = 16$

Problem Solving Reasoning

You can use what you know about solving equations to rewrite formulas. For example, $A = lw$ can be rewritten as $l = \frac{A}{w}$ and $w = \frac{A}{l}$. So $l = \frac{A}{w}$ means that you can find the length by dividing the area by the width.

13. Rewrite the formula for the circumference of a circle $C = \pi d$ for d.

$\frac{C}{\pi} = d$

14. Rewrite the formula for the perimeter of a triangle $P = a + b + c$ for b.

$b = P - (a + c)$

Test Prep ★ Mixed Review

15 If $a = ^-3$, what is the value of the polynomial $2a^2 + 3a - 4$? C; Obj. 9B

A $^-31$ **C** 5

B $^-5$ **D** 23

16 A man said that he had 4.735×10^4 pennies. How much money does he have? H; Obj. 9C

F \$4.735 **H** \$473.50

G \$47.35 **J** \$4,735

Closing the Lesson *Given a subtraction equation such as $x - 7 = 12$ or $d - \frac{1}{3} = \frac{8}{3}$, what should be done to solve the equation?* (Add the same number to each side of the equation.) *Given a multiplication problem such as $2x = 6.8$, what should be done to solve the equation?* (Divide each side of the equation by the same number.)

Name ____________________

Solving Two-Step Equations

Guided Practice: Complete Row 3, p. 261; Ex. 7, p. 262
Independent Practice: Complete pp. 260–262

A two-step equation is an equation that has two operations. When solving a two-step equation, you must follow the order of operations.

Solve: $5x + 33 = 63$

1. Original equation. $5x + 33 = 63$
2. Add $^{-}33$ to each side. $5x + (33 + {}^{-}33) = 63 + {}^{-}33$

   $5x = 30$
3. Divide each side by 5. $\frac{5x}{5} = \frac{30}{5}$
4. Simplify. $1x = 6$

   $x = 6$

√ Check by substitution.

$5x + 33 = 63$

$(5 \cdot 6) + 33 = 63$

$30 + 33 = 63$

$63 = 63$

Sometimes you need to simplify the equation before you solve for the variable.

Solve: $3 \cdot 4 + x = 17$

1. Original equation. $3 \cdot 4 + x = 17$
2. Multiply. $12 + x = 17$
3. Add $^{-}12$ to each side. $(12 + {}^{-}12) + x = 17 + {}^{-}12$
4. Simplify. $0 + x = 5$

   $x = 5$

√ Check by substitution.

$3 \cdot 4 + x = 17$

$3 \cdot 4 + 5 = 17$

$12 + 5 = 17$

$17 = 17$

Solve the equation. Remember to perform all possible calculations before solving for the variable.

1. $7 \cdot 6 + x = 45$ $x = 3$ $4 \cdot 4 + n = 25$ $n = 9$ $5 \cdot 7 + y = 39$ $y = 4$

2. $3 \cdot 6 + c = 50$ $c = 32$ $10 \cdot 8 + a = 92$ $a = 12$ $9 \cdot 8 + b = 80$ $b = 8$

Check Understanding *Solve $4x - 21 = {}^{-}6$ and $3.5 = 2n + 9.5$.* ($x = \frac{15}{4}$ and $n = {}^{-}3$) Be sure that students check their answers by substitution.

Name ____________________

Solve the equation. Show all your work. The first one is done for you.

3. $3x + 5 = 23$

$3x + (5 + {}^-5) = 23 + {}^-5$

$3x = 18$

$\frac{3x}{3} = \frac{18}{3}$

$x = 6$

$4a + 8 = 32$

$a = 6$

$8c + 6 = 62$

$c = 7$

4. $21 + 7x = 105$

$x = 12$

$7.6 + 4x = 10.4$

$x = 0.7$

$8x + 15 = {}^-89$

$x = {}^-13$

5. $2.3y + 1.2 = 10.4$

$y = 4$

$5n + {}^-11 = 24$

$n = 7$

$6y + 12 = 99$

$y = 14.5$

When you solve an equation with subtraction, you need to write it as addition before you solve for the variable.

Solve: $6x - 8 = 34$

1. Original equation. $6x - 8 = 34$
2. Rewrite the subtraction as an addition. $6x + {}^-8 = 34$
3. Add **8** to each side. $6x + ({}^-8 + 8) = 34 + 8$
4. Simplify each side. $6x + 0 = 42$

   $6x = 42$
5. Divide each side by **6**. $\frac{6x}{6} = \frac{42}{6}$
6. Simplify each side. $1x = 7$

   $x = 7$

Check by substitution.

$6x - 8 = 34$

$6(7) - 8 = 34$

$42 - 8 = 34$

Solve the equation. Show your work.

6. $9x - 8 = 55$

$x = 7$

$65 = 8 \cdot 9 - y$

$y = 7$

$12x - 6 = 90$

$x = 8$

Solve the two-step equation. Show your work.

7. $23 = 13 - 2a$ — $a = {}^-5$

$7c - 14 = 49$ — $c = 9$

$6m - 4 = 3.2$ — $m = 1.2$

8. $^-16x - {}^-7 = {}^-121$ — $x = 8$

$4.5b - {}^-1.8 = 12.15$ — $b = 2.3$

$\frac{3}{4}x - \frac{1}{8} = \frac{1}{4}$ — $x = \frac{1}{2}$

Problem Solving
Reasoning

Choose an equation that could be used to solve the problem. Then, solve the equation.

9. The difference of **4** and twice a number is **50**. What is the number?

Choose $4 - 2x = 50$ or $2x - 4 = 50$

solve $4 - 2x = 50$; $x = {}^-23$

10. The sum of $^-6$ and twice a number is **24**. What is the number?

Choose $^-6 + 24 = 2x$ or $^-6 + 2x = 24$

solve $^-6 + 2x = 24$; $x = 15$

Quick Check

Solve these equations. Show your work.

11. $^-8x = 24$ $x = {}^-3$

12. $z + 4 = {}^-12$ $z = {}^-16$

13. $4 = x - 1.5$ $x = 5.5$

14. $\frac{x}{7} = {}^-9.2$ $x = {}^-64.4$

15. $\frac{3}{4}n - 3 = 5$ $n = \frac{32}{3}$ or $10\frac{2}{3}$

16. $\frac{3x - 4}{3} = 5$ $x = \frac{19}{3}$ or $6\frac{1}{3}$

Work Space.

Item	Error Analysis
11–13	**Common Error** Watch for students who confuse negative and minus signs in simplifying equations with rational numbers. **Reteaching** Reteach 74
14–16	**Common Error** Watch for students who do not simplify the equations in the correct order. **Reteaching** Reteach 75

Closing the Lesson *Solve this two-step equation and describe your steps as you solve it:* $12x + 6 = 1$. (Add the opposite of 6 to each side of the equation: $12x + 6 + {}^-6 = 1 + {}^-6$. Simplify to get $12x = {}^-5$. Multiply each side of this equation by the reciprocal of 12: $(\frac{1}{12})12x = (\frac{1}{12})(^-5)$ Thus, $x = {}^-\frac{5}{12}$.)

Name ______________________________

Guided Practice: Ex. 1, 4, 6, 9, 13, 20 & 25, pp. 263–265
Independent Practice: Complete pp. 263–265

The word phrase "the sum of four and seven" can be written as the numerical expression "**4 + 7**." In order to understand and solve problems, it is important to be able to write word phrases as numerical or algebraic expressions and to write expressions using words.

Word Phrase	Expression
The sum of **12** and ***x***	$12 + x$
The product of **6** and ***y***	$6y$
The product of **20** and the difference of **8** and **3**	$20(8 - 3)$
The quotient of **18** and **5**	$\frac{18}{5}$ or $18 \div 5$
The difference between the opposite of **7** and **6**	$^{-}7 - 6$

Write as word phrases. Wording may vary.

1. $9 + 19$ The sum of 9 and 19

2. $58 \div x$ The quotient of 58 and x

3. $16 \div 4$ The quotient of 16 and 4

4. $\frac{y}{32}$ The quotient of *y* and 32

5. $11(7 - x)$ Eleven times the difference of *x* and 7

6. $^{-}14 - 36$ The difference of 36 and $^{-}14$

7. $36 - 11$ The difference of 11 and 36

8. $(3 + a)9$ 9 times the sum of 3 and *a*

Write an expression.

9. Six more than eleven $11 + 6$

The sum of ***a*** and thirteen $a + 13$

10. Three increased by nine $3 + 9$

The product of five and nine 5×9

11. Two times ***x*** $2x$

The quotient of thirty-two divided by ***y*** $32 \div y$

12. Eight less than fifty $50 - 8$

Ten percent of eighty-five 10% of 85

Check Understanding *Write as an equation: One third of a number equals the number decreased by 5.* ($\left(\frac{1}{3}\right)x = x - 5$) *Write as an equation or inequality: A number squared is greater than or equal to 3 more than the number.* ($x^2 \geq x + 3$)

Just as the verb in a word sentence tells you what kind of sentence you have, a symbol such as =, <, >, or ≠ tells you what kind of number sentence you have. You know that a number sentence that has an = sign in it is an equation. In an equation, the expressions on each side of the = have the same value.

Word Equation	Equation
Ten is three less than *x*.	$10 = x - 3$
The product of **6** and *y* is **30**.	$6y = 30$

Symbols

= is equal to
> is greater than
< is less than
≥ is greater than or equal to, or is at least
≤ is less than or equal to, or is at most
≠ is not equal to

A number sentence that has an <, >, ≤, ≥, or ≠ sign in it is an **inequality.** In an inequality, the expressions on each side of the symbol do not have the same value.

Word Inequality	Inequality
The sum of two and *z* is greater than seven.	$2 + z > 7$
The product of one half and *x* times the sum of negative five and three is less than or equal to **4**.	$\frac{1}{2}x(^-5 + 3) \leq 4$

Write an equation or an inequality.

13. Seventeen is greater than fifteen. $17 > 15$

14. The sum of one and three is equal to *y*. $1 + 3 = y$

15. The difference of *x* subtracted from six is less than two. $6 - x < 2$

16. The product of nine times the sum of *a* and two equals twenty. $9(a + 2) = 20$

17. Negative seven is less than the sum of *n* and four. $^-7 < n + 4$

18. The quotient of *z* divided by three is less than or equal to twelve. $z \div 3 \leq 12$

19. One fourth of a number *y* is two more than one fifth of the number. $\frac{1}{4}y = \frac{1}{5}y + 2$

20. Three times the quotient of *m* divided by **4** is at least five. $3(\frac{m}{4}) \geq 5$

21. Two thirds of a number *x* is at most five less than ten. $\frac{2}{3}x \leq 10 - 5$

22. A number *z* decreased by two is equal to the product of three and *z*. $z - 2 = 3z$

23. The quotient of three times a number *c* divided by nine is four. $3c \div 9 = 4$

24. A number *x* increased by the product of two and *y* is not equal to one. $x + 2y \neq 1$

Name ______________________

Write in words.

25. $17 > x$ Seventeen is greater than x.

26. $y + 2 = 5$ Two more than y equals 5.

27. $14 - 2 = t$ Two less than fourteen equals t.

28. $x + y = 9$ The sum of x and y equals nine.

29. $b + 3 \leq 4$ The sum of b and three is less than or equal to four or is at most four.

30. $7 - n > 1$ The difference of n subtracted from 7 is greater than 1.

31. $5x + 3 \neq 6x - 2$ The sum of five times x and three is not equal to two less than six times x.

32. $\frac{(1 + x)}{2} < 5$ The quotient of the sum of one and a number x divided by two is less than 5.

Problem Solving Reasoning **Write the expression using symbols and units of measure.**

Examples:

The number of minutes in ***x*** hours 60***x*** minutes
The number of days in ***y*** weeks 7***y*** days

33. The number of feet in ***x*** yards $3x$ feet

34. The number of ounces in ***p*** pounds $16p$ ounces

35. The number of millimeters in ***m*** meters $1{,}000m$ millimeters

36. The number of inches in ***x*** feet increased by 5 $(12x + 5)$ inches

Test Prep ★ Mixed Review

37 **If $x - 6.52 = {}^{-}4.01$, what is the value of x?** C; Obj. 9D

A $^{-}10.53$ **C** 2.51

B $^{-}2.51$ **D** 10.53

38 **If $\frac{1}{3}n - \frac{5}{6} = \frac{1}{6}$, what is the value of n?** F; Obj. 9D

F 3 **H** $\frac{1}{3}$

G 2 **J** $\frac{2}{9}$

Closing the Lesson *Translate into a sentence: $2d + 1 < 3d$.* (Twice a number increased by 1 is less than three times the number.)

Name ______________________________

Guided Practice: Ex. 1 & 7, p. 267
Independent Practice: Complete p. 267

Problem Solving Strategy: Write an Equation

To solve problems, sometimes you can write an equation.

You need to read the problem to look for the facts and what you are trying to find. You can represent what you are trying to find with a variable.

Problem

Two students are comparing their stamp collections. Ron has 109 fewer stamps than Tara. Together they have 725 stamps. How many stamps does Ron have?

1 Understand

"Asking yourself questions will help you identify the variable."

As you reread, ask yourself questions.

- What do you already know?

  Ron has **109** fewer stamps than Tara.

  Tara has **109** more stamps than Ron.

  Together Ron and Tara have **725** stamps.

- What do you need to find? how many stamps Ron has

2 Decide

"Choose a variable. Then, use it and the facts from the problem to write an equation."

Choose a method for solving.

Try the strategy Write an Equation.

- Let s = the number of stamps Ron has.

  Ron's number and Tara's number = **725**

$$s + (s + 109) = 725$$

- Write the simplified equation. $2s + 109 = 725$

3 Solve

"Is the answer to the equation the solution of the problem? Do you need to find Tara's number too?"

Solve the addition equation.

Be neat in your solution. Remember that whatever you do to one side of an equation, you must do the same to the other.

Equation:

$$2s + 109 = 725$$
$$2s + 109 - 109 = 725 - 109$$
$$2s = 616$$
$$\frac{2s}{2} = \frac{616}{2}$$
$$s = 308$$

4 Look back

"Look back at the original problem. Is your answer reasonable? Make sure you use the correct labels in the answers."

Check your answer.

Substitute your solution into the equation.

$$2s + 109 = 725$$
$$2(\mathbf{308}) + 109 = 725$$

Write your answer as a full sentence.

Answer Ron has 308 stamps.

What steps did you use to solve the problem? Possible answer: Before I could write an equation, I had to write the facts in a verbal expression; then I could use numbers, symbols, and variables to write an equation. When I solved for the variable I found the amount for Ron. I could also find the amount for Tara.

Check Understanding *Write an equation for this word problem and then solve: Dennis checked out 3 more books from the library than Mary did. Together they checked out 19 books. How many books did Dennis check out?* $\{x + (x - 3) = 19; x = 11 \text{ books.}\}$

Use the Write an Equation strategy or any other strategy you have learned.

1. A student has **13** coins, all nickels and dimes, worth **$.95.** There is **1** dime less than there are nickels. How many nickels are there?

Think: If there are *n* nickels, then how many dimes are there?

1 fewer: $n - 1$

7 nickels

2. Carlo has **$3** more than twice as many dollars as Jake. If Carlo has **$15,** then how much does Jake have?

Think: Carlo has $15 and Carlo has $3 more than twice as many dollars as Jake. What equation can you write?

$\$15 = \$3 + 2j$

$6

3. The sum of three consecutive integers is **93.** What are the integers?

30, 31, 32

4. I am thinking of a number. If I add **63** to it the result is **13.** What number am I thinking of?

$^{-}50$

5. The towns of Dory, Elba, and Faro are all in a line on the same route. The town of Dory is **52** kilometers from Elba. Dory is **3.7** kilometers closer to Elba than Faro is. How far is Faro from Elba?

55.7 km

6. Manuel scored **8** fewer points than Will scored. Together they scored **44** points. How many points did Will score?

26 points

7. A student has **12** coins, all dimes and quarters. The value of the coins is **$1.95.** How many dimes are there?

7 dimes

8. It took **8** students **3** hours to clean up after a school play. How long would it have taken **6** students?

4 hours

9. A submarine exploring the ocean floor is **300** meters below the surface. It takes **5** minutes to ascend to a depth of **100** meters. If the submarine is traveling at a constant rate, in how many more minutes will the submarine ascend to the surface?

$2\frac{1}{2}$ minutes

10. It is **13°F** now. If the temperature is dropping at a constant rate of **4°F** per hour, what was the temperature $1\frac{1}{2}$ hours ago?

19°F

Closing the Lesson *Describe the four steps used to solve word problems by writing an equation.* ((1) Choose a variable and organize the information given in the problem, (2) Write an equation based on the information, (3) Solve the equation, and (4) Check.)

Name ______________________

Solving Inequalities

Guided Practice: Ex. 4 & 5, p. 268; Ex. 11, p. 270
Independent Practice: Complete pp. 268–270

You know how to write an inequality to represent a verbal sentence. Now you will learn how to solve an inequality. Any number that makes the inequality true is a **solution of the inequality.**

What are the possible solutions for the inequality $x > 4$?

- Is **4** a solution?

  No, **4** is not greater than **4**.

- Is $4\frac{1}{2}$ a solution?

  Yes, $4\frac{1}{2}$ is greater than **4**.

- Is **4.0001** a solution?

  Yes, **4.0001** is greater than **4**.

If $x > 4$, then any rational or irrational number greater than **4** is a solution of the inequality.

To solve inequalities such as $x + 3 < 5$ or $x - 6 > 4$, you use inverse operations.

Solve: $x + 3 < 5$

1. Original inequality	$x + 3 < 5$
2. Subtract **3** from each side.	$x + 3 - 3 < 5 - 3$
3. Simplify each side.	$x + 0 < 2$
	$x < 2$

Solve: $x - 6 \geq 4$

1. Original inequality	$x - 6 \geq 4$
2. Add **6** to each side.	$x - 6 + 6 \geq 4 + 6$
3. Simplify each side.	$x + 0 \geq 10$
	$x \geq 10$

Check. Is the given value a solution of the inequality? Write *yes* or *no*.

1. $x + 20 > 25$ Yes.
Given value: **10**

$a - 8 < 18$ Yes.
Given value: **⁻4**

$y + 68 \neq 101$ Yes.
Given value: **0**

2. $b + 2 > 3$ No.
Given value: $\frac{1}{2}$

$x - 2 < {}^{-}15$ No.
Given value: **10**

$(w - 5) + 7 < 18$ Yes.
Given value: **6**

Solve.

3. $x - 3 < 9$ $x < 12$ $x + 10 > {}^{-}5$ $x > {}^{-}15$ $x + 4 < {}^{-}10$ $x < {}^{-}14$

4. $x + 8 > 3$ $x > {}^{-}5$ $x - 7 < {}^{-}5$ $x < 2$ $x - 13 < {}^{-}7$ $x < 6$

5. $x - 9 < 3$ $x < 12$ $x + 15 < {}^{-}3$ $x < {}^{-}18$ $x + 5 > {}^{-}16$ $x > {}^{-}21$

Check Understanding *When you add the same number to both sides of an inequality, is the resulting inequality still true?* (Yes.) *When you multiply both sides of an equation by a number n, is the resulting inequality still true?* (Yes if *n* is positive; no if $n \leq 0$.) *Solve this inequality:* ($-\frac{9}{8}x > 2$. ($x < -\frac{16}{9}$)

Name ______________________________

Multiply and divide each side of these inequalities by 2. Decide whether the resulting inequality is still true.

6. $6 < 8$ $12 < 16$, $3 < 4$ — True.

$6 > {}^-8$ $12 > {}^-16$, $3 > {}^-4$ — True.

${}^-6 > {}^-8$ ${}^-12 > {}^-16$, ${}^-3 > {}^-4$ — True.

Multiply and divide each side of these inequalities by ⁻2. Decide whether the resulting inequality is still true.

7. $6 < 8$ ${}^-12 < {}^-16$, ${}^-3 < {}^-4$ — False.

$6 > {}^-8$ ${}^-12 > 16$, ${}^-3 > 4$ — False.

${}^-6 > {}^-8$ $12 > 16$, $3 > 4$ — False.

From your computations in the last few exercises, you can see that:

> When both sides of an inequality are multiplied or divided by a **negative number,** the inequality sign must be reversed.

To solve inequalities such as $5x < 25$ or ${}^-8x < 4$, you use inverse operations, but when you multiply or divide by a negative number, you need to reverse the inequality sign.

Solve: $\frac{x}{3} < 5$

1. Original inequality $\frac{x}{3} < 5$
2. Multiply each side by **3.** $3 \cdot \frac{x}{3} < 3 \cdot 5$
3. Simplify each side. $1x < 15$

   $x < 15$

Solve: ${}^-8x < 4$

1. Original inequality ${}^-8x < 4$
2. Divide each side by **⁻8,** *and* reverse the inequality. $\frac{{}^-8x}{{}^-8} > \frac{4}{{}^-8}$
3. Simplify each side. $1x > \frac{1}{{}^-2}$

   $x > -\frac{1}{2}$

Solve.

8. $7x < 21$ $x < 3$ | $\frac{1}{5}x < 11$ $x < 55$ | $\frac{3}{7}x > 5$ $x > \frac{35}{3}$ or $x > 11\frac{2}{3}$

9. $3x > 20$ $x > \frac{20}{3}$ or $x > 6\frac{2}{3}$ | ${}^-2x < 10$ $x > {}^-5$ | $\frac{2}{9}x < {}^-30$ $x < {}^-135$

10. $\frac{3}{4}x > 24$ $x > 32$ | ${}^-3x > {}^-16$ $x < \frac{16}{3}$ or $x < 5\frac{1}{3}$ | $\frac{{}^-1}{4}x > {}^-15$ $x < 60$

To solve a two-step inequality, remember to always perform the operations in the correct order.

Solve: $3x + 2 \le 3$

1. Original inequality $\quad 3x + 2 \le 3$
2. Subtract **2** from each side. $\quad 3x + 2 - 2 < 3 - 2$
3. Simplify. $\quad 3x < 1$
4. Divide each side by **3**, $\quad \frac{3x}{3} < \frac{1}{3}$
5. Simplify. $\quad x < \frac{1}{3}$

Solve: $^-x + 6 < 3$

1. Original inequality $\quad ^-x - 6 < 3$
2. Add **6** to each side. $\quad ^-x - 6 + 6 < 3 + 6$
3. Simplify. $\quad ^-x < 9$
4. Multiply each side by $^-1$. Reverse the inequality. $\quad ^-1 \cdot {}^-x > {}^-1 \cdot 9$
5. Simplify. $\quad 1x > {}^-9$

$x > {}^-9$

Solve these inequalities.

11. $3x + 1 > 10$ $\underline{\quad x > 3 \quad}$ $\qquad$ $15x - 3 < 6$ $\underline{\quad x < \frac{3}{5} \quad}$ $\qquad$ $\frac{x + 1}{5} < 2$ $\underline{\quad x < 9 \quad}$

12. $4x + 3 > 9$ $\underline{\quad x > \frac{3}{2} \text{ or } x > 1\frac{1}{2} \quad}$ $\qquad$ $^-5x + 4 > 12$ $\underline{\quad x < \frac{^-8}{5} \text{ or } x < {}^-1\frac{3}{5} \quad}$ $\qquad$ $^-3x - 7 > 8$ $\underline{\quad x < {}^-5 \quad}$

Problem Solving
Reasoning

For each problem, choose a variable. Then, write and solve an inequality.

13. A number is increased by ten. The result is at least **15**. What is the number?

$n + 10 \ge 15; n \ge 5$

14. Negative **8** is added to **5** times a number. The result is less than **2**. What is the number?

$^-8 + 5n < 2; n < 2$

Quick Check

Write the expression, equation, or inequality.

15. One third of a number n and seven $\underline{\quad \frac{1}{3}n + 7 \quad}$

16. The product of a number y and three is greater than or equal to four. $\underline{\quad 3y \ge 4 \quad}$

17. The difference of negative eight from a number z is equal to negative one. $\underline{\quad z - {}^-8 = {}^-1 \quad}$

Solve the inequality.

18. $^-9x \ge {}^-18$ $\underline{\quad x \le 2 \quad}$ $\qquad$ **19.** $\frac{x + 3}{2} \ge 3$ $\underline{\quad x \ge 3 \quad}$

Work Space.

Item	Error Analysis
15–17	**Common Error** Watch for students who cannot distinguish equations from expressions. **Reteaching** Reteach 76, 77
18–19	**Common Error** Watch for students who do not reverse symbols when they multiply or divide with negative numbers. **Reteaching** Reteach 78

Closing the Lesson *Solve and show your steps:* $\frac{x + 2}{^-7} < 3$ *and* $14a - 5 > {}^-11$. ($x > {}^-23$ and $a > \frac{^-3}{7}$)

Name ______________________

Unit 9 Review

Simplify.

1. 3^{-2} $\frac{1}{9}$
2. $\left(\frac{-4}{5}\right)^2$ $\frac{16}{25}$
3. $\left(\frac{-1}{2}\right)^{-3}$ $^{-}8$
4. $\left(\frac{7}{11}\right)^0$ 1
5. $2^4 \cdot 2^{-7}$ $\frac{1}{8}$
6. $3^{-5} \cdot 3^9$ 81
7. $x^3 \div x^{-2}$ x^5
8. $(2^5 \cdot 5^3) \div (2^2 \cdot 5^4)$ $\frac{8}{5}$

Write true or false.

9. $\sqrt{16} = 4$ True.
10. $\sqrt{44}$ is between 5 and 6. False.
11. $\sqrt{3}$ is a rational number. False.
12. $\sqrt{\frac{36}{49}} = \frac{6}{7}$ True.
13. In the monomial $3x^2$, 2 is a constant. False.
14. In the monomial $3x^2$, 3 is a coefficient. True.

Simplify.

15. $9x - {}^{-}3x$ $12x$
16. $b^5 \cdot b^7$ b^{12}
17. $x^6 \div x^{10}$ $\frac{1}{x^4}$
18. $5a - 3b + 6a + {}^{-}7b - {}^{-}8a$ $19a - 10b$
19. $(6x^2 - 4x) - ({}^{-}2x^2 - {}^{-}5x)$ $8x^2 - 9x$
20. $8a^2 + 6a - 2 + 3a^2 - 5a - 7$ $11a^2 + a - 9$

Multiply or divide.

21. $4x(3x + 5)$ $12x^2 + 20x$
22. ${}^{-}2y(5 - 4y)$ ${}^{-}10y + 8y^2$
23. $\frac{15a^2 - 5a + 10}{5}$ $3a^2 - a + 2$
24. $\frac{8b^3 + 4b^2 - 12b}{4b}$ $2b^2 + b - 3$

Evaluate the expression.

25. $x^2 - 5x + 7$ for $x = 2$ 1
26. ${}^{-}3x^2 + 2x - 1$ for $x = {}^{-}1$ $^{-}6$
27. $x^3 - 4x + 2$ for $x = 3$ 17

Express in scientific notation.

28. 7,000,000 7×10^6
29. 31,408,000 3.1408×10^7
30. 9,460,000,000 9.46×10^9
31. $1{,}260 \times 10^4$ 1.260×10^7
32. 0.00825 8.25×10^{-3}
33. 0.0000068 6.8×10^{-6}
34. 0.0000519 5.19×10^{-5}
35. 0.015×10^{-2} 1.5×10^{-4}

Express in standard form.

36. 4.267×10^{-8} 0.00000004267

37. 8.228×10^{7} 82,280,000

Solve the equation. Use addition or subtraction.

38. $35 + y = 51$

$y = 16$

39. $^{-}7 + d = 15$

$d = 22$

40. $\frac{1}{6} + n = \frac{11}{18}$

$n = \frac{4}{9}$

41. $x + 15.6 = {}^{-}4.2$

$x = {}^{-}19.8$

42. $y - {}^{-}6 = {}^{-}13$

$y = {}^{-}19$

43. $^{-}9 - n = {}^{-}19$

$n = 10$

Solve the equation. Use multiplication or division.

44. $\frac{x}{10} = {}^{-}20$

$x = {}^{-}200$

45. $9 = \frac{108}{y}$

$y = 12$

46. $\frac{c}{^{-}2} = {}^{-}6$

$c = 12$

47. $\frac{b}{8} = 9$

$b = 72$

48. $\frac{13 \cdot 8}{d} = 2$

$d = 52$

49. $\frac{156}{y} = 3$

$y = 52$

Solve the two-step equation.

50. $8x + 4 = 60$

$x = 7$

51. $9b - 10 = 26$

$b = 4$

52. $\frac{2}{3}y - \frac{1}{6} = 7\frac{5}{6}$

$y = 12$

53. $^{-}15x - {}^{-}8 = 233$

$x = {}^{-}15$

54. $2.7 + 6a = {}^{-}6.3$

$a = {}^{-}1.5$

55. $9.6n - {}^{-}2.6 = 6.44$

$n = 0.4$

Name ______________________

Write an expression, an equation, or an inequality.

56. Four times the sum of six and c $4(6 + c)$

57. The difference when six is subtracted from c is fifteen. $c - 6 = 15$

58. The quotient of x plus seven divided by three is less than ten. $\frac{x + 7}{3} < 10$

Write in words. Word phrases or sentences may vary.

59. $^{-}6 + 4$ The sum of negative six and four

60. $^{-}x < 15$ The opposite of x is less than fifteen.

61. $7 + \frac{5}{c} > 4$ The sum of seven and the quotient of five and a number c is greater than or equal to four.

Solve these inequalities.

62. $3x + 4 < 7$

$x < 1$

63. $^{-}2x - 5 > 8$

$x < {}^{-}6.5$

64. $\frac{3}{5}x - 4 \leq \frac{1}{2}$

$x \leq \frac{15}{2}$ or $x \leq 7\frac{1}{2}$

Choose an equation to solve the problem. Then solve.

65. The quotient of twice a number divided by three is four. What is the number?

$\frac{2x}{3} = 4$ or $\frac{x + 2}{3} = 4$

6

66. In December the new recreation center added **16** more videos to its collection.

The new videos represent $\frac{1}{4}$ of the total number of videos. How many videos do they have in all?

$x \cdot \frac{1}{4} = 16$ or $16 = \frac{1}{4}x$

64 videos

Write an equation to solve this problem.

67. The average of two numbers is **14.6.** One of the numbers is **18.** What is the other number?

$\frac{n + 18}{2} = 14.6$; 11.2

Name ______________________

Cumulative Review
★ Test Prep

1 **What is the missing measurement?** C; Obj. 9D

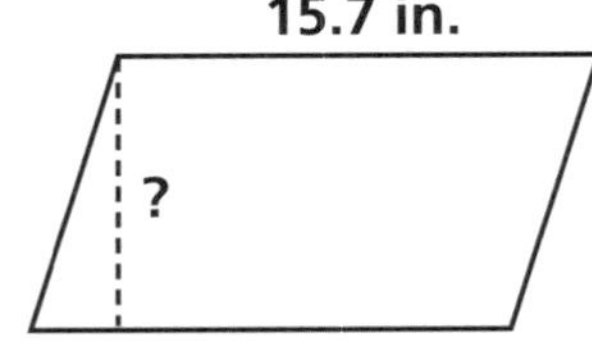

A 128.74 in. **C** 9.2 in.

B 15.7 in. **D** 7.85 in.

2 **This spreadsheet is using the formula $M = 0.037t^2 + 10$ to calculate figures for the number of movie theaters in the U.S. during certain years. What is the missing number?** G; Obj. 9B

t	t^2	$0.037t^2$	10	M
3	9	0.333	10	10.333
2	4	0.148	10	10.148
1	1	0.037	10	10.037
0	0	0	10	?

F 0 **H** 10.037

G 10 **J** 10.10

3 **Which expression is equivalent to $24r^3s^2$?** D; Obj. 1C

A $4 \cdot r \cdot s \cdot 6 \cdot r \cdot s$

B $4 \cdot r \cdot r \cdot s \cdot 9 \cdot r \cdot s$

C $7 \cdot r \cdot s \cdot r \cdot 3 \cdot s \cdot r$

D $r \cdot 8 \cdot s \cdot r \cdot 3 \cdot s \cdot r$

4 **It takes 20 workers about 2.5 days to prepare a building site. How many workers would you need to complete the job in just about 1.5 days?** H; Obj. 4C

F 12 **H** 33

G 18 **J** 50

5 **Which describes a scalene triangle?** A; Obj. 7D

A no congruent sides

B 2 or 3 congruent sides

C all angles less than 90°

D one angle greater than 90°

6 **$\frac{^-2}{3}$ and $\frac{5}{6}$ are factors of what product?** F; Obj. 8D

F $-\frac{5}{9}$

G $-\frac{9}{5}$

H $\frac{5}{9}$

J $\frac{7}{18}$

7 **At a grand opening of the arts and crafts store, every 3rd person who enters the store gets a drawing pen. Every 5th person gets a pad of paper. Every 20th person gets a gift certificate for $5. Which person is the first person to get all three gifts?** C; Obj. 2C

A the 28th person

B the 50th person

C the 60th person

D the 300th person

8 **If $a + b = 4$, and $a - b = 38$, what are the values of a and b?** G; Obj. 8B

F $a = {^-21}, b = 17$

G $a = 21, b = {^-17}$

H $a = 21, b = 17$

J $a = {^-21}, b = {^-17}$

K Not here

UNIT 10 • TABLE OF CONTENTS

Using Formulas in Geometry

We will be using this vocabulary:

area the measure of a region within a closed curve

circumference the distance around a circle

cone a space figure with a circular base and another surface that is curved

cube a rectangular prism whose faces are congruent squares

cylinder a space figure with two congruent circular bases that are joined by a curved surface

diameter of a circle a chord that goes through the center of the circle

prism a space figure with two faces that are congruent and parallel and whose other faces are parallelograms

pyramid a space figure with a polygonal base and whose other sides are triangles

rectangular prism a space figure all of whose faces are rectangles

Dear Family,

During the next few weeks, our math class will be reviewing how to find area, finding surface area, and volume.

You can expect to see homework that provides practice with these skills. Here is a sample you may want to keep handy to give help when needed.

Finding the surface area of a rectangular prism

A rectangular prism has three dimensions: length, width, and height. You can use these dimensions to find its surface area.

To find the surface area, add the areas of all six faces. The area of a rectangle is found by multiplying the length times the width.

$$\begin{aligned} SA &= lw + lw + lh + lh + wh + wh \\ &= 2(8 \cdot 12) + 2(12 \cdot 4) + 2(8 \cdot 4) \\ &= 192 + 96 + 64 \\ &= 352 \end{aligned}$$

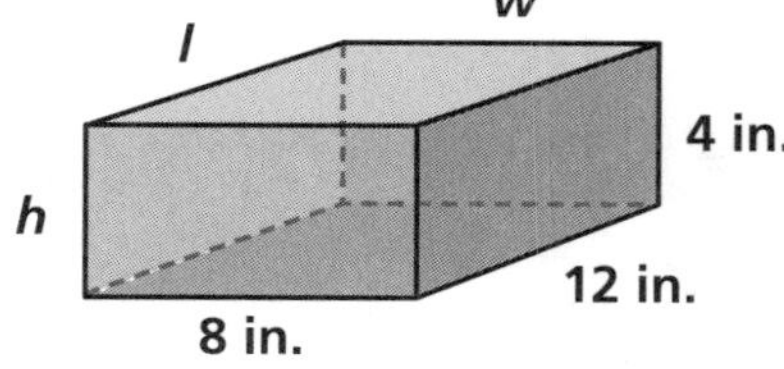

The surface area of the prism is **352** square inches.

To find the volume of the prism, multiply the length times the width times the height. This is written as the formula $V = lwh$. For this prism, the volume is **4 in. · 8 in. · 12 in. = 384** cubic inches.

During this unit, students will continue to learn new techniques related to problem solving and will continue to practice basic skills with fractions and decimals.

Sincerely,

Name ______________________________

Guided Practice: First ex. in Rows 1, 4 & 9, pp. 277–279
Independent Practice: Complete pp. 277–279

Circumference and Area of Circles

A **circle** is a plane figure with points all the same distance from a given point called the **center.**

A segment from any point on a circle to the center is a **radius (*r*).**

A segment that joins any two points on a circle is a **chord.**

Any chord that contains the center of a circle is a **diameter (*d*).** A diameter is twice as long as a radius (**$d = 2r$**).

chord
center
diameter
radius

The distance around a circle is called the **circumference.** The circumference of a circle is a little more than **3** times the length of the diameter of the circle.

The ratio $\frac{\text{circumference}}{\text{diameter}}$ was named by the Greeks as π **(pi).**
The value of pi cannot be written as an exact decimal. It is an **irrational number**, that is, its decimal form never repeats or terminates.
Use $\frac{22}{7}$ or **3.14** as close approximations for π.

You can review the formulas for finding the circumference of a circle.

$C = \pi d$ or $C = 2\pi r$

Find the circumference of the circle to the nearest tenth. Use **3.14** for π.

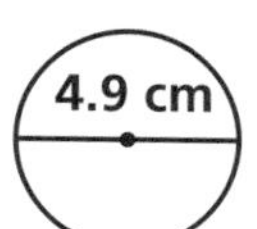

$C = \pi d$

$\approx 3.14 \cdot 4.9$ cm

≈ 15.386 cm $\rightarrow$ **15.4** cm

Find the circumference of the circle. Use $\frac{22}{7}$ for π.

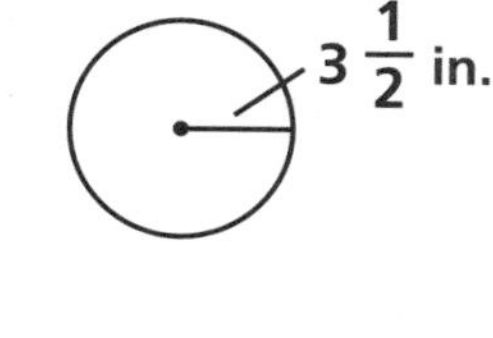

$C = 2\pi r$

$\approx 2 \cdot \frac{22}{7} \cdot 3\frac{1}{2}$ in.

$\approx 2 \cdot \frac{22}{7} \cdot \frac{7}{2}$ in.

≈ 22 in.

Find the circumference of the circle. Use $\frac{22}{7}$ for π.

	Diameter	14 m	15.4 mm	$3\frac{1}{2}$ ft	$7\frac{2}{3}$ in.	42.07 cm	$3\frac{1}{3}$ yd
1.	Circumference	44 m	48.4 mm	11 ft	$24\frac{2}{21}$ in.	132.22 cm	$10\frac{10}{21}$ yd

Find the diameter and circumference to the nearest tenth. Use 3.14 for π.

	Radius	63 cm	32 m	6 dm	5 cm	9 km	3 m
2.	Diameter	126 cm	64 m	12 dm	10 cm	18 km	6 m
3.	Circumference	395.6 cm	201.0 m	37.7 dm	31.4 cm	56.5 km	18.8 m

Check Understanding *If a circle had a radius of 3.2 m, what would its circumference be to the nearest tenth of a meter?* (20.1 m) *What would its area be to the nearest meter squared?* (32 m^2)

Here is a way to think about the area of a circle. The circle to the right has been divided into **20** sections. Half of the circle has been shaded. Separate the sections and arrange them as shown.

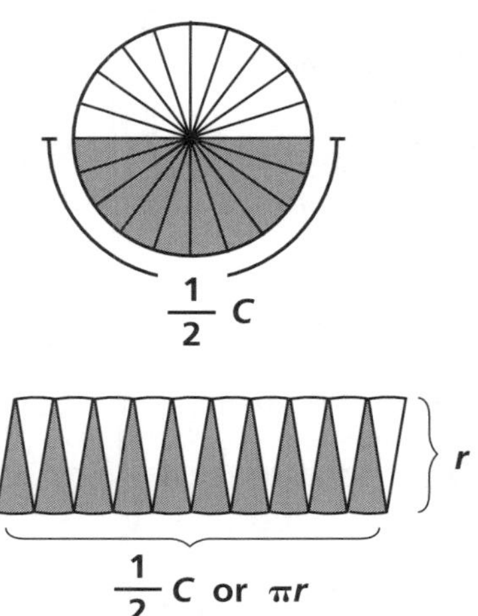

This arrangement resembles a parallelogram whose base is half the circumference of the circle and whose height is the radius.

Area of a parallelogram: $A = bh$

Area of a circle: $A = \frac{1}{2}C \cdot r$

$= \frac{1}{2}(2\pi r) \cdot r$

$= \pi r^2$

Find the area to the nearest tenth. Use **3.14** for π.

$A = \pi r^2$

$= 3.14 \cdot 15$ cm²

$= 3.14 \cdot 225$ cm²

$= 706.5$ cm²

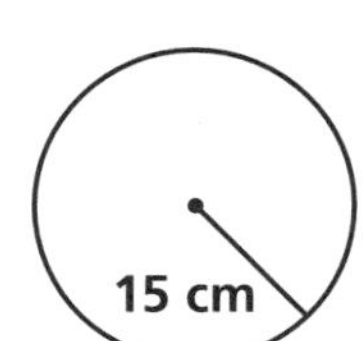

Find the area of the circle. Use $\frac{22}{7}$ for π.

$A = \pi r^2$

$= \frac{22}{7}(42 \div 2)^2$ in.²

$= \frac{22}{7} \times 21 \times 21$ in.²

$= 1{,}386$ in.²

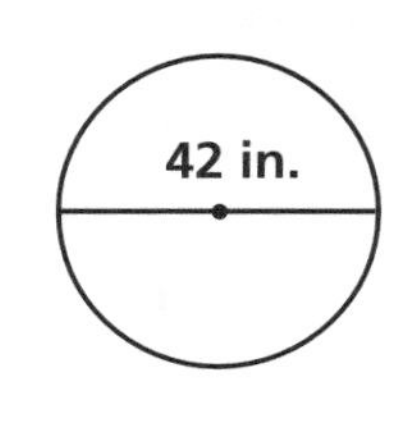

Complete the table. Use either 3.14 or $\frac{22}{7}$ as an approximation for π.

Answers may vary slightly.

4.	Radius	14 m	10.5 cm	26 ft	$1\frac{3}{4}$ yd	$1\frac{3}{4}$ in.	28 in.	63 ft	$2\frac{1}{3}$ yd
5.	Diameter	28 m	21 cm	52 ft	$3\frac{1}{2}$ yd	$3\frac{1}{2}$ in.	56 in.	126 ft	$4\frac{2}{3}$ yd
6.	Area	615.4 m²	346.2 cm²	2,122.64 ft²	$9\frac{5}{8}$ yd²	$9\frac{5}{8}$ in.²	2,461.76 in.²	12,463 ft²	$17\frac{1}{9}$ yd²

Find the area of the shaded region.

7.

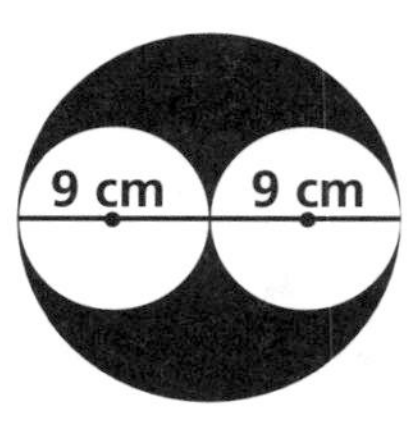

127.17 cm²

8.

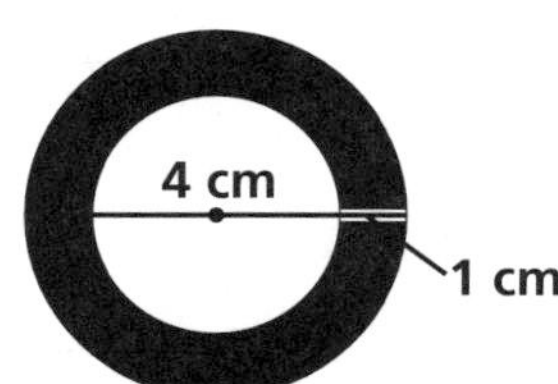

15.7 cm²

Name ____________________

If you know the circumference of a circle, you can find its diameter or radius.

What is the diameter of a circular mirror whose circumference is **44** in.?

1. Use the formula.

$C = \pi d$, so $\frac{C}{\pi} = d$

2. Substitute.

$\frac{44}{\frac{22}{7}} \approx d$

3. Evaluate.

$d \approx \overset{2}{\cancel{44}} \cdot \frac{7}{\underset{1}{\cancel{22}}}$ → **14** in.

Find the missing measures.

9.	Radius	$12\frac{1}{4}$ in.	31.5 ft	28 yd	$10\frac{1}{2}$ in.	14 mi	$12\frac{1}{11}$ yd
10.	Diameter	$24\frac{1}{2}$ in.	63 ft	56 yd	21 in.	28 mi	$24\frac{2}{11}$ yd
	Circumference	**77** in.	**198** ft	**176** yd	**66** in.	**88** mi	**76** yd

11. the area of a circular lamp base that is **20** cm in diameter 314 cm^2

12. the total television viewing area for a **51**-mile radius 8,167.14 mi^2

13. the distance a tire that is **70** cm in diameter travels in one revolution

220 cm

14. the area of the largest circle that can be cut out from a **9** in. by **12** in. piece of construction paper 63.585 $in.^2$

Problem Solving Reasoning

The decimal form of irrational numbers, such as π, are non-terminating and non-repeating. Choose the irrational number in each pair and explain your choice.

15. a. 0.010101...
b. 0.010010001...

b; the cycle of 0's and 1's keeps expanding instead of repeating.

16. a. 0.525522555222...
b. 0.5255255255...

a; the cycle of 5's and 2's keeps expanding instead of repeating.

Test Prep ★ Mixed Review

17 What is the simplest form of the expression $m^3 \cdot m^8 \cdot m^{-5}$? B; Obj. 9A

A m^{120}

B m^6

C m^{-6}

D m^{-120}

18 If $a = {}^-4$, what is the value of the polynomial $2a^2 - 3a + 4$? F; Obj. 9B

F 48

G 24

H ⁻24

J ⁻48

Closing the Lesson *If the radius of a circle is doubled, what happens to its circumference?* (It is doubled.) *If the radius of a circle is doubled, what happens to its area?* (It is quadrupled.)

Name ______________________________

Complex Plane Figures

Guided Practice: Ex. 1 & 7, pp. 280–281
Independent Practice: Complete pp. 280–282

Area is the measure of how much surface a figure covers. To find the area of a figure like the one shown at the right, you may need to use more than one formula. This figure is called a **complex figure** because it is made up of different geometric figures.

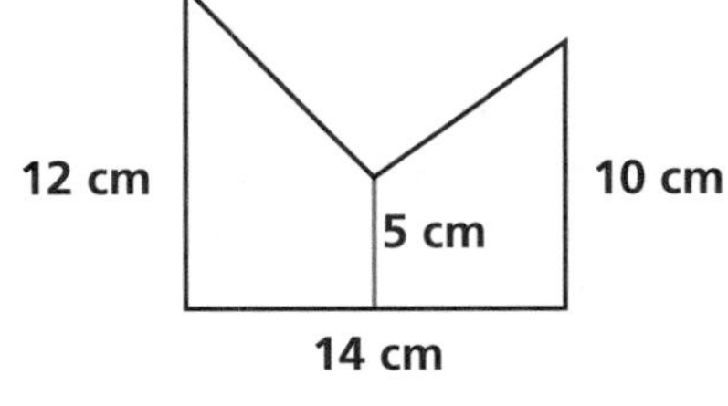

Find the area of the figure.

1. Divide the figure into different geometric figures. Draw $\overline{AB}$. Label vertices of all the figures you see. Find any missing lengths.

- Rectangle ***ABFH*** is **14** cm long and **5** cm wide.
- $\overline{DG}$ divides the base into **2** congruent segments **7** cm long.

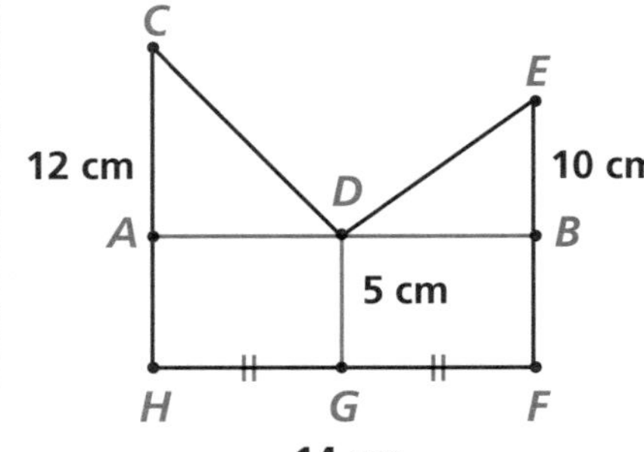

- Since $\overline{AB}$ is congruent to $\overline{HF}$, $\overline{AD}$ = **7** cm and $\overline{DB}$ = **7** cm.
- △ ***ADC*** has a base of **7** cm and a height of (**12** cm − **5** cm), or **7** cm.
- △ ***BDE*** has a base of **7** cm and a height of (**10** cm − **5** cm), or **5** cm.

---

2. Find the area of each different figure.

- Triangle ***ACD***

$$A = \frac{1}{2}bh \text{ or } \frac{b \cdot h}{2}$$
$$= \frac{7 \cdot 7}{2} \rightarrow \frac{49}{2} \text{ or } 24.5 \text{ cm}^2$$

- Triangle ***BED***

$$A = \frac{b \cdot h}{2}$$
$$= \frac{7 \cdot 5}{2} \rightarrow \frac{35}{2} \text{ or } 17.5 \text{ cm}^2$$

- Rectangle ***ABFH***

$$A = lw$$
$$= 14 \cdot 5 \rightarrow 70 \text{ cm}^2$$

---

3. Find the sum of the areas.

$A = 24.5 \text{ cm}^2 + 17.5 \text{ cm}^2 + 70 \text{ cm}^2 \rightarrow 112 \text{ cm}^2$

The total area of the complex figure above is **112** cm².

Find the area. Draw segments where needed.

1.

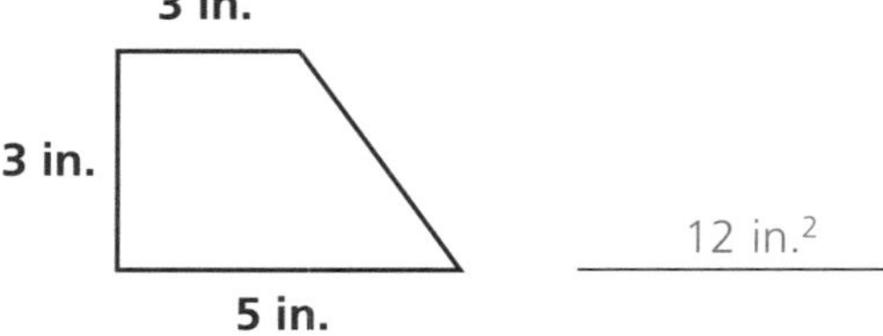

12 in.²

2.

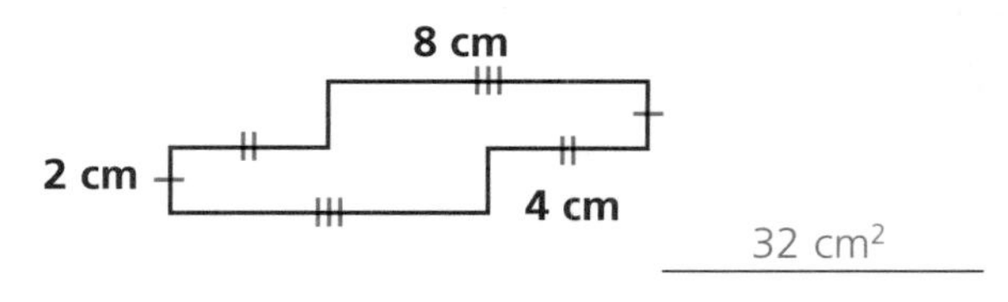

32 cm²

Check Understanding *A rectangle, which is 14 cm long and 8 cm wide, has two semicircles on each short side. What is the area of the total figure rounded to the nearest tenth?* (Multiply 14 times 8, and add 16 times 3.14 to get 162.2 cm².)

Name ___________________________

Find the area of the complex figures. Draw segments when you need to.

3.

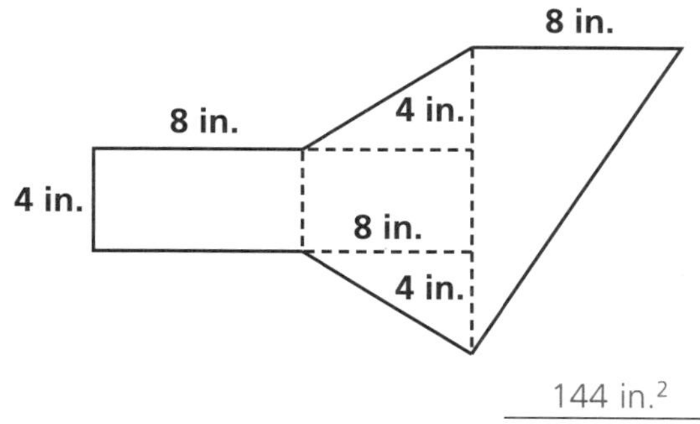

144 in.^{2}

4.

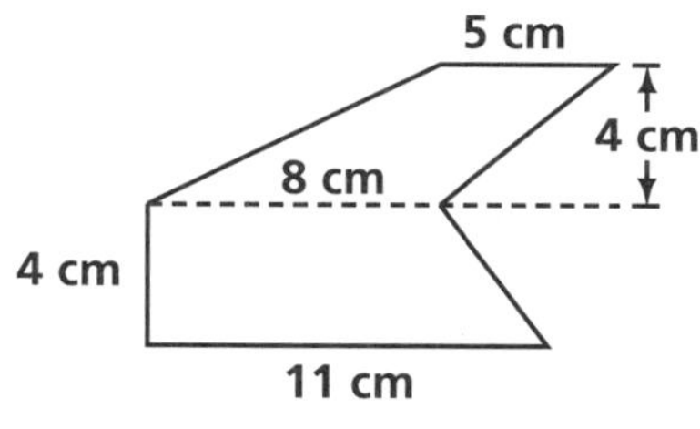

64 cm^2

5.

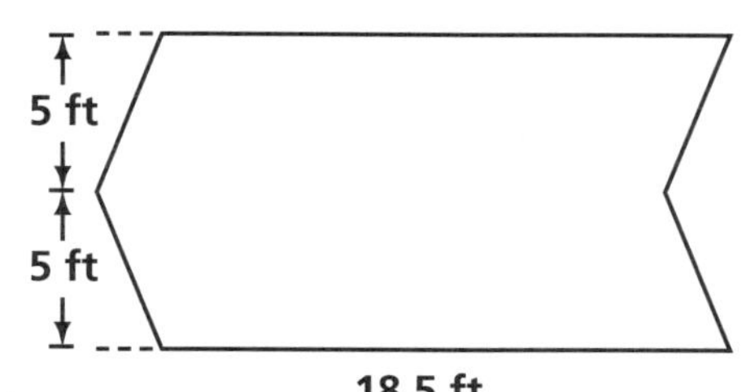

185 ft^2

6.

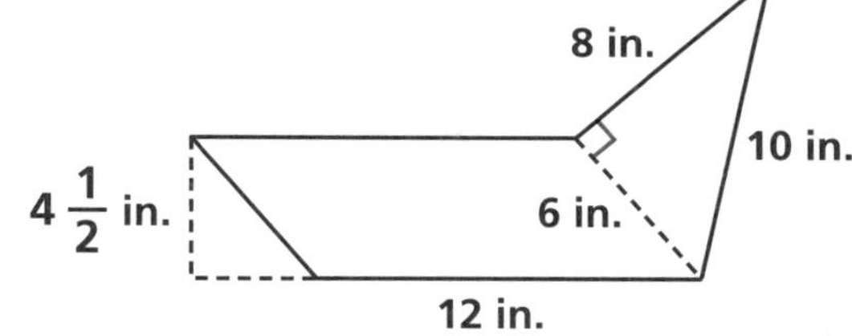

78 in.^{2}

7.

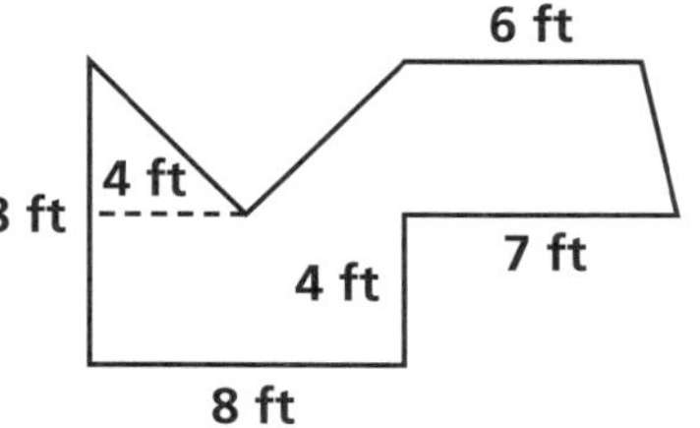

74 ft^2

8.

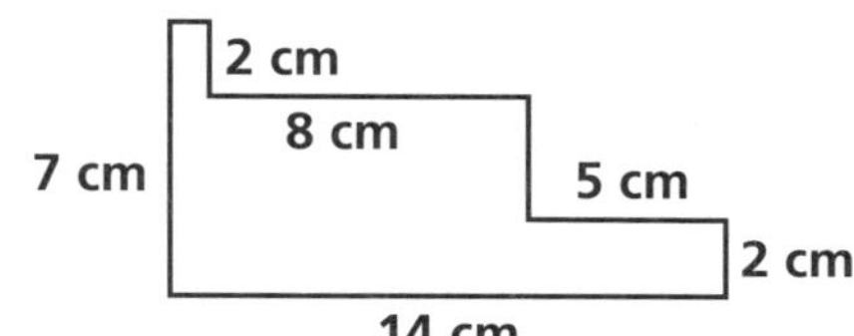

57 cm^2

9.

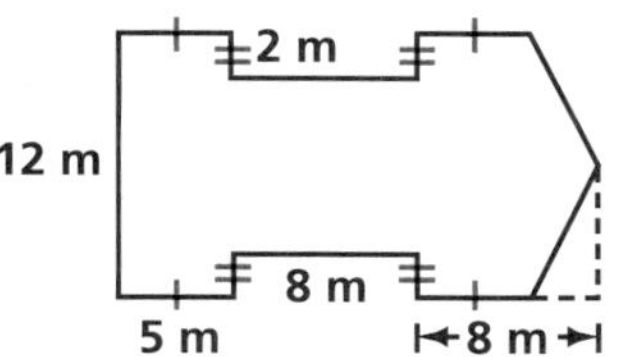

202 m^2

10.

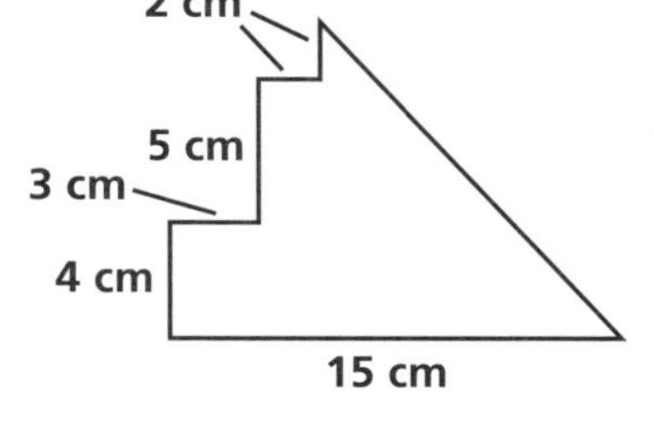

85 cm^2

Problem Solving Reasoning

Solve. Find the area of the complex figure to the nearest tenth.

11. Architects and house designers use complex figures in their work. An arched door or a *lassway* mirror looks like this.

- The shaded part of the mirror is a semicircle or half a circle. The diameter of the semicircle is the same as the length of the rectangle, or **13** in.
- The radius of the semicircle is $\frac{13}{2}$ in., or **6.5** in.

13 in.

13 in.

What is the total area of the mirror to the nearest tenth? 235.3 in.^{2}

12. What is the area of this plate?

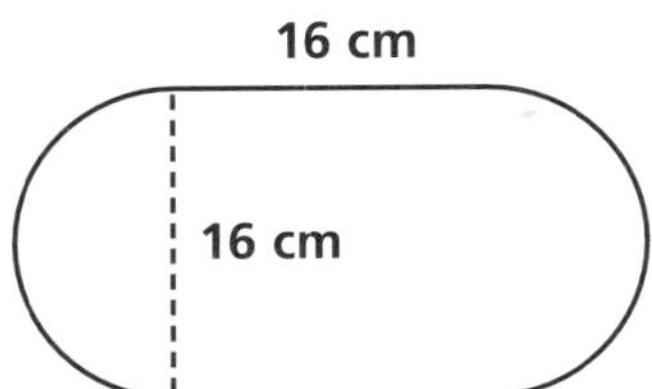

457.0 cm^2

13. The circular parts of this mirror will be covered in tiles. What is the area of the part that will be covered in tiles?

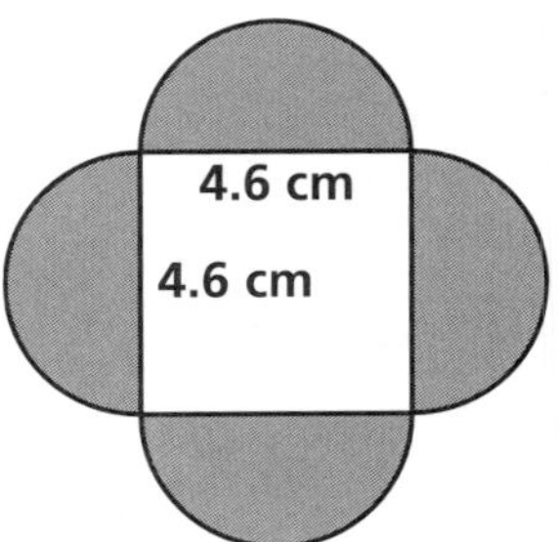

33.2 cm^2

14. In order to complete a design, you need to cut paper circles from construction paper. About what percent of the paper is wasted?

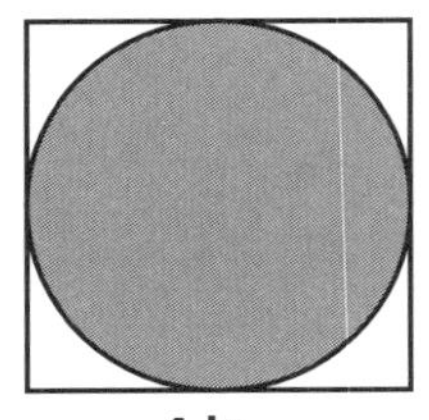

21.5%

15. A homeowner is designing paths through her flower garden. If the shaded regions represent flower beds, then what is the area of the pathways?

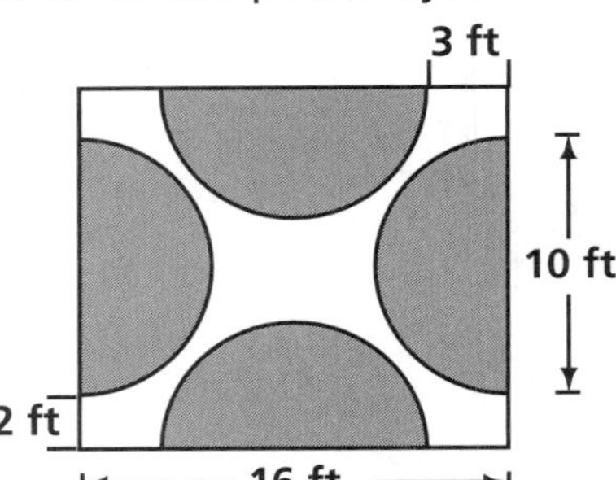

67 ft^2

Test Prep ★ Mixed Review

16 **If $a + 4.12 = {}^{-}3.01$, what is the value of a?** A; Obj. 9D

A $^{-}7.13$ **C** 1.11

B $^{-}1.11$ **D** 7.13

17 **If $\frac{1}{5}n - \frac{4}{5} = 1\frac{2}{5}$, what is the value of n?** F; Obj. 9D

F 11 **H** $2\frac{1}{5}$

G 3 **J** $\frac{3}{5}$

Closing the Lesson *Who can summarize what the strategy for finding the area of complex plane figures is?* (Possible answer: You divide the figure up into smaller simpler figures whose area can easily be found. You then add all the areas together.)

Name ______________________________

Area of a Trapezoid

Guided Practice: Ex. 1 & 11, pp. 283–284
Independent Practice: Complete pp. 283–284

A trapezoid is a quadrilateral that has one pair of parallel sides called **bases**. The bases, b_1 and b_2, are of unequal length.

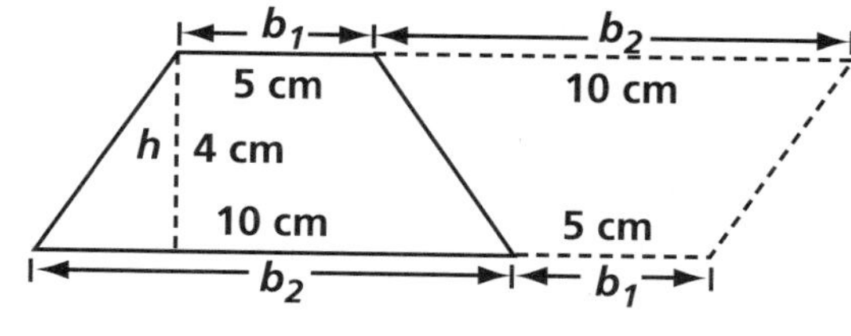

One way to find a formula for the area of a trapezoid is to arrange two congruent trapezoids to form a parallelogram.

- The parallelogram has a base of $(b_1 + b_2)$. Its height is h. The area of the parallelogram is:

$$A = bh \rightarrow A = (b_1 + b_2)\,h \rightarrow A = h\,(b_1 + b_2)$$

- The area of the trapezoid is half the area of the parallelogram.

$$A = \frac{1}{2}h(b_1 + b_2)$$

You can use the formula to find the area of the trapezoid.

1. Write the formula.

$$A = \frac{1}{2}h(b_1 + b_2)$$

2. Substitute.

$$A = \frac{1}{2} \cdot 4 \text{ cm} \cdot (10 \text{ cm} + 5 \text{ cm})$$

3. Evaluate.

$$A = \frac{1}{2} \cdot 4 \text{ cm} \cdot (15 \text{ cm})$$

$$= 30 \text{ cm}^2$$

area of the trapezoid

Find the area of the trapezoid.

	b_1	b_2	h	Area
1.	12 m	16 m	10 m	140 m²
3.	54 mm	45 mm	20 mm	990 mm²
5.	65 ft	32 ft	24 ft	1,164 ft²
7.	12 km	13 km	10 km	125 km²

	b_1	b_2	h	Area
2.	9 in.	8 in.	6 in.	51 in.²
4.	18 mm	28 mm	15 mm	345 mm²
6.	4 cm	8 cm	7 cm	42 cm²
8.	$1\frac{1}{4}$ yd	$2\frac{3}{4}$ yd	$1\frac{1}{2}$ yd	3 yd²

9. What is the area of a trapezoidal sign that has bases **12** ft and **18** ft and a height of **6** ft?

90 ft²

10. An open field is trapezoidal in shape. The bases are **21** m and **40** m. The height is **18** m. What is the area?

549 m²

Check Understanding *In order to find the area of a trapezoid, what information do you need?* (You need to know the lengths of the two parallel sides and the perpendicular distance between these sides.)

Find the area of the complex figure.

11.

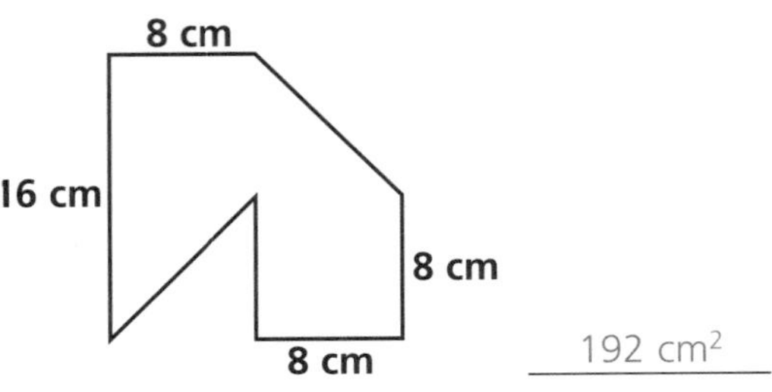

192 cm²

12.

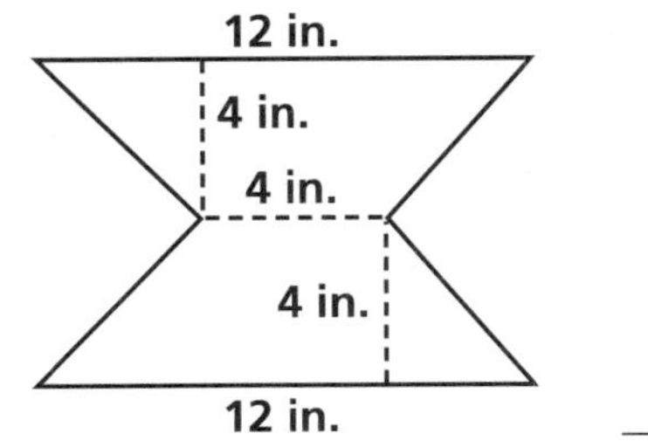

64 in.²

13.

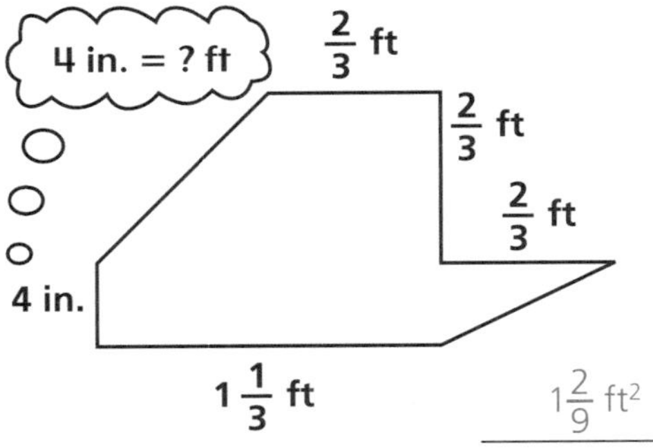

$1\frac{2}{9}$ ft²

14.

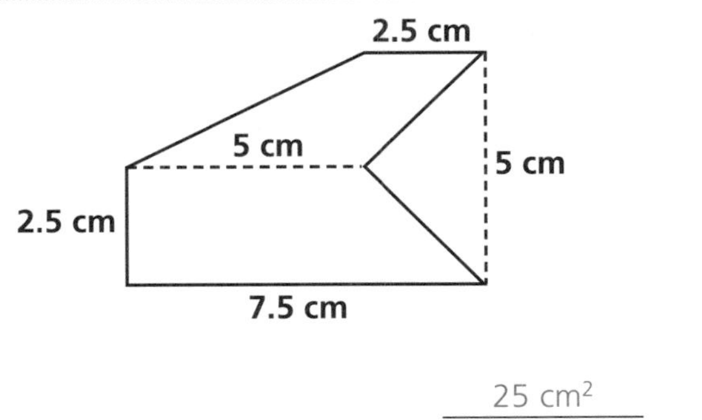

25 cm²

Problem Solving Reasoning Solve.

A flag maker is making a square flag that will have a black trapezoid and a red triangle as shown. The rest of the flag will be white.

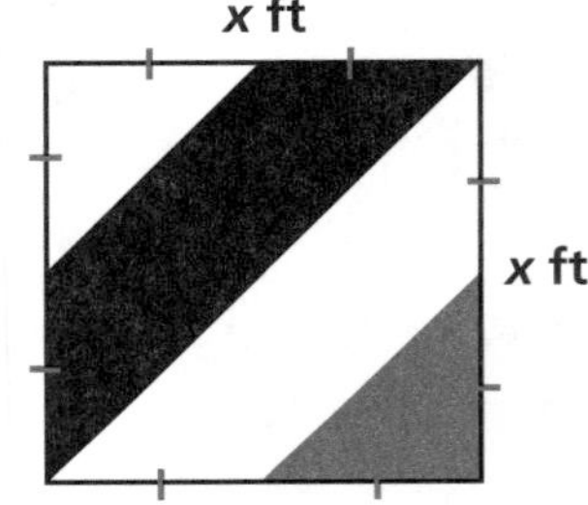

15. What is the area of the black section of the flag? $\frac{3}{8}x^2$

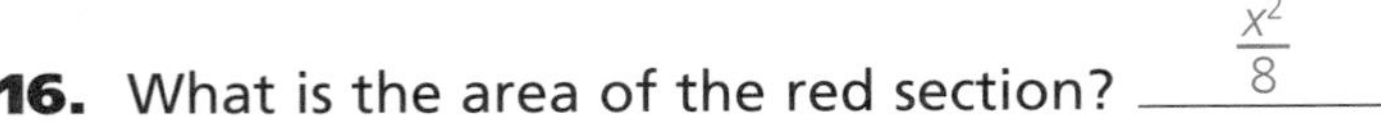

16. What is the area of the red section? $\frac{x^2}{8}$

17. What percent of the flag is white? 50%

Quick Check

Find the circumference and area to the nearest tenth. Use 3.14 for π.

18. a circle with diameter **20** m 62.8 m 314 m²

19. a circle with radius **7** in. 44.0 in. 153.9 in²

Find the area.

20.

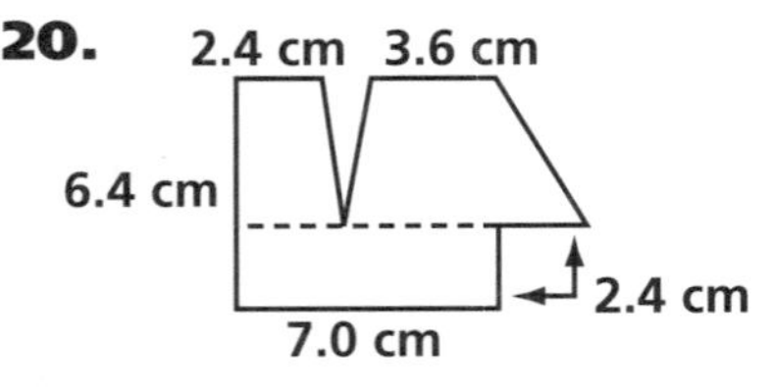

47.6 cm²

21.

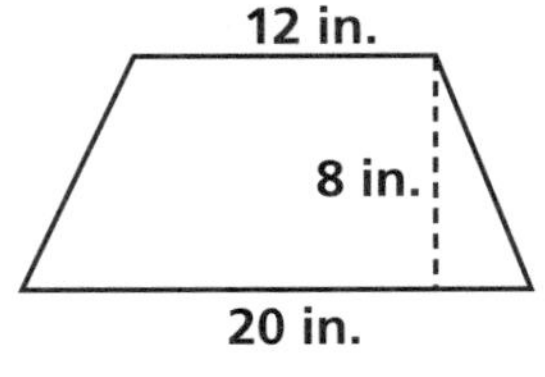

128 in.²

Work Space.

Item	Error Analysis
18–19	**Common Error** Students may confuse diameter and radius. **Reteaching** Reteach 81
20	**Common Error** They may not divide the figure into known shapes. **Reteaching** Reteach 82
21	**Common Error** They may multiply rather than add bases. **Reteaching** Reteach 83

Closing the Lesson *What is the formula for the area of a trapezoid? ($A = \frac{1}{2}(b_1 + b_2)\,h$)*

Name ____________________

Area of Regular Polygons

Guided Practice: Ex. 1 & 9, pp. 285–286
Independent Practice: Complete pp. 285–286

A **regular polygon** has all congruent sides and all congruent angles. You can use what you know about finding the area of complex figures to find the area of regular polygons. Each polygon has been divided into congruent triangles with base ***b*** and height ***h*** as shown. The number of triangles is the same as the number of sides in the figure.

Regular pentagon

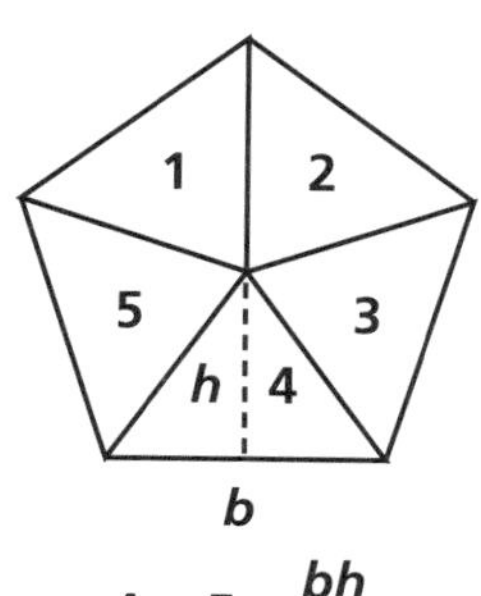

$A = 5 \bullet \frac{bh}{2}$

Regular hexagon

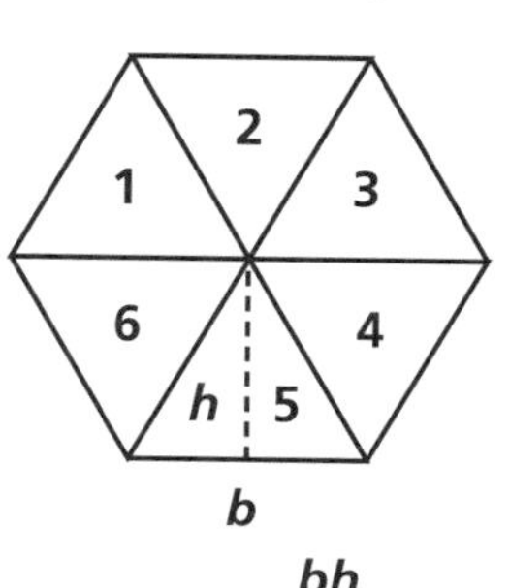

$A = 6 \bullet \frac{bh}{2}$

Regular octagon

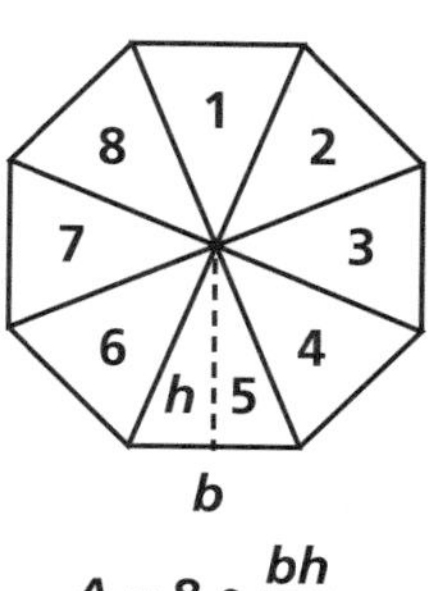

$A = 8 \bullet \frac{bh}{2}$

The area of a regular polygon of ***n*** sides is ***n*** *times the area of **1** congruent triangle, or*

$$A = n \cdot \frac{bh}{2}$$

Find the area of the regular polygon.

	Regular Polygon	Base *b*	Height *h*	Area *A*
1.	Hexagon	**11.7** in.	**8** in.	280.8 in.^{2}
2.	Decagon (**10** sides)	**3.4** cm	**5.3** cm	90.1 cm^2
3.	Octagon	**4.5** ft	$5\frac{1}{2}$ ft	99 ft^2
4.	Heptagon (**7** sides)	**8.6** m	**8.8** m	264.9 m^2
5.	Nonagon (**9** sides)	**3.7** cm	**5.2** cm	86.6 cm^2
6.	Pentagon	**9.5** yd	$6\frac{1}{2}$ yd	154.4 yd^2

Solve.

7. How much surface area is in a regular hexagonal flower bed in which each triangle has a base of **10.4** ft and a height of **9** ft? How many tons of topsoil are needed if each ton covers **4** yd^2?

280.8 ft^2; 7.8 tons

8. One regular hexagonal table mat measures **4.6** in. on a side and has a height of **4** in. How many mats can be cut from a piece of felt that is **2** ft by **4** ft?

20 mats

Check Understanding *How could you use this lesson to find the area of a square with a 2-in. side?* (Divide it into 4 triangles; each has an area of $\frac{1}{2} \times 2 \times 1 = 1$ in.^{2}; the area of all four triangles is 4 in.^{2}.)

To find the perimeter of a regular polygon with ***n*** sides, use the formula:

$$P = nb$$

Perimeter = number of sides × base

If you know the perimeter of a regular polygon, you can find its area. A regular polygon with *n* sides is made up of *n* triangles.

Its area is *n* times the area of one triangle:

$$A = n \cdot \frac{bh}{2} \rightarrow \frac{1}{2}n \cdot b \cdot h \rightarrow \frac{1}{2}Ph$$

Substitute *P* for *n* • *b*.

$$A = \frac{1}{2}Ph$$

Regular hexagon

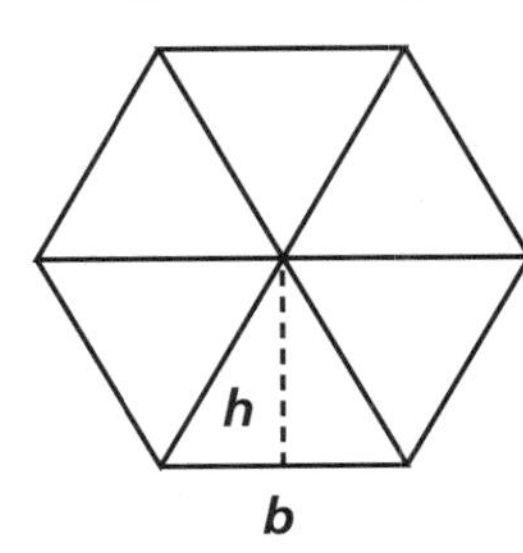

Regular octagon

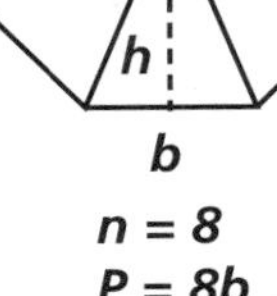

Find the area of the regular polygon.

	Regular Polygon	Height *h*	Perimeter *P*	Area *A*
9.	Hexagon	9 in.	63 in.	283.5 in^2
10.	Decagon	6.8 cm	43.5 cm	147.9 cm^2
11.	Octagon	$5\frac{2}{3}$ ft	37.4 ft	105.9 ft^2
12.	Heptagon	10 m	68.6 m	343 m^2
13.	Nonagon	7.2 cm	46.7 cm	168.12 cm^2
14.	Pentagon	$3\frac{1}{2}$ yd	25.6 yd	44.8 yd^2

Problem Solving Reasoning

Solve.

15. A quilted design, in the shape of a regular hexagon, is made up of triangles that are 6 cm high. If the area of the design is 125 cm^2, then what is the length of each side of the design? How much ribbon would you use to border the design?

7 cm; 42 cm

16. A sign, in the shape of a regular octagon, has an area in square inches that is three times the numerical value of its perimeter. What is the height (***h***) in inches of the octagon? 6 in.

Test Prep ★ Mixed Review

17 **What is the area of a circle whose radius is 8 cm? (Use $\pi \approx 3.14$.)** C; Obj. 10A

A 25.12 cm^2
B 50.24 cm^2
C 200.96 cm^2
D 803.84 cm^2

18 **A trapezoid has a height of 6.5 in., and the lengths of the bases are 4.8 in. and 10 in. What is the area of the trapezoid?** F; Obj. 10A

F 48.1 in.^{2}
G 65 in.^{2}
H 96.3 in.^{2}
J 113 in.^{2}

Closing the Lesson *How do you find the area of a regular polygon?* (Possible answer: Find the length of a side of the regular polygon, find the height of one of its triangles, compute the area of one of the triangles, and multiply that by the number of sides.)

Name ____________________

Guided Practice: Ex. 1, p. 287
Independent Practice: Complete pp. 287–288

Estimating the Area of Irregular Plane Figures on a Grid

Sometimes you may not be able to find the area of an irregular figure using a formula. To estimate the area of an irregular figure, you can use a grid.

Estimate the area of the irregular figure shown.

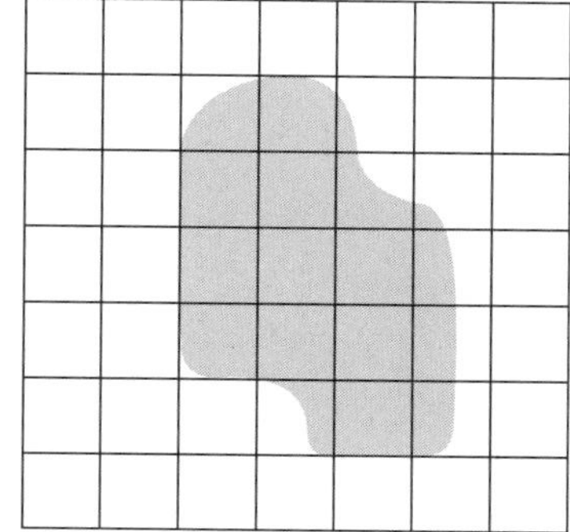

1. Count the number of whole squares.
2. Put together parts of other squares to approximate whole squares.
3. Add the area of the whole squares to the area of the partial squares.

This figure has an estimated area of about **14** square units.

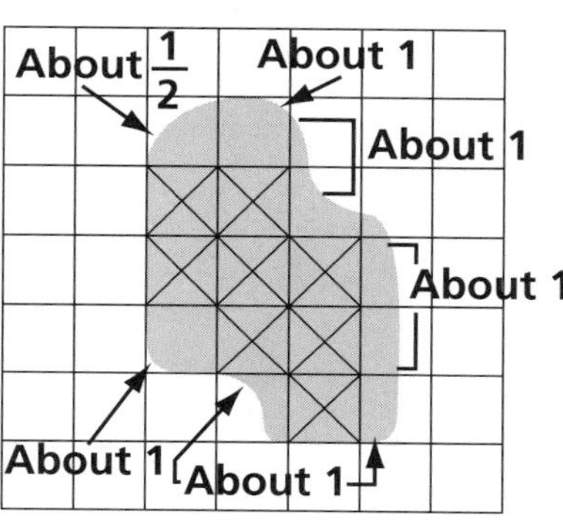

Estimate the area in square units.

1.

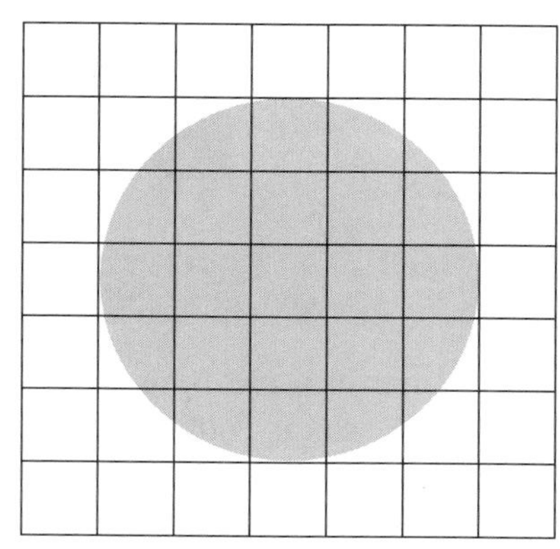

about 20 square units

2.

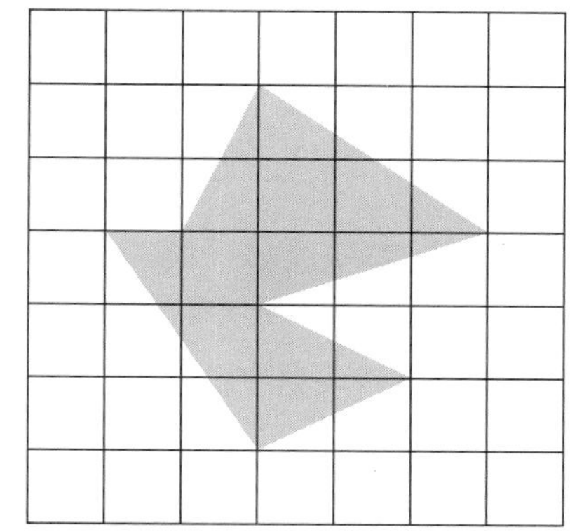

about 10 square units

Check Understanding *Could this method be used to find the area of a parallelogram?* (Yes, but formulas are usually more accurate.)

Estimate the area in square units. Estimates may vary slightly.

3.

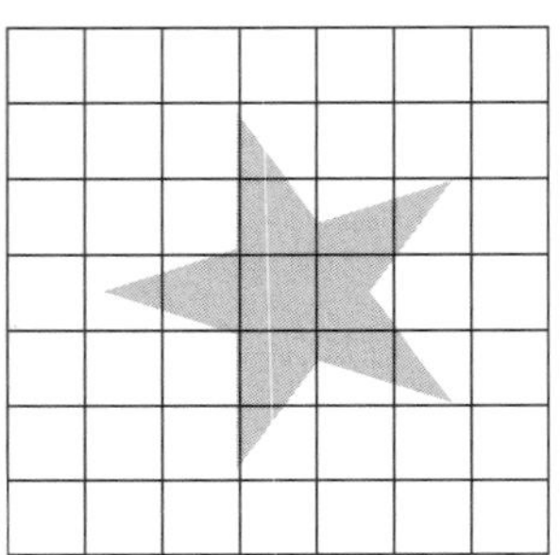

$A \approx$ 7 square units

4.

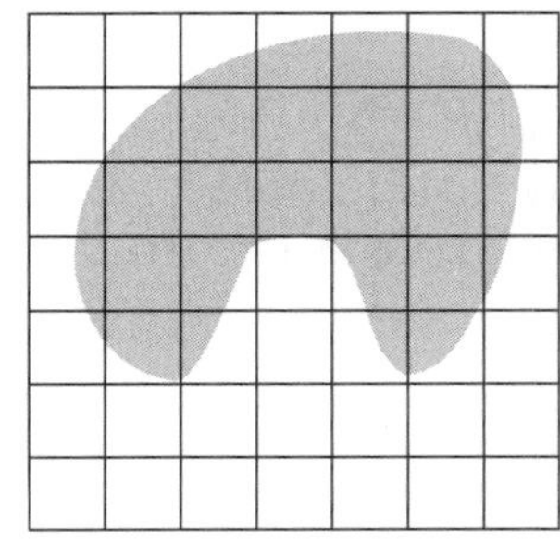

$A \approx$ 19 square units

5.

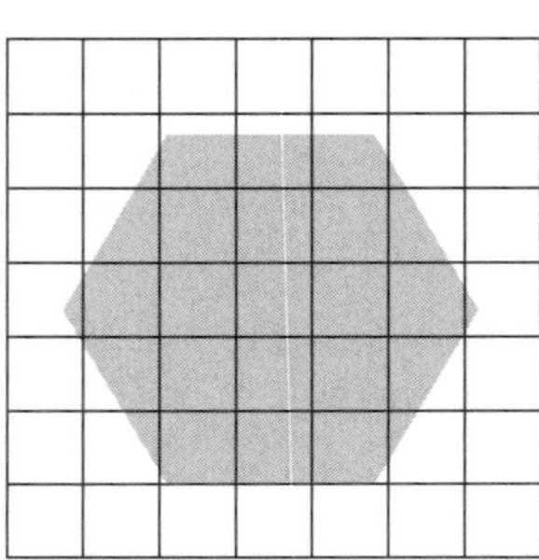

$A \approx$ 18 square units

6.

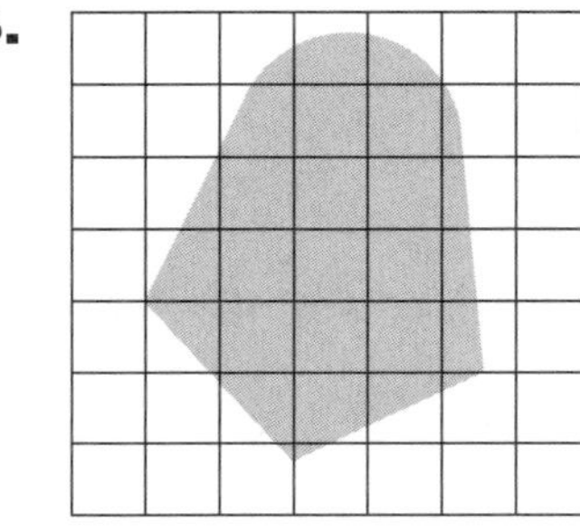

$A \approx$ 20 square units

Problem Solving Reasoning

Use what you know about area to complete. Exact answers are given in parentheses.

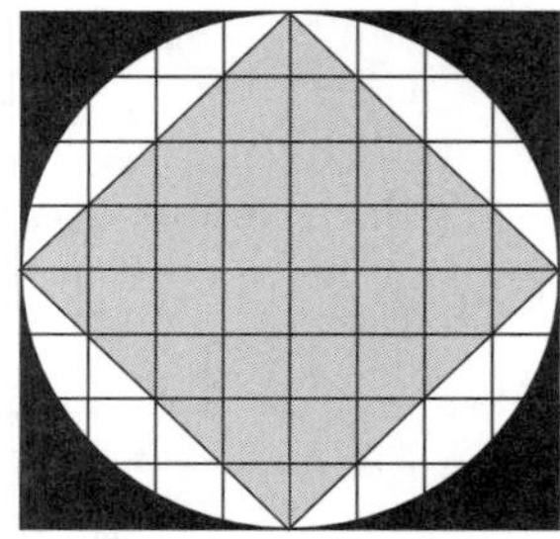

7. Find the area of the inner shaded square. 32 square units

8. Estimate the area of the circle that is outside the square. 18 (18.24) square units

9. Estimate the area of the shaded corners. 14 (13.76) square units

Test Prep ★ Mixed Review

10 **A regular pentagon is divided into 5 congruent isosceles triangles. $\triangle ABC$ is one of the triangles. It has a base *BC* that is 6 cm and a height of 4.1 cm. What is the area of the pentagon?** B; Obj. 10A

A 12.3 cm^2 **C** 129 cm^2

B 61.5 cm^2 **D** 615 cm^2

11 **A scale drawing of a running track consists of a rectangle measuring 3 in. by 12 in., with a semicircle at each of the shorter sides. What is the area of the scale drawing to the nearest square inch? (Use $\pi \approx 3.14$)** H; Obj. 10A

F 36 in.^{2} **H** 43 in.^{2}

G 40 in.^{2} **J** 64 in.^{2}

Closing the Lesson *How do you estimate area using a grid?* (Possible answer: You count all the squares and pieces of squares.)

Name ______________________________

Guided Practice: Ex. 1, p. 290

Independent Practice: Complete p. 290

Problem Solving Strategy: Solve a Simpler Problem

To solve some problems, you can work an easier problem like it and find a pattern.

When you solve a simpler problem, think about how the problem you have to solve relates to the simpler problem.

Problem

You want to enlarge a photo so that its length and width are each $3\frac{1}{2}$ times their original size. How many times greater is the area of the enlargement?

1 Understand

"Asking yourself questions will help you identify the math ideas."

As you reread the problem, ask yourself questions.

- The length and the width of the photo will increase to $3\frac{1}{2}$ times their original size.
- Do you know what the original size is? No.
- What do you need to find? the ratio of the new areas

2 Decide

"A simpler problem will help you to see a pattern in the way the area increases. It helps you think about how to solve the problem."

Choose a method for solving.

Try the Solve a Simpler Problem strategy.

- Pick any rectangle, perhaps **2** in. by **3** in. How does its area increase when the sides increase **2, 3,** and **4** times?

Rectangle	Length	Width	Area	Number of Times Larger
Original	**2**	**3**	**6**	
2 times	**4**	**6**	**24**	**4** times
3 times	6	9	54	9 times
4 times	8	12	96	16 times

3 Solve

"Is there more than one way to describe the pattern in the simpler problem?"

Answer the question.

- Complete the table.
- If the dimensions increase ***n*** times, then how many times does the area increase? n^2
- How many times as great will the area of the enlargement be? 12.25 times

4 Look back

"How does the simpler problem help to show that your answer is reasonable?"

Ask if your answers make sense.

- Write the answer as a complete sentence.

The area of the enlargement is 12.25 times greater than the original area.

Check Understanding *What kind of problems would lend themselves to using this method?* (Possible answer: ones that involve large numbers or complex ideas)

Use the Solve a Simpler Problem strategy or any other strategy you have learned.

1. What is the total number of squares of all sizes in the checkerboard below?

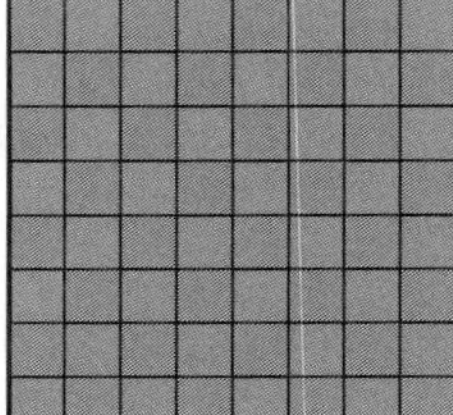

Think: What simpler problem can you use? How does the total number of squares increase as the size of the board increases?

Use smaller checkerboards or grids; Each increases by the next square number.

Answer 204 squares

2. What is the total number of triangles of all sizes in the figure below?

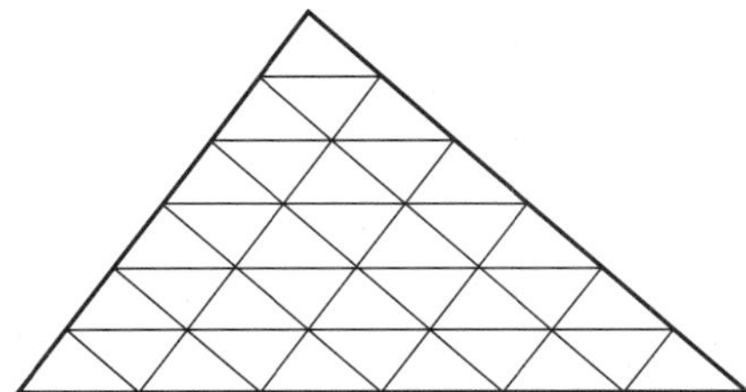

Think: What simpler problem can you use? How does the total number of triangles increase as the size of the large triangle increases?

Count the triangles by size; In increasing order, there are 36 + 21 + 11 + 6 + 3 + 1, or 78 triangles.

Answer 78 triangles

3. The sides of a square increase from **4** cm to **10** cm. How many times as large is the area of the new square?

6.25 times as large

4. The sides of a triangle are enlarged to **3.3** times their original length. How many times as large is the area of the new triangle?

10.89 times as large

5. The dot patterns below represent triangle numbers. How many dots are in the **8**th triangle number?

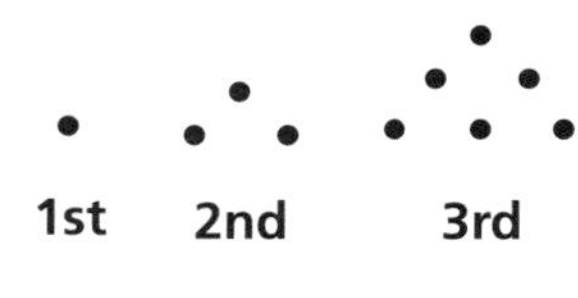

36 dots

6. With one straight cut, you can cut a pizza into **2** pieces. With two straight cuts, you can cut it into **4** pieces. What is the greatest number of pieces you can cut with **5** straight cuts? (Hint: Not all the pieces will have a curved side.)

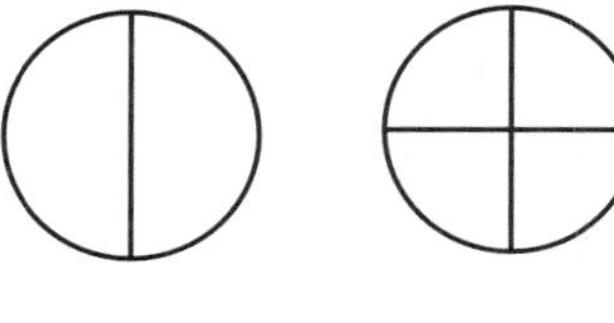

15 pieces

7. Two numbers have a sum of **8.125** and a product of **1.** What are the two numbers?

8 and $\frac{1}{8}$

8. You spend half your money on gloves. Then, you spend $\frac{1}{3}$ of what you have left on a book. You spend **$4** on lunch and have **$6** left. How much money did you start with? $30

Closing the Lesson *What does the strategy of solving a simpler problem mean?* (Possible answer: By looking at a simpler problem, you may be able to see a pattern and generalize.)

Name ______________________________

Guided Practice: Ex. 1, Create net for ex. 6, pp. 291–292
Independent Practice: Complete pp. 291–292

Spatial Visualization with Nets

Any figure that is not entirely in one plane is a space figure. For example, the figure at the right is a rectangular prism. A rectangular prism unfolded might look like this:

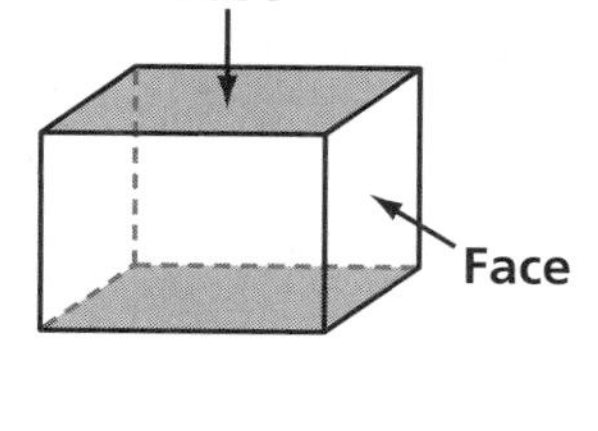

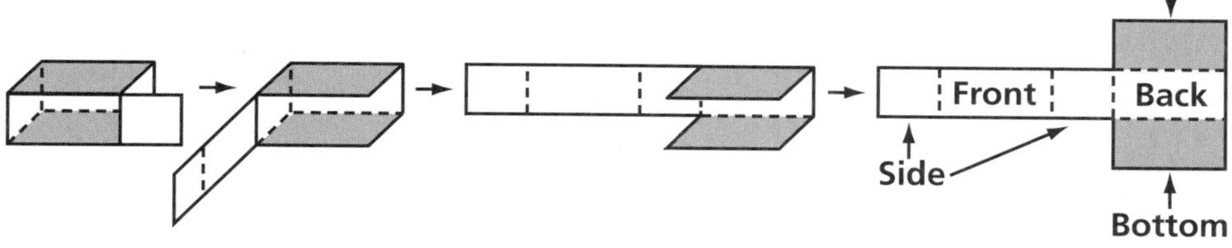

Any flat pattern that can be folded to form a space figure is a **net.** These are nets for a cube.

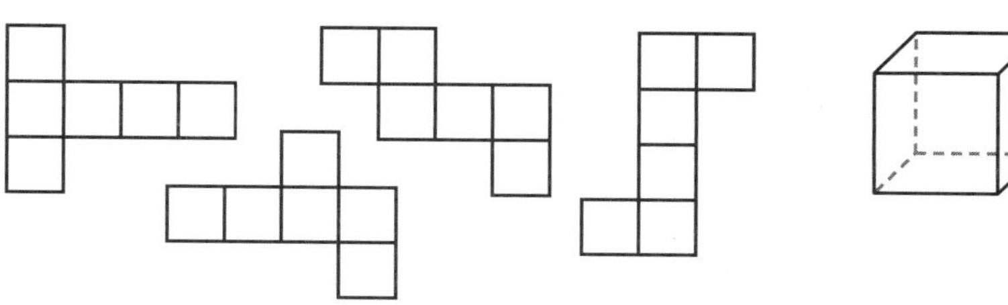

Space figures are named by the shape of their bases. A prism has two bases. A pyramid has only one base. Here are nets for a prism and a pyramid.

Rectangular prism

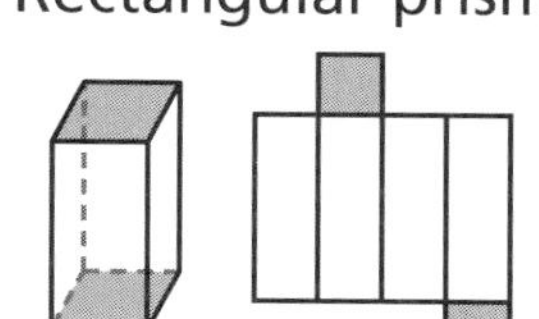

Triangular pyramid

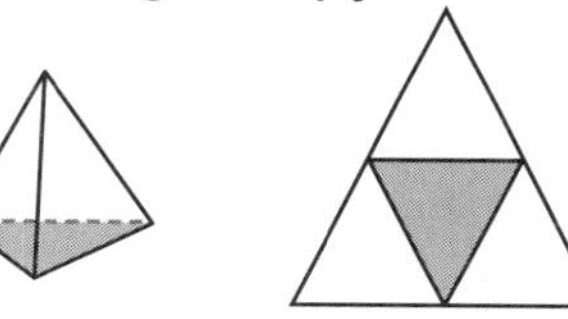

Circle the figure that can be made from the net.

1.

Cylinder

Sphere

Cone

2.

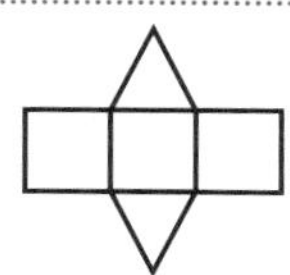

Triangular prism

Cube

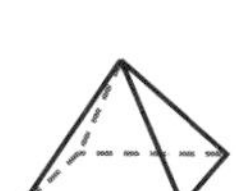

Square pyramid

3.

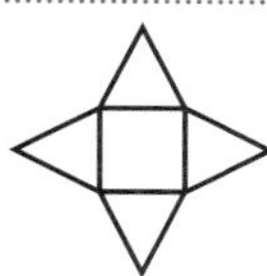

Triangular prism

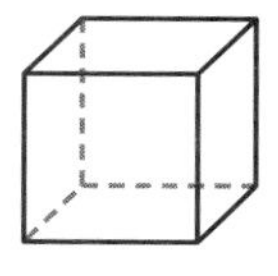

Cube

Square pyramid

Check Understanding *In what situations is the use of nets important?* (Possible answer: in the design of packages and scale models)

Sketch a net for the space figure.

4. Pentagonal prism

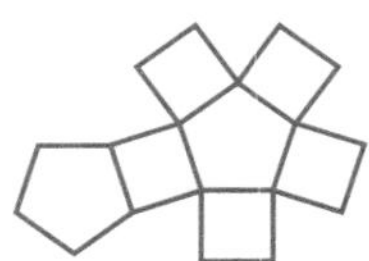

5. Pentagonal pyramid

6. There are **11** different nets that can be made for a cube. Four are shown at the beginning of the lesson. How many can you find? Hint: This net **cannot** be folded to form a cube.

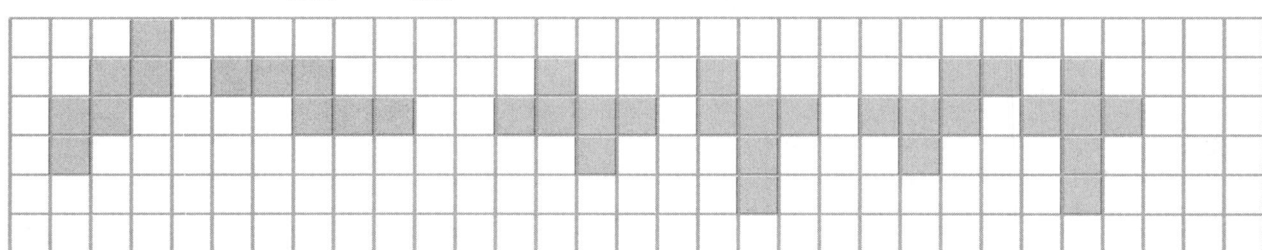

Problem Solving Reasoning

Architects use technical drawings of front, side, and top views to visualize space figures. Match the drawing to the correct figure on page 291. Explain your choice.

7.

Figure: cylinder

Explanations will vary.

8.

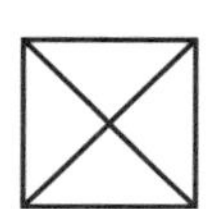

Figure: square pyramid

Explanations will vary.

Quick Check

9. Find the perimeter and area of this regular figure.

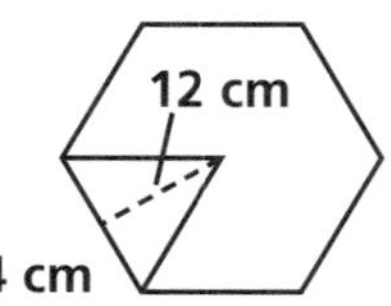

84 cm; 504 cm^2

10. Each □ is **1** square unit. Find the area.

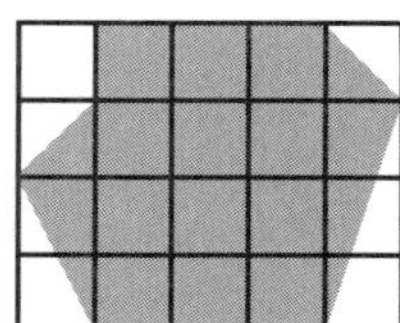

about $15\frac{1}{2}$ square units

11. What space figure can be made with this net?

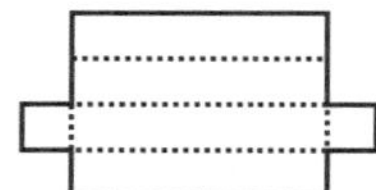

rectangular prism

Work Space.

Item	Error Analysis
9	**Common Error** Watch for students who count the wrong number of sides. **Reteaching** Reteach 84
10	**Common Error** Students may count partial squares as whole squares. **Reteaching** Reteach 85
11	**Common Error** Watch for students who confuse prisms and pyramids. **Reteaching** Reteach 86

Closing the Lesson *How many polygons make up the net for a pentagonal pyramid?* (six)

Name ______________________________

Guided Practice: Ex. 1 & 8; First ex. in Rows 14 & 19, pp. 294–295
Independent Practice: Complete pp. 294–295

The **surface area (*SA*)** of a space figure is the sum of the areas of all its surfaces. To find the surface area of a rectangular prism, find the area of each pair of opposite faces.

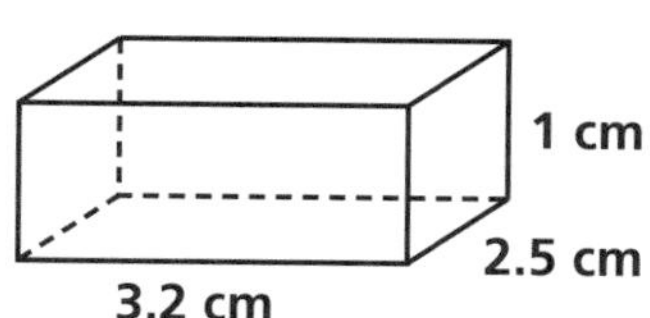

Find the surface area of the regular prism

Sides

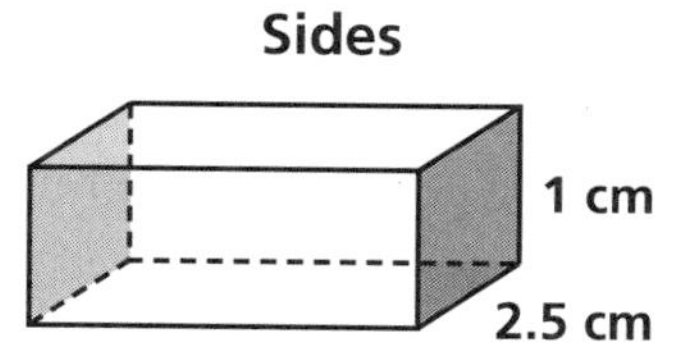

$A = 2(2.5 \text{ cm} \cdot 1 \text{ cm})$

$= 2(2.5 \text{ cm}^2)$

$= 5 \text{ cm}^2$

Front and Back

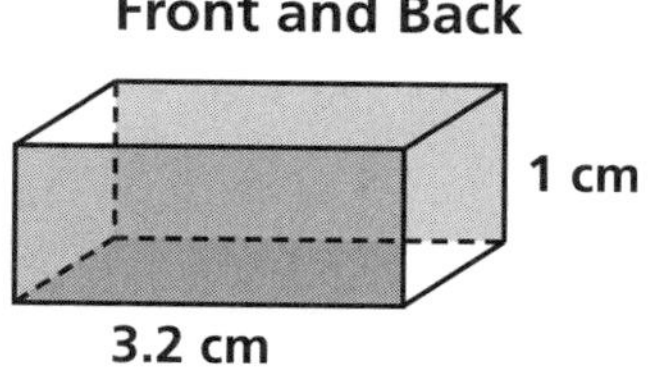

$A = 2(3.2 \text{ cm} \cdot 1 \text{ cm})$

$= 2(3.2 \text{ cm}^2)$

$= 6.4 \text{ cm}^2$

Top and Bottom

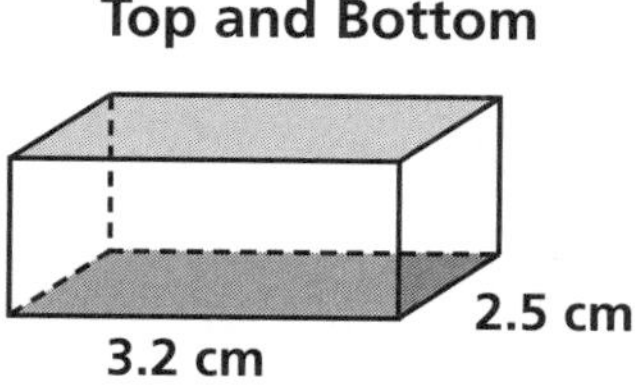

$A = 2(3.2 \text{ cm} \cdot 2.5 \text{ cm})$

$= 2(8 \text{ cm}^2)$

$= 16 \text{ cm}^2$

Total surface area $SA = 5 \text{ cm}^2 + 6.4 \text{ m}^2 + 16 \text{ m}^2$

$= 27.4 \text{ cm}^2$

The general formula for the surface area of any rectangular prism with length ***l***, width ***w***, and height ***h*** can be given as:

> Surface area of a rectangular prism: $SA = 2(lw + lh + wh)$

Other examples:

If a prism has a square base, the formula becomes simpler.

Square prism

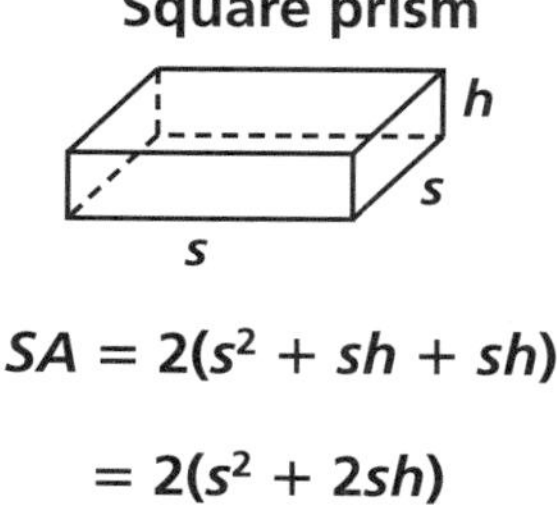

$SA = 2(s^2 + sh + sh)$

$= 2(s^2 + 2sh)$

A cube is a special kind of square prism in which $h = s$.

$SA = 2(s^2 + 2sh)$

$= 2(s^2 + 2s \cdot s)$

$= 2(s^2 + 2s^2)$

$= 2(3s^2)$

$= 6s^2$

Cube

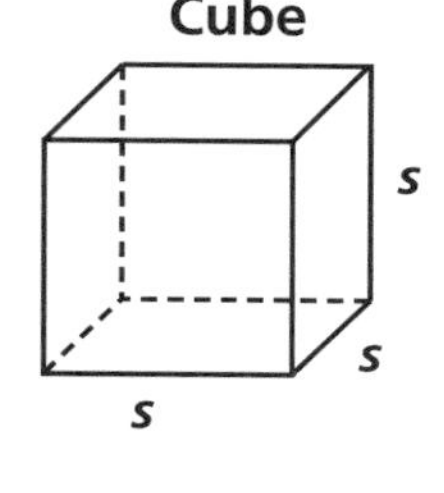

Check Understanding *What is the simple formula for the surface area of a cube? ($A = 6s^2$) What does s stand for in this formula?* (the length of the edge of a cube)

Find the surface area of the rectangular prism.

	Length l	Width w	Height h	SA
1.	3 m	2 m	2 m	32 m^2
2.	15 cm	4 cm	11 cm	538 cm^2
3.	7.2 dm	6 dm	4.6 dm	207.84 dm^2
4.	8.2 cm	9.1 cm	6.3 cm	367.22 cm^2
5.	$4\frac{1}{2}$ ft	$7\frac{3}{4}$ ft	$8\frac{1}{2}$ ft	278 ft^2
6.	$2\frac{1}{4}$ in.	$3\frac{1}{2}$ in.	4 in.	$61\frac{3}{4}$ $in.^2$
7.	l m	w m	h m	$2(lw + lh + wh)$ m^2

Find the surface area of the square prism.

	Length l	Width w	Height h	SA
8.	7 cm	7 cm	10 cm	378 cm^2
9.	16 m	16 m	12 m	1,280 m^2
10.	$3\frac{1}{2}$ ft	$3\frac{1}{2}$ ft	5 ft	$94\frac{1}{2}$ ft^2
11.	$8\frac{1}{4}$ in.	$8\frac{1}{4}$ in.	$10\frac{3}{4}$ in.	$490\frac{7}{8}$ $in.^2$
12.	3.5 m	3.5 m	5 m	94.5 m^2
13.	s in.	w in.	s in.	$2(s^2 + 2sw)$ $in.^2$

Find the surface area of the cube.

	Side s	SA	Side s	SA	Side s	SA
14.	5 mm	150 mm^2	$\frac{1}{2}$ yd	$1\frac{1}{2}$ yd^2	12 cm	864 cm^2
15.	8.5 m	433.5 m^2	$\frac{2}{3}$ ft	$2\frac{2}{3}$ ft^2	10.6 dm	674.16 dm^2

Compare the surface areas of the rectangular prisms. Write >, <, or =.

16. Prism A: $l = 6$ in., $w = 6$ in., $h = 6$ in. ___<___ Prism B: $l = 6$ in., $w = 10$ in., $h = 4$ in.

17. Prism C: $l = 2$ cm, $w = 2$ cm, $h = 2$ cm ___<___ Prism D: $l = 2$ cm, $w = 4$ cm, $h = 1$ cm

18. Prism E: $l = 3$ ft, $w = 3$ ft, $h = 2$ ft ___=___ Prism F: $l = 10$ ft, $w = 1$ ft, $h = 1$ ft

Name ______________________

To find the surface area of a triangular prism, use a net as a complex model of the figure.

Area of faces ***A*** and ***B***:

$$2(8 \cdot 5.4)\ \text{cm}^2 = 86.4\ \text{cm}^2$$

Area of face ***C***:

$$(8 \cdot 4)\ \text{cm}^2 = 32\ \text{cm}^2$$

Total area of faces: **118.4** cm²

Area of bases ***D*** and ***E***:

$$2(\tfrac{1}{2} \cdot 4 \cdot 5)\ \text{cm}^2 = 20\ \text{cm}^2$$

Total surface area: **118.4** cm² + **20** cm² = **138.4** cm²

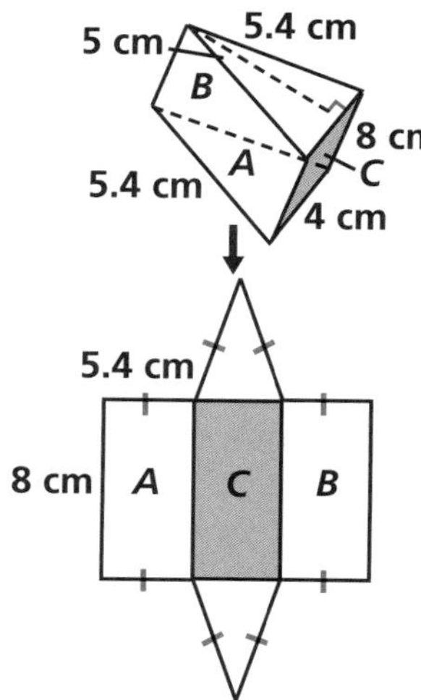

Faces ***A*** and ***B*** are congruent. So are the triangular bases.

Find the surface area of the triangular prism.

19.

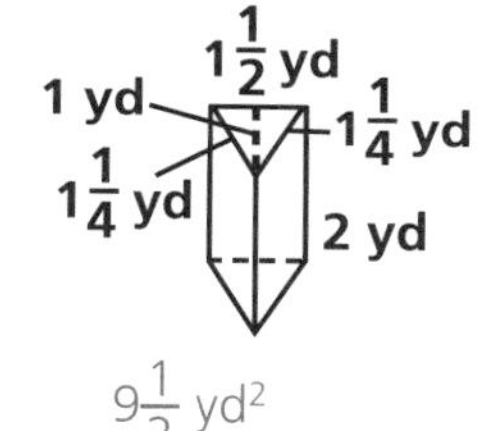

$9\frac{1}{2}$ yd²

6 cm, 5.5 cm, 5 cm, 5.5 cm, 4.5 cm

115.5 cm²

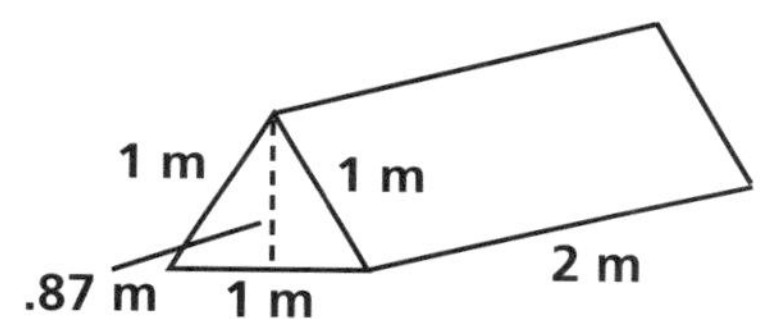

6.87 m²

Problem Solving Reasoning **Solve.**

20. What is the surface area of a cube that is twice as long, twice as wide, and twice as high as this cube? What is the ratio of the surface area of the new cube to that of the original cube?

864 cm²; 4:1

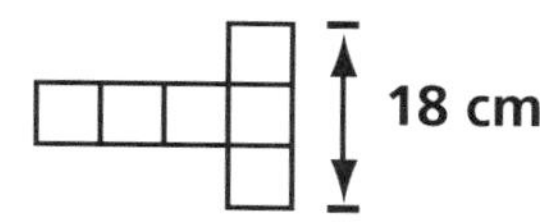

Test Prep ★ Mixed Review

21 **A regular hexagon has a side of 6 ft, and the distance from the center of the hexagon to the midpoint of each side is 5.2 ft. What is the area of the hexagon?** B; Obj. 10A

A 93.6 ft **C** 87.2 ft²

B 93.6 ft² **D** 15.6 ft²

22 **Laurie's lawn is in the shape of a rectangle measuring 18 ft by 8 ft., with a semicircle at one of the short sides. Which solution best represents the area of the lawn? (Use $\pi \approx 3.14$.)** G; Obj. 10A

F 169 ft **H** 199 ft

G 169 ft² **J** 199 ft²

Closing the Lesson *What is the surface area of a space figure?* (Possible answer: It is the total area of all the surfaces making up the space figure.)

Name ______________________________

Surface Area of Cylinders

Guided Practice: Ex. 1 & 8, pp. 296–297
Independent Practice: Complete pp. 296–297

As you can see from its net, a cylinder is a space figure that is made up of two circular bases and a rectangle.

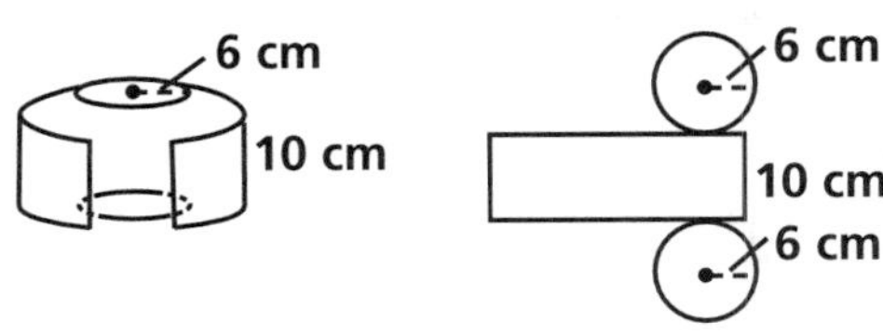

To find the surface area of a cylinder, you find the area of its parts.

The width of the rectangle is equal to the height of the cylinder. The length of the rectangle is equal to the circumference of the circular base.

Think: $A = \pi r^2$

Area of the circular bases: **2 · 3.14 · 36** cm² = **226.08** cm²

Think: $A = l \cdot w$

Area of the rectangle: **2 · (3.14 · 6** cm**) · 10** cm = **376.80** cm²

Total surface area of the cylinder: **226.08** cm² + **376.80** cm² = **602.88** cm²

Find the surface area of the cylinder. Use 3.14 for π. Answers may vary slightly.

	Radius *r*	Diameter *d*	Height *h*	*SA*
1.	3.5 m	7 m	11 m	318.71 m²
2.	$1\frac{3}{4}$ ft	$3\frac{1}{2}$ ft	15 ft	184.0825 ft²
3.	4 cm	8 cm	12 cm	401.92 cm²
4.	$1\frac{1}{2}$ in.	3 in.	4 in.	51.81 in.²

Find the surface area of the cylinder. Use 3.14 for π. Answers may vary slightly.

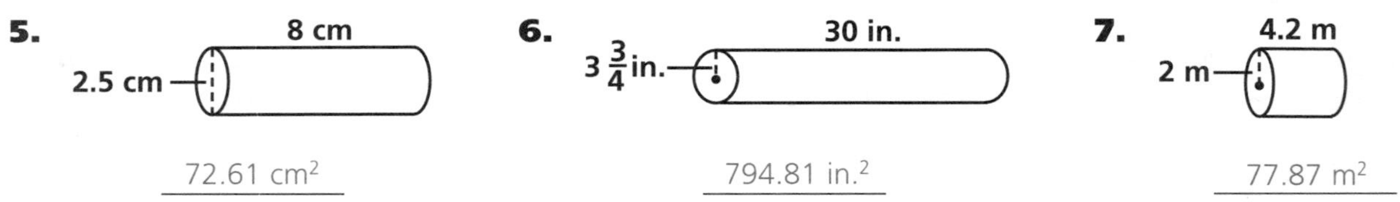

5. 72.61 cm²

6. 794.81 in.²

7. 77.87 m²

Check Understanding *What two measurements do you need in order to find the surface area of a cylinder?* (the length of the radius of the circle and the height of the cylinder)

Name ______________________

The surface of a cylinder with radius r and height h is given by the formula $SA = 2\pi r(r + h)$.

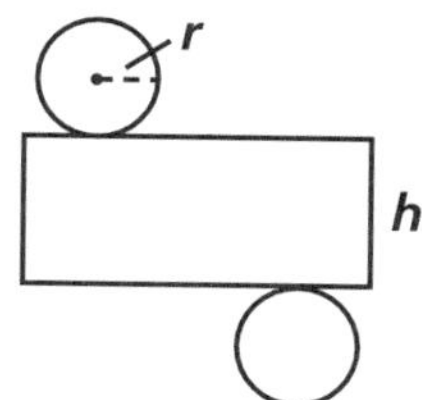

Use the formula to complete the table. Use 3.14 for π.

	h	r	$2\pi r$	$r + h$	SA
	5 in.	2 in.	12.56 in.	7 in.	87.92 in.^{2}
8.	2 cm	5 cm	31.4 cm	7 cm	219.8 cm^2
9.	3 ft	4 ft	25.12 ft	7 ft	175.84 ft^2
10.	5 m	4 m	25.12 m	9 m	226.08 m^2

Find the surface area.

11. 5 in. 20 in.

785 in.^{2}

12.

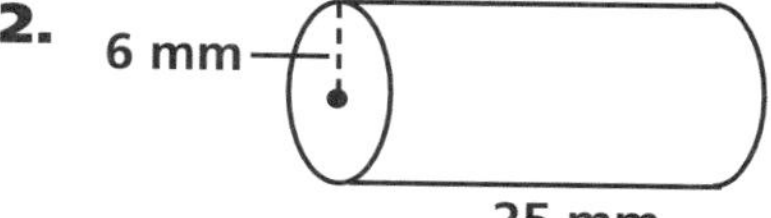

1,168.08 mm^2

13.

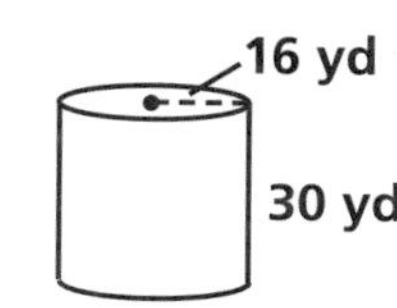

4,622.08 yd^2

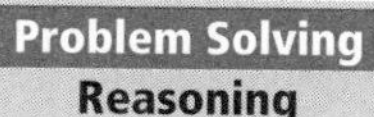

Solve.

A cylinder has a radius of **5** cm and a height of **10** cm.

14. What is the surface area of a cylinder whose radius is double the given cylinder? What is the ratio of the surface area of the new figure to the original one?

1,256 cm^2; $2\frac{2}{3}$:1

15. What is the surface area of a cylinder whose height is double the given cylinder? What is the ratio of the surface area of the new figure to the original one?

785 cm^2; $1\frac{2}{3}$:1

Test Prep ★ Mixed Review

16 Leon wants to wrap a box that measures 18 in. by 12 in. by 5 in. What is the minimum area of wrapping paper he needs? A; Obj. 10C

A 732 in.^{2} **C** 366 in.^{2}

B 732 in. **D** 366 in.

17 The base of a prism is an equilateral triangle with 4-inch sides and a height of about 3.5 in. If the height of the prism is 10 in., which best represents the surface area of the prism? H; Obj. 10C

F 120 in.^{2} **H** 134 in.^{2}

G 127 in.^{2} **J** 148 in.^{2}

Closing the Lesson *What similarities exist between finding the surface area of a cylinder and finding the surface area of a prism?* (Possible answer: In both cases, you find the areas of all the plane figures that make up the net for the space figure.)

Name ___________________________

Volume of Prisms

Guided Practice: Ex. 1 & 4, p. 298; Ex. 7, p. 299
Independent Practice: Complete pp. 298–299

The volume of a space figure is the number of cubic units it contains. Remember, volume is expressed in cubic units, for example, cm^3, m^3, or $in.^3$.

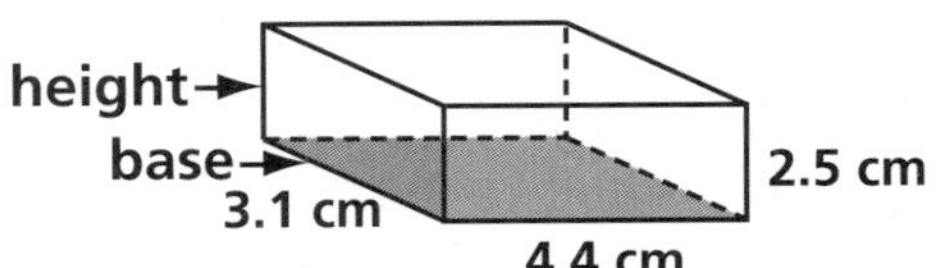

To find the volume of any prism, multiply the area of the base ***B*** by the height ***h***.

$$V = Bh$$

The volume (V) of the prism above is:

$$V = (3.1 \cdot 4.4)\ cm^2 \cdot 2.5\ cm$$

$$= 34.1\ cm^3$$

> The volume (V) of any rectangular prism with length l, width w, and height h is:
>
> $$V = lwh$$

A cube is a rectangular prism in which the length, width, and height are all equal.

$s = 4.3$ cm

4.3 cm

4.3 cm

Find the volume of the cube.

$$V = 4.3\ cm \cdot 4.3\ cm \cdot 4.3\ cm$$

$$= 4.3^3\ cm^3$$

$$= 79.5\ cm^3$$

> The volume (V) of any cube with side s is:
>
> $$V = s^3$$

Find the volume of the rectangular prism.

	Length l	Width w	Height h	Volume V
1.	5.2 cm	8.1 cm	4.5 cm	189.54 cm^3
2.	16 in.	16 in.	16 in.	4,096 $in.^3$
3.	7.2 m	3.4 m	4.5 m	110.16 m^3

Use the formula $V = Bh$ to find the volume.

	Area of rectangular base B	Height h	Volume V
4.	16 cm^2	6.5 cm	104 cm^3
5.	42 $in.^2$	$8\frac{1}{2}$ in.	357 $in.^3$
6.	26 ft^2	$5\frac{3}{4}$ ft	$149\frac{1}{2}$ ft^3

Check Understanding *If the height of a prism is doubled, what happens to its volume?* (It is doubled.)

Name ______________________________

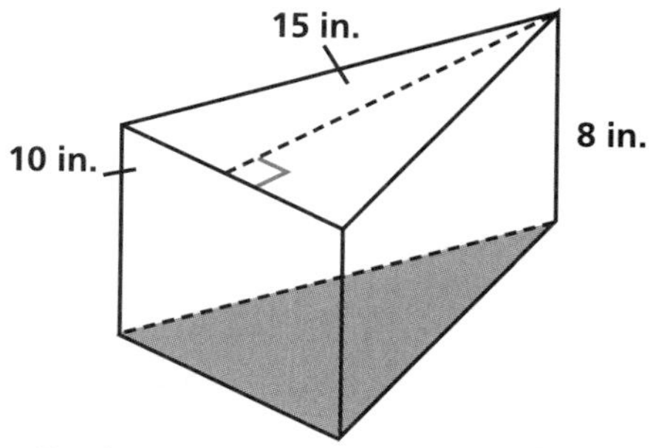

You can find the volume of a triangular prism by multiplying the area of the triangular base by the height. To find the volume of the prism at right you need two formulas.

1. First, find the area of the base.

$A = \frac{1}{2}bh$

$= \frac{1}{2} \cdot 10 \text{ in.} \cdot 15 \text{ in.}$

$= 75 \text{ in.}^2$

2. Then, find the volume.

$V = Bh$

$= 75 \text{ in.}^2 \cdot 8 \text{ in.}$

$= 600 \text{ in.}^3$

Volume of the triangular prism

Find the volume of the triangular prism.

7.

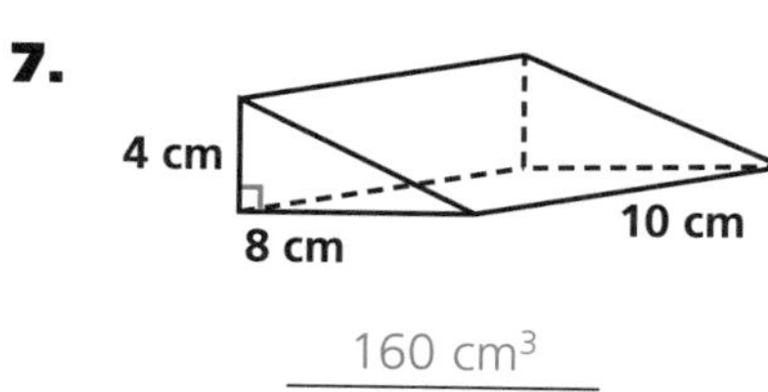

160 cm³

8. 6 m, 4 m, 12 m

144 m³

9. 11 in., 12 in., 25 in.

1,650 in.³

Solve. Draw the figure if you need to.

10. The base of a prism is a regular hexagon. The height of the prism is **10** cm. The hexagonal base can be divided into **6** triangles, each with base **8** cm and height **7** cm. Find the volume of the prism.

1,680 cm³

11. The base of a prism is a regular pentagon. The height of the prism is **5** cm. The pentagonal base can be divided into **5** triangles, each with base **6.5** cm and height **4.5** cm. Find the volume of the prism.

365.625 cm³

Quick Check

Find the surface area.

12.

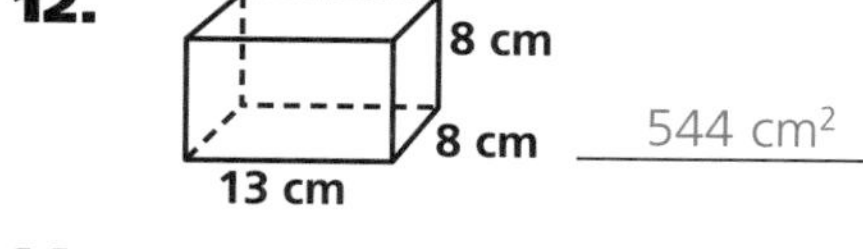

544 cm²

13.

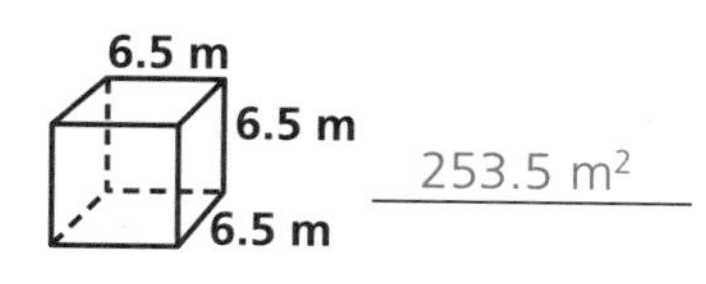

253.5 m²

14.

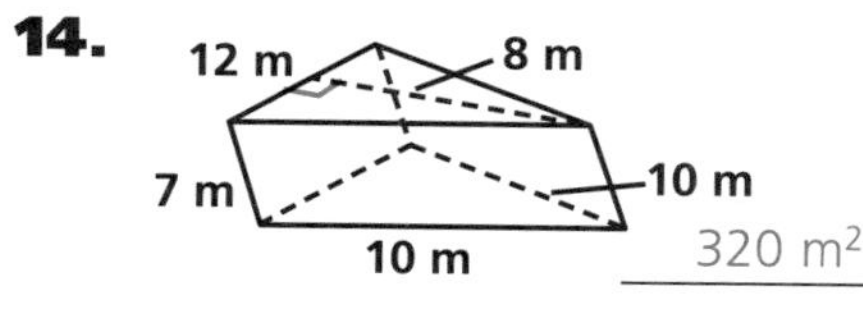

320 m²

15.

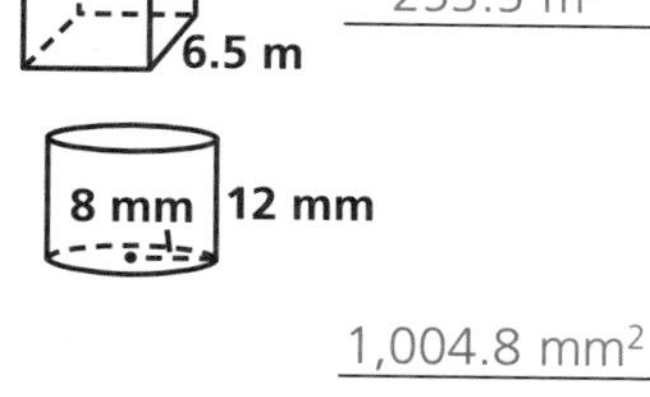

1,004.8 mm²

Find the volume of the figures in exercises 12–14.

16. Exercise 12 832 cm³

17. Exercise 13 274.625 cm³

18. Exercise 14 336 m³

Work Space

Item	Error Analysis
12–14	**Common Error** Students may forget to double the areas of corresponding faces or may not find circumference of base. **Reteaching** Reteach 87 and 88
16–18	**Common Error** Students may not recognize the bases. **Reteaching** Reteach 89

Closing the Lesson *When would you need to find the volume of a prism?* (Possible answer: When manufacturers ship objects like cereal boxes or candy bars in larger cartons, they need to find the optimum volume for the cartons.)

Name ______________________________

Guided Practice: First ex. in Rows 1 & 3, pp. 300–301
Independent Practice: Complete pp. 300–301

Volume of Composite Space Figures

Many space figures are combinations of different types of prisms. For example, the figure at the right is made up of centimeter cubes. To find its volume, you can count the number of cubes. Make sure you count any cubes that are hidden from view.

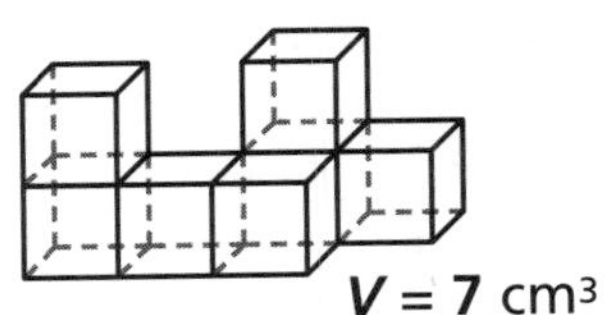

To find the volume of **composite space** figures that are made up of different space figures, you may need to use more than one formula.

Find the volume of the figure at right.

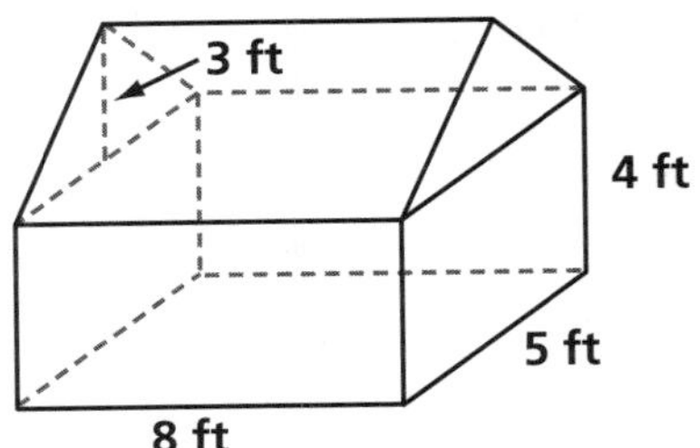

This figure is made up of a triangular prism and a rectangular prism.

1. Divide the figure into space figures you know. Then, find any missing lengths.

Rectangular prism: $l = 8$ ft $w = 5$ ft $h = 4$ ft

Triangular prism: You need the dimensions of the triangular bases.

- The *base* of the triangle is equal to the width of the rectangular prism, or **5** ft.
- The height of the triangle is **3** ft.
- The height of the triangular prism is equal to the length of the rectangular prism, or **8** ft.

2. Find the volume of each figure.

Volume of rectangular prism: $V = lwh$

or $V = 8 \text{ ft} \cdot 5 \text{ ft} \cdot 4 \text{ ft}$ or 160 ft^3

Volume of triangular prism: $V = Bh$

or $V = (\frac{1}{2} \cdot 5 \text{ ft} \cdot 3 \text{ ft}) \cdot 8 \text{ ft}$ or 60 ft^3

3. Find the sum of the volumes.

$V = 160 \text{ ft}^3 + 60 \text{ ft}^3$

$= 220 \text{ ft}^3$

The total volume of the composite figure is **220** ft³.

Count cubes to find the volume. Write the answer in cm³. Remember to count cubes that are hidden from view.

1.

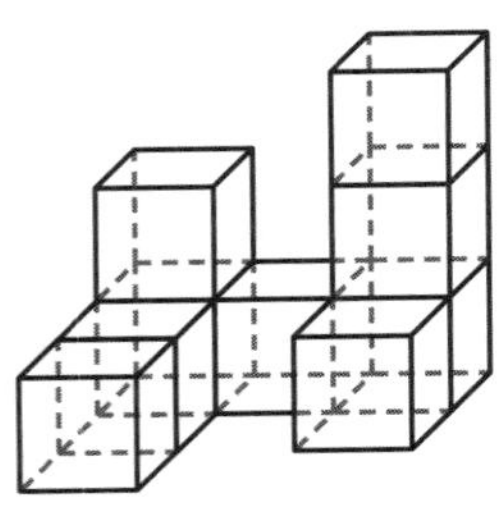

9 cm³

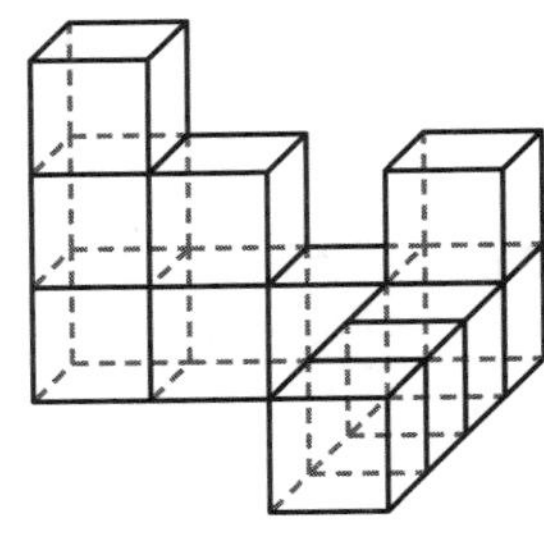

11 cm³

Check Understanding *How do you find the volume of a composite space figure?* (Break the figure down into figures such as prisms.)

Find the volume of the composite figure.

2.

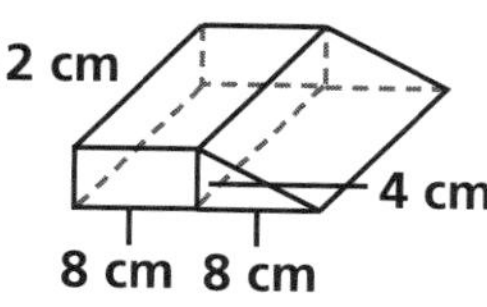

576 cm³

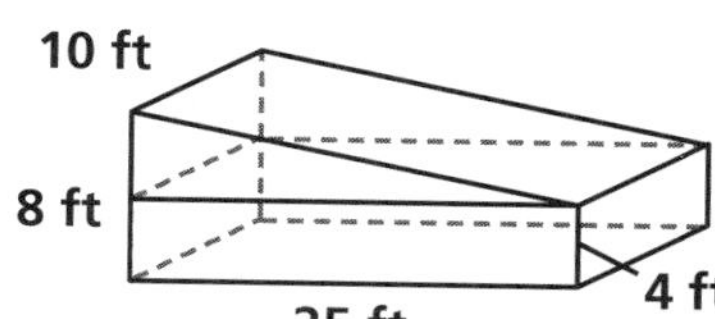

1,500 ft³

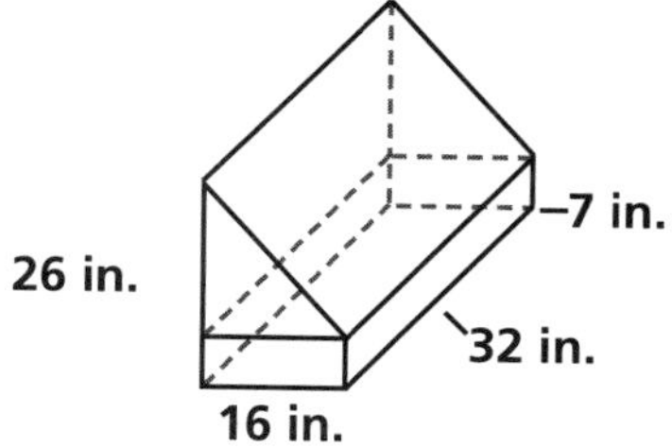

8,448 in.³

3.

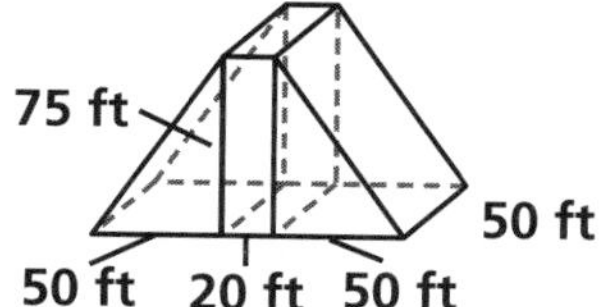

262,500 ft³

8 m
3 m
10 m
10 m

700 m³

3 cm 3 cm
3 cm
3 cm
9 cm

243 cm³

Problem Solving Reasoning Complete. You may need to use cubes to model the figure.

4. This figure is made up of centimeter cubes. You are painting the outside faces of the figure, including the bottom.

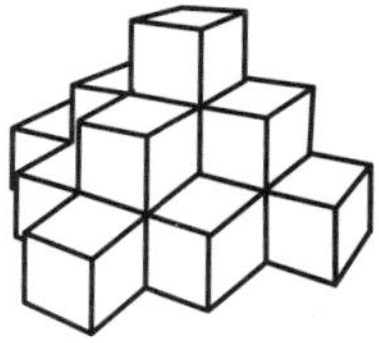

a. How many centimeter cubes make up the figure? 14

b. How many painted faces are there? 48

Test Prep ★ Mixed Review

5 **The height of a cylindrical can of paint is 7.5 in. and the diameter of its base is 6 in. Which number best represents the surface area of the can? (Use $\pi \approx 3.14$.)** C; Obj. 10C

A 45 in.²

B 170 in.²

C 198 in.²

D 508 in.²

6 **The volume of a cube-shaped box is 729 in.³. What is the area of one of its faces?** G; Obj. 10C

F 9 in.²

G 81 in.²

H 121.5 in.²

J 243 in.²

Closing the Lesson *Why would you ever need to know how to find the volume of composite space figures?* (Possible answer: Most houses and buildings are not simple prisms but are made up of two or more prisms.)

Name ______________________________

Guided Practice: Ex. 1, p. 302; Ex. 7, p. 303
Independent Practice: Complete pp. 302–303

Relating Length, Area, and Volume

Throughout this unit, you have measured geometric figures in one, two, and three dimensions. You have found perimeters, areas, and volumes. In this lesson, you will investigate relationships among length, area, and volume. You have already studied some of these relationships.

How does the area of a face, surface area, and volume of Figure *A* change when the length of a side is increased **2** times, **3** times, **4** times, and **5** times?

Figure *A*

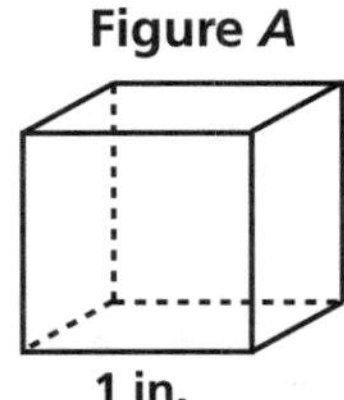

1. Record what you know about the figure.

- The area of a face is **1 × 1,** or **1** in.^{2}
- The surface area is **6 × 1,** or **6** in.^{2}
- The volume is **1 × 1 × 1,** or **1** in.^{3}

2. To look for relationships, find the area, surface area, and volume. Record the results in a table. Then, look for patterns.

Figure	Side (s)	Area of a Face	Surface Area	Volume
A	1 in.	1 in.^{2}	6 in.^{2}	1 in.^{3}
B	2 in.	4 in.^{2}	24 in.^{2}	8 in.^{3}
C	3 in.	9 in.^{2}	54 in.^{2}	27 in.^{3}
D	4 in.	16 in.^{2}	96 in.^{2}	64 in.^{3}
E	5 in.	25 in.^{2}	150 in.^{2}	125 in.^{3}

When the side is increased **2** times:

- the area of a face increases **4** times.
- the surface area increases **4** times.
- the volume increases **8** times.

Complete.

1. When the side of Figure *A* is increased **3** times, how does the area of a face, surface area, and volume change?

Area increases 9 times, surface area increases 9 times, and volume increases 27 times.

2. When the side of Figure *A* is increased **4** times, how does the area of a face, surface area, and volume change?

Area increases 16 times, surface area increases 16 times, and volume increases 64 times.

The change in the length of a side from an original figure to a new figure is called the *scale factor*. In this lesson the scale factor (*k*) is the ratio of the length of a new side to that of the previous figure. Find the scale factors.

> The scale factor for a side of Figure *C* to Figure *B* is $\frac{3}{2}$.

	Original Figure	New Figure	Scale Factor (*k*)
3.	**3** cm	**6** cm	$\frac{6}{3}$ or 2
5.	$2\frac{1}{2}$ in.	$7\frac{1}{2}$ ft	3

	Original Figure	New Figure	Scale Factor (*k*)
4.	**5** in.	**15** in.	$\frac{15}{5}$ or 3
6.	**23** mm	**92** mm	4

Check Understanding *If the volume of a cube is 27 cm^3, what is the volume of a new cube that is formed by multiplying each edge by a scale factor of 4?* (27 × 64 = 1,728 cm^3)

Use the scale factor (k) of the sides to find the surface area and volume of the new figure. The first one has been done for you.

7. $k = 6$

Original Surface Area: **1** in.^{2} (k^2)

New Surface Area: $\mathbf{6^2 \cdot 1}$ in.^{2} = **36** in.^{2}

Original Volume: **1** in.^{3} (k^3)

New Volume: $\mathbf{6^3 \cdot 1}$ in.^{3} = **216** in.^{3}

8. $k = 2$

Original Surface Area: **54** cm^2

New Surface Area: 216 cm^2

Original Volume: **27** cm^3

New Volume: 216 cm^3

9. $k = \frac{1}{4}$

Original Surface Area: **96** ft^2

New Surface Area: 6 ft^2

Original Volume: **64** ft^3

New Volume: 1 ft^3

10. $k = 3$

Original Surface Area: **30.25** cm^2

New Surface Area: 272.25 cm^2

Original Volume: **166.375** cm^3

New Volume: 4492.125 cm^3

11. $k = \frac{2}{3}$

Original Surface Area: **54** cm^2

New Surface Area: 24 cm^2

Original Volume: **27** cm^3

New Volume: 8 cm^3

Problem Solving Reasoning

Figures *A* and *B* are two different space figures. Complete the tables for the figures.

	k (A:B)	Length A	Surface Area A	Volume A	Length B	Surface Area B	Volume B
12.	$\frac{1}{16}$	4 in.	96 in.^{2}	64 in.^{3}	64 in.	24,576 in.^{2}	262,144 in.^{3}
13.	7.5	22.5 cm	11,137.5 cm^2	68,343.75 cm^3	3 cm	198 cm^2	162 cm^3

Quick Check

Find the volume.

14.

Each block is 1 cm^3.

14 cm^3

15.

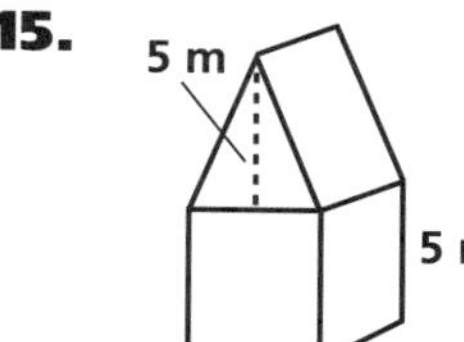

120 m^3

Complete the table for scale factor $k = 2$.

16.

	Side Length	Surface Area	Volume
New Figure	8 in.	1,536 in.^{2}	512 in.^{3}
Original Figure	4 in.	384 in.^{2}	64 in.^{3}

Work Space

Item	Error Analysis
14–15	**Common Error** Watch for students who do not count hidden cubes. **Reteaching** Reteach 90
16	**Common Error** Watch for students who do not understand what a scale factor is. **Reteaching** Reteach 91

Closing the Lesson *If the scale factor of the enlargement of a cube is 3, how does the surface area for the new cube compare to that of the old cube?* (It is 9 times the surface area of the original cube.) *How do the volumes compare?* (The new cube has a volume equal to 27 times that of the original cube.)

Name ______________________________

Volume of Cylinders

Guided Practice: First ex. in Rows 2 & 5, p. 305
Independent Practice: Complete p. 305

Remember that a cylinder is a space figure with two circular bases. You find the volume of a cylinder by multiplying the number of square units of area in the circular base by the number of units of height.

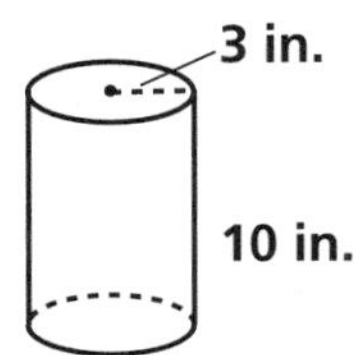

Area of base: $B = \pi \cdot 3^2 \text{ in.}^2$

$\approx 3.14 \cdot 9 \text{ in.}^2$

$\approx 28.26 \text{ in.}^2$

Volume of cylinder: $V = 28.26 \text{ in.}^2 \cdot 10 \text{ in.}$

$= 282.60 \text{ in.}^3$

$$V = Bh$$
$$= \pi r^2 h$$

You can use what you know about volume and scale factors to investigate how the volumes of different cylinders are related.

- **Volume and Height**

Cylinders ***A*** and ***B*** have the same radius. The height of Cylinder ***A*** is twice the height of Cylinder ***B***. What is the ratio of the volume of Cylinder ***A*** to Cylinder ***B***?

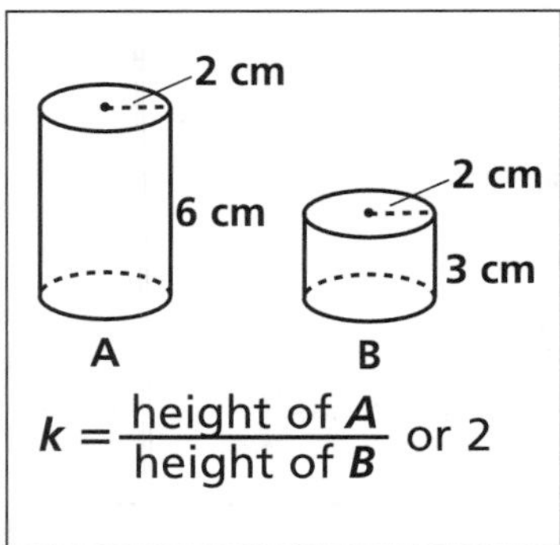

$k = \dfrac{\text{height of } A}{\text{height of } B}$ or 2

Volume of ***A***: $V_A = \pi r^2 h$

$= \pi \cdot 2^2 \cdot 6$

$\approx 75.36 \text{ cm}^3$

Volume of ***B***: $V_B = \pi r^2 h$

$= \pi \cdot 2^2 \cdot 3$

$\approx 37.68 \text{ cm}^3$

Ratio of Volumes

$\dfrac{V_A}{V_B} = \dfrac{\pi \cdot 2^2 \cdot 6}{\pi \cdot 2^2 \cdot 3}$

$\approx \dfrac{75.36 \text{ cm}^3}{37.68 \text{ cm}^3}$ or $\dfrac{2}{1}$

The ratio of volumes equals ***k***. The ratio of volumes remains the same as the ratio of heights: **2** to **1**.

- **Volume and Radius**

Cylinders ***C*** and ***D*** have the same height. The radius of Cylinder ***C*** is twice the radius of Cylinder ***D***. What is the ratio of the volume of Cylinder ***C*** to Cylinder ***D***?

4 in.
6 in.
2 in.
6 in.
C
D

$k = \dfrac{\text{radius of } C}{\text{radius of } D}$ or 2

$V_C = \pi r^2 h$

$= \pi \cdot 4^2 \cdot 6$

$\approx 301.44 \text{ in.}^3$

$V_D = \pi r^2 h$

$= \pi \cdot 2^2 \cdot 6$

$\approx 75.36 \text{ in.}^3$

Ratio of Volumes $\dfrac{\pi \cdot 4^2 \cdot 6}{\pi \cdot 2^2 \cdot 6} = \dfrac{301.44 \text{ in.}^3}{75.36 \text{ in.}^3}$ or **4** (k^2)

The ratio of radii is **2** to **1**, but the ratio of volumes is **4** to **1**.

Check Understanding *If one cylinder has a radius of 2 inches and a height of 5 inches and another has a radius of 4 inches and a height of 5 inches, how would their volumes compare?* (The first cylinder would be four times smaller than the second.)

Name ______________________________

Find the volume of the cylinder. Remember that $d = 2r$.

1.

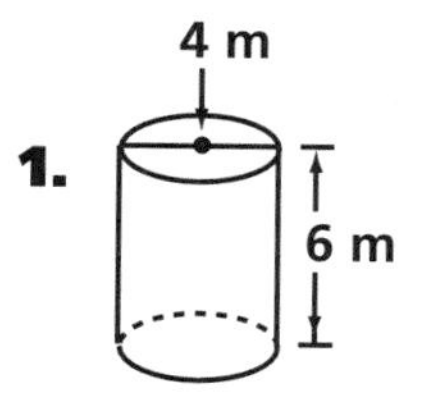

75.36 m³

8 in.
9.2 in.

462.208 in.³

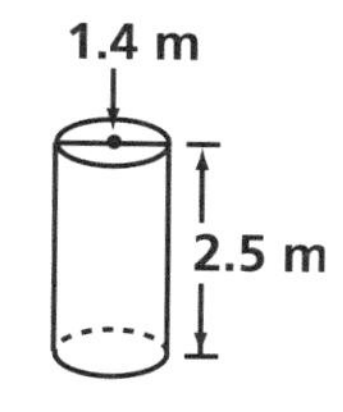

3.8465 m³

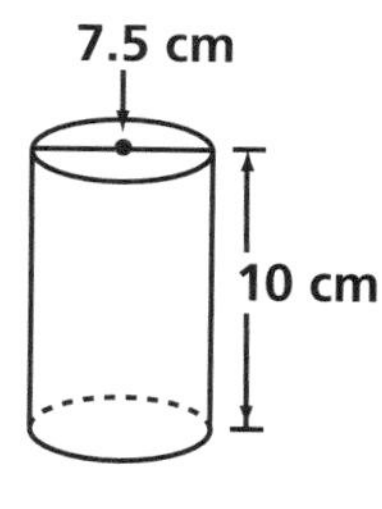

441.5625 cm³

Find the missing values.

	radius	height	volume		radius	height	volume
2. Cylinder *P*	2.5 cm	10 cm	196.25 cm³	Cylinder *Q*	5 cm	10 cm	785 cm³
3. Cylinder *R*	2.5 cm	5 cm	98.125 cm³	Cylinder *S*	5 cm	5 cm	392.5 cm³
4. Cylinder *T*	2.5 cm	20 cm	392.5 cm³	Cylinder *U*	10 cm	10 cm	3,140 cm³

Use the values from exercises 2–4 to compare the cylinders.

	ratio of radii	ratio of heights	ratio of volumes		ratio of radii	ratio of heights	ratio of volumes
5. *Q* and *P*	2	1	4	*P* and *R*	1	2	2
6. *U* and *S*	2	2	8	*T* and *R*	1	4	4

Problem Solving Reasoning Solve.

7. Remember that 1 cubic decimeter is 1 liter. About how many liters will a cylinder hold if it has a radius of 2 meters and a height of 0.5 meters?

6,280 L

8. A cylinder has a height of 8 ft and a volume of 226.08 ft³. What is its radius?

3 ft

Test Prep ★ Mixed Review

9 A cylindrical can of paint has a diameter of 6 in. and a height of 8 in. To the nearest cubic inch, how many cubic inches of paint does it hold? (Use $\pi \approx 3.14$.) D; Obj. 10C

A 72 **C** 204

B 75 **D** 226

10 If a cylindrical container can hold 452 in.³ of water, how much water could it hold if the height remained the same but the radius were doubled? G; Obj. 10E

F 2,712 in.³ **H** 904 in.³

G 1,808 in.³ **J** 452 in.³

Closing the Lesson *If the radius and height are multiplied by the same scale factor to form two different cylinders, why does the cylinder whose radius changed have more of an effect on the volume than the cylinder whose height changed?* (Changing the height only changes one dimension, but changing the radius changes the area of the base, which is a two-dimensional change.)

Name ______________________________

Problem Solving Application: Use a Diagram

Guided Practice: Problem 1, p. 306; Problem 5, p. 307
Independent Practice: Complete pp. 306–307

Problem

What is the area of the outer circle in the diagram?

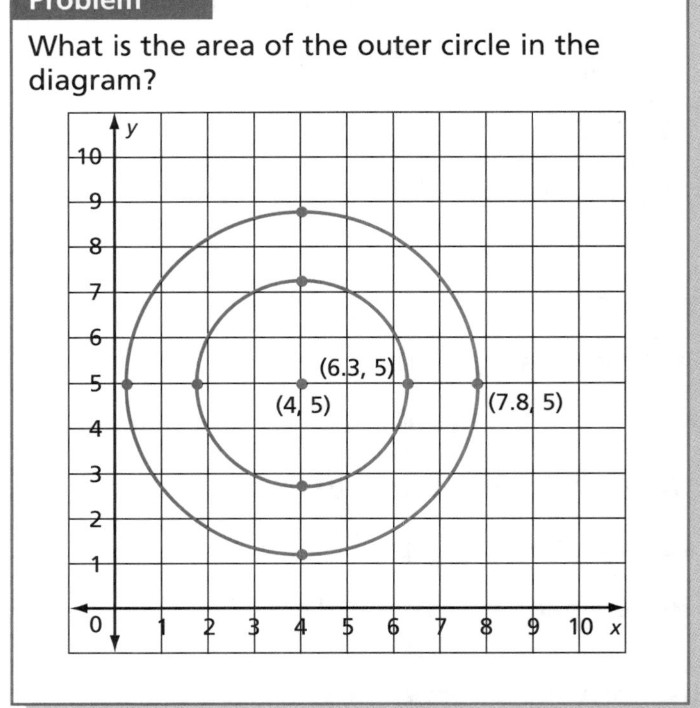

Sometimes you can use a coordinate grid to find an area.

Remember: To find the point **(4, 5)** on the coordinate plane, start at **(0, 0)**. Go right **4** and up **5.**

Tips to Remember:

1. Understand 2. Decide 3. Solve 4. Look back

- Ask yourself: What do I know? What do I need to find?
- How can I find the length of a horizontal line segment? Of a vertical line segment?
- Think about whether the area makes sense. Is it reasonable?

Use the coordinate grid shown above.

1. What is the area of the inner circle?

Think: How long is its radius? How can I use this length to find the area?

2.3 units; Square it and multiply by π.

Answer about 16.6106 sq. units

2. What is the area of the region between the two circles?

Think: I know the area of both circles. How can I use these areas to find the area of the region between them?

Subtract the smaller area.

Answer about 28.731 sq. units

Check Understanding *Why does drawing a diagram help you solve a problem?*
(It helps you see relationships and may help you generalize.)

Name ______________________________

Use the diagrams or any other strategy you have learned.

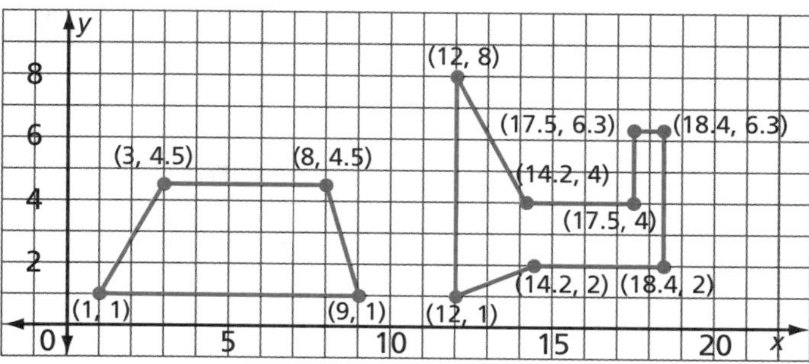

3. What is the height of the trapezoid? What is the area of the trapezoid?

h = 3.5 units; A = 22.75 sq. units

4. What is the approximate area of the figure to the right of the trapezoid?

$A \approx 20$ sq. units

5. You want to frame a picture that is **10** in. by **14** in. The width of the wooden molding you want to use is **3** in. How many inches of molding do you need? Hint: Use diagonal cuts at the corners.

72 in. of molding

6. For a math fair, tables with displays are placed around three sides of a gymnasium that is **40** feet wide and **60** feet long. Each **2**-foot by **4**-foot table is placed lengthwise **2** feet from a wall and **2** feet from each other. What is the greatest number of tables that can be set up in the gym?

25 tables

7. A **20** ft × **40** ft in-ground swimming pool is **8** ft deep. If the concrete on the bottom and sides of the pool is **12** in. thick, how many cubic feet of concrete were used to make the pool?

1,349 ft^3

8. In Mr. Keyes's math class, **14** students have one or more sisters, **15** have one or more brothers, **6** have one or more brothers and sisters, and **5** have no brothers or sisters. How many students are in the class?

28 students

Extend Your Thinking

9. The two endpoints of a radius are (**5.4, 6**) and (**5.4, 3.8**). What is the area of the circle? How did you find your answer?

15.2 sq. units; I subtracted 3.8 from 6 to find the radius; then, I used the formula.

10. How did using the coordinate grid help you to find the answer to problem **4** above?

It helped me see how long each segment was so that I could use the area formulas.

Closing the Lesson *In what kinds of problems would you use the strategy of using a diagram?* (Possible answer: ones in which the diagram might help me see relationships.)

Name ______________________________

Guided Practice: First ex. in Row 1, p. 308; Row 11, p 310
Independent Practice: Complete pp. 308–310

Pythagorean Property of Right Triangles

Over 2,500 years ago, the Greek mathematician Pythagoras made an important discovery:

In a right triangle, the square of the hypotenuse equals the sum of the squares of the legs. The **Pythagorean Property** can also be written as a formula.

$$a^2 + b^2 = c^2$$

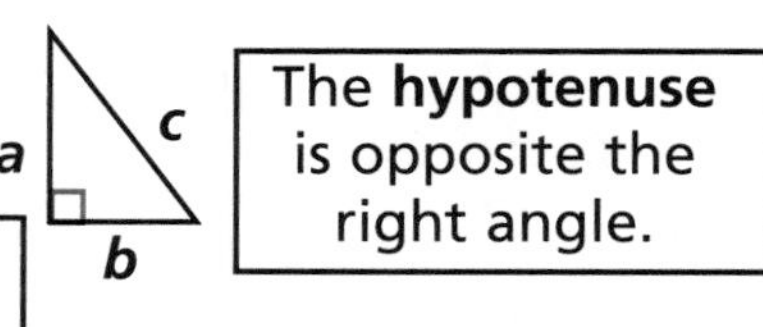

Look at the model.

- The square on side *a* has an area of 16 square units.
- The square on side *b* has an area of 9 square units.
- The square on side *c* has an area of 25 square units.

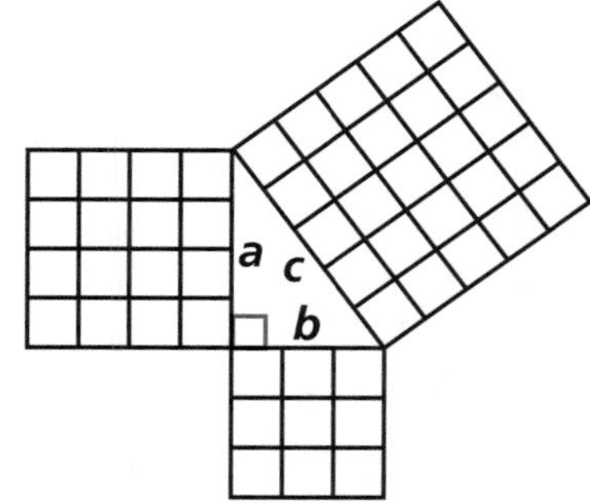

If you know the lengths of the sides of a triangle, you can use the Pythagorean Property to decide whether it is a right triangle.

$a^2 + b^2 = c^2$

$(5 \text{ cm})^2 + (12 \text{ cm})^2 \stackrel{?}{=} (13 \text{ cm})^2$

$25 \text{ cm}^2 + 144 \text{ cm}^2 \stackrel{?}{=} 169 \text{ cm}^2$ True.

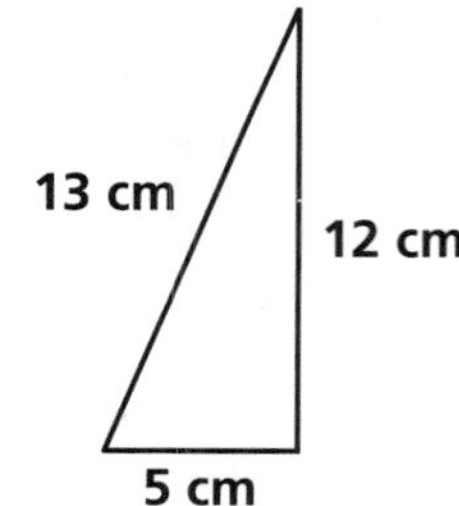

A set of three whole numbers *a, b, c* that satisfies the Pythagorean Property, such as **5, 12, 13,** is called a **Pythagorean triple.**

Use the Pythagorean Property to decide whether the triangle is a right triangle.

1.

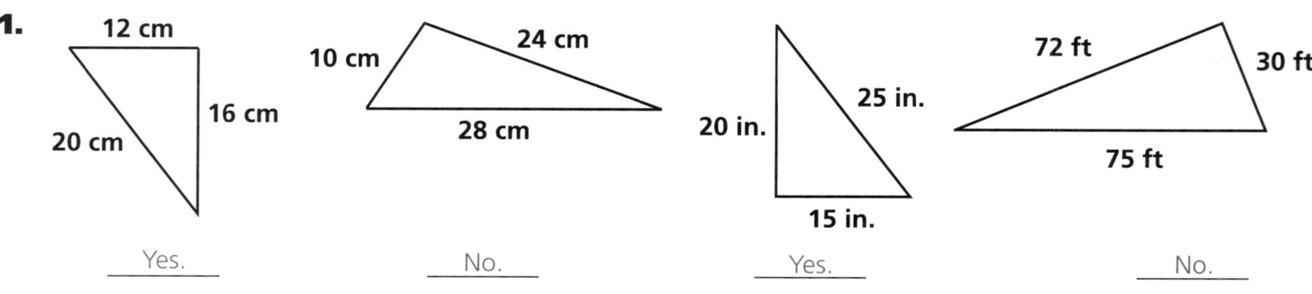

Yes. No. Yes. No.

Check Understanding *If a triangle has sides of measure 9 cm, 12 cm and 15 cm, is it a right triangle? How do you know?* (Yes. Square the two small sides and add them together and see if you get the square of the largest side. In this case you do, so it is a right triangle.)

Name ______________________________

If you know the length of two sides of a right triangle, you can use the Pythagorean Property to find the length of the third side.

1. Write the formula and substitute.

$a^2 + b^2 = c^2$

$a^2 + 16^2 = 20^2$

Remember: c is the hypotenuse.

2. Simplify.

$a^2 + 16^2 = 20^2$

$a^2 + 256 = 400$

$a^2 = 144$

3. Find the square root.

$\sqrt{144} = 12 \rightarrow a = 12$

So, the third side is 12 cm.

Sometimes the square root you need is an irrational number. It cannot be written as an exact decimal.

2 cm, 3 cm, c

$2^2 + 3^2 = c^2$

$4 + 9 = c^2$

$13 = c^2 \rightarrow c = \sqrt{13}$

To estimate this value, you can use a calculator:

Press [1] [3] [√]

$\sqrt{13} \approx 3.6055513$

Or, you can use a table.

$\sqrt{13} \approx 3.6$

N	$\sqrt{N}$	N	$\sqrt{N}$
2	1.141	225	15
13	3.606	289	17
121	11	676	26
162	12.728	1,156	34
169	13	3,025	55

Find the missing lengths to the nearest tenth.

	Side a	Side b	Side c
2.	4 in.	≈ 4.5 in.	6 in.
3.	3 cm	3 cm	≈ 4.2 cm
4.	1 m	3 m	≈ 3.2 m

	Side a	Side b	Side c
5.	4 ft	2 ft	≈ 4.5 ft
6.	8 m	6 m	10 m
7.	8 in.	15 in.	17 in.

△*XYZ* is an isosceles triangle. If we draw a line segment from point *Z* to the opposite base at point *P*, we form two right triangles.

8. Name the two right triangles. _XZP_ and _YZP_

9. What is the measure of the hypotenuse of each triangle?

_15 ft_

10. What is the measure of each side? _12 ft_ and _9 ft_

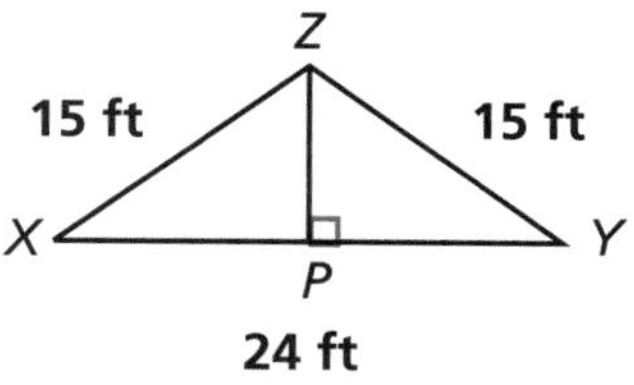

Find the measure of the diagonal.

11.

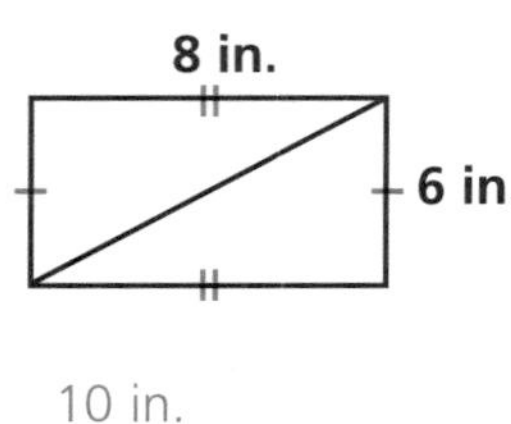

10 in.

24 cm
10 cm

26 cm

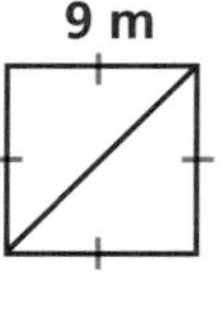

≈ 12.7 m

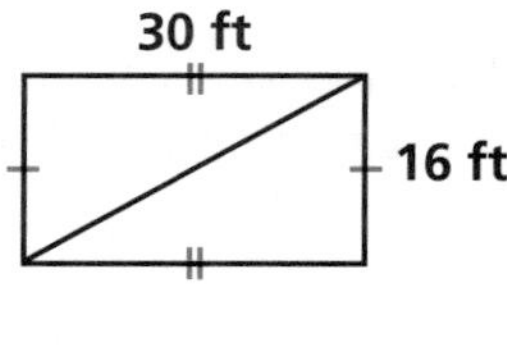

34 ft

Problem Solving Reasoning

Draw a right triangle and label the sides as indicated in the problem. Use the Pythagorean Property to compute the missing measurement.

12. A wire cable is attached to the top of a pole that is **4** meters high. How long must the cable be if it is fastened to the ground **3** meters from the base of the pole?

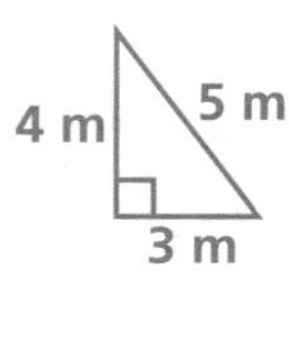

5 m

13. A ladder reaches to the top of a sign **8** feet from the ground. How long is the ladder if the bottom of it is placed **6** feet from the base of the sign?

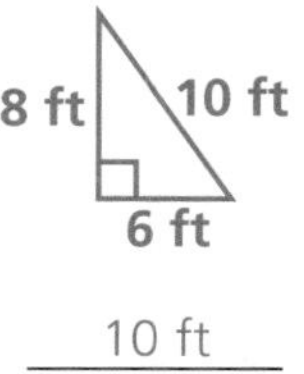

10 ft

14. Ken swims diagonally across a swimming pool that is **25** feet wide and **60** feet long. Dick swims the length of the pool. Who swims the longer distance and by how much? (A diagonal cuts a rectangle into two congruent right triangles.)

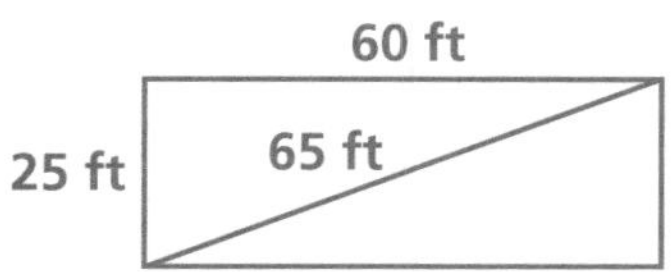

Ken swims about 5 feet farther.

Quick Check

Find the volume. Use $\pi = 3.14$.

15.

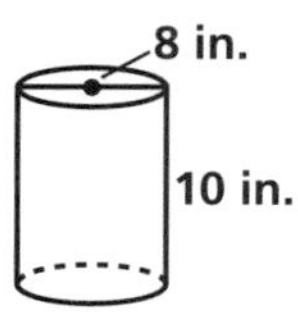

502.4 in.^{3}

16.

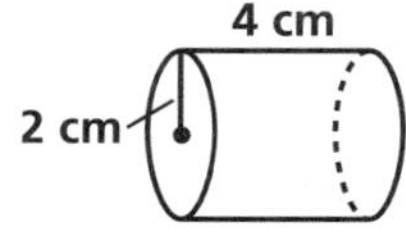

50.24 cm^3

Find the missing measure.

17.

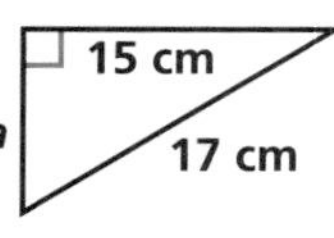

8 cm

18.

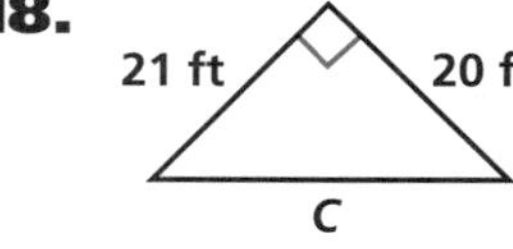

29 ft

Work Space.

Item	Error Analysis
15–16	**Common Error** Watch for students who forget to find a radius when given a diameter. **Reteaching** Reteach 92
17–18	**Common Error** Watch for students who do not find the square root. **Reteaching** Reteach 93

Closing the Lesson *Who can state the two parts to the Pythagorean Property?* (In a right triangle, the square of the hypotenuse equals the sum of the squares of the two legs. If a triangle is such that the sum of the squares of two sides is equal to the square of the third side, then it is a right triangle.)

Name ______________________

Write the formula for the area of the figure. Then, find the area. Use 3.14 for π.

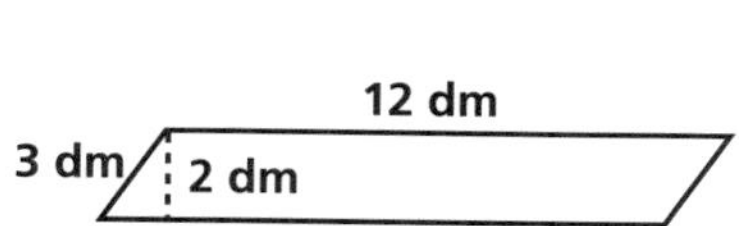

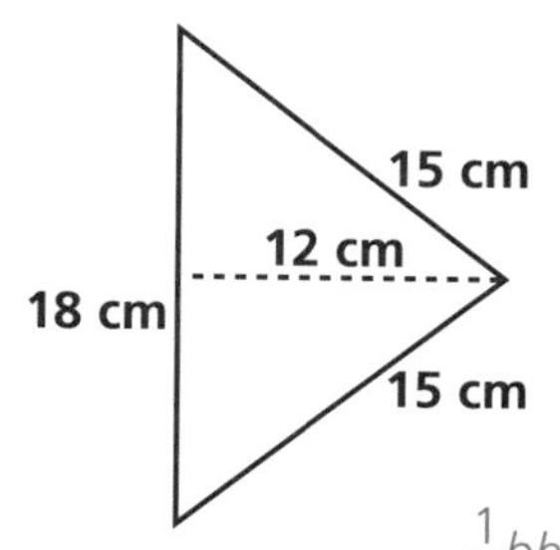

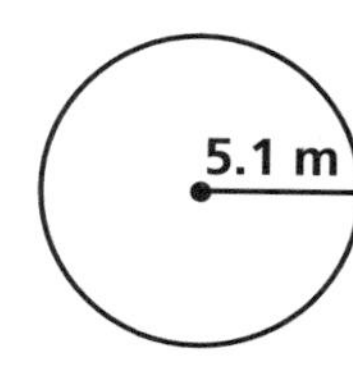

1. Formula: $A =$ bh

Area is 24 dm².

2. Formula: $A =$ $\frac{1}{2}bh$

Area is 108 cm².

3. Formula: $A =$ πr^2

Area is about 81.67 m².

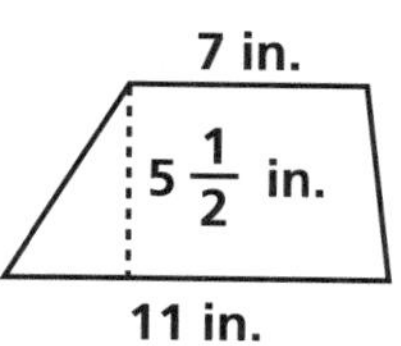

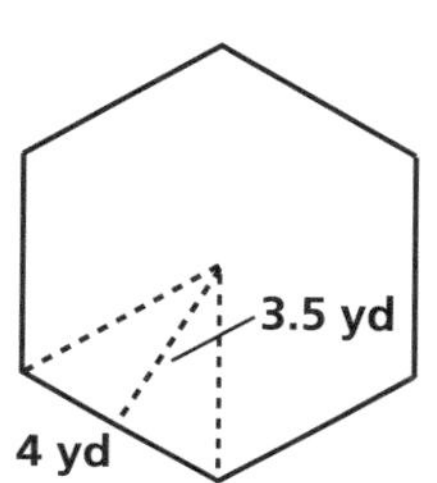

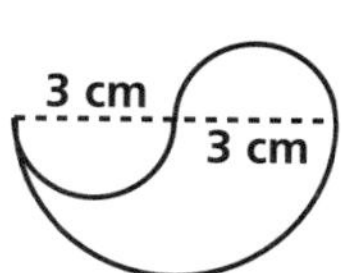

4. Formula: $A =$ $\frac{1}{2}h(b_1 + b_2)$

Area is $49\frac{1}{2}$ in.².

5. Formula: $A =$ $6\left(\frac{1}{2}bh\right)$

Area is 42 yd².

6. Area is about 14.13 cm².

Use the nets below for exercises 7–10.

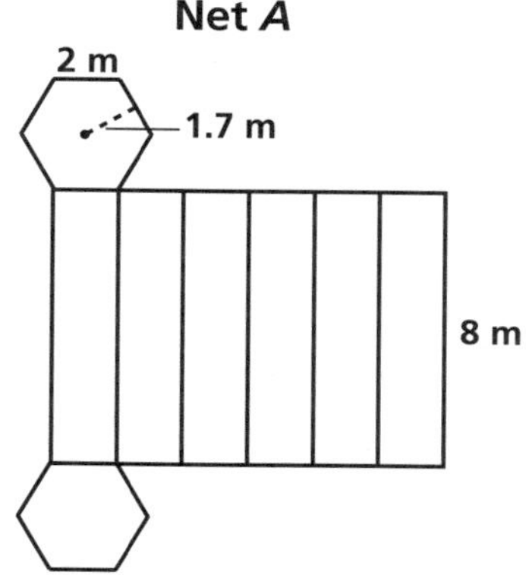

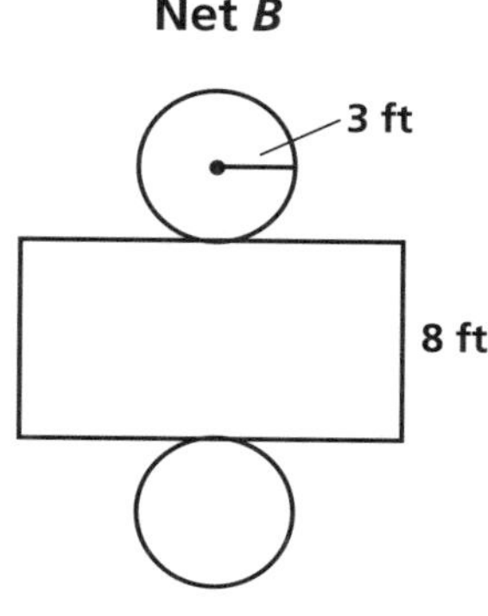

7. Net *A* will form a hexagonal prism.

8. Net *B* will form a cylinder.

9. The surface area of the figure Net *A* forms is 116.4 m².

10. The surface area of the figure Net *B* forms is about 207.24 ft².

Write the formula for the volume of the space figure. Then, compute the volume.

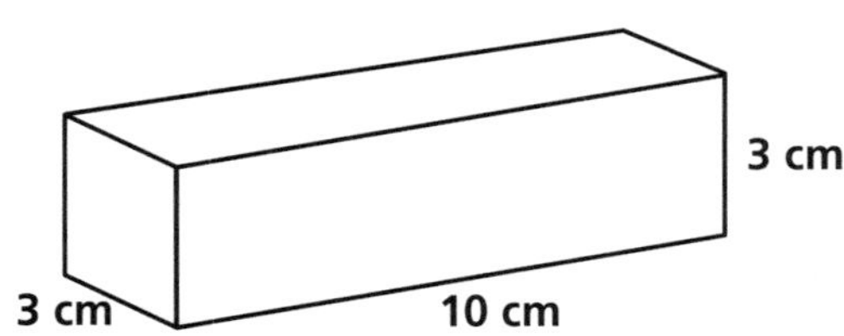

11. Formula: $V =$ <u>lwh</u>

The volume is <u>90 cm³</u>.

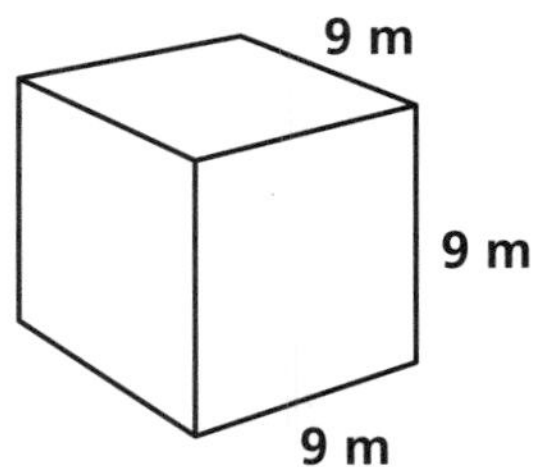

12. Formula: $V =$ <u>s^3</u>

The volume is <u>729 m³</u>.

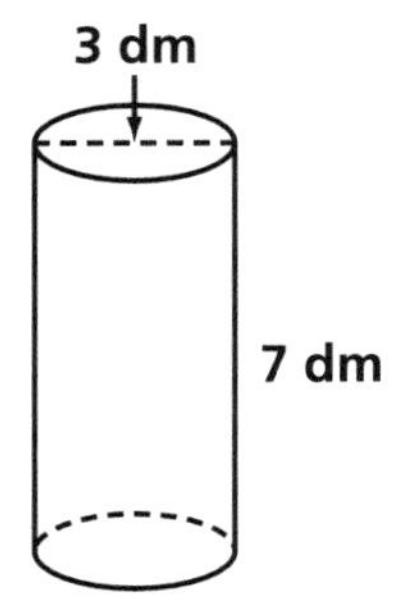

13. Formula: $V =$ <u>$\pi r^2 h$</u>

The volume is about <u>49.46 dm³</u>.

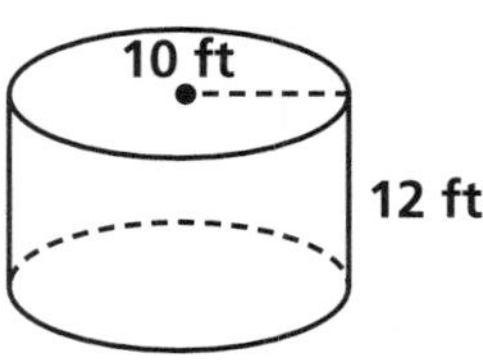

14. Formula: $V =$ <u>$\pi r^2 h$</u>

The volume is about <u>3,768 ft³</u>.

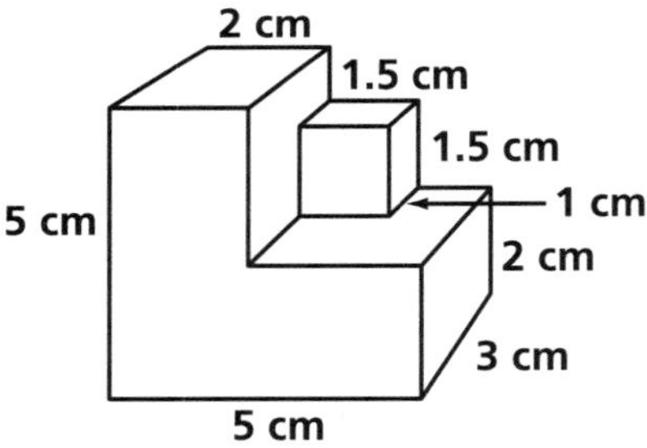

15. The volume is <u>50.25 cm³</u>.

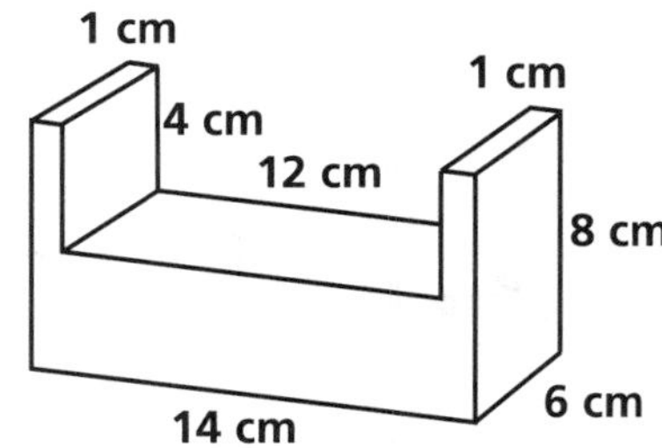

16. The volume is <u>384 cm³</u>.

Answer the question.

17. A rectangle is enlarged so that its sides are $1\frac{1}{3}$ times their original length. How many times as great is the area of the new rectangle? <u>$\frac{16}{9}$ or $1\frac{7}{9}$ times greater</u>

18. A prism is enlarged so that its edges are **3** times as long as before. How many times greater is the new surface area? <u>9 times greater</u>

19. How many times as great is the volume of the new prism in exercise **18**?

<u>27 times greater</u>

Name ______________________

Find the missing length of the triangle. Use the table on page 309.

20. $c =$ 15 in.

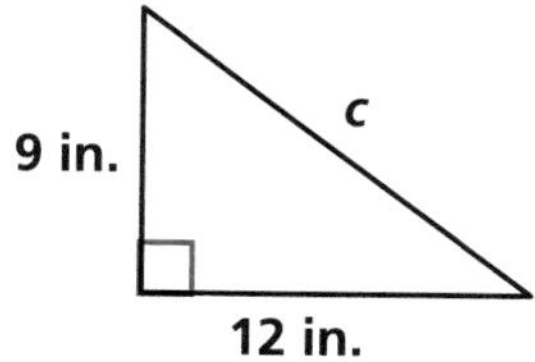

21. $c \approx$ 3.16 m

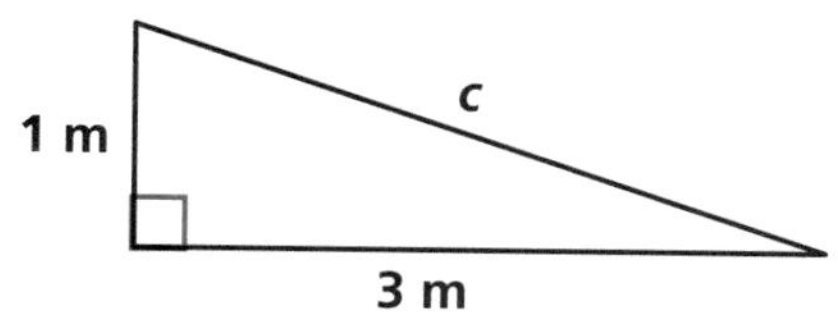

22. $a \approx$ 4.47 cm

23. $h =$ 3 ft $x \approx$ 3.61 ft

Solve. Use the figure on the coordinate grid below.

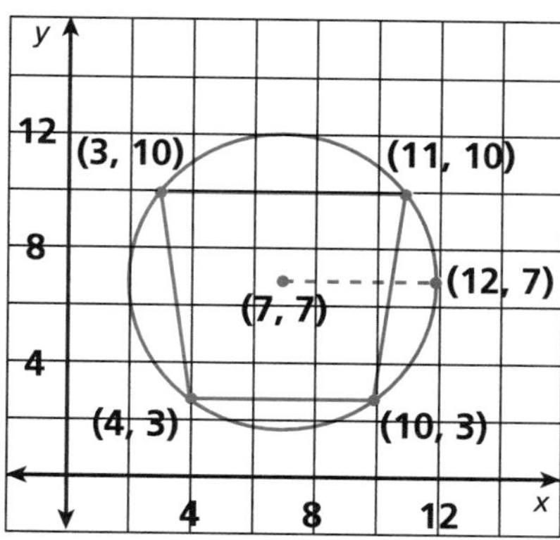

24. What are the lengths of the bases of the trapezoid? How did you find these lengths?

6 units and 8 units; subtracted the *x*-coordinates of the endpoints

25. What is the area of the region between the circle and the trapezoid?

about 29.5 square units

Name ______________________

Cumulative Review
★ Test Prep

1 **What is the area of the regular octagon?** C; Obj. 10A

7.5 cm

6 cm

A 360 cm^2

C 180 cm^2

B 180 cm

D 90 cm^2

2 **Which space figure could be assembled from this net?** G; Obj. 10B

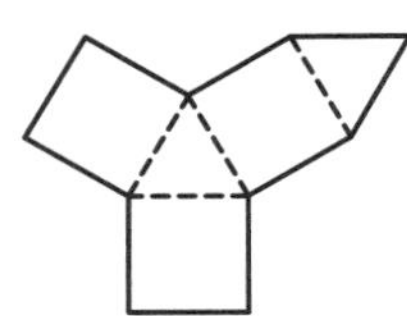

F square pyramid

G triangular prism

H tetrahedron

J pentagonal prism

3 **Which of the numbers is irrational?** C; Obj. 9A

A $\sqrt{36}$

B $\sqrt{4 \cdot 5^3}$

C $\sqrt{11}$

D $\sqrt{100}$

4 **What is the quotient when $^{-}535.5$ is divided by 8.5?** H; Obj. 8D

F 63

G 6.3

H $^{-}63$

J $^{-}6.3$

K Not here

5 **A school pennant is in the shape of a triangle. The base of the pennant is 12 inches, while the height is 30 inches. Which formula would you use to find the area of the pennant?** C; Obj. 1E

A $A = bh$

B $A = 2\,(b + h)$

C $A = \frac{1}{2}\,bh$

D $A = \frac{h}{2}\,(b_1 + b_2)$

6 **How many pieces of wood, each $1\frac{2}{3}$ feet long, can be cut from a board that is $16\frac{1}{2}$ feet long?** K; Obj. 2A

F 16

G 14

H 12

J 10

K Not here

7 **What is the simplified form of the polynomial: $^{-}2p(3p + 2q + r)$?** B; Obj. 9A

A $^{-}6p^2 + 4pq + 2pr$

B $^{-}6p^2 + {}^{-}4pq + {}^{-}2pr$

C $^{-}6p^2 + 2pq + pr$

D $^{-}6p + {}^{-}4q + {}^{-}2r$

8 **Jill is cutting strips of colored material, all of equal width, for a quilt pattern. To fit the pattern, the minimum width of each strip in inches (w) is given by the formula $5w - 2 > 7$. What values can w have?** G; Obj. 9F

F $w > 1$

G $w > 1\frac{4}{5}$

H $w > 25$

J $w > 45$

UNIT 11 • TABLE OF CONTENTS

The Coordinate Plane: Graphs and Transformations

Lesson	Page

We will be using this vocabulary:

congruent figures figures that have the same size and shape

symmetry a property of figures such that each point has a matching point on the opposite line

similar figures figures that have the same shape but not necessarily the same size

geometric transformation a procedure for moving figures in a plane

reflection a transformation that changes the position of a figure by flipping it about a line

translation a transformation that changes the position of a figure by sliding it in the same plane

solution of an equation in two variables an ordered pair of values that satisfy an equation

slope the ratio of the difference in y-coordinates (the rise) to the difference in x-coordinates (the run)

Dear Family,

During the next few weeks, our math class will be learning about and practicing how to graph geometric figures and equations in two variables in the coordinate plane. This includes solving algebraic equations to find ordered pairs as well as finding matching points for ordered pairs in symmetric, congruent, and similar polygons.

You can expect to see homework that provides practice with these skills. Here is a sample you may want to keep handy to give help if needed.

Graphing Ordered Pairs in the Coordinate Plane

x	$y = 2x - 1$
0	$^{-}1$
1	1
2	3
$^{-}1$	$^{-}3$
$^{-}2$	$^{-}5$

The table of values at the right shows some x- and y-values for the equation $y = 2x - 1$. The table values can be also written as ordered pairs and graphed in the coordinate plane.

(0, ⁻1), (1, 1), (2, 3), (⁻1, ⁻3), (⁻2, ⁻5)

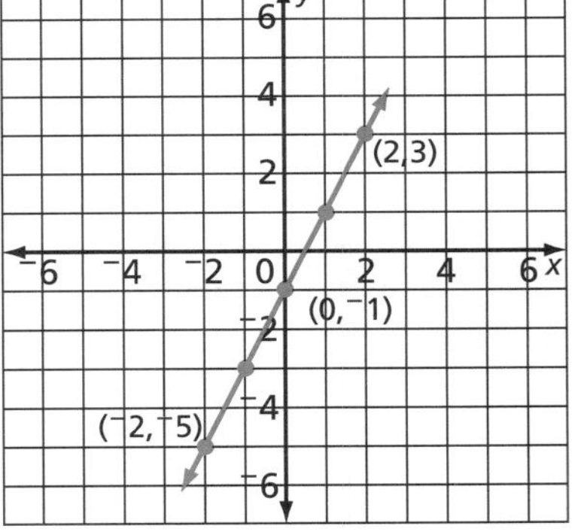

When the points are plotted on the grid, and then connected, the result is a straight line.

You can find the slope of the line by finding a ratio of the changes in y-values to the changes in x-values for any two points on the line:

$$\text{slope} = \frac{\text{change in } y\text{-values}}{\text{change in } x\text{-values}} \rightarrow \frac{3 - {}^{-}1}{2 - 0} \rightarrow \frac{4}{2} \rightarrow 2$$

Sincerely,

Name ______________________________

Graphing Polynomials

Guided Practice: First ex. in Rows 1, 3 & 4, pp. 317–319
Independent Practice: Complete pp. 317–319

You have used tables to evaluate polynomials such as $2x + 3$ and $x^2 - 5x + 1$ for certain values of x. In the tables below, the x and y columns are related to each other by rules.

Rule: $x + 1 = y$

x	y
2	3
1	2
0	1
⁻1	0
⁻2	⁻1
⁻3	⁻2

Think: $2 + 1 = 3$

Rule: $x^2 - 2 = y$

x	y
2	2
1	⁻1
0	⁻2
⁻1	⁻1
⁻2	2
⁻3	7

Think: $2^2 - 2 = 4 - 2 = 2$

For each table, you can write ordered pairs of numbers. You can then graph the set of ordered pairs for a table in the coordinate plane.

The solutions for the first table are shown on the graph at the right.

(2, 3), (1, 2), (0, 1), (⁻1, 0), (⁻2, ⁻1), and **(⁻3, ⁻2)**

You make a coordinate plane using two number lines called **axes**. The ***x*-axis** and ***y*-axis** divide the coordinate plane into four parts called **quadrants**.

- Both coordinates of the point **(2, 3)** are positive, so the point is in the first quadrant.
- Both coordinates of the point **(⁻3, ⁻2)** are negative, so the point is in the third quadrant.

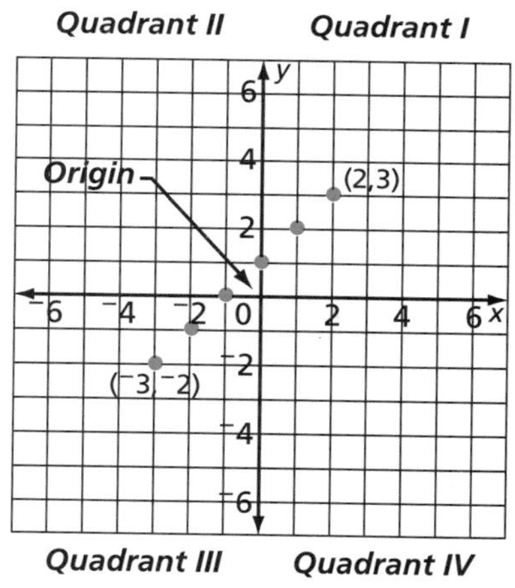

In the graph, the ordered pairs appear to be in a straight line when they are plotted. Take a straightedge, line it up with the points, and draw the line. This line is called the **graph of the polynomial**.

Complete the table of values for each rule.

1.

Rule: $-x = y$

x	y
3	⁻3
⁻2	2
⁻1	1

Rule: $x - 2 = y$

x	y
⁻2	⁻4
⁻1	⁻3
0	⁻2
1	⁻1
2	0

Rule: $2x = y$

x	y
⁻2	⁻4
⁻1	⁻2
0	0
1	2
2	4

Rule: $-2x = y$

x	y
⁻2	4
⁻1	2
0	0
1	⁻2
2	⁻4

Check Understanding *If $3x - 4 = y$, what y value would correspond to x = ⁻1? (⁻7) What y value would correspond to x = 5? (11)*

Some ordered pair solutions for the rule $x^2 - 2 = y$ are shown on the graph.

(3, 7), (2, 2), (1, ⁻1), (0, ⁻2), (⁻1, ⁻1), (⁻2, 2), and **(⁻3, 7)**

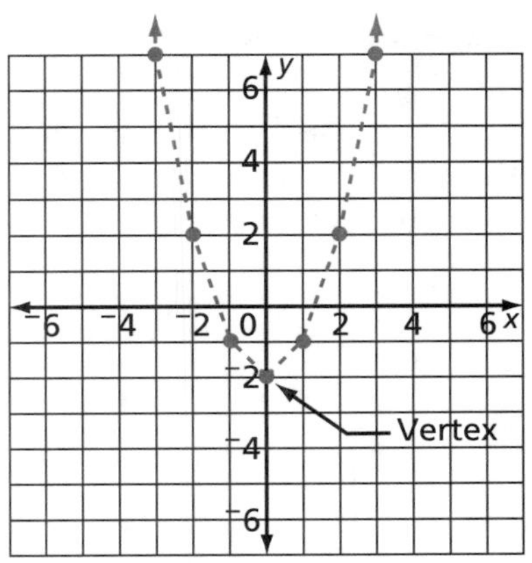

The ordered pairs from the second table form a curved figure when they are plotted.

Notice that when the ***x***-coordinates are opposites, they have the same ***y***-coordinates. When this happens, the points form a curved figure called a **parabola**.

Connect the points.

The turning point of the parabola, point **(0, ⁻2)**, is called the **vertex** of the parabola.

Find ordered pairs for *x* = ⁻2, ⁻1, 0, 1, and 2 for each rule.

2. Rule: $x + 2 = y$

x	y
⁻2	0
⁻1	1
0	2
1	3
2	4

Rule: $x^2 - 1 = y$

x	y
⁻2	3
⁻1	0
0	⁻1
1	0
2	3

Rule: $-x^2 = y$

x	y
⁻2	⁻4
⁻1	⁻1
0	0
1	⁻1
2	⁻4

Rule: $2x^2 + 1 = y$

x	y
⁻2	9
⁻1	3
0	1
1	3
2	9

Find solutions for *x* = ⁻2, ⁻1, 0, 1, and 2 for each rule. Then draw and label the graph of the pair of figures on the coordinate grid. What do you notice about the graphs?

3. Rule: $x = y$

x	y
⁻2	⁻2
⁻1	⁻1
0	0
1	1
2	2

Rule: $\frac{1}{2}x = y$

x	y
⁻2	⁻1
⁻1	$-\frac{1}{2}$
0	0
1	$\frac{1}{2}$
2	1

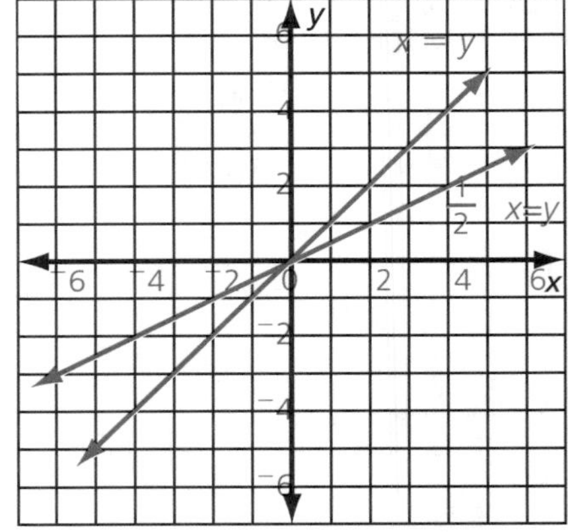

Describe the figures. Where do they intersect?

intersecting lines at (0, 0)

Name ______________________________

Find solutions for $x = {}^-2, {}^-1, 0, 1,$ and 2 for each rule. Then draw and label the graph of the pair of figures on a coordinate grid. What do you notice about the graphs?

4. Rule: $3x + 1 = y$

x	y
$^-2$	$^-5$
$^-1$	$^-2$
0	1
1	4
2	7

Rule: $-3x + 1 = y$

x	y
$^-2$	7
$^-1$	4
0	1
1	$^-2$
2	$^-5$

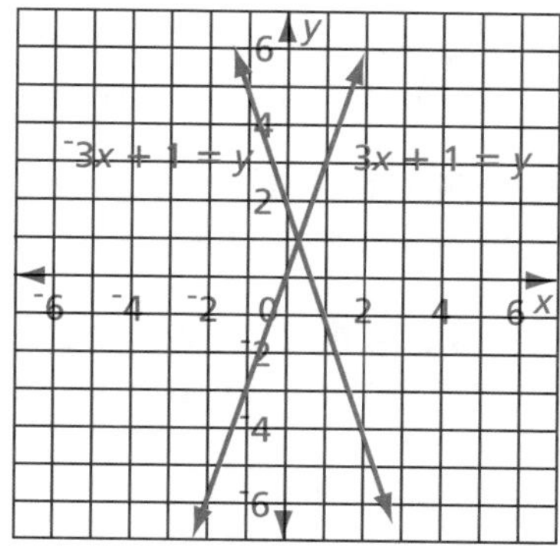

intersecting lines at (0,1)

5. Rule: $\frac{1}{2}x^2 = y$

x	y
$^-2$	2
$^-1$	$\frac{1}{2}$
0	0
1	$\frac{1}{2}$
2	2

Rule: $2x^2 = y$

x	y
$^-2$	8
$^-1$	2
0	0
1	2
2	8

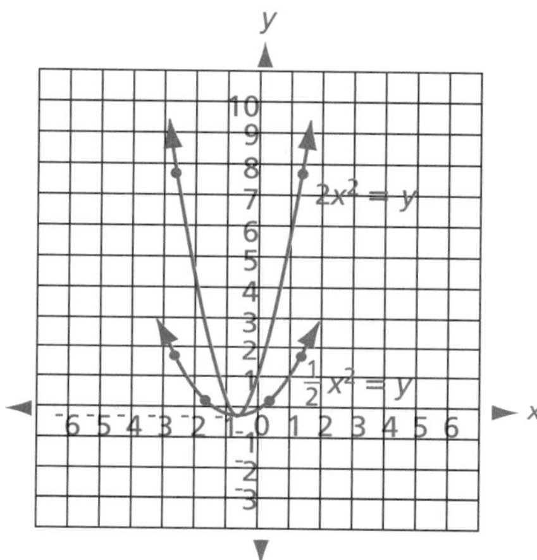

graph of $2x^2 = y$ is inside graph of $\frac{1}{2}x^2 = y$

Problem Solving Reasoning

Find some ordered pairs for these rules. Then graph them. Describe how the graphs are alike and how they are different.

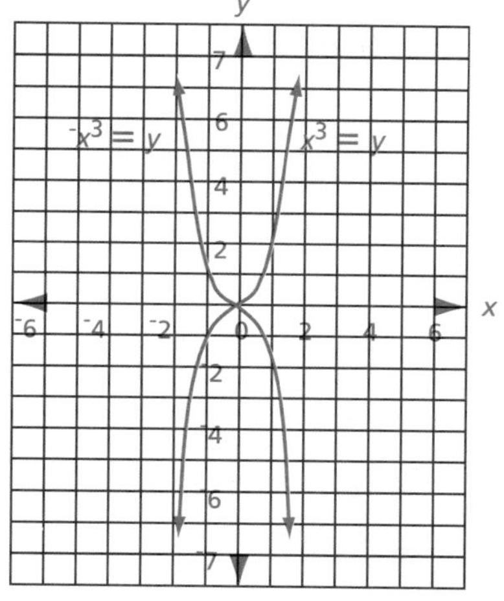

6. Rule: $x^3 = y$
Possible ordered pairs:
$(^-2, {}^-8)$, $(^-1, {}^-1)$,
$(-\frac{1}{2}, -\frac{1}{8})$, $(0, 0)$,
$(\frac{1}{2}, \frac{1}{8})$, $(1, 1)$, $(2, 8)$

Rule: $-x^3 = y$
Possible ordered pairs:
$(^-2, 8)$, $(^-1, 1)$,
$(-\frac{1}{2}, \frac{1}{8})$, $(0, 0)$,
$(\frac{1}{2}, -\frac{1}{8})$, $(1, {}^-1)$, $(2, {}^-8)$

They are both parabolas; The y-coordinates are opposites.

Test Prep ★ Mixed Review

7 Which is the standard form of the number 3.8×10^{-5}? B; Obj. 9C

A 0.0000038 **C** 380,000

B 0.000038 **D** 3,800,000

8 If $a = {}^-3$, what is the value of the polynomial $4a^2 + 2a - 10$? H; Obj. 9B

F 40 **H** 20

G 26 **J** $^-20$

Closing the Lesson *What shape is the graph of $x^2 + 5 = y$?* (a parabola) *What can you tell me about points in the second quadrant?* (The x values are negative and the y values are positive.)

Name ______________________________

Guided Practice: First ex. in Rows 1, 2 & 7, pp. 320–321
Independent Practice: Complete pp. 320–322

Symmetry in the Coordinate Plane

> **Line of symmetry** A line that divides a figure into two parts that are the same size and shape and are mirror images of one another

In the trapezoid shown at the right, the *y*-axis, or fold line, is a **line of symmetry**. Look at the relationship between pairs of points on the trapezoid.

Point ***A*, (−2, 4)**, is **2** units to the left of the *y*-axis.
Point ***B*, (2, 4)**, is **2** units to the right of the *y*-axis.

The ***x***-coordinate for Point ***A*** is the opposite of the ***x***-coordinate for Point ***B***, but the ***y***-coordinates are the same.

If the ***y***-axis is a line of symmetry for a figure, then every point on the figure has a matching point.

- The ***x***-coordinate for one point is the opposite of the ***x***-coordinate of the other point.
- The ***y***-coordinates are the same for both points.

Now look at the coordinates for point ***C*** and point ***D***.

(4, 0) and **(−4, 0)**

- The ***x***-coordinates are opposites.
- The ***y***-coordinates are the same.

D is the matching point of ***C***.

The point **(0, 4)** is on the line of symmetry. The opposite of **0** is **0**, so its matching point is itself, **(0, 4)**.

Complete the table below by finding matching points for other points on the trapezoid.

1.

Point	**(2,0)**	**(−1,4)**	**(−3,0)**	**($\frac{5}{2}$,3)**
Matching Point	(−2,0)	(1,4)	(3,0)	($\frac{-5}{2}$,3)

Complete the figure so that the *y*-axis is the line of symmetry. Write the coordinates of the matching points for *A* and *B*.

2.

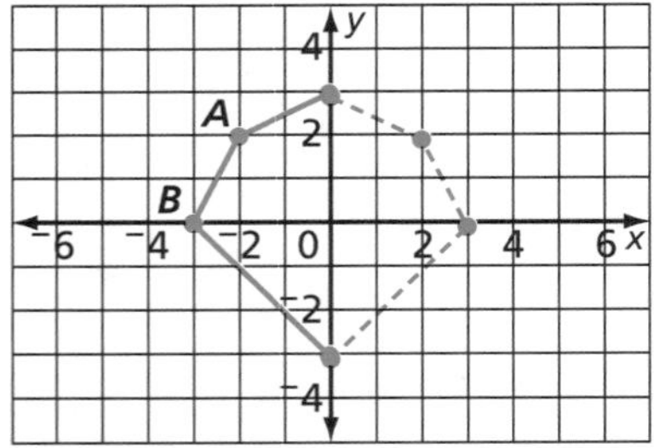

Matching point for ***A*** (2, 2)

Matching point for ***B*** (3, 0)

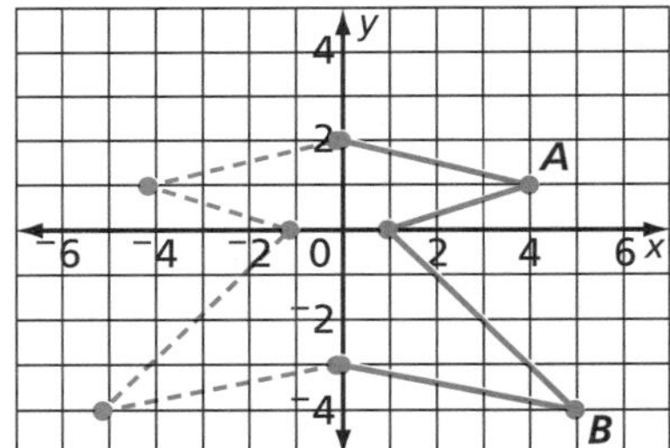

Matching point for ***A*** (−4, 1)

Matching point for ***B*** (−5, −4)

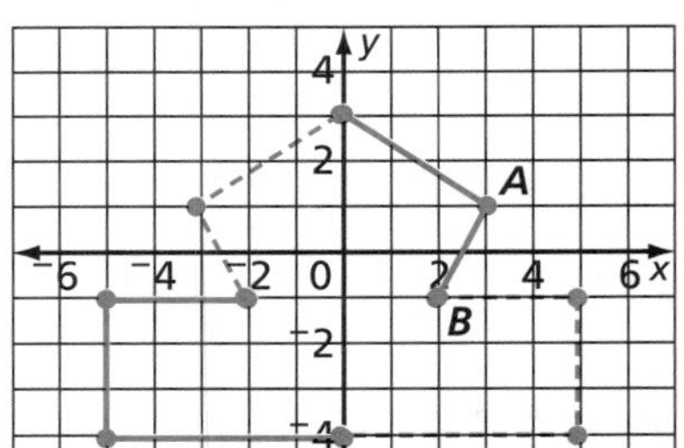

Matching point for ***A*** (−3, 1)

Matching point for ***B*** (−2, −1)

Check Understanding *Is the figure with vertices (2,1) (3,2), (2, −1), and (3, −2) symmetric about either of the axes?* (Yes. It is symmetric about the *x*-axis)

Name ______________________

In some figures, the *x*-axis is the line of symmetry.
Study the figure on the graph at the right to answer the questions.

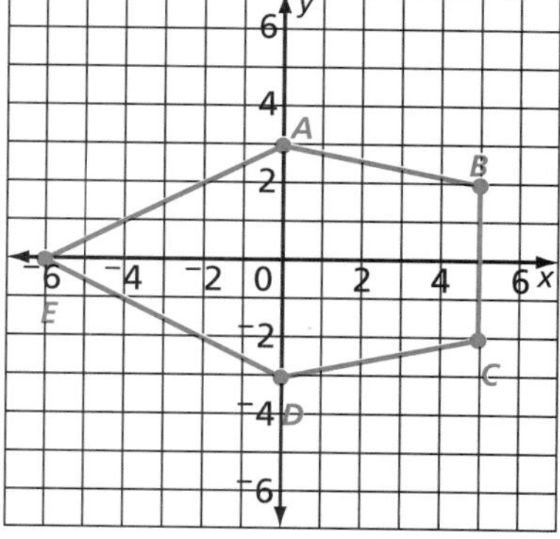

3. Point ***A*** has coordinates **(0, 3)**. Its matching point is Point ***D***, with coordinates **(0, ⁻3)**.

How far is Point ***A*** from the ***x***-axis? 3 units

How far is Point ***D*** from the ***x***-axis? 3 units

4. Another point on the figure is ***B*** **(5, 2)**.

What is its matching point? C (5, ⁻2)

Is each of these points the same distance from the ***x***-axis?

Yes.

Complete the table by finding matching points for other points on the figure. Then use the table to complete the statements.

5.

Point	(⁻2,⁻2)	(⁻4,⁻1)	(5,0)	$(4,\frac{11}{5})$
Matching Point	(⁻2,2)	(⁻4,1)	(5,0)	$(4,\frac{-11}{5})$

6. If the ***x***-axis is a line of symmetry for a figure, then every point with coordinates ***x*** and ***y*** on the figure has a "matching point" whose ***x***-coordinate is the same and whose ***y***-coordinate is the opposite of *y*.

Complete the figures so that the *x*-axis is the line of symmetry. Write the coordinates of the matching points for *A* and *B*.

7.

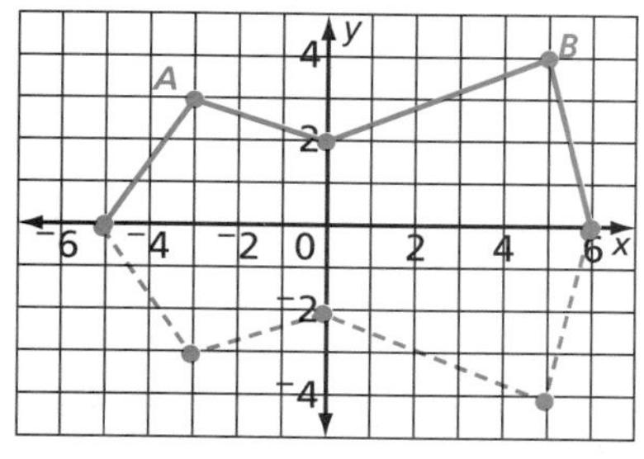

Matching point for ***A***

(⁻3, ⁻3)

Matching point for ***B***

(5, ⁻4)

Matching point for ***A***

(⁻3, 3)

Matching point for ***B***

(1, 3)

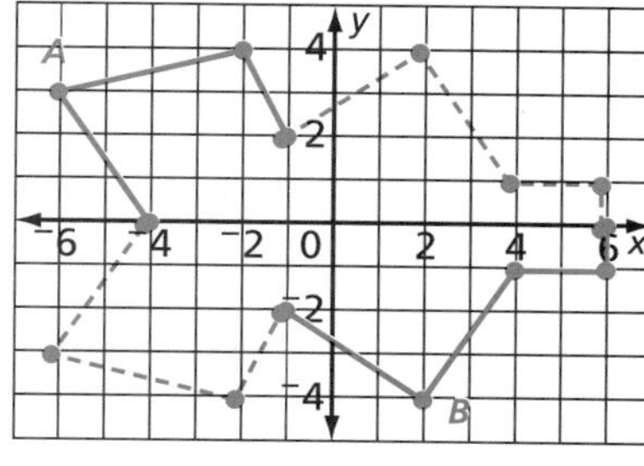

Matching point for ***A***

(⁻6, ⁻3)

Matching point for ***B***

(2, 4)

Plot the points and then connect them in order. Find the matching points to complete the symmetric figure.

8. (⁻4, 0), (⁻2, 4), (1, 1), (3, 3), (4, 1), (4, 0)

Line of symmetry: *x*-axis

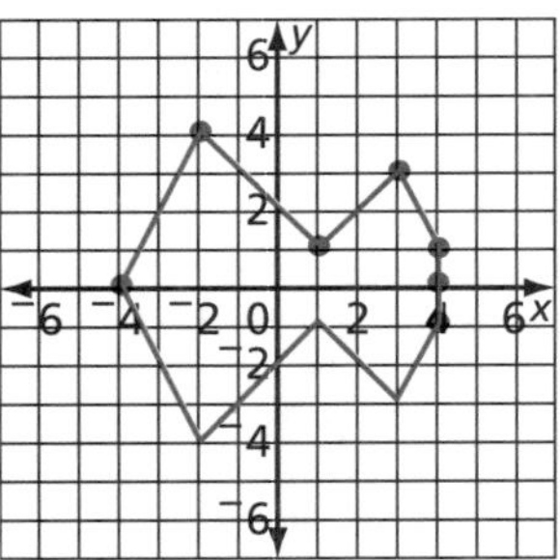

(⁻3, 0), (⁻1, ⁻2), (1, ⁻1), (1, ⁻3), (3, ⁻3), (3, 0)

Line of symmetry: *x*-axis

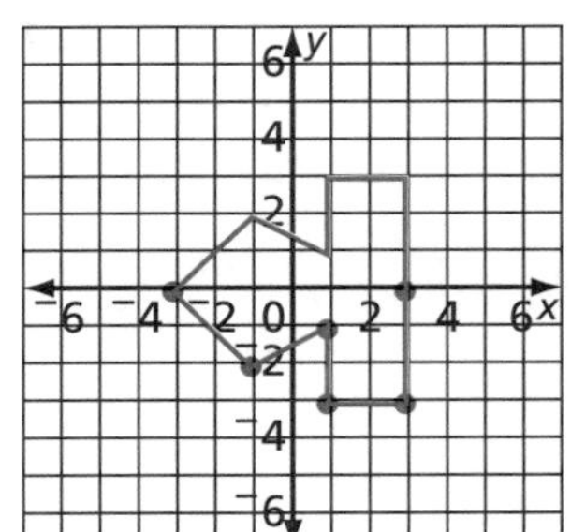

9. (0, ⁻5), (4, ⁻4), (1, ⁻3), (3, 0), (0, ⁻3)

Line of symmetry: *y*-axis

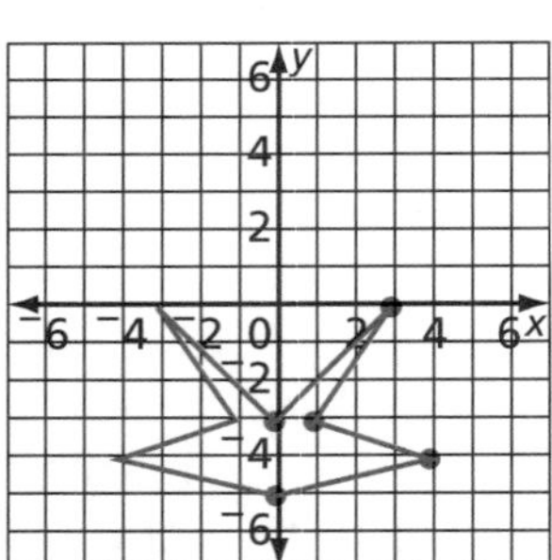

(0, ⁻4), (⁻1, ⁻4), (⁻1, ⁻3), (⁻4, ⁻1), (⁻1, 2), (0, 4)

Line of symmetry: *y*-axis

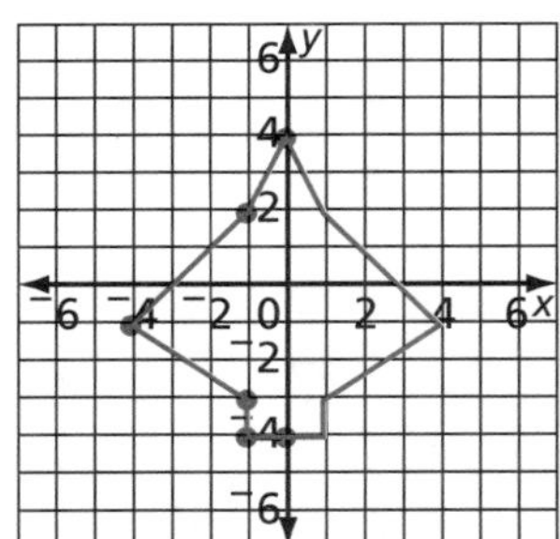

Problem Solving
Reasoning

Use the coordinate grid to graph the quadrilaterals.

10. Graph a quadrilateral ***ABCD*** that is only symmetric about the ***x***-axis.

11. Graph a quadrilateral ***EFGH*** that is only symmetric about the ***y***-axis.

12. Graph a quadrilateral ***WXYZ*** that is symmetric about both axes.

Answers will vary.

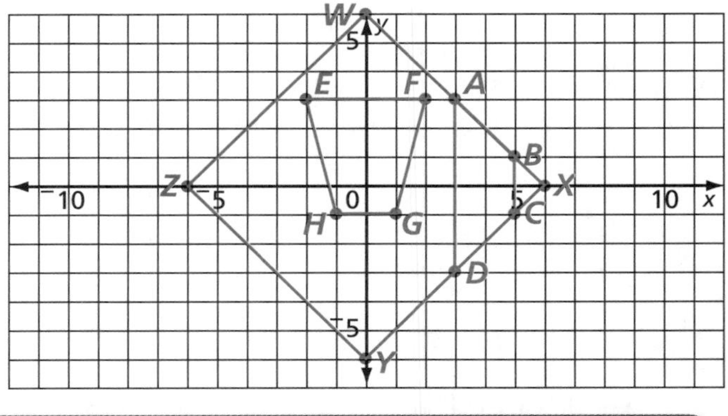

Test Prep ★ Mixed Review

13 **If the sides of a right triangle measure 7.5 cm and 9.2 cm, what is the length of the hypotenuse?** A; Obj. 10D

A 11.9 cm **C** 141 cm

B 16.7 cm **D** 119 cm

14 **The height of a can is 5.7 in. and the radius of its base is 2.5 in. Which represents the surface area? (Use $\pi = 3.14$.)** G; Obj. 10C

F 109.1 in.^{2} **H** 83.9 in.^{2}

G 128.7 in.^{2} **J** 105.2 in.^{2}

Closing the Lesson *When is a figure symmetric about both the x- and y-axis?* (Possible answer: For every ordered pair (*a*, *b*), the figure would also have to have (⁻*a*, *b*), (*a*, ⁻*b*), and (⁻*a*, ⁻*b*). Students may use a specific point to illustrate this idea.)

Name ______________________________

Congruence and Similarity

Guided Practice: Draw polygons in ex. 1 & 3, pp. 323–324
Independent Practice: Complete pp. 323–325

The quadrilaterals ***ABCD*** and ***EFGH*** shown in the coordinate grids are **congruent**.

ABCD* ≅ *EFGH

Read ≅ as "is congruent to"

Congruent figures have the same size and the same shape.

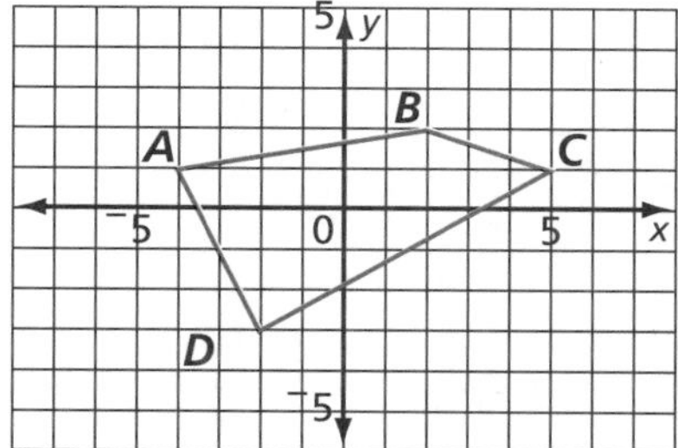

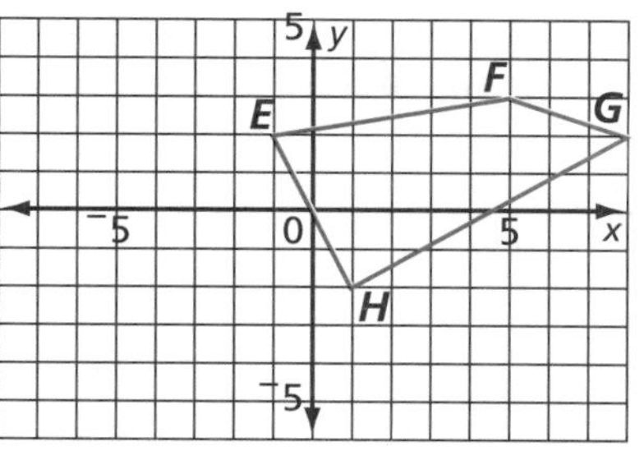

If two figures are congruent, corresponding sides and angles in the figures are also congruent. For example:

- Side $\overline{BC}$ in quadrilateral ***ABCD*** corresponds to side $\overline{FG}$ in quadrilateral ***EFGH***. So $\overline{BC} \cong \overline{FG}$.
- ∠***A*** in quadrilateral ***ABCD*** corresponds to ∠***E*** in quadrilateral ***EFGH***, so ∠***A*** ≅ ∠***E***.

All of this information lets us state a more complete definition for congruent polygons.

Two polygons are **congruent** if corresponding angles are congruent and corresponding sides are congruent.

Draw a polygon congruent to the polygon shown. One side has been given for you to start.

1.

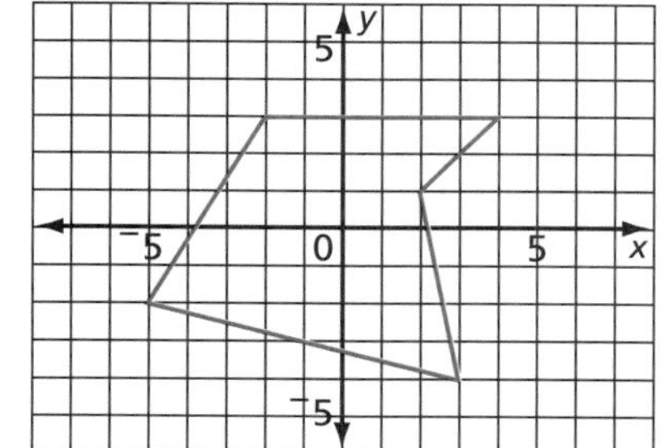

2.

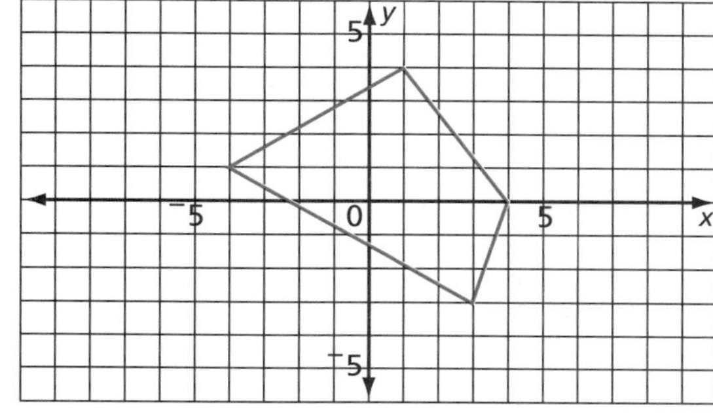

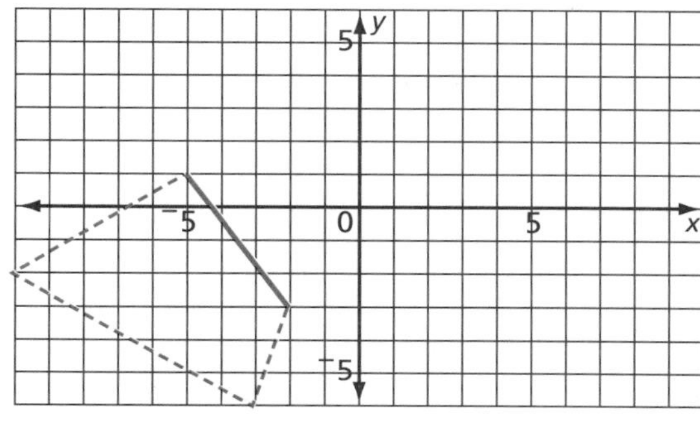

Check Understanding *If two triangles are congruent, are they similar? Explain.* (Yes. Congruent figures have congruent angles and sides that have ratio of 1 to 1.) *If two triangles are similar, are they congruent?* (Not necessarily. The corresponding angles are congruent, but the corresponding sides may not be congruent.)

The triangles ***ABC*** and ***EFG*** shown below are not congruent triangles, but they are **similar** triangles.

Similar figures have the same shape but not necessarily the same size.

Triangle ***ABC*** ~ Triangle ***EFG***

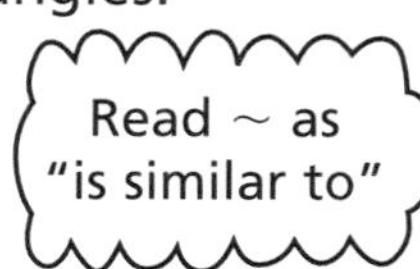

Are the corresponding sides and angles of similar figures congruent?

- Corresponding angles of similar figures are congruent. For example,

  ∠***A*** in triangle ***ABC*** corresponds to ∠***E*** in triangle ***EFG***. ∠***A*** ≅ ∠***E***

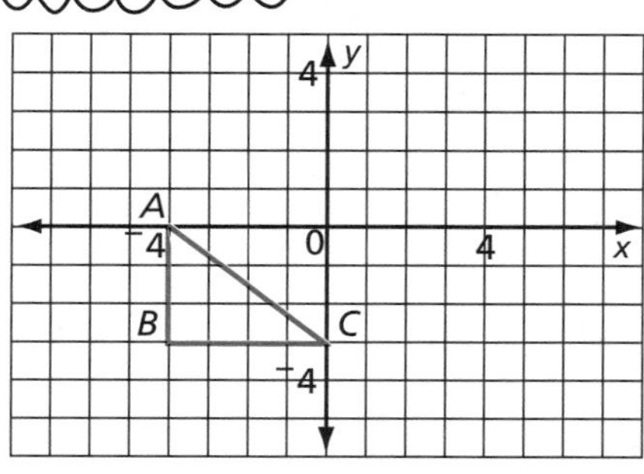

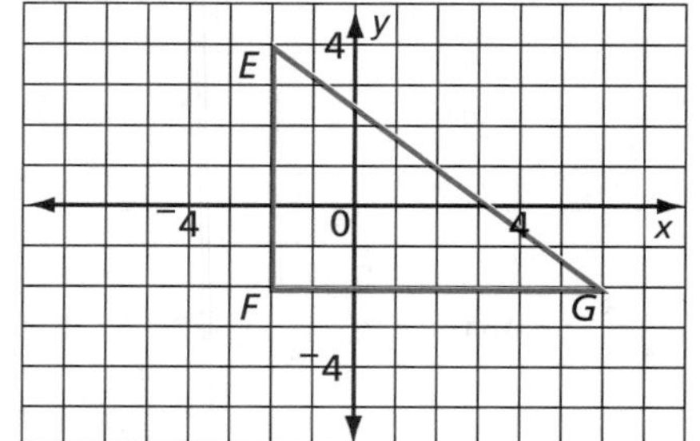

- Corresponding sides of similar figures may not be congruent, but the scale factor of the ratio of corresponding sides is the same.

Side $\overline{AB}$ is **3** units.
Side $\overline{EF}$ is **6** units.

$\frac{6}{3} = 2$

Side $\overline{BC}$ is **4** units.
Side $\overline{FG}$ is **8** units.

$\frac{8}{4} = 2$

Side $\overline{CA}$ is **5** units.
Side $\overline{GE}$ is **10** units.

$\frac{10}{5} = 2$

Triangle ***EFG*** is similar to triangle ***ABC*** by a scale factor of **2**.

All of this information lets us state a more complete definition for similar polygons.

Two polygons are **similar** if corresponding angles are congruent and corresponding sides are proportional.

A polygon is shown on the first grid below. Suppose that the scale factor is 2. Draw the enlargement of the polygon, using the origin as one vertex.

3.

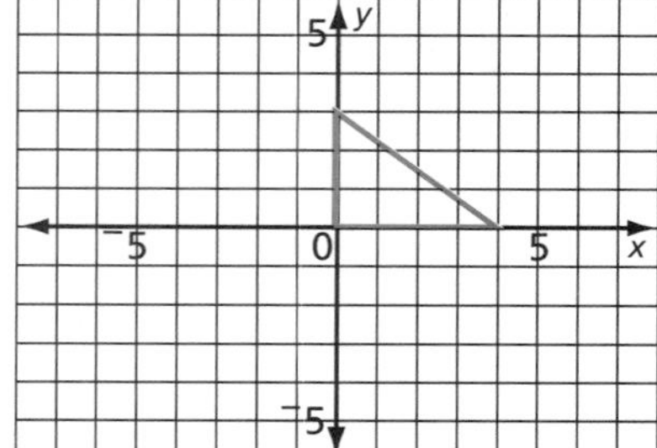

4.

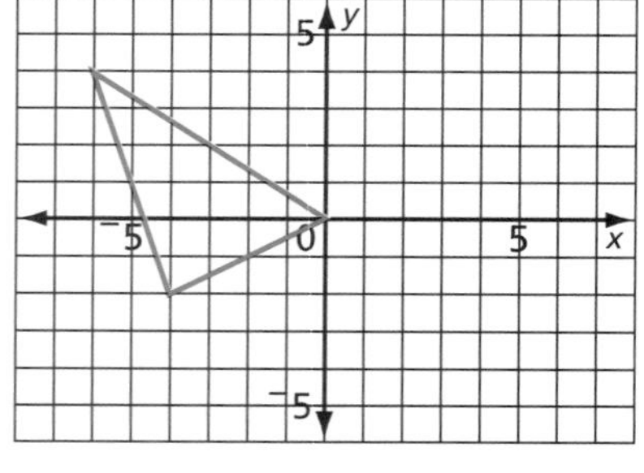

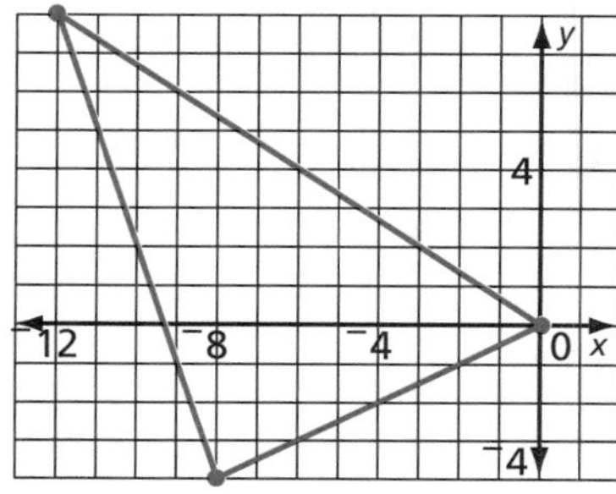

Name ____________________

You can use similar triangles to find the heights of objects that are difficult to measure directly.

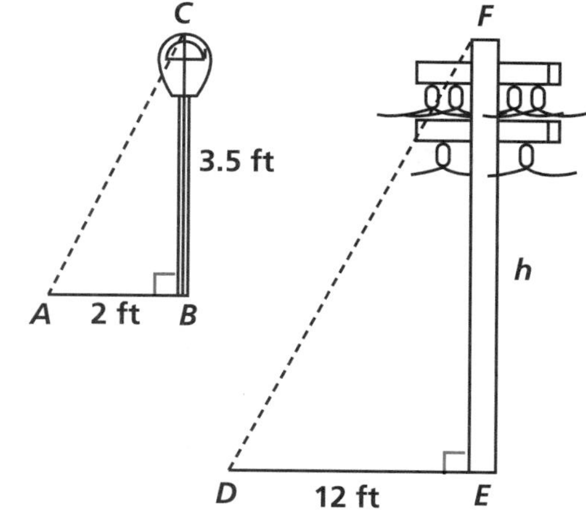

You know that a parking meter that is **3.5** feet tall casts a shadow that is **2** feet long at the same time that a telephone pole that is ***h*** feet tall casts a shadow that is **12** feet long. How tall is the telephone pole?

Since you know the sides of similar figures are proportional, you can write and solve a proportion to find ***h***.

$$\frac{3.5}{2} = \frac{h}{12}$$
$$2h = 42$$
$$h = 21$$

The telephone pole is **21** feet tall.

---

5. Find the missing measure.

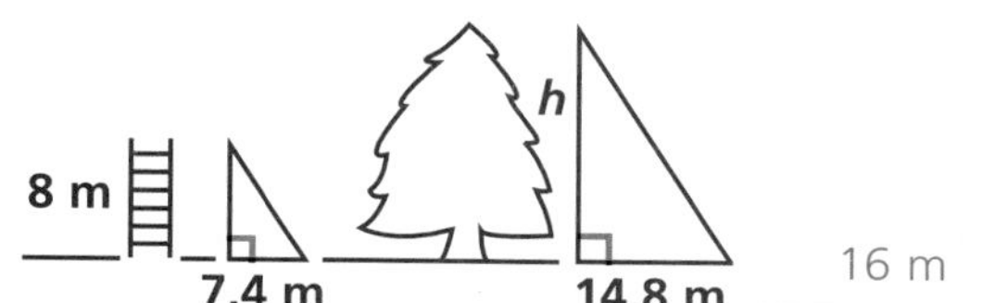

16 m

6. Some boys noticed that the flagpole cast a shadow of **28** feet. The boys asked Alan, a **4**-foot first grader, to stand beside the pole. He cast a **7**-foot shadow. How high is the flagpole?

16 ft

Quick Check

Find three ordered pairs that satisfy the rule. Answers will vary.

7. Rule: $x^2 - 3 = y$

(0, ⁻3), (1, ⁻2), (⁻2, 1)

8. Rule: $2x + 5 = y$

(0, 5), (⁻2, 1), (1, 7)

9. Tell whether the graphs of the rules in exercises **7** and **8** will be lines or parabolas. parabola, line

10. Point *A* **(2, 4)** in trapezoid *ABCD* is symmetric about the *x*-axis. What are the coordinates of its matching point?

(2, ⁻4)

11. Segment *AB* in one triangle has endpoints **(0,0)** and **(0,3)**. Its corresponding segment in another triangle has endpoints **(4,4)** and **(4,10)**. Could the triangles be congruent or similar? Explain. similar, scale factor 2

Work Space.

Item	Error Analysis
7–9	**Common Error** Students may write some pairs in wrong order. **Reteaching** Reteach 95
10	**Common Error** Students may confuse *x*- and *y*-axis symmetry. **Reteaching** Reteach 96
11	**Common Error** Students may not be able to find length using coordinates. **Reteaching** Reteach 97

Closing the Lesson *Where would you use the idea of similar figures?* (Possible answer: reducing or enlarging photographs.)

Name ____________________

Translations and Reflections

Guided Practice: First ex. in Rows 1 & 8, ex. 3, pp. 326–328
Independent Practice: Complete pp. 326–328

Some **geometric transformations** change only the position of a figure, not its size or shape. For example, imagine flipping Triangle ***ABC*** over the ***y***-axis.

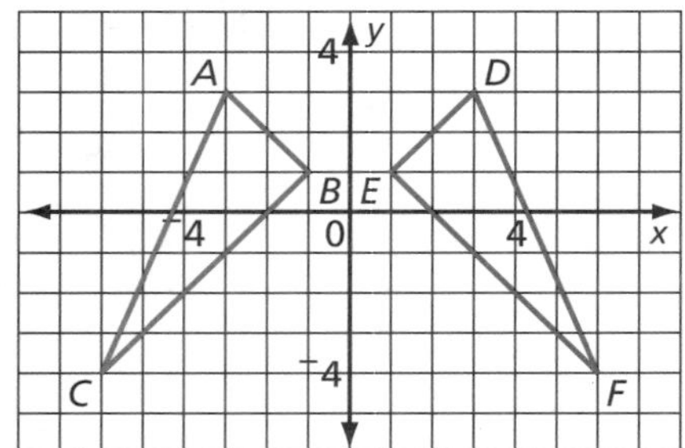

The resulting triangle, Triangle ***DEF,*** is the **line reflection image** of Triangle ***ABC*** over the ***y***-axis.

Vertex ***A*** has coordinates (**⁻3,3**). Its image, Point ***D***, has coordinates (**3,3**). Vertex ***B*** has coordinates (**⁻1,1**), and its image, Point ***E***, has coordinates (**1,1**). Finally, Vertex ***C***, with coordinates (**⁻6,⁻4**), has Point ***F*** as its image, with coordinates (**6,⁻4**).

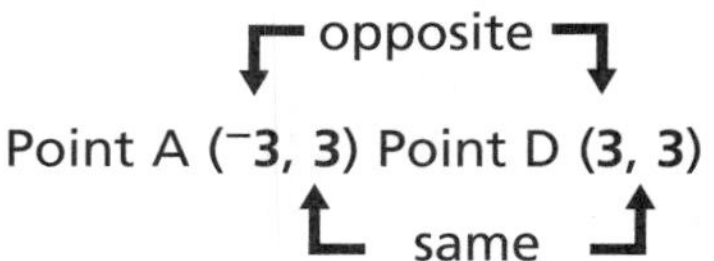

For each vertex in Triangle ***ABC***, its image has an ***x***-coordinate that is just the opposite and a ***y***-coordinate that is exactly the same.

On the coordinate grid at the right, Quadrilateral ***ABCD*** has been flipped over the ***x***-axis. Look at the coordinates of corresponding points.

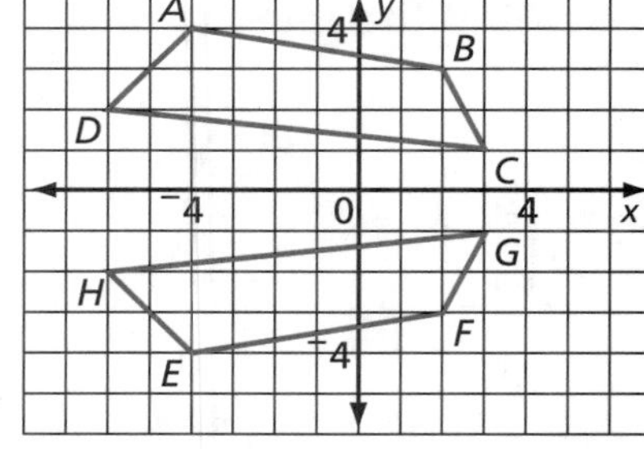

Point A: (**⁻4,4**)	Point E: (**⁻4,⁻4**)
Point B: (**2,3**)	Point F: (**2,⁻3**)
Point C: (**3,1**)	Point G: (**3,⁻1**)
Point D: (**⁻6,2**)	Point H: (**⁻6,⁻2**)

What do you notice about the coordinates of corresponding points?

The *x*-coordinates are the same. The *y*-coordinates are opposites.

Reflect the figure over the *y*-axis. Write the coordinates of each image point.

1.

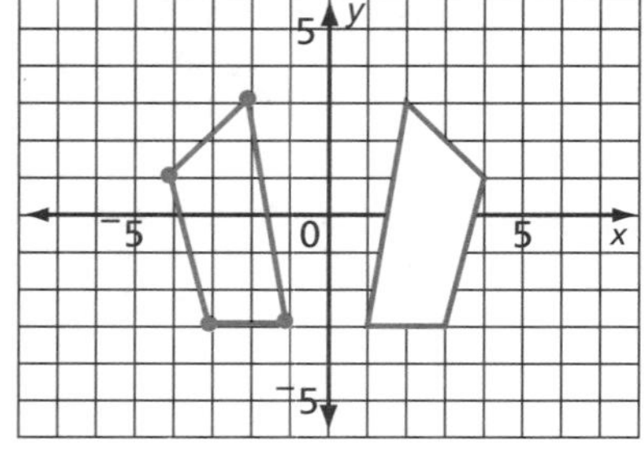

(⁻1,⁻3), (⁻2,3), (⁻4,1) (⁻3,⁻3)

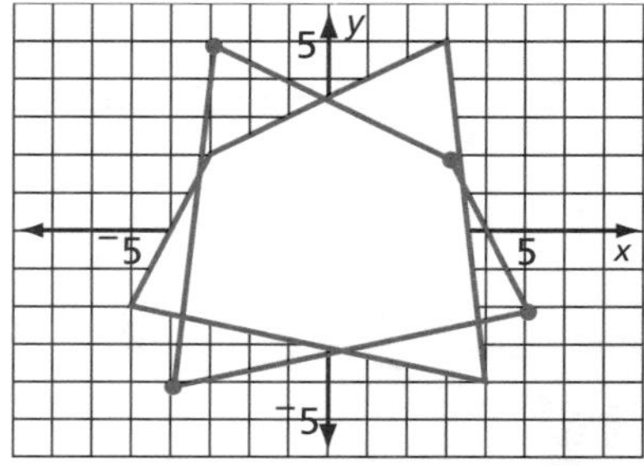

(5,⁻2), (3,2), (⁻3,5) (⁻4,⁻4)

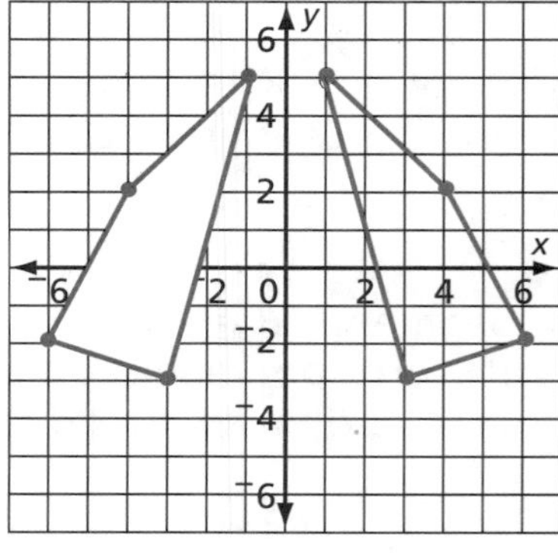

(1,5), (4,2), (6,⁻2,) (3,⁻3)

Check Understanding *If the point (⁻4,6) is translated 4 units left and 2 units up, what are its new coordinates?* (⁻8, 8)

Name ___________________________

Reflect each figure over the *x*-axis. Write the coordinates for each image point.

2.

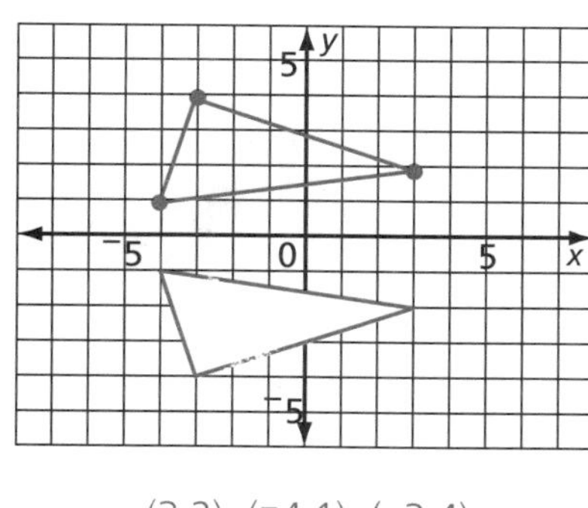

(3,2), (⁻4,1), (⁻3,4)

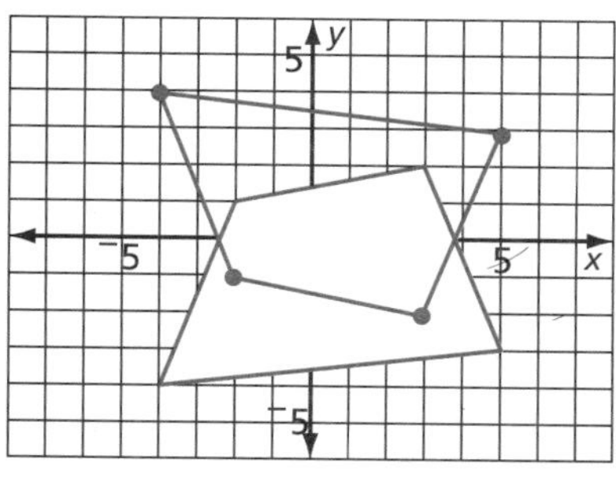

(5,3), (3,⁻2), (⁻2,⁻1), (⁻4,4)

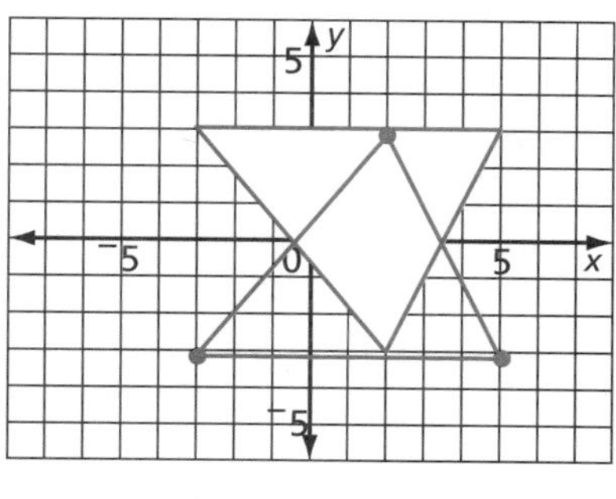

(⁻3,⁻3), (5,⁻3), (2,3)

Another geometric transformation is called a **translation** or **slide**. In a translation, the figure slides to a new position on the coordinate grid.

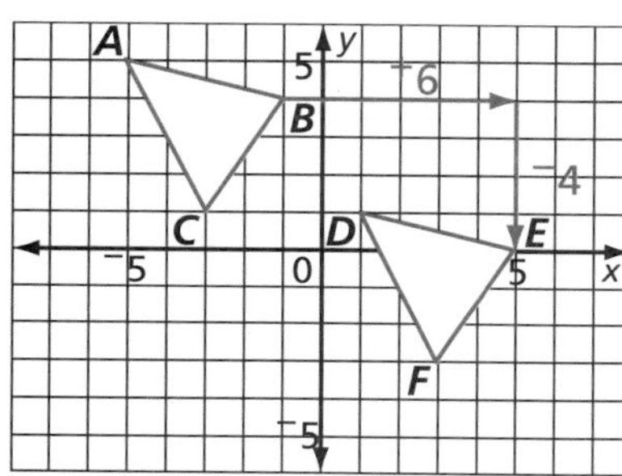

The corresponding pairs of vertices for the translation are ***A*** and ***D***, ***B*** and ***E***, and ***C*** and ***F***. The coordinates for Vertex ***B*** are **(⁻1,4)**. To find the image Point ***F***, move **6** units to the right and **4** units down. Point ***F*** has coordinates **(5,0)**.

⁻1 + 6 = 5 and **4 − 4 = 0; (5,0)** is the image.

Adding **6** to the ***x***-coordinate and subtracting **4** from the ***y***-coordinate of Points ***A*** and ***C*** will give the image Points ***D*** and ***F***.

Here is another example. To slide from Vertex ***D*** to Vertex ***H***, move **6** units to the left and then **3** units up. Point ***D*** has coordinates **(⁻1,⁻4)**. Point ***H*** has coordinates **(⁻7,⁻1)**.

⁻1 − 6 = ⁻7 and **⁻4 + 3 = ⁻1**.

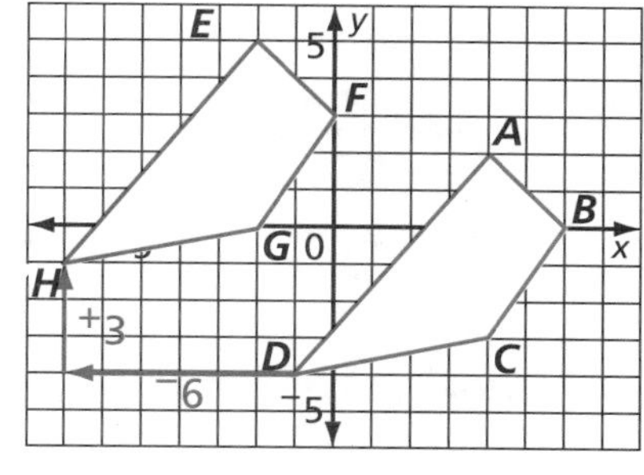

Find the coordinates of the image point if the given point is translated according to the directions.

3. **(4,5)**; translated **3** units right and **4** units up (7,9)

4. **(⁻3,1)**; translated **2** units right and **2** units down (⁻1,⁻1)

5. **(3,⁻6)**; translated **5** units left and **7** units up (⁻2, 1)

6. **(⁻2,⁻4)**; translated **3** units left and **10** units up (⁻5,6)

7. A triangle has the following vertices: **(⁻1,3)**, **(⁻5,1)**, and **(⁻2,0)**. It is translated **5** units right and **3** units down. What are the coordinates of the image triangle?

(4,0), (0,⁻2), (3,⁻3)

Translate the figures below, following the rules given.

8. Right 3 units
Up 4 units

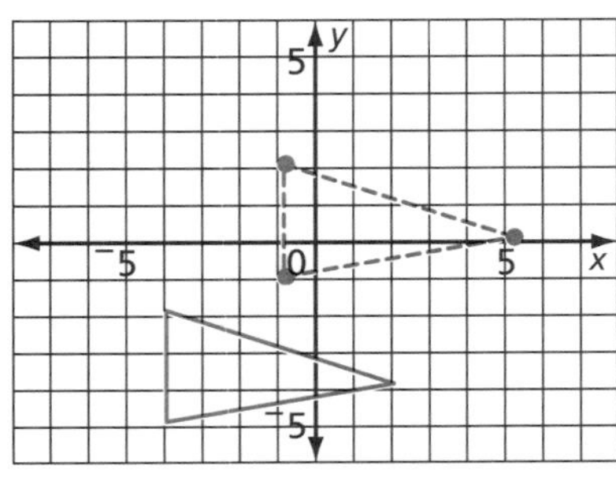

Left 5 units
Down 3 units

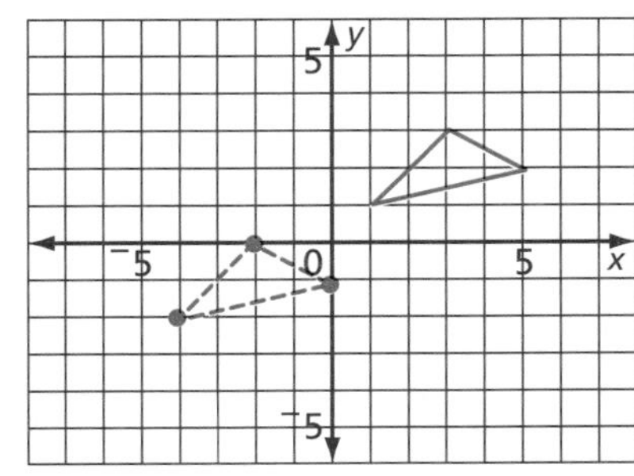

Right 1 units
Up 5 units

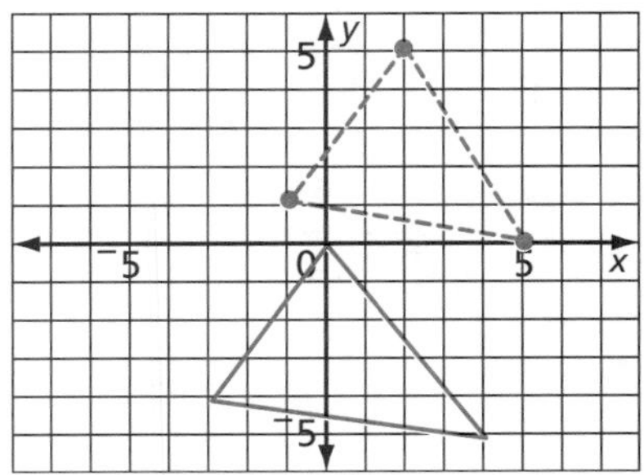

Each Triangle *ABC* shown below has been translated. The image is Triangle *DEF*.
State the directions for the slide (Right or Left __ units, Up or Down __ units).

9.

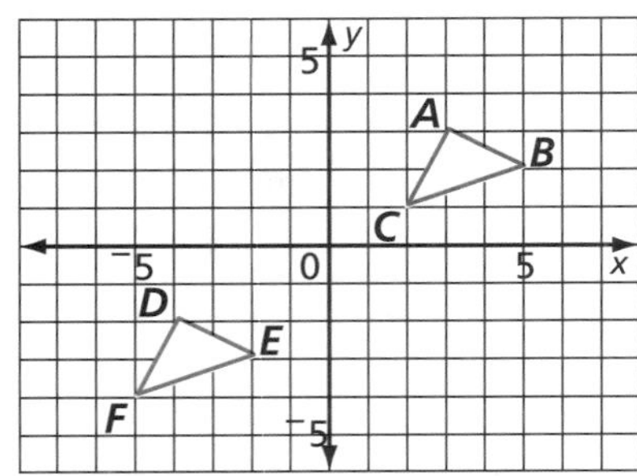

Left 7 units, Down 5 units

Right 6 units, Down 3 units

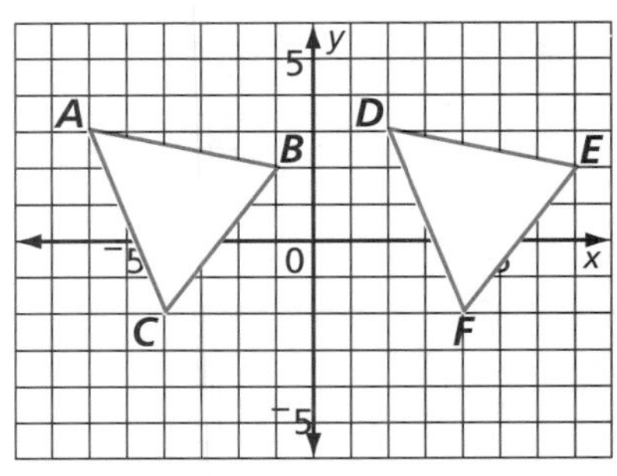

Right 8 units, Down 0 units

Problem Solving
Reasoning

10. The point (6,⁻2) is flipped over the ***y***-axis first. This result is then flipped over the ***x***-axis. What are the coordinates of this final result?

(⁻6,2)

11. A triangle with vertices **(1,⁻1)**, **(5,1)**, and **(3,4)** is flipped over the ***x***-axis first. This result is then flipped over the ***y***-axis. What are the coordinates of this final result?

(⁻1,1), (⁻5,⁻1) (⁻3,⁻4)

Test Prep ★ Mixed Review

12 **In right △*ABC*, *A* is the point (0, 5), *B* is (0, 0), and *C* (7, 0). Hal wants to draw a right △*DEF* congruent to △*ABC*. He puts point *E* at (3, 5) and point *F* at (10, 5). Where could he place point *D*?** D; Obj. 11C

A (10, 10)
B (3, 10)
C (3, 0)
D (3, 10) or (3, 0)

13 **In right △*ABC*, *A* is the point (0, 6), *B* is (0, 0), and *C* (10, 0). Maya wants to draw a right △*DEF* similar to △*ABC*. She puts point *D* at (5, 9) and point *E* at (5, 6). Where could she place point *F*?** J; Obj. 11C

F (10, 9)
G (10, 6)
H (0, 6)
J (10, 6) or (0, 6)

Closing the Lesson *If a point in the third quadrant is reflected about the x-axis, what quadrant is it in? Explain.* (It is in the second quadrant, since the *y*-coordinate changes sign and the *x*-coordinate remains the same.)

Name ______________________________

Guided Practice: First ex. in Rows 1 & 2; Ex. 5, pp. 329–331
Independent Practice: Complete pp. 329–331

Equations with Two Variables

Throughout this text you have been using equations with one variable such as $n + 2 = 3$ or $\frac{2}{3} = \frac{n}{6}$ to solve problems. What happens when an equation has two variables?

$$y = 2x + 3$$

Notice that if you substitute **1** for x and **5** for y, the resulting number sentence is true.

$$5 = 2(1) + 3$$

The ordered pair **(1, 5)** is called a **solution** of the equation. Similarly, when $x = {}^-2$ and $y = {}^-1$, the resulting number sentence, $^-1 = 2(^-2) + 3$, is true. The ordered pairs **(⁻2, ⁻1), (0, 3), (100, 203)** are other solutions of the equation.

In an ordered pair, the first number represents the value of *x* and the second number represents the value of *y*.

$$y = 2x + 3 \qquad y = 2x + 3$$

$$3 = 2(0) + 3 \qquad 203 = 2(100) + 3$$

In fact, the equation $y = 2x + 3$ and equations like it have an infinite number of ordered pair solutions. (Equally, there are an infinite number of ordered pairs that are not solutions. Try the ordered pair **(0, 0)**. What do you notice?)

Here is another example.
Find three solutions for the equation $y = 3x - 4$.

Choose a value for *x*. Then find a value for *y*.

Try $x = 2$

$y = 3(2) - 4$

$= 2$

So **(2, 2)** is a solution.

Try $x = (^-3)$

$y = 3(^-3) - 4$

$= {}^-13$

So **(⁻3, ⁻13)** is a solution.

Try $x = \frac{2}{3}$

$y = 3(\frac{2}{3}) - 4$

$= {}^-2$

So $(\frac{2}{3}, {}^-2)$ is a solution.

Complete each table of values.

1.

$y = 2x$	
x	*y*
⁻2	⁻4
⁻1	⁻2
0	0
1	2
2	4

$y = {}^-3x$	
x	*y*
⁻3	9
⁻2	6
⁻1	3
0	0
1	⁻3

$y = 5x + 1$	
x	*y*
⁻1	⁻4
0	1
1	6
2	11
3	16

$y = \frac{1}{2}x - 1$	
x	*y*
⁻2	⁻2
0	⁻1
2	0
4	1
6	2

Check Understanding *If $y = \frac{x}{2} + 3$, what does y equal if x equals 4?* (5) *What does y equal if x equals zero?* (3) *What does y equal if $x = {}^-6$?* (0)

Make a table of values showing four solutions for each equation. Answers may vary.

2.

$y = 5x + 2$	
x	y
$^-1$	$^-3$
0	2
1	7
2	12

$y = {}^-3x - 8$	
x	y
$^-1$	$^-5$
0	$^-8$
1	$^-11$
2	$^-14$

$y = \frac{1}{3}x + 4$	
x	y
$^-3$	3
0	4
3	5
6	6

$y = {}^-\frac{5}{6}x - 2$	
x	y
12	$^-12$
6	$^-7$
0	$^-2$
$^-6$	3

Write two ordered pairs that are not solutions for the equation. Answers may vary.

3. $y = 2x + 1$ (0, 0) (1, 1)

$y = {}^-\frac{4}{5}x - 2$ (0, 0) (1, 1)

4. $y = {}^-3x$ (0, 4) (1, 1)

$y = 4x - 7$ (0, 0) (1, 1)

You can use equations with two variables to express relationships between two values.
Consider these equations:

$y = 3x$

If x = number of yards, then y = number of feet.

If x = number of 3-point baskets in a basketball game, then y = number of points scored.

The value of y depends on the value of x.

$y = 12x$

If x = number of feet, then y = number of inches.

If x = number of years, then y = number of months.

Again, the value of y depends on the value of x.

Even some of the formulas you use in geometry express a relationship between two numbers.

$P = 4s$ or $y = 4x$ — If s is the length of a side of a square, then P is the perimeter. The value of P depends on the value of s.

$C = 2\pi r$ or $y = 2\pi x$ — If r is the radius of a circle, then C is the circumference of the circle. The value of C depends on the value of r.

Throughout these examples, the value of y depends on the value of x. So in an x, y equation, y is the **dependent variable**, while x is the **independent variable.**

Name ______________________________

Use the equation $y = 12x$ or the formula $C = \frac{5}{9}(F - 32)$ to find the value.

5. How many inches are in **5** feet? 60 in.

6. How many months are in **15** years? 180 months

7. If the temperature is **32°F**, what is the temperature in degrees Celsius? 0°C

8. If the temperature is **212°F**, what is the temperature in degrees Celsius? 100°C

9. If the temperature is **84°F**, what is the temperature in degrees Celsius? $28\frac{8}{9}$°C

Problem Solving
Reasoning

Solve.

10. The length of a rectangle is twice as long as the width. Write an equation to find the perimeter of the rectangle. Find five solutions. Graph them in the coordinate plane. What do you notice about the graph?

P = 6w or y = 6x; the graph is a straight line.

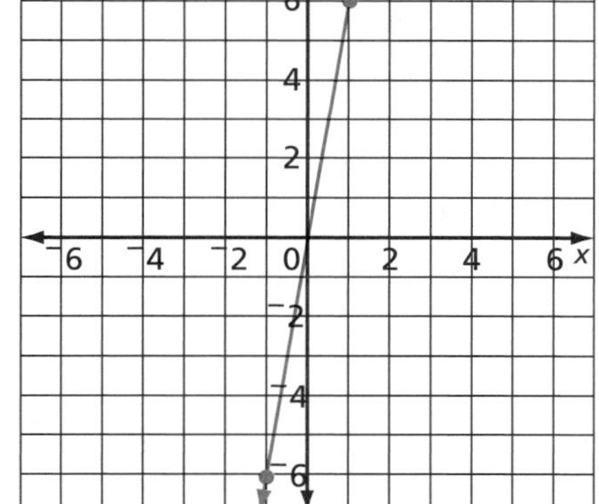

11. Think of another real-life example of a relationship between two quantities, write an equation to express that relationship, and identify the independent variable and the dependent variable in your equation.

Answers will vary.

Test Prep ★ Mixed Review

This spreadsheet computes the volumes of cylinders with height 5 in. and variable radius *r*. Use it for exercises 12 and 13.

r (in.)	r^2	$\pi = 3.14$	πr^2	*h* = 5 (in.)	$V = \pi r^2 h$ (in.^{3})
1	1	3.14	3.14	5	15.7
2	4	3.14	12.56	5	62.8
3	9	3.14	?	5	141.3
4	16	3.14	50.24	5	?

12 **What is the missing value in the fourth column?** B; Obj. 11A

A 12.56
C 3.14
B 28.26
D 9.42

13 **What is the missing value in the sixth column?** H; Obj. 11A

F 141.3
H 251.2
G 15.7
J 314.0

Closing the Lesson *How do you find solutions for an equation in two variables?* (Possible answer: You pick a value for one of the variables and substitute it into the equation and solve for the other variable.)

Name ______________________________

Problem Solving Application: Choose an Equation

Guided Practice: First problem, p. 332
Independent Practice: Complete pp. 332–333

In this lesson, you will be asked to choose an equation that models a problem situation. Clues in a table of values can help you choose an equation.

For example, you know

- The value of *l* depends on the value of *w*
- When **$w = 0$, $l = 3$**
- When **$w = 1$, $l = 4$**, and so on

Scientists often use tables of values to express relationships. For example, this table shows how a spring's length (*l*) depends on how much weight (*w*) is attached to it.

Weight *w* (pounds)	Length *l* (inches)
0	3
1	4
2	5
3	6
4	7

Understanding how to substitute ordered pairs from a table into an equation will help you choose the correct equation.

Tips to Remember:

1. Understand 2. Decide 3. Solve 4. Look back

- Ask yourself whether you have solved a problem like this before.
- Think about the relationships between the variables. Which variable is the dependent variable? Which operation do you use to relate the units or data in the problem?
- Think about the strategies you have learned and use them to help you solve a problem.

Solve.

1. Which equation below shows the same results as the table?

$w + 3 = l$ $w - 3 = l$ $3w = l$ $w \div 3 = l$

Think: Substitute some ordered pairs from the table in each equation.

Pairs will vary.

Answer $w + 3 = l$

2. Suppose a spring is **9** inches long. Use your formula to tell the weight that was attached to it.

Think: Spring length is ***l*** and weight is ***w***.

$w + 3 = 9$

Answer 6 pounds

Check Understanding *If a person worked 4 hours, he/she would earn $28. How could you use that information to verify which of these formulas is correct: $P = 7 + h$; $P = 7h$?* (Substitute 28 for *P* and 4 for *h* and see if the statement is true.)

Circle the appropriate equation for each situation. Explain why you chose the equation. Explanations will vary.

3. This table shows the weight in pounds of some containers of water. Which equation shows the same result as the table?

Gallons *g*	2	4	6	8
Weight *w*	16	32	48	64

$g + 8 = w$ $g + 14 = w$ $8g = w$

4. Which equation shows the same result as this table?

x	y
$^-2$	$^-1$
0	0
2	1

$2x = y$

$\frac{x}{2} = y$

$x + 1 = y$

$x - 1 = y$

5. The number of times a cricket chirps per minute depends on the temperature. When the temperature is **72°F**, the cricket chirps about **58** times a minute. When the temperature is **80°F**, the cricket chirps about **60** times a minute. Which equation models this situation?

$y = 2x - 100$ $y = \frac{1}{4}x + 40$

6. A salesperson who uses her own car to make deliveries collected **$9** for driving **50** miles. Which equation could be used to show how much she would be paid for an **80**-mile trip?

$\frac{9}{x} = \frac{50}{80}$ $\frac{x}{9} = \frac{50}{80}$

7. The sum of two numbers *f* and *s* is **14**. Which equation shows how *s* depends on *f*?

$s = f - 14$ $f \cdot s = 14$ $s = 14 - f$

8. Maris is **5** years older than Carl. Carl is **2** years older than Rory. Which equation shows how Maris's and Rory's ages are related?

$M = R + 5$ $C + R = M$ $M = R + 7$

Extend Your Thinking

9. Write a problem that could be modeled by a one-variable equation. Then write a problem that could be modeled by a two-variable equation. What is the difference between the situations?

Answers will vary.

10. Explain your method for choosing the correct equation in problem **5**. Which words or phrases helped you choose the equation?

Answers will vary.

Closing the Lesson *What is the process you could use to find out which equation correctly represents the data in a table?* (Substitute some of the ordered pairs from the table into the equations and see if they make true statements.)

Name ___________________________

Graphing Linear Functions

Guided Practice: First ex. in Rows 3 & 4, pp. 334–335
Independent Practice: Complete pp. 334–335

You already know how to graph ordered pairs in the coordinate plane using tables and rules. Both the table and graph at the right represent the equation $y = 2x - 3$.

The equation $y = 2x - 3$ is a **function,** because for each value of x that you substitute in the equation, there is exactly one y value. For example, for $y = 2x - 3$, when $x = 2$, then $y = 2 \cdot 2 - 3$, or **1**.

The ordered pairs of the equation $y = 2x - 3$ all lie on the **same line,** so the equation is called a **linear function.**

$y = 2x - 3$	
x	y
0	$^-3$
1	$^-1$
2	1
$^-1$	$^-5$
$^-2$	$^-7$

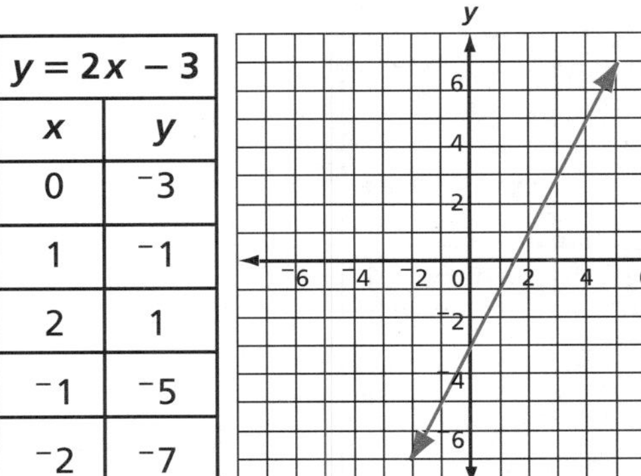

Circle the equations that define linear functions.

1. $y = 3x + 7$ (circled) $\quad y = {}^-x^3 - 2x + 1 \quad y = |x|$

2. $y = \frac{1}{x} \quad$ $y = 0.25x - 2$ (circled) $\quad y = \frac{^-3}{4}x^2 - 8$

Complete the table of values for each function. Then, graph the linear function in the coordinate plane.

3.

$y = x$	
x	y
0	0
1	1
2	2
$^-1$	$^-1$
$^-2$	$^-2$

$y = x - 3$	
x	y
0	$^-3$
1	$^-2$
3	0
$^-1$	$^-4$
$^-2$	$^-5$

$y = 2x + 1$	
x	y
0	1
1	3
2	5
$^-1$	$^-1$
$^-2$	$^-3$

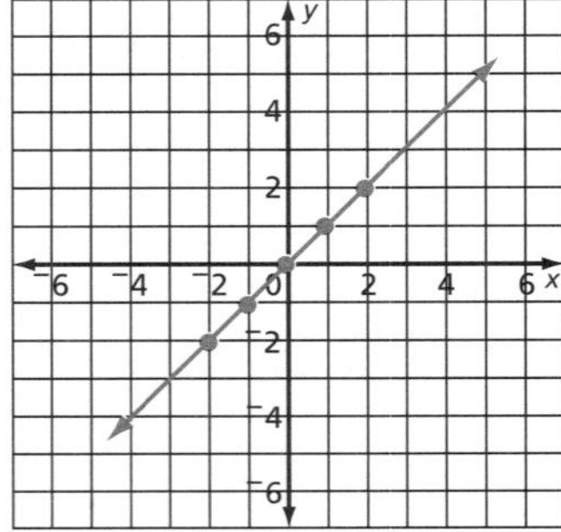

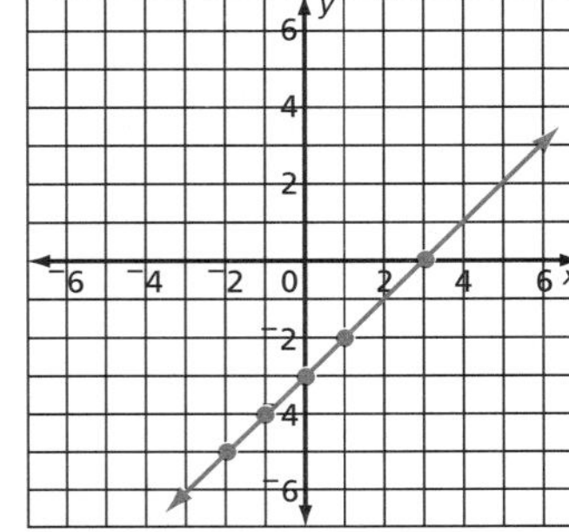

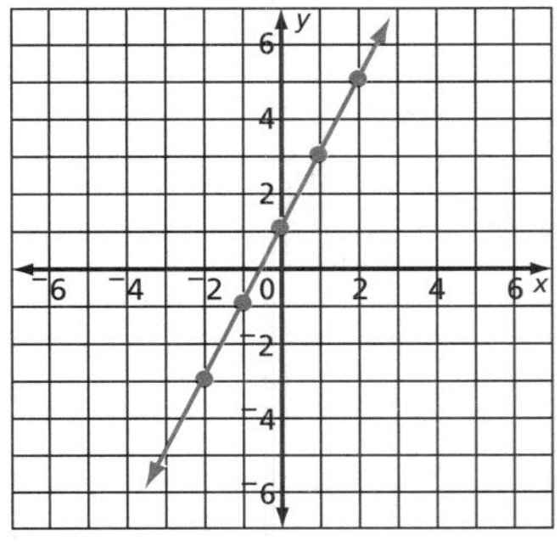

Check Understanding *If an equation is a linear function, what can you tell me about it?* (Possible answers: For every x value, there is exactly one y value. Its graph is a straight line.)

4.

$y = ^-2x$	
x	**y**
0	0
1	$^-2$
2	$^-4$
$^-1$	2
$^-2$	4

5.

$y = \frac{1}{2}x - 1$	
x	**y**
0	$^-1$
1	$^-\frac{1}{2}$
2	0
$^-1$	$^-\frac{3}{2}$
$^-2$	$^-2$

6.

$y = \frac{2}{3}x + 2$	
x	**y**
0	2
1	$2\frac{2}{3}$
2	$3\frac{1}{3}$
$^-1$	$1\frac{1}{3}$
$^-2$	$\frac{2}{3}$

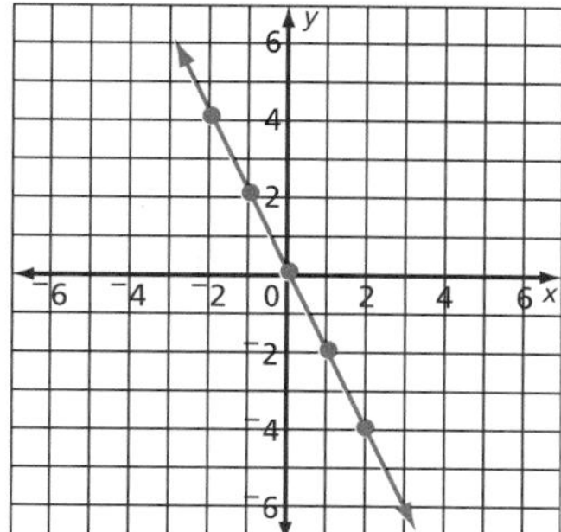

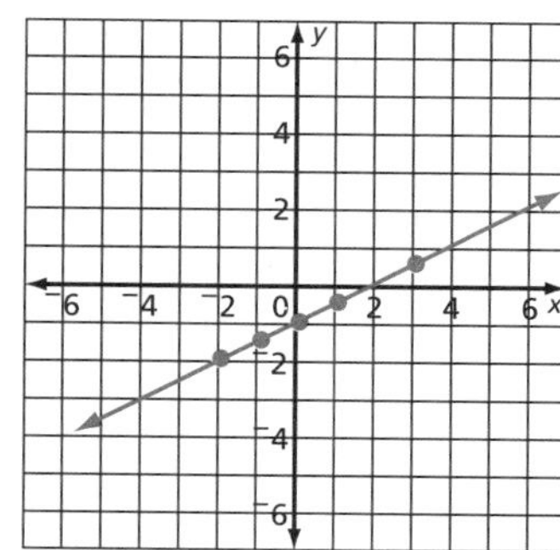

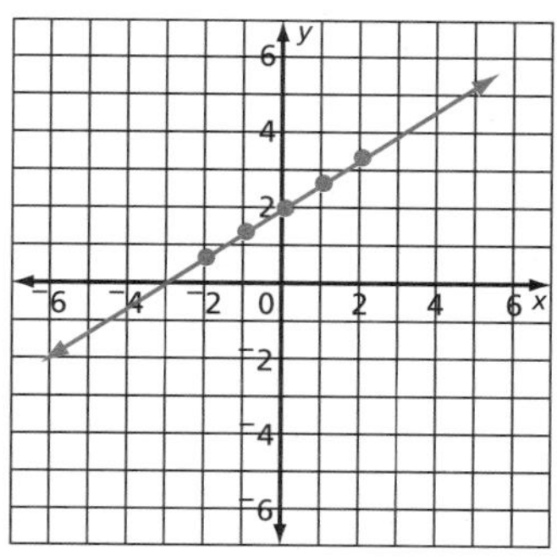

Problem Solving Reasoning **Use graph paper to draw a coordinate grid. Solve.**

Check students' graphs.

7. Plot the points (1,2), (1,$^-3$), (1,5), and (1,$^-6$). Connect the points in order. Are the points part of a function? Will its graph be a linear function? Explain.

No; There are many *y*-values for the same *x*-values.

Quick Check

Write the coordinates of the image point.

8. The point **(1, 2)** translated **2** units right and **4** units down.
(3, $^-2$)

9. The point **(1, 2)** reflected over the ***y***-axis. ($^-1$, 2)

Complete the table of values.

10. $y = x - 5$

x	y
6	1
5	0
7	2
10	5

11. $y = x + 2$

x	y
1	3
0	2
3	5
5	7

12. Which is the independent variable, ***x*** or ***y***? *x*

13. Graph the equations in exercises **10** and **11** in the coordinate plane. State whether the graphs are the graphs of linear functions or not. They are.

Work Space

Item	Error Analysis
8-9	**Common Error** Students may apply the rules to the wrong coordinate. **Reteaching** Reteach 98
10–11	**Common Error** Watch for students who cannot find *y*, given *x*. **Reteaching** Reteach 99
12–13	**Common Error** Students may not graph the points in the correct *x*-, *y*-order. **Reteaching** Reteach 100

Closing the Lesson *Do you know any formulas that are linear functions?* (Possible answers: $C = 2\pi r$; $S = (n - 2)180$ for the number of degrees in the angles of a polygon; $P = 4s$ for the perimeter P of a square of side s)

Name ______________________________

Slope of a Line

Guided Practice: First ex. in Rows 1 & 4, pp. 336–337
Independent Practice: Complete pp. 336–337

The slope of a line is its steepness. Imagine that the line in the graph below is the side of a hill. You can see that the slope is very steep. The **slope of a line** (abbreviated as ***m***) is the ratio of the change in the ***y*** values to the change in the ***x*** values between any two points on the line.

$$\textbf{slope} = \frac{\textbf{change in } y \textbf{ values}}{\textbf{change in } x \textbf{ values}}$$

The graph at the right shows the line $y = 2x - 3$. Two points on the graph are **(0, ⁻3)** and **(2, 1)**. The *y*-values change from **⁻3** to **1**. The *x*-values change from **0** to **2**.

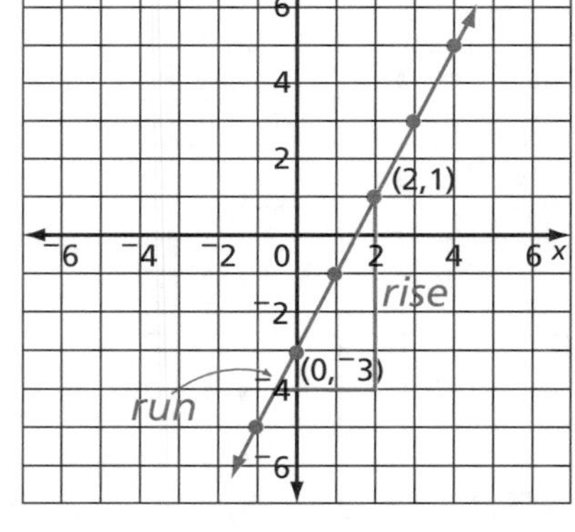

$$\text{slope } (m) = \frac{1 - (^{-}3)}{2 - 0}$$
$$= \frac{4}{2} \text{ So, } m = 2.$$

The change in the two ***y***-values is called the **rise**. The change in the two ***x***-values is called the **run**. You can think of slope as

$$\textbf{slope} = \frac{\textbf{rise}}{\textbf{run}}$$

It does not matter which two points you select on the line. The slope remains constant. For example, the points **(3,3)** and **(10,17)** are both on the line. The slope of the line is

$$\textbf{slope} = \frac{17 - 3}{10 - 3} = \frac{14}{7} \text{ So, } m = 2. \quad \text{or} \quad \textbf{slope} = \frac{3 - 17}{3 - 10} = \frac{^{-}14}{^{-}7} \text{ So, } m = 2.$$

Notice that the slope of the line is the same as the coefficient of ***x*** in the linear function $y = 2x - 3$.

Find the slope *m* of the line.

1. $y = 4x + 3$ — $m =$ 4

$y = {}^{-}\frac{3}{5}x - 2$ — $m =$ $-\frac{3}{5}$

$y = 1.2x + 5$ — $m =$ 1.2

2. $y = {}^{-}5x + 1$ — $m =$ ⁻5

$y = \frac{4}{3}x + 2$ — $m =$ $\frac{4}{3}$

$y = {}^{-}2.7x - 2$ — $m =$ ⁻2.7

3. $y = 2$ — $m =$ 0

$y = x - 5$ — $m =$ 1

$y = x$ — $m =$ 1

Name ______________________________

Find the slope m of the line shown on the coordinate grid.

4.

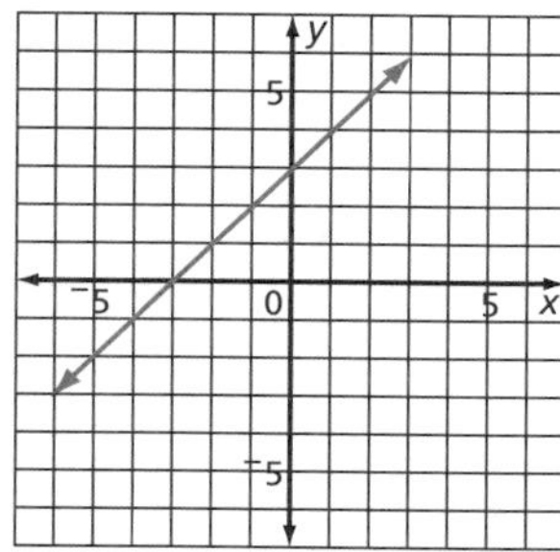

$m =$ 1

5.

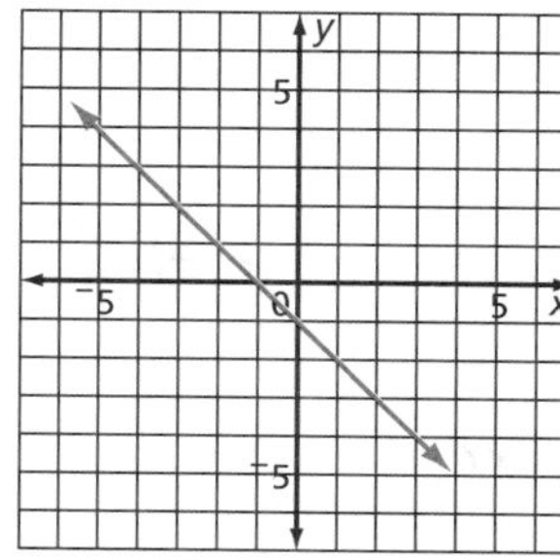

$m =$ $^-1$

6.

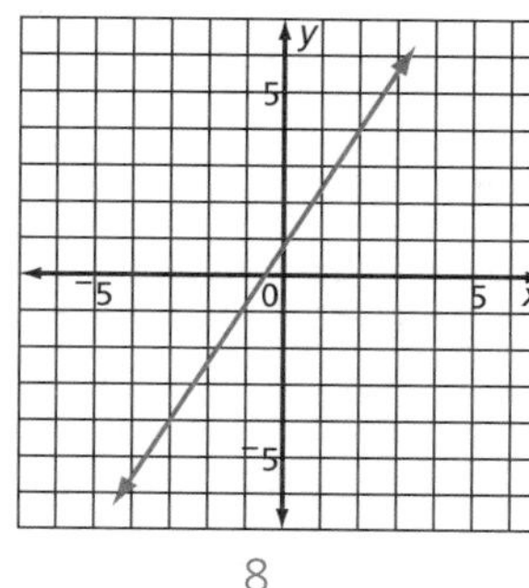

$m =$ $\frac{8}{5}$

7.

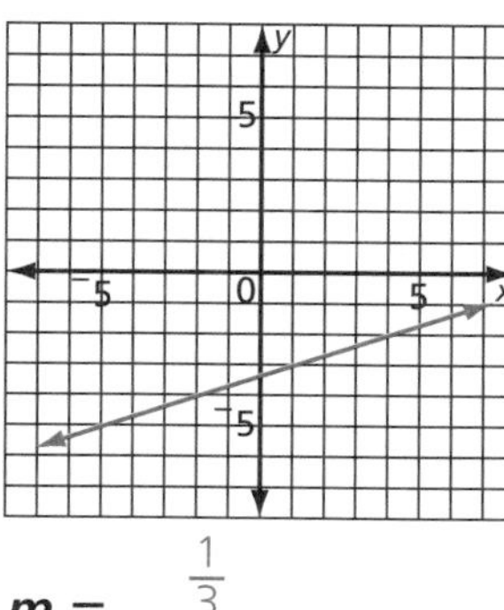

$m =$ $\frac{1}{3}$

8.

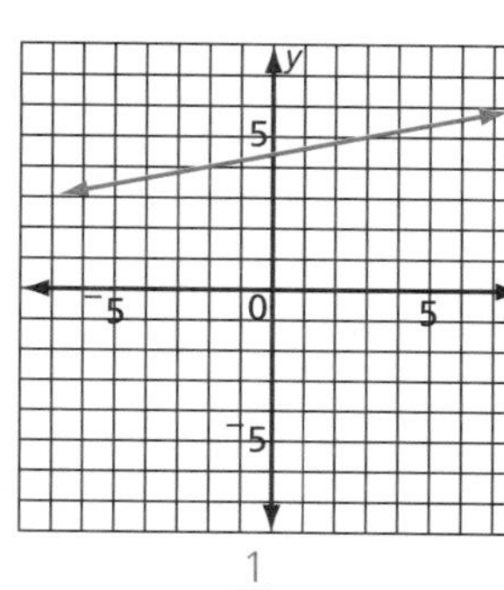

$m =$ $\frac{1}{5}$

9.

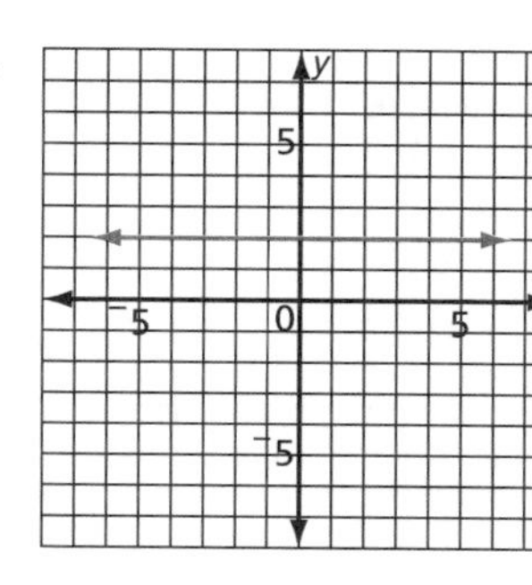

$m =$ 0

Problem Solving Reasoning Solve.

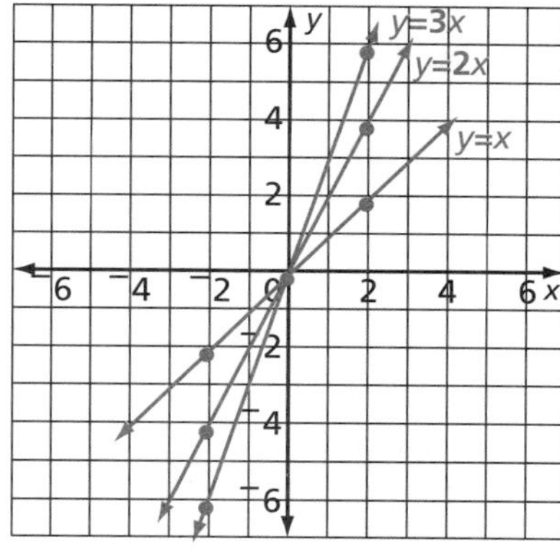

10. Graph each of the following linear functions using the values $x = 0$, $x = 1$, and $x = 2$ on the coordinate grid.

$y = x$ $y = 2x$ $y = 3x$

11. How is the steepness of the graphs related to the coefficients of x? It increases as the coefficient increases.

12. At what point do all the lines meet? (0, 0)

Test Prep ★ Mixed Review

13 Sue has used a grid to draw a geometric figure that is symmetrical about the y-axis. One of the points of the figure is ($^-3$, 4). What are the coordinates of its matching point? C; Obj. 11B

A (3, $^-4$) C (3, 4)

B ($^-3$, $^-4$) D ($^-3$, 4)

14 A rectangle *ABCD* has been drawn on a grid, and its translation image is *EFGH*. *C* is the point (3, 2) and *A* is the point (0, 4). If point *G* (the image of point *C*) has coordinates (8, 4), what are the coordinates of the point *E*? H; Obj. 11D

F (0, 6) H (5, 6)

G (6, 5) J (5, 4)

Name ______________________________

Direct Variation

Guided Practice: First ex. in Rows 1, 3 & 5, pp 338–339
Independent Practice: Complete pp. 338–339

You know that sometimes two numbers can vary in direct proportion to each other. For example, if you always leave a **15%** tip, then the amount of your tip is in direct proportion to the cost of your meal.

Cost of Meal	Amount of Tip
\$1	\$.15
\$2	\$.30
\$3	\$.45
\$4	\$.60
\$5	\$.75
x	$0.15x$

The table shows some values for this relationship.

This pattern can be written as $y = 0.15x$. *Direct variation* is another way of talking about direct proportions.

> Two variables x and y form a **direct variation** if they are related by a linear function of the form $y = mx$, where m is a non-zero constant called the **constant of variation**. It represents the rate at which the function is changing.

- Tell whether the relationship is a direct variation. If it is, state the constant of variation.

a.

x	6	7	8	9
y	9	10.5	12	13.5

Each y value is **1.5** times the x value. This is a direct variation, and the constant of variation is **1.5**.

b.

x	4	5	6	7
y	9	11	13	15

The values are related by the equation $y = 2x + 1$.

This is not a direct variation. The ratios $\frac{y}{x}$ are not constant, so there is no constant of variation.

- A variable k varies directly with t. When $t = 5$, $k = 40$. What is the constant of variation?

You know that this is a direct variation, so

$$k = mt$$

Substitute for k and t. $\quad 40 = m(5)$

Divide each side by **5**. $\quad \frac{40}{5} = \frac{m(5)}{5}$

Simplify. $\quad 8 = m$

The variable k is changing at a rate that is **8** times that of t.

State whether the relationship defines a direct variation. If it does, state the constant of variation, m.

1. $y = 3x$ yes; $m = 3$ $\qquad y = \frac{1}{2}x$ yes; $m = \frac{1}{2}$ $\qquad y = 5x + 1$ no

2. $y = 2x^2$ no $\qquad y = 0.6x - 2$ no $\qquad y = \frac{3}{4}x$ yes; $m = \frac{3}{4}$

Find the constant of variation.

3. $y = 9$ when $x = 3$ $m = 3$ $\qquad y = 210$ when $x = 30$ $m = 7$ $\qquad y = 5.6$ when $x = 0.7$ $m = 8$

4. $y = 9.6$ when $x = 4$ $m = 2.4$ $\qquad y = 16.74$ when $x = 5.4$ $m = 3.1$ $\qquad y = 1\frac{3}{4}$ when $x = \frac{1}{2}$ $m = 3\frac{1}{2}$

Check Understanding *If 2.3 is the constant of variation between two variables x and y, what would be the equation for the direct variation? ($y = 2.3x$)*

Name ________________________________

Latoya, Carlos, and Paula read at different rates. Paula reads **0.5** page per minute, Carlos reads **1** page, and Latoya reads **2** pages. You can write these relationships as

$$p = 0.5t, \quad p = t, \quad \text{and} \quad p = 2t$$

The variable p is the number of pages and t is the time spent reading, in minutes. These equations are all direct variations.

The equations are graphed at the right. Notice that the constant of variation equals the slope of the line. You can use the graph to estimate answers about the friends and their reading rates.

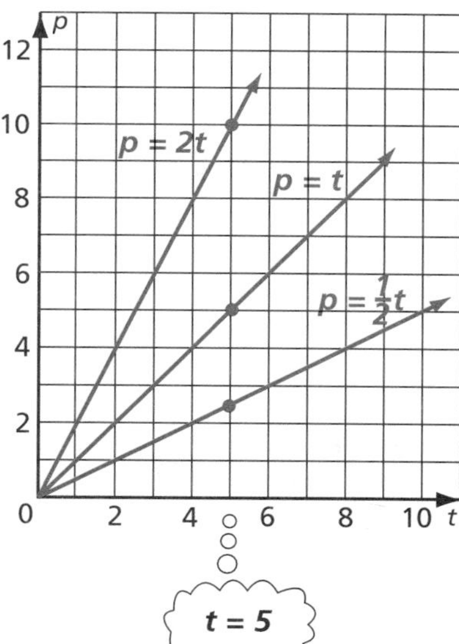

About how many pages will the three students each read in **5** minutes?

You can look at each graph at $t = 5$. You find that Paula will read about **2.5** pages, Carlos will read about **5** pages, and Latoya will read about **10** pages.

Graph the direct variation.

5. $C = 3.14d$

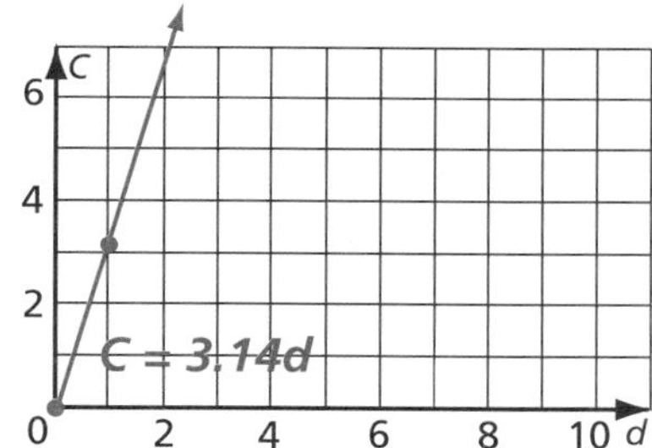

6. $s = 5t$

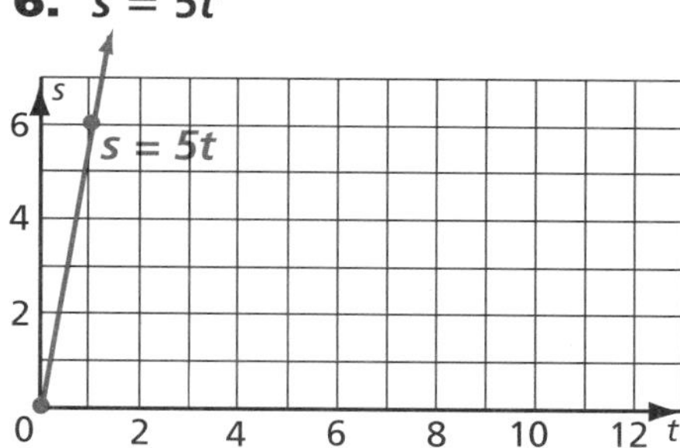

7. $y = \frac{1}{3}x$

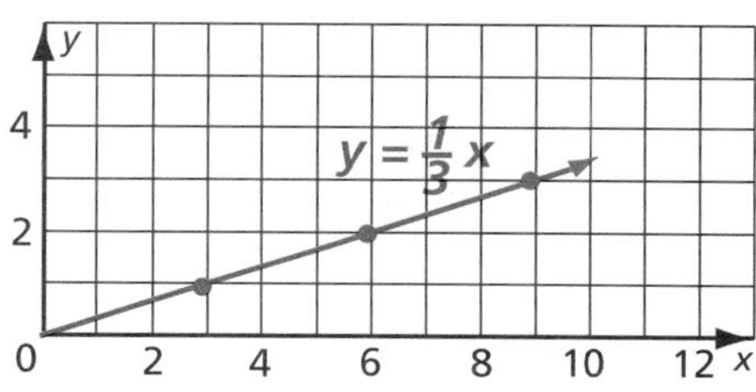

Problem Solving Reasoning Solve.

8. A car averages **27** miles per gallon of gasoline. Find the constant of variation and use it to find the number of miles it will travel on **15** gallons.

$m = 27$; 405 miles

9. A book has **48** lines of type per page. Find the constant of variation and use it to find the number of pages that **312** lines of type will fill.

$m = 48$; 6.5 pages

Test Prep ★ Mixed Review

10 **Pat repairs appliances. She charges $75 to check out the appliance and, after that, $50 per hour ($h$). Her total charge ($C$) can be written as a function: $C = 50h + 75$.**

What does she charge after $5\frac{1}{2}$ hours? A; Obj. 11E

A $350   C $300

B $325   D $275

11 **If you were to draw the graph of Pat's total charges function, what would the slope of the graph be?** G; Obj. 11E

F 75   H $5\frac{1}{2}$

G 50   J 0

Closing the Lesson *Can you think of some everyday examples of direct variation?* (Possible answers: sales taxes; the perimeter of a square versus the length of a side)

Name ____________________

Guided Practice: Problem 1, p. 341

Independent Practice: Complete pp. 340–341

Problem Solving Strategy: Write an Equation

This graph shows how the total amount Jayne is paid **(*P*)** depends on the number of lawns **(*n*)** she mows. How much will she earn if she mows **80** lawns during the summer?

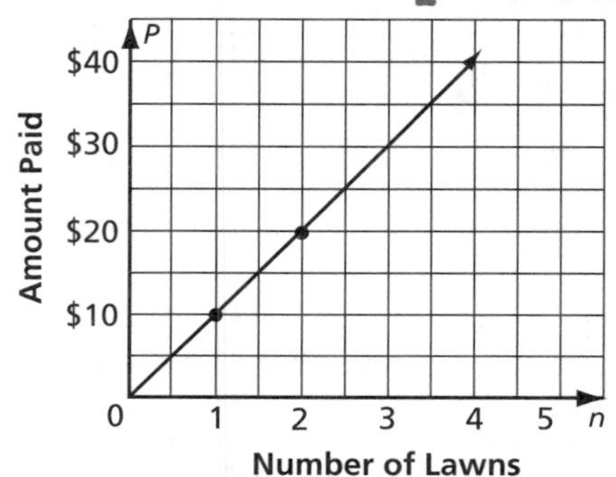

It's not always possible to extend a graph or table to answer a problem. One way to solve this problem is to write an equation that relates the variables.

1 Understand

"Asking yourself questions will help you identify which is the dependent variable and which is the independent variable."

As you read, ask yourself questions.

- What do you already know?

  Jayne is paid each time she mows a lawn, so ***n*** is the independent variable.

  The graph is the graph of a direct variation of the form ***y = mx*.** Some ordered pairs on the graph are **(1, 10)** and **(2, 20)**

- What do you need to find?

  the constant of variation that tells how the ordered pairs are related

2 Decide

"What do the variables mean? How are they related?"

Choose a method for solving.

Try the strategy Write an Equation.

- Let ***n*** be the number of lawns Jayne mows and ***P*** be the total amount she is paid.
- Find the value of ***m***, the constant of variation. 10

Write the equation. $10 \cdot n = P$

3 Solve

"Is the answer to the equation the solution of the problem?"

Use the equation to solve the problem.

Remember to keep your equal signs aligned.

Solution:

$$\begin{aligned} 10n &= P \\ 10(80) &= P \\ 800 &= P \end{aligned}$$

4 Look back

"Look back at the original graph. Is your equation reasonable? Make sure you use the correct labels in the answers."

Check your answer.

Use some other ordered pairs from the graph to check your equation.

Write your answer as a full sentence.

Answer Jayne will earn $800.00.

Check Understanding *If a fair costs $5.00 to enter and $.65 a ride, write an equation for what you spent (y) if you went on x rides.* ($y = 5 + 0.65x$)

Name ______________________

Use the Write an Equation strategy or any other strategy you have learned to solve these problems.

1. An Internet provider includes a service charge of **$18** per month (***m***) on the bill. How much will a customer pay in service charges (***S***) from April through December?

Think: How many months is it from April through December?

9 months

$s = 18m$; $162

2. A mobile phone company charges its customers a flat fee of **$10** per month and **$.19** for each minute or fraction of a minute (***x***) of use. In the month of May, Jana used her mobile phone a total of **82.5** minutes. What was her monthly bill for May (***y***)?

Think: What operations will you use in your equation?

addition and multiplication

$y = 10 + 0.19x$; $25.68

3. Saul is paid **$15** each time he mows his neighbor's yard (***n***). If he mows all summer he will also get a **$50** bonus. From June through September, Saul mowed the lawn **25** times. How much did his neighbor pay him (***P***)?

$P = 15n + 50$; $425

4. Star Bank automatically adds a **$5.00** bonus for opening a new savings account. Saul opened a new account in September and deposited **$100**. If the bank pays **0.3%** per month interest on deposits, how much does Saul have in his account at the end of September?

about $105.32

5. The ordered pairs show how the score (***s***) depends on the number of questions answered correctly (***n***). If Toria answered **25** questions correctly, what was her score?

n	0	4	8	10
s	0	16	32	40

$s = 4n$; 100 points

6. The table shows how far (***d***) a car that is traveling at a constant rate of speed goes in ***t*** hours. How long would it take the car to travel **150** miles?

t	0	0.5	4	6
d	0	27.5	220	330

$d = 55t$; $2\frac{8}{11}h$ or $2.73h$

7. The ***y***-values for a function are one less than twice the difference between the ***x***-values and **3**. If ***x* = 3**, then what is the corresponding value for ***y***?

$y = 2(x - 3) - 1$; $^{-}1$

8. The ***y***-values are one half of the difference between the ***x***-values and **4**. If ***y* = 3**, then what is the corresponding value for ***x***?

$y = \frac{1}{2}(x - 4)$; 10

Closing the Lesson *How does writing an equation help you solve a problem?* (Possible answer: It helps you generalize from particular ones.)

Name ________________________________

Guided Practice: Ex. 1, p. 345

Independent Practice: Complete pp. 345–347

Non-Linear Functions

A function in x and y is a rule that generates ordered pairs. For each x-value you substitute into the rule, there is exactly one corresponding y-value. You have learned to use ordered pairs for linear functions. However, not all functions are linear.

$A = s^2$	
s	A
0	0
0.5	0.25
1.0	1
1.5	2.25
2.0	4
2.5	6.25
3.0	9

Think about this formula for the area of a square: The area of a square is $A = s^2$, where s is the length of a side.

Look at the table of ordered pairs at the right. For each s-value, there is exactly one value for A. The formula $A = s^2$ is an example of a function. The area A depends on the length of a side s; so, A is a function of s. Notice that there are no negative values in the table, since there is no square with a side that is a negative number.

In the graph of this function, the horizontal axis is the s-axis and the vertical axis is the A-axis. Remember that you can use different scales for the axes.

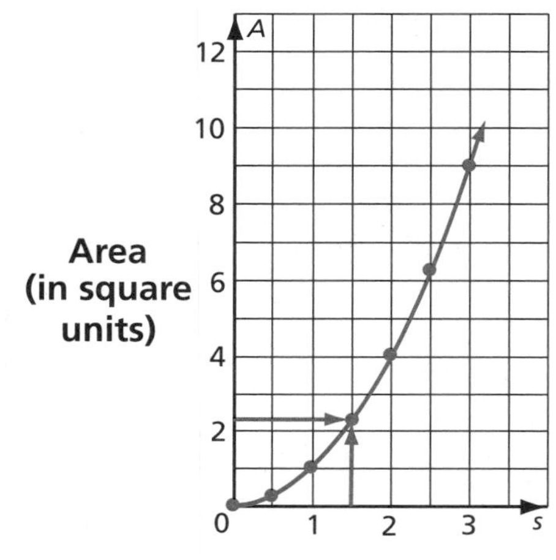

You can see that the area of a square with side **1.5** units is **2.25** square units. From the shape of the graph you can see that $A = s^2$ is the graph of a **non-linear function**.

Suppose that s could be a negative number. If $s = {}^-1$, then $A = 1$; if $s = {}^-2$, then $A = 4$, if $s = {}^-3$, then $A = 9$. If we plot the points **(⁻1, 1), (⁻2, 4), (⁻3, 9)**, the graph would be a curve called a **parabola** that is symmetric to the y-axis, and non-linear.

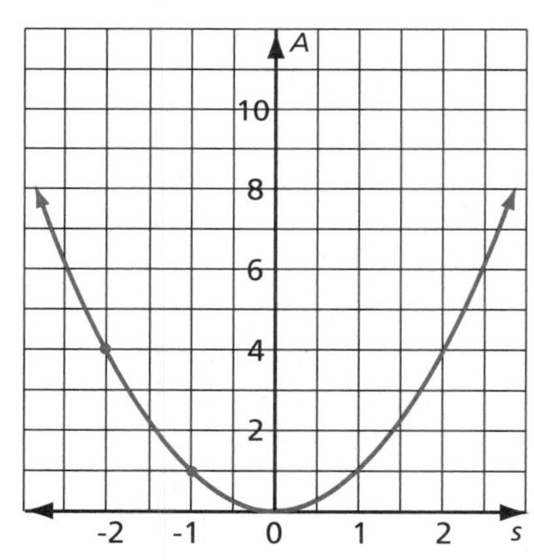

Check Understanding *Which of the following are non-linear functions?* $y = x^2 + 1$, $y = 2x - 5$, $y = 3 - x^2$. (The first and third equations are non-linear functions.)

Name ______________________

The volume of a cube is $V = s^3$, where s is the length of a side of a cube. Again, notice that there are no negative values of s in the table, since volume cannot be negative. The values of V increase very rapidly as the length of a side increases. Choosing an appropriate scale for the graph is difficult because of the rapid increase in V. In the graph, the horizontal axis represents the length of a side s and the vertical axis represents the volume V.

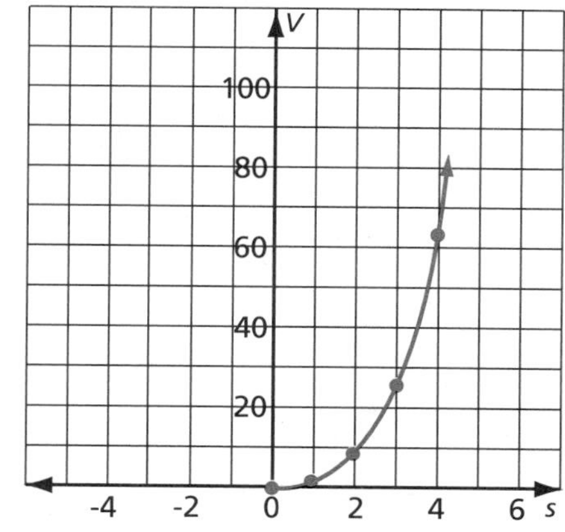

$V = s^3$	s	0	1	2	3	4	5
	V	0	1	8	27	64	125

If s could be a negative number, then the graph at the right represents $V = s^3$. It is a non-linear function that decreases very rapidly as s decreases.

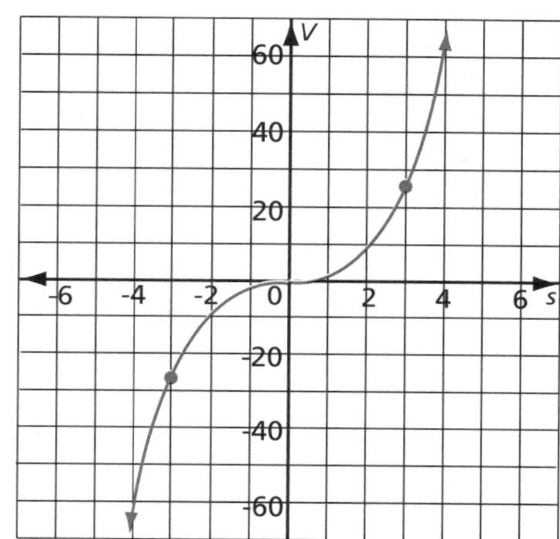

$V = s^3$	s	0	1	2	3	4	5
	V	0	1	8	27	64	125

Complete the table of values for the function. Graph the function on a coordinate grid. State whether the function is linear or non-linear. Check students' graphs.

1.

$y = x^2$	
x	**y**
0	0
⁻1	1
1	1
⁻2	4
2	4
⁻3	9
3	9

non-linear

2.

$y = 2x + 1$	
x	**y**
0	1
⁻1	⁻1
1	3
⁻2	⁻3
2	5
⁻3	⁻5
3	7

linear

3.

$y = x^3 - 1$	
x	**y**
0	⁻1
⁻1	⁻2
1	0
⁻2	⁻9
2	7
⁻3	⁻28
3	26

non-linear

The following problems involve formulas that you have used in this unit. Select appropriate values and complete a table. Graph the function on a coordinate grid. State whether the function is linear or non-linear. Table values will vary.

Area of a Circle

4. ← Formula

$A = \pi r^2$	
r	*A*
1	3.14
2	12.56
3	28.26
4	50.24
5	78.5
6	113.04

non-linear

Circumference of a Circle

5. ← Formula

$C = 2\pi r$	
r	*C*
1	6.28
2	12.56
3	18.84
4	25.12
5	31.40
6	37.68

linear

Perimeter of a Square

6. ← Formula

$P = 4s$	
s	*P*
1	4
2	8
3	12
4	16
5	20
6	24

linear

Problem Solving
Reasoning

Complete.

Two variables ***x*** and ***y*** form an **inverse variation** if there is a positive number ***k*** such that ***xy* = *k*.** Here are two tables that relate rate **(*x*)** and time **(*y*)**.

A

x	*y*
24	0.5
12	1
6	2
3	4

B

x	*y*
24	1
12	2
6	3
3	4

7. Which table shows an inverse variation? What is the value of ***k***?

table A; 12

8. Use your answer from exercise 7 to extend the table of ordered pairs (be sure to include some negative values for ***x***) and graph them. State whether the function is linear or non-linear.

Graph is a hyperbola in the first and third quadrants. Graph is non-linear.

Quick Check

Find the slope of the line.

9. $y = 3x - 8$ 3

10. $y = 0.2x + 18$ 0.2

11. $y = 3x$ 3

Find the constant of direct variation.

12. $y = 10$ when $x = 2$ 5

13. $y = 3$ when $x = 5$ $\frac{3}{5}$

14. Is the graph of $y = \frac{2}{3}x^2 - 1$ linear or non-linear? How do you know? Non-linear; The graph of a function in x^2 is a parabola.

Work Space

Item	Error Analysis
9–11	**Common Error:** Students may forget that the slope is the coefficient of *x*. **Reteaching** Reteach 101
12–13	**Common Error:** Students may reverse the order of the variables. **Reteaching** Reteach 102
14	**Common Error:** Watch for students who use x^2, not *x*. **Reteaching** Reteach 103

Closing the Lesson *What is a non-linear function?* (Possible answer: It is a function whose graph is not a straight line.)

Name ___________________________________

Translate the given figure according to the directions given.

1. Right **6** units, Down **4** units

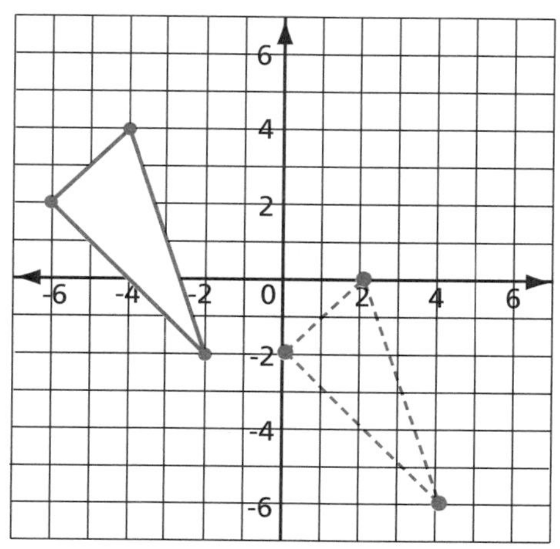

2. Left **5** units, Up **3** units

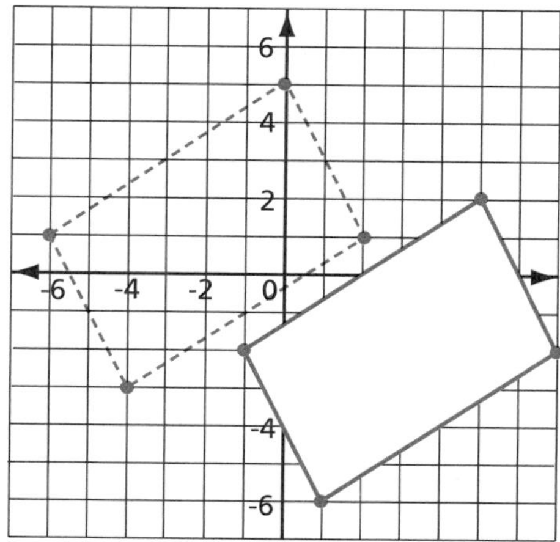

Reflect the figure over the given axis.

3. Reflect over the *y*-axis

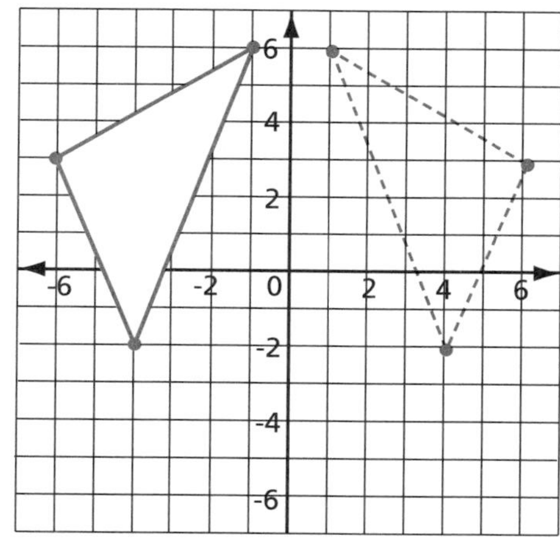

4. Reflect over the *x*-axis

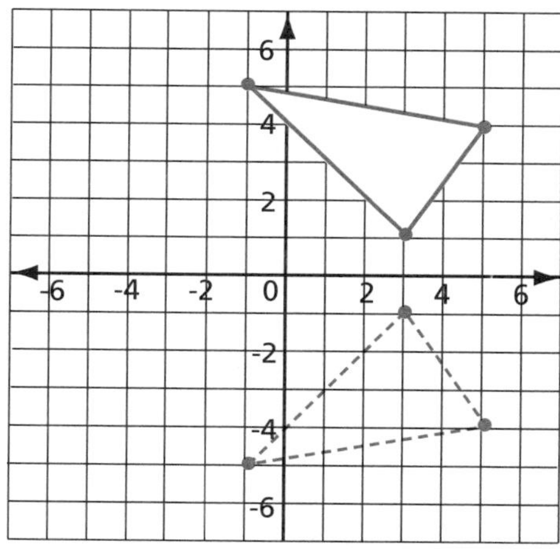

Complete the table of values for the given function. State whether the function is linear or non-linear.

5.

$y = 4x$	
x	**y**
2	8
3	12
0	0
$^-1$	$^-4$

linear

6.

$y = \frac{^-2}{3}x$	
x	**y**
0	0
3	$^-2$
$^-3$	2
$^-2$	$\frac{4}{3}$

linear

7.

$y = {}^-x + 2$	
x	**y**
4	$^-2$
$^-2$	4
1	1
0	2

linear

8.

$y = x^2 + 1$	
x	**y**
1	2
0	1
$^-2$	5
$^-1$	2

non-linear

9.

$y = x^3$	
x	**y**
0	0
$^-2$	$^-8$
1	1
$^-1$	$^-1$

non-linear

On the grid below, complete the figure so it is symmetric to the given axis.

10. Symmetric about *y*-axis

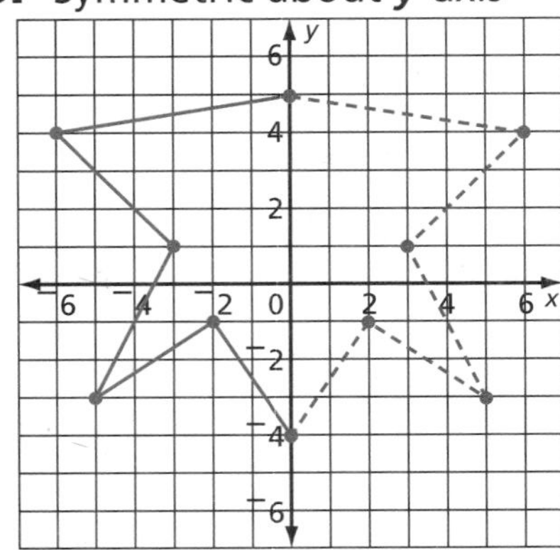

11. Symmetric about *x*-axis

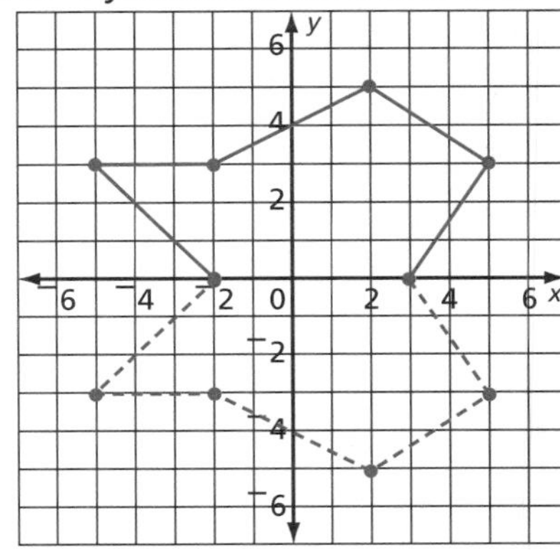

Graph the linear function on the coordinate grid.

12. $y = 2x - 5$

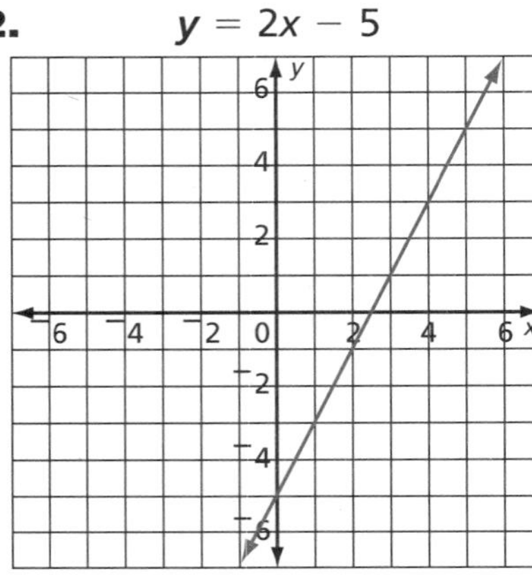

13. $y = -x + 2$

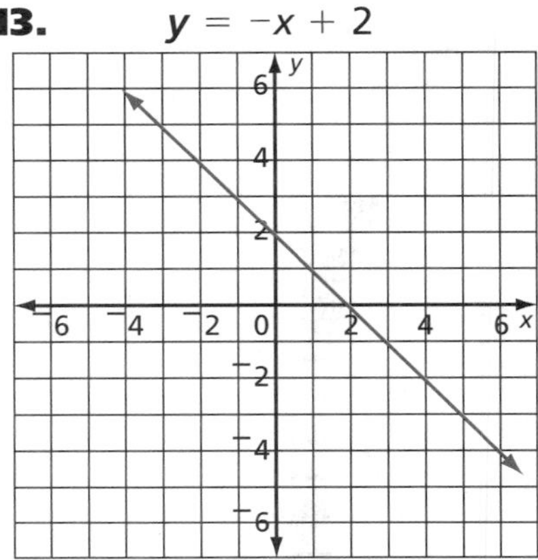

Find the slope of the linear function.

14. $y = 3x - 7$ 3

15. $y = -\frac{4}{5}x + 2$ $\frac{-4}{5}$

16. $y = {}^{-}x + 3$ $^{-}1$

17. $y = \frac{1}{3}x - 4$ $\frac{1}{3}$

Find the constant of variation.

18. $y = 15$ when $x = 3$ 5

19. $y = 2$ when $x = 10$ $\frac{1}{5}$

20. $y = 13$ when $x = 4$ $\frac{13}{4}$

The figures are similar. Find the missing lengths.

21.

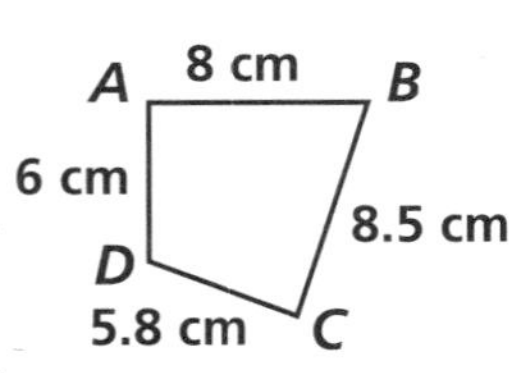

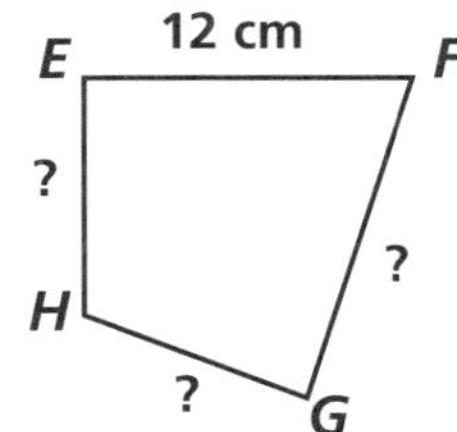

$\overline{FG}$ 12.75 cm

$\overline{GH}$ 8.7 cm

$\overline{HE}$ 9 cm

Name ______________________

Find the slope of the line.

22.

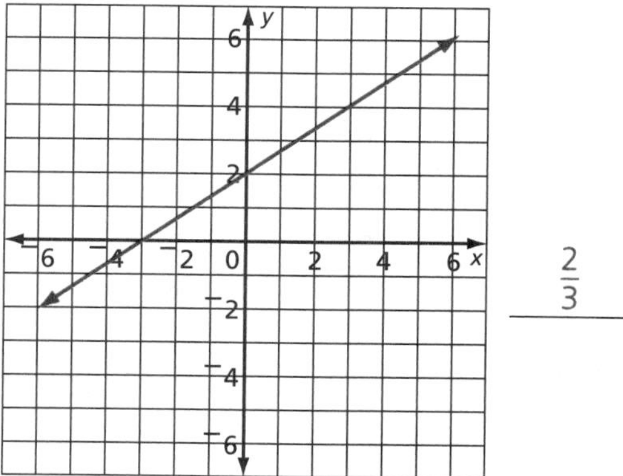

$\frac{2}{3}$

23.

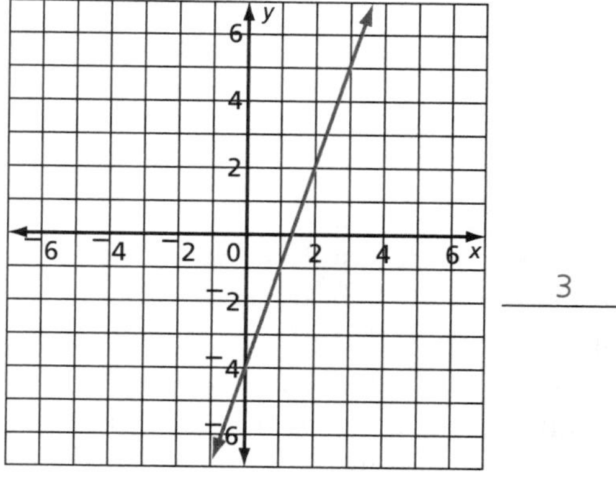

3

Graph the non-linear function.

24. $y = 2x^2 - 3$

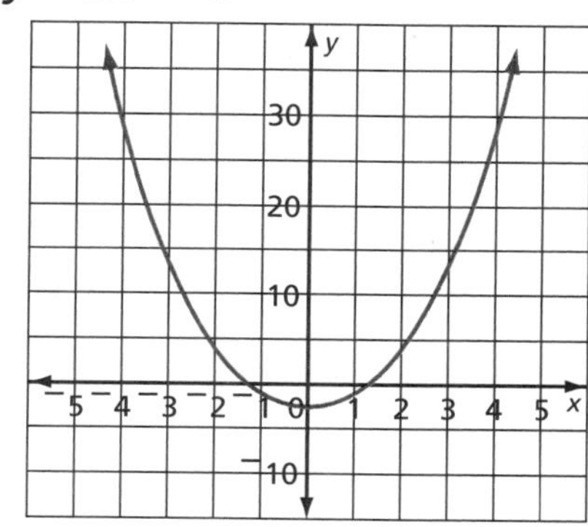

25. $y = x^2 + 1$

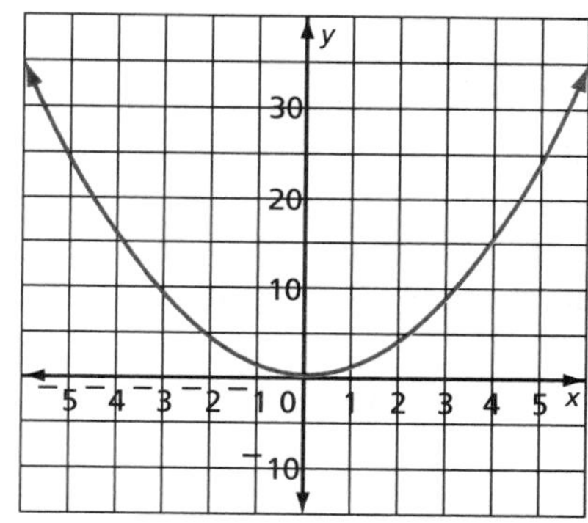

Solve.

26. A map has a scale of **1** inch:**50** miles. Two cities are $2\frac{3}{4}$ inches apart on the map. What is the actual distance between the cities? 137.5 miles

27. Practice times depend on the age of a student. The average practice time for a **5** year-old is about **13** minutes, while that for a **12** year-old is about **34** minutes. Choose the equation that shows this relationship.

(circled) $y = 3x - 2$ $\quad$ $y = x + 5 + 12$ $\quad$ $y = 12 - 3x$ $\quad$ $y = 5x + 13$

Write an equation to solve the problem.

28. The ordered pairs are part of a function that shows how much an office spent per day for paper. Write an equation that shows how the ordered pairs are related. $y = 20x$

x	0	1	2	3
y	0	$20	$40	$60

Use your equation to find out the paper cost for **250** days. $5,000

Name ______________________________

Cumulative Review ★ Test Prep

Students will need grid paper for this review.

1 **Steve is a paint supplier. He charges a flat rate of $30 for use of his spray-painting equipment and, after that, $13 per gallon (*g*) for latex paint. So his total charge (*C*) can be written as a function: $C = 13g + 30$. If you were to draw the graph of the function, what would the slope of the graph be?** B; Obj. 11E

A 30 **C** $\frac{30}{13}$

B 13 **D** $\frac{13}{30}$

2 **A triangle *ABC* has been drawn on a grid, and its translation image is △*DEF*. *A* is the point (3, 6) and *B* is the point (1, 3). If point *D* (the image of point *A*) has coordinates (8, 9), what are the coordinates of the point *E*?** G; Obj. 11D

F (4, 5) **H** (9, 3)

G (6, 6) **J** (9, 8)

3 **A light-year, the distance traveled by light in 1 year, is about five trillion, eight hundred seventy billion miles. Which of these is the closest to that number?** B; Obj. 9C

A 5.87×10^{10} **C** 5.87×10^{8}

B 5.87×10^{12} **D** 5.87×10^{18}

4 **What is the value of the expression: $|{}^-30| + {}^-25 \div {}^-5$?** G; Obj. 8A, 8B, 8C

F 25 **H** $^-25$

G 35 **J** $^-30$

5 **The differences of the four times *p* subtracted from three is at least seven. What mathematical sentence best represents this?** B; Obj. 9E

A $3 - 4p = 7$ **D** $3 - 4p > 7$

B $3 - 4p \geq 7$ **E** Not here

C $4p - 3 \geq 7$

6 **Fourteen feet from the corner of a rectangular playing field Tina fixes one end of a 15-ft rope to a peg on the side line. Then, keeping the rope fully stretched, she moves toward the goal line until her end of the rope can be pegged exactly on the goal line. How far from the corner is that end of the rope?** G; Obj. 10D

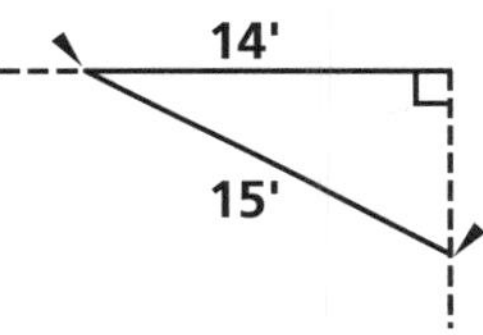

F 1 ft **H** 14.5 ft

G 5.4 ft **J** 29 ft

7 **If a cylindrical container can hold 65 ft³ of water, how much water could it hold if the radius remained the same but the height were doubled?** B; Obj. 10E

A 260 ft^3 **C** 105 ft^3

B 130 ft^3 **D** 65 ft^3

8 **A CD player was marked down from $98.98 to $84.99. About what was the percent of discount?** G; Obj. 4G

F 10% **J** 50%

G 15% **K** 86%

H 18%

Tables of Measures

Metric System

Prefixes

kilo (k)	=	1,000		
hecto (h)	=	100		
deka (da)	=	10		
deci (d)	=	0.1	=	$\frac{1}{10}$
centi (c)	=	0.01	=	$\frac{1}{100}$
milli (m)	=	0.001	=	$\frac{1}{1,000}$

Length

1 kilometer (km)	=	1,000 meters (m)
1 meter	=	10 decimeters (dm)
1 decimeter	=	10 centimeters (cm)
1 meter	=	100 centimeters (cm)
1 centimeter	=	10 millimeters (mm)
1 meter	=	1,000 millimeters
1 millimeter (mm)	=	0.001 meter

Capacity

1 kiloliter (kL)	=	1,000 liters (L)
1 centiliter (cL)	=	0.01 liter
1 liter	=	1,000 milliliters (mL)
1 milliliter (mL)	=	0.001 liter

Mass

1 metric ton (T)	=	1,000 kilograms (kg)
1 kilogram	=	1,000 grams (g)
1 centigram (cg)	=	0.01 gram
1 gram	=	1,000 milligrams (mg)
1 milligram (mg)	=	0.001 gram

Area

100 square mm (mm^2)	=	1 square cm (cm^2)
1 square m (m^2)	=	10,000 square cm
1 hectare (ha)	=	10,000 square m
1 square km (km^2)	=	1,000,000 sq m

Volume

1 cubic cm (cm^3)	=	1,000 cubic mm (mm^3)
1 cubic m (m^3)	=	1,000,000 cubic cm

Customary System

Length

1 foot (ft)	=	12 inches (in.)
1 yard (yd)	=	3 feet
1 yard	=	36 inches
1 mile (mi)	=	5,280 feet
1 mile	=	1,760 yards

Capacity

1 cup (c)	=	8 fluid ounces (fl oz)
1 pint (pt)	=	2 cups
1 quart (qt)	=	2 pints
1 gallon (gal)	=	4 quarts

Weight

1 pound (lb)	=	16 ounces (oz)
1 ton (T)	=	2,000 pounds

Area

1 square foot (ft^2)	=	144 square inches ($in.^2$)
1 square yard (yd^2)	=	9 square feet
1 acre (A)	=	4,840 square yards
1 square mile (mi^2)	=	640 acres

Volume

1 cubic foot (ft^3)	=	1,728 cubic inches ($in.^3$)
1 cubic yd (yd^3)	=	27 cubic feet

Other Measures

Time

1 minute (min)	=	60 seconds (s)
1 hour (h)	=	60 minutes
1 day (d)	=	24 hours
1 week (wk)	=	7 days
1 month (mo)	≈	4 weeks
1 year (yr)	=	12 months
1 year	=	52 weeks
1 year	=	365 days
1 leap year	=	366 days
1 decade	=	10 years
1 century	=	100 years

Counting

1 dozen (doz)	=	12 things
1 score	=	20 things
1 gross (gro)	=	12 dozen
1 gross	=	144 things

Geometric Formulas

Triangle

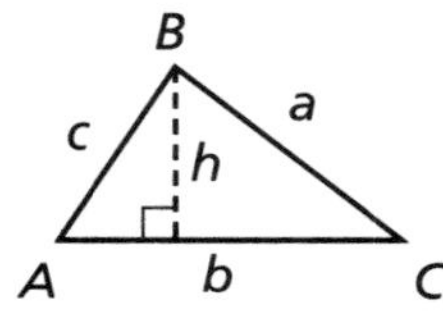

Perimeter:
$P = a + b + c$

Area:
$A = \frac{1}{2}bh$

Square

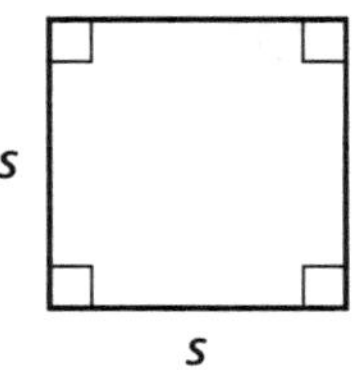

Perimeter:
$P = 4s$

Area:
$A = s^2$

Rectangle

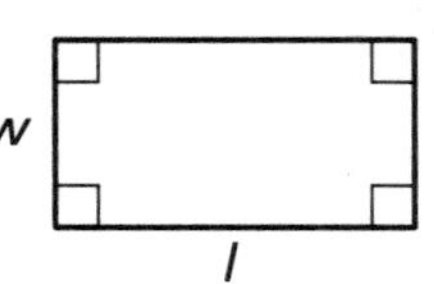

Perimeter:
$P = 2(l + w)$

Area:
$A = lw$

Parallelogram

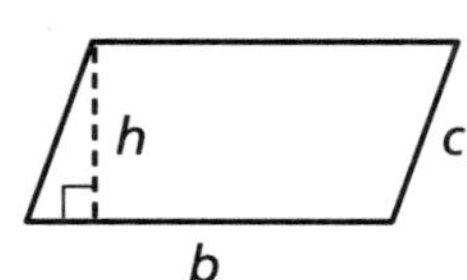

Area:
$A = bh$

Trapezoid

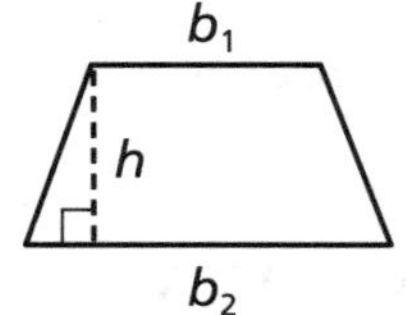

Area:
$A = \frac{1}{2}h(b_1 + b_2)$

Circle

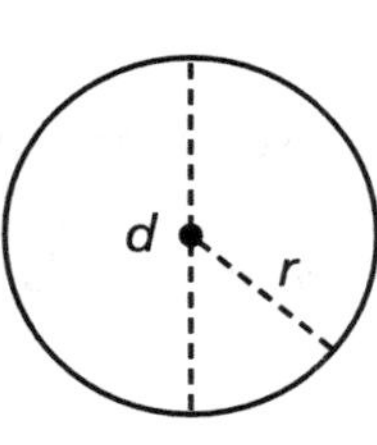

Circumference:
$C = 2\pi r$

Area:
$A = \pi r^2$

Rectangular Prism

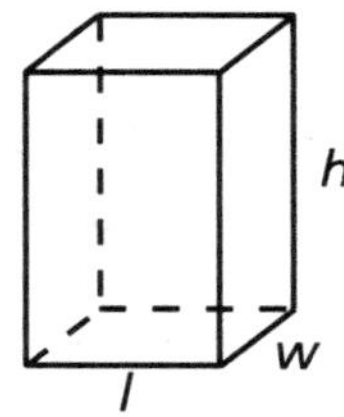

Surface Area:
$SA = 2(lw + wh + lh)$

Volume:
$V = lwh$

Cube

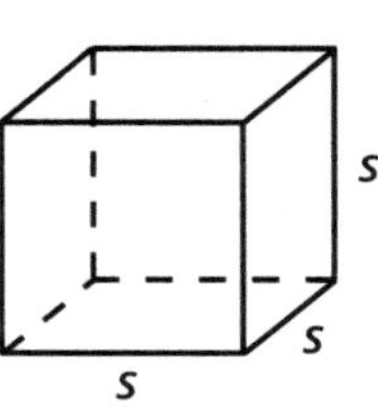

Surface Area:
$SA = 6s^2$

Volume:
$V = s^3$

Cylinder

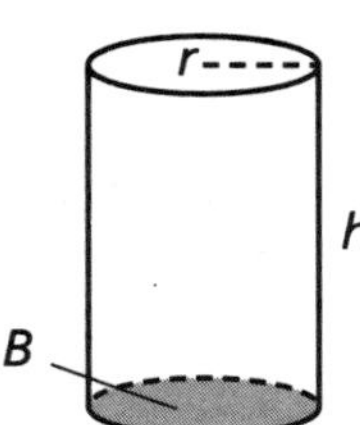

Surface Area:
$SA = 2\pi r^2 + 2\pi rh$

Other Formulas

	Distance (D) traveled	Simple Interest (I)	Percent (P) of a number
r = rate (in decimal form) t = time p = principal b = original base number	$D = rt$	$I = prt$	$P = br$

Symbols

$=$	is equal to	%	percent	$\perp$	is perpendicular to
$\neq$	is not equal to	°	degree	$\sim$	is similar to
$<$	is less than	$\angle A$	angle A	$\cong$	is congruent to
$>$	is greater than	$\overline{AB}$	line segment AB	5^4	5 to the fourth power $(5 \cdot 5 \cdot 5 \cdot 5)$
$\approx$	is approximately equal to	$\overrightarrow{AB}$	ray AB	π	pi
n, x	variables	$\overleftrightarrow{AB}$	line AB	$^{+}5$	positive 5
$0.\overline{37}$	0.37373737 . . . (repeating decimal)	$\triangle$	triangle	$^{-}5$	negative 5
$a:b$	the ratio of a to b	$\parallel$	is parallel to	$P(A)$	the probability of A

Equivalent Fractions and Percents

$50\% = \frac{1}{2}$	$16\frac{2}{3}\% = \frac{1}{6}$	$90\% = \frac{9}{10}$
$33\frac{1}{3}\% = \frac{1}{3}$	$83\frac{1}{3}\% = \frac{5}{6}$	$14\frac{2}{7}\% = \frac{1}{7}$
$66\frac{2}{3}\% = \frac{2}{3}$	$12\frac{1}{2}\% = \frac{1}{8}$	$11\frac{1}{9}\% = \frac{1}{9}$
$25\% = \frac{1}{4}$	$37\frac{1}{2}\% = \frac{3}{8}$	$9\frac{1}{11}\% = \frac{1}{11}$
$75\% = \frac{3}{4}$	$62\frac{1}{2}\% = \frac{5}{8}$	$8\frac{1}{3}\% = \frac{1}{12}$
$20\% = \frac{1}{5}$	$87\frac{1}{2}\% = \frac{7}{8}$	$5\% = \frac{1}{20}$
$40\% = \frac{2}{5}$	$10\% = \frac{1}{10}$	$4\% = \frac{1}{25}$
$60\% = \frac{3}{5}$	$30\% = \frac{3}{10}$	$2\frac{1}{2}\% = \frac{1}{40}$
$80\% = \frac{4}{5}$	$70\% = \frac{7}{10}$	$2\% = \frac{1}{50}$

Square Roots

Rational approximations are rounded to the nearest thousandth. Exact square roots are in red.

Number N	Positive Square Root $\sqrt{N}$	Number N	Positive Square Root $\sqrt{N}$	Number N	Positive Square Root $\sqrt{N}$	Number N	Positive Square Root $\sqrt{N}$
1	1	**26**	5.099	**51**	7.141	**76**	8.718
2	1.414	**27**	5.196	**52**	7.211	**77**	8.775
3	1.732	**28**	5.292	**53**	7.280	**78**	8.832
4	2	**29**	5.385	**54**	7.348	**79**	8.888
5	2.236	**30**	5.477	**55**	7.416	**80**	8.944
6	2.449	**31**	5.568	**56**	7.483	**81**	9
7	2.646	**32**	5.657	**57**	7.550	**82**	9.055
8	2.828	**33**	5.745	**58**	7.616	**83**	9.110
9	3	**34**	5.831	**59**	7.681	**84**	9.165
10	3.162	**35**	5.916	**60**	7.746	**85**	9.220
11	3.317	**36**	6	**61**	7.810	**86**	9.274
12	3.464	**37**	6.083	**62**	7.874	**87**	9.327
13	3.606	**38**	6.164	**63**	7.937	**88**	9.381
14	3.742	**39**	6.245	**64**	8	**89**	9.434
15	3.873	**40**	6.325	**65**	8.062	**90**	9.487
16	4	**41**	6.403	**66**	8.124	**91**	9.539
17	4.123	**42**	6.481	**67**	8.185	**92**	9.592
18	4.243	**43**	6.557	**68**	8.246	**93**	9.644
19	4.359	**44**	6.633	**69**	8.307	**94**	9.695
20	4.472	**45**	6.708	**70**	8.367	**95**	9.747
21	4.583	**46**	6.782	**71**	8.426	**96**	9.798
22	4.690	**47**	6.856	**72**	8.485	**97**	9.849
23	4.796	**48**	6.928	**73**	8.544	**98**	9.899
24	4.899	**49**	7	**74**	8.602	**99**	9.950
25	5	**50**	7.071	**75**	8.660	**100**	10

Glossary

A

absolute value The distance of a number from zero on the number line, regardless of direction

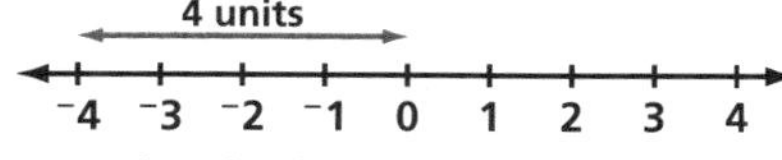

The absolute value of ⁻4 is 4.

acute angle An angle whose measure is between 0° and 90°

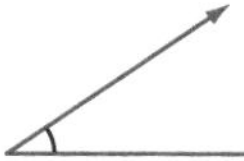

acute triangle A triangle with acute angles

addend (see *addition*)

addition The arithmetic operation that combines two numbers

Example: 23 ⟵ addend
+ 13 ⟵ addend
36 ⟵ sum

addition property of equality If two expressions are equivalent, then adding the same number to each forms two more equal expressions.
Example: If $n - 7 = 10$, then $n - 7 + 7 = 10 + 7$

additive inverse (see *opposites*)

adjacent angles Two angles that share a common vertex with a common side between them

alternate interior angles (on a tranversal) Pairs of angles that are on opposite sides of the transversal and interior to the lines

altitude A segment of a triangle, parallelogram, or trapezoid that is perpendicular to the base. In a triangle one endpoint is the vertex opposite the base.

amount due The amount you pay back to the bank; that is, principal plus interest

angle A geometric figure formed by two rays with a common endpoint called the vertex. The angle below can be named either ∠ABC or ∠B.

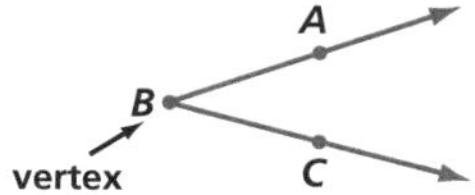

angle bisector A ray that divides an angle into two adjacent angles of equal measure

arc Two points on a circle and all the points of the circle between them.

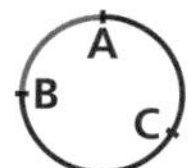

$\overset{\frown}{AB}$: *minor arc*
$\overset{\frown}{ACB}$: *major arc*

area A measure of a region or a surface. A square is used as a unit.

associative property of addition The grouping of the addends does not change the sum
Example: $(37 + 95) + 5 = 37 + (95 + 5) = 137$

associative property of multiplication The grouping of the factors does not change the product
Example:
$(25 \cdot 5) \cdot 2 = 27 \cdot (5 \cdot 2) = 270$

average A measure of central tendency. It is computed by adding all the items of data and dividing by the number of items.

axis (see *x*-axis, *y*-axis)

B

bar graph A graph that uses lengths of bars to represent the data

base (number) That part of the percent equation that represents the entire original amount.
Example: 25% of 16 is 4.
rate (*r*) × base (*b*) = percentage (*p*)

base (of a power) The number that is used as a factor when evaluating powers
Example: $3^4 = 3 \cdot 3 \cdot 3 \cdot 3$
The base is 3.

base (of a space figure) (see *cone, cylinder, prism, pyramid*)

binary operation An operation, such as addition, that is performed on two numbers at a time.

bisector A point, line, or ray that divides a figure into two parts of equal measure.

box-and-whisker plot A graph that shows how data are distributed by using the median, quartiles, maximum and minimum values

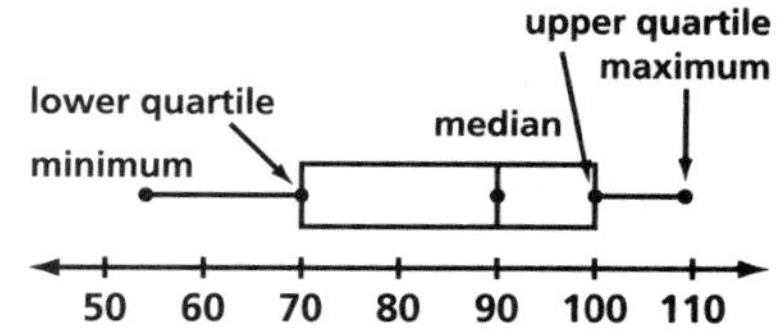

C

capacity The maximum amount of liquid that a container can hold

center (see *circle, sphere*)

central angle An angle whose vertex is the center of a circle

central tendency The most representative numbers of a set of data

chord A segment with its endpoints on a circle.

circle A plane figure that has all of its points at a fixed distance from a given point called the center

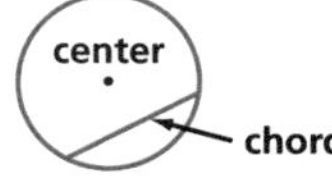

circle graph A pictorial representation of data that uses sections of a circle to show the information

circumference The distance around a circle. It is about 3.14 times the length of the diameter.

closed curve A curve that has no endpoints. If it does not cross itself, it is called a simple closed curve.

cluster Several items of data grouped into a small interval

coefficient (of a monomial) The numerical factor in each term containing a variable
Example: for $3x^2 + 2x - 1$, 3 is the coefficient of x^2, 2 is the coefficient of x.

collinear points Points that lie on the same straight line

combinations A collection of objects in which order is not important

commission The part of the total selling price that is paid to the salesperson

common denominator A denominator used when adding two or more fractions with unlike denominators.
Example: Some common denominators of $\frac{1}{2}$ and $\frac{1}{3}$ are 6, 12, 18, 24, . . .

common factor A number that is a factor of two or more whole numbers
Example: 1, 2, 3, and 6 are common factors of 12 and 18.

common multiple A number that is a multiple of two or more whole numbers
Example: Common multiples of 3 and 4 are 12, 24, 36, . . .

commutative property of addition The order of the addends does not change the sum
Example: $3 + 4 = 4 + 3 = 7$

commutative property of multiplication The order of the factors does not change the product
Example: $3 \cdot 5 = 5 \cdot 3 = 15$

compass A geometric construction tool used to draw arcs and circles

compatible numbers Two numbers that form a basic division fact. For example, 5 and 30 are compatible numbers

complementary angles Two angles whose measures total 90°

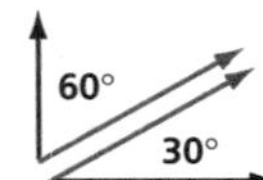

composite number A number with three or more factors
Example: 9 is composite, because its factors are 1, 3, and 9.

compound event The combination of two or more single events
Example: Rolling a "4" on one number cube and then rolling a "6" on another

cone A space figure with one flat, circular surface and one curved surface

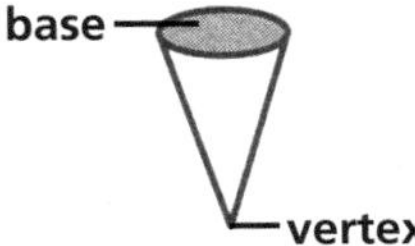

congruent figures Figures that have exactly the same size and shape. In congruent polygons, *corresponding angles* are congruent and *corresponding sides* are congruent.

constant A numerical term in a polynomial

constant of variation (see *direct variation*)

coordinate Each number of an ordered pair
Example: (4, 6) has a first coordinate of 4 and a second coordinate of 6.

coordinate plane A grid with number lines used to locate points in a plane

coplanar Two or more points, lines, or figures that are in the same plane

correlation (of scatter-plot points) A relationship between the x- and y-coordinates of points on a scatter plot such that both coordinates increase (positive correlation) or both decrease (negative correlation).

corresponding angles (on a transversal) Two angles in the same position in relation to two lines and a transversal

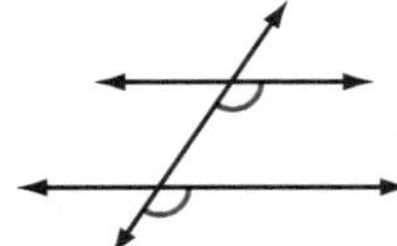

cross product property In a proportion, if $\frac{a}{b} = \frac{c}{d}$, then $a \bullet d = b \bullet c$

cross products The products obtained by multiplying the numerator of one ratio by the denominator of the other.
Example: In the proportion $\frac{5}{7} = \frac{2.5}{3.5}$, the cross products are equal: $5 \times 3.5 = 17.5$ and $7 \times 2.5 = 17.5$

cube A rectangular prism whose faces are all congruent squares

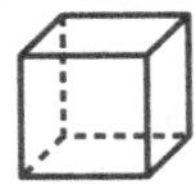

customary system of measurement The system of measurement currently used in the United States

cylinder A space figure with two congruent circular bases joined by a single curved surface

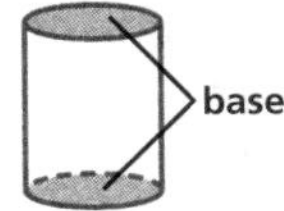

D

data Numerical information

decimal A number that uses place value to indicate parts of a whole. The decimal point separates the whole number digits from the digits representing parts of a whole.
Example: The decimal

3.67

decimal point

represents the number three and 67 hundredths.

denominator The numeral below the fraction bar in a fraction. It tells how many parts are in the whole.

dependent events Two or more events such that the results of one influences the results of the others
Example: Suppose the numbers 1, 2, and 3 are each written on a slip of paper. Choose one number, and without putting it back, choose a second number.

diagonal A segment joining two vertices of a polygon that is not a side

diagonal (of a polyhedron) A segment that joins two vertices that are not in the same face

diameter A chord of a circle that passes through the center

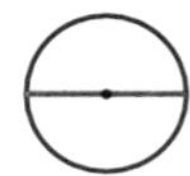

difference (see *subtraction*)

digit Any of the symbols used to write numerals. In the base 10 system, they are 1, 2, 3, 4, 5, 6, 7, 8, 9, and 0.

dimensional analysis (see *unit analysis*)

direct proportion A relationship between two quantities such that both increase simultaneously. For example, the distance *(d)* traveled by a car during a fixed time (say, 2 hours) increases as the speed *(s)* increases. $d = 2 \cdot s$

direct variation A linear function of the form $y = mx$. The non-zero number m is called the *constant of variation* and represents the rate at which the function is changing.

discount A reduction in the original or list price of a product

distributive property The same answer is obtained whether you add (or subtract) first and then multiply or multiply first and then add (or subtract).
Example:
$3 \cdot (20 + 7) = 3 \cdot 20 + 3 \cdot 7 = 81$

dividend (see *division*)

divisible A number is divisible by another number if there is no remainder when they are divided.
Example: 4, 16, and 640 are all divisible by 4.

division An operation that divides a set into equal sets
Example:
quotient → 10 R5 ← remainder
divisor → 6)65 ← dividend

division property of equality If two expressions are equal, then dividing each by the same non zero number forms two new equal expressions.
Example: If $a = b$ and $n \neq 0$, then $a \div n = b \div n$

divisor (see division)

double-line graph A line graph that compares two sets of data by using one line for each set

E

edge (see *polyhedron*)

endpoint (see *ray, line segment*)

equally likely Outcomes of an experiment that have an equal chance of occurring
Example: A spinner is divided into 6 congruent sections. Each section is an equally likely outcome of a spin.

equation A number sentence that says that two expressions have the same value. It may be true, false, or open.
Example: $3 + 7 = 10$ is true; $3 + 7 = 7$ is false, and $3 + n = 10$ is open.

equiangular Having angles of the same measure

equilateral triangle A triangle with three congruent sides

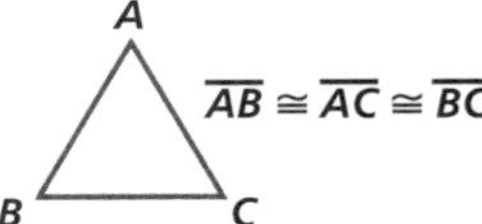

equivalent fractions Two or more fractions that represent the same number.
Example: $\frac{1}{2} = \frac{2}{4} = \frac{3}{6} = \frac{4}{8}$

estimate To find a approximate solution mentally by using numbers that are close to the original numbers and easy to work with mentally

evaluate To find the value of an expression

even number A whole number that is divisible by 2

event Any outcome or set of outcomes of an experiment

expanded form A number written so that each digit is expressed as a power of 10 instead of by its position in the numeral

Example: The expanded form of 316 is

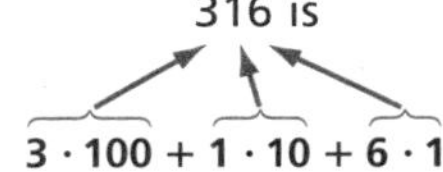

experimental probability An estimate of the probability of an event based on the results of an experiment

exponent A number that tells how many times a base is to be used as a factor
Example: 3^4 represents the product $3 \cdot 3 \cdot 3 \cdot 3$
4 factors

exponent form A number expressed as a power
Example: Exponent forms of 64 are 2^6 and 8^2

expression A combination of numbers and symbols of operation (or grouping) that represents a mathematical quantity
Examples: $(7 + 3) \div 5$ or $6 \cdot n$

F

face (see *polyhedron*)

factor (see *multiplication*)

factor tree A diagram used to help factor a composite number into its prime factors

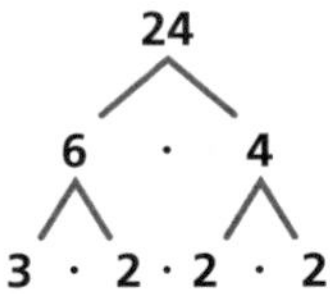

formula A general rule or relationship expressed in symbols.

fraction A number such as $\frac{1}{2}$ or $\frac{3}{4}$ that is used to express a part of a region or set

function A rule that tells how to perform one or more operations on a set of numbers so that each input value has just one output value. The rule is usually expressed as an equation.
Example: The equation $y = 3x - 7$ states that y is a function of x, and also expresses the rule of the relationship.

G

gap A characteristic of data. It is a significant interval that contains no data

graph A pictorial representation of a data set or equation

greatest common factor (GCF) The greatest number that is a factor of each of two or more numbers.
Example: The greatest common factor of 24 and 30 is 6.

H

hemisphere Half of a sphere.

heptagon A polygon that has 7 sides

regular heptagon

irregular heptagon

hexagon A polygon that has 6 sides

regular hexagon

irregular hexagon

histogram A type of bar graph. The categories are consecutive intervals along a number line. The intervals are all the same size with no gaps between them.

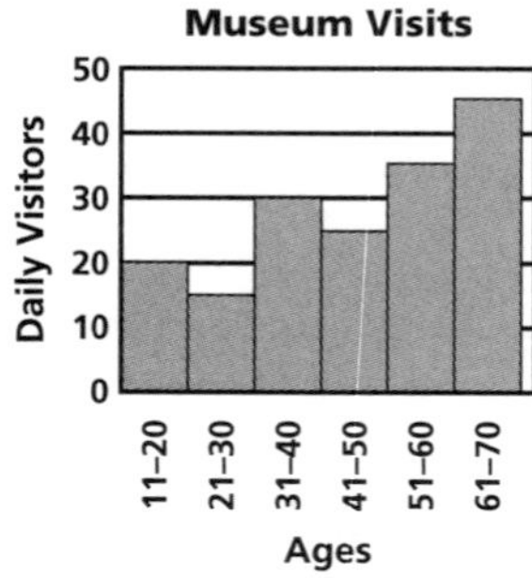

horizontal line A line that is parallel to the horizon

hypotenuse The side of a right triangle that is opposite the right angle

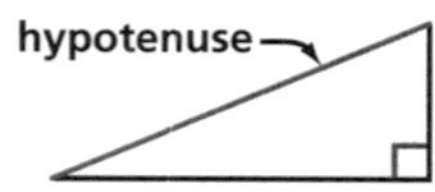

I

identity property of addition Adding zero to any number equals that number.
Examples: $7 + 0 = 7$ and $n + 0 = n$

identity property of multiplication Multiplying one by any number equals that number.
Examples: $10 \cdot 1 = 10$ and $n \cdot 1 = n$

image (see *reflection*)

improper fraction A fraction in which the denominator is either greater than or equal to the numerator

independent events Two or more events whose outcomes do not affect each other
Example: Two tosses of a coin when you are recording "heads" or "tails"

inequality A number sentence that states that two numbers or expression are not equal
Examples:
$3 + 6 < 10$ read "Three plus six is less than 10."
$5 + 7 > 10$ read "Five plus seven is greater than 10."

integer The set of numbers containing all the whole numbers and their opposites

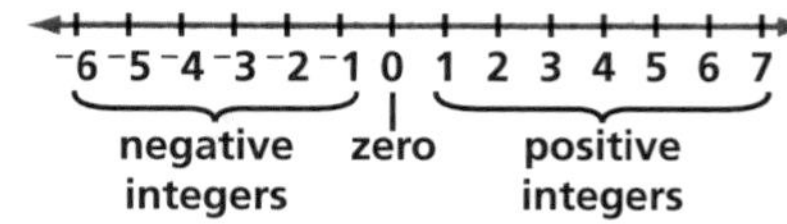

interest The amount of money charged for a loan, or earned on a savings account. Interest that is allowed to accumulate and be added to the principal at regular intervals is compound interest. Otherwise it is simple interest.

inverse operations A numerical operation that undoes the results of another operation

inverse proportion A relationship between two quantities such that as one quantity increases, the other decreases. For example, the time *(t)* taken by a car to travel a fixed distance (say 10 miles) decreases as the speed *(s)* increases.
$t = \frac{10}{s}$

irrational number A number that cannot be expressed as a ratio of two integers
Example: An infinite non-terminating, non-repeating decimal such as $\sqrt{2}$ or π.

isosceles triangle A triangle with at least two congruent sides

L

least common denominator The least number that is a common denominator of two or more fractions. It is the least common multiple of the denominators of each of the fractions.
Example: The least common denominator of $\frac{1}{2}$ and $\frac{2}{3}$ is 6.

least common multiple (LCM) The least number that is a common multiple of two or more numbers
Example: 12 is the least common multiple of 3 and 4.

like terms (*See terms of a polynomial*)

line A series of points that extends endlessly in two opposite directions along a straight path

A B Line *AB* or $\overleftrightarrow{AB}$

line graph A graph that shows changes over time using line segments

line of symmetry A line that divides a figure into two parts that are the same size and shape and are mirror images of one another
Example:

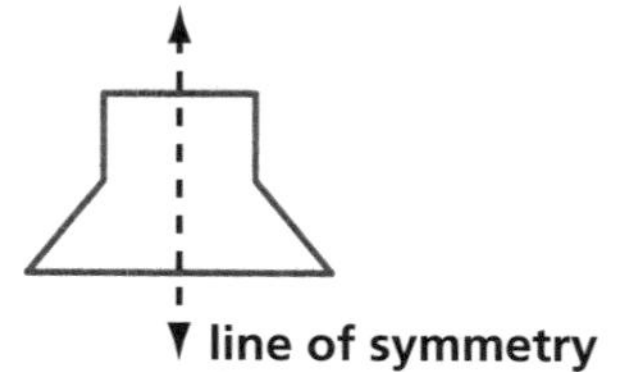

line segment A part of a line that has two endpoints

A B

linear function A function whose ordered pair solutions lie on a straight line.

line plot A pictorial representation of a small set of data. Each data item is represented with an "X" placed above a number line

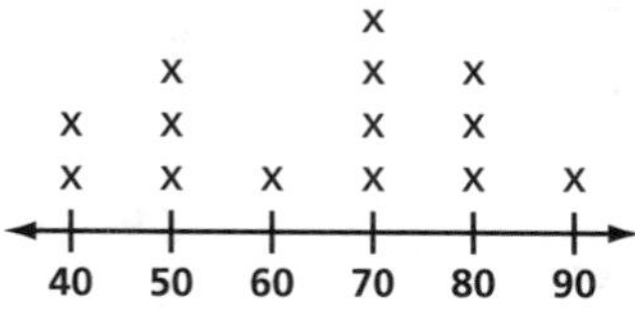

list price (marked price) The price of an item before any discount has been deducted.

M

major arc (See *arc*)

mean The average of a set of data. It is found by adding each item of data and dividing by the number of items.
Example: 4 is the mean of 2, 4, 5, 5.

median The middle point of the data when they are arranged from least to greatest. If there is an odd number of data items, it is the middle number. If there is an even number of data items, it is the mean of the two middle numbers.
Example: 4.5 is the median of 2, 4, 5, 5.

metric system of measurement An international system of measurement that uses the meter, liter, gram, and degrees Celsius as the basic units of measure

midpoint (See *segment bisector*)

minor arc (See *arc*)

mixed decimal A decimal , such as $0.83\frac{1}{3}$, that ends with a fraction

mixed number A number, such as $2\frac{2}{3}$, that is made up of a fraction less than one and a whole number

mode The number (or numbers) that occurs most often in a set of data. If every number occurs only once, the data has no mode.
Example: 5 is the mode of 2, 4, 5, 5.

monomial An expression consisting of a number, a variable, or the product of a number and one or more variables.
Examples: 5, n, $7xy$, $-3x^2$

multiple of a number The product of the number and any whole number.
Example: The multiples of 4 are 0, 4, 8, 12, 16, . . .

multiplication An operation that expresses repeated addition of the same number

Example:

12	← factor
× 4	← factor
48	← product

multiplication property of equality If two expressions are equal, then multiplying each by the same number forms two new equal expressions.
Example: If $a = b$, then $a \cdot n = b \cdot n$

multiplicative inverse (see *reciprocals*)

N

negative exponent A number that tells how many times the reciprocal of the base is to be used as a factor.
Example: 3^{-4} represents the product $\frac{1}{3} \cdot \frac{1}{3} \cdot \frac{1}{3} \cdot \frac{1}{3}$

negative integer (see *integer*)

negative slope The slope of a line that goes downward from left to right.

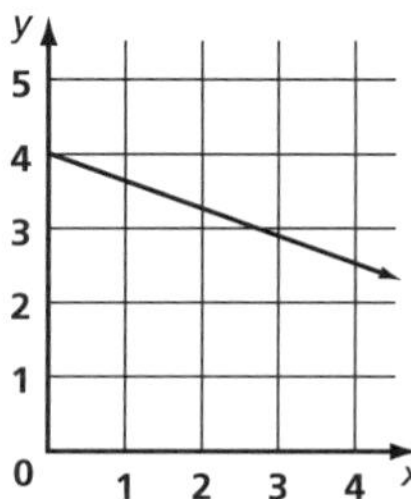

net A flat pattern that can be folded to form a space figure

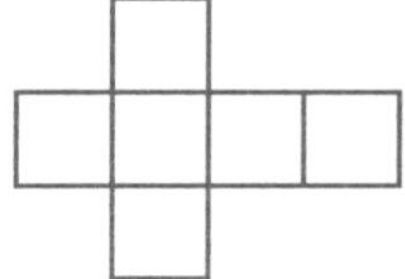

net price The price of an item after a discount has been deducted from the list price

net proceeds The difference between the amount of the sale and the commission

non-linear function A function whose ordered pair solutions do not lie on a straight line.
Example: $y = x^2$ and $V = s^3$

number line A line that has its points labeled with numbers (called coordinates) such as whole numbers, integers, fractions, and so on

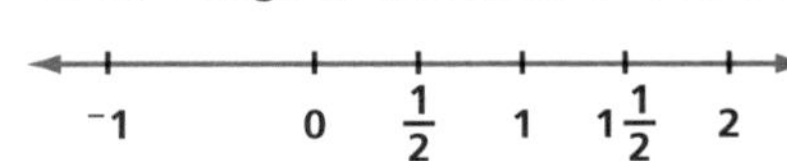

numeral A name or symbol for a number

numerator The number over the bar in a fraction. It tells how many parts of the whole are under discussion.

numerical expression An expression that contains only numbers and symbols of operation and grouping
Example: $(7 + 4) \cdot 6$

O

obtuse angle An angle whose measure is between 90° and 180°

obtuse triangle A triangle with one obtuse angle

octagon A polygon that has 8 sides

odd number A whole number that is not divisible by 2

open equation An equation that contains a variable

opposites Two numbers whose sum is 0. They are also called additive inverses.
Examples: 2 and ⁻2 are opposites; so are $\frac{-2}{3}$ and $\frac{2}{3}$.

order of operations The rules that define the order in which the operations in an expression are to be evaluated. They are

1 First work within parentheses
2 Next evaluate powers
3 Multiply and divide in order from left to right
4 Finally, add and subtract in order from left to right

ordered pair A pair of numbers used to locate a point in a coordinate plane. The first number (x-value) is the horizontal distance from the origin; the second number (y-value) is the vertical distance.

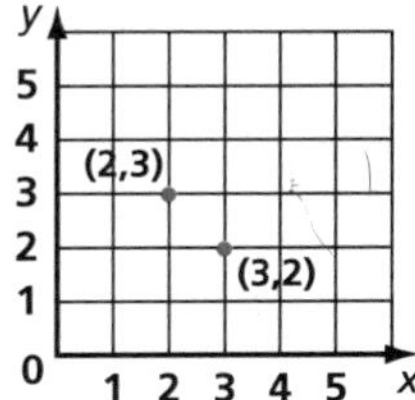

origin The point on a coordinate grid at which the two axes meet. Its coordinates are (0, 0)

outcome A result in a probability experiment

outlier An item of data that is significantly greater or less than all the other items of data

P

parallel lines Lines in the same plane that do not intersect

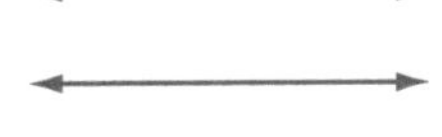

parallelogram A quadrilateral that has its opposite sides parallel and congruent

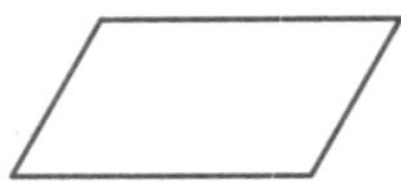

pentagon A polygon with 5 sides

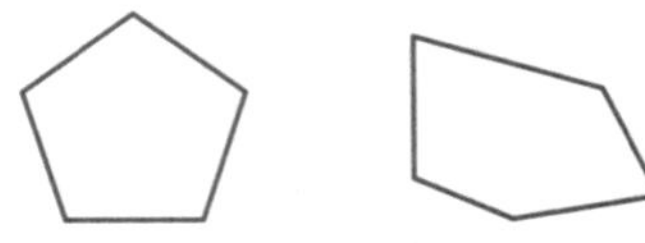

percent A ratio that compares a number to 100
Example: 39% is $\frac{39}{100}$.

percent equation An equation of the form rate (***r***) × base (***b***) = percentage (***p***)

percentage The result obtained by multiplying a quantity by a percent

perimeter The distance around a polygon. It is found by adding the lengths of all the sides.

period Each group of three digits seen in a number written in standard form
Example: In the number 306,789,245, the millions period is 306, the thousands period is 789, and 245 is the ones period.

permutation An arrangement or listing of objects in which order is important

perpendicular lines Two lines that intersect to form right angles

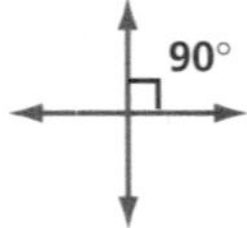

pi The number used to tell how many times a diameter will fit around the outside of a circle; the ratio of the circumference to the diameter. Its value is about 3.14.

pictograph A pictorial representation of data that uses a single symbol to represent multiples of a quantity

place-value system A system of numeration in which the value of a digit depends on its position in the numeral

plane A smooth flat surface that extends indefinitely in all directions

plane figure A figure whose points are all in the same plane

point A location in space. It is represented by a dot.

polygon A closed plane figure composed of line segments that meet only at their endpoints.

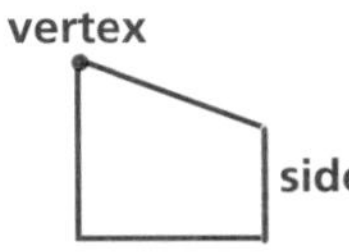

polyhedron A closed figure in space whose faces are all polygons

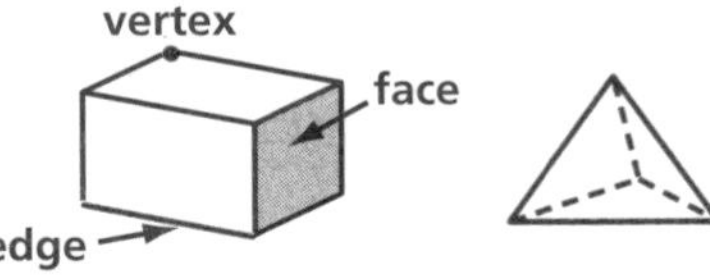

polynomial An expression that is itself a monomial or is the sum or product of monomials.
Examples: $5 \quad 7xy \quad 2(l + w) \quad \pi r^2$
$3x^2 + 9xy - y^2$

positive integer (see *integer*)

power A number that can be expressed using a single base and exponent.
Example: 32 is a power of 2; it is the fifth power of 2.

prime factorization Expressing a number as a product of prime numbers
Example: $36 = 2 \cdot 2 \cdot 3 \cdot 3$ or $2^2 \cdot 3^2$

prime number A whole number greater than 1 that has exactly two factors, itself and 1
Example: $2 = 2 \cdot 1$

principal (of a loan or savings deposit) The amount of money that is borrowed or deposited

prism A polyhedron that has two congruent, parallel bases that are joined by parallelograms. A prism is named by the shape of its bases.

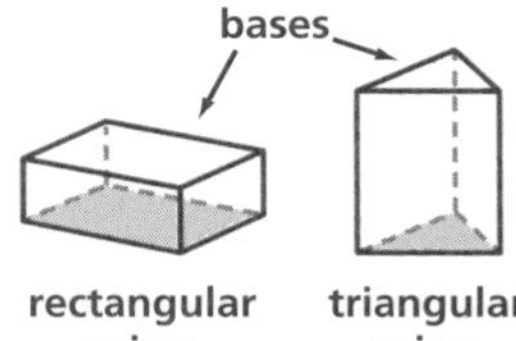

probability A number between 0 and 1 used to describe how likely an event is to happen; a measure of chance

product (see *multiplication*)

proportion An equation that states that two ratios are equal.
Example: 3 : 4 = 6 : 8 or $\frac{3}{4} = \frac{6}{8}$

protractor A tool used to measure angles

pyramid A polyhedron whose base is a polygon and whose other faces are triangles that share a common vertex. A pyramid is named by the shape of its base

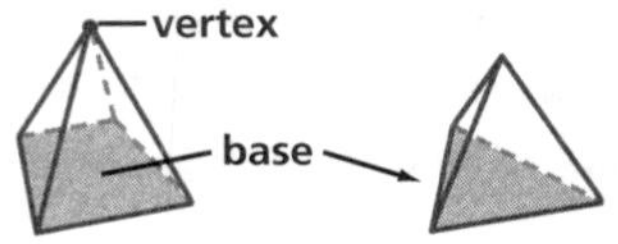

Pythagorean Property The square of the length of the hypotenuse of a right triangle is equal to the sum of the squares of the lengths of the other two sides.

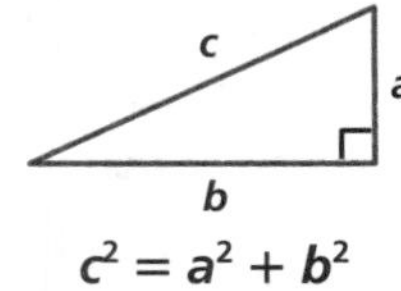

$$c^2 = a^2 + b^2$$

Q

quadrant One of the four sections of a coordinate plane formed by the axes. They are numbered counterclockwise starting from the upper right quadrant.

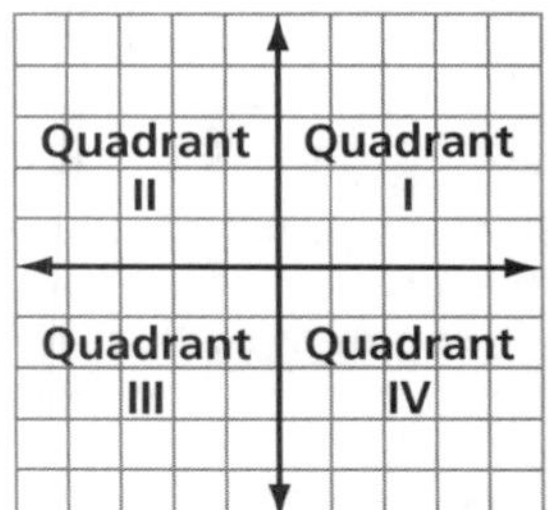

quadrilateral A polygon that has four sides and four angles

quartiles The three numbers in a data set that divide the data into four equal groups. The middle quartile is also called the median. The other two points are the upper and lower quartiles.

quotient (see *division*)

R

radius A segment from any point on a circle to its center; also the length of this segment

range The difference between the least and greatest number in a set of data
Example: The range of the data 2, 4, 5, 5 is 5 − 2 = 3.

rate A comparison by division of two unlike quantities, such as words per minute or feet per second

rate (in percent equation)(See *base*)

ratio A comparison of two like quantities using division
Example: 3 : 4, 3 to 4, or $\frac{3}{4}$

rational number A number that can be expressed as the ratio of two integers
Examples: $1.67 = \frac{167}{100}$ $^{-}5 = \frac{^{-}5}{1}$

ray A part of a line that has one endpoint. When naming it, the endpoint is used first.

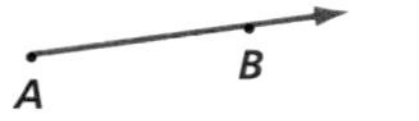

Ray *AB* or $\overrightarrow{AB}$

reciprocals Two numbers whose product is 1. They are also called multiplicative inverses.
Examples: 2 and $\frac{1}{2}$ $\frac{^{-}3}{4}$ and $\frac{^{-}4}{3}$

rectangle A parallelogram that has four right angles

reflection A transformation that changes the position of a figure by flipping it about a line to form its mirror image
Example:

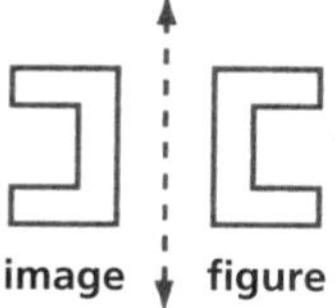

regular polygon A polygon that has all sides congruent and all angles congruent

relatively prime Two or more numbers whose only common factor is 1

remainder (see *division*)

repeating decimal A fraction whose decimal expression shows a repeating pattern of digits
Examples: $\frac{1}{3} = 0.333333...$
$\frac{1}{11} = 0.09090909....$

rhombus A parallelogram that has all of its sides congruent

right angle An angle whose measure is 90°

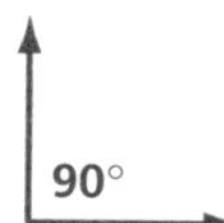

right triangle A triangle with one right angle

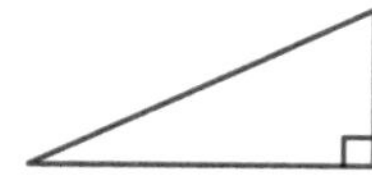

rise (see *slope*)

rounded number A number that is close to a given number in which the final digits have been replaced with zeroes.
Examples: 12,501 rounded to the nearest hundred is 12,500.
12, 501 rounded to the nearest thousand is 13,000

run (see *slope*)

S

scale drawing A picture or diagram that is an enlargement or reduction of another. Each distance in the drawing is in the same proportion as the corresponding distance in the original.

scale factor The ratio in a scale drawing or similar figures that compares the scale drawing dimensions to the actual dimensions

scalene triangle A triangle that has no congruent sides

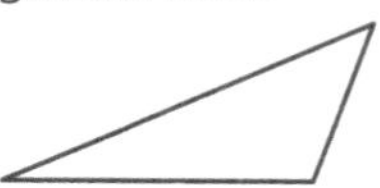

scatter plot A graph of ordered pairs that shows two measurements for each item of a set

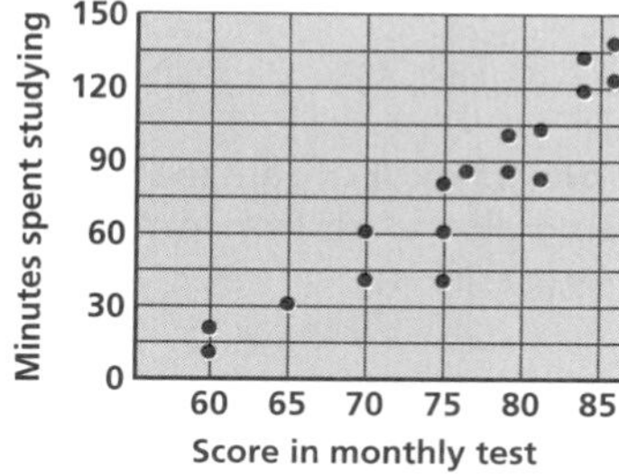

scientific notation A form for writing a number as the product of a number between 1 and 10 and a power of ten
Examples: $186.3 = 1.863 \times 10^2$
$0.0379 = 3.79 \times 10^{-2}$

segment (see *line segment*)

segment bisector A point, called a midpoint, that divides a line segment into two parts of equal measure

semicircle All points on a circle that are on the same side of a diameter, including the endpoints of the diameter; half of a circle.

side (see *angle, polygon*)

similar figures Two figures that have the same shape but not necessarily the same size. In similar polygons, corresponding angles are congruent and corresponding sides are proportional.

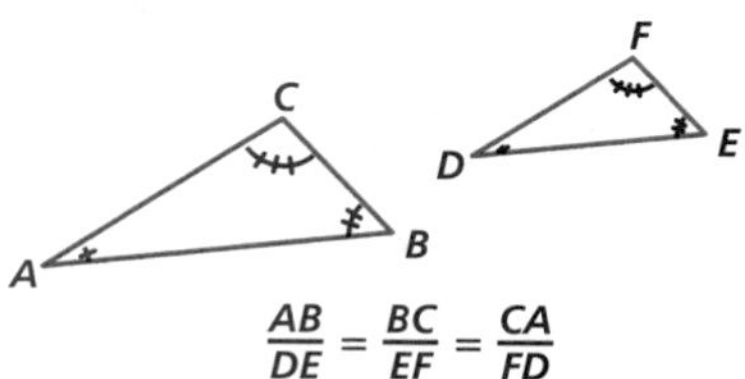

$$\frac{AB}{DE} = \frac{BC}{EF} = \frac{CA}{FD}$$

simplest form Either a fraction less than 1 in which the numerator and denominator have no common factors except 1, or a mixed number in which the fraction part is in simplest form
Examples: $\frac{5}{10} = \frac{1}{2}$ $2\frac{6}{9} = 2\frac{2}{3}$

skew lines In space figures, lines that are not in the same plane.

slope (*m*) The ratio of the difference in *y*-coordinates (the rise) to the difference in *x*-coordinates (the run) of any two points on a coordinate plane; it may be written $\frac{\text{rise}}{\text{run}}$

solution The value of the variable(s) that makes an open equation or inequality true.

space The set of all points

space figure A figure that is not entirely in one plane

sphere A space figure that has all of its points the same distance from a point, called the center.

spreadsheet A computer program that creates tables or cells of values

square A rectangle that has all its sides congruent

square root A number such that its square is a given number
Example: 5 and $^{-}5$ are the square roots of 25 because $5^2 = 25$ and $(^{-}5)^2 = 25$. They are written: $\sqrt{25} = 5$, $^{-}\sqrt{25} = {}^{-}5$.

standard form A number that is expressed as a base 10 numeral
Example: 3,126 is the standard form of the number three thousand, one hundred twenty-six

stem-and-leaf plot A convenient way of arranging a data set in order from least to greatest by making the last digit of each number a leaf and making the other digits of each number part of the stem.
Example:

**data set: 42, 37, 35, 48
56, 37, 42, 41**

stem	leaves
3	5 7 7
4	1 2 2 8
5	6

straight angle An angle whose measure is 180°.

straightedge An unmarked ruler used as a geometric construction tool

subtraction An arithmetic operation that takes away a given amount
Example:
$$\begin{array}{r} 345 \\ -\ 122 \\ \hline 223 \end{array} \longleftarrow \text{difference}$$

subtraction property of equality If two expressions are equal and the same number is subtracted from each, then the two new expressions are equal.
Example: If $n + 7 = 10$. then $n + 7 - 7 = 10 - 7$.

sum (see *addition*)

supplementary angles Two angles whose measures total 180°.

surface area The total area of all the faces or surfaces of a space figure

survey A method of gathering data about a population by recording the results of specific questions

T

term (of a ratio) Either of the two numbers of a ratio

terms (of a polynomial) Each monomial that is part of a polynomial. If terms contain the same powers of the same variables, they are *like terms*. If terms differ in at least one variable or power of a variable, they are *unlike terms*.
Example:

$2x^2 - 4x$	$3y - 2x$	$7xy + 3xy$
unlike terms	unlike terms	like terms

terminating decimal The decimal expression of a fraction whose denominator can be written using only powers of 2 and 5
Examples: $0.1 = \frac{1}{10}$ $\quad 0.675 = \frac{27}{40}$

transformations The basic motions that can be applied to a geometric figure. Two kinds of transformations are reflections and translations.

translation A transformation that changes the position of a figure by sliding it in the same plane.
Example:

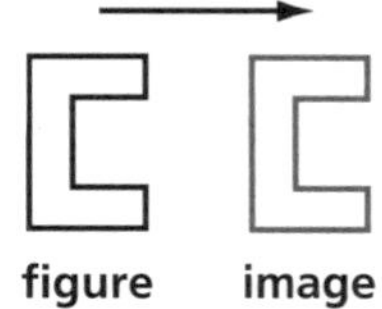

figure **image**

transversal A line that intersects two or more other lines in the same number of points as there are lines.
Example:

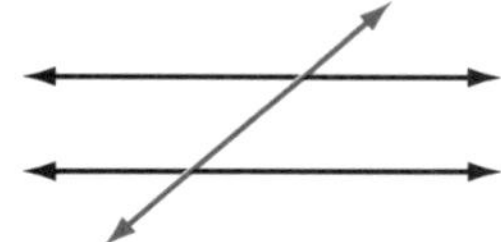

trapezoid A quadrilateral that has exactly one pair of parallel sides

tree diagram A organized way of listing all the possible outcomes of an experiment

Choice 1	Choice 2	Outcomes
red	white	1 red-white
	black	2 red-black
blue	white	3 blue-white
	black	4 blue-black

triangle A polygon that has three sides

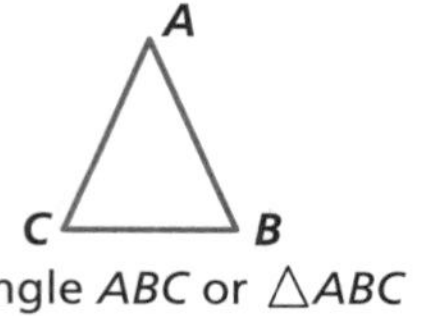

Triangle *ABC* or $\triangle ABC$

U

unit A fixed quantity used as a standard for length, area, volume, weight, and so on

unit analysis (also dimensional analysis) A technique that uses units of measure in a computation to decide what unit is appropriate in the solution.
Example:
$\frac{65 \text{ mi}}{\cancel{\text{hour}}} \cdot 2.5 \cancel{\text{hours}} \longrightarrow 162.5 \text{ mi}$

unit price The cost of a single unit of an item or service
Example: $3 per pound for hamburger meat

unit rate A rate whose second term is a single unit, such as 50 miles per hour

V

variable A letter that is used to represent one or more numbers

variable expression An expression that contains one or more variables

variation (See *direct variation*)

vertex (see *angle, polygon, polyhedron*)

vertical angles Two "opposite" angles formed by two intersecting lines

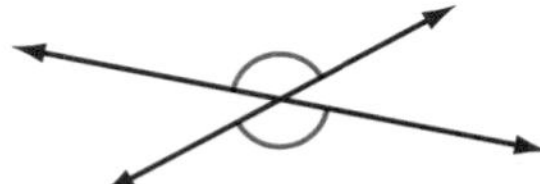

vertical line A line that is perpendicular to a horizontal line

volume A measure of the space within a closed figure in space

W–X–Y–Z

whole number Any of the numbers 0, 1, 2, 3, . . .

***x*-axis** The horizontal number line on a coordinate plane

***y*-axis** The vertical number line on a coordinate plane

zero exponent The zero power of any nonzero base is 1; in other words,
$n^0 = 1$

zero property of multiplication Multiplying zero by any number equals zero
Example: $6 \cdot 0 = 0$

Scope and Sequence

The following chart indicates the scope and sequence of the topics in *MathSteps.* Type printed in bold denotes that a topic is being introduced. Although a topic might appear at each level, the material will vary in place and depth. Use student page references to see how the instruction varies.

Number Sense

5

Common factors 69–70, 81–82, 89–90
Common multiples 97–98
Composite numbers 65–68
Decimals
 adding decimals 149–150, 151–152
 comparing and ordering 145–148
 decimals as fractions 147–148, 247–250
 decimals as percents 247–250
 dividing decimals 160–165
 estimating decimals
  decimal differences 149–152
  decimal sums 149–152
  decimal products 158
  decimal quotients 162–163
 fractions and decimals 147–148, 247–250
 measurement and decimals 181–182
 mental math and decimals 159–160
 multiplying decimals 155–158
 place value of decimals 145–146
 reading and writing decimals 145–146
 rounding decimals 149
 subtracting decimals 151–152
Divisibility rules 63–64
Estimating
 decimals 149, 151–152, 158, 162, 163
 differences 14, 49–52, 149–152
 percents 252
 products 36, 158
 quotients 77–78, 162–163
 for reasonableness of answers 13–14, 32, 43, 78, 104, 139, 150, 154, 160, 178, 179
 sums 13, 149–152
Even numbers 63–64
Exponents 9–10, 51–52, 67–68
Factor tree 67–68
Factors 65–66, 67–69, 70
Fractions
 adding fractions 91–92, 99–100
 changing fractions to mixed numbers 88
 decimals as fractions 98, 147–148, 249–250
 denominators 85–86, 97

6

Base ten numerals 3, 39–40
Common factors 69–70, 75–76
Common multiples 77, 85–86
Composite numbers 69–70
Decimals
 adding decimals 43–44
 comparing and ordering 41–42
 decimals as fractions 87–88
 decimals as mixed numbers 87–88
 decimals as percents 169–170
 dividing decimals 56–60
 estimating decimals
  decimal sums and differences 43–44
  decimal products 47–48
 measurement and decimals 55
 mental math and decimals 54–55
 multiplying decimals 45–48
 place value of decimals 39–40
 reading and writing decimals 39–40
 repeating decimals 89–90
 rounding decimals 42
 subtracting decimals 43–44
 terminating decimals 89–90
Divisibility rules 67–68
Estimating
 decimals 43–44, 47–4
 fractions 102–104, 111–112
 mixed numbers 101, 113
 percents 181–182
 products 45, 113
 quotients 19
 for reasonableness of answers 5, 12, 113, 181
 sums 43–44
 using benchmarks 101
 using compatible numbers 19, 111
Even numbers 67
Expanded notation 3–4
Exponents 71–72
 expressions and exponents 71
 least common multiple and exponents 77–78
Factor tree 73

7

Absolute value 218–220, 222
Common factors or multiples 46
Compatible numbers 121
Composite numbers 45
Decimals
 adding decimals 37–38
 comparing decimals 33–34
 decimal equations 69–70
 decimal expressions 67–68
 decimals as fractions 49–50
 decimals as percents 121–122
 dividing decimals 42–44
 estimating decimals
  decimal products 39–41
  decimal sums and differences 37–38
 fractions and decimals 49–50, 114–116
 measurement and decimals 76–77
 mental math and decimals 39–44
 multiplying decimals 39–41
 ordering decimals 33–34
 place value of decimals 33–34
 repeating and terminating 49
Estimating
 decimals 35–36, 121–122
 fractions and mixed numbers 60, 63, 121–122
 percents 121–122
 for reasonableness of answers 37–38
Exponents
 base 22
 expressions and exponents 22–23, 39, 243–245
 integer exponents 243–245
 power 22, 243
 simplifying 22–23, 244
 using order of operations to simplify 22–23, 247
Factorials 167–168
Factor tree 45–46
Factors 16, 45–46
Fractions
 adding fractions 53–54
 decimals as fractions 49–50
 dividing 62–64

oldface entry denotes the introduction of a topic.

Number Sense *continued*

5

- dividing 133–134, 135–136
- equivalent fractions 85–86
  - meaning of 85–86
  - dividing to find 85–86
  - multiplying to find 85–86, 126
- fractional parts
  - of a number 85
  - of a region or a set 85
- **fractions as decimals** 147–148, 249–250
- **fractions as percents** 243–244, 245–246
- fractions in equations 126
- fractions in expressions 137–138
- **least common denominator** 97–98
- **least common multiple** 97–98
- modeling fractions 85–86
- multiplying fractions 117–118, 119–120, 121–122
- numerators 85–86, 87
- **on a number line** 111–112, 131–132
- order of operations with fractions 137–138
- ordering fractions 87
- **percents as fractions** 243–244, 245–246
- probability and fractions 273–275
- **ratio and fractions**
  - **writing equivalent ratios** 237–238
  - **writing ratios as fractions** 233–234
- **reciprocals** 129–130
- relating fractions and mixed numbers 88–90
- **simplest form of fractions** 89–90, 234
- subtracting fractions 93–94, 103–104, 105–106

Greatest common factor (GCF) 69–70, 89–90, 123

Integers
- adding integers 289–290, 113–114
- comparing and ordering 283–286
- **dividing integers** 297–298
- **multiplying integers** 295–296
- **negative numbers** 281–284
- **on a number line** 283–284
- **opposites** 281
- **positive numbers** 281–284
- subtracting integers 291–294, 305–306

Mixed numbers
- adding mixed numbers
  - adding like denominators 91–92
  - **adding unlike denominators** 101–102
- **dividing mixed numbers** 135–136
- **multiplying mixed numbers** 123–124
- simplest form of mixed numbers 88, 90
- subtracting mixed numbers
  - subtracting mixed numbers with like

6

Factors 69–70

Fractions
- adding fractions 97–98, 100–101
- comparing fractions 85–86
- dividing fractions 117–118
- equations with fractions 125
- equivalent fractions 81–82, 83–84, 85–86
- estimating fractions 111
- expressions with fractions 125–126
- fractional parts of an inch 148
- fractions as decimals 87–88
- fractions as percents 169–170
- least common denominator 81–82
- missing numerator or denominator 83
- multiplying fractions 109–110
- modeling 85, 87, 117
- probability and fractions 255
- ratio and fractions
  - writing ratios as fractions 153–154
  - writing equivalent ratios 157–158
- reciprocals 115–116
- simplest form 83–84
- subtracting fractions 97–104
- writing fractions as mixed numbers 87–88

Greatest common factor (GCF) 75–76, 83–84

Integers
- adding integers 271–273
- comparing integers 269
- dividing integers 281–282
- **equations with integers** 287–288
- expressions with integers 287–288
- meaning of integers 267–268
- multiplying integers 279–280
- negative numbers 267–268
- on a number line 267–268, 269
- positive numbers 267–268
- subtracting integers 274–276

Mixed numbers 113–114
- adding mixed numbers 97–101
- dividing mixed numbers 121–122
- mixed numbers as fractions 113–114, 121–122
- modeling mixed numbers 87
- multiplying mixed numbers 113–114
- simplest form of mixed numbers 87–88, 97–101, 102–104
- subtracting mixed numbers 102–104
- writing mixed numbers 113–114, 121–122

Multiples 77–78
- least common multiple 77–78, 85

Odd numbers 63

Ordering
- decimals 41–42
- integers 267–268

7

- equivalent fractions 47–48
- fractional parts of an inch 83
- **fractions in equations** 69–70
- **fractions in expressions** 67–68
- least common denominator 53, 55
- least common multiple 44–46
- missing numerator 47
- multiplying fractions 59–61
- ordering fractions 52
- percents as fractions 116–122, 130
- probability and fractions 169–170
- ratio and fractions 99–100
  - writing equivalent ratios 100
  - writing ratios as fractions 99
- reciprocals 62–64
- simplest form 47–48
- subtracting fractions 55–56

Greatest common factor (GCF) 44–45

Inequalities 268–270

Integers
- **absolute value** 218
- adding integers 221–222
- dividing integers 229–230
- graphing on a number line 219
- multiplying integers 227–228
- negative numbers 217
- on a number line 217, 218, 221
- opposites and integers 217
- positive numbers 217
- subtracting integers 223–224

Irrational number 245, 277, 279, 309

Mixed numbers
- adding mixed numbers 53–54
- dividing mixed numbers 62–64
- multiplying mixed numbers 59–61
- simplest form of mixed numbers 53–54, 55–56, 62–64
- subtracting mixed numbers 55–56

Multiples
- least common multiple 45–46

Ordering
- decimals 33–34
- fractions 51–52
- integers 217–219
- rational numbers 231–232

Percents 114
- **benchmark percents** 118
- decimals as percents 115–122, 129
- estimating with percents 121–122
- fractions as percents 116–122, 130
- percent applications
  - circle graphs 204–206
  - **commission** 143–144
  - **compound interest** 146
  - discount 139–140
  - **list price** 141–142
  - **net price** 141–142

Number Sense *continued*

5

6

7

Computation and Operations

5

Addition
- adding decimals 151–152
- adding fractions
  - like denominators 91–92
  - unlike denominators 99–102
- adding integers 289–290
- adding mixed numbers 92, 101–102
- adding whole numbers 13–14, 15–16, 43–44
- addition equations 17–18, 21–22, 29–30, 51–52
- addition expressions 15–16, 21–22, 29–30, 51–52
- estimating sums 13, 43–44, 149–150
- order of operations 21–22, 51–52, 137–138
- properties 17–18, 21, 30, 33–34, 125–126

Division
- algorithm 53, 71
- averages 59–60
- checking division with multiplication 57–58, 71–72
- **dividing by powers of 10** 160
- **dividing decimals** 160–168
- **dividing fractions** 131–134
- **dividing integers** 297–298
- **dividing mixed numbers** 135–136
- dividing money amounts 55–56
- dividing whole numbers 49–54, 71–78, 129–133, 159–160
- order of operations 51–52, 137–138
- rules for division 52

Mental math 20–30, 33–34, 36, 125–126

Multiplication
- basic facts 29–32, 45–46, 125–126, 155–156, 295–296, 305–306
- composite numbers 65–66
- estimating products 158–159, 164, 166
- **factor tree** 67–68
- factors 29–30, 65–66, 67–69, 70
- **greatest common factor** 69–70
- **least common multiple** 97–98
- mental math 33–34, 36
- multiples 97–98
- **multiplication and exponents** 9–10, 67–68
- multiplication equations 29–30, 49–50
- multiplication expressions 27–28, 51–52
- **multiplying decimals** 155–158
- **multiplying fractions** 119–122
- **multiplying integers** 295–296
- **multiplying mixed numbers** 123–124
- multiplying money amounts 39–40, 41–42
- multiplying whole numbers 33–31, 39–42

6

Addition
- adding decimals 43–44
- adding fractions 100–101
  - like denominators 97–98
  - unlike denominators 100–101
  - writing sums in simplest terms 97, 100–101
- adding integers 271–273
- adding mixed numbers
  - estimating sums, using benchmarks 101
  - like denominators 98
  - unlike denominators 100–101
- adding whole numbers 5–6
- addition equations 9–11, 61–62, 125–126
- addition expressions 8, 9–11
- estimating sums 43–44, 100
- inverse operations 125
- missing addends 7, 273, 274
- order of operations 22–23
- properties
  - associative property 7–8
  - commutative property 7–8
  - identity property 7–8

Division
- averages 24–25, 26–29, 243–244
- checking division with multiplication 20–21, 51–52
- dividing decimals 56–60
  - by a decimal 56–58
  - by a whole number 51–53
  - interpreting remainders 59–60
  - metric system 55
  - powers of ten 54–55
  - **repeating decimals** 89–90
  - rounding decimal quotients 57
  - **terminating decimals** 89–90
  - zeros in the dividend 52
- dividing fractions
  - by a fraction 117–118, 120
  - **by a whole number** 119–120
  - reciprocals 115–116
  - modeling 122
- dividing integers 281–282
- dividing money amounts 51, 56–58
- dividing whole numbers 18–21
- divisibility rules 67–68
- division equations
  - solving 30–31
  - writing 61–62
- division expressions 22, 68
- estimating
  - exact or estimated answer 40
  - quotients 21
  - using compatible numbers 19–20
- inverse operations 281–282
- mixed numbers 121–122

7

Addition
- adding decimals 37–38
- adding fractions 53–54
- adding integers 221–222
- adding mixed numbers 53–54
- **adding rational numbers** 233–234
  - **writing sums in simplest form** 234
- addition equations 9–11
- addition expressions 5–6
- estimating sums 37–38
- order of operations 7–8, 23, 67
- properties
  - associative property 16–18
  - commutative property 16–18
  - identity property 16–18

Division
- averages 3–4
- checking division with multiplication 42–44
- compatible numbers 121
- dividing by powers of 10 42
- dividing decimals 42–44
  - dividing a decimal by a decimal 42
  - dividing a decimal by a whole number 44
  - powers of ten 42
- dividing fractions 62–64
- dividing integers 229–230
- dividing mixed numbers 62–64
- dividing money amounts 42, 44
- **dividing rational numbers** 235–236
  - **quotient in simplest form** 235
- division equations 12–13
- division expressions 5–6
- estimating quotients 42, 63
- order of operations 7–8, 23, 67
- reciprocals 62

Mental math
- using multiples of 10 17
  - in division 44
  - in multiplication 17, 39–41
- using properties of zero and one 16–18
  - in addition 16–18
  - in multiplication 16–18
- using the distributive property 19–21

Multiplication
- composite numbers 45
- estimating products 59–61
- factor tree 45
- factors 46
- greatest common factor 46
- least common multiple 46
- mental math strategies 16, 17, 18, 39, 227, 228
- multiple 46
- multiplication and exponents 243–245
- multiplication equations 12–13
- multiplication expressions 5–6

Computation and Operations *continued*

5

6

7

Algebra and Functions

5

6

7

Algebra and Functions *continued*

5

6

7

Algebra and Functions *continued*

5

6

- Properties
  - addition properties 7–8
  - distributive 6–17
  - multiplication properties 16–17
- Proportions
  - equivalent ratios 157–158
  - scale drawings 162–164
  - **in similar figures** 203–204
  - **solving percent equations** 177–178
  - **using cross-products to solve** 159–161
  - **using multiplicative inverse to solve** 159–161
  - **variables** 160
- **Rational numbers** 270, 309–310
- Variables 9, 17, 30–32, 61–62, 126, 157, 160

7

-
  - solving percent equations 129–130
  - using cross products to solve 104, 105–107
  - using mental math to solve 103
  - variables 103–104
- Rational numbers 232, 233, 235, 257–259
  - **density property** 232
  - **variable expressions** 236, 317–319
- **Scientific notation** 254–255
- **Square root** 245, 309
- Variables 5–9, 12, 20, 68, 106, 236, 260–261

Measurement

5

- Angles
  - **parallelogram** 207–208
  - **quadrilateral** 207–208
  - **right triangle** 203–204
  - **triangle** 203–204
- Area
  - complex figures 214–215
  - meaning of area 214–215
  - **parallelogram** 217
  - polygon 216–217
  - rectangle 214–215
  - square 214–215
  - surface area 221–222
  - **triangle** 216–217
- Capacity
  - customary units of capacity 189–190
  - metric units of capacity 179–180
- Customary system 185–190
- Decimals and measurement 181–182
- Estimating measurement 177–178, 179
- Length
  - choosing the unit 187–188
  - customary units of measure 185–186
  - metric units of measure 177–178
- Mass
  - gram (g) 179–180
  - kilogram (kg) 179–180
- Measurement, rewriting
  - customary 185–186, 189–190
  - metric 177–178, 179–180

6

- Angles
  - acute 189
  - **central angle** 193–194
  - **complementary** 191–192
  - **corresponding** 191, 195
  - obtuse 189
  - right 189
  - straight 189
  - **supplementary** 191–192
  - **vertical** 191–192
- Area
  - circle 221–222
  - complex figure 215–216
  - exponents and area 216
  - irregular figures 215–216
  - parallelogram 217–218
  - polygons 215–216
  - rectangle 215–216
  - **triangle** 123–124, 217–218
- Capacity
  - customary units of capacity 143
  - metric units of capacity 133
- **Circumference** 219–220
- Customary system 141–144
- Decimals and measurement 55
- Elapsed time 139–140
- Estimating measurement 134
- Equivalent measurements
  - customary 141–144
  - metric 131–134

7

- Angles
  - acute 185–186
  - central angle 204–206
  - complementary 189–190
  - obtuse 185–186
  - right 185–186
  - straight 185–186
  - supplementary 189–190
  - vertical 187–188
- Area 302–303
  - circle 25–26, 277–279
  - complex figures 280–282
  - parallelogram 280–282
  - rectangle 25–26, 40, 280–282
  - **regular polygon** 285–286
  - square 25–26, 280–282
  - surface area 293–297
  - triangle 25–26, 280–282
  - **trapezoid** 283–284
  - units of 79–80, 87–88
- Capacity
  - customary units of capacity 85–86
  - metric units of capacity 77–78
- Circumference 24, 277–279
- Customary system 83–86
- Decimals and measurement 76, 77
- Dimensional analysis 109–110
- Estimating measurement 75, 77–78, 287–288
- Fractions and measurement 83

Measurement *continued*

5

Metric measurement
- capacity 179–180
- **decimals and the metric system** 181–182
- length 177–178
- mass 179–180

Perimeter 214–215

Surface area 221–222

Temperature
- Celsius 184
- Fahrenheit 191

Time
- adding time 183
- elapsed time 183–184.
- subtracting time 183–184

Volume 223–224
- cube and rectangular prism 223–224
- **formulas** 223–224

Weight
- ounce (oz) 189–190
- pound (lb) 189–190
- ton (T) 189–190

6

Length
- customary units of measure 141–142
- metric units of measure 131–132

Mass
- gram, kilogram 134

Metric measurement
- capacity 133–134
- decimals and 55
- length 131–132
- mass 133–134

Perimeter 215–216, 233–234

Pi (π) 219

Rate 155–156

Surface area 225–226

Temperature
- Celsius 135–136
- Fahrenheit 145–146
- negative numbers 135

Time 139–140

Volume
- cube 230–231
- **cylinder** 230
- exponents 229–232
- formula 229
- rectangular prism 229
- **triangular prism** 230

Weight
- ounce, pound, ton 143–144

7

Length 302–303
- customary units of measure 83–84
- metric units of measure 75–76

Mass
- gram, kilogram 77–78

Measurement, rewriting
- customary 83–88
- metric 75–80

Metric measurement
- capacity 77–78
- decimals and the metric system 76–77
- length 75–76
- mass 77–78

Perimeter 24–26
- of a regular polygon 286

Pi (π) 24–25, 277–279

Relating length, area, and volume 302–303

Rate (of speed) 27–28

Surface area 293–297, 302–303

Temperature
- Celsius 27–28, 77–78
- Fahrenheit 27–28, 77–78

Time 91–92

Unit rates 101

Volume 300, 305
- of composite space figures 300–301

Weight
- ounce, pound, ton 85–86
- units of 80, 81

Geometry

5

Angles
- **measuring angles** 200–202
- naming angles 200–202
  - acute 201
  - obtuse 201
  - right 201
  - **straight** 201
- **sums of angles**
  - **quadrilaterals** 227–228
  - **triangles** 227–228

Circle
- constructing circles 211–213
- diameter 211–213

6

Angles
- acute 189–190
- **central angle** 194
- **complementary** 191–192
- **congruent angles** 191, 195
- constructing angles 195
- **corresponding (similar figurers)** 191, 195
- measuring angles 189–190
- naming angles 189–190
- obtuse 189–190
- protractor 195
- right 189–190

7

Angles
- **adjacent angles** 187
- **alternate interior** 190
- central angle 202–203
- classifying angles
  - acute 185–186
  - complementary 187–188
  - obtuse 185–186
  - right 185–186
  - supplementary 187–190
  - vertical 187–190
- congruent angles 188–190, 195, 323
- constructing angles 195–196
- corresponding angles 189, 323
- **formed by parallel lines and a transversal** 189–190
- measuring angles 185–186

Geometry *continued*

5

6

7

Geometry *continued*

5

6

7

Geometry *continued*

5

6

of an angle 187, 197
of a polygon 197
of a space figure 223–224

Volume
of a cube 229
of a cylinder 230
of a prism 229–230

7

Data Analysis, Statistics, and Probability

5

Average 59–60

Choosing an appropriate graph 261–262

Clusters 266

Data
collecting data 270, 276
comparing ways of representing data 261–262
organizing data 270–272, 276
survey 276
tables and charts 7–8, 79–80, 263, 270
tally charts 270, 275

Gaps 266

Graphs
bar graph 11–12, 128, 261–262
circle graph 253–254, 261–262
constructing circle graphs 253–254
interpreting circle graphs 253–254, 262
double line graph 191–192
histogram 259–262
line graph 184, 190, 191, 238, 261–262
line plot 59, 265–266
pictograph 127–128, 261–262
constructing pictographs 127–128
stem-and-leaf plots 259–260

Mean 59–60, 263–264, 266

Measures of central tendency
mean 59–60, 263–264, 266
median 263–264, 266
mode 263–264, 266
outliers 266
range 263–264, 266

Median 263–264, 266

Mode 263–264, 266

6

Average 27–29, 243–244

Choosing an appropriate graph 241–242

Clusters 243–244

Data
analyzing data 241–242
comparing different graphs of the same data 241–242
comparing ways of representing data 241–242
evaluating conclusions 251
interpreting data from a graph 136
organizing data 26, 91–92, 241–242, 253–254
predicting from 254
survey 26, 247–248
tables and charts 26, 253–254

Gaps 243–244

Graphs
bar graph 26, 91–92, 241–242
circle graph 179–180
double bar graph 241–242
double line graph 241–242
line graph 136
interpreting 136, 145
line plot 27–28, 243
pictograph 105–106
triple bar graph 242

Mean 27–29, 243–244

Measures of central tendency
effects of data on 26–29, 243–244
mean 27–29, 243–244
median 27–29, 243–244
mode 27–29, 243–244
outliers 243–244
range 29, 241–242

7

Average 3–4

Choosing an appropriate graph 160, 162

Data
comparing ways of representing data 157–158, 159–160
frequency table 154
listing outcomes 165–166
organizing data 3–4, 153, 154, 155, 156
tables and charts 93–94, 147–148, 153, 154, 156

Graphs
bar graph 4, 173, 237
line graph 4, 90, 174, 238
box and whisker plot 157–158
circle graph 174, 204–206
double line graph 89–90
histogram 153–154
line plot 3, 153–154
misleading 161–162
scatter plot 159–160
stem-and-leaf plot 155–156

Mean 3–4

Measures of central tendency
clusters 3–4, 159–160
gaps 159–160
mean 3–4, 159–160
median 3–4, 153, 156, 174
mode 3–4, 153, 156, 174
outliers 3–4, 155, 156, 159–160
range 3–4, 153, 156, 159–160, 174

Median 3–4, 153, 156, 174

Misleading graphs 161–162

Mode 3–4, 153, 156, 174

Outliers 3–4, 155, 159–160

Data Analysis, Statistics, and Probability *continued*

5

6

7

Mathematical Reasoning

5

Checking reasonableness of answers 13–14, 19, 37, 43–44, 72, 79, 139, 191, 209, 241, 271, 293

Drawing conclusions 7, 11–12, 18, 56, 64, 178, 184, 190–191, 236, 253–254, 260–261, 264, 267–269, 272

Explaining reasoning 6–8, 11–12, 16, 18–19, 28, 43–44, 52, 62, 64, 70, 88, 90, 94, 104, 110–112, 118, 127–128, 130, 134, 154, 156, 160, 180, 183, 222, 236, 244, 250, 252, 260–261, 267–268, 272

Generalizing 7, 11–12, 18, 56, 70, 178, 184, 190–191, 236, 244, 253, 260, 264, 268

Identifying relationships 7, 11–12, 18–19, 37–38, 209–219

Identifying relevant information 19, 43–44, 61–62, 79–80, 95–96, 183–184, 241–242, 267–268, 271–272

Justifying thinking 11–12, 16, 18–19, 28, 62, 96, 134, 156, 160, 180, 183, 222, 236, 244, 250, 252

Making decisions
- choosing a strategy 27–28, 37–38, 39–40, 49–50, 57–58, 85–86, 87–88, 107–108, 117–118, 119–120, 121–122, 137–138, 141, 149–150, 151–152, 155–156, 163–164, 160–170, 171–172, 179–180, 197–199, 200–202
- **choosing an appropriate graph** 261–262
- choosing an operation 303–304

Making predictions 35–36, 79–80, 95–96, 183–184, 191–192, 209–210, 241–242, 261, 264, 271–272, 275–276

Reasonableness of method and solution 19–20, 37–38, 79–80, 139–140, 153–154, 183–184, 191–192, 209–210, 241–242, 271–272, 293–294

Sequencing 35–36, 109–110, 185–186, 191–192, 271–272

Solving a simpler problem 139–140

Using strategies to find solutions 11–12, 19–20, 35–36, 43–44, 61–62, 79–80, 95–96, 111–112, 139–140, 153–154, 171–172, 183–184, 191–192, 209–210, 241–242, 253–254, 267–268, 271–272, 293–294, 303–304

6

Drawing conclusions 24–27, 33–34, 49–50, 59–60, 79–80, 91–92, 105–106, 108, 116, 123–124, 137–138, 145–146, 156, 165–166, 179–180, 201–202, 207–208, 227–228, 233–234, 242, 245–246, 249–254, 277–278, 289–290, 303–304, 311–312

Explaining reasoning 13, 24–25, 33–34, 44, 49–50, 59–60, 79–80, 91–92, 105–106, 108, 116, 123–124, 137–138, 165–166, 179–180, 201–202, 207–208, 216, 227–228, 233–234, 236, 245–246, 249–254, 277–278, 282, 284, 286, 288–290, 303–304, 306, 311–312

Generalizing 24–25, 33–34, 49–50, 59, 80, 92, 106, 124, 138, 148, 166, 180, 202, 208, 228, 234, 246, 254, 278, 290, 304, 312

Identifying relationships 24–25, 33–34, 49–50, 59–60, 79–80, 91–92, 105–106, 123–124, 137–138, 145–146, 165–166, 179–180, 201–202, 207–208, 227–228, 233–234, 242, 245–246, 249–254, 277–278, 289–290, 303–304, 311–312

Identifying relevant information 24–25, 33–34, 49–50, 59–60, 79–80, 91–92, 105–106, 123–124, 137–138, 145–146, 165–166, 179–180, 201–202, 207–208, 227–228, 233–234, 245–246, 253–254, 277–278, 289–290, 303–304, 311–312

Justifying thinking 13, 24–25, 33–34, 44, 49–50, 59–60, 79–80, 91–92, 105–106, 108, 116, 123–124, 137–138, 165–166, 179–180, 201–202, 207–208, 216, 227–228, 233–234, 236, 245–246, 249–250, 277–278, 282, 284, 286, 288–290, 303, 312

Making decisions
- choosing a strategy 24–25, 33–34, 59–60, 79–80, 91–92, 105–106, 123–124, 137–138, 145–146, 165–166, 179–180, 201–202, 207–208, 227–228, 233–234, 245–246, 253–254, 289–290, 303–304, 311–312
- choosing an appropriate graph 241–242
- choosing an operation 147–148, 277–278

Making predictions 25, 34, 50, 60, 80, 92, 106, 124, 138, 148, 166, 180, 208, 228, 234, 2248, 254, 278, 290, 304, 312

Sequencing 253–254

Solving a simpler problem 137–138

Using strategies to find solutions 24–25, 59–60, 79–80, 91–92, 105–106, 123–124, 125–126, 137–138, 147–148, 165–166, 179–180, 207–208, 227–228, 233–234, 245–246, 277–278, 289–290, 303–304, 311–312

7

Checking reasonableness of answers 14, 27, 57, 63, 65, 81, 93, 109, 110, 123, 135, 147, 165, 173, 193, 209, 225, 264, 289, 306, 332, 340

Drawing conclusions 57–58, 61, 65–66

Explaining reasoning 8, 11, 13, 18, 21, 23, 26, 76, 78, 80, 84, 86, 88, 90, 92, 100, 101, 104, 106, 108, 113, 116, 118, 120, 122, 130, 132, 134, 138, 222, 228, 230, 232, 234, 236, 238, 245, 247, 249, 251, 253, 259, 262, 265, 270, 275, 279, 282, 283, 284, 285, 286, 292, 295, 297, 299, 301, 305, 310, 319, 322, 328

Generalizing 57–58, 65–66

Identifying relationships 57–58, 65–66, 193–194, 319, 322

Identifying relevant information 14–15, 27–28, 57–58, 65–66, 81–82, 93–94, 123–124, 135–136, 147–148, 165–166, 173–174, 193–194, 209–210, 225–226, 237–238, 252–253, 264–265, 289–290, 306–307, 332–333, 340–341

Justifying thinking 8, 11, 13, 21, 23, 26, 76, 78, 80, 84, 86, 88, 90, 92, 100, 101, 104, 106, 108, 113, 116, 118, 120, 122, 130, 132, 134, 138, 222, 228, 230, 232, 234, 236, 238, 245, 249, 251, 253, 259, 262, 265, 270, 275, 279, 282, 283, 284, 285, 286, 292, 295, 297, 299, 301, 305

Making decisions
- choosing a strategy 14–15, 27–28, 57–58, 65–66, 81–82, 93–94, 123–124, 135–136, 147–148, 165–166, 173–174, 193–194, 209–210, 225–226, 237–238, 252–253, 264–265, 289–290, 306–307, 332–333, 340–341
- **choosing an equation** 252–253, 262, 332–333
- choosing an operation 252–253, 332–333

Making predictions 163–164, 167–172

Reasonableness of method and solution 14–15, 65–66, 81–82, 93–94, 109–110, 123–124, 135–136, 165–166, 193–194, 225–226, 252–253, 264–265, 332–333, 340–341

Solving a simpler problem 289–290

Using strategies to find solutions 14–15, 27–28, 57–58, 65–66, 81–82, 93–94, 123–124, 135–136, 147–148, 165–166, 173–174, 193–194, 209–210, 225–226, 237–238, 252–253, 264–265, 289–290, 306–307, 332–333, 340–341

Problem Solving

5

Applications
addition applications 140
decimal applications 148, 152, 156, 158, 162, 164, 166, 181
division applications 50, 56, 58, 60, 72, 76, 127, 132, 162, 164, 166
fraction applications 88, 90, 92, 94, 96, 98, 100, 104, 106, 108, 110–112, 118, 122, 124, 132, 134, 136, 138, 140, 148
geometry applications 199–207, 211–212, 215, 217, 219–220, 222
integer applications 282–283, 286, 290,
measurement applications 177–182, 185–186, 189, 200, 224, 272
money applications 43–44, 56, 58, 72, 76, 80–81, 140, 154, 156, 162, 164, 166, 182, 242
multiplication applications 36, 40, 42–44, 72, 118, 122, 124, 154, 156, 160, 222
percent applications 244, 246, 248, 250, 252, 254
place value applications 4
probability applications 269–270, 272–276
ratio applications 234, 239–241, 275
Solving a Multi-step Problem 171–172
statistics applications 263–264, 268
subtraction applications 154, 183
time applications 183–184
Too Much or Not Enough Information 61–62, 267–268
Using a Chart 208
Using a Diagram 84, 96
Using a Formula 255–256
Using a Graph 11–12, 127–128, 183–184, 190, 238, 253–254, 259–262, 264, 269, 302
Using a Number Line 87, 111–112, 132, 146–147, 187, 283, 286
Using a Table, List, or Chart 7–8, 16, 28, 79–80, 183–184, 208, 241–242, 244, 254, 259, 261, 264–265, 271–272
Using Measurement 177–182, 185–186, 189, 200, 272
Using Patterns 37–38, 209–210
Using Pictures, Graphs, or Maps 11–12, 84, 119, 127–128, 183–184, 188, 190–192, 238, 253–254, 259–260, 262, 264, 269, 302

Strategies
Conjecture and Verify 153–154
Find a Pattern 37–38, 109–110
Interpreting Remainders 54, 56, 58
Make a Graph 191–192, 262
Make a List 271–272
Make a Table 79–81, 241–242, 244

6

Applications
addition applications 24–25, 44
decimal applications 58
fraction applications 101, 110, 112, 114, 116, 120, 122, 126
geometry applications 131–134, 140–143, 190, 194, 198, 200, 205, 216, 220, 222, 226
integer applications 268, 270, 275–276, 279, 280–282, 284, 286
measurement applications 131–134, 140–143, 190
money applications 13, 24–25, 34, 44, 46, 48, 50, 51, 112, 172, 174, 182, 268, 299
multiplication applications 15, 46
percent applications 168, 170, 172, 175, 178
probability applications 255, 256, 258, 260, 261–262
proportion applications 161–164, 171, 177
ratio applications 153–154, 157, 175
Solving a Multi-step Problem 24–25
statistics applications 26, 29, 32, 241, 243, 244, 247–250, 252
subtraction applications 24–25, 44
time applications 139
Too Much or Not Enough Information 165–166
Using a Diagram 207–208
Using a Formula 215–216, 220, 222, 226, 232–234, 310
Using a Number Line 41
Using a Table, List, or Chart 26, 32, 201–202, 253–254
Using Measurement 131–134, 140–143, 190, 226
Using Patterns 227–228, 311–312
Using Graphs or Maps 26–27, 91–92, 105–106, 136, 145–146, 179–180, 241–242, 251–252, 303–304

Strategies
Conjecture and Verify 245–246
Draw a Diagram 123–124
Find a Pattern 227–228, 311–312
Make a Graph 136, 179–180, 242, 251–252
Make a List 79–80
Make a Table 201–202
Solve a Simpler Problem 137–138
Solve Multi-step Problems 24–225
Too Much or Not Enough Information 165–166
Work Backward 49–50, 51–53
Write an Equation 33–34, 126, 289–290, 308

7

Applications
addition applications 38
decimal applications 38, 40, 41, 44
fraction applications 34, 35, 36, 38, 50, 54, 56, 64
geometry applications 182, 184, 188, 195, 196, 198, 201, 203, 325, 328
integer applications 222, 228, 230
measurement applications 76, 77, 78, 80, 84, 86, 88, 90, 92, 249, 279, 281, 283, 284, 285, 286, 299
money applications 15, 21, 38, 82, 104, 106, 124, 142
percent applications 114, 116, 118, 120, 122, 130, 132, 134, 138
probability applications 165, 166, 168, 170, 172
proportion applications 103, 105, 106, 107, 108, 111
ratio applications 100, 103, 104, 113
statistics applications 3, 4, 153, 156, 174
time applications 91–92
Too Much or Not Enough Information 81–82
Using a Diagram 57–58, 207–208, 306–307
Using a Formula 24–26, 27–28, 279, 284, 286, 288, 295, 296, 298, 300, 305, 310
Using a Table, List, or Chart 3, 4, 18, 77, 78, 118, 120, 137, 139, 147–148, 173–174, 205
Using Measurement 76, 77, 78, 80, 84, 86
Using Patterns 58, 94, 124, 290
Using Graphs or Maps 112, 161, 162, 163, 173, 205

Strategies
Conjecture and Verify 135–136
Draw a Diagram 225–226
Find a Pattern 193–194
Is the Answer Reasonable? 109–110
Make a Graph 162
Make a List 165–166
Make a Table 93–94
Solve a Simpler Problem 289–290
Too Much or Not Enough Information 81–82
Work Backward 123–124
Write an Equation 14–15, 264–265, 340–341

Problem Solving *continued*

5	6	7
Solve a Simpler Problem 139–140 Solve Multi–Step Problems 171–172 Too Much or Not Enough Information 61–62, 267–268 Work Backward 293–294, 304 Write an Equation 15–16, 18–20, 28, 30, 50, 52		

Index